personality and
personal growth

SIXTH EDITION

Robert Frager
Institute of Transpersonal Psychology

James Fadiman
Institute of Transpersonal Psychology

PEARSON

Prentice
Hall

Upper Saddle River, New Jersey 07458

Library of Congress Cataloging-in-Publication Data

Frager, Robert

  Personality and personal growth/Robert Frager, James Fadiman—6th ed.
  p. cm.

  Includes bibliographical references and indexes.

  ISBN 0-13-144451-4

  1. Personality—Textbooks. 2. Psychotherapy—Textbooks.
  3. Self-actualization (Psychology)—Textbooks. I. Fadiman, James,
  II. Title.

  BF698.F22 2006
  155.2—dc22

                                                      2005028705

Senior Acquisitions Editor: Jeff Marshall
Editorial Director: Leah Jewell
Editorial Assistant: Patricia Callahan
Marketing Assistant: Julie Kestenbaum
**VP, Director of Production and
  Manufacturing:** Barbara Kittle
Managing Editor: Joanne Riker
Assistant Managing Editor:
  Maureen Richardson
Production Liaison: Nicole Girrbach
Manufacturing Manager: Nick Sklitsis
Manufacturing Buyer: Ben Smith
Designer: *The GTS Companies/*York,
  PA Campus
Cover Design: Bruce Kenselaar

Cover Photo: Lisa Fahey
Director, Image Resource Center:
  Melinda Reo
Manager, Rights and Permissions:
  Zina Arabia
Interior Image Specialist: Beth Brenzel
Photo Researcher: Nicole Girrbach
Image Permission Coordinator:
  Robert Farrell
Composition: *The GTS Companies/*
  York, PA Campus
Full-Service Project Management:
  Penny Walker
Printer/Binder: Courier Westford
Cover Printer: Lehigh Press

Credits and acknowledgments borrowed from other sources and reproduced, with permission, in this textbook appear on page 461.

Pearson Education Ltd.
Pearson Education Singapore Pte. Ltd.
Pearson Education Canada, Ltd.
Pearson Education—Japan

Pearson Education Australia Pty. Limited
Pearson Education North Asia Ltd.
Pearson Educación de Mexico, S. A. de C.V.
Pearson Education Malaysia Pte. Ltd.

10 9 8 7 6 5 4
ISBN   0-13-144451-4

To our wives, Ayhan and Dorothy, and our children, Ariel, Eddie, John, Kenan, Renee, and Maria, and to our teachers.

We also sincerely thank our contributing authors: William Brater, Christine Brooks, Jennifer Clements, Franz R. Epting, Judith V. Jordan, Larry M. Leitner, Jean Baker Miller, Bernard J. Paris, Kaisa Puhakka, Jonathan D. Raskin, Irene Pierce Stiver, Janet L. Surrey, Eugene Taylor.

brief contents

contents

3.   Alfred Adler and Individual Psychology   90

preface

After more than 30 years of writing and rewriting, we have continued to change and improve the book's readability. Our goal is to make it useful and more current as we continue the emphasis maintained since our first edition: We present each student with a book that encourages and supports them as they evaluate each theory. Every chapter gives them opportunities to understand their lives and the lives of others through a different theoretical lens.

Each chapter focuses on a theory's positive and useful aspects and reasons why it remains in wide use, rather than its limitations. We encourage students to test each theory's validity or utility against their own life experience and common sense.

We also know that relatively few students who use this text will pursue graduate work or become professional psychologists. Those who do have told us that this book served them well as a reference in their further training, while those who follow other paths tell us that their understanding of the issues raised here has enriched their lives.

For teachers and authors, it doesn't get much better than that.

Although expert proponents of each theory have pointed us to successful applications of their theory, all acknowledge that the research, while valuable and exciting, is not definitive enough to allow them to declare an opposing viewpoint invalid. Thus, we have included research data only when they clarify the theory under discussion. Research on personality has been improving constantly, and we have continually added more references to careful, creative, first-rate empirical studies of the theories we cover.

Space available and our inclusion of areas beyond the scope of many other texts have prevented us from including additional theorists whose work has moved the field forward. We have, however, included in our teaching guide several minichapters on theories and theorists sent to us by brilliant teachers whose expertise exceeded our own. Instructors can make these chapters available to their classes as they choose.

New to the Sixth Edition

Every chapter has been improved and shortened. We have reedited and trimmed each chapter, moving supplemental material to our new **web site.** Our **web site** is a rich addition to this text, and we encourage students to explore the site and instructors to feel free to assign any part of our **web site** material. (www.prenhall.com/frager)

Not totally surprising, we found errors that had eluded our own five revisions, plus five editors' suggestions, plus five proofreaders' detailed scrutiny. Please let us know what else we missed.

New Pedagogy

Web Sites.   As mentioned above, we have shortened the physical text by moving a great deal of background material to our **web site.** The chapter on Reich and the body has been moved to the **web site** in it's entirety, because many instructors have told us they bypass this chapter in class in part because of time constraints and in part because Reich is ignored in psychology today. The same is true for our chapter on Charles Kelly. If you have a special interest in a theory or tradition we have omitted, please let us know. We would be delighted to consider adding your contributions to our **web site.**

As our students have increasingly used the Web, we have offered far more challenging assignments. Students can follow more specialized interests, even with limited access to conventional academic libraries. They soon discover the wonderful quirkiness to some web sites that never could have gotten past an academic press. In addition, an ever-growing number of professors worldwide are posting their own ways of working with each of our theorists. Students can look beyond our views and the views of their instructor. We have included enough web sites for each theory to give students an easy opening set of choices. (www.prenhall.com/frager)

Please send us your favorite web sites if we have overlooked them. Contact us at either rfrager@niyet.com or Jfadiman@aol.com.

New Chapter.   We have renamed our cognitive psychology chapter "Cognitive Psychology and Its Applications" and have added a substantial new section on the work of Albert Bandura. Along with most of our colleagues, we recognize the exciting developments in both cognitive psychology and positive psychology and introduce both fields in this sixth edition.

Changes by Chapter

As we have noted, we've renewed every chapter with text editing, updated references, and material transferred to our new **web site.** We also changed the order of chapters to ensure that theorists more closely linked follow one another. Beyond that, major changes in specific chapters include the following:

- **Chapter 1—Sigmund Freud and Psychoanalysis.**   Anna Freud and the defense mechanisms have been placed in this chapter where they make the best fit with the rest of Freud's general theory. Aided by Freudian therapist Peter Carnochan, we have expanded our evaluation of Freud's ongoing influence in the general culture as well as in psychology. A more extensive discussion of psychoanalysis and more materials on Anna Freud plus excerpts from her writings have been placed on the **web site.**
- **Chapter 2—Carl Gustav Jung and Analytic Psychology.**   We have added new material by modern Jungian analysts, who continue to apply and refine Jung's ideas.
- **Chapter 4—Karen Horney and Humanistic Psychoanalysis.**   A lengthy section on Horney's methods of therapy and a discussion of her influence in the areas of literary analysis and criticism, psychobiography, and cultural studies has been placed in the Web section.
- **Chapter 5—Feminist Approaches to Personality Theory.**   Prior editions provided a discussion and description of relational cultural theory and Organic Inquiry. In the sixth edition we are grateful to Christine Brooks, who has brought in other schools that contribute to personality theory including liberal feminism, radical feminism,

socialist feminism, and cultural feminism. Brooks also considered the issues of diversity and feminist contributions to epistemology and methodology.

At last, this material does the complete job we consider critical to any book of this sort. We continue to be appalled that no other text in this area has dealt with the seemingly obvious truths of male or female differences that most theorists and much research has ignored. A full description of relational therapy, an excerpt from *Woman's Growth in Connection,* as well as a personal case study by Rebecca Caldwell, "eating the fat girl," are included in the **web site.**

- **Chapter 6—Erik Erikson and the Life Cycle.** We have added to the **web site** detailed discussion of Erikson's best-known psychobiography, *Gandhi's Truth.*
- **Chapter 7—William James: The Psychology of Consciousness.** With Eugene's Taylor's help, we have added a far more extensive and detailed overview of James's influence, not only in psychology but also in half a dozen other fields. We have also included a more far-ranging discussion of his intellectual antecedents, more evaluation, and updates in two areas of research about the nature of consciousness, emotions, and time and space perception on the Web.
- **Chapter 8—B. F. Skinner and Radical Behaviorism.** Without Skinner around to fight back, his supporters and opponents seem content to let him speak for himself, so we have retained our basic presentation. We have moved some applications of his work, including Applied Behavioral Analysis, his work on programmed learning and its eventual morphing into computer games, and a section on augmented learning to the Web.
- **Chapter 9—Cognitive Psychology and Its Applications.** We have doubled our coverage of cognitive psychology by adding a section on the work of Albert Bandura, one of today's best-known psychologists. This section includes Bandura's research and theories of observational or vicarious learning, modeling, self-efficacy, self-regulation, and moral disengagement.
- **Chapter 10—George Kelly and Personal Construct Psychology.** We have made this entire chapter far easier for students to grasp. Kelly is a wonderful theorist, but his unique writing style can make him hard to follow. The authors of this chapter, responding to teacher feedback, have made Kelly's basic ideas even more accessible and exciting than in the prior edition. We have also shortened the chapter considerably and made a larger section on our **web site** than for many other chapters.

    On the Web, we present the core of the theory, its assumptive structure, exactly as Kelly laid it out. We have new sections on ordination, fragmentation, range and modulation, which are additional aspects of his theory, plus the full section on dynamics as well as sections on diagnosis (radically different from the *DSM-IV*) and therapy that had been in the text proper in prior editions.
- **Chapter 11—Carl Rogers and the Person-Centered Perspective.** Rogers' influence is growing far more outside the United States than within. We have moved some material on Rogerian therapy and the style of group work that he developed to the **web site.**
- **Chapter 12—Abraham Maslow and Transpersonal Psychology.** We have included new material on developments in transpersonal psychology.
- **Chapter 13—Yoga and the Hindu Tradition.** We have added new material bridging Western psychology and Yoga. We hope in these last three chapters to facilitate class discussion and dialog concerning the relationship between the concepts of these spiritual traditions and the theoretical approaches and assumptions of Western psychology.
- **Chapter 14—Zen and the Buddhist Tradition.** We have added new material bridging Western psychology and Buddhism.
- **Chapter 15—Sufism and the Islamic Tradition.** We have added new material, particularly from several brilliant Iranian psychiatrists who are also serious students of Sufism.

Web Chapters

1. **The Post-Freudians.** We have taken text material infrequently assigned by instructors and moved it to the Web for easy access. We have retained the text chapter format so that instructors can assign it as such and students can use it to discover more about people trained within the Freudian tradition who did not stray far from it. Anna Freud and the defense mechanisms were added to the Freud chapter.
2. **Wilhelm Reich and Somatic Psychology.** We have moved the entire chapter to the Web. Although the field of somatic psychology has grown steadily both in theory and in clinical practice, fewer instructors use this chapter. Somatic psychology remains far from mainstream developments in psychology. We are delighted to keep this information available for those of you interested in this area.

The Teacher Guide

Instructors, make sure you have a teacher guide. If you don't, contact our publisher and complain. We have added new class and homework exercises to various chapters and, as we did with the text, edited it throughout. It has the usual wide range of exam questions and the like, but most of the guide is filled with ways for you to more easily teach each chapter, as we do not expect every instructor to know such a wide range of theorists equally well.

As ever, we remain open to your inputs, your criticisms, and your suggestions.

We thank our reviewers, whose suggestions and corrections strengthened major portions of the text. They are Eric Shiraev, George Mason University; Linda Wolfe, Webster University; Kevin Eames, Dordt College; David Fresco, Kent State University; Gerald Henkel-Johnson, The College of St. Scholastica; and Victor Shamas, University of Arizona.

Notice to Instructors:

If you have not received an Instructor's Manual, please call Prentice Hall at 1-800-922-0579.

about the authors

Robert Frager received his PhD in social psychology from Harvard University, where he was a teaching assistant to Erik Erikson. He has taught psychology at UC Berkeley and UC Santa Cruz and is the founder and first president of the Institute for Transpersonal Psychology. He is also past president of the Association for Transpersonal Psychology. Author of several books and numerous articles in psychology and related fields, he is currently director of the spiritual-guidance program at the Institute of Transpersonal Psychology in Palo Alto, California.

I am fortunate to have met and worked with many of the distinguished theorists and therapists whose work is featured in this text and have personally experienced Jungian analysis, Gestalt therapy, Reichian and neo-Reichian therapy, and Rogerian group work. I have also lived in Zen temples, Yoga ashrams, and Sufi centers and studied and practiced these traditions.

In addition to teaching psychology, I teach the Japanese martial art of Aikido. I was a personal student of the founder of Aikido. He was the first of a series of wonderful teachers who taught me what Maslow called the farther reaches of human nature. I have edited, with Jim Fadiman, a collection of Sufi stories, poetry, and teachings, *Essential Sufism* (HarperSanFrancisco, 1997), and written *Heart, Self, and Soul* (Quest, 1999), a book on Sufi psychology.

I am married to a wonderful, creative graphic artist and have four children.

James Fadiman received his PhD in psychology from Stanford University and has taught at San Francisco State University, Brandeis University, and Stanford. He has his own consulting firm and offers seminars to executives and educators in the United States and abroad. He has written or edited books on holistic health, goalsetting, and abnormal psychology, edits two journals, and sits on the board of several corporations concerned with the preservation of natural resources.

I have used the psychological and clinical skills I learned in graduate school in a variety of areas beyond psychology. Although I was a college counselor for several years and continue to teach psychology, I have spent more time working as a consultant with scientists and business people. My early research into altered states of consciousness opened me up to discovering the profound wisdom in indigenous and non-Western cultures. My delight was in finding that the ancient wisdom has turned out to be immensely practical.

This book gave me a chance to put together different points of view that I've found personally useful, even when the creators of these ideas were at sword's points with one another.

I'm currently teaching creative problem solving and invention for a major Silicon Valley electronics firm, completing a second novel, continuing to write a series of short stories, and staying involved with several environmental start-up companies.

I have been married for more than thirty years to a documentary filmmaker. We have two children.

introduction

This text is intended to provide you with a worldwide, cross-cultural body of knowledge to help you explore human nature. In every chapter of this, our sixth edition, we present a variety of tools with which you might attain a greater understanding of your own and others' personalities.

WHAT IS PERSONALITY?

Your personality can limit or expand your life. Some people are warm, pleasant to be around, sincere friends. Others are unpleasant, negative, and difficult to get along with. Difficult aspects of personality can be obstacles to success, or sources of enthusiasm, creativity, and achievement.

We have all observed **personality development** in ourselves and others. All human beings change and mature over time. Sigmund Freud described the **psychosexual stages** people go through in childhood and adolescence. Erik Erikson expanded Freud's theory and portrayed **psychosocial stages** that include the entire life span.

We are all personality psychologists in that we constantly look for regularities in others' behavior. We say, for instance, "She has her father's personality." We also make predictions about others: "You can trust him to be honest with you." We have even developed our own theories of personality: "Redheads are impulsive and emotional." Thinking about personality is an integral part of our everyday lives.

At times, a single situation evokes different responses in different people. This has given rise to the notion of **individual differences,** or variations in personality. In addition, the same situation may bring different responses from the same individual, which has led observers to look for internal states that may change over time.

Webster's unabridged dictionary (McKechnie, 1983) defines personality as, "habitual patterns and qualities of behavior of any individual as expressed by physical and mental activities and attitudes; distinctive individual qualities of a person, considered collectively." More simply, your personality is your individual pattern of thinking, feeling, and acting.

The History of Personality Study

The study of personality dates back centuries before the development of academic psychology. In 400 BCE, Hippocrates, the father of Western medicine, developed a theory of personality based on four body "humors." He theorized that physical differences were related to personality types. The melancholic (depressed) personality has a body with more black bile. The choleric (irritable, easily angered) type has more yellow bile, or adrenaline. The phlegmatic (calm, easygoing) type has more phlegm (lymph and mucous fluids). The sanguine (optimistic) temperament is associated with the humor of blood. A version of Hippocrates' model is still used today in the international Waldorf school system, as a guide to help teachers understand their students (Wilkinson, 1977).

Twenty-three hundred years ago, Plato, in his *Republic,* wrote of three major forces in the personality: intellect, emotions, and will. According to Plato, the will (or spirit, as in the phrase "a spirited horse") assists the intellect in overcoming the influences of the emotions.

In the third century BCE, Theophrastus, a student of Aristotle, asked, "Why is it that while all Greece lies under the same sky and all Greeks are educated alike, we are all different with respect to personality?" (in Frager, 1994, p. 5). Theophrastus defined thirty personality types, each organized around a central trait such as stinginess, dishonesty, or flattery. He concluded that this central trait could be found in all aspects of a person's life.

MODERN THEORIES OF PERSONALITY

Nineteenth-century Europe and America, before Freud and the other major personality theorists, showed little interest in theories of personality. Mental disorders were considered the inexplicable results of "alien" or demonic possession of otherwise rational, logical individuals. In fact, the early physicians who specialized in treating mental patients were called "alienists."

One of Freud's greatest contributions was to insist that rules and a cause-and-effect structure govern mental events. He looked at the irrational and unconscious thoughts and behaviors of his patients and noted that they fell into certain patterns. In so doing, Freud founded a "science of the irrational." Furthermore, he recognized that most of the behavior patterns found in neurotic and psychotic patients seemed to be intense versions of the mental patterns observed in normal people.

Jung, Adler, and many others built on Freud's insights. In Jung's theory, the individual's unconscious includes not only personal memories (as Freud had observed) but also material from the collective unconscious of all humanity. Alfred Adler and others focused their attention on the ego as a sophisticated mechanism of adaptation to the inner and outer environment.

Karen Horney explored ego psychology and also pioneered in the development of the psychology of women. In one sense, she expanded psychoanalytic theory to include women. Her work has been carried on by several generations of women theorists. Among the most highly regarded are the Stone Center group, who present their widely accepted theoretical work in Chapter 5, Feminist Approaches to Personality Theory

William James, a contemporary of Freud and Jung, was more interested in consciousness itself than in the contents of consciousness. In his exploration of how the mind operates, James was a precursor of the cognitive psychologists. He was also the founder of consciousness studies, a field in which researchers investigate such topics as altered states of consciousness, including dreams, meditation, and biofeedback.

Later American theorists such as George Kelly, Carl Rogers, and Abraham Maslow concerned themselves with issues of psychological health and growth. As Maslow cogently wrote, "[I]t is as if Freud supplied to us the sick half of psychology and we must now fill it out with the healthy half" (Maslow, 1968, p. 5).

Two Contemporary Approaches to Personality Study: Nomothetic and Idiographic

The *nomothetic* approach studies personality in order to develop regular laws of behavior. Typically, large groups of subjects are tested and their scores are related to regularities in behavior. Psychological research on personality has generally relied on the nomothetic approach. Most psychologists look to developing laws, or general principles, of human behavior. For example, IQ tests were developed to predict success at school. After decades of research, IQ scores have been related to success at a variety of intellectual activities. In addition, research has shown that few IQ tests are valid indicators of intellectual ability outside middle-class European and American populations.

The *idiographic* approach seeks to understand personality through a rich and detailed study of an individual's life. The idiographic approach in personality study focuses on the particular combination of life history factors that affect an individual. For example, Erik Erikson pioneered in detailed psychological studies of great figures in history, including Martin Luther and Mahatma Gandhi. Studies of individual lives are hard to compare because the pattern of each life is unique. However, from detailed studies of a variety of lives, we may eventually discern certain basic factors in human experience.

Many of the personality theorists in this text have been psychotherapists, and their theories are based on detailed, idiographic, clinical **case studies** of their clients.

Clinical case studies have two major drawbacks:

1. Clinicians cannot share all the details of their cases. They are bound by therapist–client confidentiality to protect the deeply personal details of their clients' revelations. Because we have no access to the original data, it is extremely difficult to evaluate the details of the clinicians' reports or the validity of their conclusions.
2. Therapy cases tend to distort our view of human nature to the extent they focus on pathology; most clients come to a therapist because their lives are functioning at less than optimal levels.

CHARACTERISTICS OF A GOOD THEORY OF PERSONALITY

Psychologists generally agree on the basic characteristics of good theories. As you read this text, judge for yourself how well each theory meets the following criteria. Also, even a theory that lacks some of these formal criteria may contribute a great deal to your understanding of human nature and of yourself.

Verifiability

A good theory can be tested. Verifiable theories include *clearly defined concepts*. For example, if we cannot clearly define Freud's concept of ego, how can we even begin to measure it? On the other hand, psychologists have managed to assess Adler's conception of inferiority through various measurements of self-concept.

Second, we must be able to make **operational definitions** of the theory's concepts. An operational definition specifies behavior or experience associated with a particular concept. The operational definition may not capture the full richness and complexity of the original theoretical construct, but it represents a method of applying the theory to the real world. For example, we might operationally define introversion as preference for solitude and avoidance of situations involving being with groups of people.

Another way to describe verifiability is *falsifiability,* that is, whether or not a theory can ever be proven incorrect. According to philosopher of science Karl Popper (1963), a theory must state what people are expected to do and also what they are expected *not* to do. In evaluating a theory, ask yourself if someone might in any way prove this theory false. If a theory can *never* be proven false, how can we have any confidence in its accuracy or usefulness? For example, if I assert that the experience of birth is a major factor in personality development, how could this be tested? It is impossible to find control subjects who have never been born!

Good science is always self-critical, and scientific research typically seeks to test the validity of a hypothesis. A scientific investigation sets up a research hypothesis and then seeks to prove it false. Research can never prove the truth of a hypothesis, because there can always be alternative explanations for positive research findings. However, research can prove that a particular research hypothesis is false. For example, let us suppose I seek to study Freud's concept of repression. (According to Freud, repression forces out of consciousness an anxiety-provoking event, thought, or perception.) I develop the hypothesis that people who experienced sexual trauma in childhood are likely to experience amnesia concerning the traumatic events. Then, I study a group of individuals who have reported childhood trauma. If I find that all of these people report clear and detailed memories of these events ever since childhood, I have disproved my research hypothesis.

In fact, research did support this particular hypothesis. In a careful study of 450 women and men who had reported sexual abuse before age 16, Briere and Conte (1993) found that 59% reported amnesia concerning the abuse some time before age 18. The earlier and more severe the sexual abuse, the more likely they were to have experienced amnesia. This does not *prove* Freud correct. But it does support Freud's theory of repression.

Comprehensiveness

Some theories seek to explain a broad range of human behaviors, while others focus on more specific areas. If theory uses a relatively small number of basic concepts to illuminate a wide range of behaviors, we might have greater confidence in the power and accuracy of these concepts.

Other theories are based on observations of a limited range of behavior, such as a therapist's experiences with neurotic patients, or a behaviorist's experiments with mice, monkeys, and mazes. When we extend these theories to try and explain human behavior, they may become fuzzy and poorly defined.

Only recently have psychologists become concerned with evaluating comprehensiveness in psychological theories related to their applicability to diverse populations. Virtually all personality theorists are white and come from Europe or America. Almost all are men. An Asian-American psychologist described modern psychology: "In America the overwhelming subject of research is white Americans. The U.S. constitutes less than 5 percent of the world's population, yet from that population we develop theories and principles assumed to be universal" (Sue, in McGuire, 1999, p. 26).

To make this text more comprehensive, we have included two chapters written by women and focused on the development of a psychology applicable to both women and men. We have also included three chapters on non-Western psychologies, psychologies that developed within three of the world's great religious traditions—Hinduism, Buddhism, and Islam.

Applications

We can evaluate a theory on its practical usefulness. For example Carl Rogers' theory of personality has been extraordinarily influential in modern counseling and psychotherapy. Theories may also have heuristic value, that is, they may provide important insights in understanding ourselves and others.

Personality theories have had influence beyond psychology. Carl Jung's theory has been of great interest to theologians and students of folklore and mythology. Alfred Adler's ideas have affected education and social work, and Abraham Maslow's formulations have been extremely influential in the business world.

NO SINGLE TRUTH

In this book you will discover many diverse ways of looking at personality. Various theories employ differing fundamental assumptions and dissimilar data. It is not surprising, therefore, that they come to different conclusions.

Some theories rely on an assumption of **reductionism.** They try to reduce one level of activity to a simpler or more basic level. A biologist may take as a working assumption that life is nothing but the behavior of cells, and therefore if we only understand cellular biology more deeply, we will understand all animal behavior. A Freudian might similarly propose that all human behavior can be reduced to the interaction of id, ego, and superego. A Skinnerian may argue that human behavior is completely determined by patterns of reinforcement and extinction.

Reductionism may be useful at times in driving theorists to extend their ideas as widely as possible. However, reductionism is a fundamental error in science. Biology *cannot* be reduced to single-cell behavior, even though the body is composed of single cells; similarly, psychology cannot be reduced to biology. In addition, the full range of human thought, emotion, and behavior cannot be reduced to any single set of constructs.

A CONSTRUCTIVE APPROACH TO PERSONALITY THEORY

We approach each theory as positively and as sympathetically as possible. We have avoided, as much as possible, the tendency to criticize or belittle any theory. Instead, we have highlighted the strengths and the effectiveness of each approach. We have been purposefully biased in our choices. We have included those theorists whose importance and utility are evident within psychology and left out other well-known theorists who seemed less useful or less compatible with the overall aim of this book.

Each theorist in this book offers something of unique value and relevance, isolating and clarifying various aspects of human nature. We believe that each one is essentially "correct" in his or her own area of expertise. Nevertheless, we have presented certain crucial disagreements between theorists. These disputes often resemble the famous tale of the blind men encountering an elephant. When each man touched a part of the elephant, he assumed that the part under his finger was the key to the whole animal's appearance.

In the original version of this fable, the blind men were philosophers who were sent into a pitch-dark barn by a wise king (who was probably tired of their academic bickering). Each blind philosopher insisted that his limited experience and the theory based on that experience was the sum total of the truth.

We take a different approach. We assume that each theory has something of relevance to every one of us. For example, hourly wage earners may find that B. F. Skinner's concept of schedules of reinforcement sheds light on their workplace behavior. However, it is doubtful that reading Skinner will help people understand why they attend religious services. Here, Carl Jung's writings on the power of symbols and the significance of the self are more likely to be useful. Thus, at different times or in different areas of our lives, each theory can provide guidance, enlightenment, or clarity.

You will probably feel more affinity for one or two theorists than for the others covered in this book. Each theorist is writing about certain basic patterns of human experience, often patterns that come from his or her own life. You may appreciate those theories that focus on patterns most matched to your own.

Each chapter also discusses a theory or perspective that adds to our general knowledge of human behavior. We are convinced that, in addition to our innate biological pattern of growth and development, individuals possess a tendency for psychological growth and development. Our assumption of this tendency, described by various psychologists as a striving for self-actualization—the desire to understand oneself and the need to utilize one's capacities to the fullest—has led to the unique features of this text.

EXPANDING THE SCOPE OF PERSONALITY THEORY

In recent years, three approaches to human nature and functioning have become increasingly important: cognitive psychology, the psychology of women, and non-Western approaches to psychology. Our coverage of these areas is intended to extend the limits and range of traditional perspectives on personality theory.

The Psychology of Women

In the past two editions of this volume, our chapter entitled The Psychology of Women sought to highlight research and theory developed over the past forty years that acknowledges the difference between men and women. While many mainstream personality-theory textbooks continue to sidestep this critical issue (Madden and Hyde, 1998), the psychology of women and sex-difference studies are becoming increasingly visible both in theoretical models (such as the one presented in this chapter) and research (journals such as *Psychology of Women Quarterly, Signs,* and *Journal of Gender Studies* regularly publish research related to the psychology of women). We were privileged to work with a group of eminent scholars and therapists who generously wrote an original exposition of women's studies' unique contribution to the field of personality. In this edition, we have expanded this chapter to include historical and theoretical context around the existing exposition, including the rise of the contemporary feminist movement and its influence within the field of psychology. It is appropriately renamed Feminist Approaches to Personality Theory. The feminist framework suggests that individuals must be understood in the context of living in constant relationship to her or his outer world and that sociocultural factors such as gender, race, class, and personal values must be considered in any analysis or theory building. Feminist psychology specifically adheres to the belief that all persons develop within such a multifaceted social construct. This revised chapter includes two additional sections: one underscoring the work within feminist psychology to address issues of diversity, and the other introducing feminist research methods.

Eastern Theories of Personality

The final three chapters of this book are devoted to the models of personality developed in three Eastern psychospiritual disciplines: Yoga, Zen Buddhism, and Sufism. Chapters 13, 14, and 15 represent an extension of the traditional limits of personality theory. As psychology study becomes more international and less dependent on U.S. and Western European intellectual and philosophical assumptions, these other points of view are being more broadly integrated into other parts of the educational system.

These Eastern theories have been developed in societies and value systems that are often strikingly different from Europe and the United States. The beliefs and ideals emanating from these cultures enrich our ideas of what it is to be human.

The underlying religious traditions for these systems—Hinduism, Buddhism, and Islam—represent the perspectives of nearly three billion people today in more than one hundred countries. These three traditions are embraced by the majority of the world's population and are living realities for their adherents.

Contemporary Concern with Eastern Systems

We realize that a psychology class on personality theory is not the place for the study of Eastern religions. Although we provide a simple overview of the religious contexts of three Eastern psychologies, our final three chapters focus primarily on the psychological concepts and models of human nature developed in these three non-Western psychologies. These spiritual psychologies have developed unique psychological wisdom in hundreds of years of practice and interaction between sophisticated teachers and serious students dedicated to personal change and development

The Eastern theories include powerful concepts and effective techniques of personal and spiritual development. Both practical applications and research studies of these disciplines have increased in the West.

> There is growing recognition that Western psychologists may have underestimated the psychologies and therapies of other cultures. Certain Asian disciplines contain sophisticated therapies, and experimental studies have demonstrated their ability to induce psychological, physiological, and psychotherapeutic effects. An increasing number of Westerners, including mental-health professionals, now use Asian therapies. Benefits include new perspectives on psychological functioning, potential, and pathology, as well as new approaches and techniques. In addition, the study of other cultures and practices often has the healthy effect of revealing unsuspected ethnocentric assumptions and limiting beliefs, thus leading to a broader view of human nature and therapy. . . .
>
> Asian psychologies focus primarily on existential and transpersonal levels and little on the pathological. They contain detailed maps of states of consciousness, developmental levels, and stages of enlightenment that extend beyond traditional Western psychological maps. Moreover, they claim to possess techniques for inducing these states and conditions. (Walsh, 1989, pp. 547–548)

These chapters provide you with the opportunity to consider, evaluate, and, to some extent, experience these perspectives on personality in the context of a critical and comparative psychology course. We have ample evidence of the interest and time that students are already devoting to these questions.

Yoga, Zen, and Sufism originated in a common need to explain the relationship between religious experience and everyday life. Spiritual guides were among the earliest psychologists in the West and in the East. They needed to understand the emotional and personal dynamics of their students, as well as their spiritual needs. In order to comprehend the issues their students faced, they turned first to their own experiences, a principle we find honored today in the training analysis that psychotherapists undergo.

These systems do differ from most Western personality theories in their greater concern with values, moral considerations, and psycho-spiritual development. We should live within a moral code, they argue, because a morally codified life has definite, recognizable, and beneficial effects on our consciousness and overall well-being. However, all three psychologies view morals and values in a pragmatic, even iconoclastic way. Each of these traditions stresses the futility and foolishness of valuing external form over inner function.

These psychologies, like their Western counterparts, are derived from careful observations of human experience. They are built on centuries of empirical observations of the psychological, physiological, and spiritual effects of a variety of ideas, attitudes, behaviors, and exercises.

The vitality and importance of these traditional psychologies, however, rest on the continual testing, reworking, and modifying of their initial insights to fit new settings and interpersonal situations as well as different cultural conditions. In other words, these centuries-old psychologies are still relevant, still changing and developing.

Carl Jung wrote, "The knowledge of Eastern psychology . . . forms the indispensable basis for a critique and an objective consideration of Western psychology" (in Shamdasani, 1996, p. x–xi). We believe that the development of a complete psychology rests on our study and understanding of Eastern thought.

The evaluation of the Eastern systems is no different from the personal judgments we are asking you to make of the Western theories in this book: Do they help you understand yourself and others? How do they resonate with your own experience?

CHAPTER STRUCTURE

Each chapter generally is divided into the following sections. Some chapters also feature other topics pertinent to their discussions. Personal Reflection exercises, like the one on p. 28, are peppered throughout each chapter.

Personal History
Intellectual Antecedents
Major Concepts
Dynamics
    Psychological Growth
    Obstacles to Growth
Structure
    Body
    Social Relationships
    Will
    Emotions
    Intellect
    Self
    Therapist/Teacher
Evaluation
The Theory Firsthand
Chapter Highlights
Key Concepts
Annotated Bibliography
Web Sites
References

One great difficulty in comparing and contrasting theories of personality is that not only has each major theory made its own discrete and unique contribution to the sum of human knowledge, each also has its own approach, definitions, and dynamics. Often the same word, such as *self,* varies widely in meaning from theory to theory. (Theorists have even used the same term differently within their own writings.) To make it easier, we have attempted to describe each theory in terms of its usefulness for human understanding. We approach each theory not as a researcher, not as a therapist, not as a patient, but primarily as people trying to understand ourselves and other people. Fortunately, many theories do overlap and can be easily compared. Except where it was contrary to sense, we have used this system of organization.

Personal History

Each chapter presents the personal history and the intellectual antecedents of the theorist. We outline the major influences on the theorist's thinking, influences rooted in childhood as well as pivotal later-life experiences.

We have learned that it is easier to understand a theory if we know more about the man or woman who created it. Thus, the biographies we have for each chapter are extensive enough to allow you to develop a feeling for the person before you begin to study his or her theory. You will find that Skinner's theory (or Freud's, or Rogers's, and so forth) makes much more sense once you can see how it arose from the theorist's life experience.

Intellectual Antecedents

Every theory owes part of its genesis and its elaboration to the ideas of others. Every theory was developed within a particular society, at a particular time in history, a time in which certain other theories and concepts affected the thinking of virtually all writers and investigators. An idea is actually part of an ecosystem of related theories and concepts. It is often easier to appreciate the scope of a theory if we are aware of the major intellectual currents of the time. For example, most of the theories developed in the late nineteenth century were strongly influenced by Darwin's principles of evolution, natural selection, and survival of the fittest.

Major Concepts

The bulk of each chapter explores the theory, beginning with a summary of the major concepts. These are the foundation upon which each theory rests and the elements psychologists refer to when they distinguish between theories. The concepts are also what each theorist would agree are his or her most important contributions to human understanding.

This section is called "Major Concepts," not "Major Facts." It would be encouraging to say that the major concepts covered in this book rest, after many years of research, on factual bases. Unfortunately, it is not so. Little objective evidence supports the existence of the id, archetypes, sublimation, inferiority complex, or real self (major concepts from each of the next few chapters). However, we have empirical confirmation of several important ideas, such as Erikson's concepts of identity and human development and Maslow's concept of self-actualization. More than empirical data, the field of personality theory contains a vast amount of brilliant thinking, clear observation, innovative methods of therapy, and insightful expositions of concepts that help us grasp the complex reality of who we are.

As you will see, we rarely cite research. Virtually every theorist has been highly critical of the validity and usefulness of any research done on his or her theory (Corsini & Wedding, 1989). Instead, we use our pages to make each theory as clear, as vivid, and as understandable as possible.

Dynamics

We are living systems, not static ones. The ways in which we strive to achieve greater health and awareness are discussed in the chapter sections Psychological Growth. The ways in which growth is delayed, thwarted, turned aside, prevented, or perverted are described in the sections Obstacles to Growth.

Every theory included has developed a set of interventions, variously called therapy, counseling, or spiritual practices, to help the person overcome the obstacles and return a person to normal growth. Although they are fascinating outgrowths of theory, we do not discuss these interventions in detail because this is a text on personality theory, not psychotherapy.

Structure

We work for consistency in order to help you compare and contrast different theories but try not to be so rigid as to be unfair to the theories. While every theory in the book might be said to include every major aspect of human functioning, we have found that each focuses most clearly on certain areas and almost totally neglects others. Often we say no more under a given heading than, essentially, "This theory does not discuss this."

Body.   Although this is a book of psychological theories, all rely on the study of embodied humans beings who breathe, eat, tense, and relax. Some theories pay close attention to how much the physical body influences psychological processes, others much less so.

Social Relationships.   When we call humans social animals, we suggest that we derive meaning and satisfy our basic needs by being with each other—in families, in play groups, in friendships, in work groups, in couples, and in communities. Some theories consider these groups of primary importance, while others focus on the inner world of the individual and tend to ignore social relations. For example, Karen Horney, who was deeply interested in the cultural determinants of personality, defined neurosis in terms of social relationships. She analyzed three classic neurotic patterns: moving toward people, moving against people, and moving away from people. Although almost every chapter clusters around the question of individual development, the chapter on the psychology of women looks instead at the centrality of relationships between individuals. The issues raised in that chapter reflect on every other chapter and should be kept in mind as you proceed through the book.

Will.   William James made the will a central concept in his psychology. For James, the will is a combination of attention and effort. It is an important tool for focusing consciousness. According to James, the will can be systematically strengthened and trained. In contrast, Skinner considered the will a confusing and unrealistic concept because he assumed that all actions are determined, even if we may not know enough to understand how or why. Therefore, the will has no place in Skinner's theory.

Emotions.   Descartes wrote, "I think, therefore I am." Psychology adds, "I feel, therefore I am fully human." Psychological theory is rich in ways to consider the effects of emotions on all other mental and physical activities.

Maslow and the Eastern psychologies recognize two basic kinds of emotions—positive and negative. Maslow included calmness, joy, and happiness as positive emotions. He wrote that they facilitated self-actualization. Similarly, the Yoga tradition distinguishes between emotions that lead to greater freedom and knowledge, and emotions that increase ignorance.

Intellect.   Personality theories often focus on the irrational aspects of the personality. It is of value to see how the theorists construe "rational" functioning in widely differing ways, and to discover that the theorists vary widely in the importance they place on rationality.

Self.   The self is an elusive concept, never completely captured by any of the theorists. It is more than the ego, more than the sum total of the factors that make up the individual; it is less limited than the personality but contains it. The concept of self veers most defiantly away from the world of pure science, refusing to submit to objective measurement. Sounds confusing? It can be.

Consider also the "felt sense" of self. You have a clear sense of who you are, no matter how ill you feel, how upset you might be, whatever your age. One of us asked his father, when the older man was 88, if he ever felt old. He said that although he was acutely aware of how old his body was, the felt sense of himself seemed unchanged from childhood. His attitudes, opinions, behaviors, moods, and interests had all changed over the course of his life, but this elusive something was unchanged. Some theories avoid this slippery aspect of ourselves, but others wade in and make it a central concept.

One of the greatest differences between Yoga and Buddhism, for example, is how they define the self. In Yoga, the self is the eternal, unchanging essence of each individual. Buddhism recognizes no unchanging, central self within the individual. The person is merely an impermanent collection of finite traits. (Skinner says much the same thing but from a totally different perspective.) The greater self, or Buddha-nature, is not individual but is as large as the entire universe.

Therapist/Teacher.   Each theory contains ideas to help people grow and gain more pleasure and integrity in their lives. And, in accordance with its major concepts, each theory establishes the type of training an individual would need in order to become a professional therapist or a skilled helper or guide. Acceptable preparation for such work varies widely. The U.S. psychoanalyst is generally a medical doctor who then undergoes several years of arduous training in psychoanalytic psychotherapy, whereas the Zen teacher experiences years of meditation and spiritual instruction. Each system makes specific demands on its practitioners and encourages the evolution of different skills.

Evaluation

A great temptation in reviewing a theory is to take a critical position on the value of this or that concept. We have, instead, tried to stand aside and give you the task of evaluating each theorist, not only according to traditional academic and psychological standards but also in terms of the theory's usefulness for you personally, now or in the future.

The Theory Firsthand

We include whenever possible an extended passage from the theorist's own writings or a description of the system in operation. We want you to experience the style and the personality of each theorist. We want you to read for yourself something that each one has written, to develop a sense of the theorist's "voice" and to experience firsthand what made his or her work important and sought after. The style with which the theorists present their ideas is often as unique and meaningful as the ideas themselves. In addition to these excerpts, each chapter includes margin quotes that provide useful, pithy insights into the theorists, their adherents, and, occasionally, their critics.

Chapter Highlights

To help you grasp the essential elements in every chapter, we have included a summary of the major points and central theoretical issues discussed in each theory.

Key Concepts

A second pedagogical feature is the section "Key Concepts," near the end of each chapter. This glossary-like listing provides definitions for the major terms used by each theorist.

Annotated Bibliography

Each chapter includes an annotated bibliography. The chapter is in fact only an introduction to an involved and complex system of thought. We hope you will pursue the theories you find most interesting and valuable. We have facilitated this next step by suggesting books we find most helpful in understanding each theory.

One of the kindest things a teacher can do for students is to steer them away from second-class readings and direct them to the most useful and/or best written books in a given area. (We have spent a tremendous amount of time going through the less useful books on each theory, and we don't think you should have to do the same.) Each chapter includes a guide to where to start if you want to do your own exploration.

Our Web Site

Our web site provides additional resources and supplements to this text—presentations on each theory as well as chapters not included in the text. These include Reich and the Body, and Anna Freud and the Post-Freudians. Each chapter retains the same structure as the text.

References

We have put the references at the end of each chapter rather than together in the back of the book. Students have told us that our text is a useful reference book for other classes, as well as for their personal self-study of particular theorists. On their advice we keep the references in this separated format.

Personal Reflections

In addition to this overall structure, each chapter contains, sprinkled throughout it, a series of personal reflection exercises to give you a better feel for some aspects of the theory. Experiential learning and intellectual learning are complementary rather than contradictory processes. A personal encounter with a concept adds unparalleled immediacy to the theory. The exercises have all been tested, improved, and retested until our students pronounced them helpful.

We strongly advise you to try as many of the exercises as possible. Our own students have found that doing so adds real depth to their understanding of the material, helps them remember the concepts, and adds to their knowledge of themselves and others.

QUESTIONS TO POSE TO EACH THEORY

- How much is the theorist writing primarily from his or her own life experiences? To what extent are these experiences common to most people?
- How has the theory been researched or applied in the real world? What evidence supports its validity? Has it been proved valid when applied in therapy, education, business, or health?
- Does the theory help you understand yourself and others? Has studying this theory helped you experience more insight into your own life or the lives of your friends or parents? Does the theory "ring true" to your own experience?
- To what extent did the theorist's values, religion, or social class play a role in his or her theory?
- Is the theory culturally or historically limited? Did the theorist learn from exposure to other cultures, or is the theory "culture-bound"? Which theory elements seem of universal relevance and which do not?
- Does the theory consider gender differences, or is it based primarily on men's experience? To what extent is the theory influenced by social and cultural values regarding gender?
- How much of the theory is based on the study of psychopathology, the study of animal behavior, or research on white male college sophomores? Does it focus primarily on dysfunctional, normal, or exceptional human behavior?
- Does the theory address the issue of human development? Does it discuss differences in the experiences and behaviors of children and adults?
- What are the values implicit in the theory? Is the theory deterministic, insisting that human behavior is controlled by certain internal or external factors, or does it assume choice and some level of free will? Is the theory mechanistic, assuming that human beings are passive objects responding automatically to inner or outer influences?
- Does the theory assume all people are basically conflict-ridden or neurotic, or does it assume all people are fundamentally healthy and good? What are the implications of either of these assumptions?

Working with the Questions for Each Theory

This can be used for classroom discussion, or for your own consideration as you read this book. Look over the above questions and consider the following.

1. Which questions are the most important questions you would ask of each theory? Why?
2. Are there any questions you feel are unimportant, that you can leave out?
3. Are there any additional questions you would add to this list?

KEY CONCEPTS

Case study Qualitative research in which a single subject is studied in depth.

Individual differences Individual characteristics that are stable over time and distinguish one person from another.

Operational definition The definition of a theoretical construct in terms of observable behaviors.

Personality development Formation or change in personality over time.

Psychosexual stages Freud's theory that everyone develops through five overlapping stages—oral, anal, phallic, latency, and genital. The stages are identified in terms of the bodily zone that serves as the primary source of pleasure.

Psychosocial stages Erikson's reinterpretation of Freud's psychosexual stages, which emphasizes the social aspects of each stage. Erikson's psychosocial stages include the entire human life span, from birth to old age.

Reductionism A theoretical approach that attempts to explain completely the phenomena of one field of study in terms of the dynamics of a more "basic" field, for example, to claim that psychological phenomena can be fully explained in terms of biology, or that biological phenomena can be completely explained in terms of chemistry.

REFERENCES

Brieve J., & Conte, J. (1993). Self-reported amnesia for abuse in adults molested as children. *Journal of Traumatic Stress, 6,* 21–31.

Frager, R. (1994). *Who am I? Personality types for self-discovery.* New York: Putnam.

Madden, Margaret, & Hyde, Janet (Eds.). (1998). Special Issue: Integrating gender and ethnicity into psychology courses. *Psychology of Women Quarterly,* 22.

Maslow, A. (1968). *Toward a psychology of being* (2nd ed.). New York: Van Nostrand.

McGuire, P. A. (1999, March) Multicultural summit cheers packed house. *APA Monitor,* p. 26.

McKechnie, J. (Ed.) (1983). *Webster's new twentieth century dictionary of the English language, unabridged.* (2nd edition). New York: Simon and Schuster.

Popper, K. (1963). *Conjectures and refutations.* New York: Basic Books.

Shamdasani, S. (Ed.). (1996). *The psychology of kundalini yoga: Notes of the seminar given in 1932 by C. G. Jung.* Princeton, NJ: Princeton University Press.

Walsh, R. (1989). Asian psychotherapies. In R. Corsini & D. Wedding (Eds.), *Current psychotherapies* (4th ed.). Itasca, IL: F. E. Peacock.

Wilkinson, R. (1977). *The temperaments in education.* Fair Oaks, CA: St. George Publications.

WEB SITES

http://www.psych-central.com/

Online resources for psychology students and their professors. Lots of links to places you may want to go.

http://www.findingstone.com/main.htm

A **web** site with a wide range of information, links, and practical suggestions about many areas of psychology. Try "ask a therapist." You can have serious questions answered by practicing professionals.

http://www.psywww.com/index.html

Another site designed for students and teachers of psychology. Lots of information, lots of links.

chapter 1

sigmund freud
and psychoanalysis

Sigmund Freud's work, developed from his knowledge of biology, neurology, and psychiatry, proposed a new understanding of mental life that profoundly affected Western culture. His view of the human condition, striking violently against the prevailing opinions of his era, offered a complex and compelling way to understand normal and abnormal mental functioning. His ideas were like an explosion that scattered late Victorian views of human nature in every direction. His exploration of the dark sides of the human psyche helped people understand some of the horrors of World War I and the traumatic changes it made in every country involved in the conflict. Freud explored areas of the psyche obscured by Victorian morality and philosophy. He devised new approaches to treat the mentally ill. His work challenged cultural, religious, social, and scientific taboos. His writings, his personality, and his determination to extend the boundaries of his work kept him at the center of an intense, shifting circle of friends, disciples, and critics. Freud was constantly rethinking and revising his earlier ideas. Interestingly, his harshest critics included those he had personally supervised at various stages in their careers.

It is impossible to discuss all of Freud's contributions in a single chapter. Therefore, what follows is a deliberate simplification of a complex and intricately constructed system. This overview will make later exposure to Freudian ideas more intelligible and to allow a better understanding of theorists whose works are heavily influenced by Freud.

> Sigmund Freud, by the power of his writings and by the breadth and audacity of his speculations, revolutionized the thought, the lives, and the imagination of an age. . . . It would be hard to find in the history of ideas, even in the history of religion, someone whose influence was so immediate, so broad, or so deep. (Wollheim, 1971, p. ix)

> Freud, along with Marx and Darwin, has been regarded as the most significant influence on modern Western thought. (Nolan, 1999)

PERSONAL HISTORY

Sigmund Freud was born on May 6, 1856, in Freiberg in Moravia, now part of the Czech Republic. When he was 4 years old, his family suffered financial setbacks and moved to Vienna, where Freud remained most of his life. In 1938, he fled to England to escape the German takeover of Austria.

During his childhood, Freud excelled as a student. Despite his family's limited finances, with all eight members living together in a crowded apartment, Freud, the eldest child, had his own room and even an oil lamp to study by while the rest of the family made do with candles. In gymnasium he continued his excellent academic performance. "I was at the top of my class for seven years. I enjoyed special privileges there and was required to pass scarcely any examinations" (Freud, 1925a, p. 9).

Such was the prevailing anti-Semitic climate of the time that, because Freud was Jewish, most professional careers, except medicine and law, were closed to him. He chose to enter the faculty of medicine at the University of Vienna in 1873 where he remained for eight years, three more than was customary.

During these years, he worked in the physiological laboratory of Ernst Brücke, where he did independent research in histology, the study of the minute structure of animal and vegetable tissue, and published articles on anatomy and neurology. At the age of 26, Freud received his medical degree. He continued his work under Brücke for a year, while living at home. He aspired to fill the next open position in the laboratory, but Brücke had two excellent assistants ahead of Freud. He concluded, "The turning point came in 1882, when my teacher, for whom I felt the highest possible esteem, corrected my father's generous improvidence by strongly advising me, in view of my bad financial position, to abandon my theoretical career" (1925a, p. 13). In addition, Freud had fallen in love and realized that if he ever were to marry, he would need a better-paying position.

Although he moved reluctantly to a private practice, his primary interests remained in scientific exploration and observation. Working first as a surgeon, then in general medicine, he became a "house physician" at the principal hospital in Vienna. He took

> He was profoundly a Jew, not in a doctrinal sense, but in his conception of morality, in his love of the skeptical play of reason, in his distrust of illusion, in the form of his prophetic talent. (Bruner, 1956, p. 344)

Neither at that time, nor indeed in my later life, did I feel any particular predilection for the career of a physician. I was moved, rather, by a sort of curiosity, which was, however, directed more towards human concerns than towards natural objects; nor had I grasped the importance of observation as one of the best means of gratifying it. (Freud, 1935, p. 10)

a course in psychiatry that furthered his interest in the relationships between mental symptoms and physical disease. By 1885, he had established himself in the prestigious position of lecturer at the University of Vienna. His career began to look promising.

From 1884 to 1887, Freud did some of the first research in cocaine. At first, he was impressed with its properties: "I have tested this effect of coca, which wards off hunger, sleep, and fatigue and steels one to intellectual effort, some dozens of times on myself" (1963, p. 11). He wrote about its potential therapeutic uses for both physical and mental disturbances. He later became concerned with its addicting properties and discontinued the research (Byck, 1975).

With Brücke's backing, Freud obtained a travel grant to work under Jean-Martin Charcot in Paris, where he studied hypnotic technique and served as Charcot's translator for his lectures (Carroy, 1991). Charcot gave him permission to translate his papers into German upon Freud's return to Vienna.

His work in France increased his interest in hypnosis as a therapeutic tool. In cooperation with the distinguished older physician Josef Breuer, Freud (1895) explored the dynamics of hysteria. Freud summarized their findings: "The symptoms of hysterical patients depend upon impressive, but forgotten scenes of their lives (traumata). The therapy founded thereon was to cause the patients to recall and reproduce these experiences under hypnosis (catharsis)" (1914, p. 13). He found hypnosis less effective than he had hoped. It did not allow the patient or the therapist to work with the patient's resistance to recalling the traumatic memories. Eventually, Freud abandoned hypnosis altogether. Instead, he encouraged his patients to speak freely by reporting whatever thoughts came to mind, regardless of how these thoughts related to the patients' symptoms.

In 1896, Freud first used the term *psychoanalysis* to describe his methods. His own self-analysis began in 1897. Freud's interest in the unconsciousness insights provided by dreams his patients described led to the publication, in 1900, of *The Interpretation of Dreams*. This serious treatment of the significance of dreams, radical at the time, received little attention but many now consider it his most important work. Freud followed it the next year with another major book, *The Psychopathology of Everyday Life*, which looked at the everyday moments when we reveal hidden wishes without being aware of what we are doing or saying. Eventually, Freud had a following of interested physicians that included Alfred Adler, Sandor Ferenczi, Carl Gustav Jung, Otto Rank, Karl Abraham, and Ernest Jones. The group established a society. Papers were written and a journal published. Soon psychoanalytic groups formed in a dozen countries. By 1910, Freud was invited to the United States to deliver lectures at Clark University in Worcester, Massachusetts. His works were translated into English. More and more people were becoming interested in his theories.

Even a superficial glance at my work will show how much I am indebted to the brilliant discoveries of Freud. (Jung in McGuire, 1974)

As I stepped on to the platform at Worcester to deliver my "Five Lectures" upon psychoanalysis it seemed like some incredible daydream: psychoanalysis was no longer a product of delusion, it had become a valuable part of reality. (Freud, 1925a, p. 104)

Freud spent the rest of his life developing, extending, and clarifying psychoanalysis. He tried to retain control over the psychoanalytic movement by ejecting members who disagreed with his views and by demanding an unusual degree of loyalty to his own position. Jung, Adler, and Rank, among others, left after repeated disagreements with Freud on theoretical issues and personal differences (Esterson, 2002; Kuhn, 1998). Each later founded a separate school of thought.

Freud wrote extensively. His collected works fill 24 volumes and include essays concerning the fine points of clinical practice, a series of lectures outlining the theory in full, and specialized monographs on religious and cultural questions. He attempted to build a structure that might eventually reorient all of psychiatry. He feared that analysts who deviated from the procedures he established might dilute the power and the possibilities of psychoanalysis. Above all, he wanted to prevent the distortion and misuse of psychoanalytic theory. When, for example, in 1931 Ferenczi suddenly changed his procedures to make the analytic situation one in which affection might be more freely expressed, a radical departure from Freud's methods, Freud wrote him as follows:

> I see that the differences between us have come to a head in a technical detail which is well worth discussing. You have not made a secret of the fact that you kiss your patients and let them kiss you. . . . Now I am assuredly not one of those who from prudishness or from consideration of bourgeois convention would condemn little erotic gratifications of this kind. . . . We have hitherto in our techniques held to the conclusion that patients are to be refused erotic gratifications.
>
> Now picture what will be the result of publishing your technique. There is no revolutionary who is not driven out of the field by a still more radical one. A number of independent thinkers in matters of technique will say to themselves: why stop at a kiss? (Jones, 1955, pp. 163–164)

In spite of declining health, Freud maintained a private practice, a full writing schedule, and an ever-increasing correspondence, even answering letters from total strangers asking for help (Benjamin & Dixon, 1996). However, as Freud's work became more widely available, the criticisms increased. In 1933, the Nazis, offended by his frank discussion of sexual issues, burned a pile of Freud's books in Berlin. Freud commented on the event: "What progress we are making. In the Middle Ages they would have burnt me, nowadays they are content with burning my books" (Jones, 1957).

His last book, *An Outline of Psycho-analysis* (1940), begins with a blunt warning to critics: "The teachings of psycho-analysis are based on an incalculable number of observations and experiences, and only someone who has repeated those observations on himself and others is in a position to arrive at a judgment of his own upon it" (p. 1).

Freud's last years were difficult. From 1923 on, he was in ill health, suffering from cancer of the mouth and jaws. He was in almost continual pain and had a total of 33 operations to halt the spreading cancer. When, in 1938, the Germans who had taken over Austria threatened Anna, his daughter, Freud left for London with her. He died there a year later.

Unfortunately, Freud's first biographer, Ernest Jones, also a close personal friend, wrote a sanitized account of his life (Steiner, 2000), leaving the writing of a more balanced version to a later generation (Gay, 1988). Others have criticized Freud for a possible affair with his wife's sister (O'Brien, 1991), a lack of professional honesty (Masson, 1984; Newton, 1995), and a blatant disregard of confidentiality within psychoanalysis (Goleman, 1990; Hamilton, 1991). He has also been accused of possibly misrepresenting some of his most famous cases (Decker, 1991) and even of being "the false prophet of the drug world" (Thornton, 1984).

Only the continuing importance of Freud's work supports the publication of these attacks. Freud's ultimate importance can be judged not only by the ongoing interest in and debate over aspects of psychoanalytic theory but, to a greater extent, by the number of his ideas now part of the common heritage of the West. We are all in Freud's debt for partially illuminating the world that moves beneath conscious awareness.

No one who, like me, conjures up the most evil of those half-tamed demons that inhabit the human breast, and seeks to wrestle with them, can expect to come through the struggle unscathed. (Freud, 1905b)

INTELLECTUAL ANTECEDENTS

Freud's thinking was an original synthesis of his exposure to philosophical ideas, his training in scientific rigor, and his own contact with the unconscious.

Philosophy

While still a student at the University of Vienna, Freud was influenced by the German romantic poet Clemens Brentano and introduced to the ideas of Friedrich Nietzsche as well (Godde, 1991a). Nietzsche believed, for example, that moral convictions arose from internalized aggression. Freud's ideas are also close to those of Arthur Schopenhauer. They overlap in their view of the will, the importance of sexuality in determining behavior, the domination of reason by the emotions, and the centrality of repression—the nonacceptance of what one experiences (Godde, 1991b).

Biology

Some of Freud's faith in the biological origins of consciousness may be traced to Brücke's positions. Brücke once took a formal oath to abide by the following proposition, which was open and optimistic for its time:

> No other forces than the common physical and chemical ones are active within the organism. . . . (Rycroft, 1972, p. 14)

I sometimes come out of his lectures [Charcot's] . . . with an entirely new idea about perfection. . . . No other human being has ever affected me in the same way. (Freud in E. Freud, 1961, pp. 184–185)

Charcot demonstrated that it was possible to induce or relieve hysterical symptoms with hypnotic suggestion. Freud observed, as had others, that in hysteria patients exhibit symptoms that are physiologically impossible. For example, in glove anesthesia a person's hand is without feeling, while the sensations in the wrist and arm are normal. Because the nerves run continuously from the shoulder into the hand, this symptom can have no physical cause. It became clear to Freud that hysteria required a psychological explanation.

The Unconscious

Freud did not discover the unconscious. The ancient Greeks and the Sufis, among others, recommended the study of dreams. Just before Freud's time, Johann Wolfgang von Goethe and Friedrich von Schiller "had sought the roots of poetic creation in the unconscious" (Gay, 1988, p. 128), as had many romantic poets and even Freud's contemporary, the novelist Henry James. Freud's contribution lies in his observing the origins and content of this part of the mind with the emerging tools of scientific analysis. His work and the attention it attracted has made the unconscious a part of our public lexicon.

One evening last week when I was hard at work, tormented with just that amount of pain that seems to be the best state to make my brain function, the barriers were suddenly lifted, the veil was drawn aside, and I had a clear vision from the details of the neuroses to the conditions that make consciousness possible. Everything seemed to connect up, the whole worked well together, and one had the impression that the thing was really a machine and would soon go by itself . . . all that was perfectly clear, and still is. Naturally I don't know how to contain myself for pleasure. (Freud, letter to Fliess; in Bonaparte, 1954)

Freud's final attempt to develop a neurologically based psychology (1895) may have arisen from his own earlier and highly sophisticated personal explorations with cocaine (Fuller, 1992). This model, eventually cast aside by Freud, was revived and appears to some a neglected but brilliant precursor to contemporary theories linking changes in brain chemistry to emotional states (Pribram, 1962).

MAJOR CONCEPTS

Underlying all of Freud's thinking is the assumption that the body is the sole source of all mental energy. He looked forward to the time when all mental phenomena might be explained with direct reference to brain physiology (Sulloway, 1979). Working from a biological model, Freud attempted to create a theory that encompassed all mental activity. His major concepts include a structural breakdown of the parts of the mind, its developmental stages, what it does with energy, and what drives it.

Psychic Determinism

Freud assumed that we have no discontinuities in mental life and that all thought and all behavior have meaning. He contended that *nothing* occurs randomly, least of all mental processes. There is a cause, even multiple causes, for every thought, feeling, memory, or action. Every mental event is brought about by conscious or unconscious intention and is determined by the events that have preceded it. While it appears that many mental events occur spontaneously, Freud denied this and began to search out and describe the hidden links that join one conscious event to another.

Many of the most puzzling and seemingly arbitrary turns of psychoanalytic theory . . . are either hidden biological assumptions, or result directly from such assumptions. (Halt, 1965, p. 94)

Conscious, Preconscious, Unconscious

Freud described the mind as if it were divided into three parts:

Conscious.   Consciousness is self-evident, and for that reason science most concerned itself with this part of the mind—until Freud. However, the conscious is only a small portion of the mind; it includes only what we are aware of in any given moment. Although Freud was interested in the mechanisms of consciousness, he was far more interested in the less-exposed and less-explored areas of consciousness, which he labeled the *preconscious* and the *unconscious* (Herzog, 1991).

There is no need to characterize what we call "conscious." It is the same as the consciousness of philosophers and of everyday opinion. (Freud, 1940, p. 16)

Preconscious.   Strictly speaking, the preconscious is a part of the unconscious, but a part that can easily be made conscious. Accessible portions of memory are part of the preconscious. This might include memories, for example, of everything a person did yesterday, a middle name, street addresses, the date of the Norman Conquest, favorite foods, the smell of fall leaves burning, and an oddly shaped birthday cake served at your tenth birthday party. The preconscious is like a holding area for the memories of a functioning consciousness.

Unconscious.   When a conscious thought or feeling seems unrelated to the thoughts and feelings that preceded it, Freud suggested, the connections are present but unconscious. Once the unconscious links are found, the apparent discontinuity is resolved. Within the unconscious are instinctual elements that have never been conscious and are never accessible to consciousness. In addition, certain material has been barred—censored and repressed—from consciousness. This material is neither forgotten nor lost, but neither is it remembered; it still affects consciousness, but indirectly.

There is a liveliness and an immediacy to unconscious material. "We have found by experience that unconscious mental processes are in themselves 'timeless.' That is to say to begin with: they are not arranged chronologically, time alters nothing in them, nor can the idea of time be applied to them" (Freud in Fodor & Gaynor, 1958, p. 162). Decades-old memories, when released into consciousness, have lost none of their emotional force.

Certain inadequacies of our psychic functions and certain performances which are apparently unintentional prove to be well motivated when subjected to psychoanalytic investigation. (Freud, 1901)

Impulses

Impulse (*trieb* in German) has been incorrectly translated in older textbooks as "instinct" (Bettelheim, 1982, pp. 87–88). Impulses or drives are pressures to act without conscious thought toward particular ends. Such impulses are "the ultimate cause of all activity" (Freud, 1940, p. 5). Freud labeled the physical aspects of impulses "needs" and the mental aspects of impulses "wishes." Needs and wishes propel people to take action.

There can be no question of restricting one or the other basic impulses to a single region of the mind. They are necessarily present everywhere. (Freud, 1940)

All impulses have four components: a *source,* an *aim,* an *impetus,* and an *object.* The source, where the need arises, may be a part or all of the body. The aim is to reduce the need until no more action is necessary, that is, to give the organism the satisfaction it now desires. The impetus is the amount of energy, force, or pressure used to satisfy or gratify the impulse. This is determined by the urgency of the underlying need. The object of an impulse is whatever thing or action allows satisfaction of the original desire.

Consider the way in which these components appear in a thirsty person. The body gradually dehydrates until it needs more liquids; the source is the growing need for fluids. As the need becomes greater, thirst is perceived. If this thirst is unsatisfied, it becomes more pronounced. As the intensity rises, so does the impetus or energy available to do something to relieve the thirst. The aim is to reduce the tension. The solution is not simply a liquid—milk, water, or beer—but all the acts that go toward reducing the tension. These might include getting up, going to the kitchen, choosing a beverage, and drinking it. A critical point to remember is that the impulse can be fully or partially satisfied in various ways. The capacity to satisfy needs in animals is often limited by a pattern of stereotypical behavior. Human impulses only *initiate* the need for action; they do not predetermine the particular action or how it will be completed. The number of solutions open to an individual is a summation of the initial biological urge, the mental wish (which may or may not be conscious), and a host of prior ideas, habits, and available options.

Freud assumed that a normal, healthy pattern aims to reduce tension to previously acceptable levels. A person with a need will continue seeking activities to reduce the original tension. The complete cycle of behavior from relaxation to tension and activity and back to relaxation is called a *tension-reduction* model. Tensions are resolved by returning the body to the state of equilibrium that existed before the need arose.

Basic Impulses.   Freud developed two descriptions of basic impulses. The early model described two opposing forces: the sexual (more generally, the erotic or physically gratifying) and the aggressive, or destructive. Later, he described these forces more globally as either life supporting or death (and destruction) encouraging. Both formulations presupposed a biological, ongoing, and unresolvable pair of conflicts.

Freud was impressed with the diversity and complexity of behavior that arises from the fusion of the basic drives. "The sexual impulses are remarkable for their plasticity, for the facility with which they can change their aims, for their interchangeability—for the ease with which they can substitute one form of gratification for another—and for the way in which they can be held in suspense" (1933, p. 97). What Freud noted is that the "object" can be a wide variety of things. Sexual desire, for example, can be released through sexual activity but also by watching erotic films, looking at images, reading about other people, fantasizing, eating, drinking—even exercising. The impulses are the channels through which the energy can flow, but this energy obeys laws of its own.

Libido and Aggressive Energy

A person falls ill of a neurosis if his ego has lost the capacity to allocate his libido in some way. (Freud, 1916)

Each of these generalized impulses has a separate source of energy. **Libido** (from the Latin word for *wish* or *desire*) is the energy available to the life impulses. "Its production, increase or diminution, distribution, and displacement should afford us possibilities for explaining the psychosexual phenomena observed" (Freud, 1905a, p. 118).

One characteristic of libido is its "mobility"—the ease with which it can pass from one area of attention to another. Freud pictured the volatile nature of emotional responsiveness as a flow of energy, flowing in and out of areas of immediate concern.

Aggressive energy, or the death impulse, has no special name. It has been assumed to have the same general properties as libido.

Cathexis

Cathexis is the process by which the available libidinal energy in the psyche is attached to or invested in a person, idea, or thing. Libido that has been cathected is no longer mobile and can no longer move to new objects. It is rooted in whatever part of the psyche has attracted and held it.

The German word Freud used, *Besetzung,* means both "to occupy" and "to invest." If you imagine your store of libido as a given amount of money, cathexis is the process of investing it. Once a portion has been invested or cathected, it remains there, leaving you with that much less to invest elsewhere. For example, psychoanalytic studies of mourning interpret the lack of interest in normal pursuits and the excessive preoccupation with the recently deceased as a withdrawal of libido from usual relationships while attaching it to the deceased.

Psychoanalytic theory is concerned with understanding where libido has been inappropriately cathected. Once released or redirected, this same energy is then available to satisfy other current needs. The need to release bound energies is also found in the ideas of Carl Rogers and Abraham Maslow, as well as in Buddhism and Sufism. Each of these theories comes to different conclusions about the source of psychic energy, but all agree with the Freudian contention that the identification and channeling of psychic energy is a major issue in understanding personality.

> There are certain pathological conditions which seem to leave us no alternative but to postulate that the subject draws on a specific quantity of energy which he distributes in variable proportions in his relationships with objects and with himself. (LaPlanche & Pontalis, 1973, p. 65)

STRUCTURE OF THE PERSONALITY

Freud observed in his patients an endless series of psychic conflicts and compromises. He saw impulse pitted against impulse, social prohibitions blocking biological drives, and ways of coping often conflicting with one another. Only late in his career did he order, for himself, this seeming chaos by proposing three basic structural components of the psyche: the *id,* the *ego,* and the *superego.* These are now accepted English terms, but they are artificially abstract and leave an impression different from that Freud had intended (Solms, 1998). His words for each were simple and direct: *Das es* (id) simply means "it," *das Ich* (ego) means "I," and *das uber-Ich* (superego) means "above I." It is almost too late to correct the damage done by the initial translation of Freud's work into English. His writings were made deliberately obscure so as to sound more scientific, which appealed to the predominant American mind-set of the time (Bettelheim, 1982).

The Id

The **id** is the original core out of which the rest of the personality emerges. It is biological in nature and contains the reservoir of energy for the whole personality. The id itself is primitive and unorganized. "The logical laws of thought do not apply in the id" (Freud, 1933, p. 73). Moreover, the id is not modified as one grows and matures. The id is not changed by experience because it is not in contact with the external world. Its goals are simple and direct: reduce tension, increase pleasure, and minimize discomfort. The id strives to do this through reflex actions (automatic reactions such as sneezing or blinking) and by using other portions of the mind.

> In the id there is nothing corresponding to the idea of time, no recognition of the passage of time, and (a thing which is very remarkable and awaits adequate attention in philosophic thought) no alteration of mental processes by the passage of time.... Naturally the id knows no values, no good and evil, no morality. (Freud, 1933, p. 74)

The id may be likened to a blind king who has absolute power and authority but whose trusted counselors, primarily the ego, tell him how and where to use these powers. The contents of the id are almost entirely unconscious. They include primitive thoughts that have never been conscious and thoughts that have been denied, found unacceptable to consciousness. According to Freud, experiences denied or repressed can still affect a person's behavior with undiminished intensity without being subject to conscious control.

The Ego

The **ego** is the part of the psyche in contact with external reality. It develops out of the id, as the infant becomes aware of its own identity, to serve and placate the id's repeated demands. In order to accomplish this, the ego, like the bark of a tree, protects the id but also draws energy from it. It has the task of ensuring the health, safety, and sanity of the personality. Freud postulated that the ego has several functions in relation both to the outside world and to the inner world, whose urges it strives to satisfy.

> [We] might say that the ego stands for reason and good sense while the id stands for the untamed passions. (Freud, 1933)

Its principal characteristics include control of voluntary movement and those activities that tend toward self-preservation. It becomes aware of external events, relates them to past events, then through activity either avoids the condition, adapts to it, or modifies the external world to make it safer or more comfortable. To deal with "internal events," it attempts to keep control over "the demands of the impulses, by deciding whether they shall be allowed to obtain satisfaction, by postponing that satisfaction to times and circumstances favorable in the external world or by suppressing their excitations completely" (1940, pp. 2–3). The ego's activities are to regulate the level of tension produced by internal or external stimuli. A rise in tension is felt as discomfort, while a lowering of tension is felt as *pleasure*. Therefore, the ego pursues pleasure and seeks to avoid or minimize pain.

Thus the ego is originally created by the id in an attempt to cope with stress. However, to do this, the ego must in turn control or modulate the id's impulses so that the individual can pursue realistic approaches to life.

The act of dating provides an example of how the ego controls sexual impulses. The id feels tension arising from unfulfilled sexual arousal and, without the ego's influence, would reduce this tension through immediate and direct sexual activity. Within the confines of a date, however, the ego can determine how much sexual expression is possible and how to establish situations in which sexual contact is most fulfilling. The id is responsive to needs, whereas the ego is responsive to opportunities.

The Superego

> [The superego] is like a secret police department, unerringly detecting any trends of forbidden impulses, particularly of an aggressive kind, and punishing the individual inexorably if any are present. (Horney, 1939, p. 211)

This last part of the personality's structure develops from the ego. The **superego** serves as a judge or censor over the activities and thoughts of the ego. It is the repository of moral codes, standards of conduct, and those constructs that form the inhibitions for the personality. Freud describes three functions of the superego: conscience, self-observation, and the formation of ideals. As conscience, the superego acts to restrict, prohibit, or judge conscious activity, but it also acts unconsciously. The unconscious restrictions are indirect, appearing as compulsions or prohibitions. "The sufferer . . . behaves as if he were dominated by a sense of which he knows nothing" (1907, p. 123).

The superego develops, elaborates, and maintains the moral code of an individual. "A child's superego is in fact constructed on the model, not of its parents but of its parents' superego; the contents which fill it are the same and it becomes the vehicle of tradition . . . which have propagated themselves in this manner from generation to generation" (1933, p. 39). The child, therefore, learns not only the real constraints in any situation but also the moral views of the parents as well.

Relationship Between the Three Subsystems

The overarching goal of the psyche is to maintain—and when it is lost, to regain—an acceptable level of dynamic equilibrium that maximizes the pleasure of tension reduction. The energy used originates in the primitive, impulsive id. The ego exists to deal realistically with the basic drives of the id. It also mediates between the demands of the id, the restrictions of the superego, and external reality. The superego, arising from the ego, acts as a moral brake or counterforce to the practical concerns of the ego. It sets guidelines that define and limit the ego's flexibility.

The id is entirely unconscious, whereas the ego and the superego are only partly so. "Certainly large portions of the ego and superego can remain unconscious, are, in fact, normally unconscious. That means to say that the individual knows nothing of their contents, and that it requires an expenditure of effort to make him conscious of them" (Freud, 1933, p. 69).

Psychoanalysis, the therapeutic method that Freud developed, has a primary goal to strengthen the ego, to make it independent of the overly strict concerns of the superego, and to increase its capacity to become aware of and control material formerly repressed or hidden in the id.

PSYCHOSEXUAL STAGES OF DEVELOPMENT

As an infant becomes a child, a child an adolescent, and an adolescent an adult, marked changes occur in what is desired and how desires are satisfied. The shifting modes of gratification and the physical areas of gratification are the basic elements in Freud's description of the developmental stages. Freud uses the term **fixation** to describe what occurs when a person fails to progress normally from stage to stage and remains overly involved with a particular stage. A person fixated in a particular stage will tend to seek gratification in simpler or more childlike ways.

The Oral Stage

The **oral stage** begins at birth, when both needs and gratification primarily involve the lips, tongue, and somewhat later, the teeth. The basic drive of the infant is not social or interpersonal; it is simply to take in nourishment and to relieve the tensions of hunger, thirst, and fatigue. During feeding and when going to sleep, the child is soothed, cuddled, and rocked. The child associates both pleasure and the reduction of tension with these events.

The mouth is the first area of the body that the infant can control; most of the libidinal energy available is initially directed or focused in this area. As the child matures, other parts of the body develop and become important sites of gratification. However, some energy remains permanently affixed or cathected to the means for oral gratification. Adults have well-developed oral habits and a continued interest in maintaining oral pleasures. Eating, sucking, chewing, smoking, biting, and licking or smacking one's

Psychoanalysis is the first psychology to take seriously the whole human body as a place to live in. . . . Psychoanalysis is profoundly biological. (Le Barre, 1968)

lips are physical expressions of these interests. Constant nibblers, smokers, and those who often overeat may be partially fixated in the oral stage.

The late oral stage, after teeth have appeared, includes the gratification of the aggressive instincts. Biting the breast, which causes the mother pain and leads to the actual withdrawal of the breast, is an example of this kind of behavior. Adult sarcasm, tearing at one's food, and gossip have been described as being related to this developmental stage.

It is normal to retain some interest in oral pleasures. Oral gratification can be looked upon as pathological only if it is a dominant mode of gratification, that is, if a person is excessively dependent on oral habits to relieve anxiety or tension unrelated to hunger or thirst.

The Anal Stage

As the child grows, new areas of tension and gratification come into awareness. Between the ages of 2 and 4, children generally learn to control their anal sphincter and bladder. The child pays special attention to urination and defecation. Toilet training prompts a natural interest in self-discovery. The rise in physiological control is coupled with the realization that such control is a new source of pleasure. In addition, children quickly learn that the rising level of control brings them attention and praise from their parents. The reverse is also true: parents' concern over toilet training allows the child to demand attention both by successful control and by mistakes.

Adult characteristics that are associated with partial fixation at the **anal stage** are excessive orderliness, parsimoniousness, and obstinacy. Freud observed that these three traits are usually found together. He speaks of the "anal character," one whose behavior may be linked to difficult experiences suffered during this period in childhood.

Part of the confusion that can accompany the anal stage arises from the apparent contradiction between lavish praise and recognition, on the one hand, and the idea that toilet behavior is "dirty" and should be kept a secret, on the other. The child does not initially understand that his or her bowel movements and urine are not valued. Small children love to watch the action of the toilet bowl as it flushes, often waving or saying good-bye to their evacuations. It is not unusual for a child to offer part of a bowel movement to a parent as a gift. Having been praised for producing it, the child may be surprised and confused if the parents react with disgust. No other area of contemporary life is as saddled with prohibitions and taboos as toilet training and behaviors typical of the anal stage.

The Phallic Stage

Starting as early as age 3, the child moves into the **phallic stage,** which focuses on the genitals. Freud maintained that this stage is best characterized as phallic, because it is the period when a child becomes aware either of having a penis or of lacking one. This is the first stage in which children become conscious of sexual differences.

Freud tried to understand the tensions a child experiences during sexual excitement—that is, pleasure from the stimulation of the genital areas. This excitement is linked in the child's mind with the close physical presence of the parents. The craving for this contact becomes increasingly more difficult for the child to satisfy; the child is struggling for the intimacy that the parents share with each other. This stage is characterized by the child's wanting to get into bed with the parents and becoming jealous of the attention the parents give to each other. Freud concluded from his observations that during this period both males and females develop fears about sexual issues.

Freud saw children in the phallic stage reacting to their parents as potential threats to the fulfillment of their needs. Thus, for the boy who wishes to be close to his mother, the father takes on some of the attributes of a rival. At the same time, the boy wants his father's love and affection, for which his mother is seen as a rival. The child is in the untenable position of wanting and fearing both parents.

In boys, Freud called this conflict the **Oedipus complex,** after the tragic hero in the play by the Greek dramatist Sophocles. In the most familiar version of the myth, Oedipus (knowing neither parent) kills his father and later marries his mother. When he is eventually made aware of who he has killed and who he has married, Oedipus disfigures himself by tearing out both of his eyes. Freud believed that every male child reenacts a similar inner drama. He wishes to possess his mother and kill his father to achieve this goal. He also fears his father and is afraid that he, a child, will be castrated by him. The anxiety around castration, the fear and love for the father as well as the love and sexual desire for the mother, can never be fully resolved. In childhood, the entire complex is repressed. Among the first tasks of the developing superego are to keep this disturbing conflict out of consciousness and to protect the child from acting it out.

For girls the problem is similar, but its expression and solution take a different turn. The girl wishes to possess her father, and she sees her mother as the major rival. Boys repress their feelings partly out of fear of castration. For girls the repression of their desires is less severe, less total. This lack of intensity allows the girl to "remain in the Oedipus situation for an indefinite period. She only abandons it late in life, and then incompletely" (Freud, 1933, p. 129). Freud's views about women and their psychological development remain highly controversial and will be discussed in this chapter and in other chapters as well.

The Latency Period.   Whatever form the resolution of the struggle actually takes, most children seem to modify their attachment to their parents sometime after 5 years of age and turn to relationships with peers and to school activities, sports, and other skills. This phase, from age 5 or 6 until the onset of puberty, is called the **latency period.** It is a time when the unresolvable sexual desires of the phallic stage are successfully repressed by the superego.

> From then on, until puberty, . . . sexuality makes no progress; on the contrary, the sexual strivings diminish in strength, and much that the child practiced or knew before is given up and forgotten. In this period, after the early blooming of sexual life has withered, are built up such attitudes of the ego as shame, disgust, and morality, designed to stand against the later storms of puberty and to direct the paths of the freshly-awakened sexual desires. (1926, p. 216)

For both parents and children, this is a relatively calm and psychologically uneventful time.

The Genital Stage

The final period of biological and psychological development, the **genital stage,** occurs with the onset of puberty and the consequent return of libidinal energy to the

So you too are aware that the Oedipus complex is at the root of religious feeling. Bravo! (Freud, letter to Jung; in McGuire, 1974)

PSYCHOSEXUAL STAGES

The following exercises and questions will give you a chance to experience feelings associated with each developmental stage. (If Freud is correct in his supposition that any remaining fixations from each stage will be linked to anxiety, any one of the following could prove difficult or embarrassing.)

The Oral Stage

Buy a baby bottle with a nipple. Fill it with milk, water, or fruit juice. Either alone or with other members of the class, drink from the bottle. Does drinking, or even the thought of drinking, from a bottle bring up any memories or feelings? If you go ahead and do it, what postures are you most comfortable in? Allow yourself to experience your unfiltered reactions. Share these reactions with the class. Do you encounter responses specific to men or to women?

The Anal Stage

Notice to what extent privacy is a consideration in the architecture of public lavatories, as well as your bathroom at home. How does privacy play a role in how you behave in the lavatory? Do you avoid meeting anyone's eyes or even looking at anyone else when you enter a public restroom? Can you imagine urinating in public? In a park? By the side of the highway? In a forest?

Many people have strongly conditioned toilet behaviors. For example, some people must read while they are sitting on a toilet. What might be the reason for this behavior?

Share some of your observations with others, and be aware of how it makes you feel to talk about aspects of this exercise. Joking or giggling could be a defense against anyone's discomfort with the topic.

The Phallic Stage

Can you recall what your parents said to you about your genitals when you were little? Can women in the class recall any thoughts or ideas about boys and their penises? Can the men recall any fear of losing their penises? If you have no memories of these kinds of feelings, is this sufficient reason to assume that you had no such feelings at the time?

The Genital Stage

Write down any misinformation you have had about sexual matters that has been subsequently corrected. (Examples: You were brought by the stork or found at the supermarket. Every time a person has intercourse a pregnancy results.)

Do you think your early sexual experiences have affected your attitudes or beliefs about your own sexuality? Have those experiences reinforced previously held beliefs? How did you feel about your first sexual experience? Do you feel differently now? Can you relate your current attitudes about sexual matters to earlier attitudes or beliefs?

Every aspect of the female Oedipus complex has been effectively criticized, using empirical data and methods which did not exist in Freud's lifetime. (Emmanuel, 1992, p. 27)

sexual organs. Now boys and girls are made aware of their separate sexual identities and begin to look for ways to fulfill their erotic and interpersonal needs. Freud believed that homosexuality, at this stage, resulted from a lack of adequate development, a position still voiced by some, in spite of contemporary understanding of the varieties of healthy sexual development.

FREUD'S VIEWS ABOUT WOMEN

Freud's ideas about women, based initially on biological differences between men and women, have come under an ever-increasing volume of attack. Later chapters of this text, especially Chapter 4 (Karen Horney and Humanistic Psychoanalysis) and

Chapter 5 (Feminist Approaches to Personality Theory), present current contrasting views. Here we present only Freud's position so that you understand what other theorists are arguing about. Full-fledged, pointed rebuttals by feminist scholars, for example, Miller (1984) and Sagan (1988), leave few parts of Freud's theory standing upright.

Penis envy—the girl's desire for a penis and her related realization that she is "lacking" one—is a critical juncture in female development. "The discovery that she is castrated is a turning point in a girl's growth. Three possible lines of development diverge from it: one leads to sexual inhibition and to neurosis, the second to a modification of character in the sense of masculinity complex, and the third to normal feminity" (Freud, 1933, p. 126).

This theory proposes that girl's penis envy persists as a feeling of inferiority and predisposes her to jealousy. Her perpetual desire for a penis, or "superior endowment," is, in the mature woman, converted to the desire for a child, particularly for a son, "who brings the longed-for penis with him" (1933). The woman is never decisively forced to renounce her Oedipal strivings out of castration anxiety. As a consequence, the woman's superego is less developed and internalized than the man's.

Freud viewed the little girl as a creature in whom phallic strivings were extremely important but inevitably unsatisfied, thus dooming the girl to feelings of perpetual deficiency and inferiority. Yet despite such assertions (which have, not surprisingly, received much criticism in feminist literature), Freud frequently stated that he never really felt that he understood women or the psychology of women. In fact, he reiterated time and again the tentative nature and value of his own portrayal of female sexuality and its vicissitudes.

Freud assumed that female sexuality constituted disappointed male sexuality, rather than the outcome of distinctly female tendencies. Today this view seems perhaps the weakest of suppositions in Freud's theory.

The assumption is made in most early psychoanalytic writing that a little girl's lack of a penis leads not only to envy of the boy's penis and *feelings* of inferiority but also to *actual* inferiority—that is, inferiority in terms of a woman's sense of justice, intellectual curiosity, capacity to implement her ideas independent of a man's approval, and so forth. The notion that penis envy may be a real and commonly observed clinical phenomenon is dismissed because it is so intimately connected, in the minds of many people, with the assumption of generalized female inferiority. This is unfortunate because, as Karen Horney (1926) has suggested, penis envy may be a natural experience for females in the same way that envy of pregnancy, childbirth, motherhood, and suckling is a natural experience for males. Even more important, *experiencing* envy does not doom the little girl to perpetual inferiority. Rather, its occurrence, says Horney, may present her with a complex set of feelings, the working through and mastery of which are central to her growth and development as a mature—certainly not inferior—human being.

Ernest Jones, Freud's early biographer, was one of the first psychoanalysts who argued that "the little girl's Oedipal attachment develops out of her intrinsic, innate femininity undergoing its own maturation processes" (Fliegel, 1973, p. 387). He also suggested that castration anxiety derives from a basic fear of loss of sexuality and that this fear poses as much threat to the little girl as to the little boy (Jones, 1927).

We may usefully reexamine a traditional psychoanalytic concept, one that has received considerable feminist criticism. Instead of eliminating the whole notion of penis envy (which would not explain away its frequent clinical manifestations), we

Though anatomy, it is true, can point out the characteristics of maleness and femaleness, psychology cannot. For psychology the contrast between the sexes fades away into activity and passivity, in which we far too readily identify activity with maleness and passivity with femaleness. (Freud, 1930)

may reject the idea that women feel inferior *as a result of penis envy* and look more deeply into why some women do report feelings of inferiority, especially in their teenage years. The recurring criticism in the feminist literature suggests that Freud's observations about female feelings of inferiority might be reexamined but not dismissed (Richards, 1999), even if his idea of how these feelings originated seems unrealistic.

DYNAMICS: ANXIETY, ANNA FREUD AND THE DEFENSE MECHANISMS, PSYCHOANALYSIS, AND DREAMWORK

Psychoanalysis arose naturally out of years of treating clients. The theory rested on a few central premises. One was the key role of anxiety in the maintenance of neurosis (that is, maladaptive, repetitive behavior).

Anxiety

The psyche's major problem is how to cope with anxiety. **Anxiety** is triggered by an expected or foreseen increase in tension or displeasure; it can develop in any situation (real or imagined) when the threat to some part of the body or psyche is too great to be ignored or mastered.

Events with a potential to cause anxiety include but are not limited to the following:

1. Loss of a desired object—for example, a child deprived of a parent, close friend, or pet.
2. Loss of love—for example, rejection, failure to win back the love or approval of someone who matters to you.
3. Loss of identity—for example, castration fears or loss of self-respect.
4. Loss of love for self—for example, superego disapproval of traits, as well as any act that results in guilt or self-hate.

If the ego is obliged to admit its weakness, it breaks out into anxiety—realistic anxiety in regarding the face of the external world, moral anxiety regarding the super-ego, and neurotic anxiety regarding the strength of the passions in the id. (Freud, 1933)

Humans decrease anxiety in two general ways. The first is to deal with the situation directly. We overcome obstacles, either confront or run from threats, and resolve or come to terms with problems in order to minimize their impact. In these ways, we work to eliminate difficulties, lower the chances of their recurrence, and also decrease the prospects of additional anxiety in the future. In Hamlet's words, we "take up arms against a sea of troubles and by opposing end them."

The alternative approach defends against the anxiety by distorting or denying the situation itself. The ego protects the whole personality against the threat by falsifying the nature of the threat. The ways in which we accomplish the distortions are called **defense mechanisms** (Anna Freud, 1936).

Anna Freud and the Defense Mechanisms

Freud's staunchest supporter was his daughter Anna, who not only made major theoretical contributions to psychoanalysis but also developed, taught, and encouraged this type of treatment with disturbed young children. Perhaps even more important, she pioneered the use of psychoanalytic insights in teaching and helping normal children in difficult life situations.

Anna Freud's descriptions of ego defenses passed into the therapeutic literature and from there into general use with little dissent. According to Sigmund Freud, each of us wards off anxieties with a combination of strategies that arise from our genetic predisposition, external difficulties, and the microculture of our family and community. Defenses used with awareness and self-understanding make life more endurable and more successful. However, when defenses obscure reality and impede our ability to function, they become neurotic and their effects are damaging.

The defense mechanisms described here are repression, denial, rationalization, reaction formation, projection, isolation, regression, and sublimation. All the defenses except sublimation block the direct expression of instinctual needs. Although any of these mechanisms can be and are found in healthy individuals, their presence is an indication of possible neurosis.

Repression.   **Repression** forces a potentially anxiety-provoking event, idea, or perception away from consciousness, thus precluding any possible resolution. "The essence of repression lies simply in turning something away, and keeping it at a distance, from the consciousness" (S. Freud, 1915, p. 147). Unfortunately, the repressed element is still part of the psyche, though unconscious, and remains active. "Repression is never performed once and for all but requires a constant expenditure of energy to maintain the repression, while the repressed constantly tries to find an outlet" (Fenichel, 1945, p. 150).

Hysterical symptoms are often found to have originated in earlier repression. Some psychosomatic ailments, such as asthma, arthritis, and ulcers, may be linked to repression. Excessive lassitude, phobias, and impotence or frigidity may also be derivatives of repressed feelings. For example, if you have strongly ambivalent feelings about your father, you might love him and at the same time wish he were dead. The desire for his death, the accompanying fantasies, and your resulting feelings of guilt and shame might all be unconscious because both your ego and your superego would find the idea unacceptable. Should your father actually die, these conflicting feelings would be still more rigidly repressed. To admit to your ambivalence would mean you felt pleasure at his death, a reaction even more unacceptable to your superego than the original resentment or hostility. In this situation, you might appear unaffected or unmoved by his death, the repression withholding your genuine and appropriate grief and sense of loss as well as your inexpressible hostility.

Denial.   **Denial** is the unwillingness to accept an event that disturbs the ego. Adults have a tendency to "daydream" that certain events are not so, that they didn't really happen. This flight into fantasy can take many forms, some of which seem absurd to the objective observer. The following traditional story is an illustration:

> A woman was brought into court at the request of her neighbor. This neighbor charged that the woman had borrowed and damaged a valuable vase. When it came time for the woman to defend herself, her defense was threefold: "In the first place, I never borrowed the vase. Second, it was chipped when I took it. Finally, your honor, I returned it in perfect condition."

The form of denial most often observed in psychotherapy is the remarkable tendency to remember events incorrectly. An example is the patient who vividly recalls one version of an incident, then at a later time may recall the incident differently and become suddenly aware that the first version was a defensive fabrication.

A casual scanning of Freud leads us to believe that everything in the subconscious is something nasty we have repressed, but perhaps it is the repression that caused the nastiness, rather than whatever it is that we have repressed. (L'Engle, 1995 p. 131)

If the ego employs repression the formation of symptoms relieves it of the task of mastering its conflicts. (A. Freud, 1946, p. 52)

There are times in life when you must face reality directly and then deny it. (Garrison Keillor, 1995)

Sigmund Freud did not claim that his clinical investigations, which led to his theories, were entirely original. In fact, he quotes Charles Darwin's and Friedrich Nietzsche's observations about themselves. Darwin, in his autobiography, noted

> I had during years followed a golden rule, namely, whenever I came across a published fact, a new observation or idea, which ran counter to my general results, I made a memorandum of it without fail and at once; for I had found by experience that such facts and ideas were far more apt to slip the memory than favorable ones. (Darwin in S. Freud, 1901, p. 148)

Nietzsche commented on a different aspect of the same process:

> "I have done that," says my memory. "It is impossible that I should have done it," says my pride, and it remains inexorable. Finally my memory yields. (Nietzsche in S. Freud, 1901, p. 148)

Rationalization.   Rationalization is the process of finding acceptable reasons for unacceptable thoughts or actions. A person presents an explanation that is either ethically acceptable to others or logically consistent with an attitude, action, idea, or feeling that actually arises from other motivating sources. We use rationalization to justify our behavior when in fact the reasons for our actions are not commendable nor do we even understand them. The following statements might be rationalizations (followed by possible unexpressed feelings in parentheses):

> "I'm doing this for your own good." (I want to do this to you. I don't want it done to me. I even want you to suffer a little bit.)
> "The experiment was a logical continuation of my prior work." (It started as a mistake; I was lucky that it worked out.)

Rationalization is a way of accepting pressure from the superego; it disguises our motives, rendering our actions morally acceptable. As an obstacle to growth, it prevents the person who is rationalizing (or anyone else!) from working with, observing, and understanding the genuine, less-commendable motivating forces. When we view a rationalization from the outside, as in the following story, its foolish aspect is obvious:

> "I have chosen," said the mouse, "to like cheese. Such an important decision, needless to say, cannot be arrived at without a sufficient period of careful deliberation. One does not deny the immediate, indefinable aesthetic attraction of the substance. Yet this in itself is possible only to the more refined type of individual—as an example, the brutish fox lacks the sensitive discrimination even to approach cheese.
> "Other factors in the choice are not less susceptible to rational analysis: which is, of course, as it should be.
> "The attractive colour, suitable texture, adequate weight, interestingly different shapes, relatively numerous places of occurrence, reasonable ease of digestion, comparative abundance of variety in nutritional content, ready availability, considerable ease of transport, total absence of side-effects—these and a hundred other easily defined factors abundantly prove my good sense and deep insights, consciously exercised in the making of this wise and deliberate choice." (Shah, 1972, p. 138)

Reaction Formation.   Reaction formation substitutes behaviors or feelings diametrically opposed to the actual wish; it is an explicit and usually unconscious inversion of the wish.

Like other defense mechanisms, reaction formations are developed first in childhood. "As the child becomes aware of sexual excitement which cannot be fulfilled, the sexual 'excitations' evoke opposing mental forces which, in order to suppress this unpleasure effectively, build up the mental dams of disgust, shame and morality" (S. Freud, 1905a, p. 178). Not only is the original idea repressed, but any shame or self-reproach that might arise by admitting such thoughts is also excluded from awareness.

Unfortunately, the side effects of reaction formation may cripple social relationships. The principal identifying characteristics of reaction formation are its excessiveness, its rigidity, and its extravagance. The urge being denied must be repeatedly obscured. The following letter was written to a researcher from an antivivisectionist. It is a clear example of one feeling—compassion toward all living things—used to disguise another feeling: a desire to harm and torture:

> I read [a magazine article] . . . on your work on alcoholism. . . . I am surprised that anyone who is as well educated as you must be to hold the position that you do would stoop to such a depth as to torture helpless little cats in the pursuit of a cure for alcoholics. . . . A drunkard does not want to be cured—a drunkard is just a weak-minded idiot who belongs in the gutter and should be left there. Instead of torturing helpless little cats why not torture the drunks or better still exert your would-be noble effort toward getting a bill passed to exterminate the drunks. . . . My greatest wish is that you have brought home to you a torture that will be a thousand fold greater than what you have, and are doing to the little animals. . . . If you are an example of what a noted psychiatrist should be I'm glad I am just an ordinary human being without letters after my name. I'd rather be just myself with a clear conscience, knowing I have not hurt any living creature, and can sleep without seeing frightened, terrified dying cats—because I know they must die after you have finished with them. No punishment is too great for you and I hope I live to read about your mangled body and long suffering before you finally die—and I'll laugh long and loud. (Masserman, 1961, p. 38)

Reaction formations may be evident in any excessive behavior. The homemaker who is continually cleaning her house may, in reality, be concentrating her awareness on being with and examining dirt. The parent who cannot admit his or her resentment of the children "may interfere so much in their lives, under the pretext of being concerned about their welfare and safety, that [the] overprotection is really a form of punishment" (Hall, 1954, p. 93). Reaction formation masks parts of the personality and restricts a person's capacity to respond to events; the personality may become relatively inflexible.

Projection.   The act of attributing to another person, animal, or object the qualities, feelings, or intentions that originate in oneself is called **projection**. In this defense mechanism, the individual aspects of his or her own personality displaces onto the external environment. The threat is treated as if it were an external force. A person can therefore deal with actual feelings but without admitting or being aware of the fact that the feared idea or behavior is his or her own. The following statements might be projections (the statement in parentheses could be the actual unconscious feeling):

1. All that men/women want is one thing." (I think about sex a lot.)
2. "You can never trust a wop/spic/nigger/WASP/honky/college boy/woman/priest." (I want to take unfair advantage of others.)
3. "You're mad at me." (I'm mad at you.)

personal reflection

DEFENSE MECHANISMS

Recall a time or an event that was psychologically painful—for example, the death of a close friend or relative—or a time when you were deeply humiliated, beaten up, or caught in a crime. Notice first of all your lack of interest in recalling the event clearly and, further, your resistance even to thinking about it. Your tendency may be to say, "I don't want to do this. I can skip this exercise. Why should I think about that again?" If you can, overcome your initial defenses with an act of will and try to recall the event. You may be aware of strong feelings all over again. If it is too difficult to stay focused on the memory, notice instead the ways your mind keeps diverting your attention. Can you begin to see the mechanisms people use to avoid psychic tension?

The person who has built up reaction formations does not develop certain defense mechanisms for use when an instinctual danger threatens; he has changed his personality structure as if this danger were continually present, so that he may be ready whenever the danger occurs. (Fenichel, 1945)

Whenever we characterize something "out there" as evil, dangerous, perverted, and so forth, without acknowledging that these characteristics might also be true for us, we are probably projecting. It is equally true that when we see others as powerful, attractive, capable, and so forth, without appreciating the same qualities in ourselves, we are also projecting. The critical variable in projection is that we do not see in ourselves what seems vivid and obvious in another.

Research into the dynamics of prejudice has shown that people who tend to stereotype others also display little insight into their own feelings. People who deny having a specific personality trait are more critical of that trait when they see it in, or project it onto, others (Sears, 1936).

Isolation. Isolation separates the anxiety-arousing parts of a situation from the rest of the psyche. It is the act of partitioning off, so that little or no emotional reaction remains connected to the event.

When a person discusses problems isolated from the rest of the personality, the events are recounted without feeling, as if they had happened to a third party. This stoic approach can become a dominant style of coping. A person may withdraw more and more into ideas, having less and less contact with his or her own feelings.

Children sometimes play at isolation, dividing their identities into good and bad aspects. They may have a toy animal say and do all kinds of forbidden things. The animal's personality may be tyrannical, rude, sarcastic, and unreasonable. Thus a child may be able to display, through the animal, these "splitting" behaviors that parents would not tolerate under normal circumstances.

Freud believed that the normal prototype of isolation is logical thinking, which also tries to detach the content from the emotional situation in which it is found. Isolation becomes a defense mechanism only when it is used to prevent the ego from accepting anxiety-ridden aspects of situations or relationships (S. Freud, 1926).

Regression. Regression is a reversion to an earlier level of development or to a simpler and more childlike mode of expression. It is a way of alleviating anxiety by withdrawing from realistic thinking into behaviors that have reduced anxiety in the past. Linus, in the *Peanuts* comic strip, always returns to a safe psychological situation when he is under stress; he feels secure when he is holding his blanket. A person who

personal reflection

REGRESSIVE BEHAVIORS

Regression is a primitive way of coping. Although it reduces anxiety, it often leaves the source of the anxiety unresolved. Consider the following extensive list of regressive behaviors suggested by Calvin Hall. See if it includes any of your own behaviors.

Even healthy, well-adjusted people make regressions from time to time in order to reduce anxiety, or, as they say, to blow off steam. They smoke, get drunk, eat too much, lose their tempers, bite their nails, pick their noses, break laws, talk baby talk, destroy property, masturbate, read mystery stories, go to the movies, engage in unusual sexual practices, chew gum and tobacco, dress up as children, drive fast and recklessly, believe in good and evil spirits, take naps, fight and kill one another, bet on the horses, daydream, rebel against or submit to authority, gamble, preen before the mirror, act out their impulses, pick on scapegoats, and do a thousand and one other childish things. Some of these regressions are so commonplace that they are taken to be signs of maturity. Actually they are all forms of regression used by adults. (1954, pp. 95–96)

Do you agree with Hall that all the behaviors on his list are truly regressive?

is regressing may prefer the ice cream flavor he or she was given as a child, or may reread a favorite book, as ways to withdraw from the present.

Sublimation. Sublimation is the process whereby energy originally directed toward sexual or aggressive goals is redirected toward new aims—often artistic, intellectual, or cultural. Sublimation has been called the "successful defense" (Fenichel, 1945). If we think of the original energy as a river that periodically floods, destroying homes and property, sublimation is the building of dams and diversionary channels. These, in turn, may be used to generate electric power, irrigate formerly arid areas, create parks, and open up other recreational opportunities. The original energy of the river is successfully diverted into socially acceptable or culturally sanctioned channels. Sublimation, unlike the other defenses, actually resolves and eliminates the tension.

Sigmund Freud argued that the enormous energy and complexity of civilization results from the desire to find acceptable and sufficient outlets for suppressed energy. Civilization encourages the transcendence of the original drives and, in some cases, creates alternative goals that can be more satisfying to the id than the satisfaction of the original urges. This transformation "places extraordinarily large amounts of force at the disposal of civilized activity, and it does this in virtue of its especially marked characteristic of being able to displace its aim without materially diminishing its intensity" (S. Freud, 1908, p. 187).

Summary of the Defense Mechanisms. The defenses described here are ways for the psyche to protect itself from internal or external tension. The defenses avoid reality (repression), exclude reality (denial), redefine reality (rationalization), or reverse reality (reaction formation). These mechanisms place inner feelings on the outer world (projection), partition reality (isolation), cause a withdrawal from reality (regression), or redirect reality (sublimation). In every case, libidinal energy is necessary to maintain the defense, indirectly limiting the ego's flexibility and strength.

"When a defense becomes very influential, it dominates the ego and curtails its flexibility and its adaptability. Finally, if the defenses fail to hold, the ego has nothing

People are in general not candid over sexual matters. They do not show their sexuality freely, but to conceal it they wear a heavy overcoat woven of a tissue of lies, as though the weather were bad in the world of sexuality. (S. Freud in Malcolm, 1980)

The forces that can be employed for cultural activities are thus to a great extent obtained through the suppression of what are known as the "perverse" elements of sexual excitation. (S. Freud, 1908)

The defensive methods so far discovered by analysis all serve a single purpose—that of assisting the ego in its struggle with the instinctual life.... [I]n all these situations of conflict the ego is seeking to repudiate a part of its own id." (A. Freud, 1936, p. 73)

to fall back upon and is overwhelmed by anxiety (Hall, 1954, p. 96). Each defense takes psychological energy away from more satisfying ego activities.

Psychoanalysis: The Theory

Freud's intention, from his earliest writings, was to better understand aspects of mental life that were obscure and apparently unreachable. He called both the theory and the therapy **psychoanalysis.**

> Psychoanalysis is the name (1) of a procedure for the investigation of mental processes that are almost inaccessible in any other way, (2) of a method (based upon that investigation) for the treatment of neurotic disorders, and (3) of a collection of psychological information obtained along those lines, which is gradually being accumulated into a new scientific discipline. (1923, p. 234)

The more psychoanalysis becomes known, the more will incompetent doctors dabble in it and naturally make a mess of it. This will then be blamed on you and your theory. (Jung, letter to Freud; in McGuire, 1974)

Freud believed that unconscious material remains unconscious only with considerable and continual expenditure of libido. As this material is made accessible, energy is released for the ego to use in healthier pursuits. The release of blocked materials can minimize self-destructive attitudes. The need to be punished or the need to feel inadequate can be lessened by bringing into awareness those early events or fantasies that led to the need. For example, many Americans are concerned about their sexual attractiveness: penises are too short or too thin; breasts are too small, too large, not well formed, and so forth. Most of these beliefs arise during the teenage years or earlier. The unconscious residues of these attitudes are visible in worries over sexual adequacy, desirability, premature ejaculation, frigidity, and a host of related concerns. If these unexpressed fears are explored, exposed, and relieved, the individual can experience a rise in available sexual energy as well as a lowering of overall tension.

The theory of psychoanalysis suggests that it is possible, but difficult, to come to terms with the recurring demands of the id. Analysis works to overcome the natural resistance and to bring the id's painful, repressed memories and ideas back into the conscious (Freud, 1906). "One of the tasks of psychoanalysis, as you know, is to lift the veil of amnesia which shrouds the earliest years of childhood and to bring the expressions of infantile sexual life which are hidden behind it into conscious memory" (1933, p. 28). The goals as described by Freud assume that if one is freed from the inhibitions of the unconscious, the ego establishes new levels of satisfaction in all areas of functioning. Thus the resolution of anxieties rooted in early childhood frees blocked or displaced energy for more realistic and complete gratification of one's needs.

Dreams and Dreamwork

In listening to the free associations of his patients, as well as in his own self-analysis, Freud began to scrutinize the reports and memories of dreams. In *The Interpretation of Dreams* (1900), he examined how dreams help the psyche protect and satisfy itself. Obstacles and unmitigated desires fill daily life. Dreams are a partial balance, both physically and psychologically, between instinctual urges and real-life limitations. Dreaming is a way of channeling unfulfilled desires through consciousness without arousing the physical body.

> A structure of thoughts, mostly very complicated, which has been built up during the day and not brought to settlement—a day remnant—clings firmly even during night to

the energy which it has assumed . . . and thus threatens to disturb sleep. This day remnant is transformed into a dream by the dream-work and in this way rendered harmless to sleep. (Freud in Fodor & Gaynor, 1958, pp. 52–53)

More important than the biological value of dreams are the psychological effects of dreamwork. **Dreamwork** is "the whole of the operations which transform the raw materials of the dream—bodily stimuli, day's residues, dream-thoughts—so as to produce the manifest dream" (LaPlanche & Pontalis, 1973, p. 125). A dream does not simply appear. It develops to meet specific needs, although these are not clearly described by the dream's manifest content.

Almost every dream can be understood as a **wish fulfillment**. The dream is an alternative pathway to satisfy the desires of the id. While awake, the ego strives to increase pleasure and reduce tension. During sleep, unfulfilled needs are sorted, combined, and arranged so that the dream sequences allow additional satisfaction or tension reduction. The id does not care whether satisfaction occurs in physical, sensory reality or in internal, imagined dream reality. In both cases, accumulated energies are discharged.

Repetitive dreams may occur when a daytime event triggers the same kind of anxiety that led to the original dream. For example, an active, happily married woman in her sixties may still dream, from time to time, of going to take a college exam. When she arrives at the classroom, she sees that the examination is over. She has arrived too late. She has this dream when she is anxious over some current difficulty; however, her anxiety is related neither to college nor to examinations, both of which she left behind many years ago.

Many dreams appear unsatisfying; some are depressing, some disturbing, some frightening, and many simply obscure. Many dreams seem to be the reliving of past events, whereas others appear prophetic. Through the detailed analysis of dozens of dreams, linking them to events in the life of the dreamer, Freud concluded that dreamwork is a process of selection, distortion, transformation, inversion, displacement, and other modifications of an original wish. These changes render the modified wish acceptable to the ego even if the original wish is totally unacceptable to waking consciousness. Freud suggested reasons for the permissiveness in dreams in which we act beyond the moral restrictions of our waking lives. In dreams we kill, maim, or destroy enemies, relatives, or friends; we act out perversions and take as sexual partners a wide range of people. In dreams, we combine people, places, and occasions that would be an impossible mix in our waking world.

Dreams attempt to fulfill wishes, but they are not always successful. "Under certain conditions, the dream can only achieve its end in a very incomplete way or has to abandon it entirely; an unconscious fixation to the trauma seems to head the list of these obstacles to the dream functions" (Freud, 1933, p. 29).

Within the context of psychoanalysis, the therapist aids the patient in interpreting dreams to facilitate the recovery of unconscious material. Freud made certain generalizations about special kinds of dreams (for example, falling dreams, flying dreams, swimming dreams, and dreams about fire), but he specified that the general rules are not always valid. An individual's own dream associations are more important than any preconceived set of rules of interpretation. Critics of Freud often suggest that he exaggerated the sexual components of dreams to conform to his overall theory, but Freud's rejoinder is clear: "I have never maintained the assertion which has often been ascribed to me that dream-interpretation shows that all dreams have

We recognize the soundness of the wish-fulfillment theory up to a certain point, but we go beyond it. In our view it does not exhaust the meaning of the dream. (Jung, letter to Freud; in McGuire, 1974)

A dream then, is a psychosis, with all the absurdities, delusions and illusions of a psychosis. No doubt it is a psychosis which has only a short duration, which is harmless and even performs a useful function. (Freud, 1940)

Dreams are not to be likened to the unregulated sounds that rise from a musical instrument struck by the blow of some external force instead of a player's hand; they are not meaningless, they are not absurd; . . . they can be inserted into the chain of intelligible waking mental acts; they are constructed by a highly complicated activity of the mind. (Freud, 1900)

Dreams are the true interpreters of our inclinations, but art is required to sort and understand them. (Montaigne, 1580, Essays)

Dreams are real while they last—can we say more of life? (Havelock Ellis)

personal reflection

INVESTIGATE YOUR OWN DREAMS

Make a dream journal by keeping a pad of paper by your bed. In the morning, before you do anything else, make a few notes about your dreams. Even if you have never remembered dreams before, this procedure will help you to recall them. It has been shown that students given this assignment recall dreams regularly within a few days.

Later in the day, write out your dreams in more detail. Include your associations with particular aspects of your dreams. See if these associations point to possible meanings. For example, might your dreams be attempts at wish fulfillment? Try to guess what various segments relate to in your life. Pay attention to those fragments that seem to be part of your "day residue." Do you notice anything that reflects your desires or attitudes toward others?

Keep this journal for several weeks. As you read other parts of this text, you will learn other ways to analyze dreams. From time to time, go over your dream journal, and see if you can make new interpretations. Notice especially any recurrent themes or patterns. (The chapter on Jung provides a different approach to recording dreams.)

---

a sexual content or are derived from sexual motive forces" (Freud, 1925a, p. 47). He emphasized that dreams are neither random nor accidental but a way to satisfy unfulfilled wishes.

A different kind of criticism is that Freud's ideas were severely limited by his lack of knowledge of non-European societies. In India, for example, "the self [and its dreams] are by no means so clearly limited as it is for us" (O'Flaherty, 1984, p. 22), and in Native American groups the function and the understanding of dreams stand outside Freud's speculations. "In most of the 16 Native American models, there is no distinct separation between the dreamed world and the lived world. . . . In contrast, Western models of dreaming sharply demarcate dreaming from waking, and see dreaming as a biologically driven altered state of consciousness which, none-the-less, may produce useful information in the hands of a skilled interpreter" (Krippner & Thompson, 1996). Sand (1999) charges that Freud's injunction against the use of symbolism, except for sexual content, inhibited psychoanalysts' freer use of dream interpretation. Not at all outdated, Freud's penetration of the world of dreams is still vital and a matter of concern and debate (Kramer et al., 1994).

"The first thing I heard about Freud was that there was a man in Vienna, a doctor of neurology who said in earnest that when a girl dreamed of electric light bulbs she meant in reality a penis." (Wittels, 1995, p. 28)

STRUCTURE

Freud considered almost every aspect of mental and social life. However, he treated important areas, including energy, the body, social relationships, emotions, intellect, self, and the special role of therapy, in different ways at different times in his life. What follows is an attempt to create order out of enormous complexity.

Energy

The availability of energy is at the core of Freud's concepts of the unconscious, psychological development, personality, and neurosis. "His theories on impulses deal primarily with the source of mental energy; his theories on psychosexual development and the defenses deal with the diversion of energy; and his theories of the id, ego, and superego deal with conflicts of energy and the effects of such conflict" (Cohen, 1982, p. 4).

Body

The body is the core of experience. As Sulloway points out, "It was Freud's continued appeal to biological assumptions that justified his personal conviction that he had finally created a universally valid theory of human thought and behavior" (1979, p. 419).

> The ego is first and foremost a body ego. (Freud, 1937)

Moreover, the primary focuses of energy are through the various forms of sexual expression (oral, anal, and genital). Maturity is partially defined as the capacity for achieving quality of expression in genital sexuality. It is unfortunate that many of Freud's critics never looked at his entire theory but instead became obsessed with his reintroduction of physical and sexual concerns into the field of so-called mental functioning.

In spite of Freud's recognition of the centrality of the body, his own writings on therapy rarely discuss it. Perhaps the cultural denial of the body that characterized the age in which he lived colored his own apparent lack of reporting about the gestures, postures, and physical expressions exhibited by his patients. Many later Freudians, such as Erik Erikson and Frederick Perls, as well as theorists who broke from Freud, such as Carl Jung and Wilhelm Reich, paid more attention to the actual physical body but less attention to biological theories.

Social Relationships

Adult interactions and relationships are greatly influenced by early childhood experiences. The first relationships, those that occur within the nuclear family, are often the defining ones. All later relationships are influenced by the ways those initial relationships were formed and maintained. The basic patterns of child–mother, child–father, and child–sibling are the prototypes against which subsequent encounters are unconsciously measured. Later relationships are, to some degree, recapitulations of the dynamics, tensions, and gratifications that occurred within the original family.

> The all-inclusive nature of sex energy has not yet been correctly understood by psychologists. In fact, the very term *reproductive* or *sex energy* is a misnomer. Reproduction is but one of the aspects of the life energy, of which the other theater of activity is the brain. (Krishna, 1974)

Our choices in life—of lovers, friends, bosses, even our enemies—derive from our parent–child bonds. The natural rivalries are recapitulated in our sex roles and in the way we accommodate the demands of others. Over and over again, we play out the dynamics begun in our homes, frequently picking as partners people who reawaken in us unresolved aspects of our early needs. For some, these are conscious choices. Others choose without conscious knowledge of the underlying dynamics.

> I confess that plunging into sexuality in theory and practice is not to my taste. But what have my taste and feeling about what is seemly and what is unseemly to do with the question of what is true? (Breuer in Sulloway, 1979, p. 80)

People shy away from this aspect of Freudian theory because it suggests that one's future choices are beyond one's control. The issue turns on the question of to what degree childhood experience determines adult choices. For example, one critical period in developing relationships occurs during the phallic stage, when both sexes first confront their growing erotic feelings toward their parents and the concomitant inability to gratify these urges. According to Freudian theory, even as the resulting Oedipal complications are resolved, these dynamics continue to affect the individual's relationships.

Relationships are built on a foundation of the residual effects of intense early experiences. Teenage, young adult, and adult dating, as well as friendship and marriage patterns, are partly a reworking of unresolved childhood issues.

personal reflection

PATTERNS IN YOUR LIFE

Here is a way to look at your current relationships as they relate to your relationships with your parents.

Part 1

1. Make a list of some of the people you have liked or loved most in your life—excluding your parents. List men and women separately.
2. Describe desirable and undesirable aspects of each person.
3. Notice, reflect on, or record the similarities and differences in your lists. Are there certain traits common to the men and the women?

Part 2

1. Make a list of the desirable and undesirable characteristics of your parents.
2. List the desirable and undesirable characteristics of your parents as you saw them when you were a child. (The two lists may or may not overlap.)

Part 3

Compare and contrast the list of attributes of your parents with those of the other important people in your life.

Emotions

Freud revealed, in an age that had worshiped reason and denied the value and the power of emotion, that we are not primarily rational animals but are driven by powerful emotional forces, the genesis of which is often unconscious. Emotions are our avenues for tension release and appreciation of pleasure. Emotions may also serve the ego by helping it to keep certain memories out of awareness. Strong emotional responses may actually mask a childhood trauma. A feeling of disgust about a food that one has not even tasted in years, for example, may cover the memory of an unhappy time when that food was served. A phobic reaction effectively prevents a person from approaching an object or class of objects that might trigger a more threatening source of anxiety.

Primarily through observing both the appropriate and inappropriate expressions of emotion, Freud found the keys to uncovering and understanding the motivating forces within the unconscious.

Intellect

The intellect is one tool available to the ego. The person is most free who can use reason when it is expedient and whose emotional life is open to conscious inspection. Such a person is not driven by unfulfilled remnants of past events but can respond directly to each situation, balancing individual preferences against the restrictions imposed by the culture.

The most striking and probably the strongest emotional force in Freud was his passion for truth and his uncompromising faith in reason. Freud considered reason the only human capacity that could help solve the problem of existence or at least ameliorate the suffering inherent in human life.

For Freud, as for the age in which he lived, the impact of Darwin's work cannot be underestimated. An unquestioned goal of the time was to prove that rational thought placed human beings above the beasts. Much of the resistance to Freud's work arose from the evidence that people were in fact less reasonable and less in control of their emotions than anyone had suspected. Freud's own hope and personal belief was that reason was primary and that the intellect was the most, if not the only, important tool that consciousness possessed to control its darker side.

Freud realized that any aspect of unconscious existence, raised into the light of consciousness, might be dealt with rationally: "Where id is, there let ego be" (1933, p. 80) was his shorthand way to express this insight. Where the irrational, instinctual urges dominate, let them be exposed, moderated, and dominated by the ego. If the original drive will not be suppressed, the ego, using the intellect, must devise safe and sufficient methods for gratification.

Self

The self is the total being: the body and the instincts, as well as the conscious and unconscious parts of the mind. A self not limited by the body or detached from it had no place in Freud's biological beliefs. When confronted with such a metaphysical (or spiritual) image of humankind, Freud asserted that this was not within his province as a scientist. Psychoanalysts have since moved past Freud's position and have written extensively about the self.

THERAPIST/THERAPY

We have been chiefly concerned with Freud's general theory of personality. Freud himself, however, was involved in the practical applications of his work—the practice of psychoanalysis. Psychoanalysis aims to help the patient establish the best possible level of ego functioning, given the inevitable conflicts arising from the external environment, the superego, and the relentless instinctual demands of the id. Kenneth Colby, a former trainer of analysts, describes the goal of the analytic procedure:

> In speaking of the goal of psychotherapy, the term "cure" . . . requires definition. If by "cure" we mean relief of the patient's current neurotic difficulties, then that is certainly our goal. If by "cure" we mean a lifelong freedom from emotional conflict and psychological problems, then that cannot be our goal. Just as a person may suffer pneumonia, a fracture, and diabetes during his lifetime and require particular medication and separate treatment for each condition, so another person may experience at different times a depression, impotence, and a phobia, each requiring psychotherapy. . . . (1951, p. 4)

It is useful to keep in mind that therapy, as used by any of the theorists covered in this book, does not "cure" past problems but may help prevent future ones.

The Role of the Psychoanalyst

The therapist's task is to help the patient recall, recover, and reintegrate unconscious materials so that the patient's current life can become more satisfying. Freud says:

> We pledge him to obey the *fundamental rule* of analysis which is henceforward to govern his behavior towards us. He is to tell us not only what he can say intentionally and willingly, what will give him relief like a confession, but everything else as well that comes into

Reason, so Freud felt, is the only tool—or weapon—we have to make sense of life, to dispense with illusions . . . to become independent of fettering authorities, and thus to establish our own authority. (Fromm, 1959)

To stand firm against this general assault by the patient requires the analyst to have been fully and completely analyzed himself. . . . The analyst himself . . . must know and be in control of even the most recondite weaknesses of his own character; and this is impossible without a fully completed analysis. (Ferenczi, 1955)

personal reflection

EARLY MEMORIES

Freud found that early memories often were indicative of current personal issues. You can try testing this assumption by doing the following exercise.

Find a partner. One of you will recall your earliest memory while the other records it on paper. (You will trade roles, so don't worry about who goes first.)

1. The speaker should sit so as not to be looking at the recorder. Recall your earliest memory or any very early memory. Tell it to the person who is the recorder. Talk no more than five minutes. The more clearly and vividly you can recall the memory, the more you may gain from this exercise. Other memories may emerge in addition to the one you are describing. Feel free to mention them as well. Remember, it's the recorder's task to take notes while the speaker talks about past events. Do not interrupt. Pay attention to the importance the speaker puts on any aspect of a memory.
2. After five minutes, stop. Without any discussion, switch roles. The person who was the speaker is now writing down the partner's memories. At the end of another five minutes, stop. Silently, for a minute or so, think about what you have said and what you have heard.
3. Discuss your notes with each other. Point out any implications and connections you observe. Note differences in feelings expressed by your partner. Try to relate aspects of these first memories to current events in your life.

his head, even if it is *disagreeable* for him to say it, even if it seems to him *unimportant* or actually *nonsensical.* (1940, p. 31)

See our **web** site for further discussion of this topic.

The post-Freudians, however, extended the range of clients and conditions to be treated under the psychoanalytic umbrella in many ways. See Chapter 4 on Horney who said she did not break with Freud, although many late commentators believe her work was as strong a departure from his thinking as those who formally repudiated him.

EVALUATION AND CURRENT INFLUENCE

We have presented an overview of the vast and complex theoretical structure that Freud developed. This chapter does not attempt to include the numerous shadings and elaborations of his followers, disciples, detractors, critics, and clients. Instead, we have organized and simplified the outlines of what was, at its inception, a radical and innovative point of view. Freud threw down a gauntlet that few thinkers have left unchallenged. Most of the theorists in this book acknowledge their debt to Freud, both those who agree with him and those who oppose him.

Freud's thought has had such influence that only now, a hundred years after he brought psychoanalysis into being, have we begun to treat him as a historical figure rather than as a revered, feared, or hated father. His work captured the imagination of academics in many disciplines and came to permeate our contemporary notion of what it means to be human. For years, then, writers have approached Freud either as someone to whom they owe great allegiance or as a kind of false authority who must be unmasked. Only more recently has Freud been considered in a more balanced way. A hundred years after the debut of psychoanalysis we have a greater chance to see both how progressive Freud was for his time as well as how his thoughts sometime reflect the prejudices of his era. In this way, contemporary thought can now embrace Freud's insights without a reactive need to denounce him for his limits and to appreciate the magnitude of Freud's genius while recognizing the need for revision and extension of his seminal ideas.

Freud's ideas continue to influence psychology, literature, art, anthropology, sociology, and medicine. Many of his ideas, such as the importance of dreams and the vitality of the unconscious processes, are widely accepted. Other facets of his theory, such as the relationships among the ego, the id, and the superego, or the role of the Oedipus complex in adolescent development, are extensively debated. Still other parts of his work, including his analysis of female sexuality and his theories on the origins of civilization, have been widely criticized.

Those who have followed the Freudian tradition have not stood still, and the shape of contemporary psychoanalysis is multifaceted and evolving. Over the past century this progressive dialogue has led to multiple branches of neo-Freudian analysis. To take a single example, Freud inspires, among others Melanie Klein (1957). She develops his ideas on the death instinct and the internal world of fantasy. The work of Klein inspires major thinkers including Winnicott (1971). Also see *our web site*. Meltzer (1973), Joseph (1983), Rosenfeld (1987), and Bion (1962). His work has led to the emergence of a group of Bionian analysts. And so on. A veritable torrent of books and articles about Freud's ideas continues, as well as a stream of journals and monographs about psychoanalytic therapy. More works are published about Freud and his ideas each year than on all the other Western theorists in this book combined. An international growth industry of Freudian journals, institutes, and presses constitutes a world unto themselves. While most of this community is self-involved and self-contained, Freud's large presence still reasserts itself into the general culture from time to time. In 1993, for example, he was on the cover of *Time* magazine. Later, the Library of Congress scheduled a large exhibit on the impact of his ideas. Shortly thereafter, however, that exhibit was shelved because of the amount of virulent criticism leveled against it. Still later, it was revived and hugely popular.

The current analytic world boasts numerous major schools of psychoanalysis. Areas of agreement and radical dispute arise between these different schools, yet all owe significant debts to Freud's pioneering insights. Within France, Lacan's work is a dominant influence. In England and South America, Klein and Bion are major figures. Winnicott, through his work on the emergence of the self in relationship to the mother's care, gives rise to the "middle school" of psychoanalysis. In America, all these schools are in dialogue with the two prominent American schools: American Ego psychology and American Relational psychology.

Although we cannot predict how Freudian theory will be judged historically, we maintain that Freud's ideas are of no less urgent concern today than they were during his lifetime (S. Freud, 1998). Those who choose to study the mind or try to understand other human beings must make their peace with Freud's basic assertions through an examination of their own inner experience. Freud's fundamental assumption is that all behavior is linked together, with no psychological accidents—that your choice of persons, places, foods, and amusements stems from experiences you recall or that you do not or will not remember. All thoughts and all behaviors have meaning. We recognize that at certain times in a person's life Freud's picture of the role of the conscious and unconscious seems like a personal revelation. The stunning impact of his thinking can illuminate an aspect of your own or someone else's character and send you scurrying after more of his books. At other times, he seems of no use; his ideas seem distant, convoluted, and irrelevant.

At either time, Freud is a figure to be dealt with; he cannot be treated lightly, nor dismissed as out of fashion. Whatever your response to Freud's ideas, Freud's advice would be to regard your response as an indicator of your own state of mind as well as a reasoned reaction to his work.

Psychoanalysis uses a set of tools for personal analysis that includes lengthy self-examination, reflection, and dream analysis, while also noting recurrent patterns of thought and behavior. Freud has written how he used the tools, what he discovered, and what he concluded from his discoveries. Although the conclusions remain debatable, the tools lie at the core of a dozen other systems and may be the most lasting of his contributions to the study of personality.

Contemporary analysis is increasingly aware of the subjectivity of the analyst and how this inevitably shapes the treatment process. In contrast to more traditional schools of analysis, awareness is growing of impossibility of analysts functioning as neutral and objective observers. With this awareness comes an appreciation for the potentially damaging effects that a blank-screen approach can have on treatment. Consensus also is growing that the analyst's emotional response to the patient, called *countertransference,* is not only inevitable but a necessary source of insight into the patient's subjectivity (Carnochan, 2001). Contemporary psychoanalysis is a far cry from the film stereotypes of the pipe smoking, turgid analyst. Contemporary psychoanalysis is perhaps still the most rigorous and far-reaching therapy available.

Influence

Freud's influence, though, extends well beyond the world of contemporary psychoanalysis. Over the years, numerous analysts have broken from the analytic community. Within the first circle of analysts, Jung (Chapter 2), Adler (Chapter 3), and Reich (Web Chapter) all began as favored students of Freud, but ended up falling out with him and developing their own schools of psychotherapy. Again and again, major developments within contemporary psychotherapy have been inspired and shaped by a creative and sometimes painful conflict with the Freudian tradition and establishment. In more recent years, humanistic psychotherapies have been developed by analysts who sought to further extend the range of therapeutic activity. Rollo May, Carl Rogers (Chapter 11), and others have all been inspired by and reacted against the potentials and problems of the Freudian tradition.

It is only too certain that I shall not get the Nobel Prize. Psychoanalysis has several good enemies among the authorities on whom the prize depends.... though the money would be welcome.... Anna and I have agreed that one is not bound to have everything and have decided I am to renounce the prize, and she the journey to Stockholm to collect it. (Freud in a letter to Arnold Zwieg in 1938, quoted by Benjamin, 2003, p. 738.) Freud was nominated for a Nobel Prize eleven times in medicine, once in literature.

Beyond the world of psychotherapy, Freud has shaped the intellectual terrain in significant ways. Literary critics and philosophers have taken up his work. At many universities, the English department, rather than the psychology department, may be where students may first encounter Freud. The way we read fiction has changed partly because of Freud's theories on character and development. We can no longer read Hamlet without considering his Oedipal struggle with his father and uncle. In political theory, Freudian ideas have been tied to a range of ideas. During the sixties the interface between Marx and Freud was at the forefront contemporary thought. In cinema, Freudian ideas were taken up by directors such as Hitchcock. (For example, the Norman Bates character in *Psycho* is caught in a pathological Oedipal attachment to his mother.) It is fair to say that no intellectual or cultural discipline remained untouched by the Freudian revolution. At first, these points of influence were overt, but eventually, as the first wave of excitement crested and passed, the influence became more naturally woven into the material. We can see this in a more recent film, *Being John Malkovich.* The central premise of this film involves a tunnel in an office building that allows the protagonist to inhabit

"Then why were you so frightened when you found them together? Did you understand it? Did you know what was going on?"

"Oh no. I didn't understand anything at that time. I was only sixteen. I don't know what I was frightened about."

"Fräulein Katharina, if you could remember now what was happening in you at that time, when you had your first attack, what you thought about it—it would help you."

"Yes, if I could. But I was so frightened that I've forgotten everything."

(Translated into the terminology of our "Preliminary Communication". . . , this means: "The affect itself created a hypnoid state, whose products were then cut off from associative connection with the ego-consciousness.")

"Tell me, Fräulein. Can it be that the head that you always see when you lose your breath is Franziska's head, as you saw it then?"

"Oh no, she didn't look so awful. Besides, it's a man's head."

"Or perhaps your uncle's?"

"I didn't see his face as clearly as that. It was too dark in the room. And why should he have been making such a dreadful face just then?"

"You're quite right."

(The road suddenly seemed blocked. Perhaps something might turn up in the rest of her story.)

"And what happened then?"

"Well, those two must have heard a noise, because they came out soon afterwards. I felt very bad the whole time. I always kept thinking about it. Then two days later it was a Sunday and there was a great deal to do and I worked all day long. And on the Monday morning I felt giddy again and was sick, and I stopped in bed and was sick without stopping for three days."

We (Breuer and I) had often compared the symptomatology of hysteria with a pictographic script which has become intelligible after the discovery of a few bilingual inscriptions. In that alphabet being sick means disgust. So I said: "If you were sick three days later, I believe that means that when you looked into the room you felt disgusted."

"Yes, I'm sure I felt disgusted," she said reflectively, "but disgusted at what?"

"Perhaps you saw something naked? What sort of state were they in?"

"It was too dark to see anything; besides they both of them had their clothes on. Oh, if only I knew what it was I felt disgusted at!"

I had no idea either. But I told her to go and tell me whatever occurred to her, in the confident expectation that she would think of precisely what I needed to explain the case.

Well, she went on to describe how at last she reported her discovery to her aunt, who found that she was changed and suspected her of concealing some secret. There followed some very disagreeable scenes between her uncle and aunt, in the course of which the children came to hear a number of things which opened their eyes in many ways and which it would have been better for them not to have heard. At last her aunt decided to move with her children and niece and take over the present inn, leaving her uncle alone with Franziska, who had meanwhile become pregnant. After this, however, to my astonishment she dropped these threads and began to tell me two sets of older stories, which went back two or three years earlier than the traumatic moment. The first set related to occasions on which the same uncle had made sexual advances to her herself, when she was only fourteen years old. She described how she had once gone with him on an expedition down into the valley in the winter and had spent the night in the inn there. He sat in the bar drinking and playing cards, but she felt sleepy and went up to bed early in the room they were to share on the upper floor. She was not quite asleep when he came up; then she fell asleep again and woke up suddenly "feeling his body" in the bed. She jumped up and remonstrated with him: "What are you up to, Uncle? Why don't you stay in your own bed?" He tried to pacify her: "Go on, you silly girl, keep still. You don't know how nice it is"—"I don't like your 'nice' things; you don't even let one sleep in peace." She remained standing by the door, ready to take refuge outside in the passage, till at last he gave up and went to sleep himself. Then she went back to her own bed and slept till morning. From the way in which she reported having defended herself it seems to follow that she did not clearly recognize the attack as a sexual one. When I asked her if she knew what he was trying to do to her, she replied: "Not at the time." It had become clear to her much later on, she said; she had resisted because it was unpleasant to be disturbed in one's sleep and "because it wasn't nice."

I have been obliged to relate this in detail, because of its great importance for understanding everything that followed.—She went on to tell me of yet other experiences of somewhat later date: how she had once again had to defend herself against him in an inn when he was completely drunk, and similar stories. In answer to a question as to whether on these occasions she had felt anything resembling her later loss of breath, she answered with decision that she had every time felt the pressure on her eyes and chest, but with nothing like the strength that had characterized the scene of discovery.

Immediately she had finished this set of memories she began to tell me a second set, which dealt with occasions on which she had noticed something between her uncle and Franziska. Once the whole family had spent the night in their clothes in a hay loft and she was woken up suddenly by a noise; she thought she noticed that her uncle, who had been lying between her and Franziska, was turning away, and that Franziska was just lying down. Another time they were stopping the night at the inn at the village of N———; she and her uncle were in one room and Franziska in an adjoining one. She woke up suddenly in the night and saw a tall white figure by the door, on the point of turning the handle: "Goodness, is that you, Uncle? What are you doing at the door?"—"Keep quiet. I was only looking for something."—"But the way out's by the other door."—"I'd just made a mistake" . . . and so on.

I asked her if she had been suspicious at that time. "No, I didn't think anything about it; I only just noticed it and thought no more about it." When I enquired whether she had been frightened on these occasions too, she replied that she thought so, but she was not so sure of it this time.

At the end of these two sets of memories she came to a stop. She was like someone transformed. The sulky, unhappy face had grown lively, her eyes were bright, she was lightened and exalted. Meanwhile the understanding of her case had become clear to me. The later part of what she had told me, in an apparently aimless fashion, provided an admirable explanation of her behaviour at the scene of the discovery. At that time she had carried about with her two sets of experiences which she remembered but did not understand, and from which she drew no inferences. When she caught sight of the couple in intercourse, she at once established a connection between the new impression and these two sets of recollections, she began to understand them and at the same time to fend them off. There then followed a short period of working-out, of "incubation," after which the symptoms of conversion set in, the vomiting as a substitute for moral and physical disgust. This solved the riddle. She had not been disgusted by the sight of the two people but by the memory which that sight had stirred up in her. And, taking everything into account, this could only be the memory of the attempt on her at night when she had "felt her uncle's body."

So when she had finished her confession I said to her: "I know now what it was you thought when you looked into the room. You thought: 'Now he's doing with her what he wanted to do with me that night and those other times.' That was what you were disgusted at, because you remembered the feeling when you woke up in the night and felt his body."

"It may well be," she replied, "that that was what I was disgusted at and that that was what I thought."

"Tell me just one thing more. You're a grown-up girl now and know all sorts of things . . . "

"Yes, now I am."

"Tell me just one thing. What part of his body was it that you felt that night?" But she gave me no more definite answer. She smiled in an embarrassed way, as though she had been found out, like someone who is obliged to admit that a fundamental position has been reached where there is not much more to be said. I could imagine what the tactile sensation was which she had later learnt to interpret. Her facial expression seemed to me to be saying that she supposed that I was right in my conjecture. But I could not penetrate further, and in any case I owed her a debt of gratitude for having made it so much easier for me to talk to her than to the prudish ladies of my city practice, who regard whatever is natural as shameful.

Thus the case was cleared up.—But stop a moment! What about the recurrent hallucination of the head, which appeared during her attacks and struck terror into her? Where did it come from? I proceeded to ask her about it, and, as though her knowledge, too, had been extended by our conversation, she promptly replied: "Yes, I know now. The head is my uncle's head—I recognize it now—but not from that time. Later, when all the disputes had broken out, my uncle gave way to a senseless rage against me. He kept saying that it was all my fault: if I hadn't chattered, it would never have come to a divorce. He kept threatening he would do something to me; and if he caught sight of me at a distance his face would get distorted with rage and he would make for me with his hand raised. I always ran away from him, and always felt terrified that he would catch me some time unawares. The face I always see now is his face when he was in a rage."

This information reminded me that her first hysterical symptom, the vomiting, had passed away; the anxiety attack remained and acquired a fresh content. Accordingly, what we were dealing with was a hysteria which had to a considerable extent been abreacted. And in fact she had reported her discovery to her aunt soon after it happened.

"Did you tell your aunt the other stories—about his making advances to you?"

"Yes. Not at once, but later on, when there was already talk of a divorce. My aunt said: 'We'll keep that in reserve. If he causes trouble in the Court, we'll say that too.'"

I can well understand that it should have been precisely this last period—when there were more and more agitating scenes in the house and when her own state ceased to interest her aunt, who was entirely occupied with the dispute—that it should have been this period of accumulation and retention that left her the legacy of the mnemic symbol (of the hallucinated face).

I hope this girl, whose sexual sensibility had been injured at such an early age, derived some benefit from our conversation. I have not seen her since.[2] (Breuer & Freud, 1895, pp. 125–134)

CHAPTER HIGHLIGHTS

- The body is the sole source of all consciousness.
- Nothing occurs randomly—least of all the individual's mental processes. All thoughts and all behaviors have meaning.
- The conscious is only a small part of the mind. The unconscious and the preconscious, the other components of consciousness, are less exposed and explored. A psychic process is called unconscious when its existence is inferred from its effects. The preconscious is a part of the unconscious, the section that contains the available memories.
- Human impulses do not predetermine the outcome of an action. The two basic impulses are described as the sexual (life supporting) and the aggressive, or destructive (death encouraging).
- One's personality structure is composed of the id (it), the ego (I), and the superego (above I). The overarching goal of the psyche is to maintain an acceptable level of dynamic equilibrium that maximizes the pleasure felt as tension reduction.
- The primary goal of psychoanalysis is to strengthen the ego, to make it independent of the overly strict concerns of the superego, and to increase its capacity to deal with material formerly repressed or hidden.
- Freud proposed a psychosexual description of the developmental stages. Modes of gratification of desires and physical areas of gratification shift through each developmental stage. In his sequence, the individual would pass first through the oral, anal, and phallic stages. Issues of the Oedipal phase occur within the phallic stage. The latency period follows, until the individual emerges into the genital stage of development. Fixation occurs when a person becomes overly involved in a particular stage.
- Freud, after acknowledging that he didn't fully understand women, proposed a biological reason for the feelings of inferiority reported by women undergoing psychoanalysis. His speculations, especially that female sexuality was "disappointed" male sexuality, have been roundly attacked since their first publication.
- Dreams are used in psychoanalysis as an aid to recover unconscious material. Neither random nor accidental, dreams are considered to be one way to satisfy unfulfilled wishes.
- Anxiety is the major coping problem for the psyche. If threats to the body or psyche are not dealt with directly, defense mechanisms come into play. The expenditure of energy necessary to maintain the defenses effectively limits the flexibility and strength of the ego.
- The concept of energy flow lies at the center of Freud's theories, linking concepts of the unconscious, psychological development, personality, and neurosis.
- Responses to tension are both mental and physical. Libidinal energy is derived from physical energy. Basic drives arise from somatic sources.
- Early childhood experiences greatly influence teenage, young adult, and adult patterns of interacting and relating. Relationships that occur in the nuclear family are the defining ones throughout an individual's later life.
- We are not primarily rational animals. Rather, we are often unconsciously driven by powerful emotional forces that may provide avenues for the release of tension and the appreciation of pleasure, and may serve to keep certain memories out of awareness.

[2] *(Footnote added, 1924)* I venture after the lapse of so many years to lift the veil of discretion and reveal the fact that Katharina was not the niece but the daughter of the landlady. The girl fell ill, therefore, as a result of sexual attempts on the part of her own father. Distortions like the one which I introduced in the present instance should be altogether avoided in reporting a case history. From the point of view of understanding the case, a distortion of this kind is not, of course, a matter of such indifference as would be shifting the scene from one mountain to another.

- Given the conflicts inevitably arising from the external environment, the superego, and the relentless instinctual demands of the id, the aim of therapy is to help establish the best possible level of ego functioning.
- The therapist's role is to help a patient recall, recover, and reintegrate unconscious materials, so that the patient's life can become more satisfying.

KEY CONCEPTS

Aggressive energy Energy assumed to have the same general properties as libido. It is also termed the energy of the death impulse.

Anal stage Developmental stage from ages 2 to 4. Both the anal sphincter and the bladder are brought into awareness as areas of tension and gratification. A natural interest in self-discovery is prompted by toilet training.

Anxiety The major coping problem for the psyche. Anxiety is triggered by an expected or foreseen increase in tension or displeasure, real or imagined, when a threat to the body or psyche is too great to be ignored, discharged, or mastered.

Cathexis The process by which the available libidinal energy in the psyche is attached or invested in a person, idea, or thing. Once it is released this same energy may be redirected and become available for other current needs.

Defense mechanisms Ways in which the ego attempts to protect the whole personality against threat.

- **Denial** Defense mechanism in which a person is unwilling to accept an event that disturbs the ego.
- **Isolation** Defense mechanism of partitioning, or separating, the anxiety-arousing parts of a situation from the rest of the psyche. Little or no emotional reaction remains connected to the event.
- **Projection** Defense mechanism in which a person attributes to another person, animal, or object the qualities, feelings, or intentions that originate in the self. The projection is then treated as if it were an external force.
- **Rationalization** Defense mechanism in which the individual finds acceptable reasons for unacceptable thoughts or actions. It disguises motives, rendering our actions morally justifiable, thus bowing to pressure from the superego.
- **Reaction formation** Defense mechanism that replaces behaviors or feelings with those that are diametrically opposite. The result is an explicit and usually unconscious inversion of the wish.
- **Regression** Defense mechanism that is manifested as reversion to an earlier level of development, or to a mode of expression that is simpler or more childlike.
- **Repression** Defense mechanism that forces a potentially anxiety-provoking idea, event, or perception away from consciousness, precluding possible resolution.
- **Sublimation** Differs from the other Freudian defenses in that the tension may actually be resolved and elimi-

nated by redirecting it to other channels. Intellectual, artistic, or cultural goals may receive the energies previously directed toward sexual or aggressive ends.

Dreamwork A process of distortion, selection, inversion, displacement, transformation, or other modifications of an original wish to render it acceptable to the ego, even if the original wish is not.

Ego (I) The part of the psyche that develops to ensure the health, safety, and sanity of the personality as it mediates between demands of the id and external reality. The ego is responsive to opportunities, whereas the id is responsive only to needs.

Fixation A response that occurs when there is excessive involvement in a particular developmental stage. In fixation, there is a tendency to seek gratification of needs in simpler or childlike ways, rather than as an adult.

Genital stage Developmental stage from puberty to adulthood. Libidinal energy returns to the genitals. Awareness of their separate sexual identities and the search for ways to satisfy erotic and interpersonal needs occurs for boys and girls.

Id (it) The original biological core out of which the rest of the personality emerges. Although primitive and unorganized, the id contains the reservoir of energy for all parts of the personality. It is not changed by experience, nor is it in contact with the external world. Its goals are to reduce tension, to increase pleasure, and to minimize discomfort. The id's contents are almost entirely unconscious.

Impulses (drives) Pressures to act without conscious thought toward particular ends. Needs are the physical aspects and wishes are the mental aspects of impulses. There are four components to all impulses: source, aim, impetus, and object.

Latency period Developmental period from ages 5 to 6 until the onset of puberty. The individual's focus shifts from relationship with parents to relationships with peers, and to sports, school activities, and other skills. The superego successfully represses the unresolvable sexual desires of the phallic stage.

Libido The energy of the life impulses. Characterized as a flow of energy, it easily passes from one area of attention to another, moving with the volatile nature of emotional responsiveness. Aggressive energy, or the death impulse, is assumed to have the same properties as libido.

Oedipus complex A conflict that occurs during the phallic stage of development. In boys, the father is seen as a rival for the mother's attention. Yet the boy still wants the father's love and affection, for which the mother is seen as a rival. The boy's feelings are repressed partly out of fear of castration. In girls, the problem is similar, but different in expression and solution. Because repression of desires is less total or severe, the girl is allowed to remain in this situation for an indefinite period.

Oral stage Developmental stage from birth to 2 to 4 years. Needs and gratification predominately involve lips, tongue, and, later, teeth. The basic drive is to take in nourishment to relieve the tensions of hunger and thirst.

Penis envy In Freud's view, the feelings of inferiority that result from a girl's desire for a penis, and the related realization of its lack. In the mature woman, this ongoing desire for a penis is converted to the specific desire for a male child, who comes so equipped. In Horney's theory (Chapter 4), penis envy is viewed as the complement to a boy's envy of pregnancy, childbirth, and motherhood.

Phallic stage Developmental stage from ages 3 to 5. Focus is on the genitals, with an awareness of the presence or absence of a penis. Children become conscious of sexual differences.

Psychoanalysis A procedure for investigation, a method of treatment, and an accumulated collection of psychological information used to understand those aspects of mental life that are obscure and apparently unreachable. Psychoanalytic theory suggests that although it is a difficult process, one can come to terms with the recurring demands of the id.

Superego (above I) The part of the psyche that develops from the ego and serves as a repository of moral codes, standards of conduct, and inhibitions that function as conscience, self-observation, and formation of ideals. It develops, elaborates, and maintains the moral code of an individual, and also sets out a series of guidelines that define and limit the flexibility of the ego.

Wish fulfillment An aspect of dreams that may be considered as an alternate pathway to satisfy the desires of the id.

ANNOTATED BIBLIOGRAPHY

Books by Freud

Freud, S. The interpretation of dreams. In J. Strachey (Ed. and Trans.), *The standard edition of the complete psychological works of Sigmund Freud* (Vols. 4, 5 of 24). London: Hogarth Press, 1953–1966. (Originally published, 1900.)

Freud said of it in 1931: "It contains, even according to my present-day judgment, the most valuable of all the discoveries it has been my good fortune to make." We agree. The best of Freud. Read it to appreciate his intuitive genius and his writing style. Most of Freud's writings are available in a variety of inexpensive editions.

Freud, S. Introductory lectures on psycho-analysis. In *Standard edition* (Vols. 15, 16). (Originally published, 1916.)

Two courses of lectures given at the University of Vienna. The first part of the book assumes no knowledge of the subject; the second part assumes familiarity with the first. Lectures to and for students.

Freud, S. (1957). *A general selection from the works of Sigmund Freud* (John Rickman, Ed.). New York: Doubleday.

A good set of readings taken from different parts of Freud's work. Other collections may be as good. We like this one.

Freud, S. (1963). *Three case histories.* New York: Collier Books.

Three cases that Freud analyzed. He presents material from the cases, interweaving his developing theory. This is as close to seeing Freud in action as can be gleaned from his writings.

Books About Freud and His Ideas

Crews, R. (1998). *Unauthorized Freud: Doubters confront a legend.* New York: Viking Penguin.

If you really want to reject Freud and everything he ever wrote or thought, this book will give you endless pleasure and all the arguments you will ever need to bolster your position.

Erwin, E. (Ed.) 2001. *The Freud Encyclopedia: Theory, Therapy, and Culture.* New York: Routledge.

Recent work on all aspects of Freudian theory, plus developments in twenty-five countries plus biographies plus . . . you get the idea. A huge and serious work.

Gay, P. (1988). *Freud: A life for our time.* New York: W. W. Norton.

The best biography of Freud available. Gay neither attacks nor defends Freud, avoiding the subjectivity that is the fault of most of the other biographies. He understands the era as well as the man.

Hall, C. S. (1954). *A primer of Freudian psychology.* New York: New American Library (Mentor Books).

A short, readable, and lucid exposition of the major features of Freud's theories. It is compact and accurate. The best easy introduction available.

Hall, C., & Lindzey, G. (1968). The relevance of Freudian psychology and related viewpoints for the social sciences. In G. Lindzey & E. Arronson (Eds.), *The handbook of social psychology* (2nd ed.). Menlo Park, CA: Addison-Wesley.

An intermediate-level summary of psychoanalytic thinking, with emphasis on its relevance to social psychology; a theoretical rather than clinical focus.

Rapaport, D. (1959). The structure of psychoanalytic theory. In S. Koch (Ed.), *Psychology: The study of a science: Vol. 3. Formulations of the person and the social context.* New York: McGraw-Hill.

Among the most sophisticated and complete theoretical statements of psychoanalytic thinking. Not for the fainthearted.

Roazen, P. (1993). *Meeting Freud's family.* Amherst: University of Massachusetts Press.

Good fun if you've become interested in the strange and often silly stories about the relationships at the center of the psychoanalytic world and those within Freud's household as well.

Sulloway, F. (1979). *Freud, biologist of the mind: Beyond the psychoanalytic legend*. New York: Basic Books.

> Suggests that Freud was more aligned with biology than with psychology. A more human, less heroic view of him than usual, solidly based on historical documents. Disagrees with Ernest Jones on matters of fact and opinion. Endless references.

Books About Psychoanalysis

Bergman, M., & Hartman, F. (Eds.). (1976). *The evolution of psychoanalytic technique*. New York: Basic Books.

> Collected papers from the first wave of movements and changes, arising out of Freud's original thinking. The work of those who believed they stayed within the fold. Contributors include Erikson, Fenichel, Ferenczi, Alexander, and Reich.

Bergman, M., & Hartman, F. (Eds.) (1972). *The fallacy of understanding. An inquiry into the changing structure of psychoanalysis*. New York: Basic Books.

> A delightful musing about the way in which we see and interpret Freud's work from a vantage point years later and cultures apart. Their sensible rethinking of Freud's basic ideas and how they were first expressed and understood is a fresh look that stresses utility.

Levenson, E., & Mitchell, S. (1988). *Relational concepts in psychoanalysis: An integration*. Cambridge, MA: Harvard University Press.

> A valiant and often compelling attempt to integrate several successful offshoots fromtraditional psychoanalysis, including self psychology, existential psychoanalysis, object relations theories, and interpersonal psychoanalysis. Not for the fainthearted.

Schafer, R. (1983). *The analytic attitude*. New York: Basic Books.

> An exploration of the inner workings of the mind of the analyst during therapy itself, by a professor of psychiatry at the Columbia University Medical Center for Psychoanalytic Training and Research. Widely read, used, and praised by professionals.

Psychoanalytic Books About Women

Jordan, J., Kaplan, A., Miller, J., Stiver, I., & Surrey, J. (1991). *Woman's growth in connection*. New York: Guilford Press.

> These authors are among the best post-Freudian theorists writing about women. Not limited to psychoanalytic concerns.

Mitchell, J. (1974). *Psychoanalysis and feminism*. New York: Pantheon.

> Mitchell explores at length the usefulness of psychoanalytic theory in contributing to an understanding of women's psychology in Western, male-dominated society. Mitchell is strongly and openly a feminist, and as such she examines psychoanalysis as put forth by Freud and various theorists since Freud. A critique of various feminist criticisms of these same theories—psychoanalysis in particular—is offered.

Ruitenbeck, H. (Ed.). (1966). *Psychoanalysis and female sexuality*. New Haven, CT: College and University Press.

> A collection of psychoanalytic papers on female sexuality. Included are essays by Jones, Thompson, Horney, Freud, Greenacre, Riviere, and, somewhat surprisingly, Maslow.

Web Sites

Abstracts of the complete psychological works of Sigmund Freud
http://nyfreudian.org/abstracts/

> A digital version of abstracts of the standard edition of the complete psychological works of Sigmund Freud. Detailed descriptions. Very useful.

Sigmund Freud and the Freud Archives
http://plaza.interport.net/nypsan/freudarc.html

> A master site with links to most other valuable Freud sites.

Freud chat room
http://westerncanon.com/cgibin/lecture/SigmundFreudhall/live/chat.cgi

> A distinctly informal site. If you have opinions or want to read them, this is the place.

http://www.human-nature.com/esterson/index.html

> A delightful site to see a Freudian-versus-Freudian fight. Well written and documented, it is indicative of the passion that still surrounds much of the Freudian legacy.

Anna Freud site
http://www.annafreudcentre.org/

> Start here. Leads to many related sites.

http://www.psychematters.com/bibliographies/annafreud.htm

> The full listing of all she ever wrote. Lots of links to related sites.

REFERENCES

Auden, W. H. (1945). *The collected poems of W. H. Auden*. New York: Random House.

Benjamin, L., & Dixon, D. (1996). Dream analysis by mail: An American woman seeks Freud's advice. *American Psychologist, 51*(5), 461–468.

Benjamin, L., Jr. (2003). Behavioral Science and the Nobel Prize: A history. *American Psychologist, 59*(9), p. 731–741.

Bettelheim, B. (1982, March 1). Reflections: Freud and the soul. *New Yorker*, pp. 5293.

Bion, W. R. (1962). *Learning from experience*. London: Karnac Books.

Bonaparte, M. (Ed.). (1954). *The origins of psychoanalysis: Letters to Wilhelm Fliess*. London: Imago.

Breuer, J., & Freud, S. (1953–1966). Studies in hysteria. In J. Strachey (Ed. and Trans.), *The standard edition of the complete psychological works of Sigmund Freud* (Vol. 2). London: Hogarth Press. (Originally published, 1895.)

Bruner, J. (1956). Freud and the image of man. *Partisan Review, 23*, 340–347.

Byck, R. (Ed.). (1975). Cocaine papers by Sigmund Freud. New York: New American Library.

Carnochan, P. G. (2001), *Looking for ground: Countertransference and the problem of value in psychoanalysis*. Hillsdale, N.J.: Analytic Press.

Carroy, J. (1991). "My interpreter with German readers": Freud and the French history of hypnosis. *Psychanalyse à l'Université, 16*(62), 97–113.

Cohen, M. (1982). *Putting energy back into Freud*. Unpublished doctoral dissertation, California Institute of Transpersonal Psychology.

Colby, K. M. (1951). *A primer for psychotherapists*. New York: Ronald Press.

Decker, H. (1991). *Freud, Dora, and Vienna 1900*. New York: Free Press.

Emmanuel, D. (1992). A developmental model of girls and women. *Progress: Family Systems Research and Therapy, 1*(1), 25–40.

Esterson, A. (2002). The myth of Freud's ostracism by the medical community in 1896–1905. *History of Psychology, 5*(2), 115–134.

Fenichel, O. (1945). *The psychoanalytic theory of neurosis*. New York: Norton.

Ferenczi, S. (1955). *Final contributions to the problems and methods of psychoanalysis*. London: Hogarth Press/New York: Basic Books.

Fliegel, Z. O. (1973). Feminine psychosexual development in Freudian theory: A historical reconstruction. *The Psychoanalytic Quarterly, 42*(3), 385–408.

Fodor, N., & Gaynor, F. (1958). *Freud: Dictionary of psychoanalysis*. New York: Fawcett Books.

Freud, A. (1946). *The ego and the mechanisms of defense*. London: Hogarth Press.

Freud, Ernest (Ed.). (l961). *Letters of Sigmund Freud*. New York: Dover Publications.

Freud, S. The neuro-psychoses of defense. In J. Strachey (Ed. and Trans.), *The standard edition of the complete psychological works of Sigmund Freud* (Vol. 3). London: Hogarth Press, 1953–1966. (Originally published, 1894.)

Freud, S. The interpretation of dreams. In *Standard edition* (Vols. 4, 5). (Originally published, 1900.)

Freud, S. The psychopathology of everyday life. In *Standard edition* (Vol. 6). (Originally published, 1901.)

Freud, S. Three essays on the theory of sexuality. In *Standard edition* (Vol. 7). (Originally published, 1905a.)

Freud, S. Fragment of an analysis of a case of hysteria. In *Standard edition* (Vol. 8). (Originally published, 1905b.)

Freud, S. Psycho-analysis and the establishment of the facts in legal proceedings. In *Standard edition* (Vol. 9). (Originally published, 1906.)

Freud, S. Obsessive actions and religious practices. In *Standard edition* (Vol. 9). (Originally published, 1907.)

Freud, S. "Civilized" sexuality and modern nervous illness. In *Standard edition* (Vol. 9) (Originally published, 1908.)

Freud, S. Five lectures on psycho-analysis. In *Standard edition* (Vol. 11). (Originally published, 1910.)

Freud, S. Formulations on the two principles of mental functioning. In *Standard edition* (Vol. 12). (Originally published, 1911.)

Freud, S. On the history of the psycho-analytic movement. In *Standard edition* (Vol. 14). (Originally published, 1914.)

Freud, S. On the transformations of instinct, as exemplified in anal eroticism. In *Standard edition* (Vol. 17). (Originally published, 1917.)

Freud, S. Lines of advance in psycho-analytic therapy. In *Standard edition* (Vol. 17). (Originally published, 1919.)

Freud, S. Beyond the pleasure principle. In *Standard edition* (Vol. 18). (Originally published, 1920.)

Freud, S. Two encyclopedia articles. In *Standard edition* (Vol. 18). (Originally published, 1923.)

Freud, S. An autobiographical study. In *Standard edition* (Vol. 20). (Originally published, 1925a.) (Also, *Autobiography*. New York: Norton, 1935.)

Freud, S. The question of lay analysis. In *Standard edition* (Vol. 20). (Originally published, 1926.)

Freud, S. Civilization and its discontents. In *Standard edition* (Vol. 21). (Originally published, 1930.)

Freud, S. New introductory lectures on psycho-analysis. In *Standard edition* (Vol. 22). (Originally published, 1933.) (Also, New York: Norton, 1949.)

Freud, S. Analysis terminable and interminable. In *Standard edition* (Vol. 23). (Originally published, 1937.)

Freud, S. An outline of psycho-analysis. In *Standard edition* (Vol. 23). (Originally published, 1940.) (Also, New York: Norton, 1949.)

Freud, S. (1963). *The cocaine papers*. Zurich: Duquin Press. (Papers not reprinted in *The standard edition;* originally published, 1884–1887.)

Freud, Sophie. (1998). The baby and the bathwater: Some thoughts on Freud as a postmodernist. *Families in Society, 79*(5), 455–464.

Fromm, E. (1959). *Sigmund Freud's mission: An analysis of his personality and influence*. New York: Harper & Row.

Fuller, R. (1992). Biographical origins of psychological ideas: Freud's cocaine studies. *Journal of Humanistic Psychology, 32*(3), 67–86.

Gay, P. (1988). *Freud: A life for our time*. New York: W. W. Norton.

Godde, G. (1991a). Freud's philosophical discussion circles in his student years. *Jahrbuch der Psychoanalyse, 27,* 73–113.

Godde, G. (1991b). Schopenhauer's anticipation of Freudian metapsychology. *Psyche Zeitschrift für Psychoanalyse und ihre Anwendungen, 45*(11), 944–1033.

Goleman, D. (1990, February 7). Freud's reputation shrinks a little. *New York Times, 1,* 4.

Hall, C. S. (1954). *A primer of Freudian psychology*. New York: New American Library.

Halt, R. R. (1965). A review of some of Freud's biological assumptions and their influence on his theories. In N. S. Greenfield & W. C. Lewis (Eds.), *Psychoanalysis and current biological thought*. Madison: University of Wisconsin Press.

Hamilton, J. (1991). A reconsideration of the Freud–Tausk–Deutch relationship. *Psychoanalytic Review, 78*(2), 267–278.

Herzog, P. (1991). *Conscious and unconscious: Freud's dynamic distinction reconsidered*. Madison, CT: International Universities Press.

Horney, K. (1939). *New ways in psychoanalysis*. New York: Norton.

Jones, E. (1953, 1955, 1957). *The life and work of Sigmund Freud* (3 Vols.). New York: Basic Books.

Jones, E., (1966). The early development of female sexuality. In H. Ruitenbeck (Ed.), *Psychoanalysis and female sexuality*. New Haven, CT: College and University Press. (Originally published, 1927.)

Joseph, B. (1983). On understanding and not understanding: Some technical issues. *International Journal of Psycho-Analysis, 64*, 291–298.

Kazin, Alfred. (1956). The Freudian Revolution Analyzed. *New York Times Magazine*, May 6, 1956.

Keillor, G. (1995, April 19): A prairie home companion. *National Public Radio*.

Klein, M. (1957). *Envy and Gratitude*. New York: Delacorte Press.

Kramer, M., et al. (1994). 13 book reviews of Freud's The Interpretation of Dreams. *Dreaming, 4*(1), 43–88.

Krippner, S., & Thompson, A. (1996). A 10-facet model of dreaming applied to dream practices of sixteen Native American cultural groups. *Dreaming 6*(2), 71–96.

Krishna, G. (1974). *Higher consciousness: The evolutionary thrust of kundalini*. New York: Julian Press.

Kuhn, Phillip. (1998). 'A pretty piece of treachery': The strange case of Dr. Stekel and Sigmund Freud. *International Journal of Psychoanalysis, 79*(6), 1151–1171.

La Planche, J., & Pontalis, J. B. (1973). *The language of psychoanalysis* (D. Nicholson-Smith, Trans.). New York: Norton.

Lauzan, G. (1962). *Sigmund Freud: The man and his theories* (P. Evans, Trans.). New York: Fawcett.

Le Barre, W. (1968). Personality from a psychoanalytic viewpoint. In E. Lothane, Zvi. (1998). *The feud between Freud and Ferenczi over love. American Journal of Psychoanalysis, 58*(1), 21–39.

L'Engle, M. (1995). *Walking on Water: Reflections on Faith and Art*. New York: North Point Press.

Malcolm, J. (1980, November 24 and December 1). The impossible profession. *The New Yorker*.

Masson, J. (1984). *The assault on truth: Freud's suppression of the seduction theory*. New York: Farrar, Straus & Giroux.

McGuire, W. (Ed.). (1974). *The Freud/Jung letters*. Bollingen Series XCIV. Princeton, NJ: Princeton University Press.

Meltzer, D. (1973). *Sexual states of mind*. Perthshire, England: Clunie Press.

Miller, A. (1984). *Thou shalt not be aware*. New York: Farrar, Straus & Giroux.

Newton, Peter M. (1995). *Freud: From youthful dream to mid-life crisis*. New York: Guilford.

Norbeck, R., Price-Williams, D., & McCord, W. (Eds.). (1997). *The study of personality: An interdisciplinary appraisal* (pp. 65–87). New York: Holt, Rinehart and Winston.

O'Brien, M. (1991). Freud's affair with Minna Bernays: His letter of June 4, 1896. *American Journal of Psychoanalysis, 51*(2), 173–184.

O'Flaherty, W. (1984). *Dreams, illusions, and other realities*. Chicago: University of Chicago Press.

Pribram, K. (1962). The neuropsychology of Sigmund Freud. In A. Bachrach (Ed.), *Experimental foundations of clinical psychology* (pp. 442–468). New York: Basic Books.

Richards, Arlene K. (1999). Freud and feminism: a critical appraisal. *Journal of the American Psychoanalytic Association, 47*(4), 1213–1237.

Rosenfeld, H. (1987). *Impasse and interpretation*. London: Tavistock.

Rycroft, C. (1972). *Wilhelm Reich*. New York: Viking Press.

Sagan, E. (1988). *Freud, women and morality: The psychology of good and evil*. New York: Basic Books.

Sand, Rosemarie. (1999). The interpretation of dreams: Freud and the Western dream tradition. *Psychoanalytic Dialogues, 9*(6), 725–747.

Sears, R. T. (1936). Experimental studies of projection. I: attribution of traits. *Journal of Social Psychology, 7*, 151–163.

Solms, Mark. (1998). Controversies in Freud translation. *Psychoanalysis and History, 1*(1), 28–43.

Steiner, Ricardo. (2000). Nostalgia for the future: Biographies of myths and heros. . . ? Remarks on Jones' Freud Biography. *Psyche: Zeitschrift fuer Psychoanalyse und ihre Anwendungen, 54*(3), 242–282.

Sulloway, F. (1979). *Freud, biologist of the mind: Beyond the psychoanalytic legend*. New York: Basic Books.

Thornton, E. M. (1984). *The Freudian fallacy*. Garden City, NY: Dial Press.

Volosinov, V. (1987). *Freudianism, a critical sketch* (I. R. Titunik, Trans.). Bloomington: Indiana University Press. (Originally published in Russian.)

Winnicott, D. W. (1971). *Playing and Reality*. New York: Basic Books.

Wollheim, R. (1971). *Sigmund Freud*. New York: Viking Press.

carl gustav jung and
analytic psychology

Carl Jung is one of the most important, most complex, and most controversial psychological theorists. Jungian psychology focuses on establishing and fostering the relationship between conscious and unconscious processes. Dialogue between the conscious and the unconscious aspects of the psyche enriches the person, and Jung believed that without this dialogue, unconscious processes can weaken and even jeopardize the personality.

In this chapter we will take a careful look at the basic concepts of Jungian psychology and examine some brief references to the philosophical underpinnings of this psychology. We will explore such concepts as individuation, archetype, the nature of the symbolic, and Jung's structure of the psyche, which includes ego, shadow, anima/animus, and the self.

One of Jung's central concepts is **individuation,** his term for a process of personal development that involves establishing a connection between the ego and the self. The ego is the center of consciousness; the self is the center of the total psyche, including both the conscious and the unconscious. Jung recognized constant interplay between the two. They are not separate but are two aspects of a single system. Individuation is the process of developing wholeness by integrating all the various parts of the psyche.

Jung's analysis of human nature includes investigations of Eastern and Western religions, alchemy, parapsychology, and mythology. His initial impact was greater on philosophers, folklorists, and writers than on psychologists or psychiatrists. Today, however, growing concern with human consciousness and human potential has caused a resurgence of interest in Jung's ideas.

> Everything in the unconscious seeks outward manifestation, and the personality too desires to evolve out of its unconscious conditions and to experience itself as a whole. (Jung, 1961, p. 3)

PERSONAL HISTORY

Any theory is best understood in the context of the theorist's worldview. Jung's theory is no exception. Thus an appropriate beginning to our study of Jung is a look at the personal, historical, and cultural influences that touched him.

> My life is a story of the self-realization of the unconscious. (Jung, 1961, p. 1)

Carl Gustav Jung was born in Switzerland on July 26, 1875. Until the age of 9, when his sister was born, Jung experienced a somewhat isolated childhood, which he filled with solitary play and a rich inner world: "I did not want to be disturbed [at play]. I was deeply absorbed in my games and could not endure being watched" (1961, p. 18). His father was a pastor in the Swiss Reformed Church and a scholar in Asian languages. Even as a child, Jung was deeply concerned with religious and spiritual questions. In his autobiography, *Memories, Dreams, Reflections* (1961), Jung relates two powerful early experiences that strongly influenced his attitude toward religion. Between the ages of 3 and 4, he dreamed of a terrifying phallic image standing on a throne in an underground chamber. The dream haunted Jung for years. Not until many years later did he realize that the image was a ritual phallus; it represented a hidden, "subterranean God" that was more frightful yet much more real and more powerful for Jung than the conventional church images of Jesus.

The second experience occurred when Jung was 11. He came out of school at noon and saw the sun sparkling on the roof of the Basel church. He reflected on the beauty of the world, the splendor of the church, and the majesty of God sitting high up in the sky on a golden throne. Suddenly gripped with terror, Jung refused to let himself pursue this train of thought, which he felt was highly sacrilegious. For several days he struggled desperately to suppress the forbidden thought. Finally Jung gave in: he saw the beautiful cathedral and God seated on his throne high above the world, and from under the throne came an enormous piece of excrement, which fell on the cathedral roof, shattering it and destroying the walls of the cathedral.

Reflecting on this experience, Jung wrote:

> A great many things I had not previously understood became clear to me. In His trial of human courage God refuses to abide by tradition no matter how sacred. . . . One must be utterly abandoned to God; nothing else matters but fulfilling His will. Otherwise all is folly and meaninglessness. (1961, pp. 38–40)

It is hard for us today to grasp the terrifying power of Jung's vision. Given the conventional piety and lack of psychological sophistication of society in 1887, such thoughts were not merely unutterable; they were unthinkable. However, following his vision, Jung felt an enormous relief and a sense of grace, instead of the expected guilt. He interpreted what he saw as a sign from God. It was God's will that Jung go against the traditions of the church. From that time on, Jung felt far removed from the conventional piety of his father and his pastoral relatives. He saw how most people cut themselves off from direct religious experience by remaining bound by the letter of church convention, instead of seriously considering the spirit of God as a living reality.

Partly as a result of his inner experiences, Jung felt himself isolated from other people; sometimes he felt almost unendurably lonely. School bored him; however, he developed a passion for reading, an "absolute craving . . . to read every scrap of printed matter that fell into my hands" (1961, p. 30).

From childhood on, Jung had been aware of two personalities within him. One was the local parson's son, insecure and uncertain. The other was a wise old man, "skeptical, mistrustful, remote from the world of men, but close to nature, the earth, the sun, the moon, the weather, all living creatures, and above all close to the night, to dreams, and to whatever 'God' worked directly in him" (Jung, 1961, pp. 44–45). The parson's son lived an ordinary daily existence as a child growing up in a particular time and place. The wise old man lived in a timeless and boundless world of wisdom, meaning, and historical continuity. The interaction of these two personalities, Jung said, occurs in everyone, only most people are unconscious of the second figure. This figure was of major significance in his life. In many ways, Jung's personality theory, especially his concepts of individuation and the self, stems from his longtime awareness of this inner wisdom.

When it came time to enter the university, Jung chose to study medicine as a compromise between his interests in both science and the humanities. He became attracted to psychiatry as the study of "diseases of the personality," though in those days psychiatry was relatively undeveloped and undistinguished. He realized that psychiatry in particular involved both scientific and humanistic perspectives. Jung also developed an interest in psychic phenomena and began an investigation of the messages received by his cousin, a local medium. This investigation became the basis for his thesis: "On the Psychology and Pathology of So-called Occult Phenomena."

In 1900, Jung became an intern at the Burghölzli Medical Hospital in Zurich, one of the most progressive psychiatric centers in Europe. Zurich became his permanent home.

Four years later, Jung set up an experimental laboratory at the psychiatric clinic and developed the word association test for psychiatric diagnostic purposes. In this test, the subject is asked to respond to a standard list of stimulus words; any inordinate delay between the stimulus and the response is taken as an indicator of emotional

Nobody could rob me of the conviction that it was enjoined upon me to do what God wanted and not what I wanted. . . . [O]ften I had the feeling that in all decisive matters I was no longer among men but was alone with God. (Jung, 1961, p. 48)

In the last analysis, most of our difficulties come from losing contact with our instincts, with the age-old unforgotten wisdom stored up in us. (Jung in McGuire & Hull, 1977, p. 89)

stress related in some way to the stimulus word. Jung also became skillful at interpreting the psychological meanings behind the various associations produced by the subjects. In 1905, at age 30, he became lecturer in psychiatry at the University of Zurich and senior physician at the psychiatric clinic. At this time, Jung had already discovered the writings of a man who would become an important teacher and mentor, Sigmund Freud.

Freud was the first man of real importance I had encountered. (Jung, 1961, p. 149)

Despite the strong criticism leveled at Freud in scientific and academic circles, Jung became convinced of the value of Freud's work. He sent Freud copies of his articles and of his first book, *The Psychology of Dementia Praecox* (1907). Freud responded by inviting him to Vienna. At their first meeting, the two men talked virtually without pause for 13 hours. They corresponded weekly after that, and Freud came to consider Jung his logical successor.

Despite their close friendship, the two men had fundamental disagreements. Jung never accepted Freud's insistence that the causes of repression are always sexual trauma. Freud, for his part, remained uneasy with Jung's interest in mythological, spiritual, and occult phenomena. The two men had a philosophical and personal break when Jung published *Symbols of Transformation* (1912), which challenged some of Freud's basic ideas. For example, Jung considered libido to be generalized psychic energy, whereas Freud was adamant that libido was sexual energy.

In his preface to the book, Jung wrote, "The whole thing came upon me like a landslide that cannot be stopped. . . . [I]t was the explosion of all those psychic contents which could find no room, no breathing space, in the constricting atmosphere of Freudian psychology and its narrow outlook" (1912, p. xxiii). It was not easy for Jung to risk the loss of his friend and mentor. "For two months I was unable to touch my pen, so tormented was I by the conflict" (1961, p. 167). The break with Freud was a painful, traumatic one for Jung, but he was determined to stand behind his own convictions.

Dreams bring to light material which cannot have originated either from the dreamer's adult life or from his forgotten childhood. We are obliged to regard it as part of the archaic heritage which a child brings with him into the world, before any experience of his own, influenced by the experiences of his ancestors. We find the counterpart of this philogenetic material in the earliest human legends and in surviving customs. (Freud, 1964, p. 177)

For Jung, this break with Freud precipitated a powerful confrontation with the unconscious. In an effort to contain and grow from these intense experiences, Jung began to document them in his personal journals as a kind of self-analysis.

Jung gradually developed his own theories of unconscious processes and dream-symbol analysis. He came to realize that his procedures for analyzing the dream symbols of his patients could also be applied to the analysis of other forms of symbolism—that he held the key to the interpretation of myths, folktales, religious symbols, and art.

His interest in fundamental psychological processes turned Jung to the study of the ancient Western traditions of alchemy and gnosticism (a Hellenistic mystical and philosophical tradition), as well as to the investigation of non-European cultures. He was also a serious student of Indian, Chinese, and Tibetan thought. Jung made two trips to Africa, visited India, and traveled to New Mexico to visit the Pueblo Indians.

In 1944, when he was 69, Jung nearly died following a severe heart attack. In the hospital, he experienced a powerful vision in which he seemed to be floating high in space, 1,000 miles above the earth, with Ceylon below his feet, India lying ahead of him, and the desert of Arabia off to the left. Jung then entered a great block of stone that was also floating in space. A temple had been hollowed out of the giant block. As he approached the steps leading to the entrance, Jung felt that everything had been left behind him. All that remained of his earthly existence was his own experience, his life's history. For the first time, he saw his life as part of a great historical matrix. Before he could enter the temple, Jung was confronted by his doctor, who told him that he had no right to leave the earth at that time. At that moment, the vision ceased.

For weeks after, as Jung gradually recovered from his illness, he felt weak and depressed by day, but would awaken each night around midnight with a feeling of ecstasy. He felt as if he were floating in a blissful world. His nightly visions lasted for about an hour and then he would again fall asleep.

After he recovered, Jung entered a highly productive period in which he wrote many of his most important works. His visions gave him the courage to formulate some of his most original ideas. These experiences also changed Jung's personal outlook to a more deeply affirmative attitude toward his own destiny.

> I might formulate it as an affirmation of things as they are: an unconditional "yes" to that which is, without subjective protests—acceptance of the conditions of existence as I see them and understand them, acceptance of my own nature, as I happen to be. . . . In this way we forge an ego that does not break down when incomprehensible things happen; an ego that endures the truth, and that is capable of coping with the world and with fate. (1961, p. 297)
>
> A few days before his death, Jung had a dream. He saw a great round stone in a high place, a barren square, and on it were engraved the words: "And this shall be a sign unto you of Wholeness and Oneness." Then he saw many vessels . . . and a quadrangle of trees whose roots reached around the earth and enveloped him and among the roots golden threads were glittering. (von Franz, 1975, p. 287)

Jung died on June 6, 1961, at the age of 86. His work has had a great impact on psychology, anthropology, history, and religious studies.

INTELLECTUAL ANTECEDENTS

Throughout his life, Jung was a scholar and a seeker after knowledge. He read widely in contemporary science and philosophy, the Greek and Latin classics, and Eastern thought, and also studied obscure Western traditions such as alchemy and gnosticism. His most important early influence, however, was Sigmund Freud.

Freud

Although Jung was already a practicing psychiatrist before he met Freud, Freud's theories were clearly among the strongest influences on Jung's thinking. Freud's *The Interpretation of Dreams* (1900) inspired Jung to attempt his own approach to dream and symbol analysis. Freud's theories of unconscious processes also gave Jung his first glimpse into the possibilities of systematically analyzing the dynamics of mental functioning, rather than relying on the superficial classification schemes that typified psychiatry at the time.

Jung acknowledged the validity of Freud's accomplishments in the area of psychopathology; however, he believed that he could devote his own theoretical efforts more to issues concerning positive growth and individuation. Jung wrote that

> Freud's greatest achievement probably consisted in taking neurotic patients seriously and entering into their peculiar individual psychology. He had the courage to let the case material speak for itself, and in this way was able to penetrate into the real psychology of his patients. . . . By evaluating dreams as the most important source of information concerning the unconscious processes, he gave back to mankind a tool that had seemed irretrievably lost. (1961, pp. 168–169)

The unconscious is on no account an empty sack in which the refuse of consciousness is collected.... [I]t is the whole other half of the living psyche. (Jung, 1973, p. 143)

Jung formulated a theory that included both the personal and collective unconscious. The personal unconscious is composed of forgotten memories, repressed experiences, and subliminal perceptions. It is similar to Freud's conception of the unconscious.

The contents of the collective unconscious, also known as the impersonal or transpersonal unconscious, are universal and not rooted in our personal experience. This concept is perhaps Jung's greatest departure from Freud, as well as his most significant contribution to psychology. (See Major Concepts in this chapter.)

Goethe and Nietzsche

Disappointed with the one-sided books of his father's theology, Jung almost gave up early on searching to understand God and God's Creation. His mother suggested to him that he read Goethe's *Faust*. This work had a major influence on Jung's understanding of the psyche and provided insight into the power of evil and its relation to growth and self-insight. An avid student, Jung became extremely well-read in philosophy and literature.

Nietzsche also had a profound effect on Jung. He believed that Nietzsche's work possessed great psychological insight even though Nietzsche's fascination with power tended to distort his portrait of the mature and free human being. Jung saw Nietzsche and Freud as representatives of the two greatest themes in Western culture—power and eros. He believed that both men had unfortunately become so deeply involved in these two vital themes that they were almost obsessed by them.

Alchemy and Gnosticism

When people say I am wise, or a sage, I cannot accept it. A man once dipped a hatful of water from a stream. What did that amount to? I am not that stream. I am at the stream, but I do nothing. (Jung, 1961, p. 355)

Jung searched for Western traditions that dealt with the development of consciousness. He was especially interested in the symbols and concepts used to describe this process. Jung found invaluable ideas in gnosticism, a mystical movement from early Christianity. (See Segal, Singer, & Stein, 1995.) Jung also discovered the Western alchemical literature, long dismissed as magical, prescientific nonsense. He interpreted the alchemical treatises as representations of inner change and purification disguised in chemical and magical metaphors: "Only after I had familiarized myself with alchemy did I realize that the unconscious is a process, and that the psyche is transformed or developed by the relationship of the ego to the content of the unconscious" (Jung, 1936b, p. 482). Jung interpreted the transformation of base metals into gold as a metaphor for the reformation of the personality and consciousness in the process of individuation.

Eastern Thought

In pursuing his research into myth and symbolism, Jung developed his own theories concerning individuation, or personality integration. Subsequently, Jung became deeply impressed with various Eastern traditions that provided the first outside confirmation of many of his own ideas.

The path to wholeness is made up of fateful detours and wrong turnings. (Jung, 1961, p. 325)

Jung discovered that Eastern descriptions of spiritual growth, inner psychic development, and integration closely corresponded to the process of individuation that he had observed in his Western patients. Jung was particularly interested in the mandala as an image of the self and of the individuation process. (*Mandala* is the Sanskrit word for circle, or a circular design or diagram frequently used in meditation and other spiritual practices.) He found that his patients spontaneously produced mandala drawings even though they were completely unfamiliar with Eastern art or philosophy. Mandalas tend to appear in the drawings of patients who have made considerable progress in their own individuation. The center of the drawing stands for the self, which comes to replace the limited ego as the center of the personality, and the circular diagram as a whole represents the balance and order that develops in the psyche as the individuation process continues.

Jung's ideas were strongly affected by India and Indian thought (Kakar, 1994). However, he was careful to point out important differences between Eastern and Western paths of individuation. The social and cultural framework in which the process of growth takes place differs greatly between the East and the West, as do the prevailing attitudes toward the concept of individuation and toward those who actively seek individuation. The desirability of inner development and enlightenment is widely accepted in the East, where there exist clearly recognized paths and techniques for facilitating the process. Jung strongly held that most spiritual traditions have become rigid systems imposed on the individual rather than ways of eliciting each individual's own unique pattern of inner growth.

MAJOR CONCEPTS

This section begins with Jung's theory of personality typology—the two basic attitudes, introversion and extraversion, and the four functions, thinking, feeling, intuition, and sensation. Next comes Jung's model of the unconscious and his concept of archetype, followed by the archetypes of the personality—ego, persona, shadow, anima and animus, and self. Finally, we include a discussion of Jung's exploration of symbols and two applications of this work—in active imagination and in dreams.

The Attitudes: Introversion and Extraversion

Among all of Jung's concepts, **introversion** and **extraversion** have probably gained the widest general use. Jung found that individuals can be characterized as either primarily inward-oriented or primarily outward-oriented. The introvert is more comfortable with the inner world of thoughts and feelings. The extravert feels more at home with the world of objects and other people.

No one is a pure introvert or a pure extravert. Jung compared the two processes to the heartbeat, with its rhythmic alternation between the cycle of contraction (introversion) and the cycle of expansion (extraversion). However, each individual tends to favor one or the other attitude and operates more often in terms of the favored attitude. Introverts see the world in terms of how it affects them, and extraverts are more concerned with their impact upon the world.

A balance exists also between conscious and unconscious emphases on these qualities:

> If you take an extravert you will find his unconscious has an introverted quality, because all the extraverted qualities are played out in his consciousness and the introverted are left in the unconscious. (Jung in McGuire & Hull, 1977, p. 342)

Follow that will and that way which experience confirms to be your own, i.e., the true expression of your individuality. (Jung in Serrano, 1966, p. 83)

At times, introversion is more appropriate; at other times, extraversion is more suitable. The two are mutually exclusive; you cannot hold both an introverted and an extraverted attitude concurrently. Neither one is better than the other. The ideal is to be flexible and to adopt whichever attitude is more appropriate in a given situation—to operate in dynamic balance between the two and not develop a fixed, rigid way of responding to the world.

Introverts are interested primarily in their own thoughts and feelings, in their inner world; they tend to be introspective. One danger for such people is that as they become immersed in their inner world, they may lose touch with the world around them. The absent-minded professor is a clear, if stereotypical, example.

Extraverts are actively involved in the world of people and things; they tend to be more social and more aware of what is going on around them. They need to guard against becoming dominated by external events and alienated from their inner selves. The hard-driving business executive who has no understanding of feelings or relationships is a classic stereotype of unbalanced extraversion.

The Functions: Thinking, Feeling, Sensation, Intuition

One of Jung's greatest contributions to psychology is his theory of type. Jung found that different people think, feel, and experience the world in fundamentally different ways. His type theory is a powerful tool to help us understand how people function.

Jung identified four fundamental psychological functions: thinking, feeling, sensation, and intuition. Each function may be experienced in an introverted or an extraverted fashion. Generally, one of the functions is more conscious, developed, and dominant. Jung called this the *superior* function. It operates out of the dominant attitude (either extraversion or introversion). One of the other three remaining functions is generally deep in the unconscious and less developed. Jung called this the *inferior* function.

Thinking and feeling are alternative ways of forming judgments and making decisions. Thinking is concerned with objective truth, judgment, and impersonal analysis. *Thinking* asks the question "What does this mean?" Consistency and abstract principles are highly valued. Thinking types (those individuals in whom the thinking function predominates) are the greatest planners; however, they tend to hold on to their plans and abstract theories even when confronted by new and contradictory evidence.

Feeling is focused on value. It may include judgments of good versus bad and right versus wrong (as opposed to decision making according to the criteria of logic or efficiency, as in thinking). Feeling asks the question "What value does this have?"

Jung classified sensation and intuition together as ways of gathering information, as distinct from ways of making decisions. *Sensation* refers to a focus on direct sense experience, perception of details, and concrete facts: what one can see, touch, and smell. Tangible, immediate experience is given priority over discussion or analysis of experience. Sensation asks the question "What exactly am I perceiving?" Sensing types tend to respond to the immediate situation and deal effectively and efficiently with all sorts of crises and emergencies. They generally work better with tools and materials than do any of the other types.

Intuition is a way of comprehending perceptions in terms of possibilities, past experience, future goals, and unconscious processes. Intuition asks the question "What might happen, what is possible?" The implications of experience are more important to intuitives than the actual experience itself. Strongly intuitive people add meaning to their perceptions so rapidly that they often cannot separate their interpretations from the raw sensory data. Intuitives integrate new information quickly, automatically relating past experience and relevant information to immediate experience. Because it often includes unconscious material, intuitive thinking appears to proceed by leaps and bounds.

Jung has called the least-developed function in each individual the *inferior function*. It is the least conscious and the most primitive, or undifferentiated. For some people it can represent a seemingly demonic influence because they have so little understanding of or control over it. For example, strongly intuitive types who are not in touch with their sensation function may experience sexual impulses as mysterious or even dangerous. Since it is less consciously developed, the inferior function may also serve as a way into the unconscious. Jung said that it is through our inferior function, that which is least developed in us, that we see God. By struggling with and confronting inner obstacles, we can come closer to the Divine.

For the individual, a combination of all four functions results in a well-rounded approach to the world:

> In order to orient ourselves, we must have a function which ascertains that something is there (sensation); a second function which establishes what is (thinking); a third function which states whether it suits us or not, whether we wish to accept it or not (feeling); and a fourth function which indicates where it came from and where it is going (intuition). (Jung, 1942, p. 167)

Unfortunately, no one develops all four functions equally well. Each individual has one dominant function and one partially developed auxiliary function. The other two functions are generally unconscious and operate with considerably less effectiveness. The more developed and conscious the dominant and auxiliary functions, the more deeply unconscious are their opposites. (See Figure 2.1.)

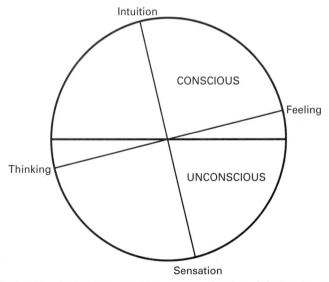

An intuitive-feeling type (intuition strongly developed; feeling less so)

FIGURE 2.1 An Example of Jung's Functional Typology
Functions above the horizontal line are the better developed, more conscious functions, and those below the line are the less developed, less conscious functions.

One's function type indicates the relative strengths and weaknesses and the style of activity one tends to prefer. Jung's typology is especially useful in helping us understand social relationships; it describes how people perceive in alternate ways and use different criteria in acting and making judgments. For example, intuitive–feeling speakers will not share the logical, tightly organized, and detailed lecture style of thinking–sensation lecturers. The former are more likely to ramble, to include stories, and to give the sense of a subject by approaching it from many different angles, rather than to develop it systematically.

The Unconscious

Our unconscious mind, like our body, is a storehouse of relics and memories of the past. (Jung, 1968, p. 44)

Jung emphasizes that, because of its very nature, the unconscious cannot be known and thus must be described in relationship to consciousness. Consciousness, he believes, theoretically has no limit.

Further, Jung divides the unconscious into the personal unconscious and the collective unconscious.

Personal Unconscious.   The material in the **personal unconscious** comes from the individual's past. This formulation corresponds to Freud's concept of the unconscious. The personal unconscious is composed of memories that are painful and have been repressed, as well as memories that are unimportant and have simply been dropped from conscious awareness. The personal unconscious also holds parts of the personality that have never come to consciousness.

It [the collective unconscious] is more like an atmosphere in which we live than something that is found in us. It is simply the unknown quantity in the world. (Jung, 1973, p. 433)

Collective Unconscious.   The **collective unconscious** is Jung's boldest and most controversial concept. Jung identifies the collective, or transpersonal, unconscious as the center of all psychic material not derived from personal experience. Its contents and images appear to be shared with people of all time periods and all cultures. Some psychologists, such as Skinner, implicitly assume that each individual is born as a blank slate, a *tabula rasa;* consequently, psychological development can come only from personal experience. Jung postulates that the infant mind already possesses a structure that molds and channels all further development and interaction with the environment. This basic structure is essentially the same in all infants. Although we develop differently and become unique individuals, the collective unconscious is common to all people and is therefore one (Jung, 1951a).

Jung's approach to the collective unconscious can be seen in the following passage from a letter to one of his patients:

> You trust your unconscious as if it were a loving father. But it is *nature* and cannot be made use of as if it were a reliable human being. It is *inhuman* and it needs the human mind to function usefully for man's purposes. . . . It always seeks its collective purposes and never your individual destiny. Your destiny is the result of the collaboration between the conscious and the unconscious. (Jung, 1973, p. 283)

We are . . . fully justified in speaking of an unconscious psyche. It is not directly accessible to observation—otherwise it would not be conscious. (Jung in Campbell, 1971, p. 28)

We are born with a psychological heritage as well as a biological heritage, according to Jung. Both are important determinants of behavior and experience: "Just as the human body represents a whole museum of organs, each with a long evolutionary period behind it, so we should expect to find that the mind is organized in a similar way. It can no more be a product without history than is the body in which it exists" (1964, p. 67).

The collective unconscious, which results from experiences that are common to all people, also includes material from our prehuman and animal ancestry. It is the source of our most powerful ideas and experiences.

Archetype

The archetype is probably Jung's most difficult concept. **Archetypes** are inherited predispositions to respond to the world in certain ways. They are primordial images, representations of the instinctual energies of the collective unconscious.

Jung postulated the idea of archetypes from experiences his patients reported, dreams and fantasies that included remarkable ideas and images whose content could not be traced to the individual's past experience. Jung suggested a level of imagery in the unconscious common to everyone. He also discovered a close correspondence between patients' dream contents and the mythical and religious themes found in many widely scattered cultures.

According to Jung, the archetypes are structure-forming elements within the unconscious. These elements give rise to the archetypal images that dominate both individual fantasy life and the mythologies of an entire culture. The archetypes exhibit "a kind of readiness to produce over and over again the same or similar mythical ideas" (1917, p. 69). They tend to appear as certain patterns—as recurring situations and figures. Archetypal situations include the hero's quest, the night-sea journey, and the battle for deliverance from the mother. Archetypal figures include the divine child, the double, the old sage, and the primordial mother.

A wide variety of symbols can be associated with a given archetype. For example, the mother archetype embraces not only each individual's real mother but also all mother figures and nurturant figures. This archetype group includes women in general, mythical images of women, such as Venus, the Virgin Mary, and Mother Nature, and supportive and nurturant symbols, such as the church and paradise. The mother archetype encompasses positive features and also negative ones, such as the threatening, domineering, or smothering mother. In the Middle Ages, for instance, negative aspects of the archetype became crystallized into the image of the witch.

Each of the major structures of the personality is also an archetype. These structures include the *ego,* the **persona,** the **shadow,** the **anima** (in men), the **animus** (in women), and the **self.**

The archetypes themselves are forms, without content of their own, that serve to organize or channel psychological material. They are somewhat like dry stream beds whose shape determines the characteristics of a river once water begins flowing through them. The archetypes are carriers of energy. When an archetype is activated, it generally unlocks a tremendous amount of energy. All creativity has an archetypal element.

Generally, archetypal images will have a contemporary form. People today are more likely to dream about fighting with their in-laws than about slaying a dragon.

Archetypes form the infrastructure of the psyche. Archetypal patterns are similar to the patterns found in crystal formation. No two snowflakes are exactly alike, but every single snowflake has the same basic crystalline structure. Similarly, the contents of each individual's psyche, as well as each individual's experiences, are unique. However, the general patterns into which these experiences fall are determined by universal parameters and generating principles, or archetypes: "The archetypes of the unconscious are manifestations of the organs of the body and the powers. Archetypes are biologically grounded" (Campbell, 1988, p. 51).

Primordial means "first" or "original"; therefore a primordial image refers to the earliest development of the psyche. Man inherits these images from his ancestral past, a past that includes all of his human ancestors as well as his prehuman or animal ancestors. (Jung in Hall & Nordby, 1973, p. 39)

It is essential to insist that archetypes are not mere names, or even philosophical concepts. They are pieces of life itself—images that are integrally connected to the living individual by the bridge of the emotions. (Jung, 1964, p. 96)

personal reflection

ARCHETYPES IN YOUR OWN LIFE

What has been the major archetypal image or theme in your life?

In what ways has it influenced you and those around you? Give some specific examples of how it has actually operated in your life.

Be aware that the first archetype that comes to mind isn't necessarily the most significant one. One way to discover what archetypes are meaningful for you is to think about the themes in literature and film that most appeal to you. Do you find a character particularly captivating? Or do you find a certain kind of situation particularly alluring—for instance, a doomed great love or a dangerous journey into the unknown?

> The term archetype is often misunderstood as meaning certain definite mythological images or motifs. . . . The archetype is a tendency to form such representations of a motif—representations that can vary a great deal in detail without losing their basic pattern. (Jung, 1964, p. 67)

In his *Hero with a Thousand Faces* (1949), Joseph Campbell, a Jungian scholar, outlines the basic archetypal themes and patterns in the stories and legends of heroes found in cultures throughout history. Several excellent studies have articulated aspects of the heroic archetype into orphan, warrior, sage, fool (Pearson, 1989, 1991) and also into king, warrior, magician, and lover (Moore & Gillette, 1990). The story of Oedipus is a good illustration of an archetypal situation that deals with a son's deep love for his mother and conflict with his father. The same basic structure can be found as a theme in many myths and legends and also as a psychological pattern in many

The Sphinx

individuals. You may recognize numerous related situations, such as a daughter's relationship to her parents, parents' relationship to children, relationships between men and women, brothers and sisters, and so forth.

Several books have discussed the Greek gods and goddesses as archetypes that describe various aspects of the personality. These include the work of Jean Shinoda Bolen (1984, 1989, 2002) and *The Goddess Within* (Woolger & Woolger, 1989).

It is important to remember that only the *contents* of an archetype can enter consciousness. The archetype itself is a pattern that channels our psychic energies. We can never become fully conscious of this underlying pattern, just as we can study thousands of snowflake crystals but can never actually see the underlying pattern that generates their common crystalline structure. More information on archetypes is available on our **web** site.

The Ego

The *ego* is the center of consciousness and one of the major personality archetypes. The ego provides a sense of consistency and direction in our conscious lives. It tends to oppose whatever might threaten this fragile consistency of consciousness and tries to convince us that we must always consciously plan and analyze our experiences.

According to Jung, the psyche at first consists only of the unconscious. Similar to Freud's view, Jung's ego arises from the unconscious and brings together various experiences and memories, developing the division between unconscious and conscious. The ego has no unconscious elements, only conscious contents derived from personal experience. We are led to believe that the ego is the central element of the psyche, and we come to ignore the other half of the psyche, the unconscious. (See Figures 2.2 and 2.3 for descriptions of the structure of the personality.)

> The ego wants explanations always in order to assert its existence. (Jung, 1973, p. 427)

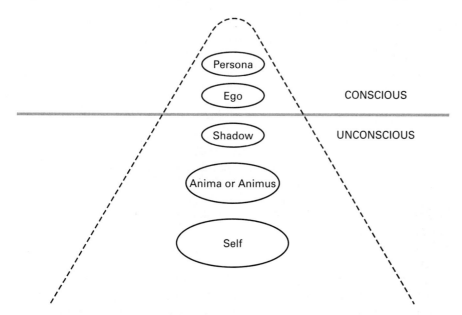

FIGURE 2.2 The Structure of the Personality
This diagram depicts the order in which the major archetypes generally appear in Jungian analysis. However, any two-dimensional representation of Jungian theory is bound to be misleading or even inaccurate. The self, for example, is more deeply unconscious than the other structures of the personality, but, at the same time, it is also the center of the total personality. (Adapted from Thomas Parker)

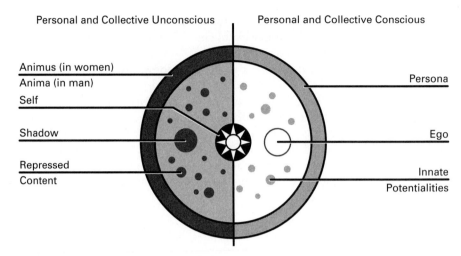

FIGURE 2.3 General Scheme of the Psyche
Source: From *The "I" and the "Not-I"* (Diagram 1, Appendix) by M. E. Harding. 1965. New York: Bollingen. Copyright 1965 by Bollingen. Adapted by permission.

The Persona

Our **persona** is the appearance we present to the world. It is the character we assume; through it, we relate to others. The persona includes our social roles, the kind of clothes we choose to wear, and our individual styles of expressing ourselves. The term *persona* comes from the Latin, meaning "mask," or "false face," as in the mask worn by an actor on the Roman stage through which he spoke. In order to function socially at all, we have to play a part in ways that define our roles. Even those who reject such adaptive devices invariably employ other roles, roles that represent rejection.

The persona has both negative and positive aspects. A dominant persona can smother the individual, and those who identify with their persona tend to see themselves only in terms of their superficial social roles and facades. In fact, Jung called the persona the "conformity archetype." As part of its positive function, it protects the ego and the psyche from the varied social forces and attitudes that impinge on them. The persona is, in addition, a valuable tool for communication. In Roman drama the actors' boldly drawn masks informed the entire audience clearly, if somewhat stereotypically, of the personality and attitudes of the role each actor was playing. The persona can often be crucial to our positive development. As we begin to play a certain role, our ego gradually comes to identify with it. This process is central to personality development.

This process is not always positive, however. As the ego identifies with the persona, people start to believe that they are what they pretend to be. According to Jung, we eventually have to withdraw this identification and learn who we are in the process of individuation. Minority group members and other social outsiders in particular are likely to have problems with their identities because of cultural prejudice and social rejection of their personas (Hopcke, 1995).

The persona may be expressed by objects we use to cover ourselves (clothing or a veil) and by the tools of an occupation (shovel or briefcase). Thus ordinary

personal reflection

THE PERSONA

List your favorite articles of clothing, jewelry, or other possessions that you generally carry, a purse or backpack, for example. Choose the one article that you feel most represents you, that somehow is an integral part of your self-image. Choose something that you wear or carry most of the time.

1. Go without the item for a week and note your reactions to its absence.
2. Lend the item to a friend. How does it feel to you to see a favorite possession worn or used by someone else?

items become symbols of the individual's identity. The term *status symbol* (car, house, or diploma) conveys society's understanding of the importance of image. All of these symbols can be found in dreams as representations of the persona. For example, someone with a strong persona may appear in a dream as overdressed or constricted by too much clothing. A person with a weak persona might appear naked and exposed. One possible expression of an inadequate persona would be a figure that has no skin.

The Shadow

The **shadow** is an archetypal form that serves as the focus for material that has been repressed from consciousness; its contents include tendencies, desires, and memories rejected by the individual as incompatible with the persona and contrary to social standards and ideals. The shadow contains all the negative tendencies the individual wishes to deny, including our animal instincts, as well as undeveloped positive and negative qualities.

> How can I be substantial without casting a shadow? I must have a dark side too if I am to be whole; and by becoming conscious of my shadow I remember once more that I am a human being like any other. (Jung, 1931c, p. 59)

The stronger our persona is and the more we identify with it, the more we deny other parts of ourselves. The shadow represents what we consider inferior in our personality and also that which we have neglected and never developed in ourselves. In dreams, a shadow figure may appear as an animal, a dwarf, a vagrant, or any other low-status figure.

In his work on repression and neurosis, Freud focused primarily on aspects of the shadow. Jung found that repressed material is organized and structured around the shadow, which becomes, in a sense, a negative self, or the shadow of the ego. The shadow is often experienced in dreams as a primitive, hostile, or repellent figure because the contents of the shadow have been forcibly pushed out of consciousness and appear antagonistic to the conscious outlook. If the material from the shadow is allowed back into consciousness, it loses much of its primitive and frightening quality.

The shadow is most dangerous when unrecognized. Then the individual tends to project his or her unwanted qualities onto others or to become dominated by the shadow without realizing it. Images of evil, the devil, and the concept of original sin are all aspects of the shadow archetype. The more the shadow material is made conscious, the less it can dominate. But the shadow is an integral part of our nature, and it can never be simply eliminated. A person who claims to be without a shadow is not a complete individual but a two-dimensional caricature, denying the mixture of good and evil that is necessarily present in all of us.

personal reflection

THE SHADOW

One aspect of the shadow can be personified by a small demon, an imp dedicated to harming you or foiling your best-laid plans. It may appear as an implacable inner critic or as a demanding judge. The following is intended to help you better understand this aspect of your shadow.

1. Think about how you would describe in detail your personal demon and how it operates in your life. When does it appear? Do any triggers seem to bring it out?
2. If you were to personify this aspect of the shadow, what would it look like? Does it have a name? How would it dress? What would some of its favorite expressions be?
3. Communicate with this figure. Discuss its good qualities. How has it helped you? Also examine how it has fostered or arrested your personal change or growth.
4. What inner figure would be the opposite of the personal demon? With this opposite figure in mind, review steps 1 to 3.

Modern Jungians have written about the "light shadow," the positive aspects of our personality seen as incompatible with our sense of self. This often includes qualities like charm, beauty, intelligence, qualities we then tend to project onto others.

The Jungian approach to the shadow has been the subject of many popular books and articles. (See, for example, Abrams & Zweig, 1991, and Abrams, 1994, for a look at the shadow in America.)

The ancient Chinese sage Chuang-tzu (369–286 BC) provides an approach to dealing with the shadow remarkably similar to Jung's approach:

> There was a man
> who was so disturbed
> by the sight of his own shadow
> and so displeased with his own footsteps
> that he determined to get rid of both.
> The method he hit upon was to run away from them.
> So he got up and ran.
> But every time he put his foot down
> there was another step,
> while his shadow kept up with him
> without the slightest difficulty.
> He attributed his failure
> to the fact that he was not running fast enough.
> So he ran faster and faster, without stopping,
> until he finally dropped dead.
> He failed to realize
> that if he merely stepped into the shade,
> his shadow would vanish,
> and if he sat down and stayed still,
> there would be no more footsteps. (In Merton, 1965, p. 155)

Each repressed portion of the shadow represents a part of ourselves. To the extent that we keep this material unconscious, we limit ourselves. As the shadow is made more conscious, we regain previously repressed parts of ourselves. Also, the shadow is not simply a negative force in the psyche. It is a storehouse for instinctual energy, spontaneity, and vitality, and a major source of our creative energies. Like all archetypes, the shadow is rooted in the collective unconscious, and it can allow the individual access to much of the valuable unconscious material rejected by the ego and the persona.

The following passage from one of Jung's letters provides a clear illustration of Jung's concept of the shadow and of the unconscious in general:

> It is a very difficult and important question, what you call the technique of dealing with the shadow. There is, as a matter of fact, no technique at all, inasmuch as technique means that there is a known and perhaps even prescribable way to deal with a certain difficulty or task. It is rather a dealing comparable to diplomacy or statesmanship. There is, for instance, no particular technique that would help us to reconcile two political parties opposing each other. . . . If one can speak of a technique at all, it consists solely in an attitude. First of all, one has to accept and to take seriously into account the existence of the shadow. Secondly, it is necessary to be informed about its qualities and intentions. Thirdly, long and difficult negotiations will be unavoidable. . . .
>
> Nobody can know what the final outcome of such negotiations will be. One only knows that through careful collaboration the problem itself becomes changed. Very often certain apparently impossible intentions of the shadow are mere threats due to an unwillingness on the part of the ego to enter upon a serious consideration of the shadow. Such threats diminish usually when one meets them seriously. (1973, p. 234)

Just when we think we understand it, the shadow will appear in another form. Dealing with the shadow is a lifelong process of looking within and honestly reflecting on what we see there (von Franz, 1995).

Anima and Animus

Jung postulated an unconscious structure that complements the persona—the **anima** in man and the **animus** in woman. This basic psychic structure serves as a focus for all the psychological material that does not fit with an individual's conscious self-image as a man or as a woman. Thus to the extent that a woman consciously defines herself in feminine terms, her animus will include those unrecognized tendencies and experiences that she has defined as masculine.

For a woman the process of psychological development entails entering into a dialogue between her ego and her animus. The animus may be pathologically dominated by identification with archetypal images (for example, the bewitched prince, the romantic poet, the ghostly lover, or the marauding pirate) and/or by an extreme father fixation.

The animus or anima initially seems to be a wholly separate personality. As the animus/anima and its influence on the individual is recognized, it assumes the role of liaison between conscious and unconscious until it gradually becomes integrated into the self. Jung views the quality of this union of opposites (in this case, masculine and feminine) as the major step in individuation.

As long as our anima or animus is unconscious, not accepted as part of our self, we will tend to project it outward onto people of the opposite sex:

> Every man carries within him the eternal image of woman, not the image of this or that particular woman, but a definitive feminine image. This image is . . . an imprint or "archetype" of all the ancestral experiences of the female, a deposit, as it were, of all the impressions ever made by woman. . . . Since this image is unconscious, it is always unconsciously projected upon the person of the beloved, and is one of the chief reasons for passionate attraction or aversion. (Jung, 1931b, p. 198)

personal reflection

SEEING OURSELVES IN OTHERS

List all the qualities you admire in the person you love or respect most. Next, list all the qualities you dislike in the person you respect the least. The first list most likely contains your anima or animus projections—those qualities you have inside you that you can develop. The second list contains your shadow projections—those qualities that you must confront within yourself.

According to Jung, the child's opposite-sex parent is a major influence on the development of the anima or animus. All relations with the opposite sex, including parents, are strongly affected by the projection of anima or animus fantasies. This archetype is one of the most influential regulators of behavior. It appears in dreams and fantasies as figures of the opposite sex, and it functions as the primary mediator between unconscious and conscious processes. It is oriented primarily toward inner processes, just as the persona is oriented to the outer. (For example, the creative influence of the anima can be seen in male artists who have traditionally attributed their inspiration to the muses—female demigoddesses.) Jung also called this archetype the "soul image." Because it has the capacity to bring us in touch with our unconscious forces, it is often the key to unlocking our creativity.

The Self

The archetype of the individual is the Self. The Self is all-embracing. God is a circle whose center is everywhere and whose circumference is nowhere. (Jung in McGuire & Hull, 1977, p. 86)

The **self** is the most important personality archetype and also the most difficult to understand. Jung has called the self the *central archetype,* the archetype of psychological order and the totality of the personality. The self is the archetype of centeredness. It is the union of the conscious and the unconscious that embodies the harmony and balance of the various opposing elements of the psyche. The self directs the functioning of the whole psyche in an integrated way. According to Jung, "[C]onscious and unconscious are not necessarily in opposition to one another, but complement one another to form a totality, which is the self" (1928b, p. 175). Jung discovered the self archetype only after his investigations of the other structures of the personality.

The self is depicted in dreams or images impersonally (as a circle, mandala, crystal, or stone) or personally (as a royal couple, a divine child, or other symbol of divinity). Great spiritual teachers, such as Christ, Muhammed, and Buddha, are also symbols for the self. These are all symbols of wholeness, unification, reconciliation of polarities, and dynamic equilibrium—the goals of the individuation process (Edinger, 1996). Jung explains the function of the self:

> The ego receives the light from the Self. Though we know of this Self, yet it is not known. . . . Although we receive the light of consciousness from the Self and although we know it to be the source of our illumination, we do not know whether it possesses anything we would call consciousness. . . . If the Self could be wholly experienced, it would be a limited experience, whereas in reality its experience is unlimited and endless. . . . If I were one with the Self I would have knowledge of everything, I would speak Sanskrit, read cuneiform script, know the events that took place in pre-history, be acquainted with the life of other planets, etc. (1975, pp. 194–195)

The self is a deep, inner, guiding factor, which can seem to be quite different, even alien, from the ego and consciousness. "The self is not only the centre, but also the whole circumference which embraces both conscious and unconscious; it is the centre of this totality, just as the ego is the centre of consciousness" (1936b, p. 41). It may first appear in dreams as a tiny, insignificant image, because the self is so unfamiliar and undeveloped in most people. The development of the self does not mean that the ego is dissolved. The ego remains the center of consciousness, an important structure within the psyche. It becomes linked to the self as the result of the long, hard work of understanding and accepting unconscious processes.

Symbols

According to Jung, the unconscious expresses itself primarily through symbols. Although no specific symbol or image can ever fully represent an archetype (which is a form without specific content), the more closely a symbol conforms to the unconscious material organized around an archetype, the more it evokes a strong, emotionally charged response.

> The symbol has a very complex meaning because it defies reason; it always presupposes a lot of meanings that can't be comprehended in a single logical concept. The symbol has a future. The past does not suffice to interpret it, because germs of the future are included in every actual situation. That's why, in elucidating a case, the symbolism is spontaneously applicable, for it contains the future. (Jung in McGuire & Hull, 1977, p. 143)

As a plant produces its flower, so the psyche creates its symbols. (Jung, 1964, p. 64)

Jung is concerned with two kinds of symbols: individual and collective. By individual symbols Jung means "natural" symbols that are spontaneous productions of the individual psyche, rather than images or designs created deliberately by an artist. In addition to the personal symbols found in an individual's dreams or fantasies, there are important collective symbols, often religious images such as the cross, the six-pointed Star of David, and the Buddhist wheel of life.

Symbolic terms and images represent concepts that we cannot completely define or fully comprehend. Symbols always have connotations that are unclear or hidden from us. For Jung, a sign *stands for* something else, but a symbol, such as a tree, *is* something in itself—a dynamic, living thing. A symbol may represent the individual's psychic situation, and it is that situation at a given moment.

Active Imagination.   Jung valued the use of active imagination as a means of facilitating self-understanding through work with symbols. He encouraged his patients to paint, sculpt, or employ other art forms as ways to explore their inner depths. Active imagination is not passive fantasy but an attempt to engage the unconscious in a dialogue with the ego, through symbols.

Active imagination refers to any conscious effort to produce material directly related to unconscious processes, to relax our usual ego controls without allowing the unconscious to take over completely. The process of active imagination differs for each individual. Some people use drawing or painting most profitably, whereas others prefer to use conscious imagery, or fantasy, or another form of expression.

Jung himself used a variety of outlets to explore his unconscious. He designed his retreat house in Bollingen according to his inner needs, and, as he himself developed,

personal reflection

ACTIVE IMAGINATION

Drawing

Start a sketch diary, a daily collection of sketches and drawings. As you work with the diary, you will gradually see how major changes in your psychological life relate to your drawings. As you draw, you will probably find that you frequently associate certain colors or forms with certain emotions and people, and your drawings will become a clearer medium for self-expression.

Another approach to drawing is to sit down with a pad and crayons and ask your unconscious a question. Then let your imagination find an image; put the image on paper. Do not think an answer.

Other Media

Technology can serve as an aid in active imagination. Photography and video recording offer many possibilities, including a wide range of special effects. Audio recording also is a readily available vehicle for active imagination. Choose one medium and experiment with it, allowing your unconscious to express itself in the form you have chosen.

Conscious Imaging

Start with a dream image or any image that is particularly powerful or meaningful for you. Contemplate it and observe how it begins to change or unfold. Do not try to make anything happen; just observe what seems to occur spontaneously. Hold to your first image and avoid jumping from one subject to another. You can eventually choose to step into the picture yourself and to address the image and listen to what it has to say.

---

he added wings to the house. Jung also painted murals on the walls at Bollingen; he inscribed manuscripts in Latin and high German script, illustrated his own manuscripts, and carved in stone.

Dreams.　For Jung, dreams play an important complementary (or compensatory) role in the psyche. The widely varied influences in our conscious life tend to distract us and to mold our thinking in ways often unsuitable to our personality and individuality. "The general function of dreams," Jung wrote, "is to try to restore our psychological balance by producing dream material that re-establishes, in a subtle way, the total psychic equilibrium" (1964, p. 50).

Jung approached dreams as living realities that must be experienced and observed carefully to be understood. He tried to uncover the significance of dream symbols by paying close attention to the form and content of the dream, and he gradually moved away from the psychoanalytic reliance on free association in dream analysis. "Free association will bring out all my complexes, but hardly ever the meaning of a dream. To understand the dream's meaning I must stick as close as possible to the dream images" (1934, p. 149). In analysis, Jung would continually bring his patients back to the dream images and ask them, "What does the *dream* say?" (1964, p. 29).

Dreams deal with symbols that have more than one meaning, which prevents a simple, mechanical system for dream interpretation. Any attempt at dream analysis must take into account the attitudes, experiences, and background of the dreamer. It is a joint venture between analyst and analysand. The dreamer interprets the dream with the help and guidance of the analyst. The analyst may be vitally helpful, but in the end only the dreamer can know what the dream means.

> The image is a condensed expression of the psychic situation as a whole, not merely, nor even predominantly, of unconscious contents pure and simple. (Jung, 1921, p. 442)

DREAM JOURNAL

Keep a journal of the dreams you have each night. Review the dreams at the end of each week, looking for recurring patterns or symbolism. You can also sketch the symbols and images of your dreams. Remember that the language of dreams is one of symbols and metaphors, and that the same dream may have several meanings. As you consider your dreams and dream images, ask yourself, "What does this dream have to say to me?"

Jeremy Taylor, a well-known authority on Jungian dreamwork, postulates certain basic assumptions about dreams (1992, p. 11):

1. All dreams come in the service of health and wholeness.
2. No dream comes simply to tell the dreamer what he or she already knows.
3. Only the dreamer can say with certainty what meanings a dream may hold.
4. There is no such thing as a dream with only one meaning.
5. All dreams speak a universal language, a language of metaphor and symbol.

More important than the cognitive understanding of dreams is the act of experiencing the dream material and taking this material seriously. Jung encourages us to befriend our dreams and to treat them not as isolated events but as communications from the unconscious. This process creates a dialogue between conscious and unconscious and is an important step in the integration of the two (Singer, 1972, p. 283).

DYNAMICS

Psychological Growth: Individuation

According to Jung, every individual naturally seeks individuation, or self-development. Jung believed that the psyche has an innate urge toward wholeness. This idea is similar to Maslow's concept of self-actualization, but it is based on a more complex theory of the psyche than Maslow's. "Individuation means becoming a single, homogeneous being, and, insofar as 'individuality' embraces our innermost, last, and incomparable uniqueness, it also implies becoming one's own self. We could therefore translate individuation as 'coming to selfhood' or 'self-realization'" (Jung, 1928b, p. 171).

Individuation is a natural, organic process. It is the unfolding of our basic nature, and is a fundamental drive in each of us. As Jung has written, "it is what makes a tree turn into a tree" (in McGuire & Hull, 1977, p. 210). Like any natural process, it can be blocked or interfered with, just as a tree may become stunted in an unfavorable environment.

Individuation is a process of achieving wholeness and thus moving toward greater freedom. The process includes development of a dynamic relationship between the ego and the self, along with the integration of the various parts of the psyche: the ego, persona, shadow, anima or animus, and other archetypes. As people become more individuated, these archetypes may be seen as expressing themselves in more subtle and complex ways.

> The more we become conscious of ourselves through self-knowledge, and act accordingly, the more the layer of the personal unconscious that is superimposed on the collective unconscious will be diminished. In this way there arises a consciousness which is no

To understand is my one great passion. But I also possess the physician's instinct. I would like to help people. (Jung, 1961, p. 322)

longer imprisoned in the petty, oversensitive, personal world of objective interests. This widened consciousness is no longer that touchy, egotistical bundle of personal wishes, fears, hopes, and ambitions. . . . [I]nstead, it is a function of relationship to the world of objects, bringing the individual into absolute, binding, and indissoluble communion with the world at large. (Jung, 1928b, p. 176)

As an analyst, Jung found that those who came to him in the first half of life were concerned primarily with external achievement, and the attainment of the goals of the ego. Older patients, who had fulfilled such goals reasonably well, tended to seek individuation—to strive for inner integration rather than outer achievement—and to seek harmony with the totality of the psyche.

From the ego point of view growth and development consist of integrating new material into one's consciousness; this process includes acquiring knowledge of the world and of oneself. Growth, for the ego, is essentially expanding conscious awareness. Individuation, by contrast, is the development of the self, and self's goal is to unite consciousness and the unconscious.

Unveiling the Persona.   Early in the individuation process, we must begin unveiling the persona we have developed and learning to view it as a useful tool rather than as an essential part of ourselves. Although the persona has important protective functions, it is also a mask that hides the self and the unconscious.

> When we analyze the persona we strip off the mask, and discover that what seemed to be individual is at bottom collective; in other words, that the persona was only a mask for the collective psyche. Fundamentally the persona is nothing real: it is a compromise between individual and society as to what a man should appear to be. He takes a name, earns a title, represents an office, he is this or that. In a certain sense all this is real, yet in relation to the essential individuality of the person concerned it is only secondary reality, a product of compromise, in making which others often have a greater share than he. (Jung, 1928b, p. 156)

In becoming aware of the limitations and distortions of the persona, we become more independent of our culture and our society.

Confronting the Shadow.   We can become free of the shadow's influence to the extent that we accept the reality of the dark side in each of us and simultaneously realize that we are more than the shadow.

Confronting the Anima or Animus.   A further step is to confront the anima or animus. We must deal with this archetype as a real person or persons that we can communicate with and learn from. For example, Jung would ask the anima figures that appeared to him about the interpretation of dream symbols, like a patient consulting an analyst. We also become aware that anima or animus figures have considerable autonomy and that they are likely to influence or even dominate us if we either ignore them or blindly accept their images and projections as our own.

Developing the Self.   The goal and culmination of the individuation process is the development of the self. "The self is our life's goal, for it is the completest expression of that fateful combination we call individuality" (Jung, 1928b, p. 238). The self replaces the ego as the midpoint of the psyche. Awareness of the self brings unity

Everything that happens to us, properly understood, leads us back to ourselves; it is as though there were some unconscious guidance whose aim it is to deliver us from all this and make us dependent on ourselves. (Jung, 1973, p. 78)

The unconscious mind of man sees correctly even when conscious reason is blind and impotent. (Jung, 1952b, p. 386)

to the psyche and helps to integrate conscious and unconscious material: "The aim of individuation is nothing less than to divest the self of the false wrappings of the persona on the one hand, and of the suggestive power of primordial images on the other" (Jung, 1945, p. 174). The ego is still the center of consciousness, but it is no longer seen as the nucleus of the entire personality. Jung wrote that

> one must be what one is; one must discover one's own individuality, that centre of personality, which is equidistant between the conscious and the unconscious; we must aim for that ideal point towards which nature appears to be directing us. Only from that point can one satisfy one's needs. (In Serrano, 1966, p. 91)

Although it is possible to describe individuation in terms of stages, the process is considerably more complex than the simple progression outlined here. All of the steps listed overlap, and each of us continually returns to old problems and issues (we hope from a different perspective). Individuation might be represented as a spiral in which we keep confronting the same basic questions, each time in a more refined form. (This concept relates closely to the Zen Buddhist conception of enlightenment, in which an individual never solves a personal *koan*, or spiritual problem, and the searching is seen as a goal in itself.)

Obstacles to Growth

Individuation, consciously undertaken, is a difficult task, and the individual must be relatively psychologically healthy to handle the process. The ego must be strong enough to undergo tremendous changes, to be turned inside out in the process of individuation:

> One could say that the whole world with its turmoil and misery is in an individuation process. But people don't know it, that's the only difference. . . . Individuation is by no means a rare thing or a luxury of the few, but those who know that they are in such a process are considered to be lucky. They get something out of it, provided they are conscious enough. (Jung, 1973, p. 442)

This process is especially difficult because it is an individual enterprise, often carried out in the face of the rejection or, at best, indifference of others. Jung writes that

> nature cares nothing whatsoever about a higher level of consciousness; quite the contrary. And then society does not value these feats of the psyche very highly; its prizes are always given for achievement and not for personality, the latter being rewarded for the most part posthumously. (1931a, p. 394)

The Persona.   Each stage in the individuation process has its difficulties. First is the danger of identification with the persona. Those who identify with the persona may try to become "perfect," unable to accept their mistakes or weaknesses, or any deviations from their idealized self-concepts. Individuals who fully identify with the persona tend to repress any tendencies that do not fit their self-image and attribute such behaviors to others; the job of acting out aspects of the repressed, negative identity is assigned to other people.

The Shadow.   The shadow can also become a major obstacle to individuation. People who are unaware of their shadows can easily act out harmful impulses without

Mohandas Gandhi: An individuated leader

Filling the conscious mind with ideal conceptions is a characteristic feature of Western theosophy. . . . One does not become enlightened by imagining figures of light, but by making the darkness conscious. (Jung, 1954a, pp. 265–266)

ever recognizing them as wrong or without any awareness of their own negative feelings. In such people, an initial impulse to harm or do wrong is instantly rationalized as they fail to acknowledge the presence of such an impulse in themselves. Ignorance of the shadow may also result in an attitude of moral superiority and projection of the shadow onto others. For example, some of those loudly in favor of the censorship of pornography seem to be fascinated by the materials they want to ban; they may even convince themselves of the need to "study" carefully all the available pornography in order to be effective censors.

The Anima/Animus. Confronting the anima or animus brings with it the problem of relating to the collective unconscious. In the man, the anima may produce sudden emotional changes or moodiness. In the woman, the animus may manifest itself as irrational, rigidly held opinions. Jung's discussion of anima and animus is not a description of masculinity and femininity in general. The content of the anima or animus is the complement of our conscious conception of ourselves as masculine or feminine—which, in most people, is strongly determined by cultural values and socially defined sex roles.

An individual exposed to collective material faces the danger of becoming engulfed by it. According to Jung, this outcome can take one of two forms. First is the possibility of ego inflation, in which the individual claims all the virtues and knowledge of the collective psyche. The opposite reaction is that of ego impotence; the person feels that he or she has no control over the collective psyche and becomes acutely aware of unacceptable aspects of the unconscious—irrationality, negative impulses, and so forth.

Ego Inflation. As in many myths and fairy tales, the greatest obstacles are those found closest to the goal (von Franz, 1995). When the individual deals with the anima and animus, tremendous energy is unleashed. This energy can be used to build up the ego instead of developing the self. Jung has referred to this as identification with the archetype of the mana-personality. (*Mana* is a Melanesian word for the energy or power that emanates from people, objects, or supernatural beings; it is energy that has an occult or bewitching quality.) The ego identifies with the archetype of the wise man or wise woman, the sage who knows everything. (This syndrome is not uncommon among older university professors, for example.) The mana-personality is dangerous because it is a false exaggeration of power. Individuals stuck at this stage try to be both more and less than they really are: more, because they tend to believe they have become perfect, holy, or even godlike; but actually less, because they have lost touch with their essential humanity and the fact that no one is infallible, flawless, and perfectly wise.

Jung sees temporary identification with the archetype of the self or the mana-personality as being almost inevitable in the individuation process. The best defense against the development of ego inflation is to remember one's essential humanity and to stay grounded in the reality of what one can and must do, not what one *should* do or be.

> Not perfection, but completeness is what is expected of you. (Jung, 1973, p. 97)

STRUCTURE

Body

In his voluminous writings, Jung did not deal explicitly with the role of the body but chose to direct his efforts to analyzing the psyche. He has argued that physical processes are relevant to us only to the extent that they are represented in the psyche. The physical body and the external world can be known only as psychological experiences: "I'm chiefly concerned with the psyche itself, therefore I'm leaving out body and spirit. . . . Body and spirit are to me mere aspects of the reality of the psyche. Psychic experience is the only immediate experience. Body is as metaphysical as spirit" (1973, p. 200). For Jung, the *experience* of the body is all-important (Conger, 1988).

> Psyche and body are not separate entities, but one and the same life. (Jung, 1917, p. 113)

Social Relationships

Jung stresses that individuation is essentially a personal endeavor; however, it is also a process that develops through relationships with other people:

> As nobody can become aware of his individuality unless he is closely and responsibly related to his fellow beings, he is not withdrawing to an egoistic desert when he tries to find himself. He only can discover himself when he is deeply and unconditionally related to some, and generally related to a great many, individuals with whom he has a chance to compare, and from whom he is able to discriminate himself. (Jung in Serrano, 1966, pp. 83–84)

Individuation does not isolate, it connects. I never saw relationships thriving on unconsciousness. (Jung, 1973, p. 504)

Social interaction is important in forming and developing the major personality structures: persona, shadow, and anima or animus. The contents of social experiences help determine the specific images and symbols associated with each structure; at the same time, these basic archetypal structures mold and guide our social relationships.

Will

Jung considered individual will a relatively recent human development. In primitive cultures, rituals (such as hunting dances) work tribal members into a state of action, a state that substitutes for our modern willpower:

> The will was practically nonexistent and it needed all the ceremonial which you observe in primitive tribes to bring up something that is an equivalent to our word "decision." Slowly through the ages we have acquired a certain amount of willpower. We could detach so much energy from the energy of nature, from the original unconsciousness, from the original flow of events, an amount of energy we could control. (Jung in McGuire & Hull, 1977, p. 103)

Jung defines the will as the energy at the disposal of consciousness or the ego. The development of the will is associated with learning cultural values, moral standards, and the like. Will has power only over conscious thought and action and cannot directly affect instinctual or other unconscious processes, although it has substantial, indirect power over them through conscious processes.

Emotions

In my medical experience as well as in my own life I have again and again been faced with the mystery of love, and have never been able to explain what it is. (Jung, 1961, p. 353)

Jung stresses the central role that study of the emotions must play in psychology:

> Psychology is the only science that has to take the factor of value (i.e., feeling) into account, because it is the link between psychical events and life. Psychology is often accused of not being scientific on this account; but its critics fail to understand the scientific and practical necessity of giving due consideration to feeling. (1964, p. 99)

Psychic material directly related to the archetypes tends to arouse strong emotions and often has an awe-inspiring quality. When Jung discusses symbols, he is not writing about lifeless words or empty forms but about powerful, living realities by which men and women live their lives and for which many have died. According to Jung, emotion is the force behind the process of individuation; "Emotion is the chief source of consciousness" (1954b, p. 96). All real, inner change has an emotional component.

Intellect

For Jung, the intellect refers to directed, conscious thought processes. Jung distinguishes intellect from intuition, which draws strongly on unconscious material. The intellect has an important, but limited, role in psychological functioning. Jung stresses that a purely intellectual understanding cannot be complete: "A psychology that satisfies the intellect alone can never be practical, for the totality of the psyche can never be grasped by intellect alone" (1917, p. 117). The intellect works best in conjunction with intuition and feeling.

Therapist

According to Jung, therapy is a joint effort between analyst and patient working together as equals. Because the two form a dynamic unit, the analyst must also be open to change as a result of the interaction. Jung believed that therapy involves primarily the interaction of the analyst's unconscious with that of the patient, who can advance in therapy only as far as the analyst has:

> It is a remarkable thing about psychotherapy: you cannot learn any recipes by heart and then apply them more or less suitably, but can cure only from one central point; and that consists in understanding the patient as a psychological whole and approaching him as a human being, leaving aside all theory and listening attentively to whatever he has to say. (1973, p. 456)

Jung tried to avoid reliance on theory and on specific techniques in the process of therapy. He believed that such reliance tends to make the analyst mechanical and out of touch with the patient. The therapist does not merely treat parts of the psyche like a mechanic patching up an old car that needs a new carburetor or muffler. Therapy aims to approach the client as a whole individual through a genuine relationship.

Jung emphasized that the analyst is deeply involved, consciously and unconsciously, in the therapeutic situation. He insisted that there is an inevitable intermingling of patient and analyst at an unconscious level. Jung also pioneered in the use of dreams, fantasies, and metaphor in analysis, based on his conception of the unconscious as "primordial" and "natural" and also energized and purposeful (Sedgwick, 2000).

Jung generally saw people only once or twice a week. To foster a sense of autonomy in his patients, he would often give them homework—for example, he might ask them to analyze their own dreams. At his insistence, his clients would take occasional vacations from analysis in order to avoid becoming dependent on him and on the analytic routine.

Jung often spoke of his approach to psychotherapy as "analyzing from the Self," a way of directly addressing his patients' deepest issues. He contrasted this approach with "prestige analysis," which is based on the persona, and "ego-centered analysis," which is driven by fear of the unconscious (Haule, 2000).

Jung outlined two major stages of the therapeutic process, each of which has two parts. First comes the *analytic stage*. It consists initially of *confession*, in which the individual begins to recover unconscious material. Ties of dependency on the therapist tend to develop at this stage. Next comes *elucidation* of the confessional material, in which greater familiarity and understanding of psychic processes develop. The patient remains dependent on the therapist.

The second stage of therapy is the *synthetic*. First comes *education*, in which Jung stressed the need to move from psychological insight to actual new experiences that result in individual growth and the formation of new habits. The final part is the *transformation*. The patient–analyst relationship is integrated, and dependency is reduced as the relationship becomes transformed. The individual experiences a highly concentrated individuation process, though archetypal material is not necessarily

A therapist who has a neurosis does not deserve the name, for it is not possible to bring the patient to a more advanced stage than one has reached oneself. (Jung, 1973, p. 95)

Any of my pupils could give you so much insight and understanding that you could treat yourself if you don't succumb to the prejudice that you receive healing through others. In the last resort every individual alone has to win his battle, nobody else can do it for him. (Jung, 1973, p. 126)

The serious problems in life, however, are never fully solved. If ever they should appear to be so it is a sure sign that something has been lost. The meaning and purpose of a problem seem to lie not in its solutions but in our working at it incessantly. (Jung, 1931a, p. 394)

confronted. This is the stage of self-education, in which patients take increasing responsibility for their own development.

EVALUATION

Jung has often been criticized for his lack of a coherent, clearly structured system of thought. His writing sometimes seems to go off on tangents, rather than present ideas in a formal, logical, or even systematic fashion. Also, at different times Jung may use varying definitions for the same term. He was aware of this difficulty in his writing but did not see it as a drawback. Jung believed that life rarely follows the logical, coherent pattern that has become the standard for scientific and academic writing, and believed that his own style may be closer to the rich complexity of psychological reality.

Jung deliberately developed a loose, open system, one that could admit new information without distorting it to fit a closed theoretical framework. He never believed that he knew all the answers or that new information would merely confirm his theories. Consequently, his theorizing lacks a tight, logical structure that categorizes all life in terms of a few theoretical constructs.

It has been argued that Jung's work remains extremely relevant today and that his writings align with the postmodern critiques of contemporary culture (Hauke, 2000). Also, Jung's nonobjectivist, yet empirically based epistemology puts him in the psychological traditional of William James (Kotsch, 2000).

Religion and Mysticism

> I am a researcher and not a prophet. What matters to me is what can be verified by experience. But I am not interested at all in what can be speculated about experience without any proof. (Jung, 1973, p. 203)

Because he dealt with religion, alchemy, spirituality, and the like, some critics have labeled Jung a mystic rather than a scientist. For Jung, mystical traditions and beliefs were important expressions of human ideals and aspirations. He treated spiritual experiences as data that no one concerned with the full range of human thought and behavior should ignore. But it is clear that Jung's attitude was always that of an investigator rather than that of a believer or a disciple.

> I am and remain a psychologist. I am not interested in anything that transcends the psychological content of human experience. . . . But on the psychological level I have to do with religious experiences which have a structure and a symbolism that can be interpreted. For me, religious experience is real, is true. I have found that through such religious experiences the soul may be "saved," its integration hastened, and spiritual equilibrium established. (Jung in McGuire & Hull, p. 229)

Jung saw clearly that a religious approach to life related closely to psychological health:

> Among all my patients in the second half of life—that is to say, over thirty-five—there has not been one whose problem in the last resort was not that of finding a religious outlook on life. It is safe to say that every one of them fell ill because he had lost what the living religions of every age have given to their followers, and none of them has been really healed who did not regain his religious outlook. (1932, p. 334)

Jung believed that all human beings have a religious instinct and a longing for wholeness. He held that God is a part of every human being (Dyer, 2000).

Jung's stress on the practical importance of spirituality is evident in a letter that he wrote to Bill Wilson, the cofounder of Alcoholics Anonymous. In the letter, Jung wrote about an alcoholic patient, Roland H., saying that Roland's addiction to alcohol was hopeless unless "he could become the subject of a spiritual or religious experience—in short a genuine conversion." Jung greatly influenced Wilson in his own conversion and cure as well as in his cofounding AA in 1934. The following is an excerpt from the letter Jung wrote to Wilson:

> I had no news from Roland H. and often wondered what has been his fate. . . . His craving for alcohol was the equivalent, on a low level, of the spiritual thirst of our being for wholeness, expressed in medieval language: the union with God.
>
> How could one formulate such an insight in a language that is not misunderstood in our days?
>
> The only right and legitimate way to such an experience is that it happens to you in reality, and it can only happen to you when you walk on a path which leads you to higher understanding. You might be led to that goal by an act of grace or through a personal and honest contact with friends, or through a higher education of the mind beyond the confines of mere rationalism. . . .
>
> You see, "alcohol" in Latin is *spiritus*, and you use the same word for the highest religious experience as well as for the most depraving poison. The helpful formula therefore is: *spiritus contra spiritum*. (1984, pp. 197–198)

Jung's inspiration in the founding of Alcoholics Anonymous and the 12-step movement may have been one of his greatest contributions to modern society.

The Analysis of Symbols

Jung's recognition of the importance of symbols and his detailed analysis of symbols and their interpretations are his most important contributions to psychology. Jung was deeply aware of the complexity of symbolism and of the need to analyze symbols without oversimplifying. He was drawn to mythology, folklore, and alchemy because they provided various contexts that shed light on the complex symbolic productions he encountered in analysis.

Although Jung's writing is difficult to comprehend, it is perhaps more valuable than simpler or more logical prose because it conveys the richness of his thinking. His flexibility and open-mindedness, and his concern for the deeper truths of human existence, give Jung's work a breadth and complexity virtually unmatched in psychology.

RECENT DEVELOPMENTS: JUNG'S INFLUENCE

Jung's ideas have been growing steadily in popularity and influence. The Jung Institute in Zurich still trains analysts from around the world. Jungian institutes in various countries and in major U.S. cities provide extensive research materials, lecture series, weekend workshops, and long-term training in Jungian analysis. The practice of Jungian analysis has continued to develop since Jung's death (see Stein, 1995, 1998). Serious biographical studies of Jung are still being published; one of the most recent is by award-winning biographer Deirdre Blair (2003).

The Myers-Briggs Type Indicator, based on Jung's theory of types, has become one of the most popular psychological tests in the world (Myers, 1980). Widely used

The main interest of my work is not concerned with the treatment of neuroses but rather with the approach to the numinous [a sense of the holy]. But the fact is that the approach to the numinous is the real therapy and inasmuch as you attain to the numinous experiences you are released from the curse of pathology. (Jung, 1973, p. 377)

Psychic development cannot be accomplished by intention and will alone; it needs the attraction of a symbol. (Jung, 1928a, p. 25)

I can only hope and wish that no one becomes "Jungian." . . . I proclaim no cut-and-dried doctrine and I abhor "blind adherence." I leave everyone free to deal with the facts in his own way, since I also claim this freedom for myself. (Jung, 1973, p. 405)

today in business and in education, it has been taken by millions of people. Each individual is scored on introversion versus extraversion, thinking versus feeling, intuition versus sensation, and also perception versus judgment. This final category was added to Jung's basic scheme. Perception refers to an openness to new evidence and new experience. Judgment refers to the shutting out of new perceptions and coming to a quick decision. In one study, the MBTI has been used to increase the effectiveness of diversity training (Most white males prefer Thinking, while virtually everyone else uses more Feeling function.) (Sheill, 1999).

Among the many prominent writers and scholars who have elaborated on Jung's ideas, Joseph Campbell applied Jungian concepts to topics including myth (1985, 1988) and the hero archetype (1949). James Hillman (1975, 1989), strongly influenced by Jung, developed an approach he calls archetypal psychology. Jean Shinoda Bolen (1984, 1989) has written two best-selling books on the archetypes of the goddesses in women and the gods in men. In their book *King, Warrior, Magician, Lover,* Robert Moore and Douglas Gillette (1990) describe the "archetypes of mature masculinity." One of the founders of the men's movement, Robert Bly (1990), has been strongly influenced by Jung's ideas.

A whole literature relates Jungian psychology and spirituality, primarily from a Christian perspective. This literature includes writings by Kelsey (1974, 1982) and by Sanford (1968, 1981). Caprio and Hedberg's (1986) *Coming Home: A Handbook for Exploring the Sanctuary Within* is a practical guide for spiritual work in the Christian tradition. It contains striking personal stories, excellent illustrations, and useful exercises.

For a fine look at the relationship between Jungian psychology and Buddhism, see Spiegelman and Miyuki (1985). Spiegelman (1982) has also written on the links between Jungian psychology and Jewish mysticism, as well as on the relationship between Jungian psychology and Hinduism (Spiegelman & Vasavada, 1987). Others have related Jungian psychology to the Kabbalah (Drob, 1999) and to a wide variety of topics in phenomenology (Brooke, 2000).

Jung's rich, complex, and sophisticated ideas are gradually gaining the widespread acceptance they so well deserve.

> Everything men assert about God is twaddle, for no man can know God. (Jung, 1975, p. 377)

The Theory Firsthand

EXCERPTS FROM *ANALYTICAL PSYCHOLOGY*

Word Association

Jung's first introduction to depth psychology came with his experiments in word association. He developed great expertise at interpreting associations. His intuitive abilities were often astonishing.

Many years ago, when I was quite a young doctor, an old professor of criminology asked me about the experiment [in word association] and said he did not believe it. I said: "No, Professor? You can try it whenever you like." He invited me to his house and I began. After ten words he got tired and said: "What can you make of it? Nothing has come of it." I told him he could not expect a result with ten or twelve words; he ought to have a hundred and then we would see something. He said: "Can you do something with these words?" I said: "Little enough, but I can tell you something. Quite recently you have had worries about money, you have too little of it. You are afraid of dying of heart disease. You must have studied in France, where you had a love affair, and it has come back to your mind, as often, when one has thoughts of dying, old sweet memories come back from the womb of time." He said: "How do you know?" Any child could have seen it! He was a man of 72 and he had associated *heart* with *pain*—fear that he would die of heart failure. He associated *death* with *to die*—a natural reaction—and with *money* he associated *too little,* a very usual reaction.

Then things became rather startling to me. To *pay*, after a long reaction time, he said *La Semeuse*, though our conversation was in German. That is the famous figure on the French coin. Now why on earth should this old man say La Semeuse? When he came to the word *kiss* there was a long reaction time and there was a light in his eyes and he said: *Beautiful.* Then of course I had the story. He would never have used French if it had not been associated with a particular feeling, and so we must think why he used it. Had he had losses with the French franc? There was no talk of inflation and devaluation in those days. That could not be the clue. I was in doubt whether it was money or love, but when he came to *kiss/beautiful* I knew it was love. He was not the kind of man to go to France in later life, but he had been a student in Paris, a lawyer, probably at the Sorbonne. It was relatively simple to stitch together the whole story. (Jung, 1968, p. 57)

Dream Analysis

The following excerpt illustrates Jung's approach to dream analysis:

I remember the case of a young girl who had been with two analysts before she came to me, and when she came to me she had the identical dream she had had when she was with those analysts. Each time at the very beginning of her analysis she had a particular dream: *She came to the frontier and she wanted to cross it, but she could not find the custom-house where she should have gone to declare whatever she carried with her.* In the first dream she was seeking the frontier, but she did not even come to it. That dream gave her the feeling that she would never be able to find the proper relation to her analyst; but because she had feelings of inferiority and did not trust her judgment, she remained with him, and nothing came of it at all. She worked with him for two months and then she left. [Then, she worked with another analyst for three months and left him as well.] . . .

When she came to me—she had seen me before at a lecture and had made up her mind to work with me—she dreamed that *she was coming to the Swiss frontier. It was day and she saw the custom-house. She crossed the frontier and she went into the custom-house, and there stood a Swiss customs official. A woman was in front of her and he let that woman pass, and then her turn came. She had only a small bag with her, and she thought she would pass unnoticed. But the official looked at her and said: "What have you got in your bag?" She said: "Oh, nothing at all," and opened it. He put his hand in and pulled out something that grew bigger and bigger, until it was two complete beds.* Her problem was that she had a resistance against marriage; she was engaged and would not marry for certain reasons, and those beds were the marriage-beds. I pulled that complex out of her and made her realize the problem, and soon after she married.

These initial dreams are often most instructive. Therefore I always ask a new patient when he first comes to me: "Did you know some time ago that you were coming? Have you met me before? Have you had a dream lately, perhaps last night?"—because if he did, it gives me most valuable information about his attitude. And when you keep in close touch with the unconscious you can turn many a difficult corner. (Jung, 1968, pp. 168–169)

CHAPTER HIGHLIGHTS

- Establishing and encouraging the relationship between the conscious and the unconscious processes is essential to achieving individual wholeness.
- Individuation is the process of personal development toward wholeness. It involves establishing a connection between the ego and the self, and integrating the various parts of the psyche.
- The ego is the center of consciousness, and the self is the center of the total psyche, including both the conscious and the unconscious processes.
- Thinking, feeling, sensation, and intuition are the four fundamental psychological functions. Each is available to experience in either introverted or extraverted fashion. The superior function is more conscious, more developed. The inferior function is the most primitive, and the least conscious, function. The inferior function may also serve as a way into the unconscious. A well-rounded approach to the world results from a combination of all four functions.
- Forgotten memories, repressed experiences, and subliminal perceptions make up the personal unconscious. The contents of the collective unconscious are not rooted in personal experience but are universal across time and cultures.

■ Archetypal imagery may be seen in many cultures and during many historical eras, as evidenced by common themes in world myths, folktales, and legends.

■ The major structures of the personality are archetypes: the persona, the ego, the shadow, the anima and the animus, as well as the self.

■ Symbols are the primary form of expression of the unconscious. As with the unconscious processes, there are two forms of symbols, the individual and the collective.

■ Dreams help restore psychological balance, reestablish one's total psychic equilibrium. We should approach dreams as living entities that must be observed carefully and experienced fully to be understood.

■ The psyche has an innate urge toward wholeness, and every individual has a tendency toward self-development or individuation.

■ Jung considered the full range of human thought and behavior to contain data from spiritual experiences. He viewed mystical belief systems as important expressions of human aspirations and ideals.

■ Jung's most important contributions to psychology are his recognition of the psychological importance of symbols and his detailed analysis of their interpretations.

KEY CONCEPTS

Active imagination Drawing, painting, sculpting, conscious imagery, fantasy, and other forms of expression. It is an attempt, through the use of symbols, to engage the unconscious in dialogue with the ego.

Anima/Animus A basic psychological structure in the unconscious. The anima or animus complements the persona and focuses all the psychological material that does not fit with an individual's conscious self-image as man or woman. Initially present as a separate personality of the opposite sex, it becomes a liaison between the conscious and the unconscious, and gradually becomes integrated into the self.

Archetypes Formless and primordial a priori structures of the psyche that act as structure-forming elements in the unconscious.

Collective unconscious The center of all the psychic material that does not come from personal experience. It extends across cultures and across time. An inborn psychological entity that structures the individual's development, the collective unconscious contains the heritage of humankind's spiritual evolution.

Extraversion The preferred attitude of one whose primary orientation is outward, who is more at ease with the world of other people and objects.

Individuation The process of developing a dynamic relationship between the ego and the self, along with the integration of the various parts of the psyche. The union of consciousness and the unconscious is the goal of individuation.

Introversion The preferred attitude of one whose primary orientation is inward, who is more comfortable with the world of feelings and thoughts.

Persona The character we assume in relating to others. It includes the clothing we wear and our individual style of expression.

Self The archetype of centeredness and psychological order. It directs the functioning of the whole psyche in an integrated way. The self embodies the balance and harmony of the various opposing elements of the psyche.

Shadow The archetype that serves as focus for material that has been repressed from consciousness. It may include material contrary to social standards, as well as desires, tendencies, memories, and experiences the individual rejects. The shadow is also a storehouse of creative and instinctual energy, spontaneity, and vitality.

ANNOTATED BIBLIOGRAPHY

Primary Sources

Jung, C. G. (1961). *Memories, dreams, reflections.* New York: Random House (Vintage Books).

An autobiography that helps place Jung's multifaceted thinking in perspective and provides an excellent introduction to Jung's thought. Includes a glossary with discussions of Jung's major concepts.

Jung, C. G. (Ed.). (1964). *Man and his symbols.* New York: Doubleday.

Contains an extremely clear essay by Jung called "Approaching the Unconscious." The book is amply illustrated, one of the best integrations of text and pictures in psychology. There is an inexpensive Dell paperback edition, but the Doubleday hardcover edition has more photos, many in color.

Jung, C. G. *Collected works of C. G. Jung* (H. Read, M. Fordham, & G. Adler, Eds.). Princeton, NJ: Princeton University Press, 1967. (Published under the sponsorship of the Bollingen Foundation; English edition, London: Routledge & Kegan Paul; American edition, volumes issued 1953–1967, Pantheon Books.)

For those seriously interested in exploring Jung in depth, this work includes virtually all of Jung's writings.

Jung, C. G. (1968). *Analytical psychology, its theory and practice.* New York: Pantheon Books.

A clear account of Jung's theories, containing transcripts of a series of lectures he gave in London. Many of Jung's essays are now available in paperback editions. Of special interest are Two Essays on Analytical Psychology, an overview of the entire theoretical system, and Psychological Types, especially Chapter 10, "General Descriptions of Types," and Chapter 11, "Definitions," both of which discuss the major Jungian concepts.

Secondary Sources

Dry, A. (1961). *The psychology of Jung.* New York: Wiley.

Fordham, F. (1953). *An introduction to Jung's psychology.* London: Penguin Books.

Hall, C., & Nordby, V. (1973). *A primer of Jungian psychology.* New York: New American Library (Mentor Books).

Clear and well-written overview of Jungian psychology.

Jacoby, J. (1959). *Complex, archetype, symbol in the psychology of C. G. Jung.* New York: Pantheon Books.

Serrano, M. (1966). *C. G. Jung and Hermann Hesse: A record of two friendships.* London: Routledge & Kegan Paul.

Includes fascinating conversations between Jung and Serrano, a Chilean poet and novelist who lived in India for several years.

Singer, J. (1972). *Boundaries of the soul: The practice of Jung's psychology.* New York: Doubleday.

A clear account of the dynamics of Jungian theory and therapy by a modern Jungian analyst.

Web Sites

The C. G. Jung Page
www.cgjungpage.org/

Includes three major areas:
1. Introduction to Jung, including a Jung lexicon, Jungian events, training, books, and Jungian organizations.
2. A library of articles on Jungian analysis.
3. Discussions of psychology and culture, including Jungian looks at technology, ecology, and popular culture.

C. G. Jung Bibliography
psychematters.com.bibliographies/jungbib.htm

Extensive listing of books by and about Jung. Includes reference books and also books on Jungian psychology, Jung and religion, Jung and literature, and other applications of Jungian theory.

Mythology and Folklore
http://www.mythinglinks.org/

A wonderfully illustrated and annotated collection of Jungian-related material. Includes links to sites on Jung, Campbell, Hillman, and other depth psychologists. Sections provide links to sites on symbols, shamanism, creation myths, and a wide variety of mythological themes. This site is meant as a reference for student research on mythology and folklore.

REFERENCES

Abrams, J., & Zweig, C. (Eds.). (1991). *Meeting the shadow.* Los Angeles: Tarcher.

Abrams, J. (Ed.). (1994). *The shadow in America.* Novato, CA: Nataraj.

Blair, D. (2003). *Jung: A biography.* New York: Little, Brown.

Bly, R. (1990). *Iron John.* Menlo Park, CA: Addison-Wesley.

Bolen, J. (1984). *The goddesses in everywoman.* San Francisco: Harper & Row.

Bolen, J. (1989). *The gods in everyman.* San Francisco: Harper & Row.

Bolen, J. (2002). *Goddesses in older women.* New York: HarperCollins.

Brooke, R. (Ed.). (2000). *Pathways into the Jungian world.* New York: Routledge.

Campbell, J. (1949). *Hero with a thousand faces.* New York: Harcourt Brace Jovanovich.

Campbell, J. (1985). *The inner reaches of outer space: Metaphor as myth and as religion.* New York: A. van der Marck.

Campbell, J. (1988). *The power of myth.* New York: Doubleday.

Campbell, J. (Ed.). (1971). *The portable Jung.* New York: Viking Press.

Caprio, B., & Hedberg, T. (1986). *Coming home: A handbook for exploring the sanctuary within.* New York: Paulist Press.

Conger, J. (1988). *Jung and Reich: The body as shadow.* Berkeley, CA: Atlantic Books.

Drob, S. (1999). Jung and the Kabbalah. *History of psychology, 2,* 102–118.

Dyer, D. (2000). *Jung's thoughts on God.* York Beach, ME: Nicholas-Hays.

Edinger, E. (1996). *The Aion lectures.* Toronto: Inner City Books.

Freud, S. The interpretation of dreams. In J. Strachey (Ed. and Trans.), *The standard edition of the complete psychological works of*

Sigmund Freud (Vols. 4, 5). London: Hogarth Press, 1953–1966. (Originally published, 1900.)

Hall, C., & Nordby, V. (1973). *A primer of Jungian psychology*. New York: New American Library (Mentor Books).

Hauke, C. (2000). *Jung and the post modern*. New York. Routledge.

Haule, J. (2000). Analyzing from the Self. In R. Brooke. (Ed.), *Pathways into the Jungian world*. New York: Routledge.

Hillman, J. (1975). *Re-visioning psychology*. New York: Harper & Row.

Hillman, J. (1989). *A blue fire: Selected writings by James Hillman*. New York: Harper & Row.

Hopcke, R. (1995). *Persona: Where sacred meets profane*. Boston: Shambhala.

Jung, C. G. The psychology of dementia praecox. In H. Read, M. Fordham, & G. Adler (Eds.), *Collected works of C. G. Jung* (Vol. 3). Princeton, NJ: Princeton University Press, 1967. (Published under the sponsorship of the Bollingen Foundation; English edition, London: Routledge & Kegan Paul; American edition, volumes issued 1953–1967, Pantheon Books.) (Originally published, 1907.)

Jung, C. G. Symbols of transformation. In *Collected works* (Vol. 5). (Originally published, 1912.)

Jung, C. G. The psychology of the unconscious. In *Collected works* (Vol. 7). (Originally published, 1917.)

Jung, C. G. Psychological types. In *Collected works* (Vol. 6). (Originally published, 1921.)

Jung, C. G. On psychic energy. In *Collected works* (Vol. 8). (Originally published, 1928a.)

Jung, C. G. The relations between the ego and the unconscious. In *Collected works* (Vol. 7). (Originally published, 1928b.)

Jung, C. G. The stages of life. In *Collected works* (Vol. 8). (Originally published, 1931a.)

Jung, C. G. Marriage as a psychological relationship. In *Collected works* (Vol. 17). (Originally published, 1931b.)

Jung, C. G. Problems of modern psychotherapy. In *Collected works* (Vol. 16). (Originally published, 1931c.)

Jung, C. G. Psychotherapists or the clergy. In *Collected works* (Vol. 11). (Originally published, 1932.)

Jung, C. G. The practical use of dream analysis. In *Collected works* (Vol. 16). (Originally published, 1934.)

Jung, C. G. Individual dream symbolism in relation to alchemy. In *Collected works* (Vol. 12). (Originally published, 1936b.)

Jung, C. G. The archetypes and the collective unconscious. In *Collected works* (Vol. 9, Part 1). (Originally published, 1936c.)

Jung, C. G. Psychology and religion. In *Collected works* (Vol. 2). (Originally published, 1938.)

Jung, C. G. Conscious, unconscious, and individuation. In *Collected works* (Vol. 9, Part 1). (Originally published, 1939.)

Jung, C. G. A psychological approach to the dogma of the Trinity. In *Collected works* (Vol. 11). (Originally published, 1942.)

Jung, C. G. The relations between the ego and the unconscious. In *Collected works* (Vol. 7). (Originally published, 1945.)

Jung, C. G. A study in the process of individuation. In *Collected works* (Vol. 9, part 1). (Originally published, 1950.)

Jung, C. G. Aion. In *Collected works* (Vol. 9, Part 2). (Originally published, 1951a.)

Jung, C. G. Answer to Job. In *Collected works* (Vol. 12). (Originally published, 1952b.)

Jung, C. G. The philosophical tree. In *Collected works* (Vol. 13). (Originally published, 1954a.)

Jung, C. G. Psychological aspects of the mother archetype. In *Collected works* (Vol. 9, Part 1). (Originally published, 1954b.)

Jung, C. G. (1961). *Memories, dreams, reflections*. New York: Random House (Vintage Books).

Jung, C. G. (1968). *Analytical psychology, its theory and practice*. New York: Pantheon.

Jung, C. G. (Ed.). (1964). *Man and his symbols*. New York: Doubleday.

Jung, C. G. (1973). *Letters* (G. Adler, Ed.). Princeton, NJ: Princeton University Press.

Jung, C. G. (1975). *Letters, Vol. II: 1951–61*. (G. Adler, Ed.). Princeton, NJ: Princeton University Press.

Jung, C. G. (1984). *Selected letters of C. G. Jung, 1909–1961*. (G. Adler, Ed.). Princeton, NJ: Princeton University Press.

Kakar, S. (1994). Encounters of the psychological kind: Freud, Jung, and India. In L. Boyer, R. Boyer, & H. Stein (Eds.), *Essays in honor of George A. DeVos*. Hillsdale, NJ: Analytic Press.

Kelsey, M. (1974). *God, dreams, and revelation: A Christian interpretation of dreams*. Minneapolis: Augsburg.

Kelsey, M. (1982). Christo-psychology. New York: Crossroad.

Kotsch, W. (2000). Jung's mediatory sciences as a psychology beyond objectivism. *Journal of Analytic Psychology, 45*, 217–244.

McGuire, W., & Hull, R. F. C. (Eds.). (1977). *C. G. Jung speaking*. Princeton, NJ: Princeton University Press.

Merton, C. (Trans.). (1965). *The way of Chuang Tzu*. New York: New Directions.

Moore, R., & Gillette, D. (1990). *King, warrior, magician, lover: Rediscovering the archetypes of mature masculinity*. San Francisco: HarperCollins.

Myers, I. (1980). *Gifts differing*. Palo Alto, CA: Consulting Psychologists Press.

Pearson, C. (1989). *The hero within: Six archetypes we live by*. New York: Harper & Row.

Pearson, C. (1991). *Awakening the heroes within*. San Francisco: HarperSanFrancisco.

Sanford, J. A. (1968). *Dreams: God's forgotten language*. Philadelphia: Lippincott.

Sanford, J. A. (1981). *The man who wrestled with God: Light from the Old Testament on the psychology of individuation*. Ramsey, NY: Paulist Press.

Sedgwick, D. (2000). Answers to nine questions about Jungian psychology. *Psychoanalytic Dialogues, 10*, 457–472.

Segal, R., Singer, J., & Stein, M. (Eds.). (1995). *The allure of gnosticism: The gnostic experience in Jungian psychology and contemporary culture*. Chicago: Open Court.

Serrano, M. (1966). *C. G. Jung and Hermann Hesse: A record of two friendships.* London: Routledge & Kegan Paul.

Sheill, R. (1999). The Jungian decision-making process and its relationship to diversity training. *Dissertation Abstracts, 60.*

Singer, J. (1972). *Boundaries of the soul: The practice of Jung's psychology.* New York: Doubleday.

Spiegelman, J. (1982). *Jungian psychology and the tree of life.* Phoenix, AZ: Falcon Press.

Spiegelman, J., & Miyuki, M. (1985). *Buddhism and Jungian psychology.* Phoenix, AZ: Falcon Press.

Spiegelman, J., & Vasavada, A. (1987). *Hinduism and Jungian psychology.* Phoenix, AZ: Falcon Press.

Stein, M. (Ed.). (1995). *Jungian analysis.* Chicago: Open Court.

Stein, M. (1998). *Jung's map of the Jungian analysis.* Chicago: Open Court.

Suzuki, D. T. (1964). *An introduction to Zen Buddhism.* New York: Grove Press.

Taylor, J. (1992). *Where people fly and water runs uphill: Using dreams to tap the wisdom of the unconscious.* New York: Warner Books.

von Franz, M. (1975). *C. G. Jung: His myth in our time.* New York: Putnam.

von Franz, M. (1995). *Shadow and evil in fairy tales.* Boston: Shambhala.

Whitmont, E. (1969). *The symbolic quest.* New York: Putnam.

Woolger, J., & Woolger, R. (1989). *The goddess within.* New York: Fawcett Columbine.

Wilhelm, R., & Jung, C. G. (1962) *The secret of the golden flower.* London: Routledge & Kegan Paul.

alfred adler and
individual psychology

Alfred Adler is the founder of a holistic system that seeks to understand each person as an integrated totality within a social system. He called his approach *Individual Psychology* because it stresses the uniqueness of the individual rather than the universalities of behavior described by Freud.

Adler's followers established centers throughout Europe, England, and the United States, and many of his original ideas have become widely accepted in psychology and psychotherapy today. Probably more people have heard of Adler's concept of the **inferiority complex** than of any other single idea in psychology.

The four major principles of Adler's system are holism, the unity of the individual's style of life, social interest or community feeling, and the importance of goal-directed behavior. Adler's argument that goals and expectations have a greater influence on behavior than do past experiences was a major cause of his break with Freud. Adler also believed that individuals are motivated primarily by the goal of superiority, or conquest of their environment. He stressed both the effect of social influences on individuals and the importance of social interest: a sense of community, cooperation, and concern for others. For Adler, life is essentially a movement toward more successful adaptation to the environment, greater cooperation, and altruism.

Adler's individual psychology is similar to behaviorism in its stress on overt behaviors and their consequences as well as in its assertion that concepts must be concrete and related to actual behavior. In contrast to most of the other psychological theories covered in this text, individual psychology is not a *depth psychology;* that is, it does not postulate intangible forces and constructs deep within the psyche. Rather, Adler developed a context psychology in which behavior is understood in terms of the physical and social environment, a context of which the individual generally is not aware. Adler was the first to practice family therapy, which he introduced in 1920. Adlerians have made important contributions to group therapy, to *brief therapy,* and to applications of psychology in education, parenting, and social work.

PERSONAL HISTORY

Alfred Adler was born in a suburb of Vienna on February 7, 1870, the son of a middle-class Jewish merchant. The Adler family was extremely musical. Alfred's sister was an excellent pianist, one brother became a violin teacher, and Alfred himself had such a beautiful voice that he was often encouraged to seek a career in the opera. As a child, he suffered from a number of serious illnesses, including rickets. He also suffered from rivalry with his older brother. He once commented, "My elder brother . . . was always ahead of me—he is *still* ahead of me!" (Adler in Bottome, 1957, p. 27).

Adler struggled hard to overcome his physical weakness. Whenever possible, young Alfred ran and played with other children, with whom he was quite popular. He seemed to gain a sense of equality and self-esteem from his friends that he did not find at home. These experiences can be seen later in Adler's work, in his stress on the community sharing of feelings and values, which he called **social interest** and through which, he believed, individuals can achieve their potential as productive members of society.

During his sickly youth, Adler read voraciously. In his adult years, his familiarity with literature, the Bible, psychology, and German philosophy made him popular in Viennese society and later as a lecturer throughout the world.

As a child, Adler was confronted by death on several occasions. When Alfred was 3 years old, his younger brother died in the bed they shared. In addition, Adler twice

The hardest things for human beings to do is to know themselves and change themselves. (Adler, 1928, p. 11)

narrowly escaped being killed in street accidents; and, at the age of 5, he contracted a severe case of pneumonia. The family physician believed the case to be hopeless, but another doctor managed to save him. As a result of this experience, Adler decided that he wanted to be a doctor.

At the age of 18, Adler entered the University of Vienna to study medicine. He was deeply interested in socialism and attended political meetings. At one of these meetings he met his future wife, Raissa, a Russian student attending the university.

Adler received his medical degree in 1895. He established a practice first in ophthalmology and then in general medicine. Because of his growing interest in nervous-system functioning and adaptation, Adler's professional interests later shifted to neurology and psychiatry. In 1901, Adler, a rising young physician, strongly defended in print Freud's new book, *The Interpretation of Dreams*. Although Freud had never met Adler, he was deeply touched by Adler's courageous defense of his work, and he wrote to thank Adler and invite him to join a newly formed discussion group on psychoanalysis.

Adler entered this group (which later became the Vienna Psychoanalytic Society) as an accomplished young professional who was already developing his own theoretical orientation. He was not a follower of Freud. He was never Freud's "pupil" and never underwent a training analysis. Nevertheless, in 1910, Adler became president of the psychoanalytic society and coeditor of one of its journals.

Just one year later, Adler's increasingly divergent theoretical orientation had become unacceptable to Freud and to many other members of the society. Two major differences were Adler's emphasis on power rather than on sexuality as a central human drive and Adler's focus on the social environment and his deemphasis on unconscious processes. Adler resigned as president and left the society along with 9 like-minded colleagues who also considered psychoanalysis too rigid and intolerant of independent thinking. A group reduced to 14 remained with Freud. Adler founded his own organization, the Association for Individual Psychology, which gradually spread throughout Europe.

Adler and his followers became active in the field of education, especially in teacher training, because of their belief in the importance of working with those who shaped the minds and characters of the young. Endorsed by the minister of education, Adler and his associates established child guidance centers in the public schools, where children and their families could receive counseling. By the 1930s, 30 such clinics operated in Vienna alone. From 1921 until 1927, when he went to teach in the United States, Adler lectured and took demonstration cases twice a month to colleagues, parents, and teachers alike. He would often explain someone's life pattern after hearing only a few basic facts about the individual, as well as his or her earliest memories or dreams.

An eminent medical colleague stated, "The whole approach of the Viennese School of Medicine to their patients was altered . . . by Adler's teaching. I do not believe a single doctor of any standing in Vienna failed to attend, at one time or another, Adler's lectures and to profit by them" (Bottome, 1957, p. 209).

Adler's wisdom and deep understanding of human nature were evident to virtually everyone who came in contact with him. The desk clerk at a hotel in which Adler often stayed mentioned to one of Adler's colleagues, "You can hardly keep the bell-boys or the porter out of his room. They'll take any excuse to talk to him, and as far as that goes, I'm not much better myself!" (Bottome, 1957, p. 54).

Adler published numerous papers and monographs and also devoted a great deal of time to lecture tours throughout Europe and the United States. Between the first and second world wars, Adlerian groups formed in 20 European countries and in the

United States. In 1927, Adler was appointed lecturer at Columbia University. In 1928, he lectured at the New School for Social Research in New York, and a year later returned to give a series of lectures and clinical demonstrations. Adler left Vienna permanently in 1932 because of the rise of Nazism. He settled in the United States and accepted a visiting professorship in medical psychology at the Long Island Medical College. Adler died in Scotland in 1937, at age 67, while on a European lecture tour.

INTELLECTUAL ANTECEDENTS

Adler based his theories on a variety of sources, but especially significant were Darwinian evolution, Freud's psychoanalytic theories, Nietzsche's will to power, Vaihinger's fictional goals, and the theory of holism.

Evolution

Adler was strongly influenced by Darwin's theory of evolution, as were most of his contemporaries. His concept of individual psychology is based on the Darwinian premise that adaptation to the environment is the most fundamental aspect of life.

> Individual Psychology stands firmly on the ground of evolution and in the light of evolution regards all human striving as a struggle for perfection. (Adler, 1964a, pp. 36–37)

Most psychological theorists are primarily concerned with intrapsychic dynamics. Adler was not. He focused on the relations *between* individual and environment. Adler's early book on organ inferiority and compensation was largely an application of the Darwinian view of medicine. It was considered a medical complement to psychoanalytic theory and was well received by Freud. Adler's later work can be viewed as a refutation of social Darwinism, which emphasizes the survival of the fittest and elimination of the unfit. According to Adler, organic inferiority can stimulate us to superior attainments, instead of necessarily causing defeat in the struggle of life. Also, Adler argued, cooperation and community feeling are more important than competition in the process of human evolution.

Psychoanalysis

Adler had begun his own theoretical work and had already published papers in the areas of social medicine and education before he met Freud. Although he never really accepted the concepts of libido or the Oedipus complex, Adler was profoundly influenced by psychoanalytic theory, especially the importance of early childhood experiences and the mother–child relationship, the purposefulness of neurotic symptoms, and the meaningfulness of dreams.

Freud considered Adler to have been his pupil, an assertion that Adler consistently denied. Rather than building upon psychoanalytic theory, Adler developed an independent theoretical position, often in response to Freud's views. The two men had fundamentally different approaches to the exploration of human nature. Freud was interested in the analysis of parts and stressed division, whereas Adler insisted that the individual's "wholeness" was the key to understanding that person. Symptoms had significance only as an aspect of the individual personality.

> All neurotic symptoms are safeguards of persons who do not feel adequately equipped or prepared for the problems of life. (Adler, 1964b, p. 95)

Adler disagreed with Freud on several major points. He could never accept Freud's theory that the repressed, unconscious, sexual material of childhood was the core of all neuroses. Adler, who viewed sexuality as an expression of one's personality and not as its fundamental motivator, opposed Freud's assertion of the primacy of the libido. Adler suggested a different fundamental drive, the drive for power. The child, Adler explained, strives to become strong and exert power over others. The major biological fact for Adler was not the child's instinctive sexual behavior but the child's smallness and helplessness in relation to the surrounding adult world. According to Adler, children's early attempts to adapt to their environment may result in their choosing to dominate others as a means of gaining self-esteem and of achieving success.

Adler was highly critical of Freudian analysis, which he believed lacked moral orientation and produced antisocial, selfish individuals: "It is a spoilt child psychology, but what can be expected from a man who asks, 'Why should I love my neighbor?'" (Adler in Bottome, 1957, p. 256). Adler strongly believed that psychological health must be built on healthy social relationships.

Friedrich Nietzsche

Like virtually all intellectuals of his generation, Adler was affected by Friedrich Nietzsche's influential writings. However, he was not a superficial imitator of Nietzsche, as some critics have maintained. Although his earliest conceptualization of the aggressive instincts did have much in common with Nietzsche's will to power, Adler's later formulation of the striving for superiority is a much broader concept than the striving for power; it emphasizes the role of creative growth and development. In addition, Adler's concept of social interest stands in diametric opposition to Nietzsche's individualistic perspective.

Fictional Goals

Adler was significantly influenced by the writings of Hans Vaihinger, a philosopher who proposed the concept of social *fictions,* which have no basis in reality but become critical determinants of human behavior. Vaihinger believed that people, confronted by a welter of facts and experiences, create systems to organize their experiences. They then assume that these mere systems are the truth. These fictions become some of the most important influences on our behavior. According to Vaihinger, people are more affected by their expectations than by their actual experiences. He called this approach *fictionalism,* or the *philosophy of "as if."* In *The Neurotic Constitution* (1912), Adler suggests that all human behavior, thought, and feeling proceed along *as if* lines. Beginning in childhood, we attempt to adapt to our environment and overcome any felt weakness. We create for ourselves an idealized goal of perfect adaptation, then struggle toward it *as if* the goal equals success, happiness, and security.

Holism

There is a logic from the head; there is also a logic from the heart; and there is an even deeper logic from the whole. (Adler in Bottome, 1957, p. 80)

Fifteen years after his exposure to Vaihinger, Adler's thinking was affected by the holistic philosophy of Jan Smuts. Smuts was a South African military leader, statesman, and philosopher, whose work on *holism* influenced many contemporary thinkers. The two men corresponded, and Adler was instrumental in having Smuts's work published in Europe. Smuts believed that whole systems often have properties distinct from the properties of their parts—that each of us has an impulse toward increasing organization, toward wholeness. Adler used to say, "You must not only ask yourself what effect a bacillus has on a body—it is also important to know what is the effect of the body on the bacillus!" (Adler in Bottome, 1957, p. 72). He found in holistic philosophy a confirmation of many of his own ideas and an important philosophical basis for individual psychology.

personal reflection

POWER

Adler wrote a great deal about having a sense of power and mastery in one's environment.

1. Where and when have you felt powerless in your life? What was it like? Do you still feel powerless in any way? How might you change that?
2. Give a specific example of a time you sought personal superiority instead of constructive self-improvement. What were the results? How did you feel?
3. Imagine that you had the power to accomplish almost anything. What would you do? How would having real power affect your life? Would you be likely to have more friends or fewer friends? Would you be happier or sadder—in what ways?

MAJOR CONCEPTS

One of Adler's greatest contributions to psychology was his postulation of the inferiority complex and of our need to compensate for our feelings of inferiority. In the Adlerian system, the process of striving for superiority was a significant reformulation of Nietzsche's concept of will to power. The concepts of life goals, lifestyle, and the creative power of the individual are important holistic contributions to psychology. Adler's emphasis on social interest, cooperation, and the effects of society on gender differences keeps his theory rooted in a social context.

Inferiority and Compensation

In his monograph on **organ inferiority,** which first appeared in 1907, Adler attempted to explain why illness affects different people in different ways. At the time, Adler wrote as a physician concerned primarily with physiological processes. He suggested that in each individual, certain weaker organs are particularly susceptible to diseases. Adler also noted that organic weaknesses can be overcome through diligent training and exercise. In fact, a weak organ can be developed to such a degree that it becomes a person's greatest strength. Adler wrote, "In almost all outstanding people we find some organ imperfection; and we gather the impression that they were sorely confronted at the beginning of life but struggled and overcame their difficulties" (1931, p. 248).

Adler extended his investigation of organ inferiority to the study of the psychological sense of inferiority. He coined the term *inferiority complex.* According to Adler, children are deeply affected by a sense of inferiority, which is an inevitable consequence of the child's size and lack of power. Adler's own childhood experiences led him to stress the importance of this concept:

> One of my earliest recollections is of sitting on a bench, bandaged up on account of rickets, with my healthy elder brother sitting opposite me. He could run, jump and move about quite effortlessly, while for me movement of any sort was a strain and an effort. (Adler in Bottome, 1957, p. 30)

Adler believed that the life experiences of all children involve feelings of weakness, inadequacy, and frustration. Children are relatively small and helpless in the world of adults. For children, controlling their own behavior and breaking free from adult

The important thing is not what one is born with, but what use one makes of that equipment. (Adler, 1964b, p. 86)

domination is a primary concern. From this perspective, power is the first good and weakness the first evil. The struggle to attain power is the child's earliest compensation for a sense of inferiority.

Moderate feelings of inferiority can motivate the individual to constructive achievements. However, a deep sense of inferiority impedes positive growth and development:

Inferiority feelings are not in themselves abnormal. They are the cause of all improvements in the position of mankind. (Adler, 1956, p. 117)

> He [the child] realizes at an early age that there are other human beings who are able to satisfy their urges more completely, and are better prepared to live. . . . [H]e learns to overvalue the size and stature which enable one to open a door, or the ability to move heavy objects, or the right of others to give commands and claim obedience to them. A desire to grow, to become as strong or even stronger than all others, arises in his soul. (Adler, 1928, p. 34)

For Adler, virtually all progress is the result of our attempts to compensate for inferiority feelings. These feelings motivate us in our most significant achievements.

Aggression and Striving for Superiority

In his early writings, Adler emphasized the importance of aggression and striving for power. He did not equate aggression with hostility, however, but with a sense of initiative in overcoming obstacles—for example, as in aggressive marketing. Adler asserted that human aggressive tendencies have been crucial in individual and species survival. The Latin root of aggression means to step or move forward. Aggression may manifest itself in the individual as the *will to power,* a phrase of Nietzsche's that Adler used. In contrast to Freud's emphasis on the sexual roots of all behavior, Adler pointed out that both men and women often use sexuality to satisfy the urge for power.

In his later theorizing, Adler viewed aggression and will to power as manifestations of a more general motive, the goal of superiority or perfection—that is, motivation to improve ourselves, to develop our capacities and potential. Adler believed that all healthy individuals are motivated to strive for perfection, to seek continuous improvement: "The striving for perfection is innate in the sense that it is a part of life, a striving, an urge, a something without which life would be unthinkable" (1956, p. 104).

The feeling of personal worth can only be derived from achievement, from the ability to overcome. (Adler, 1964b, p. 91)

The goal of superiority can take either a positive or a negative direction. When the goal includes social concerns and an interest in the welfare of others, it develops in a constructive and healthy direction. Individuals motivated by such a goal strive to grow, to develop their skills and abilities, and to work for a constructive way of living. However, some people seek personal superiority—to achieve a sense of superiority by dominating others rather than by becoming more useful to others. Adler considered striving for personal superiority a neurotic perversion, the result of a strong sense of inferiority and a lack of social interest. Personal superiority generally fails to bring the recognition and personal satisfaction that the individual seeks.

To live means to develop. (Adler, 1964b, p. 31)

The goal of superiority has its roots in the evolutionary process of continuous adaptation to the environment. All species must evolve toward more effective adaptation or else suffer extinction, and thus individuals are driven to seek a more harmonious relationship with the environment: "If this striving were not innate to the organism, no form of life could preserve itself. The goal of mastering the environment in a superior way, which one can call the striving for perfection, consequently also characterizes the development of man" (1964b, p. 39).

Adler once said to a patient,

> What do you first do when you are learning to swim? You make mistakes, do you not? And then what happens? You make other mistakes, and when you have made *all* the mistakes you possibly can without drowning—and some of them many times over—what do you find? That you can swim? Well—life is just the same as learning to swim! Do not be afraid of making mistakes, for there is no other way of learning how to live! (Adler in Bottome, 1957, p. 37)

According to Adler, the "supreme law" of life is that "the sense of worth of the self shall not be allowed to be diminished" (Adler, 1956, p. 358). Everyone *needs* a sense of success and self-worth.

Life Goals

To Adler, the goal of mastering the environment was too broad a concept to explain logically how people choose a direction in life. Therefore, Adler turned to the idea that individuals develop a specific **life goal** that serves as a focus for achievement. The individual's life goal is influenced by personal experiences, values, attitudes, and personality. The life goal is not a consciously chosen aim.

> The goal of superiority with each individual is personal and unique. It depends upon the meaning he gives to life. This meaning is not a matter of words. It is built up in his style of life and runs through it. (Adler, 1956, p. 181)

The formation of life goals begins in childhood as compensation for feelings of inferiority, insecurity, and helplessness in an adult world. Life goals generally serve as a defense against feelings of impotence, as a bridge from the unsatisfying present to a bright, powerful, and fulfilling future. As adults, we may have definite, logical reasons for our career choices. However, the life goals that guide and motivate us were formed early in childhood and remain somewhat obscured from consciousness. For example, Adler mentions that many physicians chose their careers in childhood, as he did, as a means of coping with their insecurity concerning death.

Life goals are always somewhat unrealistic and may become neurotically overinflated if inferiority feelings are too intense. Neurotic patients generally reveal a wide gap between conscious aims and unconscious, self-defeating life goals. Fantasies of great personal superiority and high self-esteem receive more attention than goals involving real achievement. Adler's favorite question to his patients was, "What would you do if you had not got this trouble?" In their answers, he usually discovered what his patients' symptoms helped them to avoid.

> Man is but a drop of water ... but a very conceited drop. (Adler in Way, 1950, p. 167)

Life goals provide direction and purpose for our activities; they enable an outside observer to interpret aspects of our thought and behavior in terms of these goals. Adler points out that our character traits are neither innate nor unalterable but are adopted as integral facets of our goal orientation: "They are not primary but secondary factors, forced by the secret goal of the individual, and must be understood teleologically" (1956, p. 219). For example, someone who strives for superiority by seeking personal power will develop various character traits necessary to attain this goal—traits such as ambition, envy, and distrust.

Style of Life

Adler emphasized the need to analyze individuals as a unified totality. **Lifestyle** is the unique way that an individual chooses to pursue his or her life goal. It is an integrated means of adapting to and interacting with life in general.

personal reflection

UNDERSTANDING GOALS

Adler emphasized more the pull of the future than the pressure of the past. For Adler, where we hope to go is more important than where we have been. In order to discover the relationship between your life goals and daily activities, try the following exercises.

Set aside 15 minutes for this exercise. Sit down with four sheets of paper and a pen or pencil. Write at the top of the first sheet, "What are my lifetime goals?" Take 2 minutes to answer this question. Write down whatever comes into your mind, no matter how general, abstract, or trivial it may seem. You may want to include personal, family, career, social, community, or spiritual goals. Then give yourself an additional 2 minutes to go over your list and make any additions or alterations. Set aside this first sheet.

Take your second sheet and write at the top, "How would I like to spend the next three years?" Take 2 minutes to answer this question. Then take 2 more minutes to go over your list. This question should help you pinpoint your goals more specifically than you did with the first question. Again, set aside this list.

For a different perspective on your goals, write on your third sheet, "If I knew my life would end six months from today, how would I live until then?" The purpose of this question is to find out what may be important to you that you are not doing or even considering now. Again, write for 2 minutes; go back over your answers for another 2 minutes, and set this sheet aside.

On your fourth sheet of paper, write down the three goals you consider most important out of all the goals you have listed. Compare all four lists. Do any themes run through the various goals you have given? Are most of your goals in one category, such as social or personal? Do some goals appear on the first three lists? Do the goals you have chosen as most important differ in some way from the other goals on your lists?

Although this method does not fully uncover the unconscious life goals that Adler discussed, it can be a powerful way of discovering the relationship between your goals and your daily activities. It is also a useful exercise to repeat every six months or so in order to see what changes may have occurred. (Adapted from Lakein, 1974)

The foremost task of Individual Psychology is to prove this unity in each individual—in his thinking, feeling, acting; in his so-called conscious and unconscious—in every expression of his personality. (Adler, 1964b, p. 69)

According to Adler, the key to understanding a person's behavior is found in the hidden purposes to which all his or her energies are directed. These purposes reveal far more than external facts or situations. For example, if I believe that my father mistreated me as a child and blame a life of failure on this construction of events, then I have orchestrated my own failure. How I was actually treated is immaterial. My belief that I was abused is true psychologically. Further, I have made the mistreatment a reality to fit my chosen style of life, a life of failure:

> It is, as we have already seen, in the first four or five years of life that the individual is establishing the unity of his mind and constructing the relationship between mind and body. He is taking his hereditary material and the impressions he receives from the environment and is adapting them to his pursuit of superiority. By the end of the fifth year his personality has crystallized. The meaning he gives to life, the goal he pursues, his style of approach, and his emotional disposition are all fixed. They can be changed later; but they can be changed only if he becomes free from the mistake involved in his childhood crystallization. Just as all his previous expressions were coherent with his interpretation of life, so now, if he is able to correct the mistake, his new expressions will be coherent with his new interpretation. (Adler, 1931, p. 34)

Seemingly isolated habits and behavior traits gain meaning as an element of the individual's lifestyle and goals, and thus psychological and emotional problems must be treated within this context. The whole style of life must be addressed in treatment because a given symptom or trait is but an expression of the unified lifestyle of the individual.

Mosak (1989) has listed the following dimensions of lifestyle:

1. **Self-concept**—conceptions about oneself, who one is.
2. **Self-ideal**—notions of what one should be. (Adler developed this concept in 1912.)
3. **Image of the world**—convictions about such things as the world, people, and nature as well as about what the world demands.
4. **Ethical convictions**—a personal ethical code.

The Creative Power of the Individual

Adler pointed out that we respond actively and creatively to the various influences affecting our lives. We are not inert objects, passively accepting all outside forces; we actively seek out certain experiences and reject others. We selectively codify and interpret experience, developing an individualized schema of apperception and forming a distinct pattern of relating to the world:

> The science of Individual Psychology developed out of the effort to understand that mysterious creative power of life which expresses itself in the desire to develop, to strive, to achieve. . . . This power is *teleological*, it expresses itself in the striving after a goal, and, in this striving, every bodily and psychological movement is made to cooperate. It is thus absurd to study bodily movements and mental conditions abstractly without relation to an individual whole. (Adler, 1956, p. 92)

Each individual, Adler believed, has a center where he or she is free. Because we are free, we are responsible for our actions and for our lives.

Adler always stressed the individual's positive, creative, healthy capacities. When a patient came to see him, Adler did not ask himself, "How ill is she?" but always "How much in her is healthy?" He believed that the basis of any cure lay not in the strength of the illness but in the individual's power of resistance (Bottome, 1957).

At the core of Adler's model of human nature is creativity—the capacity to formulate (consciously or unconsciously) goals and the means of achieving them. This culminates in the development of a life plan, which organizes one's life into a self-consistent lifestyle.

For Adler, the formation of a life goal, lifestyle, and schema of apperception is essentially a creative act. It is the creative power of the personality, or of the self, that guides and directs the individual's response to the environment. To all individuals, Adler attributes uniqueness, awareness, and control over their own destiny—qualities he believed Freud failed to emphasize sufficiently in his conception of human nature. "Every individual represents both a unity of personality and the individual fashioning of that unity. The individual is thus both the picture and the artist. He is the artist of his own personality" (Adler, 1956, p. 177). Adler emphasized that we are not powerless pawns of external forces. We mold our own personalities.

Social Interest

Adler's theories regarding aggression and the striving for power have been oversimplified and overemphasized by many critics. Adler's concept of *social interest* is central to his later writing. (A better translation of his original German term, *Gemeinschaftsgefühl*,

> It is futile to attempt to establish psychology on the basis of drives alone, without taking into consideration the creative power of the child which directs the drive, molds it into form, and supplies it with a meaningful goal. (Adler, 1956, p. 177)

> Each individual arrives at a concrete goal of overcoming through his creative power, which is identical with the self. (Adler, 1956, p. 180)

personal reflection

THREE WISHES

You have found an old sealed bottle that has washed up on shore. When you open it, a genie appears and grants you three wishes. As you contemplate your wishes, remember that they should be within the realm of the humanly attainable. They should be exciting yet believable.

1. Write out your three wishes.
2. Choose the one that is the most important to you.
3. Write out your wish clearly and in detail, as a central life goal.
4. What are you doing or planning to do in order to attain this goal?
5. What are the obstacles to your attaining your goal?
6. What feelings come up when you write out your goals and take them seriously?
7. If you wish, repeat steps 3–6 for your other two wishes.

might be "community feeling.") By social interest, Adler means "the sense of human solidarity, the connectedness of man to man . . . the wider connotation of a 'sense of fellowship in the human community'" (Wolfe in Adler, 1928, p. 32n). *Community feeling* refers to the interest we take in others not simply to serve our own purposes but to develop "an interest in the interests" of others.

From his holistic perspective, Adler saw the individual not only as a unified whole but as a part of larger wholes—family, community, society, and humanity. Our lives and all our activities are carried out within a social context:

> Any man's value is determined by his attitude toward his fellow man, and by the degree in which he partakes of the division of labor which communal life demands. His affirmation of this communal life makes him important to other human beings, makes him a link in a great chain which binds society, the chain which we cannot in any way disturb without also disturbing human society. (Adler, 1928, p. 121)

In one sense, all human behavior is social because, as Adler argued, we develop in a social environment and our personalities are socially formed. Social interest is more than concern for our immediate community or society. In its broadest sense it refers to concern for "the ideal community of all mankind, the ultimate fulfillment of evolution" (Adler, 1964b, p. 35). Social interest includes feelings of kinship with all humanity and relatedness to the whole of life.

Cooperation

One important aspect of social interest is the development of cooperative behavior. From an evolutionary point of view, the ability to cooperate in food gathering, hunting, and defense against predators has been a vital factor in the survival of the human race and the most effective form of adaptation to the environment.

Adler believed that only by functioning as cooperative, contributing members of society can we overcome our sense of inferiority or our actual inferiorities. On the other hand, lack of cooperation and the resulting sense of inadequacy and failure are at the root of all neurotic or maladaptive styles of life. "If a person cooperates," Adler wrote, "he will never become a neurotic" (1964b, p. 193). Those who have made the most valuable contributions to humanity have been the most cooperative individuals, and the works of the great geniuses have always been oriented in a social direction (Adler, 1931).

All failures . . . are products of inadequate preparation in social interest. They are all noncooperative, solitary beings who run more or less counter to the rest of the world; beings who are more or less asocial if not antisocial. (Adler, 1964b, p. 90)

The only individuals who can really meet and master the problems of life, however, are those who show in their striving a tendency to enrich all others, who go ahead in such a way that others benefit also. (Adler, 1956, p. 255)

personal reflection

PRACTICING COOPERATION

In order to understand more clearly what Adler meant by cooperation and social interest, devote as much time in one week as you can to helping others. Keep a record of your behavior and of your feelings. Resolve that you will not refuse any reasonable requests from others, even if these requests take up some of your valuable time, energy, or even money. (If you want to make the exercise more demanding, let all your friends know that you are carrying out this exercise and that you will be available to serve them for a week!) Don't simply wait for someone to ask you, but actively look for opportunities to offer your help to others.

At the end of the week, review your experiences. How did other people react to you? What were your reactions to helping others? What did you learn from the exercise?

Basic Principles of Adlerian Theory

The basic concepts of Adlerian psychology (Mosak, 1989; Grey, 1998) are as follows:

1. *All behavior occurs in a social context.* People cannot be studied in isolation.
2. *Cooperation is a biological necessity.* Because human beings are relatively weak and slow to develop, cooperation is a biological necessity, not just a social one. We are confronted by many different life choices. We may choose healthy, socially useful goals or neurotic, socially useless ones.
3. *The need to belong is fundamental to human nature.* The focus is on interpersonal psychology. Most important for the individual is the development of a feeling of being an integral part of a larger social whole.
4. *Holism is more important than reductionism.* All functions are subordinate to the person's goals and style of life. The central motivation for each individual is to strive for perfection or for superiority. (This is comparable to Horney's concept of self-realization and Maslow's self-actualization.)
5. *The term "unconscious" is an adjective not a noun.* Unconscious processes are purposeful and serve the individual's goals, as do conscious processes. The difference is only in levels of awareness.
6. *Behavior is based on our perception of reality, not necessarily reality itself.* To understand the individual, you must understand his or her style of life, or cognitive organization. This is the lens through which people view themselves and their lives.
7. *We believe in accord with what we want, not what we are.* Always look for the goal behind a given behavior rather than a label.
8. *All behavior is purposive.* Individuals are motivated by self-selected goals, which they believe will bring them success and happiness.
9. *The cure is reeducation.* Whatever meaning life has derives from what we attribute to it ourselves, and therapy is a process of unlearning mistaken perceptions. A healthy conception of life includes a sense of the importance of helping others and contributing to society. The style of life and long-range goals of the individual remain relatively constant, unless the individual's fundamental convictions are transformed, one of the main tasks of therapy.

DYNAMICS

Psychological Growth

Psychological growth is primarily a matter of moving from the self-centered goal of personal superiority to an attitude of constructive mastery of the environment and socially useful development. Constructive striving for superiority, plus strong social interest and cooperation, is the basic trait of the healthy individual.

Life Tasks.   Adler discussed three major life tasks that confront the individual: work, friendship, and love. They are determined by the basic conditions of human existence:

> These three main ties are set by the facts that we are living in one particular place in the universe and must develop with the limits and possibilities which our circumstances set us; that we are living among others of our own kind to whom we must learn to adapt ourselves; and that we are living in two sexes with the future of our race dependent on the relations of these two sexes. (Adler, 1931, p. 264)

Work includes activities useful to the community, not simply those occupations for which we receive an income. Adler believed that work provides a sense of satisfaction and self-worth only to the extent that it benefits others. The importance of our work is ultimately based on our dependence on the physical environment:

> We are living on the surface of this planet, with only the resources of this planet, with the fertility of its soil, with its mineral wealth, and with its climate and atmosphere. It has always been the task of mankind to find the right answer to the problem these conditions set us. . . . [I]t has always been necessary to strive for improvement and further accomplishments. (Adler, 1956, p. 131)

Friendship is an expression of our membership in the human race and of our constant need to adapt to and interact with others of our species. Our specific friendships provide essential links to our communities because no individual relates to society in the abstract. Friendly, cooperative endeavor is also an important element in constructive work.

Adler discusses *love* in terms of heterosexual love. It involves a close union of mind and body and the utmost cooperation between two people of the opposite sex. Love comes from intimacy, which is essential to the continuance of our species. Adler writes that the close bond of marriage represents the greatest challenge to our ability to cooperate with another human being, and a successful marriage creates the best environment for promoting cooperation and social interest in children.

To Adler, these three tasks (work, friendship, and love) are interrelated. Success at one leads to success at the others. In fact, these three tasks are all aspects of the same problem—how to live constructively in our environment.

Obstacles to Growth

In discussing the major obstacles to human growth and development, Adler first stressed three negative childhood conditions—organ inferiority, pampering, and neglect. He emphasized that adult neurosis is rooted in an attempt to overcome a feeling of inferiority that results in increasing isolation and estrangement from society. Neurosis and virtually all other psychological problems occur when we strive for personal superiority instead of for healthy, constructive achievement.

Organ Inferiority, Pampering, and Neglect.   The childhood situations that tend to result in a lack of social interest, isolation, and a noncooperative lifestyle, based on the unrealistic goal of personal superiority, are organ inferiority, pampering, and neglect.

The life of the human soul is not a "being" but a "becoming." (Adler, 1929, p. ix)

No act of cruelty has ever been done which has not been based upon a secret weakness. The person who is really strong has no inclination to cruelty. (Adler, 1956, p. 390)

Children who suffer from illnesses often become highly self-centered. They tend to withdraw from social interaction out of a sense of inferiority and inability to compete successfully with other children. However, some children may overcompensate for their original weakness and develop their abilities to an unusual degree.

Pampered or spoiled children also have difficulties in developing a sense of social interest and cooperation. They lack confidence in their own abilities because others have always done for them what they could have done for themselves. Rather than cooperate with others, they tend to make one-sided demands on friends and family. Social interest is usually minimal, and Adler found that pampered children usually have little genuine feeling for the parents they manipulate so well.

Neglect is the third situation that may impede a child's development. A neglected or unwanted child has never known love and cooperation in the home and therefore finds it extremely difficult to develop these capacities. Such children have no confidence in their ability to be useful and to gain affection and esteem from others. They tend to become cold and hard as adults.

> The traits of unloved children in their most developed form can be observed by studying the biographies of all the great enemies of humanity. Here the one thing that stands out is that as children they were badly treated. Thus they developed hardness of character, envy and hatred; they could not bear to see others happy. (Adler, 1956, p. 371)

As a result of organ inferiority, pampering, and neglect, children often have distorted worldviews, which lead to faulty lifestyles. Again, Adler stressed that it is not the children's "experience" but their perceptions and conclusions about their experience that determine the way they pursue their lives.

Basic Dynamics of Neurosis. In 1913, Adler and his group published an Adlerian approach to neurosis (Bottome, 1957). The main points are summarized as follows:

1. Every neurosis can be understood as an attempt to overcome a feeling of inferiority and to gain a feeling of competence.
2. Neurosis tends to isolate the individual because it leads away from social functioning and the solving of real-life problems.
3. The neurotic individual's relations with others are severely limited by a combination of hypersensitiveness and intolerance.
4. Estranged from reality, the neurotic tends to live a life of imagination and fantasy, avoiding responsibilities and service to society.
5. Illness and suffering become a substitute for the original, healthy goal of superiority.
6. The neurosis represents an attempt to be free of all the constraints of society by establishing a *counter-compulsion*. This may take the form of anxiety attacks, sleeplessness, compulsions, hallucinations, hypochondria, and so forth.
7. Even logical thinking becomes dominated by the counter-compulsion.
8. Logic, love, compassion, and the will to live all arise from social life. Neurotic isolation and striving for power are directed against this.
9. The neurotic is constantly seeking personal power and prestige, looking for excuses to leave real-life problems unsolved, and consequently never develops social interest.
10. To cure a neurosis, the therapist helps to change completely the individual's orientation, which results from his or her whole upbringing, and enable the patient to become an active, involved member of society.

> There must be uncovered, step by step, the unattainable goal of superiority over all; the purposive concealment of this goal; the all-dominating, direction-giving power of the goal; the patient's lack of freedom and his hostility toward mankind, which are determined by the goal. (Adler, 1956, p. 333)

This list illustrates how Adler's main ideas can be applied to understanding and working with human problems. He clearly emphasizes the importance of living constructively and cooperatively in society.

Striving for Personal Superiority. When inferiority feelings predominate or when social interest is underdeveloped, individuals tend to seek personal superiority, because they lack confidence in their ability to function effectively and to work constructively with others. The trappings of success, prestige, and esteem become more important than concrete achievements. "They have turned away from the real problems of life and are engaged in shadow-fighting to reassure themselves of their strength" (Adler, 1956, p. 255). Such individuals contribute nothing of real value to society and become fixed in self-centered behavior patterns that inevitably lead to a sense of failure.

STRUCTURE

Body

To Adler, the body is a major source of inferiority feelings in the child, who is surrounded by those who are bigger and stronger and who function more effectively physically. However, what is most important is our attitude toward our bodies (Adler, 1964b). Many attractive men and women have never resolved childhood feelings of ugliness and unacceptability, and they still behave as if they were unattractive. On the other hand, those who have physical deficiencies may, through compensation, strive hard and develop their bodies to a greater than average extent.

Social Relationships

Social relationships are of central importance in Adler's theories. They are a direct expression of social interest and are essential in developing a fulfilling, constructive lifestyle. Adler never forgot that we are social beings. Without society and social relationships, the individual would have no language and would enjoy extremely limited thinking and functioning.

Will

For Adler, *will* is another name for the striving for superiority and the actualizing of life goals. As such, it is a central element in his theory. What is crucial for Adler is that the will be used constructively for individual growth and social cooperation. The will is misused when it is directed toward self-centered, self-aggrandizing goals.

Emotions

Adler writes of two kinds of emotions: socially disjunctive emotions, which are related to individual goal attainment, and socially conjunctive emotions, which promote social interaction. *Disjunctive emotions,* such as anger, fear, or disgust, are intended to bring about a positive change in the life situation of the individual, although sometimes at the expense of others. They result from a sense of failure or inadequacy and serve to mobilize the individual's strength to make fresh efforts (Adler, 1956). *Conjunctive*

Arnold Schwarzenegger during his body-building career. Many bodybuilders have overcompensated for weak, sickly childhoods.

emotions tend to be socially oriented, as in the desire to share our joy and laughter with others. The emotion of sympathy is "the purest expression of social interest" and reveals the extent to which we can relate to others (1956, p. 228).

Intellect

Adler distinguishes between reason and intelligence. Neurotics, criminals, and others who fail to function successfully in society are often quite intelligent. Frequently, they give perfectly logical arguments and justifications for their behavior. However, Adler has called this kind of intelligence *personal intelligence,* or thinking that is bound by the individual's goal of personal superiority rather than by socially useful considerations.

Reason is "the kind of intelligence which contains social interest and which is thus limited to the generally useful" (1956, p. 150). Reason is in accord with common sense, which comes out of basic cultural attitudes and values.

Self

The *self* is the individual's style of life. It is the personality viewed as an integrated whole.

> In real life we always find a confirmation of the melody of the total self, of the personality, with its thousandfold ramifications. If we believe that the foundation, the ultimate basis of everything has been found in character traits, drives, or reflexes, the self is likely to be overlooked. Authors who emphasize a part of the whole are likely to attribute to this part all the aptitudes and observations pertaining to the self, the individual. They show "something" which is endowed with prudence, determination, volition, and creative power without knowing that they are actually describing the self, rather than drives, character traits, or reflexes. (Adler, 1956, p. 175)

Adler considered the self a dynamic, unitary *principle* rather than a structure to be found within the psyche. "[In Adlerian psychology] the self is not considered as an entity. . . . There is literally no self to actualize but through transactions with its world" (Ansbacher, 1971, p. 60). Adler's position concerning the self strongly resembles the concept of *selflessness* in Buddhist psychology.

Therapist

"The map is not the territory."
(Alfred Korzybski, founder of *General Semantics*)

The aim of Adlerian psychotherapy is to help the individual reconstruct assumptions and goals in accord with greater social usefulness. Adler defines three major aspects of therapy: understanding the specific lifestyle of the patient, helping patients understand themselves, and strengthening social interest.

Understanding the Lifestyle.   Therapy requires cooperation. One of the first tasks is to address the goals and expectations of each patient. Patients often expect from the therapist the kind of response they have gotten from everyone else. The patient may feel misunderstood, unloved, or unfairly treated. The therapist must carefully avoid meeting these unconscious expectations.

Because the lifestyle forms a basically consistent whole, the therapist looks for themes that run through the individual's behavior. In order to determine their lifestyles, Adler asked patients for their earliest memories, the most salient events from early childhood: "There are no 'chance memories'; out of the incalculable number of impressions which meet an individual, he chooses to remember only those which he feels, however darkly, to have a bearing on his situation" (1931, p. 73).

Even when a patient lies it is of value to me. . . . [I]t is his lie and nobody else's! What he cannot disguise is his own originality. (Adler in Bottome, 1957, p. 162)

Adler also emphasized the importance of expressive behavior, including posture and intonation: "I have found it of considerable value to conduct myself as during pantomime, that is, for a while not to pay any attention to the words of the patient, but instead to read his deeper intention from his bearing and his movements within a situation" (1956, p. 330).

Adler assumed that the patient's life plan had developed under negative conditions, so the therapist should be sensitized to look for organ inferiority, pampering, or neglect in childhood.

Promoting Self-understanding. Adler viewed the major problem of most patients as being their erroneous schema of apperception, determined by an unattainable and unrealistic goal of superiority over others. One of the major tasks of the therapist is to help patients understand their own lifestyles, including their basic approaches to life. Only after self-understanding is reached can people correct their nonadaptive style of life: "A patient has to be brought into such a state of feeling that he likes to listen, and wants to understand. Only then can he be influenced to live what he has understood" (1956, p. 335). *Self-understanding* means learning to see the mistakes we make in coping with daily situations. It involves gaining a better understanding of the world and of our place in it.

According to Adler, success in therapy is always up to the patient.

> The actual change in the nature of the patient can only be his own doing. . . . One should always look at the treatment and the cure not as the success of the consultant but as the success of the patient. The adviser can only point out the mistakes, it is the patient who must make the truth living. (1956, p. 336)

Adler placed greater value on learning to understand the consequences of our behavior than on learning more about our inner experience. For Adler, insight is not merely intellectual understanding. It is understanding translated into constructive action.

Strengthening Social Interest. Therapy is a cooperative enterprise between therapist and patient, a supportive relationship that helps the patient develop a sense of cooperation and social interest: "The task of the physician or psychologist is to give the patient the experience of contact with a fellow man, and then to enable him to transfer this awakened social interest to others" (Adler, 1956, p. 341).

> We can succeed only if we are genuinely interested in the other. We must be able to see with his eyes and listen with his ears. He must contribute his part to our common understanding. . . . Even if we felt we'd understood him we should have no witness that we were right unless he also understood. (Adler, 1929, p. 340)

Adler pointed out that the therapist often has to provide the care, support, and sense of cooperation that the patient never received from his or her parents. Adler was convinced that concern for self rather than for others is at the core of most psychological problems. He considered it the therapist's major task to gradually guide the patient away from exclusive interest in self toward working constructively for others as a valuable member of the community. In caring for the patient, the therapist serves as a role model for social interest.

Role of the Therapist. As a therapist, Adler worked to establish a sense of equality between patient and therapist. He preferred facing the patient to sitting behind the reclining patient, as was Freud's practice. Adler would also engage in a free discussion, not free association. His beliefs and attitudes concerning the therapeutic relationship seem to foreshadow the client-centered approach of Carl Rogers.

Adler strongly believed in empowering others. Patients, he believed, had to work to change themselves. The therapist could provide insight and support. "A patient is like a person in a dark room. He complains to me, 'I cannot get out.' I switch on the

Psychotherapy is an exercise in cooperation and a test of cooperation. We can succeed only if we are genuinely interested in the other. (Adler, 1956, p. 340)

I tell [patients] "You can be cured in fourteen days if you follow this prescription. Try to think every day how you can please someone." (Adler, 1956, p. 347)

light and point out the door-handle. If he still says that he cannot get out—I know that he does not wish to get out!" (Adler in Bottome, p. 101).

Adlerian psychology distinguishes between psychotherapy and counseling. Therapy seeks to bring about a fundamental change in an individual's unhealthy lifestyle. Counseling is aimed at changing behavior within an existing lifestyle.

EVALUATION

Adler's theories have had a great impact on humanistic psychology, psychotherapy, and personality theory. Many of his concepts have been integrated into other schools of thought. Adler's stress on social interest has made psychotherapy much more social in orientation. Also, his concern with conscious, rational processes has created the first ego psychology. In fact, it has been suggested that *neo-Adlerian* is a more accurate term than *neo-Freudian* for theorists such as Erich Fromm, Karen Horney, and Harry Stack Sullivan (Wittels, 1939). In the words of one writer, "most observations and ideas of Alfred Adler have subtly and quietly permeated modern psychological thinking to such a degree that the proper question is not whether one is Adlerian but how much of an Adlerian one is" (Wilder, 1959, p. xv). Adler's thoughts have had a major influence on many other eminent psychologists, yet, astonishingly, he is relatively unknown outside the field.

Viktor Frankl and Rollo May, noted existential analysts, have regarded Adler's psychology as an influential precursor to existential psychiatry (Frankl, 1970; May, 1970), and Adler's interest in holism, goal-directedness, and the role of values in human behavior anticipated many of the developments of humanistic psychology. Abraham Maslow writes:

> For me Alfred Adler becomes more and more correct year by year. As the facts come in, they give stronger and stronger support to his image of man. . . . [I]n one respect especially the times have not yet caught up with him. I refer to his holistic emphasis. (1970, p. 13)

However, Adler has failed to receive the credit he really deserves. Concepts original to Adler are often seen as derivatives of psychoanalytic theory or as self-evident or trivial. In his survey of major psychiatric schools of thought, Ellenberger argues:

> It would not be easy to find another author from which so much has been borrowed from all sides without acknowledgment than Alfred Adler. His teaching has become . . . a place where anyone and all may come and draw anything without compunction. An author will meticulously quote the source of any sentence he takes from elsewhere, but it does not occur to him to do the same whenever the source is individual psychology; it is as if nothing original could ever come from Adler. (1970, p. 645)

Albert Ellis, the founder of rational-emotive therapy, goes even further in his assessment of Adler's contributions:

> Alfred Adler, more even than Freud, is probably the true father of modern psychotherapy. Some of the reasons are: He founded ego psychology, which Freudians only recently rediscovered. He was one of the first humanistic psychologists. . . . He stressed holism,

goal-seeking, and the enormous importance of values in human thinking, emoting, and acting. He correctly saw that sexual drives and behavior, while having great importance in human affairs, are largely the result rather than the cause of man's non-sexual philosophies. It is difficult to find any leading therapist today who in some respect does not owe a great debt to the Individual Psychology of Alfred Adler. (1970, p. 11)

One reason for Adler's relative lack of popularity lies in his writing style. He was an excellent speaker and much preferred lecturing to writing. Except for *The Neurotic Constitution* (1912), most of Adler's later books were written for the lay public. His writing is not always precise, and his theorizing tends to be phrased in a simple, commonsensical manner that often seems superficial or shallow. Adler was more interested in practice than in theory. He was at his best in dealing with actual case materials; thus his work has tended to be most popular among teachers, social workers, clinical practitioners, and others who require practical psychological skills in their professional work. Adler's seminal contributions to the development of modern psychology include the idea of the inferiority complex, examination of the role of power and aggression in human behavior, the concept of unity of the personality, and stress on the significance of nonsexual factors in development.

RECENT DEVELOPMENTS: ADLER'S INFLUENCE

Many of Adler's pioneering ideas have become so well accepted that they are taken for granted today. His work on the interaction of psychological and physical elements in organ inferiority was instrumental in establishing psychosomatic medicine, and his writings laid the foundations of the increasingly popular field of parenting. Almost every modern book on parenting makes use of Adler's principles of child discipline, generally without giving him much credit. Adler's student Rudolf Dreikurs has had a powerful influence on this field. His book *Children: The Challenge* (1964) has become a classic.

Adlerian training institutes, family education centers, study groups, and professional societies are growing in size and influence (Mosak, 1989). The first Adlerian psychology textbook written in English, *Individual Psychology* (Manaster & Corsini, 1982), has generated widespread interest, as has *Alfred Adler, The Forgotten Prophet* (Grey, 1998), a major summary of Adler's life and ideas. *A Bibliography of Adlerian Psychology,* in two volumes, covers more than ten thousand references to the literature of Adlerian psychology (Mosak & Mosak, 1975a, 1975b).

Adlerian psychology is flourishing. Adler's influence on leading psychologists, such as Abraham Maslow and Rollo May, has been well documented (Ansbacher, 1990). Carl Rogers was an intern under Adler, and Adler's concept of social interest closely resembles Rogers's core conditions for therapeutic change (Watts, 1998). Major biographies of Adler have appeared in 1994 (Hoffman) and 1998 (Grey). Adlerian theory has been shown to be a precursor to cognitive theory in many ways (Scott, Kelly, & Tolbert, 1995) and continues to influence educational psychology (Carlson, 1995; Pryor & Tollerud, 1999), counseling (Kern, 1993; Nystul, 1995; Sweeny, 1998), cross-cultural counseling (Roberts et al., 1998), and child therapy (Mosak & Maniacci, 1993; Kottman, 1995). Adlerian theory has also found cross-cultural application among Native Americans (Kawulich & Curlette, 1998) and Mexican Americans (Martinez, 1998).

The Theory Firsthand

EXCERPT FROM *SOCIAL INTEREST*

The following passage provides an example of Adler's analytic methods.

A woman thirty-two years of age complained of a violent pain around the left side of her left eye and of double vision which compelled her to keep her left eye closed. The patient had had attacks like that for eleven years; the first occurred when she became engaged to her husband. . . . She blamed a cold bath for her last attack and believed that her former attacks were caused by cold draughts. . . .

Before her marriage she had taught the violin, had also appeared at concerts, and liked her work; but she had given it up after her marriage. She was now living with her brother-in-law's family, to be nearer to the doctor, as she said, and she was quite happy there. . . .

She is undoubtedly the ruling partner in her marriage, but she comes up against her husband's indolence and his desire for peace. He works hard, comes home tired late in the evening, and is not inclined to go out with his wife or carry on a conversation with her. If she has to play in public she suffers from violent stage-fright. The question introduced by me as an important one, What would she do if she were in good health?—a question the answer to which shows clearly the reason for the patient's timid retreat—she answers evasively with a reference to her perpetual headaches. . . . The patient persists in asserting that cold in any form hurts her and brings about all sorts of attacks. Nevertheless, before her last attack she took a cold bath, which, as she says, promptly caused the attack. . . .

It appeared that the patient ever since she had witnessed with the utmost horror the birth of a younger sister had had an insane anxiety about childbearing. . . . When she was eleven years old her father had accused her unjustly of having sexual intercourse with a neighbor's son. This premature contact with the sexual relationship, closely associated with terror and anxiety, made her protest against love more vigorous, and this protest appeared during her marriage as frigidity. Before entering into the marriage she asked a binding declaration from her bridegroom that he would permanently deny himself any children. Her attacks of migraine and the fear of them that constantly possessed her made it easier for her to assume a relationship that reduced conjugal intercourse to a minimum. . . .

She certainly esteems her husband highly, but she is far from being in love with him; indeed she has never really been in love. When asked repeatedly what she would do if she were permanently cured she answered at length that she would remove to the capital, give violin lessons there, and play in an orchestra. Any one who has acquired the art of guessing taught by Individual Psychology would have no difficulty in understanding that this meant separation from her husband, who was tied to the provincial town. . . . Since her husband has a great admiration for her and gives her incomparably the best opportunity to ride her craving for power at full gallop, it is naturally very difficult for her to separate from him. . . .

A complete cure was effected within a month. Previous to that came the explanation of the exogenous factor that had led to the last attack. She found in her husband's coat pocket a letter from a girl containing merely a few words of greeting. Her husband was able to allay her suspicion. None the less she continued to be suspicious and entertained a jealousy of her husband she had never felt before. From that time she kept watch on him. It was during this period that she took the cold bath and her attack began. . . . In explanation she says that she has never been jealous, that her pride has forbidden her that vice, but that since the discovery of the letter she had considered the possibility of her husband's being unfaithful to her. When she thought of the likelihood of this her wrath increased—against the assumed dependence of the wife on the husband. Her cold bath was therefore really the revenge of her style of life for what she imagined to be the unquestionable dependence of her worth upon her husband, and for his failure to appreciate that worth. Had she not had her attack of migraine—the result of her shock—then she would have had to admit that she was worthless. This however would have been the worst that could have happened to her. (Adler, 1964a, pp. 75–85)

CHAPTER HIGHLIGHTS

- Adler's main contributions to modern psychology are the significance of nonsexual factors in the environment, the concept of the unity of the personality, the role of power and aggression in human behavior, and the concept of the inferiority complex.
- Adler stressed the uniqueness of the individual, the importance of understanding the unity of the person, and the context of a social system.

- For the individual, conquest of the environment is a primary goal, but this drive is balanced by the importance of social interest, or community feeling and cooperation.
- As in behaviorism, concepts in Adlerian psychology are related to actual, concrete behavior and emphasize overt behaviors and their consequences.
- Individual Psychology focuses on the relations between the environment and the individual rather than on intrapsychic dynamics.
- The individual's attempts to compensate for organ inferiority or inferiority feelings result in virtually all progress and underlie humankind's most significant achievements.
- The drive for power is fundamental. A later formulation of this principle is the concept of striving for superiority, which includes the role of development and creative growth.
- The evolutionary process of conscious adaptation to the environment is the foundation for the individual's striving for perfection, or mastering of the environment in a superior way.
- The goal of superiority or perfection motivates healthy individuals to seek continuous improvement and growth. Such striving is positive if it includes social concerns and interest in the welfare of others. It is negative if the focus is on personal superiority through domination of others.
- To become a worthy human being is a goal of the individual. Life's supreme law makes diminishment of the sense of self-worth unacceptable.
- Behavior is determined by the individual's conception of the world.
- Psychological and emotional problems must be considered and treated in the context of the individual's life goals and lifestyle. The unified lifestyle of the individual is manifest in every trait or symptom.
- Creativity—the capacity to formulate both goals and the means of achieving them—is at the core of the individual. The life goal provides self-consistent organization of one's life; it is a creative response to the environment.
- Community feeling, or social interest, is the sense of the larger social context and of the connectedness of the individual to family, community, society, and humanity.
- Cooperation is a key facet in social interest. Feelings of inferiority can be overcome only through the individual's active participation as a contributing and valuable member of society.
- At the root of maladaptive or neurotic styles of life are a lack of cooperation and the resulting sense of failure and inadequacy.
- The healthy individual is cooperative, has strong social interest, and constructively strives for superiority.
- Every neurosis is an attempt to gain a feeling of competence and to overcome feelings of inferiority. Neurosis isolates the individual; it leads away from social functioning and the solving of real-life problems. To cure a neurosis, the therapist helps the patient completely change his or her orientation, to direct the patient back into society.
- Personal superiority is sought by individuals who are lacking in the confidence that they can function effectively and constructively with others. Feelings of inferiority predominate.
- It is more important to understand the consequences of behavior than to focus on one's inner experience. Insight is not simply intellectual understanding but understanding translated into constructive action.
- At the core of most psychological problems is concern for self rather than concern for others.

KEY CONCEPTS

Inferiority complex The feeling of inadequacy that results from children's sense of their small size and powerlessness. Adler looked at the psychological aspects of inferiority, which he believed touched the life experiences of all children. (See Organ inferiority.)

Life goal An individual's focus for achievement. Formation begins in childhood as a compensation for inferiority feelings, and continues as a defense against feelings of impotence.

Life tasks Basic life tasks for everyone are work, friendship, and love.

Lifestyle The individual's unique manner of interacting with and adapting to life in general, in pursuit of his or her life goal.
Organ inferiority The concept that in each person's biological structure, some organs are weaker, more susceptible to disease than others. Through training and exercise, the individual can make the weak organ become his or her greatest strength or asset. (See Inferiority complex.)
Social interest The community sharing of values and feelings. In its broadest sense, the term refers to feelings of relatedness and kinship with all humanity as well as to the whole of life.

ANNOTATED BIBLIOGRAPHY

Adler, A. (1929). The practice and theory of individual psychology. London: Routledge & Kegan Paul.

   A collection of essays and discussions on neurosis and psychological problems, including considerable case material.

Adler, A. (1931). *What life should mean to you.* Boston: Little, Brown.

   A clearly written exposition of Adler's basic concepts, for the layperson.

Adler, A. (1956). *The individual psychology of Alfred Adler: A systematic presentation in selections from his writings* (H. L. Ansbacher & R. R. Ansbacher, Eds.). New York: Harper & Row.

   The best introduction to Adler's work; it includes materials that are not available elsewhere in English. Two major sections: personality theory and abnormal psychology.

Adler, A. (1964). *Superiority and social interest: A collection of later writings* (H. L. Ansbacher & R. R. Ansbacher, Eds.). New York: Viking Press.

   Includes sections on theory, case studies, religion, and various applications of individual psychology. Also contains an essay on the increasing recognition of Adler, a biography, and a definitive bibliography of Adler's writings.

Dreikurs, R. (1957). Psychology in the classroom: A manual for teachers. New York: Harper & Row.

   An application of Adler's theories to education, including extensive case material.

Manaster, G. J., & Corsini, R. J. (1982). Individual psychology. Itasca, IL: F. E. Peacock.

   The first textbook of Adlerian psychology written in English. It includes a complete Adlerian psychotherapy case summary and also a section on research in Adlerian psychology.

Web Sites

Alfred Adler Institute of San Francisco
ourworld.compuserve.com/homepages/hstein/

   Database of articles explaining the Adlerian approach, discussion of Adlerian philosophy, theory and practice, parenting and teaching, classic Adlerian quotes, questions and answers, and a referral service. Plus, information on a distance training program in Adlerian psychotherapy.

North American Society of Adlerian Psychology
www.alfredadler.org

   Includes listings of conferences, other events, training programs, and publications.

Journal of Individual Psychology
www.utexas.edu/utpress/journals/jip.html

   A forum for dialog on Adlerian practices, principles, and theory.

REFERENCES

Adler, A. (1912). *The neurotic constitution.* New York: Moffat, Yard.

Adler, A. (1928). *Understanding human nature.* London: Allen & Unwin.

Adler, A. (1929). *The practice and theory of individual psychology.* London: Routledge & Kegan Paul.

Adler, A. (1931). *What life should mean to you.* Boston: Little, Brown.

Adler, A. (1956). *The individual psychology of Alfred Adler: A systematic presentation in selections from his writings* (H. L. Ansbacher & R. R. Ansbacher, Eds.). New York: Harper & Row.

Adler, A. (1964a). *Social interest: A challenge to mankind.* New York: Capricorn Books.

Adler, A. (1964b). *Superiority and social interest: A collection of later writings* (H. L. Ansbacher & R. R. Ansbacher, Eds.). New York: Viking Press.

Ansbacher, H. L. (1971). Alfred Adler and humanistic psychology. *Journal of Humanistic Psychology, 2,* 53–63.

Ansbacher, H. L. (1990). Alfred Adler's influence on the three leading cofounders of humanistic psychology. *Journal of Humanistic Psychology, 30,* 45–53.

Bottome, P. (1957). *Alfred Adler: A portrait from life.* New York: Vanguard Press.

Carlson, J. (1995). Adlerian parent consultation. In A. Dougherty (Ed.), *Case studies in human services consultation.* Pacific Grove, CA: Brooks/Cole.

Dreikurs, R. (1964). *Children: The challenge.* New York: Dutton.

Ellenberger, H. (1970). *The discovery of the unconscious: The history and evolution of dynamic psychiatry.* New York: Basic Books.

Ellis, A. (1970). Tributes to Alfred Adler on his hundredth birthday. *Journal of Individual Psychology, 26,* 11–12.

Frankl, V. (1970). Tributes to Alfred Adler on his hundredth birthday. *Journal of Individual Psychology, 26,* 12.

Grey, L. (1998). *Alfred Adler, the forgotten prophet.* Westport, CT: Praeger.

Hoffman, E. (1994). *The drive for self: Alfred Adler and the founding of individual psychology.* Reading, MA: Addison-Wesley.

Kawulich, B., & Curlette, W. (1998). Life tasks and the Native American perspectives. *Journal of Individual Psychology, 54,* 359–367.

Kern, C. (1993). Adlerian counseling. *TCA Journal, 21,* 85–95.

Kottman, T. (1995). *Partners in play: An Adlerian approach to play therapy.* Alexandria, VA: American Counseling Association.

Lakein, A. (1974). *How to get control of your time and your life.* New York: New American Library.

Manaster, G. J., & Corsini, R. J. (1982). *Individual psychology.* Itasca, IL: F. E. Peacock.

Martinez, D. (1998). Transcending cultures: the American process. *Journal of Individual Psychology, 54,* 346–358.

Maslow, A. (1970). Tributes to Alfred Adler on his hundredth birthday. *Journal of Individual Psychology, 26,* 13.

May, R. (1970). Tributes to Alfred Adler on his hundredth birthday. *Journal of Individual Psychology, 26,* 13.

Mosak, H. (1989). Adlerian psychotherapy. In R. Corsini & D. Wedding (Eds.), *Current psychotherapies* (4th ed.). Itasca, IL: F. E. Peacock.

Mosak, H., & Maniacci, M. (1993). Adlerian child psychotherapy. In R. Kratochwill & J. Morris (Eds.), *Handbook of psychotherapy with children and adolescents.* Boston: Allyn & Bacon.

Mosak, H., & Mosak, B. (1975a). *A bibliography of Adlerian psychology* (Vol. 1). Washington, DC: Hemisphere.

Mosak, H., & Mosak, B. (1975b). *A bibliography of Adlerian psychology* (Vol. 2). Washington, DC: Hemisphere.

Nystul, M. (1995). A problem solving approach to counseling. *Elementary School Guidance and Counseling, 29,* 297–302.

Pryor, D., & Tollerud, T. (1999). Applications of Adlerian principles in school settings. *Professional School Counseling, 2,* 299–304.

Roberts, R., Harper, R., Tuttle-Eagle-Bull, D., Heideman, P., & Heideman, L. (1998). The Native American medicine wheel and Individual Psychology. *Journal of Individual Psychology, 54,* 135–145.

Scott, C., Kelly, F., & Tolbert, B. (1995). Realism, constructivism, and the individual psychology of Alfred Adler. Individual Psychology *Journal of Adlerian Theory, Research and Practice, 51,* 4–20.

Sweeny, T. (1998). *Adlerian counseling: A practitioner's approach* (4th ed.). Philadelphia: Accelerated Development.

Watts, R. (1998). The remarkable parallel between Rogers's core conditions and Adler's social interest. *Journal of Individual Psychology, 54,* 4–9.

Way, L. (1950). *Adler's place in psychology.* London: Allen & Unwin.

Wilder, J. (1959). Introduction. In K. Adler & D. Deutsch (Eds.), *Essays in individual psychology.* New York: Grove Press.

Wittels, F. (1939). The neo-Adlerians. *American Journal of Sociology, 45,* 433–445.

karen horney
and humanistic psychoanalysis

Bernard J. Paris

Because her thought went through three distinct phases, Karen Horney has come to mean different things to different people. Some think of her primarily in terms of her essays on feminine psychology, written in the 1920s and early 1930s, in which she tried to modify Freud's ideas about penis envy, female masochism, and feminine development while remaining within the framework of orthodox theory. These essays were too far ahead of their time to receive the attention they deserved, but they have been widely read since their republication in *Feminine Psychology* in 1967, and consensus is growing that Karen Horney was the first great psychoanalytic feminist.[1]

Those who are attracted to the second stage of Horney's thought identify her primarily as a neo-Freudian member of the cultural school, which also included Erich Fromm, Harry Stack Sullivan, Clara Thompson, and Abraham Kardiner. In *The Neurotic Personality of Our Time* (1937) and *New Ways in Psychoanalysis* (1939), Horney broke with Freud and developed a psychoanalytic paradigm in which culture and disturbed human relationships replaced biology as the most important causes of neurotic development. *The Neurotic Personality of Our Time* made Horney famous in intellectual circles. It created a heightened awareness of cultural factors in mental disturbance and inspired studies of culture from a psychoanalytic perspective. Because of its criticism of Freud, *New Ways in Psychoanalysis* made Horney infamous among orthodox analysts and led to her ostracism from the psychoanalytic establishment. Although it paid tribute to Freud's genius and the importance of his contribution, it rejected many of his premises and tried to shift the focus of psychoanalysis from infantile origins to the current structure of the personality. It laid the foundations for the development of present-oriented therapies, which have become increasingly important in recent years (Wachtel, 1977).

In the 1940s, Horney developed her mature theory, which many consider her most distinctive contribution. In *Our Inner Conflicts* (1945) and *Neurosis and Human Growth* (1950), she argued that individuals cope with the anxiety produced by feeling unsafe, unloved, and unvalued by disowning their real feelings and developing elaborate strategies of defense. In *Our Inner Conflicts,* she concentrated on the interpersonal defenses of moving toward, against, and away from other people and the neurotic solutions of compliance, aggression, and detachment to which they give rise. In *Neurosis and Human Growth,* she emphasized intrapsychic defenses, showing how self-idealization generates a search for glory and what she called the pride system, which consists of neurotic pride, neurotic claims, tyrannical shoulds, and self-hate. The range and power of Horney's mature theory have been shown by both the theory's clinical applications and also its use in such fields as literary criticism, biography, and the study of culture and gender.

The object of therapy for Horney is to help people relinquish their defenses—which alienate them from their true likes and dislikes, hopes, fears, and desires—so that they can get in touch with what she called the real self. Her emphasis on self-realization as the source of healthy values and the goal of life, established Horney as one of the founders of humanistic psychology.

PERSONAL HISTORY

Karen Horney was born Karen Danielsen in a suburb of Hamburg on September 15, 1885. Her father was a sea captain of Norwegian origin; her mother was of Dutch–German extraction. Karen had a brother, Berndt, four years older than she. Karen

[David Letterman's] neurosis has achieved classical dimensions. I happened to be reading Dr. Karen Horney's "The Neurotic Personality of Our Time" recently, and (except for the pages that reminded me of me) almost every chapter cried out, Dave, Dave, Dave.... As Horney writes of this kind of highfalutin' defeatist, "He tends to feel that he is nothing, but is irritated when he is not taken for a genius." (James Wolcott, "Letterman Unbound: Dave's No. 2 and Trying Harder," *New Yorker,* June 3, 1996, p. 82)

---

[1] Some material in this chapter is adapted from *Karen Horney: A Psychoanalyst's Search for Self-Understanding,* by Bernard J. Paris (1994).

sided with her mother in fierce conflicts between her parents, who were ill-matched in age and background, and her mother supported Karen's desire for an education, against her father's opposition.

When she was 13, Karen decided that she wanted to be a physician, and she was one of the first women in Germany to be admitted to medical school. She received her medical education at the universities of Freiburg, Göttingen, and Berlin. In 1909 she married Oskar Horney, a social scientist she had met while both were students in Freiburg. In 1910 she entered analysis with Karl Abraham, a member of Freud's inner circle and the first psychoanalyst to practice in Germany. Karen decided to become an analyst herself and in 1920 was one of the six founding members of the Berlin Psychoanalytic Institute. She taught there until 1932, when Franz Alexander invited her to become associate director of the newly formed Chicago Psychoanalytic Institute. She joined the faculty of the New York Psychoanalytic Institute in 1934 but was driven out in 1941 after publication of *New Ways in Psychoanalysis*. She founded the American Institute for Psychoanalysis the same year and was dean until her death in 1952. She was also founding editor of the *American Journal of Psychoanalysis*.

Karen Horney was introspective and self-analytical in her youth, partly because of her temperament and partly because of her unhappy childhood. She had felt unwanted and that her brother was much more highly valued than she, principally because he was a male. Because she disliked her father, whom she regarded as a religious hypocrite, and her mother confided in her brother, she felt alone and unsupported in the family. To compensate for this, she tried to attach herself to her brother, with whom she seems to have engaged in some kind of sex play between the ages of 5 and 9. When her brother distanced himself from her on reaching puberty, Karen felt rejected and tried to gain a sense of worth by becoming fiercely competitive in school.

As a child, Karen was bitter, angry, and rebellious, but when she reached puberty, she could no longer tolerate her isolation and won a position in the family by joining the circle of her mother's admirers. At the age of 13, she began keeping a diary (Horney, 1980) in which she expressed adoration of her mother and brother. Her buried hostility toward them erupted when she was 21, however, and her relations with them were strained thereafter. The diaries written while Karen was repressing her anger give a misleading picture of her relations with her family and must be read in light of the Clare case in *Self-Analysis* (1942), which is highly autobiographical and explains her behavior during adolescence.

Although Karen's diaries are misleading about her relations with her family, they reveal her emotional problems quite clearly. She suffered from depression, timidity, and paralyzing fatigue, could not bear being without a boyfriend, was insecure about her mental abilities, and felt like an ugly duckling who could not compete with her beautiful mother. She had great difficulty focusing on her work and succeeded academically only because of her exceptional intelligence.

Karen's diaries were mostly devoted to her relationships with males, from whom she desperately needed attention. The typical pattern of her relationships was first idealization of the male, followed by disappointment, depression, and efforts to comprehend why the relationship failed. Because of her disappointments, she moved from man to man, often trying to hold on to several at once because each satisfied different demands. She hoped to find a great man who could fulfill her conflicting needs for dominance and

---

[Horney writes at the age of 17:] I asked this morning whether I might join a class in animal dissection, and I was turned down. . . . Et voilà a substitute: I shall take myself to pieces. That will probably be more difficult, but also more interesting. (Horney, 1980, p. 58)

If she, too, admired the mother she need no longer feel isolated and excluded but could hope to receive some affection, or at least be accepted. . . . [She] was no longer the disregarded ugly duckling, but became the wonderful daughter of a wonderful mother. . . . [But] by admiring what in reality she resented, she became alienated from her own feelings. She no longer knew what she herself liked or wished or feared or resented. (From the Clare case, Horney, 1942, pp. 50–51)

Neurotic girls cannot love a "weak" man because of their contempt for any weakness; but neither can they cope with a "strong" man because they expect their partner always to give in. Hence what they secretly look for is the hero, the superstrong man, who at the same time is so weak that he will bend to all their wishes. . . . (Horney, 1937, p. 170)

submission, crude force and refined sensibility, but she was perpetually disappointed. Deeply unhappy, she tried to understand the sources of her misery, first in her diaries and then in her psychoanalytic writings, many of which are covertly autobiographical.

At first, Karen thought that Oskar Horney was the great man for whom she had been looking, but he was not forceful enough, and the marriage was soon in trouble. She sought help in her analysis with Karl Abraham, but her symptoms were the same after two years of treatment as they had been when she began. The failure of her analysis is one reason why she began to question orthodox theory, especially with respect to the psychology of women.

After having three children, Karen and Oskar separated in 1926 and divorced in 1938. Karen never remarried, but she had many troubled relationships of the kind she describes in her essays on feminine psychology and the Clare case in *Self-Analysis*.

Although she had begun to emphasize culture in her writings of the 1920s, her move to the United States in 1932 convinced her that Freud had given too much importance to biology and too little to social factors. First in Chicago and then in New York, she found patients whose problems differed dramatically from those she had encountered in Germany. This experience, combined with her reading in the burgeoning sciences of sociology and anthropology, made her doubt the universality of the Oedipus complex and led her to explore culture's impact on individual psychology. In 1935 she lectured on this topic at the New School for Social Research and was invited by W. W. Norton to write the book that became *The Neurotic Personality of Our Time*. As Horney's disagreements with Freud deepened, she believed it important to contrast her thinking with his in a systematic way, and this she did in *New Ways in Psychoanalysis*.

Horney's third book, *Self-Analysis* (1942), was an outgrowth of the breakdown of her relationship with Erich Fromm. She had known Fromm when he was a student at the Berlin Psychoanalytic Institute (he was 15 years younger than she), and she met him again when he lectured at the University of Chicago in 1933. They became lovers when both moved to New York in 1934. Their relationship was intellectual as well as emotional, with Fromm teaching Horney sociology and Horney teaching Fromm psychoanalysis. The relationship deteriorated in the late 1930s, after Horney sent her daughter Marianne, who was specializing in psychiatry, to Fromm for a training analysis. When Marianne's hostilities toward her mother emerged in the course of analysis, as was to be expected, Horney blamed Fromm. The breakdown of the relationship was extremely painful to Horney and led to a period of intense self-analysis. This issued in the writing of *Self-Analysis*, in which the story of Clare and Peter is a fictionalized account of what happened between Horney and Fromm. Despite their estrangement, Fromm became a member of the American Institute for Psychoanalysis when it was founded in 1941, but Horney drove him out in 1942, using his status as a lay analyst (he had a PhD rather than an MD) as a pretext.

The 1930s were a turbulent period for Horney, culminating in the hostile reaction of her colleagues at the New York Psychoanalytic Institute to her criticisms of Freud and her split with Erich Fromm. The 1940s were equally turbulent, since many of Horney's most distinguished colleagues left the American Institute, one group (including Fromm, Harry Stack Sullivan, and Clara Thompson) to form the William Alanson White Institute and another to join the New York Medical College. These splits were partly the result of Horney's need for dominance and her

Won't I ever be getting well, completely well? I am beginning to despair of it. . . . I often feel as though I were paralyzed. . . . When I waken in the morning, I wish the day were already over. (Letter to Karl Abraham, after two courses of analysis— Horney, 1980, p. 270)

[S]he was described [by people whom her biographer interviewed] variously—and contradictorily—as both frail and strong, open and reticent, aloof and "with you," distant and close, caring, motherly and uncaring, unsympathetic, loving and unloving, dominating and self-effacing, manipulative and compliant, a leader and a follower, fair and mean. . . . The impression emerged that she . . . needed to encompass and unify many diverse and conflicting traits, apparently with constant struggle. (Rubins, 1978, pp. xiii–xiv)

She created in spite of her problems, because of her problems, and through her problems. (Harold Kelman in Paris, 1994, p. 176)

It is probably fair to say that she poured all her creative energy into work, into search, in part as a genuine creative effort and in part as a rescue . . . from interpersonal difficulties. She was a tremendously conflicted person who found a successful, eminently satisfying creative way of life. I think she would always want her books to speak for her, as justifying her existence. (Marianne Eckardt, Horney's daughter, in Paris, 1994, p. 178)

inability to grant others the kind of academic freedom she had demanded for herself at the New York Psychoanalytic Institute. Horney continued to have difficulties in her love life, and these often contributed to dissention at her institute, since she tended to place men with whom she was having relationships in positions of power. Despite the political turmoil it involved, heading her own institute enabled Horney to flourish. It gave her the intellectual freedom she had always sought and facilitated the development of her mature theory. Toward the end of the decade, Horney became interested in Zen, and not long before her death in 1952, she traveled to Japan with D. T. Suzuki, who had written and lectured about Zen in the United States, to visit Zen monasteries.

Although Horney was a brilliant clinician, she suffered all her life from not having had an analyst who could really help her. After her disappointing experiences, first with Karl Abraham and then with Hanns Sachs in the early 1920s, she turned to self-analysis in an effort to gain relief from her emotional difficulties. Combined with her clinical experience, her self-analysis generated many of her psychoanalytic ideas. Her constant struggle to obtain relief from her problems was largely responsible for the continual evolution of her theory and the deepening of her insights. Horney had a remarkable ability to see herself clearly and to be brutally honest about her own problems. With the exception of her earliest essays, she did not construct a theory that universalized or normalized her difficulties.

Although Horney made little progress with some of her problems, she was remarkably successful with others. As a young woman, she had suffered severely from depression, fatigue, and inability to work, but she became extraordinarily creative, energetic, and productive. Like Clare in *Self-Analysis,* she was a late bloomer, since she wrote little until her forties. The last 15 years of her life were remarkable: she published five groundbreaking books; she was in great demand as an analyst, supervisor, and speaker; she founded and directed the American Institute for Psychoanalysis; she founded and edited the *American Journal of Psychoanalysis;* she taught at the New School on a regular basis; she read widely; she learned how to paint; she had many eminent friends and a busy social life; she spent much time in the summers with her daughters; and she traveled a great deal. Her failure to overcome certain problems made her realistic, while her successes were the source of her famous optimism. Her belief both in the human potential for growth and in the difficulty of achieving it was based on her own experience.

INTELLECTUAL ANTECEDENTS

Sigmund Freud and Psychoanalysis

Although a reviewer described *New Ways in Psychoanalysis* as "a fourteen-round ring battle between the 'new ways' (Horney) and the 'old ways' (Freud)" (Brown, 1939, p. 328), Horney acknowledged her deep debt to Freud, who had provided the foundation for all subsequent psychoanalytic thought. It is not difficult to see why the young Karen Horney was attracted to psychoanalysis. She suffered from many mysterious complaints and impaired ability to function. Of an introspective temperament, she had been in the habit of seeking relief by scrutinizing her feelings and motivations. Psychoanalysis offered the most powerful tools available for such an enterprise. She frequently recognized herself, moreover, in Freud's description of women's problems. Given her suffering, her temperament, and her craving for self-understanding, psychoanalysis as a theory and a therapy must have seemed to be exactly what she was looking for.

Although certain aspects of Freudian theory fit Horney's experience well, others did not. By the early 1920s she began to propose modifications in the light of her observations of her female patients and her own experiences as a woman. Perhaps the most important factor in Horney's initial dissent was that she came to see psychoanalytic theory as reproducing and reinforcing the devaluation of the feminine, from which she had suffered in childhood.

Disturbed by the male bias of psychoanalysis, she dedicated herself to proposing a woman's view of the differences between men and women and the disturbances in the relations between the sexes. This eventually led to development of a psychoanalytic paradigm quite different from Freud's. However, Horney always paid tribute to what she regarded as Freud's enduring contributions. These included the doctrines "that psychic processes are strictly determined, that actions and feelings may be determined by unconscious motivations, and that the motivations driving us are emotional forces" (1939, p. 18). She valued Freud's accounts of repression, reaction formation, projection, displacement, rationalization, and dreams; and she believed Freud had provided indispensable tools for therapy in the concepts of transference, resistance, and free association (1939, p. 117).

> As psychology has been until now mostly worked at from the side of men, it seems to me to be the given task for a woman psychologist—or at least I think it to be mine—to work out a fuller understanding for specifically female trends and attitudes in life. (Horney in Paris, 1994, p. 55)

Alfred Adler

Fritz Wittels (1939) argued that neo-Freudians like Horney were really closer to Adler than to Freud and should really be called neo-Adlerians. Horney began reading Adler as early as 1910, and despite the fact that she gave him little credit as an intellectual antecedent, important similarities arise between her later thinking and his.

Adler's influence first appears in a diary entry in 1911. In her work with Karl Abraham, Horney struggled to understand her fatigue, and in her diary she recorded the numerous explanations he proposed, most of which had to do with unconscious sexual desires. In one entry, however, she looked at herself from an Adlerian perspective and arrived at an explanation that sounds much like her own analysis of Clare, written 30 years later. She wondered whether her fear of productive work stemmed not only from her mistrust of her own capacity but also from the need to be first that Adler considered characteristic of neurotics.

> [F]rom a feeling of uncertainty and inferiority, I am afraid that I will not be able to do anything first class, above average, and therefore prefer not to attempt it at all, perhaps trying to create a special position for myself through this exaggerated refusal. (Horney, 1980, p. 250)

Horney was especially intrigued by Adler's account of the *masculine protest* that develops in every woman in response to her sense of physical inferiority to men. She had no difficulty in identifying the masculine protest in herself. She "envied Berndt because he could stand near a tree and pee" (Horney, 1980, p. 252), she liked wearing pants, she played the prince in charades, and at the age of 12 she cut off her hair to the neckline. She compensated for her physical inferiority to males by excelling in school, taking great pride that she was a better student than her brother. In the terms of her culture, she was behaving like a man by studying medicine and believing in sexual freedom. According to Horney's Adlerian self-analysis, she needed to feel superior because of her lack of beauty and her feminine sense of inferiority, which led her to try to excel in a male domain. But her low self-esteem made her afraid she would fail, so she avoided productive work, as do "women in general" (Horney, 1980, p. 251), and experienced disproportionate anxiety over exams. Her fatigue was at once a product of her anxiety, an excuse for withdrawing from competition with men, and a means of concealing her inferiority and gaining a special place for herself by arousing concern.

Horney set aside this Adlerian way of thinking for the next two decades, but she returned to it in the 1930s and 1940s, when it became highly congruent with her own approach to psychoanalysis. Although she tended to characterize Adler as superficial, she recognized his importance as an intellectual antecedent, acknowledging that he was the first to see the search for glory "as a comprehensive phenomenon, and to point out its crucial significance in neurosis" (1950, p. 28).

Other Intellectual Influences

Georg Simmel says . . . that historically the relations of the sexes may be crudely described as that of master and slave. Here, as always, it is "one of the privileges of the master that he has not constantly to think that he is master, while the position of the slave is such that he can never forget it." (Horney, 1967, p. 69)

While still in Germany, Horney began to cite ethnographic and anthropological studies, as well as the writings of the philosopher and sociologist Georg Simmel, with whom she developed a friendship. After she moved to the United States, her sense of the differences between central Europe and America made her receptive to the work of such sociologists, anthropologists, and culturally oriented psychoanalysts as Erich Fromm, Max Horkheimer, John Dollard, Harold Lasswell, Edward Sapir, Ruth Benedict, Ralph Linton, Margaret Mead, Abraham Kardiner, and Harry Stack Sullivan, with most of whom she had personal relationships. In response to these influences, Horney argued not only that culture is more important than biology in the generation of neuroses but also that pathogenic conflict between the individual and society is the product of a bad society rather than inevitable, as Freud had contended. Following Bronislaw Malinowski, Felix Boehm, and Erich Fromm, Horney regarded the Oedipus complex as a culturally conditioned phenomenon; and following Harry Stack Sullivan, she saw the needs for "safety and satisfaction" as more important than sexual drives in accounting for human behavior.

[I]n the terms of William James: [the real self] . . . is the source of spontaneous interest and energies, "the source of effort and attention from which emanate the fiats of will"; . . . it is the part of ourselves that wants to expand and grow and to fulfill itself. It produces the "reactions of spontaneity" to our feelings or thoughts, "welcoming or opposing, appropriating or disowning, striving with or against, saying yes or no." (Horney, 1950, p. 157)

Although at first she saw conceptions of psychological health as relative to culture, in the late 1930s she developed a definition of health universal in nature. Drawing on W. W. Trotter's *Instincts of the Herd in Peace and War* (1916), she described emotional well-being as "a state of inner freedom in which 'the full capacities are available for use'" (1939, p. 182). The central feature of neurosis was now self-alienation, loss of contact with "the spontaneous individual self" (1939, p. 11). Horney gave Erich Fromm primary credit for this new direction in her thinking, but other important influences were William James and Søren Kierkegaard. In her descriptions of the "real self," she was inspired by James's account of the "spiritual self" in *Principles of Psychology* (1890), and in her discussions of loss of self, she drew on Kierkegaard's *The Sickness unto Death* (1849). Horney also cited Otto Rank's (1978) concept of "will" as an influence on her ideas about the real self, and in her later work she invoked the Zen concept of "wholeheartedness."

[Despite his despair, a man may] be perfectly well able to live on . . . and perhaps no one notices that in a deeper sense he lacks a self . . . for a self is a thing the world is least apt to inquire about. . . . The greatest danger, that of losing one's own self, may pass off as quietly as if it were nothing; every other loss, that of an arm, a leg, five dollars, a wife, etc., is sure to be noticed. (Kierkegaard in Horney, 1945, p. 185)

It is difficult to determine why Horney shifted from an emphasis on the past to one on the present, but she acknowledged the influence of Harald Schultz-Henke and Wilhelm Reich, analysts whom she knew from her days in Berlin. The Adlerian mode of analysis she had employed in her diary and to which she returned also focused on the present.

MAJOR CONCEPTS

Since Horney's thought went through three phases, it will be best to discuss the major concepts of each phase separately. We shall look first at her ideas about feminine psychology, then at the new psychoanalytic paradigm she developed in the 1930s, and finally at her mature theory.

Feminine Psychology

Nancy Chodorow locates the "political and theoretical origins" of psychoanalytic feminism with Karen Horney, whose theories form the basis "for most of the recent revisions of psychoanalytic understandings of gender and for most psychoanalytic dissidence on the question of gender in the early period as well" (1989, pp. 2–3). Horney's ideas were ignored for many years but now seem remarkably astute.

The Male View of Women. In her earliest essays on feminine psychology, Horney strove to show that girls and women have intrinsic biological constitutions and patterns of development to be understood in their own terms and not just as products of difference from and presumed inferiority to men. She argued that psychoanalysis regards women as defective men because it is the product of a male genius (Freud) and a male-dominated culture. The male view of the female has been incorporated into psychoanalysis as a scientific picture of woman's essential nature.

An important question for Horney is why men see women as they do. She contended that male envy of pregnancy, childbirth, and motherhood, and of the breasts and suckling, gives rise to an unconscious tendency to devalue women and that men's impulse toward creative work is an overcompensation for their small role in procreation. The **womb envy** of the male must be stronger than the so-called **penis envy** of the female, because men need to depreciate women more than women need to depreciate men.

In later essays, Horney continued to analyze the male view of woman in order to expose its lack of scientific foundation. In "The Distrust Between the Sexes" (1931), she argued that woman is seen as "a second-rate being" because "at any given time, the more powerful side will create an ideology suitable to help maintain its position. . . . In this ideology the differentness of the weaker one will be interpreted as inferiority, and it will be proven that these differences are unchangeable, basic, or God's will" (1967, p. 116). In "The Dread of Woman" (1932), Horney traced the male dread of woman to the boy's fear that his genitalia is inadequate in relation to his mother. The threat posed by woman is not castration but humiliation; the threat is to his masculine self-regard. As he grows up, the male continues to have a deeply hidden anxiety about the size of his penis or his potency, an anxiety that has no counterpart for the female, who "performs her part by merely being" (1967, p. 145) and is not obliged to go on proving her womanhood. There is, therefore, no corresponding female dread of men. The male deals with his anxiety by erecting an ideal of efficiency, by seeking sexual conquests, and by debasing the love object.

Cultural Factors. In her essays on feminine psychology, Horney moved steadily away from Freud's belief that "anatomy is destiny" and toward a greater emphasis on cultural factors as a source of women's problems and of gender identity. She acknowledged that little girls envy the male plumbing but regarded this as psychologically insignificant. What women chiefly envy is male privilege, and what they need is greater opportunity to develop their human capacities. The patriarchal ideal of woman does not necessarily correspond to her inherent character, but the cultural power of that ideal often makes women behave in accordance with it.

In "The Problem of Feminine Masochism" (1935), Horney challenged the idea that "masochistic trends are inherent in, or akin to, the very essence of female nature"

[T]he psychology of women has hitherto been considered only from the point of view of men. It is inevitable that the man's position of advantage should cause objective validity to be attributed to his subjective, affective relations to the woman, and according to Delius the psychology of women hitherto actually represents a deposit of the desires and disappointments of men. (Horney, 1967, p. 56)

She is said to be at home only in the realm of eros. Spiritual matters are alien to her innermost being, and she is at odds with cultural trends. She therefore is, as Asians frankly state, a second-rate being. . . . [She is] prevented from real accomplishment by the deplorable, bloody tragedies of menstruation and childbirth. And so every man silently thanks his God, just as the pious Jew does in his prayers, that he was not created a woman. (Horney, 1967, p. 114)

"[Men are] doing what they were meant to do—patrolling the borders, protecting the house. Men have vision. They build bridges. We'd still be sitting on the edge of the river without them. But two thousand years of second-class citizenship is enough! Enough!" (Lauren Hutton, in Sherrill, 2003, p. 44)

(1967, p. 214). This is the position of psychoanalysis, which reflects the stereotypes of male culture, but Horney identified social conditions that have made women more masochistic than men. Moreover, comparative studies show that these conditions have not been universal and that some societies have been more unfavorable to women's development than others.

The Masculinity Complex. Horney did not deny that women often envy men and are uncomfortable with their feminine role. Indeed, many of her essays deal with the **masculinity complex** (similar to Adler's *masculine protest*), which she defined as "the entire complex of feelings and fantasies that have for their content the woman's feeling of being discriminated against, her envy of the male, her wish to be a man and to discard the female role" (1967, p. 74). Although she initially argued that women are bound to have a masculinity complex because of their need to escape the guilt and anxiety that result from their Oedipal situation, Horney soon identified the masculinity complex not as inevitable but as the product of a male-dominated culture and of particular kinds of family dynamics. The fact that "a girl is exposed from birth onward to the suggestion—inevitable, whether conveyed brutally or delicately—of her inferiority" is an experience "that constantly stimulates her masculinity complex" (1967, p. 69).

In discussing family dynamics, Horney focused at first on the girl's relationship with male members of the family, but later she derived the masculinity complex and all the phenomena traditionally associated with penis envy—such as feelings of inferiority, vindictiveness, and competitiveness toward men—from the girl's relationship with females in the family, particularly the mother. In "Maternal Conflicts" (1933), she brought together the separate features of childhood to which she had attributed the masculinity complex in previous essays: "A girl may have reasons to acquire a dislike for her own female world very early, perhaps because her mother has intimidated her, or she has experienced a thoroughly disillusioning disappointment from the side of the father or brother; she may have had early sexual experiences that frightened her; or she may have found that her brother was greatly preferred to herself" (1967, p. 179). All of these features were present in Karen Horney's childhood.

The Overvaluation of Love. "The Overvaluation of Love" (1934) is the culmination of Horney's attempt to analyze herself in terms of feminine psychology. The essay draws on the cases of seven women whose family histories, symptoms, and social backgrounds resemble Horney's, and she may well have included herself in her clinical sample. Most of the essay is devoted to trying to explain why these women have an obsessive need for a male but are unable to form satisfactory relationships. Their obsession is traced to a childhood situation in which each "had come off second best in the competition for a man" (1967, p. 193). It is the typical fate of the girl to be frustrated in her love for her father, but for these women the consequences are unusually severe because of the presence of a mother or sister who dominates the situation erotically.

The girl responds to her sense of defeat either by withdrawing from the competition for a male or developing a compulsive rivalry with other women in which she tries to demonstrate her erotic appeal. The conquest of men provides not only what Horney would later call a "vindictive triumph" but is also a way of coping with anxiety and self-hate. The insecure girl develops an anxiety about being abnormal that

Our culture, as is well known, is a male culture, and therefore by and large not favorable to the unfolding of woman and her individuality. . . . [N]o matter how much the individual woman may be treasured as a mother or as a lover, it is always the male who will be considered more valuable on human and spiritual grounds. The little girl grows up under this general impression. (Horney, 1967, p. 82)

personal reflection

A MATTER OF PHILOSOPHY

In the beginning of *Neurosis and Human Growth* (1950, pp. 14–15), Horney distinguishes three concepts of morality that rest on three views of human nature:

1. If the human being is by nature sinful or ridden by primitive impulses, the goal of morality must be to curb them, tame them, overcome them.
2. If there is something inherently "good" in human nature and something inherently "bad," the goal of morality must be to ensure the eventual victory of the good by suppressing the bad and directing or reinforcing the good elements, using will, reason, and strength.
3. If human nature is seen as inevitably evolving toward self-realization by an intrinsic tendency, not by will, then the goal of morality becomes one of removing obstacles in the way of that evolution, in order to provide maximum opportunity for the spontaneous forces of growth to manifest.

Having read Horney's three concepts, try the following exercise.

1. In a group of at least three students, discuss the three positions and tentatively choose one to support.
2. Horney embraced the third concept of morality. Discuss what implications this philosophy had on her attitude toward psychotherapy.
3. Whichever position you have chosen, ask yourself whether you actually live by this position. How do you behave that shows your response to be true? Share your answers with the group.

> [W]e should stop bothering about what is feminine. . . . Standards of masculinity and femininity are artificial standards. . . . Differences between the two sexes certainly exist, but we shall never be able to discover what they are until we have first developed our potentialities as human beings. Paradoxical as it may sound, we shall find out about these differences only if we forget about them. (Horney, 1935, in Paris, 1994, p. 238)

often manifests itself as a fear that something is wrong with her genitals or that she is ugly and cannot possibly be attractive to men. As a defense, she may pay an inordinate amount of attention to her appearance or may wish to be a male. The most important defense is proving that, despite her disadvantages, she *can* attract a man. To be without a man is a disgrace, but having one proves that she is "normal": "Hence the frantic pursuit" (1967, pp. 197–198).

The situation of these women is sad because although their relationships with men are paramount, they are never satisfactory. They tend to lose interest in a man as soon as he is conquered, because they have "a profound fear of the disappointments and humiliations that they expect to result from falling in love" (1967, p. 205). Having been rejected by father or brother in childhood, they simultaneously need to prove their worth through erotic conquests and to make themselves invulnerable by avoiding deep emotional bonds. They tend to change partners frequently, since, after securing a man, they need to get out of the relationship before they get hurt. However attractive they are, they do not believe that a man can actually love them. Moreover, they have a "deep-seated desire for revenge" because of their original defeat: "[T]he desire is to get the better of a man, to cast him aside, to reject him just as she herself once felt cast aside and rejected" (1967, p. 206).

> The experience [of childhood sexual excitation] left certain traces in its wake . . . of a pleasure far in excess of that from any other source, and of something strangely vitalizing to the whole organism. I am inclined to think that these traces cause these particular women . . . to conceive of sexual gratification as a kind of elixir of life that only men are able to provide and without which one must dry up and waste away. . . . (Horney, 1967, p. 204)

Gender Neutrality.   Although Horney had devoted most of her professional life to writing about feminine psychology, she abandoned the topic in 1935 because she determined that culture's role in shaping the female psyche makes it impossible to determine what is distinctively feminine. In a lecture entitled "Woman's Fear of Action" (1935), she argued that only when women have been freed from the conceptions of femininity fostered by male-dominated cultures can we discover how they really differ from men psychologically. Our primary objective must not be to identify what is essentially feminine but to foster "the full development of the human personalities of all"

(Paris, 1994, p. 238). After this, Horney developed a theory that she considered to be gender neutral, one that applied equally to males and to females.

HORNEY'S NEW PARADIGM

In *The Neurotic Personality of Our Time* and *New Ways in Psychoanalysis,* Horney subjected Freud's theories to a systematic critique and developed her own version of psychoanalysis. Its distinguishing features were a greater emphasis on culture, the conception of neurosis as a set of defenses devised to cope with basic anxiety, and a focus on present character structure rather than on infantile origins.

It seems that the person who is likely to become neurotic is one who has experienced the culturally determined difficulties in an accentuated form, mostly through the medium of childhood experiences, and who has consequently been unable to solve them, or has solved them only at great cost to his personality. We might call him a stepchild of our culture. (Horney, 1937, p. 290)

[Basic anxiety develops when] the environment is dreaded as a whole because it is felt to be unreliable, mendacious, unappreciative, unfair, unjust, begrudging, and merciless. . . . The child . . . feels the environment as a menace to his entire development and to his most legitimate wishes and strivings. He feels in danger of his individuality being obliterated, his freedom taken away, his happiness prevented. In contrast to the fear of castration this fear is not fantasy, but is well-founded on reality. (Horney, 1939, p. 75)

The Role of Culture.   Horney argued that his overemphasis on the biological sources of human behavior had led Freud to incorrectly assume the universality of the feelings, attitudes, and kinds of relationships common in his culture. Not recognizing the importance of social factors, he attributed neurotic egocentricity to a narcissistic libido, hostility to a destruction instinct, an obsession with money to an anal libido, and acquisitiveness to orality. But anthropology shows that cultures vary widely in their tendency to generate these characteristics, and the Oedipus complex as well, and Horney's own experience of cultural difference after she moved to the United States confirmed this point of view.

Horney rejected Freud's derivation of neurosis from the clash between culture and instinct. In Freud's view, we must have culture in order to survive, and we must repress or sublimate our instincts in order to have culture. Horney did not believe that collision between the individual and society is inevitable but rather that it occurs when a bad environment frustrates our emotional needs and inspires fear and hostility. Freud depicts human beings as inherently insatiable, destructive, and antisocial; according to Horney, these are not expressions of instinct but neurotic responses to adverse conditions.

The Structure of Neurosis.   Horney did not reject the significance of childhood in emotional development, as is sometimes thought, but she emphasized the pathogenic conditions in the family that make children feel unsafe, unloved, and unvalued rather than the frustration of libidinal desires. As a result of these conditions, children develop **basic anxiety,** a feeling of helplessness in a potentially hostile world, which they try to reduce by adopting such strategies of defense as the pursuit of love, power, or detachment.

Horney considered these defensive strategies doomed to failure because they generate **vicious circles** in which the means employed to allay anxiety tend to increase it. For example, frustrating the need for love makes that need insatiable, and the demanding jealousy that follows makes it even less likely that the person will receive affection. Unloved people develop a feeling of being unlovable that leads them to discount any evidence to the contrary. Being deprived of affection makes them dependent on others, but they fear that dependency because it makes them too vulnerable. Horney compared such a situation with that "of a person who is starving for food yet does not dare to take any for fear that it might be poisoned" (1937, p. 114).

Although Horney devoted much of *The Neurotic Personality of Our Time* to the neurotic need for love, she gave a good deal of space to the quest for power, prestige, and possession that develops when a person feels hopeless about gaining affection.

Horney's paradigm for the structure of neurosis is one in which disturbances in human relationships generate a basic anxiety that leads to the development of defensive strategies that are not only self-defeating but in conflict with each other because people adopt not just one but several of them. This paradigm formed the basis of Horney's mature theory.

Structure Versus Genesis.   Perhaps the most significant aspect of Horney's new version of psychoanalysis was her shift in emphasis, both in theory and in clinical practice, from the past to the present. She replaced Freud's focus on genesis with a structural approach, arguing that psychoanalysis should be less concerned with infantile origins than with the current constellation of defenses and inner conflicts. This feature of her theory sharply differentiated it from classical psychoanalysis, which seeks to explain the present by trying to recover the past.

In *New Ways in Psychoanalysis*, Horney distinguished between her own "evolutionistic" thinking and what she called Freud's "mechanistic-evolutionistic" thought. Evolutionistic thinking presupposes "that things which exist today have not existed in the same form from the very beginning, but have developed out of previous stages. These preceding stages may have little resemblance to the present forms, but the present forms would be unthinkable without the preceding ones." Mechanistic-evolutionistic thinking holds that "nothing really new is created in the process of development," that "what we see today is only the old in a changed form" (1939, p. 42). For Horney, the profound influence of early experiences does not preclude continued development, whereas for Freud nothing much new happens after the age of 5, and later reactions or experiences are repetitions of earlier ones.

At the heart of Freud's conception of the relation between childhood experiences and the behavior of the adult is the doctrine of the timelessness of the unconscious. Fears and desires, or entire experiences repressed in childhood remain uninfluenced by further experiences or growth. This gives rise to the concept of *fixation,* which may pertain to a person in the early environment, such as father or mother, or to a stage of libidinal development. The concept of fixation views later attachments or other behaviors as repetitions of the past, which has remained encapsulated and unchanged in the unconscious.

Horney did not attempt to refute the doctrine of the timelessness of the unconscious, or the cluster of concepts related to it, but rather built her own theory on a different set of premises. The "non-mechanistic viewpoint is that in organic development there can never be a simple repetition or regression to former stages" (1939, p. 44). The past is always contained in the present, but through a developmental process rather than through repetition. The way in which lives "really develop," said Horney, is that "each step condition[s] the next one." Thus "interpretations which connect the present difficulties immediately with influences in childhood are scientifically only half truths and practically useless" (1935, pp. 404–405).

In Horney's model, early experiences profoundly affect us not by producing fixations that cause us to repeat earlier patterns but by conditioning the ways in which we respond to the world. These in turn are influenced by subsequent experiences and eventually evolve into our adult defensive strategies and character structures. Early experiences may have a greater impact than later ones because they determine the direction of development, but the character of the adult is the evolved product of *all* previous interactions between psychic structure and environment.

My conviction, expressed in a nutshell, is that psychoanalysis should outgrow the limitations set by its being an instinctivistic and a genetic psychology. (Horney, 1939, p. 8)

In short, then, libido theory in all its contentions is unsubstantiated. . . . What is offered as evidence are unwarranted and often gross generalizations of certain good observations. Similarities existing between physiological functions and mental behavior or mental strivings are used to demonstrate that the former determine the latter. Peculiarities in the sexual sphere are off-hand assumed to engender similar coexisting peculiarities in character traits. (Horney, 1939, p. 68)

[T]he theoretical expectation that progress is to be gained by obtaining childhood memories constitutes a temptation to make use of unconvincing reconstructions or of vague memories which leave an unresolvable doubt as to whether they concern real experiences or merely fantasies. When the real picture of childhood is befogged, artificial attempts to penetrate through the fog represent an endeavor to explain one unknown—the actual peculiarities—by something still less known—childhood. (Horney, 1939, p. 146)

The same anxiety which may compel a person to masturbate may compel him to play solitaire. It is not at all self-evident that the shame in playing solitaire results from the fact that in the last analysis he is pursuing a forbidden sexual pleasure. If he is, for instance, a type for whom the appearance of perfection is more important than anything else, the implication of self-indulgence and the lack of self-control may be sufficient to determine his self-condemnation. (Horney, 1939, p. 61)

Another important difference between Horney and Freud is that whereas Freud considered the determining experiences in childhood relatively few in number and mostly of a sexual nature, Horney believed the sum total of childhood experiences is responsible for neurotic development. Things go wrong because of events and individuals in the culture, in the relations with peers, and especially in the family that make the child feel unsafe, unloved, and unvalued and give rise to basic anxiety. This anxiety leads to the development of defensive strategies that form a neurotic character structure, and it is this character structure from which later difficulties emanate. Horney sees sexual difficulties as the result rather than the cause of personality problems.

Horney's Mature Theory

According to Horney, people have a real self that requires favorable conditions to be actualized. When they are motivated by their defensive strategies instead of their genuine feelings, they become alienated from their real selves. Horney divided defensive strategies into two kinds: interpersonal, which we use in our dealings with other people, and intrapsychic, which we employ in our own minds. She focused mainly on interpersonal strategies in *Our Inner Conflicts* and on the intrapsychic in *Neurosis and Human Growth*.

[The real self] is what we refer to when we say that we want to find ourselves. . . . [It is] the possible self—in contrast to the idealized self, which is impossible of attainment. (Horney, 1950, p. 158)

The Real Self.   Horney came to see the central feature of neurosis as alienation from the **real self** because of oppressive forces in the environment. The object of therapy is to "restore the individual to himself, to help him regain his spontaneity and find his center of gravity in himself" (1939, p. 11). The real self is not a fixed entity but a set of intrinsic potentialities—including temperament, talents, capacities, and predispositions—that are part of our genetic makeup and need a favorable environment in which to develop. It is not a product of learning, because one cannot be taught to be oneself; but neither is it impervious to external influence, because it is actualized through interactions with an external world that can provide many paths of development.

People can actualize themselves in different ways under different conditions, but everyone requires certain conditions in childhood for self-realization. These include "an atmosphere of warmth" that enables children to express their own thoughts and feelings, the goodwill of others to supply their various needs, and "healthy friction with the wishes and will" of those around them. When their own neuroses prevent parents from loving the child or even thinking "of him as the particular individual he is," the child develops a feeling of basic anxiety that prevents him "from relating himself to others with the spontaneity of his real feelings" and forces him to develop defensive strategies (1950, p. 18).

To my surprise I have to admit that I don't know who I am. I haven't the vaguest idea. . . . As far back as I can remember I've been obedient, adaptable, almost meek. . . . I had one or two violent outbursts of self-assertion as a little girl. But . . . Mother punished all such lapses from convention with exemplary severity. For my sisters and me our entire upbringing was aimed at our being agreeable. (Marianne in Ingmar Bergman's *Scenes from a Marriage*)

Interpersonal Strategies of Defense.   According to Horney, people try to cope with their basic anxiety by adopting a compliant or self-effacing solution and moving *toward* people, by adopting an aggressive or expansive solution and moving *against* people, or by becoming detached or resigned and moving *away from* people. Healthy people move appropriately and flexibly in all three directions, but in neurotic development these moves become compulsive and indiscriminate. Each solution involves a constellation of behavior patterns and personality traits, a conception of justice, and a set of beliefs about human nature, human values, and the human condition. Each also involves a "deal" or bargain with fate in which obedience to the dictates of that solution is supposed to be rewarded.

personal reflection

THE REAL SELF

Horney says a child moves further and further from his or her real self because of basic anxiety, which makes spontaneity feel dangerous and leads to the development of self-alienating defensive strategies. Test the applicability of this idea in your own life with the following exercise.

1. Close your eyes, relax, and remember a typical day when you were 13 or 14 years old. From the time you woke up in the morning, recall your experience as you worked and played at school and the quality of your contact with family and friends in the afternoon and evening. Write down a description of that day, including specific thoughts and feelings as well as your general mood.

2. Now do the same for a day when you were 4 or 5 years old. Take a few minutes to relax to help you remember.

3. Compare the two days. Is there any difference in the degree of your spontaneity? Did your interests become less or more your own as you grew up? Did your life become constricted by conflicting *shoulds,* or were you able to keep a genuine sense of what was right for you? Did your love for yourself and others change?

4. Form groups of up to six people. Each person can describe and compare his or her own two days and listen to the accounts of others.

The Compliant Solution.   People in whom the **compliant solution** is dominant try to overcome their basic anxiety by gaining affection and approval and controlling others through their dependency. Their values "lie in the direction of goodness, sympathy, love, generosity, unselfishness, humility; while egotism, ambition, callousness, unscrupulousness, wielding of power are abhorred" (1945, p. 54). They embrace Christian values, but in a compulsive way, because these are necessary to their defense system. They must believe in turning the other cheek, and they must see the world as displaying a providential order in which virtue is rewarded. Their bargain is that if they are good, loving people who shun pride and do not seek their own gain or glory, they will be well treated by fate and other people. If their bargain is not honored, they may despair of divine justice, they may conclude that they are at fault, or they may have recourse to belief in a justice that transcends human understanding. They need to believe not only in the fairness of the world order but also in the goodness of human nature, and here, too, they are vulnerable to disappointment. Self-effacing people must repress their aggressive tendencies in order to make their bargain work, but they are frequently attracted to expansive people through whom they can participate vicariously in the mastery of life. They often develop a "morbid dependency" on their partner.

Expansive Solutions: Narcissistic, Perfectionistic, and Arrogant-Vindictive.   People in whom the **expansive solutions** are predominant have goals, traits, and values opposite to those of the self-effacing solution. What appeals to them most is not love but mastery. They abhor helplessness, are ashamed of suffering, and need to achieve success, prestige, or recognition. In *Neurosis and Human Growth,* Horney divided the expansive solutions into three distinct kinds—narcissistic, perfectionistic, and arrogant-vindictive. There are thus five major solutions in all.

People who are drawn to the **narcissistic solution** seek to master life "by self-admiration and the exercise of charm" (1950, p. 212). They were often favored and admired children, gifted beyond average, who grew up feeling the world to be a fostering

... our friend William Dobbin, who was personally of so complying a disposition that if his parents had pressed him much, it is probable he would have stepped down into the kitchen and married the cook, and who, to further his own interests, would have found the most insuperable difficulty in walking across the street.... (Thackeray, *Vanity Fair,* Chapter 23)

When the rain came to wet me once, and the wind to make me chatter; when the thunder would not peace at my bidding; there I found 'em, there I smelt 'em out. Go to, they are not men o' their words! They told me I was everything. 'Tis a lie—I am not ague-proof. (King Lear in Shakespeare, *King Lear,* Act 4, scene 6)

parent and themselves to be favorites of fortune. They have an unquestioned belief in their abilities and feel that there is no game they cannot win. Their insecurity is manifested in the fact that they may speak incessantly of their exploits or wonderful qualities and need endless confirmation of their estimate of themselves in the form of admiration and devotion. Their bargain is that if they hold on to their dreams and their exaggerated claims for themselves, life is bound to give them what they want. If it does not, they may experience a psychological collapse, being ill equipped to cope with reality.

The **perfectionistic solution** is the refuge of people with extremely high standards, moral and intellectual, on the basis of which they look down upon others. They take great pride in their rectitude and aim for a "flawless excellence" in the whole conduct of life. Because of the difficulty of living up to their standards, they tend to equate knowing about moral values with being a good person. While they deceive themselves in this way, they may insist that others live up to their standards of perfection and may even despise them for failing to do so, thus externalizing their self-condemnation. Perfectionists have a legalistic bargain in which being fair, just, and dutiful entitles them "to fair treatment by others and by life in general. This conviction of an infallible justice operating in life gives [them] a feeling of mastery" (1950, p. 197). Through the height of their standards, they compel fate. Ill-fortune or errors of their own making threaten their bargain and may overwhelm them with feelings of helplessness or self-hate.

The **arrogant-vindictive solution** suits people who are motivated chiefly by a need for vindictive triumphs. Whereas narcissists received early admiration and perfectionists grew up under the pressure of rigid standards, arrogant-vindictive people were harshly treated in childhood and have a need to retaliate for the injuries they have suffered. To them, "the world is an arena where, in the Darwinian sense, only the fittest survive and the strong annihilate the weak" (1945, p. 64). The only moral law inherent in the order of things is that might makes right. In their relations with others they are competitive, ruthless, and cynical. They want to be hard and tough, and they regard all manifestation of feeling as a sign of weakness. Their bargain is essentially with themselves. They do not count on the world to give them anything but are convinced that they can reach their ambitious goals if they remain true to their vision of life as a battle and do not allow themselves to be influenced by traditional morality or their softer feelings. If their expansive solution collapses, self-effacing trends may emerge.

Detachment. Those in whom **detachment** is the predominant solution pursue neither love nor mastery but rather worship freedom, peace, and self-sufficiency. They disdain the pursuit of worldly success and have a profound aversion to effort. They have a strong need for superiority and usually look on their fellows with condescension, but they realize their ambition in imagination rather than through actual accomplishments. They handle a threatening world by removing themselves from its power and shutting others out of their inner lives. In order to avoid being dependent on the environment, they try to subdue their inner cravings and to be content with little. They do not usually rail against life but resign themselves to things as they are and accept their fate with ironic humor or stoic dignity. Their bargain is that if they ask nothing of others, others will not bother them; that if they try for nothing, they will not fail; and that if they expect little of life, they will not be disappointed.

Table 4.1 lists the ways in which we adapt our behavior based on neurotic drives. As an exercise in understanding yourself, see if any of these needs and solutions is an issue for you now or was in the past. Most of us can identify somewhat with all of them at one time or another.

The idea of undeserved fortune, whether good or bad, is alien to [the perfectionist]. His own success, prosperity, or good health is therefore less something to be enjoyed than a proof of his virtue. Conversely, any misfortune befalling him . . . may bring this seemingly well-balanced person to the verge of collapse. (Horney, 1950, p. 197)

Others there are
Who, trimmed in forms and
    visages of duty,
Keep yet their hearts attending
    on themselves,
And throwing but shows of
    service on their lords,
Do well thrive by them, and
    when they have lined their
    coats,
Do themselves homage. These
    fellows have some soul;
And such a one do I profess
    myself.

(Iago in Shakespeare, *Othello,* Act I, scene I)

[M]y lodging was my private solitude, my shell, my cave, in which I concealed myself from all mankind. . . . (Dostoevski, "Notes from the Underground," Part 2, section 8)

TABLE 4.1   Neurotic Needs—Neurotic Solutions

NEUROTIC NEED	NEUROTIC SOLUTIONS
For affection and approval	A blanket desire to please others and live up to their expectations
For a "partner" to take over one's life	Overdependence, parasitical behavior, terror of being deserted by one's partner
To restrict one's life within narrow borders	Behaving in undemanding and inconspicuous ways that lack ambition
For power	Craving power for its own sake, lack of respect for others, glorifying strength and superiority
To exploit others	Belief that success is possible only through taking advantage of others
For prestige	Basing one's self-esteem solely on recognition and others' opinions
For personal admiration	Holding an inflated self-image and needing to be admired for one's façade rather than for who one really is
For personal achievement	Compulsion to excel, driven from a sense of basic insecurity
For self-sufficiency and independence	Disappointment in attempts to find satisfying relationships, followed by remaining apart from others and refusing any form of commitment
For perfection and unassailability	Fear of criticism, attempting to seem infallible and to cover up any flaws before others might notice

Intrapsychic Strategies of Defense.   While interpersonal difficulties are creating the moves toward, against, and away from people, and the conflicts between them, concomitant intrapsychic problems are producing their own defensive strategies. Self-idealization generates what Horney calls the *pride system*, which includes neurotic pride, neurotic claims, tyrannical shoulds, and increased self-hate.

The Idealized Image and the Search for Glory.   To compensate for feelings of weakness, worthlessness, and inadequacy, we create, with the aid of our imagination, an **idealized image** of ourselves that we endow with "unlimited powers and exalted faculties" (1950, p. 22). The process of self-idealization must be understood in relation to the interpersonal strategies, since the idealized image is based on our predominant defense and the attributes it exalts. The idealized image of self-effacing people "is a composite of 'lovable' qualities, such as unselfishness, goodness, generosity, humility, saintliness, nobility, sympathy." It also glorifies "helplessness, suffering, and martyrdom" and deep feelings for art, nature, and other human beings (1950, p. 222). Arrogant-vindictive people see themselves as invincible masters of all situations. They are smarter, tougher, more realistic than other people and therefore can get the better of them. They take pride in their vigilance, foresight, and planning and feel that nothing can hurt them. The narcissistic person is "the anointed, the man of destiny, the prophet, the great giver, the benefactor of mankind" (1950, p. 194). Narcissists see themselves as having unlimited energies and as being capable of great achievements, effortlessly attained. Perfectionists see themselves as models of rectitude whose performance is invariably excellent. They have perfect judgment and are just and dutiful in their human relationships. The idealized image of detached or resigned people "is a composite of self-sufficiency, independence, self-contained serenity, freedom from

"You know, it was like this! This was it: I wanted to make myself a Napoleon, and that is why I killed her. . . . Now do you understand?" (Raskolnikov in Dostoevski, *Crime and Punishment*, Part 5, Chapter 4)

personal reflection

DO I MAKE NEUROTIC CLAIMS?

Horney suggested that studying your own reactions can lead you to observe your own neurotic patterns. She said, "It is in our real interest to examine our own reactions when we become preoccupied with a wrong done to us, or when we ponder the hateful qualities of somebody or when we feel the impulse to get back at others" (1950, p. 57).

The following questions may help you to explore your own patterns:

1. Can you recall a time when you asked for something that was unrealistic and you became upset because you did not get what you wanted?
2. Can you recall a time when you agreed to do something that you really did not want to do?
3. Can you recall a time when you were highly critical of someone else because that person did not meet your own standards of right and wrong?
4. Can you recall a time when your pride was hurt?

One patient was, in his image, a benefactor of mankind, a wise man who had achieved a self-contained serenity, and a person who could without qualms kill his enemies. These aspects—all of them conscious—were to him not only uncontradictory but also even unconflicting. In literature this way of removing conflicts by isolating them has been presented by Stevenson in *Doctor Jekyll and Mr. Hyde*. (Horney, 1950, p. 22)

We have reason to wonder whether more human lives—literally and figuratively—are not sacrificed on the altar of glory than for any other reason. (Horney, 1950, pp. 29–30)

desires and passions," and stoic indifference to the slings and arrows of outrageous fortune (1950, p. 277). They aspire to be free from restraint and impervious to pressure. In each solution, the idealized image may be modeled in whole or in part on a religious or cultural ideal or an example from history or personal experience.

The idealized image does not ultimately make us feel better about ourselves but rather leads to increased self-hate and additional inner conflict. Although the qualities with which we endow ourselves are dictated by our predominant interpersonal strategy, the subordinate solutions are also represented; and since each solution glorifies a different set of traits, the idealized image has contradictory aspects, all of which we must try to actualize. Moreover, because we can feel worthwhile only if we *are* our idealized image, everything that falls short is deemed worthless, and we develop a *despised image* that becomes the focus of self-contempt. A great many people shuttle, said Horney, between "a feeling of arrogant omnipotence and of being the scum of the earth" (1950, p. 188).

With the formation of the idealized image, we embark on a **search for glory,** the object of which is to actualize our idealized self. What is considered glorious will vary with each solution. The search for glory constitutes a private religion, the rules of which are determined by our particular neurosis, but we may also participate in the glory systems prominent in every culture. These include organized religions, various forms of group identification, wars and military service, and competitions, honors, and hierarchical arrangements of all kinds.

The Pride System.   The creation of the idealized image produces not only the search for glory but also the **pride system:** neurotic pride, neurotic claims, tyrannical shoulds, and self-hate, all of which will vary with our predominant solution.

Neurotic pride substitutes a pride in the attributes of the idealized self for realistic self-confidence and self-esteem. Threats to pride produce anxiety and hostility; its collapse results in self-contempt and despair. On the basis of our pride, we make **neurotic claims** on the world, demanding to be treated in accordance with our grandiose conception of ourselves. The claims are "pervaded by expectations of magic" (1950, p. 62). They intensify our vulnerability, for their frustration deflates our pride and confronts us with the sense of powerlessness and inadequacy from which we are fleeing.

The idealized image generates not only pride and claims but also what Horney calls the **tyranny of the shoulds.** The shoulds compel us to live up to our grandiose conception of ourselves. The shoulds are determined largely by the character traits and values associated with our predominant solution, but because our subordinate trends are also represented in the idealized image, we are often caught in a "crossfire of conflicting shoulds." For example, the self-effacing person wants to be good, noble, loving, forgiving, generous; but he has an aggressive side that tells him to "go all out for his advantage" and to "hit back at anybody who offends him. Accordingly he despises himself at bottom for any trace of 'cowardice,' or ineffectualness and compliance. He is thus under a constant crossfire. He is damned if he does do something, and he is damned if he does not" (1950, p. 221). This is a good description of Hamlet. (See Paris, 1991a.) "It is the threat of a punitive self-hate that lurks behind [the shoulds]," observed Horney, that "truly makes them a regime of terror" (1950, p. 85).

The shoulds are the basis of our **bargain with fate.** No matter what the solution, our bargain is that our claims will be honored if we live up to our shoulds. We seek magically to control external reality by obeying our inner dictates. We do not see our claims as unreasonable, of course, but only as what we have a right to expect, given our grandiose conception of ourselves, and life will seem unfair if our expectations are frustrated. Our **sense of justice** is determined by our predominant solution and the bargain associated with it.

Self-hate is the end product of the intrapsychic strategies of defense, each of which tends to magnify our feelings of inadequacy and failure. Self-hate is essentially the rage the idealized self feels toward our actual self for not being what it "should" be. Horney sees self-hate as "perhaps the greatest tragedy of the human mind. Man in reaching out for the Infinite and Absolute also starts destroying himself. When he makes a pact with the devil, who promises him glory, he has to go to hell—to the hell within himself" (1950, p. 154).

DYNAMICS

Horneyan theory has a dynamic quality: solutions combine, conflict, become stronger or weaker, need to be defended, generate vicious circles, and are replaced by others when they collapse. Conflicts between the defenses cause oscillations, inconsistencies, and self-hate. The pride system contains a seesawing between the idealized and despised selves and a crossfire of conflicting shoulds.

The Basic Conflict. In each interpersonal defense, one element involved in basic anxiety is overemphasized: *helplessness* in the compliant solution, *hostility* in the aggressive solution, and *isolation* in the detached solution. Under pathogenic conditions, all these feelings are likely to occur, leading individuals to make all three of the defensive moves and giving rise to what Horney calls the **basic conflict.**

To gain some sense of wholeness, they will emphasize one move more than the others and will become predominantly self-effacing, expansive, or detached. Which move they emphasize will depend on the particular combination of temperamental and environmental factors at work in their situation. The other trends will continue to exist but will operate unconsciously and manifest themselves in disguised and devious ways. The basic conflict will not have been resolved but will simply have gone underground. When the submerged trends for some reason rise closer to the surface, individuals will experience severe inner turmoil and may be unable to move in any direction at all. Under the impetus of a powerful influence or the dramatic failure of their predominant solution, they may embrace one of their repressed defensive strategies. They will experience this as conversion or education, but it will be merely the substitution of one neurotic solution for another.

The shoulds are in fact self-destructive in their very nature. . . . They put a person into a strait jacket and deprive him of inner freedom. Even if he manages to mold himself into a behavioristic perfection, he can do so only at the expense of his spontaneity and the authenticity of his feelings and beliefs. The shoulds aim in fact, like any political tyranny, at the extinction of individuality. (Horney, 1950, p. 118)

I love little pussy, her coat is so warm
And if I don't hurt her, she'll do me no harm.
I'll sit by the fire and give her some food,
And pussy will love me because I am good. (Mother Goose)

[T]he easy way to infinite glory is inevitably also the way to an inner hell of self-contempt and self-torment. By taking this road, the individual is in fact losing his soul—his real self. (Horney, 1950, p. 39)

The Relation Between Interpersonal and Intrapsychic Defenses

In *Neurosis and Human Growth* (1950), Horney warned against "a one-sided focus on either intrapsychic or interpersonal factors," contending that the dynamics of neurosis can be understood "only as a process in which interpersonal conflicts lead to a peculiar intrapsychic configuration, and this in turn depends on and modifies the old patterns of human relations" (p. 237). Although she sometimes overemphasized the intrapsychic herself, her theory as a whole maintained the balance she prescribed.

In reviewing the evolution of her theory at the end of *Neurosis and Human Growth,* Horney observed that, at first, she saw neurosis as essentially a disturbance in human relationships. This disturbance creates basic anxiety, against which we defend ourselves by employing the interpersonal strategies of defense. In her earlier books she had been aware of intrapsychic factors but had not recognized their extent and importance. She came to realize, however, that the formation of the idealized image marks a turning point in development, as our energies shift from developing our real potentialities to actualizing our grandiose conception of ourselves. The idealized image generates the pride system, which becomes a kind of Frankenstein's monster that hates and seeks to destroy its creator. Neurosis is a disturbance not only in our relationships with others but also in our relationship with ourselves.

The disturbance in the relationship with ourselves makes it nearly impossible for us to form better relationships with others, and even if we could form such relationships, they would not undo the original damage. The pride system is the logical outgrowth of early development and the beginning of a new one. Once in existence, it has a dynamic of its own that is to a large degree independent of external events. The pride system affects how we interact with others. It poisons all our relationships and makes it extremely difficult for them to be a source of healing or growth. To deal successfully with the pride system, analysts must recognize its manifestations in the transference and understand its structure and function.

> Although human relations are of signal importance, they do not have the power to uproot a firmly planted pride system in a person who keeps his real self out of communication. In this crucial matter the pride system again proves to be the enemy of our growth. (Horney, 1950, p. 308)

The Central Inner Conflict

In the course of successful therapy, an intrapsychic conflict develops beween the pride system and the emerging real self, which now becomes a target of self-hate. Horney calls this the **central inner conflict.** Living from the real self involves accepting a world of uncertainty, process, and limitation. It means giving up the search for glory and settling for a less-exalted existence. The proud self therefore senses the real self as a threat to its very existence and turns upon it with scorn.

Although the central inner conflict occurs at a rather late stage in psychological growth, it is extremely difficult to resolve. People who have focused their lives on dreams of glory may never be able fully to free themselves from the habit of self-idealization. If they have made progress in therapy, they may seize on their improvement as "the last chance to actualize [their] idealized self in the shining glory of perfect health" (1950, p. 358). They may look down on others for being neurotic, drive themselves to behave in what they consider healthy ways, and rage at themselves when they realize that they will always have problems and imperfections. Horney's hope is that patients will "feel sympathetic" toward themselves and experience themselves "as being neither particularly wonderful nor despicable but as the struggling and often harassed" human beings they are (1950, p. 359).

> The release of the real self from the seesawing of the pride system is, I suggest, a triumph of the ordinary. . . . In simply being herself with all her capabilities and flaws, a person comes to realize that she does not have to be extraordinary in order to be worthwhile. (Westkott, 1986, p. 211)

<u>personal reflection</u>

SELF-ANALYSIS

Try this exercise in self-analysis. In a quiet, private place, with this textbook and a notebook, take a half hour to do the following:

1. Identify one personal issue for you. After you have made your choice, write it down as succinctly as possible.
2. With as much of the objectivity of an outside observer as you can muster, write a paragraph or two describing your behavior in regard to this issue.
3. Reread the section entitled *Interpersonal Strategies of Defense (pp. 126–129)* on moving toward, moving against, and moving away from others. Note if these trends and their compulsive shoulds enter into your problem.
4. Is the issue a relatively minor difficulty that arises only under special conditions? Or is it ever-present, ongoing, and entangled with other conflicts?
5. Make a list of the benefits or costs involved in the issue, in terms of both psychological and other real-life losses and gains.
6. Imagine yourself in the middle of this problem. Have you ever felt this way before? If memories arise, make a note of them.
7. If possible, read your notes to another person. Notice what happens when you communicate your self-analysis: How do you feel during different parts of the reading? What do you censor? What do you feel a need to explain further?

NONCLINICAL APPLICATIONS OF HORNEY

Karen Horney's theories have proven valuable not only for clinical practice but as an explanatory system for use in other disciplines. In recent years they have been increasingly employed in the study of gender. Also her work has been utilized to better understand literature, biography, and culture. See our **web** site for more on this.

They are also applicable to religion (Huffman, 1982; Paris, 1986; Rubins, 1980; Wood, 1980; Zabriskie, 1976) and philosophy (Mullin, 1988; Paris, 1986; Tigner, 1985).

Gender Study

Horney has been rediscovered in recent years by feminists, many of whose positions she anticipated. Although most attention has been given to her early essays, her mature theory also has important implications for understanding gender identity and masculine and feminine psychology. Impressive work has been done along these lines by Alexandra Symonds, a Horneyan analyst, and Marcia Westkott, a social psychologist. Horney's mature theory has also been used to address gender issues in popular books by Helen De Rosis and Victoria Pelligrino (1976) and Claudette Dowling (1981).

Symond's essays (1974, 1976, 1978, 1991) are based largely on her clinical experience with women who were suffering from their feminine role, or who were trying to escape that role but finding it difficult, or who seemed to have escaped but were having trouble dealing with the consequences. In every case, the starting point was a culture that conditioned girls to be self-effacing and dependent, while boys were encouraged to be autonomous and aggressive. While focusing on the plight of girls, Symonds recognized that boys develop difficulties of their own as a result of cultural stereotyping.

In *The Feminist Legacy of Karen Horney* (1986), Marcia Westkott explored the implications of Horney's mature theory for feminine psychology, with chapters on the sexualization and devaluation of women and the dependency, anger, and detachment they feel as a consequence. In addition, she developed a Horneyan critique of a major strand of feminist theory. Jean Baker Miller, Nancy Chodorow, Carol Gilligan, and the Stone Center group have associated an array of personality traits specifically with women. These include a need for affiliation, a nurturing disposition, a sense of responsibility for other people, and a relational sense of identity. Westkott observed that although these traits are regarded in a positive way, they emerged from "a historical setting in which women are less highly valued than men" (Westkott, 1986, p. 2). She proposed that these traits are defensive reactions to subordination, devaluation, and powerlessness and that, however desirable they may seem from a social point of view, they are inimical to women's self-actualization. Westkott thus demythified the celebration of female relationality, arguing that it has provided "a contemporary theoretical justification for traditionally idealized femininity" (1989, p. 245). She contended, with Horney, that being deprived is not ennobling but damaging and that the self-effacing qualities many women develop in order to cope with devaluation are destructive.

EVALUATION

Horney was the first, and perhaps the best, critic of Freud's ideas about women. Her early essays on female psychology have an astonishing immediacy. . . . Many of Horney's other ideas, which so enraged the New York Society in 1941, have since been incorporated into psychoanalytic thinking. . . . (Quinn, 1987, p. 14)

Karen Horney is important for her contributions to feminine psychology, which although forgotten for many years have been highly influential since their republication in *Feminine Psychology* in 1967. They are especially notable for their exploration of female development from a woman's point of view and for their emphasis on the cultural construction of gender. Unlike her essays on feminine psychology, Horney's first two books had a great impact in their day, and their case for the importance of culture and for a structural model of neurosis continues to have an influence. The growing emphasis on present-oriented therapies owes something to Horney's teachings. Her third book, *Self-Analysis* (1942), inspired the Institute for Self-Analysis in London and remains the most thorough discussion of the possibilities and techniques of successful self-exploration. It should be noted that Horney believed that self-analysis has the best chance of success when it is employed in conjunction with therapy or as a way of continuing to work on oneself after termination.

Although each stage of Horney's thought is important, her mature theory represents her most significant contribution. Most of Horney's early ideas have been revised or enriched—by Horney herself or by others—or have been absorbed or discovered anew by later writers. This is not the case with her mature theory. *Our Inner Conflicts* (1945) and *Neurosis and Human Growth* (1950) provide explanations of human behavior in terms of currently existing constellations of defenses and inner conflicts that can be found nowhere else. Horney does not account for the whole of human psychology, since, like every theorist, she describes only part of the picture, but her mature theory is highly congruent with frequently occurring patterns of behavior. Although Horney objected to the instinctivistic nature of Freudian theory, her own theory has a biological basis, since the movements against, away from, and toward other people are human elaborations of the basic defenses of the animal kingdom—fight, flight, and submission. All the strategies are encoded in almost every culture; but each culture has its characteristic attitudes toward the different strategies, its own formulations of and variations upon them, and its own structure of inner conflicts. Horney is often thought of as having described the neurotic personality of her time, but, as its interdisciplinary uses show, her mature theory has wide applicability.

CONCLUSION

Most psychoanalytic theory has followed Freud in focusing on early origins as a means of explanation and therapy. Well in advance of many recent critics of psychoanalysis, Karen Horney believed this practice results in circular reasoning, in the conversion of analogies into causes, and in a variety of other epistemological problems. She also considered it therapeutically ineffective. Horney doubted that early childhood could ever be accurately recovered, since we are bound to reconstruct it from the perspective of our present needs, beliefs, and defenses. We have a natural desire to explain things in terms of their origins, but Horney saw as many myths of origin as she did psychoanalytic theories. It is more profitable, she argued, "to focus on the forces which actually drive and inhibit a person; there is a reasonable chance of understanding these, even without much knowledge of childhood" (1939, p. 146). Horney tried to explain behavior in terms of its function within the current constellation of defenses and to account for contradictory attitudes, actions, and beliefs by seeing them as part of a structure of inner conflicts.

Karen Horney is perhaps the first humanistic psychoanalyst. Her theories are entirely compatible with those of Abraham Maslow, who was influenced by her. Both theories are based on the idea of a *real self* that life seeks to actualize. Horney focused on what happens when we become alienated from our real selves as a result of a pathogenic environment, while Maslow focused on what we require for healthy growth and the characteristics of self-actualizing people. Horney described the defensive strategies we employ when our healthy basic needs for safety, love and belonging, and esteem have been turned into insatiable neurotic needs as a result of having been thwarted. The theories of Horney and Maslow are complementary and, taken together, provide a more comprehensive picture of human behavior than either provides by itself.

> Albert Schweitzer uses the terms "optimistic" and "pessimistic" in the sense of "world and life affirmation," and "world and life negation." Freud's philosophy, in this deep sense, is a pessimistic one. Ours, with all its cognizance of the tragic element in neurosis, is an optimistic one. (Horney, 1950, p. 378)

The Theory Firsthand

EXCERPT FROM *SELF-ANALYSIS*

The following excerpt is from Horney's account of the self-analysis of her "patient" Clare, who is a fictionalized version of herself. It deals with Clare's efforts to free herself from her "morbid dependency" on her lover, Peter, a fictionalized version of Erich Fromm, who has left her.

She wavered between times in which the experience with Peter and all that it entailed appeared as part of a far-distant past, and others in which she desperately longed to win him back. Solitude, then, was felt as an unfathomable cruelty perpetrated on her.

In one of these latter days, going home alone from a concert, she found herself thinking that everyone was better off than she.... She recognized that a tendency must be at work which made her talk herself into an exaggerated misery.... She had an expectation that great distress would bring about help. And for the sake of this unconscious belief she made herself more miserable than she was. It was shockingly silly, yet she had done it, and had done it frequently.... She remembered any number of occasions when she had felt herself the most abused of mortals, only to realize some time later that she had made matters much worse than they actually were. When she had been in the spell of such unhappiness, however, the reasons for it looked, and even felt, real....

Yes, there was a clear pattern that repeated itself—exaggerated misery and at the same time an expectation of help, consolation, encouragement, from her mother, from God, from Bruce [her first love], from her husband, from Peter. Her playing the martyr role, apart from everything else, must have also been an unconscious plea for help.

Clare was thus on the verge of recognizing another important clue to her dependency.... She recognized that a belief that she could command help through misery actually had a strong hold upon her.

Within the next months she saw with a gradually increasing measure of lucidity and in great detail what this belief did to her. She saw that she unconsciously tended to make a major catastrophe out of every difficulty that arose in her life, collapsing into a state of complete helplessness, with the result that despite a certain front of bravery and independence her prevailing feeling toward life was one of helplessness in the face of overwhelming odds. She recognized that this firm belief in forthcoming help had amounted to a kind of private religion, and that not unlike a true religion it had been a powerful source of reassurance.

Clare also acquired a deepened insight as to the extent to which her reliance on someone else had taken the place of reliance on herself. If she always had someone who taught her, stimulated her, advised her, helped her, defended her, gave her affirmation of her value, there was no reason why she should make any effort to overcome the anxiety involved in taking her life into her own hands. . . . The dependency had not only perpetuated her weakness by stifling her incentive to become more self-reliant but it had actually created an interest in remaining helpless. If she remained humble and self-effacing all happiness, all triumph would be hers. Any attempt at greater self-reliance and greater self-assertion was bound to jeopardize these expectations of a heaven on earth. . . . The compulsive modesty had not only given her the sheltering cloak of inconspicuousness, but it had also been the indispensable basis for her expectations of "love."

She realized it was merely a logical consequence, then, that the partner to whom she ascribed the godlike role of magic helper—to use a pertinent term of Erich Fromm's—became all important, and that to be wanted and loved by him became the only thing that mattered. . . . [Peter's] importance lay in the fact that he was an instrument whose services she could demand by making her need for them sufficiently great.

As a result of these insights she felt much more free than ever before. The longing for Peter, which at times had been excruciatingly strong, started to recede. More important, the insight brought about a real change in her objectives in life. She had always consciously wanted to be independent, but in her actual life had given this wish mere lip service and had reached out for help in any difficulty that arose. Now to become able to cope with her own life became an active, alive goal. (pp. 233–238)

CHAPTER HIGHLIGHTS

- There were three distinct phases in the development of Karen Horney's thought: (1) her early essays on feminine psychology, (2) her recognition that culture and disturbed human relationships are more important than biology as causes of neurotic development, and (3) her study of the interpersonal defenses and the intrapsychic defenses developed to cope with anxiety.

- Horney was one of the founders of humanistic psychology, which is based on her emphasis that healthy values and the goals of life grow from self-realization. Drawing on her own experience, she believed in the human potential for growth and recognized the difficulty of achieving it.

- Horney acknowledged that she was deeply indebted to the foundation Freud provided. However, she came to see the male bias in psychoanalysis as reinforcing and reproducing devaluation of the feminine.

- She proposed a women's view of disturbances in the relations between the sexes and differences between women and men, and she suggested that girls and women have patterns of development we must understand in their own terms, not simply in relation to those of men.

- Horney saw that male privilege more than penises was what women envied and that both men and women need greater opportunity to develop their human capacities.

- Horney's version of psychoanalysis looks at neurosis as a set of defenses against basic anxiety. It places a greater emphasis on the role of culture and shifts the focus from the infantile origins of character structure, as described by Freud.

- Her emphasis on a structural approach, in both theory and practice, looks to the individual's current constellation of inner conflicts and defenses to explain the present, rather than trying to recover the past in order to explain the present.

- In contrast to Freud's view that nothing much new happens after the age of 5, Horney suggested that development does not stop at that point and that the individual's later reactions or experiences evolve from the preceding ones.

- It is through a developmental process rather than through repetition that past events are contained in the present. Early experiences affect us profoundly by determining the direction of development and by conditioning the ways in which we respond to the world, rather than by producing fixations that cause us to repeat earlier patterns.
- Horney suggests three basic strategies that people use to cope with basic anxiety: by moving toward people and adopting a self-effacing or compliant solution; moving against people and adopting an aggressive or expansive solution; and moving away from people and becoming detached and resigned. Within the expansive solution are three divisions: narcissistic, perfectionistic, and arrogant-vindictive.
- Horney identified the pride system, which includes neurotic pride, neurotic claims, tyrannical shoulds, and increased self-hate and is generated by self-idealization.
- There is a dynamic quality to Horney's theory, as conflicts follow their own cycle, causing oscillations, inconsistencies, and self-hate. Within the pride system, there is a crossfire of conflicting shoulds and a seesawing between the despised and idealized selves.
- As our energies shift from developing our real potentialities to actualizing our grandiose conception of ourselves, our behavior is marked by the formation of the idealized image. This, in turn, generates the pride system.
- Horney's theories have been applied nonclinically as well, providing a useful explanatory system in the fields of literature, culture, biography, and gender studies, as well as religion and philosophy.
- Horney tried to account for contradictory actions, attitudes, and beliefs by seeing them as part of a structure of inner conflict, and to explain behavior in terms of its function within the individual's current defenses.

KEY CONCEPTS

Arrogant-vindictive solution One of the expansive interpersonal solutions to basic anxiety. People using this strategy are motivated by a need for vindictive triumphs. Their bargain is essentially with themselves. These individuals regard life as a tough battle with goals to be won if they do not allow themselves to be distracted by their softer feelings or traditional morality.

Bargain with fate The belief, formed from the shoulds, that our claims will be honored, regardless of our type of solution, if we live up to our shoulds. By obeying our inner dictates, we seek magically to control external reality.

Basic anxiety Response that develops in a child when the environment appears to threaten physical survival, as well as the survival of wishes and strivings. Feeling helpless in a potentially hostile world, the child pursues power, love, or detachment as an interpersonal strategy of defense.

Basic conflict The choice of which of the three defensive moves an individual emphasizes—to become self-effacing, expansive, or detached. The selection depends on the specific combination of environmental and temperamental factors in the situation. All three will occur, though one will become predominant. The others will go underground to operate unconsciously, manifesting themselves in devious and disguised ways.

Central inner conflict The intrapsychic conflict that develops between the emerging real self and the pride system. The real self is sensed as a threat to the proud self, which turns on it with a vengeance. This conflict occurs at a relatively late stage of psychological growth.

Compliant solution Interpersonal strategy of coping with basic anxiety by controlling others through their dependency, and by gaining affection and approval. The bargain made by users of this solution is that they will be well treated by fate and other people if they do not seek their own gain or glory and are good, humble, and loving.

Detachment Interpersonal strategy of coping with basic anxiety by moving away from people. The bargain made by individuals who employ this solution is threefold: others will not bother them if they ask for nothing; they will not fail if they try for nothing; and they will not be disappointed if they expect little of life.

Expansive solutions Interpersonal strategies of coping with basic anxiety by moving against people and adopting an aggressive stance. Not love, but mastery, appeals to the individuals who use this solution. Because they are ashamed of suffering, helplessness is anathema to them. There are three distinct divisions within this solution: narcissistic, perfectionistic, and arrogant-vindictive.

Idealized image A self-conception based on our predominant interpersonal defense and the attributes it exalts. Imaginatively created to compensate for feelings of inadequacy, worthlessness, and weakness, it is endowed with expansive powers and exaggerated faculties. Its creation produces the search for glory, neurotic claims, neurotic pride, tyrannical shoulds, and self-hate.

Masculinity complex   The constellation of feelings and fantasies built around the woman's feeling of being discriminated against, envy of the male, and the wish to discard the female role. Horney believed that the conflict is the product of particular kinds of family dynamics in a male-dominated culture.

Narcissistic solution   One of the expansive interpersonal solutions to basic anxiety. Narcissists seek to master life by the exercise of charm and self-admiration. Their bargain is that life is bound to give them what they want if they hold to their dreams and their exaggerated claims for themselves.

Neurotic claims   Our demands, based on our pride, to be treated in accordance with our grandiose conception of ourselves. Permeated with an air of magic, these claims intensify our vulnerability.

Neurotic pride   Pride in the attributes of the idealized self, which replaces realistic self-confidence and self-esteem.

Penis envy   Feelings of inferiority, competitiveness toward men, and vindictiveness, said to arise in women when their lack of a penis is realized, in classical psychoanalytic theory. See Freud, p. 29 for different view.

Perfectionistic solution   One of the expansive interpersonal solutions to basic anxiety. The high intellectual and moral standards of perfectionists provide the vantage point from which they look down on others. Being just, fair, and dutiful, according to their bargain, entitles them to fair treatment by life in general and specifically by other people.

Pride system   A product—consisting of neurotic pride, tyranny of the shoulds, and self-hate—of our idealized image. It affects how we work with others, poisons all relationships, and makes it highly unlikely for them to be a source of growth

or healing. It is generated by the idealized self-image, is a logical outgrowth of early development, and has its own dynamic largely independent of external events.

Real self   The possible self, in contrast to the idealized self. It is a set of intrinsic potentialities—which include temperament, capacities, talents, and predispositions—that are part of our genetic makeup and need a favorable environment in which to develop. Actualized through interactions with the external world, it is not impervious to external influence. It is not a product of learning, however, as one cannot be taught to be oneself.

Search for glory   A pursuit whose object is the actualization of our idealized self. It follows the formation of the idealized image. Our particular neurosis will determine the rules of this private religion. Every culture has its own featured glory systems.

Self-hate   The rage that the idealized self feels toward the actual self for not being what it "should" be. As a despised image develops and becomes the focus for self-contempt when we inevitably fall short of being our idealized image, additional inner conflict arises and self-hate increases.

Sense of justice   Our expectation determined by the bargain associated with our predominant solution.

Tyranny of the shoulds   Our compulsions to live up to our grandiose conception of ourselves. Self-destructive by their very nature, they aim at the complete eradication of individuality. They are determined largely by the values and character traits associated with our predominant solution.

Vicious circles   A situation in which the defensive strategies employed to alleviate anxiety instead tend to increase it.

Womb envy   The male envy of pregnancy, childbirth, and motherhood, which results in the unconscious depreciation of women. Men's impulse toward creative work may be an overcompensation for their small role in procreation.

ANNOTATED BIBLIOGRAPHY

Most of Horney's books, unlike her articles, were written for the layperson. All of Horney's books are in print and available in paperbound editions.

Horney, K. (1937). *The neurotic personality of our time*. New York: Norton.

Argues for the influence of culture on personality and sets up a new paradigm for the structure of neurosis.

Horney, K. (1939). *New ways in psychoanalysis*. New York: Norton.

Systematic critique of Freud's theory, especially its emphasis on biological factors and infantile origins. Emphasizes environmental factors, current character structure, and self-realization as the object of therapy.

Horney, K. (1942). *Self-Analysis*. New York: Norton.

Describes the possibilities, techniques, and difficulties of both dyadic analysis and self-analysis. Contains Horney's most fully developed case history, that of Clare, which is highly autobiographical.

Horney, K. (1945). *Our inner conflicts*. New York: Norton.

Focuses on the interpersonal strategies of compliance (moving toward), aggression (moving against), and detachment (moving away from) and the conflicts between these strategies (the basic conflict). A good place to start reading Horney.

Horney, K. (1950). *Neurosis and human growth*. New York: Norton.

Focuses on the intrapsychic strategies of self-idealization, the search for glory, neurotic pride, neurotic claims, and tyrannical shoulds, all of which simultaneously defend against and increase self-hate. Integrates the interpersonal strategies into a complete system, but in an occasionally confusing manner. Horney's most complex and important book. Written for fellow analysts but lucid and accessible to laypersons.

Horney, K. (1967). *Feminine psychology.* (H. Kelman, Ed.). New York: Norton.

Essays on women's problems and the relations between the sexes. In their emphasis on the cultural construction of gender, these essays were decades ahead of their time.

Horney, K. (1999). *The therapeutic process: Essays and lectures.* (B. Paris, Ed.). New Haven: Yale University Press.

The lectures constitute a version of the book Horney was preparing to write at her death and provides the most complete record of Horney's ideas about the practice of psychotherapy.

Horney, K. (2000). *The unknown Karen Horney: Essays on gender, culture, and psychoanalysis.* (B. Paris, Ed.). New Haven: Yale University Press.

In presenting eighteen previously unpublished pieces, four essays that have not been available in English, and other texts that have been difficult to locate, this collection makes accessible an important segment of Horney's work.

Paris, B. (1994). *Karen Horney: A psychoanalyst's search for self-understanding.* New Haven, CT: Yale University Press.

Combines biography with a full account of Horney's theories. Argues that the evolution of her ideas is a product of her lifelong effort to solve her problems by understanding herself. More a character portrait of Horney than a conventional biography.

Quinn, S. (1987). *A mind of her own: The life of Karen Horney.* New York: Summit Books.

The best account of Horney's social and cultural context and the events of her life. Less good on her inner life and her ideas, especially her mature theory.

Weiss, F. (1991). Karen Horney: A bibliography. *American Journal of Psychoanalysis, 51,* 343–347.

Quinn and Paris also contain much bibliographic information.

Westkott, M. (1986). *The feminist legacy of Karen Horney.* New Haven, CT: Yale University Press.

The most sustained effort to show how Horney's mature theory illuminates feminist issues.

Web Sites

A web search for "Horney," will produce numerous porn sites. Search for "Karen Horney" instead.

www.karenhorneycenter.org.

This leads you to all the important Karen Horney sites.

http://grove.ufl.edu/~biparis/links.html

Links to The International Karen Horney Society and to papers by Bernard Paris.

REFERENCES

Brown, J. F. (1939, September 23). Review of new ways in psychoanalysis. *Nation,* pp. 328–329.

Chodorow, N. (1989). *Feminism and psychoanalytic thought.* New Haven, CT: Yale University Press.

De Rosis, H., & Pelligrino, V. (1976). *The book of hope: How women can overcome depression.* New York: Macmillan.

Dowling, C. (1981). *The Cinderella complex: Woman's hidden fear of independence.* New York: Summit Books.

Horney, K. (1935). Conceptions and misconceptions of the analytical method. *Journal of Nervous and Mental Disease, 81,* 399–410.

Horney, K. (1937). *The neurotic personality of our time.* New York: Norton.

Horney, K. (1939). *New ways in psychoanalysis.* New York: Norton.

Horney, K. (1942). *Self-Analysis.* New York: Norton.

Horney, K. (1945). *Our inner conflicts.* New York: Norton.

Horney, K. (1950). *Neurosis and human growth.* New York: Norton.

Horney, K. (1967). *Feminine psychology.* (H. Kelman, Ed.). New York: Norton.

Horney, K. (1980). *The adolescent diaries of Karen Horney.* New York: Basic Books.

Horney, K. (1989). Young man Johnson. *American Journal of Psychoanalysis, 49,* 251–265.

Horney, K. (1991). The goals of analytic therapy. *American Journal of Psychoanalysis, 51,* 219–226. (Originally published, 1951.)

Horney, K. (2000). *The unknown Karen Horney: Essays on gender, culture, and psychoanalysis.* (B. Paris, Ed.) New Haven: Yale University Press.

Huffman, J. (1982). A psychological critique of American culture. *The American Journal of Psychoanalysis, 42,* 27–38.

James, W. (1890). *Principles of Psychology.* New York: Holt.

Kierkegaard, S. (1980/1849). *The Sickness Unto Death: A Christian Psychological Exposition for Upbuilding and Awakening.* Edited and translated by H. Hong and E. Hong. Princeton, NJ: Princeton University Press.

Mullin, H. (1988). Horney's contribution to a rational approach to morals. *American Journal of Psychoanalysis, 48,* 127–137.

Paris, B. (Ed.). (1986). *Third force psychology and the study of literature.* Rutherford, NJ: Fairleigh Dickinson University Press.

Paris, B. (1994). *Karen Horney: A psychoanalyst's search for self-understanding.* New Haven, CT: Yale University Press.

Quinn, S. (1987). *A mind of her own: The life of Karen Horney.* New York: Summit Books.

Rank, O. (1936/1978). *Will Therapy.* New York: Norton.

Rubins, J. (1978). *Karen Horney: Gentle rebel of psychoanalysis.* New York: Dial Press.

Rubins, J. (1980). Discussion of Barry G. Wood: The religion of psychoanalysis. *American Journal of Psychoanalysis, 40,* 23–26.

Sherrill, M. (2003). Walk on the wild side. (Article/interview about Lauren Hutton) *AARP,* November/December, 42–48.

Symonds, A. (1974). The liberated woman: Healthy and neurotic. *American Journal of Psychoanalysis, 34,* 177–183.

Symonds, A. (1976). Neurotic dependency in successful women. *Journal of the American Academy of Psychoanalysis, 4,* 95–103.

Symonds, A. (1978). The psychodynamics of expansiveness in the success-oriented woman. *American Journal of Psychoanalysis, 38,* 195–205.

Symonds, A. (1991). Gender-issues and Horney's theory. *American Journal of Psychoanalysis, 51,* 301–312.

Tigner, J. (1985). An analysis of Spinoza's pride and self-abasement. *American Journal of Psychoanalysis, 45,* 208–220.

Trotter W. (1916). *Instincts of the herd in peace and war.* London: T. Fischer Unwin.

Wachtel, P. (1977). *Psychoanalysis and behavior therapy: Toward an integration.* New York: Basic Books.

Westkott, M. (1986). *The feminist legacy of Karen Horney.* New Haven, CT: Yale University Press.

Westkott, M. (1989). Female relationality and the idealized self. *American Journal of Psychoanalysis, 49,* 239–250.

Wittels, F. (1939). The neo-Adlerians. *American Journal of Sociology, 45,* 433–445.

Wolcott, J. (1996, June 3). Letterman Unbound: Dave's No. 2 and Trying Harder. *New Yorker,* pp. 80–92.

Wood, B. (1980). The religion of psychoanalysis. *American Journal of Psychoanalysis, 40,* 13–22.

Zabriskie, C. (1976). A psychological analysis of biblical interpretation pertaining to women. *Journal of Psychology and Theology, 4,* 304–312.

feminist approaches
to personality theory

Jean Baker Miller, Irene Pierce Stiver,
Judith V. Jordan, Janet L. Surrey,
Christine Brooks, and Jennifer Clements

The field of feminist psychology has grown tremendously in the thirty years since its inception. This chapter will serve as an introduction to the major feminist personality theories, an overview of how these theories are put into practice, and an introduction to alternative research methodologies grounded in feminist theory. In addition, this chapter will illustrate ways in which feminist theories have contributed to new perspectives in personality theory.

Earlier editions of this book used the chapter title "The Psychology of Women." The present title is a more accurate portrayal of the material presented in the following pages.

FEMINIST PSYCHOLOGY

Christine Brooks

Feminist theory moves beyond the traditional examination of psychology as a study of individuals. Instead, feminist theorists believe that individuals should be understood in relation to the sociopolitical context in which one lives: the structures around the individual are viewed as having a much greater influence on her/his understanding of the "self" than traditionally proposed (Brown, 1994; Jordan & Hartling, 2002; Suyemoto, 2002).

While the primary mandate of feminist psychology is to bring a better understanding of gender into the field, it is by no means the only element feminists consider. Rising from the political and civil movements of the 1960s and 1970s, feminist psychology seeks to examine people in relation to their actual, lived lives. Thus, factors such as class, race, social and cultural beliefs, and personal values are also major factors of study for feminist psychologists. "By adding gender and diversity to the list of important variables to be evaluated . . . no longer can we strip context from the understanding of who we are, what we do, and why we do it" (Walker, p. vii).

Thus, a central focus of feminist psychology is that a person must be understood in the context of living in constant relationship to her/his outer world: familial relationships, community and/or national affiliation, religious affiliation, and any other interpersonal affiliative group.

Psychotherapist and feminist theorist Laura S. Brown's (1992) comments underscore the power inherent in interrelatedness. She writes:

> Feminist analysis has developed significantly over the last 3 decades. Building from early concepts of the second wave of U.S. feminism—such as "the personal is political," the pervasiveness of sexism, the importance of lived experience found in "consciousness raising," and the centrality of gender as a category for analysis—have evolved into a complex and sophisticated perspective. For example, "the personal is political" was originally used to emphasize that one's own experience is important and is, in some measure, caused by external factors. Currently feminist psychologists use this notion as a starting point for understanding the formative influence of sociocultural structures and forces on the individual and his or her sense of self, hence the reformulation: "the political is personal." (p. xii.)

The Pioneers

Karen Horney is viewed as a major inspiration for contemporary feminist psychological theory. A detailed overview of her work comprises Chapter 4 of this text. Horney's development of a "feminine psychology" was a critical first step toward understanding developmental and personality theory through the lens of gender. Most notably, Paludi (1998) points out, that, "whereas Freud argued that women were the result of the social conditions; Horney argued that the social conditions were the cause of women's behavior" (p. 80). Horney's work was an early attempt to interface an individual's sense of self with the sociocultural factors that influence one's development.

Clara Thompson (1942), working within the interpersonal school of psychoanalysis, noted the "centrality of relationships in development" and encouraged "women to define themselves on the basis of their own strengths" (in Enns, 1997). Both of these women sought to understand the unique perspective of women and the developmental issues women face on their own terms. Traditional models of psychology place men, with the social and cultural values associated with being male, at the core of theory—male is the norm. Anything that deviates from this norm is viewed as deviating from normal development or behavior. Thus, if normal, healthy women develop differently or behave in other ways, they are pathologized as deviant. These early theorists pointed out the absence of logic in this early work. They began to write women into psychology and define additional ways for women to define themselves.

A Brief History of Feminism

The contemporary women's movement, referred to as Women's Liberation and synonymous with the term *second wave feminism,* was greatly influenced by the U.S. civil rights, antiwar, and youth activism movements during the 1960s. The movement was "driven by a wide variety of women's concerns, including sex discrimination; limited opportunities in employment; restraints on reproductive freedom; and concerns about domestic violence, sexual victimization, and women's unpaid labor" (Biaggio, 2000, p. 3).

Several pivotal books written in the late 1950s, 1960s, and early 1970s became the foundational texts of early feminism: *The Second Sex* (de Beauvoir, 1953), *The Feminine Mystique* (Friedan, 1963), *Sexual Politics* (Millet, 1970) and *Sisterhood Is Powerful* (Morgan, 1970). Each of these books reexamined the cultural, political, and social positions of women. Assumptions about women's "position" in society as well as what had traditionally been assumed gender roles for women began to be dismantled (Ruth, 1990). As these texts gained readership, the feminist movement gained grassroots momentum, most notably through the formation of "consciousness raising" (CR) groups. These groups were collectives of women gathered together, "focused on facilitating personal awareness of a central tenet of the movement: the personal is political" (Biaggio, p. 6). Biaggio succinctly sums up the general attitudes and motivations of the women involved in early CR groups:

> All across the country, as if by spontaneous combustion, women were meeting to discuss their personal plights and arriving at the same conclusion: that their problems were not unique or isolated phenomena, but rather reflections of a political environment that devalued and subjugated women. . . . This is how the movement caught fire; women bonded around the new insight that they were being treated like second-class citizens. They realized that they had grown so accustomed to this status that they had been blind to its very existence. This awareness and the fervent sense of sisterhood it gave rise to fueled the movement. (Biaggio, p. 6)

Minnie Bruce Pratt's account of her own process of consciousness raising, "Identity: Skin, Blood, Heart" (1988), is an example of the unfolding of the empowerment process.

Feminism—I myself have never known what feminism is. I only know that people call me a feminist whenever I express sentiments that differentiate me from a doormat. (Rebecca West, 1913)

When a woman becomes a scholar there is usually something wrong with her sex organs. (Nietzsche)

I count myself lucky to have come into my maturity during a time when the second wave of American feminism was rising steadily. Because it deepened my understanding of myself as a person born into the wrong sex, feminism clarified immensely the lifelong task of sorting out "What is me? What is the world? What is being done to me? What am I doing to myself?" (Vivian Gornick)

The ideas of women's liberation came rushing toward me, arrived at the town through the writings of feminist and lesbian-feminist groups . . . and through individual women . . . who had worked in the civil rights movement . . . who had learned the principles of liberation in the homes and at the sides of Black women, young and old, who were the political organizers in their communities.

When I found myself in the market town, where the circle of my life was becoming more and more narrow: I felt like I was being brick-walled in: the ideas that I'd learned from . . . the other women became personal to me. I began to feel the restrictions around me as woman, through the pressure of neighbors and country-club social friends about how I should act as a wife. . . .

For being a woman was the constriction that I felt. There I was in a place so much like home: grown-up and I didn't want to be there: curfewed by night, watched by day, by some of the twenty-five thousand more men than women in the town. I felt surrounded. I wanted to go some place where I could just be; I was homesick with nowhere to go. (p. 24)

Realizations like Pratt's consciousness raising also often led to personal and public confrontations of long-held personal views on race, class, and social injustice.

The Second Wave and Psychology

As second wave feminism gained momentum in the 1960s, psychologists acknowledged the absence of women from the majority of psychological research: both as researchers and as subjects (Gilligan, 1982; Marecek and Kravetz, 1977; Rice and Rice, 1973; Tennov, 1973; Weisstein, 1968/1993). Psychologists began to question if results of studies conducted exclusively on men could be true for women. Later in this chapter, research related to this question will be addressed. The question of sex differences has now become a major focus of study within feminist psychology on both theoretical and applied levels.

The traditional study of psychology set norms and definitions of psychopathology with little or no regard to issues of gender. Freud's now-famous quotation, "biology is destiny" points directly to the deep roots of the primacy of science and empiricism upon which psychology is founded; it has traditionally been viewed as a hard science, one that relies on empirical information methods and quantitative measures for its data. Within the traditional paradigm, the self is an isolated, individualistic entity whose ultimate goal is separation from the mother through a process of individuation. The norms of human development have been based upon those subjects chosen for study by the primary theorists in the field: white, highly educated men who chose to study other white, highly educated men. At the time, the development of these norms seemed appropriate and unquestionable; male was equated with human. However, this focus on the individual tended to occlude the interrelatedness of sociocultural elements in human development. Feminist psychological theory has sought to clarify the multiplicity of developmental factors inherent in personality development as it questioned traditional norms. One conclusion is development must be viewed as an organic, kaleidoscopic process, grounded in each individual's experience (Maracek, 2002; Suyemoto, 2002).

Feminism Now

Today, feminism is a collection of movements with four major subcategories: **liberal feminism, radical feminism, socialist feminism,** and **cultural feminism.** Like political parties, each branch of feminism has a particular platform and mandate upon which the

Whenever a man encounters a woman in a mood he doesn't understand, he wants to know if she is tired. (George Jean Nathan)

members of the group operate. The boundaries between these groups are fluid, and many feminists hold beliefs from more than one group.

Liberal Feminism.

Liberal feminists seek reform within existing structures and inclusion of women in arenas where they have traditionally been excluded. The work of the liberal feminists generally focuses on legal and social change, most notably the effort to pass the Equal Rights Amendment in the 1970s. The amendment was passed by Congress in 1972, but had failed to be ratified by the requisite thirty-eight states in 1982, rendering the amendment essentially dead. Even with this defeat, however, liberal feminists continued to seek social reform and changes including "affirmative action, reproductive rights legislation, educational reforms, and equal opportunity legislation" (Enns, 1997, p. 44). The National Organization for Women (**www.now.org),** and the Feminist Majority Foundation (owner of *Ms.* magazine, **www.feminist.org**) are examples of feminist groups generally associated with the liberal feminist camp. Both of these groups actively seek reform, legislation, and empowerment for women through political and social campaigns.

Radical Feminism.

Radical feminists believe that the patriarchal structure of our society oppresses women and that a new vision for society based upon the dismantling of patriarchy is the only way to free women from this oppression. The theory behind the radical feminist stance was initially grounded in the writing of Simone de Beauvoir (1953), who believed that women were relegated to second-class status in relation to men. Groups agreeing with de Beauvoir's stance, including the Redstockings (1969) and the Feminists (1973), sought complete liberation for all women. "From a radical feminist perspective, women's oppression is the most fundamental and pervasive form of oppression. It is rooted in patriarchy, which is characterized by male dominance, competition, and heterosexism" (Enns, 1997, p. 61). Some of the most sacred cultural institutions including marriage and childbearing or care were excoriated as mechanisms of control and domination (Rich, 1980/1989; Firestone, 1970). However, the most prominent social and political work of radical feminism is related to violence against women and issues of sexuality—most notably the issues of rape and pornography and the effects these two elements have on women (Dworkin, 1981; MacKinnon, 1982/1993). Some of the anti-pornography rhetoric of radical feminists has been criticized for creating a polarized view of women's reality (Weitzer, 1999) that "ignore[s] the multilayered nature of human experience" (Barton, 2002, p. 586). Nonetheless, amid the criticism, radical feminists have been at the forefront of antiviolence legislation and were among the first to develop rape crisis centers and battered women's shelters (Echols, 1989).

Socialist Feminism.

Socialist feminists also believe that the firmly entrenched gender roles of society oppress women. However the fundamental structures of the oppression are found in the institutional structures of society including work, education, family structures, and sexuality as opposed to the radical feminist belief that the oppression is a direct result of male privilege within patriarchy. Socialist feminists believe, for example, that "capitalism promulgates oppressive economic practices by subordinating people on the basis of gender, race, and class. Capitalistic systems exploit the labor of many powerless persons for the benefit of a few powerful ones" (Biaggio, 2000, p. 8). Pioneers in the socialist feminist movement included Margaret Sanger, the founder of Planned Parenthood, and Emma Goldman, who denounced marriage as a system of "enslavement" of women (Enns, 1997). Early socialist feminists and their contemporary daughters fundamentally believe that economic and social institutions must be re-created in order to abolish power differentials between people in both private and public spheres, so that all of society—women and men—would benefit in a more egalitarian and supportive society (Enns, 1992).

Cultural Feminism.   *Cultural feminists* are generally less focused on political issues and seek rather to resurrect, reconsider, and re-vision the cultural meanings of female qualities and the concept of "the feminine." At the core of the cultural feminist movement is the belief that women hold special, unique qualities such as intuition, emotionality, and relationality for which they have traditionally been oppressed. "Cultural feminists . . . have tended to embrace the biological and psychological understandings of the differences between men and women. From their perspective, the social problem women encounter is not the differences per se, but rather the differential value placed on those differences" (Whalen, 1996, p. 23). Three major contributions of cultural feminism are

1. The celebration and honoring of motherhood
2. A resurgence of women's spirituality, including the resurrection of goddess traditions
3. Re-evaluations and reformation of traditional philosophies of knowledge including *logical positivism,* or the "scientific" approach, which values objectivity and empirical proof (Alpert 1973, Lips 1999; Starhawk 1979/1999).

Male and female are really two cultures and their life experiences are utterly different. (Kate Millett)

Cultural feminists have been criticized for being "essentialist," which means adhering to belief in "essential qualities in females and males, resulting from universal experiences in infancy and early childhood—namely, the early intense bond between mother and infant and the father's relative absence from these early relationships. These theories have been criticized for presuming universality and ignoring diversity in human experience" (DeLamater & Hyde 1998) (see also Bohan 1993; Lorber & Farrell, 1991).

Women are equal because they are not different any more. (Erich Fromm)

The issues of sex difference or gender difference and the large body of research arguing both for and against the belief of said differences has been explored widely (Bohan, 1993; Halpern, 2000; Maracek, 2001; Katz, Boggiano & Silvern, 1993). Some of this research cites biological or cognitive sources for such difference, while other research suggests that reducing the sex difference debate to strict biology is reductivist. "All the reasons people give for . . . differences are both right and wrong. . . . We cannot expect to find simple answers to what are very difficult questions" (Diane Halpern, as quoted in Kersting, 2003, p. 55).

Feminist Contributions to Personality Theory

Early Contributions.   During the early stages of second wave feminism, researchers and theorists were dedicated to uncovering the inequities, biases, and/or historical invisibility of women in the field of psychology. Scholars (Carlson, 1972; Chesler, 1972; Doherty, 1973; Gilligan, 1982) brought into question the universal validity of traditional theory in virtually every arena of psychology, most notably developmental and personality theory. Feminist theorists began to question the core assumptions of Western developmental models, including those of Erickson (1968)(see Chapter 6) and Levinson (1978), who both placed great primacy upon separation and individuation as hallmarks of a healthy person. In addition, feminist psychologists set out to specifically research women in an attempt to validate the assumption that androcentric (male-centered) models did not universally apply to all people. Work by Nancy Chodorow (1978) regarding the structure of the nuclear family unit and its effect upon individuals' perception of self pointed directly to the fact that men and women are products of their social, economic, and cultural environments and develop differently in response to these factors. This early research was among the first to suggest the possibility of two developmental models in operation: a separation/individuation model for boys and a relational/connection model for girls.

On the heels of publication of Chodorow's work, Carol Gilligan (1982) published an in-depth study examining differences in the moral development of girls. Her work has been viewed as a corrective to Kohlberg's (1981) study of moral development in which he studied all boys and created his model of a *morality of justice and fairness.* Gilligan's work produced and alternative model of *connected moral development,* or an "injunction to care" (Gilligan, 1982, p. 19) in which women are concerned with how their actions and decisions will affect others, thus influencing their decision-making process. In the two decades since the publication of Gilligan's findings, a debate about the soundness and applicability of her theories has ensued (Daniels, D'Andrea, & Heck, 1995; Gould, 1988; Karniol, Grosz, & Schorr, 2003; Keefer & Olson, 1995). While the debate continues regarding the replicability of Gilligan's original findings, the body of research that has unfolded from her initial investigation speaks to the value of her work regarding the development of personality and gender theories in the field of feminist psychology. Gilligan's work has especially influenced the cultural feminist camp, including the development of *Relational-Cultural Theory (RCT)* examined in detail below.

In addition to original theory building, feminist psychologists have also critiqued and revamped the processes through which theory is formed. In 1986 Hannah Lerman suggested six major factors critical in the creation of feminist personality theory:

1. The theory must place women as a central subject (as opposed to either being an "other" or interchangeable with a male subject) and women should be viewed in a fundamentally positive manner.
2. The theory should arise from women's experience—recognizing the diversity and multiplicity of views this method of theory building entails.
3. As theory is created, it should remain close to the data of experience underlying it. In other words, the theory should originate from information gained in research. Care should be taken not to overgeneralize theory in an attempt to make it "true" for all women, but should rather reflect actual lived experience for the subjects studied.
4. The theory must acknowledge that the internal and external worlds of subjects intermingle, and take into consideration the interplay between these two perspectives of reality.
5. Theory must be written in particularistic language. Generalizations, universal assumptions, and sexist, racist, or classist language should be avoided.
6. The theory should support feminist, or nonsexist, psychotherapy. It should be possible to put any theory created into practice with real clients in real therapeutic environments.

Lerman suggests that adherence to these six criteria is fundamental for feminist personality theory to truly represent the lived experience of women.

Contemporary Contributions.   A central question for feminist psychologists revolves around whether feminist personality theory can modify and reconstruct traditional theoretical frameworks such as psychoanalytical, Jungian, or object relations

Psychologists have set about describing the true nature of women with a certainty and a sense of their own infallibility rarely found in the secular world. . . . Psychology has nothing to say about what women really are like, what they need, and what they want, essentially because psychology does not know. (Naomi Weisstein, 1968)

theory, or if an entirely new framework must be created in order to achieve a more inclusive theory. Theorists, researchers, and practitioners operate on both sides of this debate within each branch of feminism (liberal, radical, socialist, and cultural). Excellent sources of information on feminists working within traditional theoretical frameworks can be found in Enns (1997), Brown & Ballou (1992), and Ballou & Brown (2002). The following is an exploration of those feminists who have chosen to eschew traditional theory in favor of the creation of something entirely new.

> . . . I believe that we can continue to borrow from mainstream developmental theories only at our peril. The feminist clinical psychologist and theoretician Rachel Hare-Mustin has aptly noted that feminist personality theorists continue to "stand on the bellies of dead white men" in building our theories (personal communication, July, 1993) . . . A feminist theory of personality requires starting afresh, departing from the patriarchal universe of knowledge, standing on our own feminist feet, and allowing our politically oriented way of knowing to represent good personality theorizing. (Brown, 1994, pp. 231–232)

Brown is dedicated to questioning, dismantling, and restructuring theory, practice, and even "the patriarchy inside ourselves" in an effort to create a "vision of the just society in which oppression and domination are no longer the norm" (Brown, 1994, pp. 233–234). Brown's passionate voice displays the intermingling of theory and politics that most often characterizes the radical feminist perspective. In relation to personality theory, Karen Suyemoto (2002) asks of traditional theorists: "Who gets to decide? Who determines what my . . . personality is or is not . . . what is or is not healthy or pathological in personality" (p. 74)? Grounded in *social constructionism* (a theory examined in detail in a later section, but in brief meaning that human experience is influenced, defined, and/or interpreted within and by sociocultural structures), Suyemoto (2002) suggests that personality is not fixed within a person. Instead, she adopts a theory of **identity** development that is fluid and changeable within each individual.

> Identity is the continual process of constructing and integrating the meanings considered and chosen within a constantly changing social, cultural, political, and historical context. Identity is always created in social context, and is therefore inherently affected by ingroup and outgroup meanings, references, comparisons, exclusions, and boundaries. . . .
>
> Theorizing identity rather than personality challenges the ideas of self-organization (personality or identity) as deterministic and individualistic, the imposition of outside judgments and constructions, and the myth that all individuals have the same options for personal development and organization structures. (pp. 92–93)

In addition to radical feminists, cultural feminists have actively participated in the creation of new personality theory. Dedicated to the revaluing of those traits most commonly associated as feminine, cultural feminists have sought to create personality theory that speaks directly to the experience of women. The originality of Relational-Cultural Theory has influenced a great deal of current feminist personality theory and psychotherapeutic practice.

Relational-Cultural Theory

Initially referred to as *relational theory,* Relational-Cultural Theory (RCT) "suggests that all growth occurs in connection, that all people yearn for connection, and that growth-fostering relationships are created through mutual empathy and mutual empowerment"

(Jordan & Hartling, 2002, p. 49). RCT was developed by members of the Stone Center group, an organization established in 1981 and housed at Wellesley College. The founding members of the group included Jean Baker Miller, whose 1976 book *Toward a New Psychology of Women* is considered a core text of feminist personality theory. The following is an explication of the theory written specifically for this text by members of the Stone Center.

A RELATIONAL APPROACH

Jean Baker Miller, Irene Pierce Stiver, Judith V. Jordan, and Janet L. Surrey

Major Concepts

A Relational Approach.   In a reframed psychology of women, Jean Baker Miller presented three central themes in the context of a relational approach—the cultural context, relationships, and pathways to growth.

The Cultural Context.   The first theme recognizes the significance of the **cultural context** in women's lives. In a patriarchal culture, where women have less power than men, women must often adapt to relationships that are unequal and essentially nonmutual. As a result, women often feel insufficiently empowered to have an impact on the important relationships in their lives or, by extension, on society. In such settings, the ways in which the less powerful group differs from and adapts to the dominant group are apt to be unnoticed or misunderstood. This dynamic perpetuates the disempowered status of the subordinate group.

Increasingly, we, as authors of this chapter, are trying to undo an acknowledged bias in our early theory work; while we sought to better understand women and represent women's special paths of development, we worked from within our largely white, middle-class, heterosexual, educated experience. Wary of the dangers of any subgroup speaking as if *its* reality is *the* reality, we tried to stay aware of our own blind spots. We could not claim to be speaking for "all women." Our appreciation of diversity needed to deepen and broaden. Several recent study groups of both lesbians and women of color have begun to do this crucial piece of work.

While all women suffer in a patriarchal society in which our reality is not represented in the dominant discourse, women in various cultural and ethnic groups suffer additional marginalization based on race, sexual orientation, socioeconomic standing, able-bodiedness, and age. Women who are marginalized also develop strengths that may differ from those of white, privileged, heterosexual women. Engaging with difference in relationship can be a source of enlargement and growth. However, when differences are organized hierarchically by dominant groups, with some characteristics viewed as "normal" or "desirable" and others as "deviant" or "undesirable," diversity can be a source of disempowerment and pain. As Alexandra Kaplan has written, those in a dominant position often "presume the right to determine which aspects of identities are core, and by which aspects others will be known. . . . People are known only in terms of where they fit in an arbitrary hierarchy of worth as defined by the dominant culture" (1991, p. 6).

The Stone Center relational model emphasizes the centrality of connection in women's lives. Disconnection is viewed as the source of most human suffering. In particular, we suggest that women develop through growth-fostering relationships. As a

Women have a profound stake, beyond the personal, of describing our reality as candidly and as fully as we can to each other. (Adrienne Rich)

personal reflection

THE CENTRALITY OF RELATIONSHIPS

To better understand the importance of relationships in your life, try this exercise.

1. Think of five to seven important relationships or relational contexts in your life (for example, parents, grandparents, siblings, friends, teachers, groups, classes, clubs, or teams).
2. Describe how each relationship has affected your development. How have you changed through each relationship, either positively or negatively? How have you contributed to each relationship?
3. How do you think these relationships will contribute to shaping your future? Specifically, how do you predict they will shape your sense of self, self-esteem, career development, relational capacities, and personal values?

result of our culture's handling of difference, through a system of hierarchy and dismissal, chronic and painful disconnections occur. Racism, sexism, heterosexism, classism, and ageism all become forces in creating disconnection rather than connection. Differences that could be sources of growth and expansion lead instead to defeat and withdrawal, fear, shame, and disconnection. Empathy across difference is one of the most compelling paths to personal and relational growth.

> While some mutual empathy involves an acknowledgment of sameness in the other, an appreciation of the differentness of the other's experience is also vital. The movement toward the other's differentness is actually central to growth in relationship and also can provide a powerful sense of validation for both people. Growth occurs because as I stretch to match or understand your experience, something new is acknowledged or grows in me. (Jordan, 1986, p. 89)

Humanity has been held to a limited and distorted view of itself—from its interpretation of the most intimate of personal emotions to its grandest vision of human possibilities—precisely by virtue of its subordination of women. (Miller, 1976)

Relationships.   The second theme stresses the importance of **relationships** as the central, organizing feature in women's development. Instead of engaging in the struggle toward independence and autonomy that characterizes most developmental models of growth and maturity, women more often search for participation and connection with others. Traditionally, these relationships have sought to foster the development of others—children, certainly, but also other adults. The relational perspective on human experience posits that

1. We grow in, through, and toward relationship;
2. For women, especially, connection with others is central to psychological well-being;
3. Movement toward relational mutuality optimally occurs throughout life, as a result of mutual empathy, responsiveness, and contribution to the growth of each individual and to the relationship. (Jordan, 1983; Miller, 1984, 1986; Stiver, 1984; Surrey, 1985)

The need for connection and emotional joining is a primary need; much of human suffering arises from disconnection and isolation. Miller has used the phrase *condemned isolation* (1986) to capture the sense of immobilization and self-blame that characterizes the pain of being disconnected from others. Jordan has described the feeling of being cut off from empathic possibility; that is, one cannot imagine that another person will be able to join one in empathic mutuality (1989). When people are unable to move from disconnection to connection, the resulting combination of immobilization and isolation may in fact become like a prison and contribute to psychological anguish.

Often it is accompanied by a sense of shame, a feeling that one is unworthy of connection at the same time that one experiences a deep yearning to connect. The desire to bring oneself fully into relationship just when one fears the impossibility of such a move creates tension, distortion of one's ability to represent feelings, and thoughts of inauthenticity and fragmentation (Jordan, 1989). Women's relational style and collaborative approach is drawing considerable attention in the workplace as well (Godfrey, 1992; Helgesen, 1990; Rosener, 1990).

Pathways to Growth.   Miller's third theme acknowledges women's relational qualities and activities as potential strengths that provide pathways to healthy growth and development. This theme stands in stark contrast to the prevailing view that interpreted many of women's most valuable qualities as defects or deficiencies. In traditional theory, women's ability to express emotions more freely and their greater attention to relationships often led to pathologizing women with labels like "hysterical" or "too dependent" (Chesler, 1972; Houck, 1972). A review of the criteria for diagnosis of "mental illness" in psychiatry's official *Diagnostic and Statistical Manual of Mental Disorders* demonstrates how biased against women these categories really are. Taking issue with this bias, Kaplan humorously suggests adding two new characterizations more applicable to male psychopathology, the *independent personality disorder* and the *restricted personality disorder* (1983).

More recently, we have begun to explore the ways in which traditional theories of development also misinterpret men's experience. Bergman (1991) observes that society pressures boys to move away from a more connected and empathic relational context into one of competition, power, and disconnection.

Gilligan notes that women's sense of self and morality revolves around issues of responsibility for, and care of, other people. It is embedded in a compelling appreciation of context. While women's orientation is toward relationships, men's tends toward separation. Gilligan also portrays the woman's dilemma of trying to find a way to include her perspectives and desires in her relationships.

Gilligan's work has expanded over the years to explore the importance of relationships for women at many ages (Brown & Gilligan, 1992; Gilligan, Lyons, & Hammer, 1990). In particular, her research highlights the crisis girls face at adolescence. She demonstrates how hard it is for girls to maintain a strong sense of self and inner "voice," when doing so means risking disconnection in a world that does not honor women's relational desires and needs.

A Paradigm Shift.   Reframing the central ideas in the psychology of women has broader implications for understanding women and women's place in our societal institutions—especially in the workplace and in the family. Women's experiences in work settings often reflect the tensions between their natural relational style and the focus on independence and hierarchy that dominates many work environments (Stiver, 1991c). In the family, although conflict often arises in the mother–daughter relationship, mothers and daughters nevertheless exhibit strong yearnings for connection. While this struggle was formulated in terms of Freud's female Oedipus complex, today the relational model offers another way of looking at this and other family relationships (Lewis & Herman, 1986; Stiver, 1991a).

Another misunderstood area in the psychology of women is the struggle for power. Miller (1982) observed the extent to which women feel that they are not supposed to have power. Yet, she notes, women exert enormous power in their role of fostering the

When you cease to make a contribution, you begin to die. (Eleanor Roosevelt)

personal reflection

EXPLORING PARENTAL RELATIONSHIPS

Try these exercises as a means of exploring parental relationships.

1. Describe to another person a recent interaction you had with your mother (or father). Now describe the interaction again, but this time imagine that your parent is in the room listening to you. Does your description change? How? What accounts for the differences?
2. With a partner or in a small group, role-play one of your parents. Tell the story of that parent's life from his or her perspective, noting in particular the major events and transitions. Reflect on your presentation. How did the events and transitions you described affect your feelings and your understanding of your mother or father?

growth of others. For women, empowering others is seen as enhancing the growth of others in addition to the self. This is a counterpoint to the notion that power means "power over," the controlling and directing of others (Jordan, 1991a). In other words, in a relational model, empowering another assists that person in developing a sense of confidence and self-worth, which will allow him or her to move into the world with increased vitality and a personal sense of creativity.

When individuals exercise "power over" others, they seek to ensure their position of dominance and control. Individuals are interested in attaining only their own self-defined goals, with little consideration or respect for the values and goals of others. Often this position is predicated on the use of force—social (silencing and shaming minority opinions), psychological (creating self-doubt or fear), or physical (threatening or actually using physical force).

By applying the relational approach to the psychology of women, every prior description of women benefits from reexamination. For example, the diagnosis of *dependent personality disorder,* and the more general use of the word **dependent** as pejorative and often pathological, are recast (Stiver, 1991b). Women's search for connection and the relative ease with which they express their vulnerabilities and needs are often mislabeled as dependent—and, thus, neurotic, regressed, and infantile. As the empowering value of relationships for women is recognized, dependency is seen as a positive movement along the path of healthy growth and development. This reframing removes a value-laden and blaming mode and is replaced by an empowering mode. The blaming mode originates in overvaluing independence and self-sufficiency and devaluing relationships, which are collaborative and mutually empowering.

Model of Self. This reexamination serves to reconceptualize notions of the self, not just in women but in all people. Traditional theories of development have emphasized the growth of an autonomous self with firm boundaries, separated from context and moving toward greater use of abstract logic and self-sufficiency. (For examples, see Chapter 1, Freud; Chapter 3, Adler; and Chapter 6, Erikson.) Miller (1976), Gilligan (1982), and Jordan et al. (1991) have posited a contextual, relational paradigm for the study of what has traditionally been called *self-experience.* Rather than focus on the "bounded" and contained self, these approaches emphasize the connected and relationally emergent nature of human experience. The movement of relating, of mutual initiative and responsiveness, is the ongoing, centrally organizing dynamic in women's lives. Because of this shift in paradigm, the self is no longer the primary target of interest and study. Instead, relational development is at the center of the examination (Jordan, 1989).

Mutual empathy and mutual empowerment are at the core of growth-enhancing relationships. **Empathy** involves a *motivational* component (the desire to know the other), a *perceptual* component (the ability to perceive verbal and nonverbal signals), an *affective* component (the capacity to resonate with another person's feelings), and a *cognitive* component (the ability to make sense of this joining resonance).

Empathy always involves a movement toward understanding; it is never a perfect matching, or "mirroring," of another person's experience. *Mutuality,* another characteristic of "good" connection, involves openness to change and growth in both people. Each person remains respectful of the other's experience (Jordan, 1986). The focus for our interest is not just the development of self but equally the movement of relationship,

The relational approach has been found helpful in understanding broader cultural contexts. The reframing of the concept of dependency has suggested a different explanation of certain characteristics of the Japanese culture (Kobayashi, 1989). Turner (1987) explored the ways in which the relational approach reflects and validates African American women's experience. It also illuminates some of the specifics of lesbian development. For instance, the relational model offers a new perspective on the concept of *fusion* when applied to lesbian women as well as other issues in lesbians' lives. In lesbian relationships fusion has been pathologized and viewed pejoratively, in models of human development that emphasize the separation of the individual; however, the intense intimacy, sense of equality, value placed on communication, and emotional support by both partners—which have been seen as indications of fusion—seem to contribute to high levels of satisfaction in such relationships (Mencher, 1990). Mencher suggests that these indications of fusion point to intense relational engagement, a sign of health, not pathology.

Dynamics

Key Features in Psychological Growth and Development: Connections and Empathy. The experience of connection, the capacity for empathy, and consequences of disconnection are the central issues in this way of reviewing personality development.

Connection. **Connection** is the experience of relating to others so that both the individual and the others believe that the interaction was beneficial. Healthy development depends on the growth and extension of this inherent human capacity.

Empathy. Connection arises naturally from **empathy.** Jordan, Kaplan, and Surrey (1982) describe empathy as a complex cognitive-affective ability rather than as the mysterious, intuitive, and even regressive experience that others have suggested. Jordan later developed its implications for psychological maturation, along with an extension of the concept of mutuality (1986).

Mutual empathy experientially alters the sense of a separate self. In true empathic interaction, each person is engaged in affecting and being affected, knowing and being known, assisting the other in coming more fully into clarity and relatedness. Surrey (1991b) suggested that the underlying processes of psychological development are mutual engagement, mutual empathy, and mutual empowerment. The goal of psychological development is participation in mutually empathic and mutually empowering relationships rather than separation from others. The following vignette of two women interacting illustrates how mutual empathy also develops mutual empowerment.

A major reaction began to take place when Heinz Kohut came out, like Luther, with postulates of a psychoanalytic "reformation," one whose centerpiece was empathy. . . . (Grotstein, 1999, p. 123)

> Ann has just heard from her friend Emily that Emily may have a serious illness. Ann is telling another friend, Beth, about this. Tears are in Ann's eyes and her voice sounds sad and fearful. Beth says, "Oh, how sad." Ann then adds, "Yes, sad, but I have this other awful feeling—like fear. Like I'm scared—as if it could happen to me." Beth replies, "Me, too. It is frightening to hear this. Maybe we all feel as if it's happening to us when we hear things like this."

As they continue, both Ann and Beth feel more in touch with what they suspect Emily may be feeling. In so doing, they come to a fuller appreciation of Emily's feelings.

This example may sound ordinary, as if it describes an experience that people frequently have. Such communication *does* take place often, especially among women, but it is not ordinary in terms of its value. Furthermore, the valuable actions Ann and Beth demonstrate are often unrecognized. We believe that these interactions contain the key features that make for psychological growth and development in children and adults.

Psychological Growth. The process of psychological growth requires the participants to respond empathically to each other. Because each feels this empathic response, each can "take off" from this empathic base and add thoughts and feelings as they arise. These additions create the interplay, the flow. This mutually empathic interplay is created by both people and builds new psychological experience—that is, growth for both.

The result of this process is that both people develop psychologically in at least five important ways (Miller, 1986):

1. Both feel a connection with the other that gives them a sense of increased zest, or energy. This is familiar to those who know the feeling of a sense of connection to another person. Its opposite is also familiar, the *down* sort of feeling that follows when one has been unable to connect with another person.
2. Both are active in the immediate relationship, and they feel more empowered to act beyond the relationship.
3. Each person has a bit more self-knowledge as well as knowledge of the other person; more is learned about feelings and thoughts and how they are for each person.
4. Because these processes have occurred, both people feel a greater sense of self-worth.
5. As a result, both desire more connections in the future.

It is important to note that in mutual interactions it is not a question of giving or getting, of helping or being helped, or of being dependent or depended upon. It is a question of whether both people participate, whether both people grow, and whether both therefore want more of the same.

Disconnections. Because women rely so heavily on relationships in the process of psychological growth, **disconnections** can lead to serious consequences in their lives. Disconnections occur whenever a child or adult is prevented from participating in a mutually responsive and mutually enhancing relationship. Clearly, disconnections exist when a child or an adult suffers mistreatment, such as sexual or physical abuse, or when the individuals who play an important role in the child's or adult's life are grossly unresponsive. However, many disconnections occur throughout childhood and adult life. Most do not lead to serious trouble, especially if there are sufficient empowering connections. The key ingredients that allow for growth from a threat of disconnection are the possibilities (1) that the child or adult can take action within the relationship to represent her experience, and (2) that the others in the relationship can respond in a way that leads back toward a reconnection (Miller, 1988).

To take a familiar example, suppose a 9-month-old infant is playing and suddenly, for no apparent reason, starts to scream and cry. The parents don't deal with this behavior well initially and respond with angry rebukes. The infant may now feel startled and afraid, in addition to the original distress. However, if the infant can reach out again to the parents and, in this second effort, find that they are more responsive to the expression of distress, the infant will feel more effective in communicating with them. Indeed, the infant has played a part in turning the interaction around, and so have the parents. Several researchers into infant behavior have documented this ability in infants as young as 3 months (Gianino & Tronick, 1985; Stern, 1985).

A more serious disconnection can be seen in a variation on the previous vignette involving Emily, Ann, and Beth. Substitute Tom, Ann's husband, for her friend Beth. Tom's response to Ann's tearful sadness and fearful voice is, "Well, it's a terrible thing. In the end, she'll have to do the best she can. She should get a second opinion. Have you called her back yet? Did you call my sister Helen about the birthday party she's arranging for my mother for next week?"

One incident like this, of course, does not lead to psychopathology, but this kind of disconnection can produce serious immediate and long-term consequences if it continues, over time, without a change in direction. Using this example, assume for a moment that the topic did arouse sadness and fear in Tom. The difference, then, between Tom's and Ann's reactions is that Tom has not learned how to experience these feelings in connection with others. In fact, he becomes angry if anyone threatens to evoke these feelings in him. Ann may sense some of Tom's feelings, but, in contrast to her interaction with Beth, the feelings and thoughts cannot be *between them* or *with both of them*. Instead, she begins to feel as if the emotions are all hers.

In addition, Ann now feels angry. First, she picks up Tom's fear, but then she also becomes angry at his response. The anger becomes tied to and confused with her other feelings. Ann is now in greater distress. Precisely because she feels in more distress, she wants even more to connect with the other person. Suppose, again for the sake of example, that she tries to express some of this to Tom. In response, he becomes more angry and attacking or withdrawn. Now Ann's confused feelings and their intensity only increase.

Here, Ann has failed to influence or alter the course of the interaction, and the person in her relational context has been unresponsive to her attempts to represent her experience. She believed that her feeling-thoughts helped to create a better connection that would, in turn, lead to more empowerment. Instead, she begins to believe that something is deeply wrong with her important feelings, because they lead to such trouble. Ann feels the problem is in her.

In contrast to the good things that flow from mutually empowering connections, Ann, in this instance, will feel less energetic (more depleted), less self-worth, less clear about her feeling-thoughts, less able to take action, and less motivated to seek other connections. Most important, she feels that her actions, feelings, and thoughts lead to less connection with the most significant person in her life; she feels not only less connection but a confusing sense of disconnection and isolation.

Clinical experience suggests that perhaps one of the most terrifying human experiences is psychological isolation. This is not isolation just in the sense of loneliness. It is the feeling of being locked out of the possibility of human connection. This feeling of desperate isolation is usually accompanied by the feeling that the individuals, themselves,

I understand the rising up of women in this century to be the human race's response to the threat of its own self-annihilation and the destruction of the planet. (Sally Miller Gearheardt)

are the reason for the exclusion. It is because of who they are. They feel helpless, powerless, unable to better the situation. People will go through amazing psychological maneuvers to escape this combination of condemned isolation and powerlessness.

Psychological Consequences of Repeated Disconnections.   In the face of the terror of condemned isolation and powerlessness, people in Ann's position try even harder to make connections with the other individuals in their lives. This effort leads to the next set of consequences, consequences that often proceed over many years.

If a woman cannot find ways to affect available relationships, she will take the only other possible step. She will attempt to change the only person possible to change, herself. Specifically, she tries to alter her internal image of herself and others, as well as her view of the connections between herself and others. She must attempt this alteration alone, since the available relationships preclude doing it in interaction with others.

In essence, the child or adult tries to construct an image of herself and others that will allow her to enter into relationships with the people available. In order to twist herself into a person acceptable in "unaccepting" relationships, she has to move away from and redefine a large part of her experience—those parts that she believes are not allowed. (See Horney, Chapter 4, to better understand interpersonal strategies of defense.)

We can think of this process occurring in a child within a family. It takes place with varying degrees of complexity, depending on the child's age. In consistently nonresponsive settings that violate the child's experience, the child learns that the only way to connect to the significant figures in her life is to become what she thinks others want her to be. For example, she may learn that only a bad person has feelings such as sadness, fear, and the like. Therefore, she tries to become a person who never allows herself to feel such feelings. When events occur that would likely cause any of the unacceptable emotions, she becomes greatly upset; she cannot be certain what she is experiencing, except that she should not be feeling whatever it is she is feeling.

Along with confusion about many feelings, certain emotions become prominent over time. One is anxiety. A child growing up in anxiety-provoking settings becomes increasingly anxious about other people. Any person is likely to evoke "forbidden" thoughts and feelings that threaten narrowly constructed images of herself and others. One feeling that threatens these images is anger. No one can withstand violations of her experience and long-term threats to connection without eventually feeling intense anger.

Most important, this process leads to a major contradiction, the **paradox of connection-disconnection.** In order to connect in the only relationships available, the child keeps more and more of her authentic self out of her relationships. She maintains relationships at the cost of failing to represent her own experience in them. In this process, she is moving further and further away from connection with her own experience—and she is losing the main source of psychological growth: interactions within relationships. The parts of herself that she has excluded cannot change from experience. That is, her construction of a sense of herself and of others cannot benefit from the interchange provided by relationships—precisely the source of knowledge and clarity needed for the development of an accurate image of self and of others. She is constructing images of relational possibilities—and impossibilities—with less and less learning from events within relationships. It is striking to note that in studying girls moving into adolescence, Gilligan (Brown & Gilligan, 1992) described a similar paradox.

This process of repeated disconnections sometimes (though not always) leads to anxious, depressive immobilization and complete disconnection (Hamilton & Jensvold,

personal reflection

EXPERIENCE OF CONNECTION AND DISCONNECTION

Think about a time in your life when you felt a sense of connection in an important relationship. Also think about a time when you felt a sense of disconnection in a relationship. In each kind of relationship:

1. What led up to your feelings?
2. What were your feelings?
3. What was the outcome?
4. How did your feelings change you or the relationship?

1992). This immobilizing path probably exists for almost all women in patriarchal societies to some degree. It underlies many of women's psychological troubles, including phobias, addictions, eating disorders, depression, dissociative states, and paranoid ideas, as well as many of the problems labeled as personality disorders (Brown, 1992). In each of these situations, the woman elaborates specific images of herself and others, and specific forms of behavior, that come to seem the only ones possible in the framework of the relationships she is in.

Implications for Personality Development.   We have found that framing psychological development and problems in terms of this central paradox helps us to understand both sexes better, and also helps us to explain how psychological troubles arise. Most important, it helps us to find clarifying and empowering ways to work. That is, *psychological problems represent the mechanisms people construct that keep them out of connection while they simultaneously seek connection.*

Stiver (1990a, 1990b) has shown how this paradox develops in families labeled *dysfunctional* (for example, alcoholic, incestuous, and Holocaust-survivor families). Several theorists have elucidated other problems with this paradox in mind. Surrey (1991a), Steiner-Adair (1991), and Mirkin (1990) have reported on adolescents' development of eating disorders and have illustrated how this connection-disconnection construct unfolds in individual and family therapy. In the same way, Jack (1991), Kaplan (1984), and Stiver and Miller (1988) have described a relational understanding in the treatment of depression. Saunders and Arnold (1990) have recast the major characteristics and treatment of women who are diagnosed with borderline personality disorders. They have depicted ways of working that differ from the pejorative and destructive treatment methods formerly applied.

Kilbourne and Surrey (1991) and Gleason (1992) have discussed the origins of, prevention of, and recovery from addictions using this more relational approach. Kaplan and Klein (1990) have examined women's suicides and suicide attempts as they differ from men's and have suggested explanations for these findings in the contrasting relational experiences of women and men.

Beyond specific clinical formulations, a relational model alters our perception of numerous overarching concepts, such as conflict, anger, and shame. Conflict and anger are seen as necessary features occurring in the movement of all relationships (Jordan, 1990; Miller & Surrey, 1989). Jordan (1989) describes shame as the feeling of being excluded from connection and the sense of loss of empathic possibility. For all of these authors, a relational approach leads to a reframing of central concepts in women's therapy (Miller & Stiver, 1991).

See our **web** site for a discussion of relational therapy and a case study.

personal reflection

A RELATIONAL INVENTORY

Take a relational inventory by making a special appointment with a friend or lover to discuss the qualities of your relationship.

Thinking of particular examples in your relationship, discuss the following relational concepts described in this chapter: empathy, authenticity, mutual empathy, mutual empowerment, connection, disconnection, reconnection, anger, conflict, isolation.

Evaluation

Without a rigorous and consistent evaluation of what kind of a future we wish to create, and a scrupulous examination of the expressions of power we choose to incorporate into all our relationships, including our most private ones, we are not progressing, but merely recasting our own characters in the same old weary drama. (Audre Lourde)

The emphasis on connection and disconnection in a relational approach speaks to the core of the human condition, a core that has remained out of focus in traditional psychodynamic approaches. Traditional theories have spoken about relationships. However, the core of these theories remains obscure because they emerge from an underlying preoccupation with individual gratification and power, disguised by terms such as *separation* and *individuation*. Such a preoccupation distorts the total human condition. Once we examine more accurately the lives of all people, we find ourselves moving toward a recognition of the need for human connection and of the sources and consequences of disconnection.

We suggest instead that human behavior is not about *self-development,* but about *relational development,* a constant movement of energy and meaning between people, a deeply contextual experience of personhood. In this perspective, the enhancement of relatedness may constitute a greater goal than individual gratification and, ironically, may lead to greater individual fulfillment (Jordan, 1987). Stated more strongly, perhaps the most basic human need is *the need to participate in relationship.*

Issues of Diversity

Feminism must be on the cutting edge of real social change if it is to survive as a movement in any particular country. (Audre Lourde)

A basic understanding of the variety of perspectives held under the umbrella term *feminism* is useful in conceptualizing the multiplicities of viewpoints, theories, and practices embraced by feminists. A critique has arisen, within feminist camps, however, because much of the early theory and research was conducted by and generally only included white, middle-class women (Yoder and Kahn, 1993). Scholars such as Patricia Hill Collins (1990), bell hooks (1981, 1989), and Johnnetta B. Cole (1986) have underscored the exclusion of women of color from the creation of core feminist theory and research. Cole (1986) grounds this phenomenon in a "chauvinism among white women" that "takes the form of attitudes and behaviors which ignore or dismiss as insignificant differences in class, race, age, sexuality, ethnicity, and physical ability" (p. xiii). Peggy McIntosh (1989) writes about *white chauvinism,* which she calls the "weightless knapsack" of white **privilege** that is the "invisible package of unearned assets which I can count on cashing in each day, but about which I was 'meant' to remain oblivious" (p. 10). McIntosh admits the difficulty with which, she, as a white woman, recognized her own privilege and how this process of consciousness raising stripped away the "myth of meritocracy":

> For me white privilege has turned out to be an elusive and fugitive subject. The pressure to avoid is great. . . . If these things [white privilege] are true, this is not such a free country; one's life is not what one makes it; many doors open for certain people through no virtues of their own. (pp. 359–360)

This privilege, according to Espin and Gawelek (1992):

> . . . leads white women to make the assumption that their experiences are universal, normative, and representative of others' experiences, although well-motivated, white, middle-class feminist scholars have fallen into the trap of presenting the experiences of "mainstream" women as the yardsticks of women's experiences. Therefore the impacts of racial, cultural, and class-based factors are ignored, not only for women of color, but also for white women. (p. 91)

Collins (1990) has brought forth a critique of existing feminist psychological theory about mother–daughter relationships to explicate the ways in which research done solely within one ethnic or racial group skews the outcome in much the same way that feminists earlier illustrated the problems inherent with all-male test subjects. As Enns (1997) points out in her extensive assessment of issues of diversity in relation to psychology and personality theory:

> Too frequently, the attitudes and behaviors of women of color have been interpreted on the basis of their similarity and divergence from white women's values and attitudes. Furthermore, dichotomous comparisons between women of color and white women may provide a foundation for forming new stereotypes and can erase information about differences within specific groups of women. In other words, feminist psychologists have sometimes inadvertently practiced the very ethnocentrism that they have accused male psychologists of enacting. (pp. 251–252)

The motto should not be: forgive one another; rather: understand one another. (Emma Goldman)

Over the past three decades, feminist psychological theory has begun to move beyond a consideration of gender in "a vacuum," recognizing that intersections and interplay of gender, race, class, physical ability, sexual orientation, and other sociocultural factors create matrices through which people experience their lives. Espin and Gawelek (1992) propose four factors that must be present in order to create diverse, flexible, and inclusive personality theory:

1. All women's experiences must be heard, understood and valued.
2. Attention to the contextual influences is essential. [Social, class, ethnic, or other variables which influence one's status must be taken into consideration]
3. The psychology of women must be pluralistic.
4. Egalitarian relationships must be at the base of the development of the theory. (p. 103)

The principles above point to a recognition in feminist theory that in order to be a truly inclusive movement, theory and research must take all perspectives and possibilities into consideration. While there is certainly greater challenge in an attempt to hold multiple viewpoints at once, the promise of even richer theory has proven this endeavor worthwhile to many scholars and researchers in the field (Ballou, Matsumoto, & Wagner, 2002; Brown, 1994; Espin & Gawelek, 1992; hooks, 1989).

Feminist Contributions to Epistemology and Methodology

In addition to radically changing the face of personality theory, feminist psychologists have also explored and critiqued the ways in which knowledge is collected, interpreted, and transmitted within psychology. Issues of **epistemology,** or the study of the nature of knowledge, and **methodology,** or the methods or rules employed by a discipline, are powerful tools often controlled by those in dominant positions (Brown & Ballou,

We ought to distrust anyone who cautions us to "let the facts speak for themselves." If you find a speaking fact, look right away for the ventriloquist. (Laura Sabatini and Faye Crosby)

1992). Much has been written about "scientism" (Beutler & Moleiro, 2001) or *logical positivism,* a methodology that posits that reality is independent of the one who knows and that this it is part of a wider, objective reality. But, as Ballou and Brown (2002) point out, "epistemologies deriving from . . . psychologies such as postmodern, multicultural, and ecological are more commonly utilized and more broadly understood" (p. xiii) among feminist psychologists as more inclusive and flexible, and thus better able to hold the manifold criteria studied in models such as Relational-Cultural Theory.

Social Constructionism

A widely accepted epistemological framework is **social constructionism.** Inquiry grounded in social constructionism takes into consideration ways of knowing other than empirical or objectively gathered data including intuition, hermeneutics (a process of interpretation), and phenomenology (Anderson, 2000; Ballou, 1992). It does not seek to do away with empirical methods of data gathering (Bohan, 1993). Rather social constructionism's main value is that it reminds theorists to remain "skeptical of received truths and taken-for-granted frames of reference . . . knowledge is never innocent, but always value-laden and predicated on specific sociopolitical conditions that it serves to legitimize" (Maracek, 2002, p. 6).

New methodologies embracing alternative epistemologies are springing up throughout feminist psychology. *Intuitive inquiry* is a process through which objective and subjective data is analyzed through successive cycles of data collection and reflection (Anderson, 2000). *Organic inquiry,* a methodology grounded in feminist and transpersonal theory, is another methodology that seeks to understand and legitimize ways of knowing traditionally dismissed in mainstream psychological research. The following section is a description of organic inquiry, written for this text by one of its founding theorists, Jennifer Clements.

ORGANIC INQUIRY: A TRANSPERSONAL/FEMINIST RESEARCH METHODOLOGY

Jennifer Clements

Concepts like *connection, women's ways of knowing,* and *diversity* have played a role in the development of an emerging research methodology called **organic inquiry.** In the early 1990s, four doctoral students and I realized we needed a better way to do our research. Dorothy Ettling (1994), Dianne Jenett (1999), Lisa Shields (1995), Nora Taylor (1996), and I met weekly and were inspired to look for a methodology where women's experience could reinforce the positive values of connection and dependency. We wanted a methodology where diversity would make us equals rather than separating us into leaders and followers, a methodology that included intuition and feeling as legitimate ways of gathering and evaluating experience (Behar, 1996; Belenky, et al., 1986; Brown & Gilligan, 1992; Gilligan, 1982; Miller, 1986; Nielsen, 1990; Reinharz, 1992; Shepherd, 1993). Out of this process organic inquiry was born (Clements, 2000; in Clements, Ettling, Jenett & Shields, 1998).

Intellectual Antecedents

The development of this methodology grew out of the introduction of feminine values into research by researchers such as Carol Gilligan (1982, in Brown & Gilligan, 1992) and Shulamit Reinharz (1992), the self-as-instrument focus of the heuristic research of Clark Moustakis (1990), the rites of passage model of Arnold van Gennep (1909) and Victor Turner (1987), the concept of the transcendent function of Carl Jung (1957), the model of transpersonal development by Michael Washburn (1995), the mystical teachings of Emanuel Swedenborg and Wilson Van Dusen (1996), the experiential and transformative orientation of the curriculum at the Institute of Transpersonal Psychology, and, in particular, the students whose work has shown the value of this way of working.

A Fundamental Metaphor

The methodology is sacred, personal, chthonic, related, and transformative. These characteristics may be understood by envisioning the growth of a tree.

An organic inquiry is *sacred*. Just as a gardener prepares to plant by clearing the ground of old roots and stones, the organic researcher prepares to study a chosen topic by rooting out habits and expectations that might interfere with an ongoing attitude of reverence, respect, and responsibility for the work. The researcher's *personal* experience of the topic is the seed for the study and will become the catalyst for the analysis. An organic inquiry is *chthonic* (from the Greek *chthon* meaning "earth") because, like the roots of a tree, much of the work is done underground in the greater realm of the unconscious. Work with participants is *related* as their stories form intertwining branches joining the trunk story of the researcher. Finally, organic inquiry is *transformative*, becoming fruitful in the life of the participants, the researcher, and hopefully those who read the results.

The following story is an example of what we mean by *transformative change*. One busy day, I needed to finish reading a story from a student's dissertation, so I took it with me to lunch in a nearby restaurant. As I read, I went from feeling burdened to unexpected pleasure, and then to feeling enraptured because it reminded me of my own childhood experience. However, the story I was reading had an outcome I hadn't even dreamed was possible. I realized I was sitting in the front window of the restaurant sobbing happy tears. I was being changed by this story, not merely intellectually, but on an *affective* level. This is the change that organic inquiry aims for: inner transformation.

The Process

In order to intentionally invite this to happen, the researcher repeatedly follows a three-step process: traveling to the deep unconscious, gathering experience, and returning to intellectually blend it into the ongoing research process. The psyche of the researcher becomes the willing setting for a working partnership between the researcher's intellect and his or her experiences of inner wisdom. This process reoccurs at all stages of the study, from choosing the topic and developing the method to collecting and analyzing the data. This threefold process involves a merging of affective personal and spiritual experience with cognitive assessment. When effective, it can result in discernible shifts in the researcher's psyche that, in turn, reframes and redirects the research.

To return to the previous example—first, I released feeling burdened and willingly began to read; second, the story carried me into my own unconscious; and third, when I realized I was crying, I found new meaning in that psychological corner of my life. I now see my childhood experience in a new way and have released an old and limiting view of myself. The presentation of an organic study offers not only an intellectual analysis, but also includes the researcher's own transformative experience and the subsequent changes in story form. This invites the reader to repeat a similar process in the context of the reader's own previous encounters with the issue. Organic studies are undertaken by and for individuals who have made a commitment to personal and spiritual growth. In organic inquiry, change occurs when affective unconscious experience integrates with the intellect, first in the researcher and later in the reader, should he or she choose to participate on this level.

Following the classic models of initiation (Turner, 1987; van Gennep, 1909), the organic model of transformative change includes three steps: preparation, inspiration, and integration.

In the first step, **preparation,** the researcher pauses on the threshold of the journey and completes several tasks. He or she clarifies an intent, persuades the conscious mind to take a position of curious ignorance, acknowledges her or his role as the setting and screen of the research, and intentionally steps over the threshold. The second step is **inspiration,** a dive to the inner richness of the unconscious. The exact experience is unpredictable, but it often includes an affective or emotional reaction. The actual response will depend on the personality of the researcher, previous life experience, and the situation itself. Finally, the psyche returns with the fruits of the spiritual encounter and delivers them to the intellect for **integration.** This depends, like Carl Jung's description of the transcendent function (1957), on the intentional marriage of the intellect with the material brought back from beyond the threshold of normal awareness. The result of this integration is not only an intellectual synthesis, but a wholly new formulation that leads to change to the self, opening it inward toward psychospiritual self-knowledge and outward toward increased connection with humanity and the desire to be of service.

The Methodology in Action

The hands-on completion of an organic study involves blending the individual practice of preparation, inspiration, and integration into the cooperative arena of connection, dependency, diversity, empathy, and equality.

The researcher chooses a topic that has been personally transformative with an eye to offering a similar impact to others. This echoes the action orientation of most feminist research. For example, Shirley Loffer (1999) chose to study the experience of women who, like her, had rheumatoid arthritis and could say their lives were better than before they were ill. Caryl Gopfert (1999) studied those who shared her experience of feeling betrayal in their encounters with Zen teachers.

The first step involves the researcher's writing of her or his personal story related to the topic. The story grows and changes over the course of collecting, analyzing, interpreting, and presenting the data. Reports of this change offer a window into the researcher's transformative change. The researcher serves as the instrument of the study, walking a fine line between solipsism and generosity, repeatedly asking the question, "Is this story self-indulgent or is it serving the needs of my intended audience?"

The researcher may gather data in individual interviews or in a group format. Gathering stories in a group allows each story to affect the others. This cumulative effect encourages participants to come to a greater level of intimacy as they spend time together. Follow-up interviews help the researcher seed a question and let it gestate before it is answered. Data may be verbal, pictorial, visceral, or imaginal, or it may take other forms.

The initial analysis includes editing and interpreting the participants' individual stories. These stories are intended to allow the reader an immediate experience of the participants' encounter with the topic. Nonrational modes of evaluation may be used to find meaning in these stories. For example, Caryl Gopfert (1999) used an ikebana flower arrangement and Dea Cioflica (2000) used collages to inform themselves more fully about each participant's story.

The second level of analysis is telling the group story, how the individual stories relate to each other. The three-step process of visiting the inner realm and bringing back meaning is essential in this step as the overlap between the stories begins to suggest insights about the topic. Robin Seeley (2000) took her stories to the desert, where she fasted in order to open to a deeper level of reflection. Sophie Giles (2000) used dreams as an analytical tool.

The third level is the description of transformative change. Participants and the primary researcher report what inner and outer change they have experienced from the study. For example, many of those who have done organic inquiry find that by the end of their research, they have radically changed their ideas about their chosen careers.

The final task of organic inquiry is presentation of the study, which may include still or moving visual images as well as the more usual modes of presentation. Transformative change can only happen if the study allows the individual reader to personally identify with the participants' and the researcher's stories of personal, spiritual, and social change.

CHAPTER HIGHLIGHTS

FEMINIST PSYCHOLOGY: HISTORY AND CONTRIBUTIONS

- Feminist psychology recognizes that sociocultural factors such as gender, race, class, as well as personal values influence a person's lived experience.
- Individuals must be understood in the context of living in constant relationship to her/his outer world: individuals are interdependent, affiliative beings, and these relationships affect one's conception of the "self."
- The feminist movement consists of four interlocking schools of thought: liberal, radical, socialist, and cultural. The boundaries between each branch of feminism are fluid and many feminists hold beliefs from more than one group.
- Feminist psychological theory seeks to clarify the myriad factors inherent to personality development. One conclusion is that development is an organic process, grounded in each individual's experience and may not adhere to traditionally set universal norms.
- A major ongoing topic of research within feminist psychology revolves around the concept of sex and/or gender difference. Arguments both for and against inherent difference continue to unfold in this field.
- Early second wave feminist psychology was dedicated to uncovering the inequities, biases, and/or historical invisibility of women in the field—both as practitioners and as subjects of research.
- Hannah Lerman suggested six pillars inherent to feminist personality theory including the necessity of women as central subject of research and the importance of validating one's lived experience through particularistic language.
- Many feminists today are creating new models of personality and identity theory that break from traditional universal models. Suyemoto suggests that identity is fluid and changeable within each individual and is directly influenced by one's environment.

- Nancy Chodorow was one of the first researchers to suggest two models of personality development might be in operation: an individuation/separation model for boys and a relational/connection model for girls.
- Carol Gilligan's pioneering work investigating the intellectual and interpersonal thought processes of girls inspired the development of Relational-Cultural Theory (RCT).

RELATIONAL-CULTURAL THEORY

- The relational approach presented by Jean Baker Miller has three related themes: the impact of the cultural context on the lives of women, the importance of relationships for women, and the legitimate strength of women's activities and relational qualities.
- Women grow in, through, and toward relationship.
- Women, especially, find connection with others central to psychological well-being.
- Traditional theories of development have also done disservice to men's experience, as boys are pressured to move toward competition, disconnection, and power, away from a more empathic and connected relational context.
- A relational model of the psychology of women affirms the powers of connection and the terrors of disconnection for women at all ages. This has implications for understanding women's role in the workplace and in the family.
- Dependency is seen as a positive movement along the path of healthy development and growth. This reframing, in turn, allows movement into an empowering mode, out of a blaming mode, which originates in overvaluing self-sufficiency and independence.
- The centrally organizing dynamic in women's lives is the ongoing movement of relating, of mutual responsiveness and initiative.
- A person's sense of zest, clarity, capacity for action, and worth increases in a growth-fostering relationship. In such a relationship each person feels more connected to the other person and experiences a greater motivation for connections with other people beyond those in the specific relationship.
- The central issues in personality development are the experiences of connection and disconnection. Basic to this new understanding of the importance of the human connection is the concept of empathy.
- Rather than separation from others, participation in mutually empowering and empathic relationships is considered the goal of psychological development.
- Being prevented from participating in such relationships as a child or as an adult can produce disconnections.
- The paradox of connection-disconnection, on one level or another, is reflected in, and underlies, all the problems that emerge in therapy.
- Psychological problems represent mechanisms people construct that keep them out of connection while they simultaneously seek connection.
- Concepts such as anger, shame, and conflict have a different framing in a relational model. Anger and conflict are seen as a necessary part of movement in relationship. Shame is described as the sense of loss of empathic possibility and the feeling of being excluded from connection.
- Children from what are typically characterized as dysfunctional families develop a range of strategies to make connections, including role-playing, replication, and emotional disengagement, while holding important parts of themselves out of connection.
- Therapy requires a setting of safety and mutuality. This situation comes about through the therapist's empathic, authentic, and engaged participation in the relationship, rather than the neutral stance advocated by classical Freudians, among others.
- Relational being rather than a separate self is at the core of experience.

ISSUES OF DIVERSITY

- Feminism has been criticized in the past for a lack of ethnic and economic diversity within the movement.

- Patricia Hill Collins, bell hooks, and Johnetta B. Cole have been at the forefront of the diversity movement pointing out where feminist theory has fallen into outmoded traps of creating universal models based upon the experience of one group: white, highly educated women.
- Discussions about diversity continue to broaden the field of psychology and underscore the importance of creating theory that is, according to Espin and Gawelek, diverse, flexible, and inclusive of all people.

FEMINIST CONTRIBUTIONS TO EPISTEMOLOGY AND METHODOLOGY

- Feminist psychologists explore and critique the ways in which knowledge is collected, interpreted, and transmitted.
- Models such as social constructionism suggest that in addition to empirical and/or objective data, psychologists must take into consideration other ways of gathering data such as hermeneutics, phenomenology, and organic inquiry.

ORGANIC INQUIRY

- Organic inquiry developed from a desire to include feminist values such as connection, diversity, and women's ways of knowing in psychological research.
- The five characteristics of the methodology—sacred, personal, chthonic, related, and transformative—may be compared to the metaphor of a growing tree.
- Organic inquiry seeks to engage the individual reader intellectually and on the deeper level of transformative change, defined as movement toward personal, spiritual, and social transformation.
- Transformative change takes place through a three-step process of inviting unconscious influence, including preparation, inspiration, and integration.
- An organic researcher begins by writing her or his own story. Reports of how the research process has changed the researcher's story is a critical part of the research project.
- Analysis of the data includes interpreting the individual stories, the group story, and the transformative change.
- The presentation of the research is aimed at inviting the individual reader into a direct experience of the study so that the reader may be similarly changed.

KEY CONCEPTS

FEMINIST PSYCHOLOGY

Liberal feminism Seeks reform within existing institutional structures and inclusion of women in arenas where they have traditionally been excluded.

Radical feminism Believes that the patriarchal structure of our society in inherently oppressive for all people. Male dominance, competition, and heterosexism must be abolished.

Socialist feminism Places the oppression of women within the economic and political structures of culture and seeks reform of social institutions.

Cultural feminism Endeavors to revalue the unique qualities associated with womanhood and femininity.

Identity A process rather than a construct that is constantly developing in relationship to the cultural, social, familial, spiritual, and historical context of one's environment.

RELATIONAL-CULTURAL THEORY

Connection The experience of participating with others for the benefit of all. Connection is fundamental to psychological development. The extended concept of empathy is basic to this understanding. Connection also includes increased mutuality, engagement, and empowerment.

Cultural context The unequal and essentially nonmutual power dynamics of patriarchal societies as they impact the lives and development of personality of men and of women alike.

Dependence A positive characteristic helping to promote healthy development and growth.

Disconnection An experience that occurs whenever a child or adult is prevented from participating in a mutually enhancing and mutually responsive relationship. Repeated disconnections can have major impact, as the individual moves further and further away from connection with his or her own experience.

Empathy A sensitivity to others that involves motivational, perceptual, affective, and cognitive components, and always has a movement toward understanding, rather than a mirroring, or matching, of another's experience.

Paradox of connection-disconnection The contradictory situation in which a child or adult, in order to connect in available relationships, withholds the authentic self. On one level or another, this paradox is reflected in, and underlies, all the problems that emerge in therapy.

Relationships Women's search for ways of connection with others. It is the central organizing feature in their development. A relational model differs from most developmental models, which are characterized by an emphasis on the struggle for autonomy and independence.

ISSUES OF DIVERSITY

Privilege The invisible sociocultural phenomenon through which one group assumes that their lived experience can stand in for the lived experience of others, that is, the acceptance of the notion of "mainstream" culture as a norm of society, without defining *mainstream* as white, middle-class, and educated.

FEMINIST CONTRIBUTIONS TO EPISTEMOLOGY AND METHODOLOGY

Social Constructionism A theoretical model that posits that human experience is influence, defined, and/or interpreted within and by sociocultural structured. This model is a major foundation of much feminist discourse.

Epistemology The study of the nature of knowledge.

Methodology The methods or rules employed by a discipline for gathering information, data, and/or knowledge.

ORGANIC INQUIRY: A TRANSPERSONAL/FEMINIST RESEARCH METHODOLOGY

Inspiration The second step in transformative change, in which unpredictable and often affective experience occurs.

Integration The third step in transformative change. The psyche delivers the newly discovered material to the intellect where it is synthesized into a wholly new formulation.

Organic inquiry A sacred qualitative research methodology, which aims to inform its individual reader not only intellectually but also on a deeper and potentially transformative level.

Preparation The first step in the model of organic transformative change in which one clarifies an intent, adopts a position of curious ignorance, acknowledges one's role as the setting for transformative change, and opens to the deeper realm of the mind.

ANNOTATED BIBLIOGRAPHY

FEMINIST PSYCHOLOGY

Ballou, M., & Brown, L. S. (Eds.) (2002). *Rethinking mental health and disorder: Feminist perspectives.* New York: Guilford Press.

A collection of current feminist research and theory that reframes what is deemed normal and what is pathological. Excellent examples of how feminist theory is utilized in the field of psychology to create more flexible, inclusive models of mental health.

Biaggio, M., & Hersen, M. (Eds.). (2000). *Issues in the psychology of women.* New York: Kluwer Academic/Plenum Publishing.

A detailed overview of the field including a detailed history of the women's movement and special topics of interest for feminist psychologists including epistemology and methodology.

Brown, L. S., & Ballou, M. (Eds.). (1992). *Personality and psychopathology: Feminist reappraisals.* New York: Guilford Press.

The precursor of *Rethinking Mental Health and Disorder,* this edition collected together some of the most important feminist theory in the field to date. This book is one of the best primers on how feminism enables psychologists to move beyond universals and rigid norms toward new models of psychology and personality theory.

Enns, C. Z. (1997). *Feminist theories and feminist psychotherapies: Origins, themes, and variations.* Binghamton, NY: Hayworth Press.

A balanced, detailed overview of the four major branches of feminism and how each has contributed to feminist psychology. An excellent introductory book for those interested in delving further into the field.

RELATIONAL-CULTURAL THEORY

Belenky, M., Clinchy, B., Goldberger, N., & Tarule, J. (1986). *Women's ways of knowing.* New York: Basic Books.

This book explores the basic patterns of knowing and interacting with the world that characterize women's experience. Based on interviews with 100 women, the book also delineates the ways in which women are silenced by male standards of knowing and learning.

Brown, L. M., & Gilligan, C. (1992). *Meeting at the crossroads: Women, psychology and girls' development.* Cambridge, MA: Harvard University Press.

Delineates the dilemmas faced by adolescent girls when they believe that they must withhold their true selves in order to participate in relationships. Also describes the idea that the authenticity and vitality available to young girls in relationships is often lost as girls attempt to meet standards of femininity that silence their real knowledge of the world of relationships.

Gilligan, C. (1982). *In a different voice.* Cambridge, MA: Harvard University Press.

Already a classic in the rethinking of the psychology of women, this book reexamines the differing paths of moral development in girls and boys. It explores the differences between a morality of justice and a morality of care. It is a must for anyone interested in new understandings of women's development.

Jordan, J. (Ed.). (1997). *Women's growth in diversity.* New York: Guilford Press.

This book continues the theory building begun in *Women's Growth in Connection* but also focuses on questions of diversity in women's development.

Jordan, J. V., Kaplan, A. G., Miller, J. B., Stiver, I. P., & Surrey, J. L. (1991). *Women's growth in connection.* New York: Guilford Press.

A collection of the early papers out of the Stone Center at Wellesley College. This book introduces the reader to core concepts of a relational model of development: mutuality, empathy, mutual empowerment, the sense of self in women, and dependency.

Miller, J. B. (1976). *Toward a new psychology of women.* Boston: Beacon Press.

A groundbreaking work that has been described as revolutionary, this book forms the core of the Stone Center's approach to understanding women. It addresses the societal forces that have shaped women's development, and it notes the considerable, although often devalued, strengths that women bring to relationships and the culture. Essential reading for anyone who wishes to understand women and the cultural dynamics shaping women's lives.

Stone Center Working Paper Series (1982–1997). Stone Center Works in Progress (Nos. 1–78). (Available from Stone Center, Wellesley College, Wellesley, MA 02181-8268.)

A wide-ranging series of papers covering the issues of power, courage, lesbian perspectives, developmental pathways of women of color, psychotherapy, and more. Considered by many to be at the cutting edge of approaches to the psychology of women.

ISSUES OF DIVERSITY

Cole, J. B. (Ed.). (1986). *All American women: Lines that divide, ties that bind.* New York: Free Press.

Collected essays addressing racism and women's lived experience of race, class, and gender in American culture.

Collins, P. H. (1990). *Black feminist thought: Knowledge, consciousness, and the politics of empowerment.* Boston: Unwin Hyman.

A major contribution to the development of the intersection of race, gender, and class. Collins uses her personal experiences, her academic training, and sharp social analysis to provide an in-depth framework through which issues of diversity and exclusion or inclusion can be further explored.

Espin, O. M., & Gawelek, M. A. (1992). Women's diversity: Ethnicity, race, class, and gender in theories of feminist psychology. In L. S. Brown & M. Ballou (Eds.), *Personality and psychopathology: Feminist reappraisals* (pp. 88–107). New York: Guilford Press.

An important article that develops four factors necessary to include a consideration of race, class, and additional diverse elements into feminist frameworks.

hooks, b. (1989). *Talking back: Thinking feminist, thinking black.* Boston: South End Press.

Essays from a pivotal author in the feminist movement on being black and feminist in America. Firsthand accounts and compelling, controversial discourse that brings the conversation about diversity to life.

McIntosh, P. (2002) White privilege: Unpacking the invisible knapsack. In A. Kesselman, L. McNair, & N. Schneidewind (Eds.), *Women: Images, and realities* (3rd ed.) (pp. 358–361). New York: McGraw Hill.

An article that speaks into consciousness the mechanisms of underlying privilege prevalent in American culture—much of which, according to the author, is kept out of public awareness as a tool of manipulation and power.

FEMINIST CONTRIBUTIONS TO EPISTEMOLOGY AND METHODOLOGY

Bohan, J. S. (1993). Regarding gender: Essentialism, constructionism, and feminist psychology. *Psychology of Women Quarterly, 17,* 5–21.

This is the article that brought the social constructionist paradigm into feminist psychological theory.

DeLamater, J. D., & Hyde, J. S. (1998). Essentialism versus social constructionism in the study of human sexuality. *Journal of Sex Research, 35*(1), 10–18.

A good secondary article that helps explain the social constructionist framework as well as providing useful ways in which the theory can be practically applied.

ORGANIC INQUIRY

Baring, A., & Cashford, J. (1991). *The myth of the goddess: Evolution of an image.* London: Viking Arkana.

Extensively complete, this book is a classic reference to the history of feminine spirituality from its ancient origins to its place in our current world.

Braud, W., & Anderson, R. (1998). *Transpersonal research methods for the social sciences: Honoring human experience.* Thousand Oaks, CA: Sage.

This thoughtful and innovative guide to transpersonal research methods demonstrates the forward edge of research technique and theory.

Clements, J., Ettling, D., Jenett, D., & Shields, L. (1998). *Organic inquiry: If research were sacred.* Unpublished manuscript, Institute of Transpersonal Psychology, Palo Alto, CA.

This is the latest edition of the still-evolving description of organic origins, theory, and practice. Available at **Serpentina.com.**

Reinharz, S. (1992). *Feminist methods in social research.* New York: Oxford University Press.

This book continues to be the best view into theory and practice of feminist research.

Seeley, R. (2000). *Sacred callings: The process of moving into vocation at midlife as seen through story and reflection in a council of nine women.* Unpublished doctoral dissertation, Institute of Transpersonal Psychology, Palo Alto, CA.

This doctoral dissertation offers a hands-on view of organic research at its best and most recent.

WEB SITES

http://www.apa.org/divisions/div35/

Society for the Psychology of Women (APA Div. 35).

http://www.nimh.nih.gov/

National Institute of Mental Health.

http://www.wellesley.edu/WCW/scsub.html

Stone Center, Wellesley Centers for Women (founded by Jean Baker Miller).

http://www.femina.com/

Comprehensive listing of women-centered and feminist **Web** sites.

http://www.feminista.com/issues/front.php

Articles, art, and information on feminist issues.

http://www.cddc.vt.edu/Feminism/

Feminist Theory **Web** site. Extensive introductory information and bibliographies.

REFERENCES

Alpert, J. (1973, August) Mother right: A new feminist theory. *Ms., 2*(2), 52–55, 88–94.

Anderson, R. (2000). *Intuitive inquiry: Interpreting objective and subjective data. ReVision, 22*(4), 31–39.

Ballou, M. (1992). Introduction. In L. S. Brown and M. Ballou (Eds.), *Personality and psychopathology: Feminist reappraisals* (pp. 3–7). New York: Guilford Press.

Ballou, M., & Brown, L. S. (Eds.) (2002). *Rethinking mental health and disorder: Feminist perspectives.* New York: Guilford Press.

Ballou, M., Matsumoto, A., & Wagner, M. (2002). Toward a feminist ecological theory of human nature: Theory building in response to real-world dynamics. In M. Ballou & L. S. Brown (Eds.), *Rethinking mental health and disorder: Feminist perspectives* (pp. 99–141). New York: Guilford Press.

Barton, B. (2002). Dancing on the möbius strip: Challenging the sex war paradigm. *Gender & Society, 16,* 585–602.

Behar, R. (1996). *The vulnerable observer: Anthropology that breaks your heart.* Boston: Beacon.

Belenky, M., Clinchy, B., Goldberger, N., & Tarule, J. (1986). *Women's ways of knowing.* New York: Basic Books.

Bergman, S. (1991). *Men's psychological development: A relational perspective.* Work in progress (No. 48). Wellesley, MA: Stone Center Working Paper Series.

Beutler, L. E., & Moleiro, C. (2001). Clinical versus reliable and significant change. *Clinical Psychology: Science and Practice, 8,* 44–59.

Biaggio, M. (2000). History of the contemporary women's movement. In M. Biaggio & M. Hersen (Eds.), *Issues in the psychology of women* (pp. 3–14). New York: Kluwer Academic/Plenum.

Bohan, J. S. (1993). Regarding gender: Essentialism, constructionism, and feminist psychology. *Psychology of Women Quarterly, 17,* 5–21.

Brown, L. M., & Gilligan, C. (1992). *Meeting at the crossroads: Women, psychology and girls' development.* Cambridge, MA: Harvard University Press.

Brown, L. S. (1992). A feminist critique of the personality disorders. In L. S. Brown & M. Ballou (Eds.), *Personality and psychopathology: Feminist reappraisals* (pp. 206–228). New York: Guilford Press.

Brown, L. S. (1994). *Subversive dialogues: Theory in feminist therapy.* New York: Basic Books.

Brown, L.S., & Ballou, M. (Eds.). (1992). *Personality and psychopathology: Feminist reappraisals.* New York: Guilford Press.

Carlson, R. (1972). Understanding women: Implications for personality theory and research. *Journal of Social Issues, 28,* 17–31.

Chesler, P. (1972). *Women and madness.* New York: Doubleday.

Chodorow, N. J. (1978). *The reproduction of mothering.* Berkeley, CA: University of California Press.

Cioflica, D. M. (2000). *The sacred search for voice: An organic inquiry into the creative mirroring process of collage and story.* Unpublished doctoral dissertation, Institute of Transpersonal Psychology, Palo Alto, CA.

Clements, J. (2000). *Organic inquiry: Theory.* Unpublished paper, Institute of Transpersonal Psychology, Palo Alto, CA.

Clements, J., Ettling, D., Jenett, D., & Shields, L. (1998). Organic research: Feminine spirituality meets transpersonal research. In W. Braud & R. Anderson, *Transpersonal research methods for the social sciences: Honoring human experience* (pp. 114–127). Thousand Oaks, CA: Sage.

Cole, J. B. (Ed.). (1986). *All American women: Lines that divide, ties that bind*. New York: Free Press.

Collins, P. H. (1990). *Black feminist thought: Knowledge, consciousness, and the politics of empowerment*. Boston: Unwin Hyman.

Daniels, J., D'Andrea M., and Heck, R. (1995). Moral development and Hawaiian youths: Does gender make a difference? *Journal of Counseling and Development 74*(1), 90–98.

de Beauvoir, S. (1953). *The second sex* (H. M. Parshley, Trans.). New York: Knopf.

DeLamater, J. D., & Hyde, J. S. (1998). Essentialism versus social constructionism in the study of human sexuality. *Journal of Sex Research, 35*(1), 10–18.

Doherty, M. A. (1973). Sexual bias in personality theory. *Counseling Psychologist, 4*, 67–74.

Dworkin, A. (1981). *Pornography: Men possessing women*. New York: Perigee.

Echols, A. (1989). *Daring to be bad: Radical feminism in America*. Minneapolis: University of Minnesota Press.

Enns, C. Z. (1992). Toward integrating feminist psychotherapy and feminist philosophy. *Professional Psychology, 23*, 453–466.

Enns, C. Z. (1997). *Feminist theories and feminist psychotherapies: origins, themes, and variations*. Binghamton, NY: Hayworth Press.

Erickson, E. H. (1968). *Identity: Youth and crisis*. New York: Norton.

Espin, O.M., & Gawelek, M. A. (1992). Women's diversity: Ethnicity, race, class, and gender in theories of feminist psychology. In L. S. Brown & M. Ballou (Eds.), *Personality and psychopathology: Feminist reappraisals* (pp. 88–107). New York: Guilford Press.

Ettling, D. (1994). *A phenomenological study of the creative arts as a pathway to embodiment in the personal transformation process of nine women*. Unpublished doctoral dissertation, Institute of Transpersonal Psychology, Palo Alto, CA.

The Feminists (1973). The Feminists: A political organization to annihilate sex roles. In Koedt, E. Levine, & A. Rapone (Eds.), *Radical feminism* (pp. 368–378). New York: Quadrangle Books.

Firestone, S. (1970). *The dialectic of sex*. New York: Morrow.

Friedan, B. (1963). *The feminine mystique*. New York: Norton.

Gianino, A., & Tronick, E. (1985). The mutual regulation model: The infant's self and interactive regulation and coping defensive capacities. In P. Field, P. McCabe, & N. Schneiderman (Eds.), *Stress and coping*. Hillsdale, NJ: Erlbaum.

Giles, S. P. (2000). *The unnested woman: An investigation of dreams of midlife women who have experienced divorce from a longtime mate*. Unpublished doctoral dissertation, Institute of Transpersonal Psychology, Palo Alto, CA.

Gilligan, C. (1982). *In a different voice*. Cambridge, MA: Harvard University Press.

Gilligan, C., Lyons, N., & Hammer, T. J. (Eds.). (1990). *Making connections*. Cambridge, MA: Harvard University Press.

Gleason, N. (1992). *Towards a model for preventing alcohol abuse by college women: A relational perspective*. Washington, DC: U.S. Dept. of Education (Fund for the Improvement of Post-secondary Education).

Godfrey, J. (1992). *In our wildest dreams*. New York: HarperCollins.

Gopfert, C. (1999). *Student experiences of betrayal in the Zen Buddhist teacher/student relationship*. Unpublished dissertation proposal, Institute of Transpersonal Psychology, Palo Alto, CA.

Gould, K. H. (1988). Old wine in new bottles: A feminist perspective on Gilligan's theory. *Social Work 33*(5), 411–416.

Grotstein, J. (1999). Melaine Klein and Heinz Kohut: An odd couple or secretly connected? In *Pluralism in self psychology: Progress in self psychology,* Vol. 15 (pp. 123–146). Hillsdale, NJ: Analytic Press.

Halpern, D. F. (2000). *Sex Differences in Cognitive Abilities* (3rd ed.). Mahuah, NJ: Erlbaum.

Hamilton, J. A., & Jensvold, M. (1992). Personality, psychopathology and depression in women. In L. S. Brown & M. Ballou (Eds.), *Personality and psychopathology: Feminist reappraisals* (pp. 116–143). New York: Guilford Press.

Helgesen, S. (1990). *The female advantage: Women's way of leadership*. New York: Doubleday.

hooks, b. (1981). *Ain't I a woman*. Boston: South End Press.

hooks, b. (1989). *Talking back: Thinking feminist, thinking black*. Boston: South End Press.

Houck, J. H. (1972). The intractable female patient. *American Journal of Psychiatry, 129*, 27–31.

Jack, D. J. (1991). *Silencing the self: Women and depression*. Cambridge, MA: Harvard University Press.

Jenett, D. E. (1999). *Red rice for Bhagavati: Cooking for Kannaki: An ethnographic/Organic Inquiry of the Pongala ritual at the Attukal Temple in Kerala, South India*. Unpublished doctoral dissertation, California Institute of Integral Studies, San Francisco, CA.

Jordan, J. (1983). *Women and empathy: Implications for psychological development and psychotherapy*. Work in progress (No. 2). Wellesley, MA: Stone Center Working Paper Series.

Jordan, J. (1986). The meaning of mutuality. In J. V. Jordan, A. G. Kaplan, J. B. Miller, I. P. Stiver, & J. L. Surrey, *Women's growth in connection* (pp. 81–86). New York: Guilford Press.

Jordan, J. (1987). *Clarity in connection: Empathic knowing, desire and sexuality*. Work in progress (No. 29). Wellesley, MA: Stone Center Working Paper Series.

Jordan, J. (1989). *Relational development: Therapeutic implications of empathy and shame*. Work in progress (No. 39). Wellesley, MA: Stone Center Working Paper Series.

Jordan, J. (1990). *Courage in connection: Conflict, compassion, creativity*. Work in progress (No. 45). Wellesley, MA: Stone Center Working Paper Series.

Jordan, J. (1991a). *The movement of mutuality and power*. Work in progress (No. 53). Wellesley, MA: Stone Center Working Paper Series.

Jordan, J. V., & Hartling, L. M. (2002). New developments in relational-cultural theory. In M. Ballou & L. S. Brown (Eds.), *Rethinking mental health and disorder: Feminist perspectives* (pp. 48–70). New York: Guilford Press.

Jordan, J. V., Kaplan, A. G., Miller, J. B., Stiver, I. P., & Surrey, J. L. (1991). *Women's growth in connection*. New York: Guilford Press.

Jordan, J. V., Kaplan, A. G., & Surrey, J. L. (1982). *Women and empathy*. Work in progress (No. 2). Wellesley, MA: Stone Center Working Paper Series.

Jung, C. G. (1957). The transcendent function. In *Collected Works*, vol. 8, 67–91. New York: Pantheon, 1960.

Kaplan, A. G. (1991). *Some misconceptions and reconceptions of a relational approach*. Work in progress (No. 49). Wellesley, MA: Stone Center Working Paper Series.

Kaplan, A. G. (1984). *The "self-in-relation": Implications for depression in women*. Work in progress (No. 14). Wellesley, MA: Stone Center Working Paper Series.

Kaplan, A. G., & Klein, R. (1990). *Women and suicide: The cry for connection*. Work in progress (No. 46). Wellesley, MA: Stone Center Working Paper Series.

Kaplan, M. (1983). A woman's view of DSM III. American Psychologist, 38, 786–792.

Karniol, R., Grost, E., & Schorr, I. (2003). Caring, gender role orientation, and volunteering. *Sex Roles 49*(112), 11–20.

Katz, P. A., Boggiano, A., & Silvern, L. (1993). Theories of female personality. In F. L. Denmark & M. A. Paludi (Eds.), *Psychology of women: A handbook of issues and theories* (pp. 247–280). Westport, CT: Greenwood Press.

Keefer, M. W., & Olson, D. R. (1995). Moral reasoning and moral concerns: An alternative to Gilligan's gender based hypothesis. *Canadian Journal of Behavioural Science 27*(4), 420–437.

Kersting, K. (2003). Cognitive sex differences: A "political minefield." *Monitor on Psychology, 34*(3), 54–55.

Kilbourne, J., & Surrey, J. (1991). *Women, addiction, and codependency*. Colloquium Presentation. Stone Center, Wellesley College.

Kobayashi, J. S. (1989). Depathologizing dependency: Two perspectives. *Psychiatric Annals, 19,* 653–658.

Kohlberg, L. (1981). *The philosophy of moral development*. San Francisco: Harper and Row.

Lerman, H. (1986). *A mote in Freud's eye*. New York: Springer.

Levinson, D. (1978). *The seasons of a man's life*. New York: Knopf.

Lewis, H. B., & Herman, J. L. (1986). Anger in the mother-daughter relationship. In T. Bernay & D. W. Cantor (Eds.), *The psychology of today's woman: New psychoanalytic visions* (pp. 139–163). Hillsdale, NJ: Lawrence Erlbaum.

Lips, H. M. (1999). *A new psychology of women: Gender, culture, and ethnicity*. Mountain View, CA: Mayfield.

Loffer, S. L. (1999). *Returning to ourselves: Women thriving with chronic illness*. Unpublished doctoral dissertation, Institute of Transpersonal Psychology, Palo Alto, CA.

Lorber, J. & Farrell, S. A. (1991). *The social construction of gender*. Newbury Park, CA: Sage.

MacKinnon, C. A. (1993). Feminism, Marxism, method, and the State: Toward a feminist jurisprudence. In P. B. Bart & E. G. Moran (Eds.), *Violence against women: The bloody footprints* (pp. 201–227). Newbury Park, CA: Sage (Originally published in 1982).

Maracek, J. (2001). After the facts: Psychology and the study of gender. *Canadian Psychology, 42,* 254–267.

Maracek, J. (2002). Unfinished business: Postmodern feminism in personality psychology. In M. Ballou & L. S. Brown (Eds.), *Rethinking mental health and disorder: Feminist perspectives* (pp. 3–28). New York: Guilford Press.

Maracek, J., & Kravetz, D. (1977). Women and mental health: A review of feminist change efforts. *Psychiatry, 40,* 323–329.

McIntosh, P. (2002) White privilege: Unpacking the invisible knapsack. In A. Kesselman, L. McNair, & N. Schneidewind (Eds.), *Women: Images, and realities* (3rd ed.) (pp. 358–361). New York: McGraw-Hill.

Mencher, J. (1990). *Intimacy in lesbian relationships: A critical reexamination of fusion*. Work in progress (No. 42). Wellesley, MA: Stone Center Working Paper Series.

Miller, J. B. (1976). *Toward a new psychology of women*. Boston: Beacon Press.

Miller, J. B. (1982). Women and power. In J. V. Jordan, A. G. Kaplan, J. B. Miller, I. P. Stiver, & J. L. Surrey, *Women's growth in connection* (pp. 197–205). New York: Guilford Press.

Miller, J. B. (1984). *The development of women's sense of self*. Work in progress (No. 12). Wellesley, MA: Stone Center Working Paper Series.

Miller, J. B. (1986). *What do we mean by relationships?* Work in progress (No. 22). Wellesley, MA: Stone Center Working Paper Series.

Miller, J. B. (1988). *Connections, disconnections and violations*. Work in progress (No. 33). Wellesley, MA: Stone Center Working Paper Series.

Miller, J. B., & Stiver, I. P. (1991). *A relational reframing of therapy*. Work in progress (No. 52). Wellesley, MA: Stone Center Working Paper Series.

Miller, J. B., & Surrey, J. L. (1989). *Revisioning women's anger: The personal and the global*. Work in progress (No. 43). Wellesley, MA: Stone Center Working Paper Series.

Millett, K. (1970). *Sexual politics*. Garden City, NY: Doubleday.

Mirkin, M. (1990). Eating disorders: A feminist structural family therapy perspective. In M. Mirkin (Ed.), *The social and political contexts in family therapy*. Boston: Allyn & Bacon.

Morgan. R. (Ed.). (1970). *Sisterhood is powerful: An anthology of writings from the women's liberation movement*. NY: Random House.

Moustakis, C. (1990). *Heuristic research: Design, methodology and applications*. Newbury Park, CA: Sage.

Nielsen, J. M. (1990). *Feminist research methods*. Boulder, CO: Westview Press.

Paludi, M. A. (1998). *The psychology of women*. Upper Saddle River, NJ: Prentice Hall.

Pratt, M. (1988). Identity: Skin, blood, heart. In E. Bulkin, B. Smith, & M. Pratt (Eds.), *Yours in struggle: Three feminist perspectives on anti-Semitism and racism* (pp. 11–61). Ann Arbor, MI: Firebrand Books.

Redstockings Manifesto (1969). In B. Roszak & T. Roszak (Eds.), *Masculine/feminine: Readings in sexual mythology and the liberation of women* (pp. 272–274). New York: Harper Colophon Books.

Reinharz, S. (1992). *Feminist methods in social research*. New York: Oxford University Press.

Rice, J. K., & Rice, D. G. (1973). Implications of the women's liberation movement for psychotherapy. *American Journal of Psychiatry, 130*, 191–196.

Rich, A. (1989). Compulsory heterosexuality and lesbian existence. In L. Richardson & V. Taylor (Eds.), *Feminist frontiers II* (pp. 120–141). New York: McGraw-Hill (Originally published in 1980).

Rosener, J. (1990). Ways women lead. *Harvard Business Review, 90,* 119–125.

Ruth, S. (1990). *Issues in feminism: An introduction to women's studies* (2nd ed.). Mountain View, CA: Mayfield.

Rutter, V. B. (1993). *Woman changing woman: Feminine psychology reconceived through myth and experience.* New York: HarperSanFrancisco.

Saunders, E. A., & Arnold, F. (1990). *Borderline personality disorder and childhood abuse: Revisions in clinical thinking and treatment approach.* Work in progress (No. 51). Wellesley, MA: Stone Center Working Paper Series.

Seeley, R. (2000). *Sacred callings: The process of moving into vocation at midlife as seen through story and reflection in a council of nine women.* Unpublished doctoral dissertation, Institute of Transpersonal Psychology, Palo Alto, CA.

Shepherd, L. J. (1993). *Lifting the veil: The feminine face of science.* Boston: Shambhala.

Shields, L. (1995). *The experience of beauty, body image and the feminine in three generations of mothers and daughters.* Unpublished doctoral dissertation, Institute of Transpersonal Psychology, Palo Alto, CA.

Starhawk (1999). *Spiral dance: A rebirth of the ancient religion of the goddess* (20th anni. ed.). San Francisco: HarperSanFrancisco (Originally published in 1979).

Steiner-Adair, C. (1991). New maps of development, new models of therapy: The psychology of women and treatment of eating disorders. In C. Johnson (Ed.), *Psychodynamic treatment of anorexia nervosa and bulimia.* New York: Guilford Press.

Stern, D. (1985). *The interpersonal world of the infant.* New York: Basic Books.

Stiver, I. (1984). *The meaning of "dependency" in female–male relationships.* Work in progress (No. 11). Wellesley, MA: Stone Center Working Paper Series.

Stiver, I. (1990a). *Dysfunctional families and wounded relationships, Part I.* Work in progress (No. 41). Wellesley, MA: Stone Center Working Paper Series.

Stiver, I. (1990b). *Dysfunctional families and wounded relationships, Part II.* Work in progress (No. 44). Wellesley, MA: Stone Center Working Paper Series.

Stiver, I. (1991a). Beyond the Oedipus complex: Mothers and daughters. In J. V. Jordan, A. G. Kaplan, J. B. Miller, I. P. Stiver, & J. L. Surrey, *Women's growth in connection* (pp. 97–121). New York: Guilford Press.

Stiver, I. (1991b). The meanings of "dependency" in female-male relationships. In J. V. Jordan, A. G. Kaplan, J. B. Miller, I. P. Stiver, & J. L. Surrey, *Women's growth in connection* (pp. 143–161). New York: Guilford Press.

Stiver, I. (1991c). Work inhibitions in women: Clinical considerations. In J. V. Jordan, A. G. Kaplan, J. B. Miller, I. P. Stiver, & J. L. Surrey, *Women's growth in connection* (pp. 223–236). New York: Guilford Press.

Stiver, I. P., & Miller, J. B. (1988). *From depression to sadness in the psychotherapy of women.* Work in progress (No. 36). Wellesley, MA: Stone Center Working Paper Series.

Surrey, J. L. (1985). *Self-in-relation.* Work in progress (No. 13). Wellesley, MA: Stone Center Working Paper Series.

Surrey, J. L. (1991a). Eating patterns as a reflection of women's development. In J. V. Jordan, A. G. Kaplan, J. B. Miller, I. P. Stiver, & J. L. Surrey, *Women's growth in connection* (pp. 237–249). New York: Guilford Press.

Surrey, J. L. (1991b). The "self-in-relation": A theory of women's development. In J. V. Jordan, A. G. Kaplan, J. B. Miller, I. P. Stiver, & J. L. Surrey, *Women's growth in connection* (pp. 51–66). New York: Guilford Press.

Suyemoto, K. L. (2002). Constructing identities: A feminist, culturally contextualized alternative to "personality." In M. Ballou & L. S. Brown (Eds.), *Rethinking mental health and disorder: Feminist perspectives* (pp. 71–98). New York: Guilford Press.

Taylor, N. (1996). *Women's experience of the descent into the underworld: The path of Inanna. A feminist and heuristic inquiry.* Unpublished doctoral dissertation, Institute of Transpersonal Psychology, Palo Alto, CA.

Tennov, D. (1973). Feminism, psychotherapy, and professionalism. *Journal of Contemporary Psychotherapy, 5,* 107–111.

Thompson, C. (1942). Cultural pressures on the psychology of women. *Psychiatry, 5,* 331–339.

Turner, C. (1987). *Clinical applications of the Stone Center theoretical approach to minority women.* Work in progress (No. 28). Wellesley, MA: Stone Center Working Paper Series.

Turner, V. (1987). Betwixt and between: The liminal period in rites of passage. In L. Mahdi, S. Foster, & M. Little (Eds.), *Betwixt & between: Patterns of masculine and feminine initiation* (pp. 3–19). La Salle, IL: Open Court.

Van Dusen, W. (1996). *Returning to the source: The way to the experience of God.* Moab, UT: Real People Press.

Van Gennep, A. (1909/1960). *The rites of passage.* Chicago: University of Chicago Press.

Walker, L. E. A. (1992). Foreward. In L. S. Brown & M. Ballou (Eds.), *Personality and psychopathology: Feminist reappraisals* (pp. xii–x). New York: Guilford Press.

Washburn, M. (1995). The ego and the dynamic ground: A transpersonal theory of human development. (2d ed.). Albany: State University of New York.

Weisstein, N. (1968/1993). Psychology constructs a female; or the fantasy life of the male psychologist. *Feminism and Psychology, 3,* 195–210.

Weitzer, R. (1999). *Sex for sale: Prostitution, pornography, and the sex industry.* New York: Routledge.

Whalen, M. (1996). *Counseling to end violence against women: A subversive model.* Thousand Oaks, CA: Sage.

Yoder, J. D., & Kahn, A. S. (1993). Working toward an inclusive psychology of women. *American Psychologist, 48,* 846–850.

erik erikson and
the life cycle

Erik Erikson is the most widely read and influential post-Freudian theorist, both in psychology and in the popular press. His books have sold hundreds of thousands of copies, and, in 1970, Erikson was featured on the covers of both *Newsweek* and the *New York Times Magazine*. His psychobiography of Mohandas Gandhi (1969) was awarded the Pulitzer Prize and the National Book Award.

Erik Erikson has extended the insights of psychoanalysis through cross-cultural studies of child rearing, psychological biographies of great men and women, and by analyzing the interaction of psychological and social dynamics. Erikson's *life-span theory* of ego development has had enormous influence within psychology and related fields. He is also the founder of modern **psychohistory.**

Erikson's work is solidly based on psychoanalytic theory; no one else since Freud has done as much to elaborate on and apply the principles of psychoanalysis to new fields and to the problems of today's world. In the process, Erikson developed an original theory rooted in psychoanalytic understanding, yet significantly different in scope, concept, and emphasis. He has been called a "nondogmatic, emancipated Freudian." Erikson's concepts of *identity* and *identity crisis* have had major professional influence throughout the social sciences. They have also become household words.

Erikson is a brilliant, insightful theorist and an elegant writer. At the core of his work is his theory of the human life cycle, a model that integrates human growth and development from birth to old age. He made three major contributions to the study of personality: (1) that along with Freud's psychosexual developmental stages, the individual simultaneously goes through psychosocial and ego-development stages, (2) that personality development continues throughout life, and (3) that each stage of development can have both positive and negative outcomes.

PERSONAL HISTORY

Erikson has unusual, even obscure, roots. He was born on June 15, 1902. His Danish Jewish mother left Denmark for Germany while pregnant, and married a German Jewish physician, Dr. Homburger. Erikson considered himself German in spite of his Danish parentage, yet his German classmates rejected him because he was Jewish. At the same time, his Jewish friends called him the *goy* (the non-Jew) because of his blond, Aryan appearance.

Erikson grew up as Erik Homburger and first published under that name. Later he wrote under the name Erik Homburger Erikson, and eventually settled on Erik Erikson (literally, Erik, son of Erik—Erikson was not the name of his biological father). A Dane by parentage and a German by upbringing, he later became an American by choice. Raised as a Jew, he married a Christian and converted to Christianity.

Erikson's formal academic education lasted until he was 18, when he graduated from a classical *gymnasium*. There he had studied Latin, Greek, German literature, and ancient history. He was not a particularly devoted student. After graduation, Erikson traveled through Europe for a year. Then, he returned home and enrolled in art school. He studied art in Munich, then went to live in Florence. The artist's life was good for a young man not ready to settle down; it gave him great latitude and time for self-exploration.

Erikson returned home at age 25, intending to find a job teaching art. He was invited to Vienna to teach at a new school for the children of families that had come to Vienna for psychoanalysis. He taught art, history, and various other subjects. Erikson was given a free hand to create an ideal educational program.

The psychoanalytic community was much less formal in the 1920s. Analysts, patients, and their families and friends attended picnics and other social events together. At these affairs, Erikson became acquainted with Anna Freud and other prominent psychoanalysts. Erikson was screened informally and judged a suitable candidate for analytic training. In 1927, Erikson began daily analysis with Anna Freud in the house she shared with her father.

When he expressed doubts about the possibility of an artist becoming a psychoanalyst, Anna Freud replied that psychoanalysis would need people who help others see. Much of Erikson's long and rich career can be viewed as an attempt to do just that: drawing exquisite word pictures of new concepts and perspectives.

Erikson also studied the Montessori system and was one of only two men who graduated from the Montessori Teachers' Association at that time. His interest in play therapy and child analysis came from his ongoing teaching, influenced by his Montessori education.

In 1929, at a Mardi Gras masked ball in a Viennese castle, Erikson met a young woman, Joan Serson, and fell in love almost immediately. They were married several months later. Serson's interests were similar to Erikson's. A teacher of modern dance, she had received a bachelor's degree in education and a master's degree in sociology, and had also been in psychoanalysis.

Although she is credited as a coauthor only in Erikson's last books (Erikson, Erikson, & Kivnick, 1986; Erikson & Erikson, 1997), it is now clear that Joan Erikson was an active intellectual partner in Erik's work. "In the late 1940's *we* . . . received an invitation to present a paper on the developmental stages of life. . . . The paper *we* were to contribute . . . was 'Growth and Crises of the Healthy Personality.' *We* went to work with great enthusiasm" (J. Erikson, 1997, p. 2; italics added).

Erikson finished his analytic training in 1933 and was accepted as a full member of the Vienna Psychoanalytic Society. The growth of fascism in Europe led Erikson, as well as many other psychoanalysts, to leave for the United States. The move was made easier by his wife's Canadian-American ancestry. The Eriksons settled in Boston, where he became the city's first child psychoanalyst. He was offered positions at Harvard Medical School and at the prestigious Massachusetts General Hospital. In addition, he began private practice and became associated with Harvard's Psychological Clinic, run by Henry Murray. During these years, he associated with brilliant and influential thinkers, including Murray, anthropologists Ruth Benedict and Margaret Mead, and social psychologist Kurt Lewin.

In 1936, Erikson accepted a position at Yale Medical School. While at Yale, he took his first anthropological field trip to observe Sioux Indian children in South Dakota. His paper on the Sioux combines the cultural richness of an anthropological field report with the psychologically rich perspective of a highly trained clinician. Among the Sioux, Erikson observed a new phenomenon. He noticed psychological symptoms, including the lack of clear self-image or identity, that were related to a sense of loss of cultural tradition. Erikson later observed a similar confusion of identity among emotionally disturbed World War II veterans. Erikson's own identity crises and his life-long quest to discover who his father was made him particularly sensistive to this concept (Friedman, 1999).

The Eriksons moved to California in 1939 and spent ten years in the San Francisco area. Erikson continued his analytic work with children and conducted research projects at the University of California at Berkeley.

Erikson's first and best-known book, *Childhood and Society,* was published in 1950. This book contains the fundamental formulations of virtually all of Erikson's

To be surprised belongs to the discipline of a clinician. (Erikson, 1963, p. 100)

major ideas: identity, the life cycle, cross-cultural studies, and psychobiography. *Childhood and Society* has been translated into a dozen languages and is used as a textbook at psychiatric training centers, in psychology courses, and in many other disciplines at undergraduate and graduate levels. The eight-stage model of the human life cycle grew from the birth of the Eriksons' third son, who was born developmentally handicapped.

That same year Erikson left Berkeley because he would not sign a state loyalty oath. Erikson, along with many other liberal scholars, refused to sign because to him the mandatory oath represented a kind of communist witch-hunt in an era of hyper-patriotism and paranoia. The Eriksons returned to Massachusetts to the Austin Riggs Center, a leading institution for psychoanalytic training and research. While at Austin Riggs, Erikson did a psychological study of Martin Luther, entitled *Young Man Luther* (1958). An exciting and innovative combination of psychoanalysis, biography, and history, the book stirred great interest among psychoanalysts, psychologists, historians, and other social scientists.

In 1960, Erikson was appointed a professor at Harvard. Two years later, he visited India and met Indians who had known Gandhi and who had been personally involved, on both sides, in his first nonviolent protest in India. Erikson became deeply interested in Gandhi, the spiritual leader and political revolutionary who transformed a negative Indian identity of powerlessness into an active, effective political technique. In 1969, while at Harvard, Erikson published his study of Gandhi.

After retiring from Harvard, Erikson and his wife moved back to the San Francisco area in 1975. Their writing and research, which they continued collaboratively until his death in 1994, focused primarily on old age and the last stage of the life cycle. Joan Erikson passed away in 1997.

INTELLECTUAL ANTECEDENTS

Two principal influences on Erikson that shaped his theories were psychoanalysis and his study of life and childrearing in other cultures.

Psychoanalysis

Throughout his career, Erikson viewed himself as a psychoanalyst. His application of psychoanalysis to new areas and his incorporation of recent advances in anthropology, psychology, and other social sciences, inevitably led Erikson to develop ideas significantly different from Freud's basic theories. However, Erikson's writings reveal his indebtedness to Freud. Rather than label himself *neo-Freudian,* Erikson preferred the more neutral term *post-Freudian.*

Erikson's work on in-depth psychological biographies and on child and adult development was essentially psychoanalytic in nature. "I spoke of 'insight,' rather than knowledge or fact, because it is so difficult to say in the study of human situations what you can really call knowledge" (Erikson in Evans, 1969, p. 89). As he dealt with new material, Erikson reshaped and expanded his psychoanalytic understandings.

> Psychoanalysis is unique. It is the treatment situation in which intellectual insight is forced to become emotional insight under very carefully planned circumstances defined by technical rules. But outside of that situation, interpretations cannot do what they can do within a disciplined setting. (Erikson in Evans, 1969)

When I started to write about twenty-five years ago, I really thought I was merely providing new illustrations for what I had learned from Sigmund and Anna Freud. I realized only gradually that any original observation already implies a change in theory. An observer of a different generation, in a different scientific climate, cannot avoid developing in a field if it is a vital one. Even a great breakthrough like Freud's is characterized by a passionate concern to bring order into data which "haunted him," to use Darwin's phrase, for very complex reasons of his own and of his time. One can follow such a man only by doing likewise, and if one does so, one differs. I say this because some workers want to improve on Freud, as if his theories were opinions, and because they prefer nicer or nobler ones. (Erikson in Evans, 1969, p. 13)

In a sense, Erikson developed psychoanalytic theory for the second half of the twentieth century.

Other Cultures

In 1937 Erikson traveled to South Dakota to investigate the cause of apathy among Sioux schoolchildren. He discovered that they were caught between conflicting value systems: the traditional tribal values they learned in early childhood and the white middle-class values taught in school. Sioux culture valued neither property nor competition. The Sioux had been buffalo hunters, and successful hunters traditionally shared freely with their villages.

Several years later, Erikson visited the Yurok Indians, who lived by the Klamath River in northern California. He was particularly interested in comparing the childhood training and personality styles in this relatively sedentary fishing society with the lifestyles of the Plains hunters he had studied earlier. Erikson found acquisition of possessions a continuing preoccupation among the Yuroks. Acquisitiveness was learned early in childhood, as Yurok children were taught to be frugal, to value long-term gain over immediate impulses, and to engage in fantasies of catching salmon and accumulating money. The Yurok differed significantly from the Sioux; their culture was much closer to middle-class American values.

Erikson's work with the Sioux and Yuroks had an important influence on his thinking. His field studies also reveal his remarkable ability to enter the worldviews and modes of thinking of cultures far different from his own. On both field trips, Erikson was accompanied by anthropologists who had developed long-standing friendships with the older people of the tribes. With their assistance, Erikson encountered informants and rich, firsthand information never before available to a psychoanalyst. Before going into the field, he read anthropological reports on both tribes. Erikson found virtually no details on childhood training in these reports. A good part of his field research consisted of asking the grandmothers, "Before the white men came, how were your children brought up?" He found they loved to talk about the subject, and they had wondered why no one ever asked.

Erikson's later theoretical developments evolved partly from his cross-cultural observations. He found that Freud's theories of pregenital stages of development were intrinsically related to the technology and worldview of Western culture. Erikson's own theoretical focus on healthy personality development strongly reflected his firsthand knowledge of other cultures.

MAJOR CONCEPTS

The core of Erikson's work is his eight-stage model of human development, a model that extends psychoanalytic thinking beyond childhood to cover the entire human life cycle. Each stage has psychological, biological, and social components, and each stage builds on the stages that precede it.

Another significant contribution of Erikson's was his pioneering work on psychohistory and psychobiography, which applied his clinical insight to the study of major historical personalities and their impact on their societies.

An Epigenetic Model of Human Development

Erikson's model of the stages of human development—a model he called *epigenetic*—is the first psychological theory to detail the human life cycle from infancy to adulthood and old age. According to Erikson, the psychological growth of the individual proceeds in a manner similar to that of an embryo. *Epigenesis* suggests that each element develops on top of other parts (*epi* means "upon" and *genesis* means "emergence"). Erikson's model is structurally similar to that of embryonic growth in that the emergence of each successive stage is predicated on the development of the previous one.

Each organ system of the body has its own special time for growth and development, which follows a predetermined sequence. Erikson explains the epigenetic principle as "anything that grows has a *ground plan,* and that out of this ground plan the *parts* arise, each part having its *time* of special ascendancy, until all parts have arisen to form a *functioning whole*" (Erikson, 1980a, p. 53).

Erikson's scheme of human development has two basic underlying assumptions:

> (1) That the human personality in principle develops according to steps predetermined in the growing person's readiness to be driven forward, to be aware of, and to interact with a widening social radius; and (2) that society, in principle, tends to be so constituted as to meet and invite the succession of potentialities for interaction and attempts to safeguard and to encourage the proper rate and the proper sequence of their unfolding. (1963, p. 270)

Each stage is characterized by a specific developmental task, or crisis, that must be resolved in order for the individual to proceed to the next stage. The strengths and capacities developed through successful resolution at each stage affect the entire personality. They can be influenced by either later or earlier events. However, these psychological capacities are generally affected most strongly during the stage in which they emerge. Each stage is systematically related to all the others, and the stages must occur in a given sequence.

Table 6.1 is taken from Erikson's first discussion of the eight stages, in *Childhood and Society.* It illustrates the progression from one stage to another over time. Also, each attribute exists in various forms before and after its critical stage. *Trust,* for example, takes one form in adolescence and yet another in old age; both are based on a sense of trust developed in infancy.

Crises in Development.   Each stage has a period of **crisis** in which the strengths and skills that form essential elements of that stage are developed and tested. By crisis, Erikson means a turning point, a critical moment, such as the crisis in a fever. When it is resolved successfully, the fever breaks and the individual begins to recover. Crises are special times in the individual's life, "moments of decision between progress and regression, integration and retardation" (Erikson, 1963, pp. 270–271). Each stage is a crisis in learning—allowing for the attainment of new skills and attitudes. The crisis may not seem dramatic or critical; often, the individual can see only later that a major turning point was reached and passed.

Erikson has pointed out that successful resolution of the crisis at each stage of human development promotes a certain psychosocial strength or virtue. Erikson uses the term *virtue* in its old sense, as in the *virtue* of a medicine. It refers more to potency

With each passage from one stage of human growth to the next we must shed a protective structure. We are left exposed and vulnerable—but also yeasty and embryonic again, capable of stretching in ways we hadn't known before. (Sheehy, 1977, p. 29)

In Chinese, the word for *crisis* is composed of two characters, *danger* and *opportunity.*

TABLE 6.1   Erikson's Eight Stages and Related Virtues

	1	2	3	4	5	6	7	8
VIII Old Age								Integrity vs. Despair WISDOM
VII Adulthood							Generativity vs. Stagnation CARE	
VI Young Adulthood						Intimacy vs. Isolation LOVE		
V Adolescence					Identity vs. Identity Confusion FIDELITY			
IV School Age				Industry vs. Inferiority COMPETENCE				
III Play Age			Initiative vs. Guilt PURPOSE					
II Early Childhood		Autonomy vs. Shame, Doubt WILL						
I Infancy	Basic Trust vs. Basic Mistrust HOPE							

Source: From Erikson, 1982, pp. 56–57.

than morality. Ideally, the individual emerges from each crisis with an increased sense of inner unity, clearer judgment, and greater capacity to function effectively.

Eight Stages of Human Development.   Erikson's first three stages are essentially an amplification of Freud's work. Freud discussed four major stages: oral, anal, phallic, and genital, which are tied to specific organs and also to specific cultural patterns. Erikson expands these to universal issues of human development.

1. Basic Trust Versus Basic Mistrust.   The first stage, **basic trust versus basic mistrust,** occurs at a time when we are the most helpless and dependent on others for physical and emotional nourishment. When infants begin life, they develop a relative sense of trust and mistrust of the world around them. Crucial to this balance between security and insecurity is the infant's experience with the mother. Development of a strong sense of basic trust "implies not only that one has learned to rely on the sameness and continuity of the outer providers, but also that one may trust oneself and the capacities of one's own organs to cope with urges" (Erikson, 1963, p. 248). If a mother, or primary caregiver, is sensitive and responsive to her child, the infant's sense of security increases and the frustrations of hunger and discomfort are tolerable.

Babies control and bring up their parents as much as they're controlled by them. (Erikson, 1963, p. 69)

personal reflection

TRUST

Share a "trust walk" with a classmate or friend. Blindfold yourself and have your partner guide you for at least 15 to 20 minutes. Your partner should try to give you a variety of experiences—different surfaces to walk on, objects to touch, smell, and even taste. Then switch roles.

After you have both finished, take a little time to discuss your experiences. Was it difficult to trust your partner at times? How did it feel to be so dependent on another person?

The relationship between mother and child focuses on the mouth and the experience of nursing. This relationship is tested during the biting stage, which is the beginning of the infant's ability to cause pain. The capacity to express anger and rage as well as the desire to harm are also connected to the pain of teething, a pain the infant must learn to endure because it cannot be alleviated as simply as can hunger. According to Erikson, this inner discomfort and the growing ability to inflict pain are the child's first experiences of a sense of evil and malevolence.

A sense of trust develops not so much from the relief of hunger or from demonstrations of love as from the quality of maternal care. Mothers who feel secure in their ability to care for their babies and who trust that their babies will develop into healthy children communicate their feelings, creating the infant's sense of trust in self and in the world.

The virtue or strength that results from achieving a balance between basic trust and mistrust is *hope*. "Hope is the enduring belief in the attainability of fervent wishes, in spite of the dark urges and rages which mark the beginning of existence" (Erikson, 1964, p. 118). Hope lays the foundation for the development of faith.

Hope is established as a basic strength, relatively independent of specific expectations, goals, and desires. As the individual continues to mature, this strength is verified at each stage; rewarding experiences inspire new hopefulness. At the same time, the individual attains a capacity for renunciation and an ability to cope with disappointment. Also, the individual develops realistic dreams and expectations.

The strength of hope emerges from three essential sources. First is the mother's relation to her own childhood—her desire and need to pass on the hope transmitted from her mother and from her culture. Second is the mother–child relationship itself, the mutuality and sensitivity that can grow when this bond is healthy. Finally, the infant's hope is maintained through social institutions that confirm and restore it, by religious ritual, inspired advice, or otherwise. The mature form of an infant's hope is faith. The rituals and practices of religion are designed to support, deepen, and restore faith.

2. Autonomy Versus Shame and Doubt. The next stage, **autonomy versus shame and doubt**, occurs at the time of muscular maturation and the accompanying ability to hold on or let go. At this stage, children rapidly acquire a variety of mental and physical abilities. They begin to walk, climb, hold on, and communicate more effectively. The child interacts with the world in new ways—in grasping and dropping objects and in toilet training. The child starts to exert control over self and also over parts of the outside world.

The basic modalities of this stage are to hold on and to let go. Freud focused on one aspect of this in his writings on the anal stage. Holding on and letting go have both positive and negative aspects. Holding on can become cruel restraint or it can be a pattern of caring. Letting go can be a release of destructive forces or it can be a relaxed allowing, a letting be.

personal reflection

AUTONOMY

Make an agreement with a partner that, for at least half a day, you will follow his or her directions in whatever you are told to do. In a sense, your partner gets to play "parent" and you agree to be an obedient "child." (Make some clear limits. For example, you will not be made to do anything that is illegal, unethical, or embarrassing to yourself or someone else.)

How does it feel to have someone tell you what to do—what to eat, when to sit down or stand up, how to act, and so on? In many ways, you are duplicating the experience of the average 2-year-old, who has little say in his or her life.

Discuss your experience with your partner when you are done. It may be better not to switch roles afterward. Knowing that you are going to switch may inhibit your partner from being really creative in ordering you around. (And, after all, few parents anticipate switching roles with their children.)

A sense of autonomy develops with the sense of free choice. It is promoted by a feeling of being able to choose what to keep and what to reject. The infant's basic faith in existence, a lasting result of the first stage, is tested in sudden and stubborn wishes to choose—to grab demandingly or to eliminate inappropriately. Parenting experts have called this age the *terrible twos*. The two-year-old's favorite word is *no*, a clear bid for increased autonomy.

Some children turn this urge to control against themselves by developing a rigid, demanding conscience. Rather than mastering the outer environment, they judge and manipulate themselves, which often results in a strong sense of shame or self-doubt.

Shame stems from a sense of self-exposure, a feeling that one's deficiencies are visible to others and that one is, in colloquial terms, "caught with one's pants down." Shame is also associated with the child's first experience of standing upright, in which the child feels small, wobbly, and powerless in an adult world.

Doubt is more closely related to the consciousness of having a front and a back. Our front is the acceptable face that we turn toward the world. The child cannot see the back part of his or her body. It is unknown and unexplored territory and yet, at the stage of toilet training, the child's backside can be dominated by the will of others. Unless the split between front and back is reduced, the child's feelings of autonomy will become tinged with doubt.

The strength acquired at this stage is *will*. To have will does not mean to be willful but to control one's drives with judgment and discrimination. The individual learns to make decisions and to act decisively in spite of inevitable frustration. "Will, therefore, is the unbroken determination to exercise free choice as well as self-restraint, in spite of the unavoidable experience of shame and doubt" (Erikson, 1964, p. 119).

Infant will develops into the adult ability to control drives and impulses. Ideally, the individual's will joins with others in a way that permits both self and others to retain a sense of power, even when restrained by rules and reason.

Will forms the basis of our acceptance of law and external necessity. It is rooted in an appreciation that parental training is guided and tempered by a spirit of justice. The law is a social institution that gives concrete form to our ego's control of our drives. We surrender our willfulness to the power of the law with ambivalence and inevitable small transgressions.

personal reflection

INITIATIVE

This exercise is much like the previous autonomy experience. Again, with a partner, agree to follow his or her directions. Only this time, you can say no. Your partner gets to make all the suggestions about possible activities. You can respond with a yes or no, but you cannot suggest any ideas on your own.

For instance, if the two of you are in a restaurant, your partner can suggest various foods that you might like. You can accept or refuse, but you cannot make any suggestions on your own. Or, if the two of you are going out to a movie, your partner can suggest films to go to. You can agree or disagree, but you cannot suggest any specific films on your own.

After you have finished, discuss how it felt to be deprived of a sense of initiative.

3. Initiative Versus Guilt. At this stage, identified as **initiative versus guilt,** the child experiences greater mobility and inquisitiveness, significant growth in language and imagination, and an expanding sense of mastery and responsibility. Play is the most basic activity of this stage. The child is "into everything," finding joy in attack and conquest over the environment. This stage is analogous to Freud's phallic stage. The child is eager to learn and to perform well. The favorite word at this stage is *why?* There is tremendous curiosity and openness to new learning. The child learns the value of planning ahead and starts to develop a sense of direction and purpose.

This new sense of mastery is tempered by feelings of guilt. The child's new freedom and assertion of power almost inevitably create anxiety. The child develops a conscience, a parental attitude that supports self-observation, self-guidance, and also self-punishment. At this stage, the child can do more than ever before and must learn to set limits.

Purpose, the virtue of this stage, is rooted in play and fantasy. Play is to the child what thinking and planning are to the adult. It provides the rudiments of purpose: focus and direction given to concerted activity. "Purpose, then, is the courage to envisage and pursue valued goals uninhibited by the defeat of infantile fantasies, by guilt and by the foiling fear of punishment" (Erikson, 1964, p. 122). Purpose provides aim and direction, fed by fantasy yet rooted in reality, limited but not inhibited by guilt. The development of fantasy forms the roots of dance, drama, and ritual in adult life.

4. Industry Versus Inferiority. At this stage, **industry versus inferiority,** the child makes his or her entrance into life outside the family. This period corresponds to Freud's latency stage. In our culture, school life begins. In other social systems, the child may become an apprentice or a working assistant to the father or mother.

This is a stage of systematic instruction, a shift from play to a sense of work. Earlier, the child could *play* at activities. No attention was given to the quality of results. Now the child needs to achieve and to derive a sense of satisfaction from a job well done. At this stage, children are expected to master tasks and skills valued in society. The attitudes and opinions of others are particularly important. Children who don't achieve—and thus fail to earn the respect of their parents, teachers, and peers—may develop a sense of inferiority or inadequacy.

The virtue of this stage is *competence,* which is based on a sense of workmanship, the development of practical skills, and general capacities. "Competence, then, is the free exercise of dexterity and intelligence in the completion of tasks, unimpaired by infantile inferiority" (Erikson, 1964, p. 124). Competence is the psychological basis for technology. At this stage, we have started to become productive members of our culture; we have just begun to master our culture's technology.

> The adult once was a child and a youth. He will never be either again; but neither will he ever be without the heritage of those former states.
> (Erikson, 1987, p. 332)

personal reflection

Erikson's Stages: A Personal Assessment

Which of Erikson's stages is the most significant (or powerful, or difficult) for you? What combination of factors makes this stage so important for you? What are the personality elements, family events, environmental influences, societal forces, and so on, that are the most significant in your experience?

How does your own experience of this stage relate to your earlier and later development? How does it relate to the stage and the growth crisis you find yourself in now?

5. Identity Versus Identity Confusion.   As childhood ends, adolescents enter the stage known as **identity versus identity confusion,** in which they integrate their past experiences into a new whole. They question role models and identifications from childhood and try out new roles. The great question of this stage is "Who am I?" A new sense of ego identity develops.

This sense of identity includes the individual's ability to integrate past identifications and present impulses, aptitudes, and skills, as well as opportunities offered by society. "The sense of ego identity, then, is the accrued confidence that the inner sameness and continuity prepared in the past are matched by the sameness and continuity of one's meaning for others, as evidenced in the tangible promise of a 'career'" (Erikson, 1963, pp. 261–262).

Adolescence, the transition between childhood and adulthood, is a crucial stage, Erikson believes. Adolescents at this point in life often call a psychological moratorium and take "time out" to devote to role experimentation. During this period, social limitations and pressures can have a strong impact. The adolescent, already likely to suffer from role confusion, may have difficulty envisioning an appropriate occupational role or finding a meaningful place in society. Doubts about sexual attractiveness and sexual identity are also common. An inability to "take hold" and develop a sense of identification with an individual or cultural role model who provides inspiration and direction can lead to a period of floundering and insecurity. Another common reaction is overidentification (to the point of apparent loss of identity) with youth-culture heroes or clique leaders. The individual often feels isolated, empty, anxious, or indecisive. Under pressure to make important life decisions, the adolescent feels unable to do so, even resistant.

The basic strength of this stage is *fidelity*. At the threshold of adulthood, the individual faces a need for commitment to a career and a lasting set of values. "Fidelity is the ability to sustain loyalties freely pledged in spite of the inevitable contradictions of value systems" (Erikson, 1964, p. 125). Fidelity is the cornerstone of identity; it requires the validation of acceptable social ideologies and the support of peers who have made similar choices.

During this stage we incorporate our culture's ethical values and belief systems. At the same time, the culture itself is renewed by the affirmation of each generation; it is revitalized as adolescents selectively offer their loyalties and energies, supporting some traditions and changing others. Those who cannot pledge their loyalties either remain deviant or commit themselves to revolutionary goals and values.

6. Intimacy Versus Isolation.   This stage, **intimacy versus isolation,** generally occurs in young adulthood. It is a time for achieving a sense of independence from parents and school, establishing friendships and intimate relationships, and developing a sense of adult responsibility.

Only after we have established a relatively firm sense of identity are we capable of developing a close and meaningful relationship with another. Only then can we

> For most of those in the twenties, a fantastic mystery story waits to be written over the next two decades. It races with excitement and jeopardy . . . and leads us down secret passageways in search of our missing personality parts. (Sheehy, 1977, p. 166)

personal reflection

THE LATER STAGES OF THE LIFE CYCLE

Rent a videotape of the Ingmar Bergman classic motion picture *Wild Strawberries* (Wilmette, IL: Janus Films, 1957). Give your own analysis of Dr. Borg's dream, and look at the events in the film from the perspective of the stages of the life cycle, especially the last three life stages—intimacy/isolation, generativity/stagnation, and integrity/despair.

Next, read Erikson's analysis, which is published as a chapter in *Vital Involvement in Old Age* (Erikson, Erikson, & Kivnick, 1986). This is a unique chance to compare your own analysis of a case study with that of a gifted clinician. You are using the same data, as presented in the film. (For many years, Erikson assigned this exercise to his own students in his Harvard course the Human Life Cycle.)

think of committing ourselves to partnership, affiliation, and intimacy with another person. The critical commitment that generally occurs at this stage is based on true mutuality with a love partner. This level of intimacy is significantly different from earlier sexual exploration and intense search for sexual identity.

Without a sense of intimacy and commitment, we may become isolated, unable to sustain nourishing personal relationships. If our sense of identity is weak and threatened by intimacy, we may turn away from or even attack whatever encroaches.

The virtue developed in this stage is *love*. Erikson (1964) argues that this is the greatest virtue. "Love, then, is mutuality of devotion forever subduing the antagonism inherent in divided functions" (Erikson, 1964, p. 129). He points out that it takes many forms. Early in life, it is the infant's love for its mother, the child's love for parents, and adolescent infatuation. When real intimacy develops between adults, love includes a shared identity and the validation of each partner in the other. This virtue can manifest itself in a romantic, sexual relationship, but also in deep ties developed in joint service to ideals, home, or country. It includes true mutuality and intimacy.

7. Generativity Versus Stagnation. This stage, **generativity versus stagnation,** generally spans most of our adult years. Intimate commitment to others widens to a more general concern for guiding and supporting the next generation. Generativity includes concern for our children and for the ideas and products we have created. It includes productivity and creativity in work and in our personal lives.

We are teaching as well as learning beings. Creation is important, as is ensuring the ongoing health and maintenance of our creations, ideals, and principles. Unless the sphere of our care and productivity widens, we fall prey to a sense of boredom and stagnation.

> The mere fact of having and wanting children does not achieve generativity. (Erikson, 1963, p. 267)

Erikson (1982) writes that social institutions tend to reinforce the function of generativity. They provide a continuity of knowledge and structure from one generation to another. Those with a healthy sense of generativity actively participate in these institutions, seeking to maintain and enhance future generations.

The strength developed at this stage is *care*. "Care is the widening concern for what has been generated by love, necessity, or accident; it overcomes the ambivalence adhering to irreversible obligation" (Erikson, 1964, p. 131). The nurturing of children is at the core of this virtue. It includes the care not only of offspring but also of the children of our minds and hearts—our ideas, ideals, and creations. Our species is unique in that we care for and education our young over a remarkably long period.

As adults, we need to be needed, or else we suffer from narcissism and self-absorption. In terms of human psychosocial evolution, we are essentially a teaching species. We must teach to fulfill our identity and to keep alive our skills and knowledge.

personal reflection

EXAMPLES OF ERIKSON'S STAGES

Think of three people who you believe are in different Eriksonian stages. You may wish to include a parent, yourself, and someone much younger. Does each person seem to fit his or her designated stage? What central issue do you see in the life of each? What major strengths? Major weaknesses? Can you see how the current life of each person relates to the past? How has each evolved from past strengths and past issues?

In what ways does framing the concerns, strengths, and critical issues for the three people help you understand these individuals, their differences, and possible difficulties in communication?

8. Integrity Versus Despair.   The final stage of life, the period of **integrity versus despair,** comes with old age. It is a time of dealing with what Erikson has called *ultimate concerns.* The sense of *ego integrity,* which includes our acceptance of a unique life cycle with its own history of triumphs and failures, provides a sense of order and meaning in our personal lives and in the world around us. With a sense of ego integrity comes an awareness of the value of many other lifestyles, including those that differ widely from our own. Integrity brings with it a perspective of wholeness—an ability to see our lives as a unity and to view human problems in a comprehensive way. Ego integrity is the development of the capacity for "postnarcissistic love" (Sheehy, 1995).

If we have not gained a measure of self-acceptance, we are likely to plunge into despair over the feeling that time is short—too short to start over. Those who end up in despair may become bitter over what might have been, constantly lamenting "if only. . . ." Despair may manifest itself in fear of death or may result in contempt and rejection of other values, institutions, and lifestyles.

Erikson (1982) noted the changing role of old age. When *Childhood and Society* was first published, in 1950, the cultural view of old age was different from what it is today. Then, the predominant model was that of the *elders,* those few who lived to a relatively decrepit old age but embodied the values of dignity, wisdom, and integrity. Today, as life expectancy increases, we have an ever-growing population of healthy and active elderly. Our model of old age will evolve as the parameters of aging continue to change. One of Erikson's most significant contributions has been to help develop a new theory of aging (Weiland, 1994). He has enriched our understanding of ongoing psychosocial development in later life. Erikson has outlined the central themes in old age, including dynamic balance of opposites, vital involvement, process in time, and integrity with despair (Kivnick, 1998).

The strength of *wisdom* develops out of encounters with both integrity and despair as the individual is confronted with ultimate concerns. "Wisdom, then, is detached concern with life itself, in the face of death itself" (Erikson, 1964, p. 133). Wisdom maintains the integrity of the individual's accumulated knowledge and experience. Those who have developed wisdom are models of wholeness and completeness. They are inspirational examples to younger generations who have adopted similar values and lifestyles. This sense of wholeness and meaning can also alleviate the feelings of helplessness and dependence that mark old age.

Table 6.2 (p. 185) summarizes the various dimensions of Erikson's eight stages. Each stage is associated with a particular crisis, social environment, strength, and various other dimensions.

TABLE 6.2 Eight Stages of Human Development

STAGES	PSYCHOSEXUAL STAGES AND MODES	PSYCHOSOCIAL CRISES	RADIUS OF SIGNIFICANT RELATIONS	BASIC STRENGTHS	CORE PATHOLOGY BASICS ANTIPATHIES	RELATED PRINCIPLES OF SOCIAL ORDER	BINDING RITUALIZATIONS	RITUALISM
I Infancy	Oral-Respiratory, Sensory-Kinesthetic (Incorporative Modes)	Basic Trust vs. Basic Mistrust	Maternal Person	Hope	Withdrawal	Cosmic Order	Numinous	Idolism
II Early Childhood	Anal-Urethral, Muscular (Retentive-Eliminative Modes)	Autonomy vs. Shame, Doubt	Parental Persons	Will	Compulsion	"Law and Order"	Judicious	Legalism
III Play Age	Locomotor (Intrusive, Inclusive Modes)	Initiative vs. Guilt	Basic Family	Purpose	Inhibition	Ideal Prototypes	Dramatic	Moralism
IV School Age	"Latency"	Industry vs. Inferiority	"Neighborhood," School	Competence	Inertia	Technological Order	Formal (Technical)	Formalism
V Adolescence	Puberty	Identity vs. Identity Confusion	Peer Group and Outgroups; Models of Leadership	Fidelity	Repudiation	Ideological Worldview	Ideological	Totalism
VI Young Adulthood	Genitality	Intimacy vs. Isolation	Partners in Friendship, Sex, Competition, Cooperation	Love	Exclusivity	Patterns of Cooperation and Competition	Affiliative	Elitism
VII Adulthood	(Procreativity)	Generativity vs. Stagnation	Divided Labor and Shared Household	Care	Rejectivity	Currents of Education and Tradition	Generational	Authoritism
VIII Old Age	(Generalization of Sensual Modes)	Integrity vs. Despair	"Mankind," "My Kind"	Wisdom	Disdain	Wisdom	Philosophical	Dogmatism

Source: From Erikson, 1982, pp. 32–33.

[A man] may equally absorb the "milk of wisdom" where he once desired more tangible fluids from more sensuous containers. (Erikson, 1963, p. 62)

Modes of Relating to the Environment.   Whereas Freud based his description of the stages of human development on specific organ-related experiences, Erikson's stages are based on more general styles of relating to and coping with the environment. Although, according to Erikson, these styles of behavior are often initially developed through a particular organ, they refer to broad patterns of activity. For instance, the mode learned in the first stage, basic trust versus basic mistrust, is *to get*— that is, the ability to receive and to accept what is given. (This stage corresponds to Freud's oral stage.) At this time, the mouth is the primary organ of interchange between the infant and the environment. However, an adult who is fixated on *getting* may exhibit forms of *dependency* unrelated to orality.

In the second stage, autonomy versus shame and doubt, the modes are *to let go* and *to hold on*. As with Freud's anal stage, the modes fundamentally relate to retention and elimination of feces; however, the child also alternates between possessing and rejecting parents, favorite toys, and so on.

The mode of the third stage, initiative versus guilt, Erikson calls *to make*. In one sense, the child is "on the make," focused on the conquest of the environment. Play is important, from making mud pies to imitating the complex sports and games of older children.

The fourth stage, industry versus inferiority, includes the modes *to do well* and *to work*. No single organ system associates with this stage; rather, productive work and accomplishment are central.

Erikson does not discuss in detail the modes involved in the remaining stages. These later stages, not as closely related to Freud's developmental stages, seem less rooted in a particular activity or organ mode.

Identity

Erikson developed the concept of identity in greater detail than the other concepts he incorporated in the eight stages. He first coined the phrase ***identity crisis*** to describe the mental state of many of the soldiers he treated at Mt. Zion Veterans Rehabilitation Clinic in San Francisco in the 1940s. These men were easily upset by any sudden or intense stimulus. Their egos seemed to have lost any shock-absorbing capacity. Their sensory systems were in a constant "startled" state, thrown off by external stimuli, as well as by a variety of bodily sensations, including hot flashes, heart palpitations, intense headaches, and insomnia. "Above all, the men felt that they 'did not know who they were': There was a distinct loss of ego identity. The sameness and continuity and the belief in one's social role were gone" (Erikson, 1968, p. 67).

Approaches to Identity.   The term *identity* brings together the theories of depth psychology with those of cognitive psychology and ego psychology (Erikson, 1993). Early Freudian theory tended to ignore the important role of the ego as, in Erikson's terms, "a selective, integrating, coherent and persistent agency central to personality function" (Erikson, 1964, p. 137). The concept of identity also provides a meeting place for psychology, sociology, and history. Because of its complexity, Erikson has wisely avoided giving the term *identity* a single definition:

> I can attempt to make the subject matter of identity more explicit only by approaching it from a variety of angles. . . . At one time, then, it will appear to refer to a conscious *sense*

of individual identity; at another, to an unconscious striving for a *continuity of personal character;* at a third, as a criterion for the silent doings of *ego synthesis;* and, finally, as a maintenance of an *inner solidarity* with a group's ideals and identity. (1980a, p. 109)

Erikson spells out these aspects of identity as follows (adapted from Evans, 1969, pp. 218–219):

1. *Individuality*—a conscious sense of one's uniqueness and existence as a separate, distinct entity.
2. *Sameness and continuity*—a sense of inner sameness, a continuity between what one has been in the past and what one promises to be in the future, a feeling that one's life has consistency and meaningful direction.
3. *Wholeness and synthesis*—a sense of inner harmony and wholeness, a synthesis of the self-images and identifications of childhood into a meaningful whole that produces a sense of harmony.
4. *Social solidarity*—a sense of inner solidarity with the ideals and values of society or a subgroup within it, a feeling that one's identity is meaningful to significant others and corresponds to their expectations and perceptions.

Further, in the following excerpt, Erikson describes identity in the transition from childhood to adulthood:

Like a trapeze artist, the young person in the middle of vigorous motion must let go of his safe hold on childhood and reach out for a firm grasp on adulthood, depending for a breathless interval on a relatedness between the past and the future, and on the reliability of those he must let go of, and those who will "receive" him. Whatever combination of drives and defenses, of sublimations and capacities has emerged from the young individual's childhood must now make sense in view of his concrete opportunities in work and love . . . [and] he must detect some meaningful resemblance between what he has come to see in himself and what his sharpened awareness tells him others judge and expect him to be. (Erikson, 1964, p. 90)

The concept of identity has become particularly popular because it is generally recognized as the major life crisis in the United States today—and perhaps in all of modern society. Our cultural emphasis on extended education, as well as the complexity of most contemporary vocations, makes the development of a sense of identity especially difficult in our society. The struggle to gain a healthy, clear sense of identity frequently continues beyond adolescence, erupting later in midlife crises.

Years ago, most children took on their parents' roles. Children began to learn adult skills, attitudes, and functions early in life; their parents' vocations were generally integrated into family life. Today, given our changing values and social roles, not only are children unlikely to assume their parents' roles, but they may have no clear adult role models. The adolescent's childhood identifications and experiences are clearly inadequate for the task of anticipating a career and making a major vocational commitment.

Erikson found that the development of a sense of identity frequently follows a "psychosocial moratorium," a period of time-out in which the individual may be occupied with study, travel, or a clearly temporary occupation. This provides time to reflect, to develop a new sense of direction, new values, new purpose. The moratorium may last for months or even years.

personal reflection

IDENTITY

To get an idea of how your identity develops, try this exercise.

1. Relax and think of a time when you felt a strong sense of identity. Describe that time. What were the components of that identity (for example, captain of the high school football team, oldest daughter in a large family, good student)?
2. List ten words that describe you then—your sense of self, crucial life issues, and so on.
3. How would you describe your present identity? Make a second list.
4. Have you experienced significant changes? What continuity do you notice in your sense of self over this period of time? What changes?
5. Was the transition from one sense of identity to another smooth and gradual or abrupt?
6. Do you believe that your present identity will remain relatively stable, or do you foresee major changes? If you foresee major changes, why might these occur?

Identity Development.   Erikson (1980a, pp. 120–130) emphasized that the development of a sense of identity has both psychological and social aspects:

1. The individual's development of a sense of personal sameness and continuity is based, in part, on a belief in the sameness and continuity of a worldview shared with significant others.
2. Although many aspects of the search for a sense of identity are conscious, unconscious motivation may also play a major role. At this stage, feelings of acute vulnerability may alternate with high expectations of success.
3. A sense of identity cannot develop without certain physical, mental, and social preconditions (outlined in Erikson's developmental stages). Also, achievement of a sense of identity must not be unduly delayed, because future stages of development depend on it. Psychological factors may prolong the crisis as the individual seeks to match unique gifts to existing social possibilities. Social factors and historical change may also postpone adult commitment.
4. The growth of a sense of identity depends on the past, present, and future. First, the individual must have acquired a clear sense of identification in childhood. Second, the adult's choice of vocational identification must be realistic in light of available opportunities. Finally, the adult must retain a sense of assurance that his or her chosen roles will be viable in the future, in spite of inevitable changes, both in the individual and in the outside world.

Erikson has pointed out that problems of identity are not new, though they may be more widespread today than ever before. Many creative individuals have wrestled with the question of identity as they carved out new careers and social roles for themselves. Some especially imaginative people were responsible for major vocational innovations, thus offering new role models for others. Freud, for example, began his career as a conventional doctor and neurologist. Only in midcareer did he devise a new role for himself (and for many others) by becoming the first psychoanalyst.

Table 6.3 (p. 189) illustrates the role of earlier life cycle stages as developmental precursors to a healthy sense of identity (the vertical dimension). It shows, also, how each of the stages of development is engaged during the period of identity crisis (the horizontal dimension).

TABLE 6.3 Identity and the Eight Stages of Development

	1	2	3	4	5	6	7	8
VIII Old Age								INTEGRITY vs. DESPAIR, DISGUST
VII Adulthood							GENERATIVITY vs. STAGNATION	
VI Young Adulthood						INTIMACY vs. ISOLATION		
V Adolescence	Temporal Perspective vs. Time Confusion	Self-Certainty vs. Self-Consciousess	Role Experimentation vs. Role Fixation	Apprenticeship vs. Work-Paralysis	IDENTITY vs. IDENTITY CONFUSION	Sexual Polarization vs. Bisexual Confusion	Leadership and Fellowship vs. Authority Confusion	Ideological Commitment vs. Confusion of Values
IV School Age				INDUSTRY vs. INFERIORITY	Task Identification vs. Sense of Futility			
III Play Age			INITIATIVE vs. GUILT		Anticipation of Roles vs. Role Inhibition			
II Early Childhood		AUTONOMY vs. SHAME, DOUBT			Will to Be Oneself vs. Self-Doubt			
I Infancy	BASIC TRUST vs. BASIC MISTRUST				Mutual Recognition vs. Autistic Isolation			

Source: Identity, Youth and Crisis (p. 94) by E. Erikson, 1968, New York: Norton. Copyright 1968 by Norton. Reprinted by permission.

Psychohistory

Erikson expanded psychoanalysis by studying major historical personalities. By analyzing their psychological growth and development, he came to understand the psychological impact they had on their generation.

Psychobiography.   Erikson made a major contribution to historical research by applying the methods used in psychoanalytic case histories to a reconstruction of the life of historical figures. He combined clinical insight with historical and social analysis in developing the new form of **psychobiography.** Erikson realized that in making the transition from case history to life history, the psychoanalyst must broaden his or her concerns and take into account the subject's activities in the context of the opportunities and limitations of the outside world. This appreciation of the interaction of psychological and social currents in turn affected Erikson's theoretical work. In addition to his books on Martin Luther and Mohandas Gandhi, Erikson's psychobiographies included studies of Maxim Gorky, Adolf Hitler, George Bernard Shaw, Sigmund Freud, Thomas Jefferson, and Woodrow Wilson.

One major difference exists between psychological biographies and case histories. In a case history, the therapist usually tries to determine why the patient has developed mental or emotional problems. In a life history, the investigator tries to understand the subject's creative contributions, often made in spite of conflicts, complexes, and crises.

And then, there are the great adults who are adult and are called great precisely because their sense of identity vastly surpasses the roles foisted upon them, their vision opens up new realities, and the gift of communication revitalizes actuality. (Erikson, 1987, p. 335)

The Study of "Great Individuals."   Erikson brought to his psychobiographical work the insights of a trained psychoanalyst to the careful study of critical periods in the lives of influential individuals. He was particularly interested in men and women whose identity conflicts mirrored the conflicts of their era and whose greatness lay in their finding a personal solution to their own identity crisis, a solution that became a model for others. Often these individuals had deep personal struggles. The crisis of the age seemed intensified in each of them; each brought a special urgency and focus to the solution of the crisis.

In his first major psychobiography, Erikson laid out his fundamental approach to the study of great men and women. To Erikson, Luther should be admired most for his struggle "to lift his individual patienthood to the level of a universal one and to try to solve for all what he could not solve for himself alone" (Erikson, 1958, p. 67).

In studying Gandhi, Erikson returned, in a sense, to his early reverence for Freud. He believed that Gandhi and Freud both sought to liberate others, that both men created new social forms, new roles and identities, and both were deeply motivated by their love of truth.

Although all were creative, energetic, and powerful people, they were not without fear, anxiety, and unhappiness. Their lives were often dominated by a sense, stemming from childhood, that they needed to *settle* or *live down* something. They were generally tied to their fathers in a way that precluded overt rebellion; they also learned a great deal from and felt needed and chosen by their fathers. These individuals frequently had early, highly developed consciences and paid early attention to ultimate values, sometimes convinced they carried special responsibility for part of humankind. These productive men and women might have simply become misfits and cranks except for their ability, energy, concentration, and spiritual devotion.

DYNAMICS

Positive Growth

The focus on positive characteristics developed at each stage distinguishes Erikson's schema from Freud's and from those of many other personality theorists. Erikson views basic strengths, or virtues, as more than psychological defenses against mental illness or negativity and more than simply as attitudes of nobility or morality. These virtues are *inherent* strengths and are characterized by a sense of potency and positive development. As mentioned earlier in the chapter, *hope* is the virtue of the first stage, trust versus mistrust. *Will* is the strength that arises from the crisis of autonomy versus shame and doubt. *Purpose* is rooted in the initiative versus guilt stage. *Competence* is the strength resulting from the stage of industry versus inferiority. *Fidelity* comes from identity versus identity confusion. *Love* is the virtue that develops from intimacy. *Care* originates in generativity. *Wisdom* is derived from the crisis of integrity versus despair.

Obstacles to Growth

The individual can successfully resolve the crisis at each stage, or leave the crisis unresolved in some ways. Erikson points out that successful resolution is always a dynamic balance of some sort. A clear example of an unsuccessful resolution is the formation of a sense of negative identity.

   Ratio and Balance.   Each stage features a dynamic ratio between two poles. Erikson's terms for these opposite poles tend to be misleading because, inevitably, one seems extremely desirable and the other extremely undesirable. However, both poles at each stage are *undesirable* because they tend to be rigid and unrealistic. (See Figure 6.1.)

   Erikson has been frequently misunderstood as concerned with only the positive pole for each stage. He has pointed out that "people often take away mistrust and doubt and shame and all of these not so nice, 'negative' things and try to make an Eriksonian achievement scale out of it all, according to which in the first stage trust is 'achieved'" (Erikson in Evans, 1969, p. 15). However, an individual who develops an unbalanced sense of trust can become a "Pollyanna" figure, as out of touch with reality as the individual paralyzed with extreme mistrust. We must be able to discriminate between situations in which we can trust and those in which some mistrust, or anticipation of danger or discomfort, is appropriate. Healthy ratios vary widely from relative trust to relative suspicion, but in every case elements of both trust and mistrust are present.

   Similarly, unbalanced autonomy can become unreasonable stubbornness. Unbalanced initiative is a self-centered preoccupation with one's own goals and concerns. A sense of industry without a sense of limitation leads to an inflated appreciation of one's abilities. An overdeveloped sense of identity is rigid and inflexible and is likely to clash with external reality, and so on.

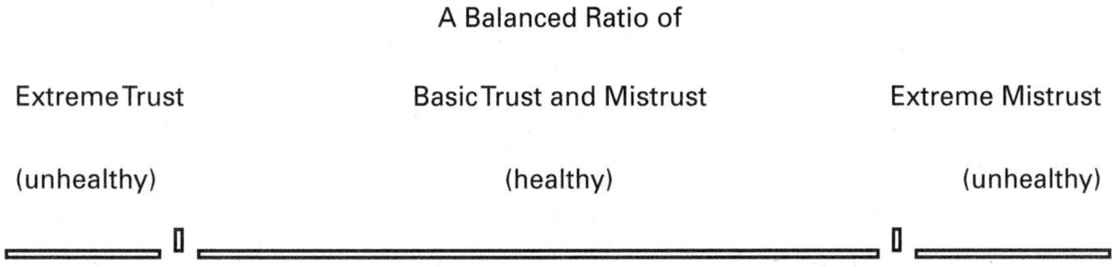

A Balanced Ratio of

Extreme Trust	Basic Trust and Mistrust	Extreme Mistrust
(unhealthy)	(healthy)	(unhealthy)

FIGURE 6.1 Balanced Ratio in Erikson's Stages

Negative Identity.   Our sense of identity always comprises positive and negative elements. These elements include what we want to become and others we do not want to be or know we should not be. Under extremely negative social conditions, it may be impossible for the majority of healthy young men and women to commit to positive social values. The Nazi era in Germany is an example.

Lack of a healthy sense of identity may be expressed in hostility toward available social goals and values. This hostility can include any role aspect: one's sexuality, nationality, class, or family background. Children of immigrant families may display contempt for their parents' backgrounds, and descendants of established families may reject everything American and overestimate everything foreign.

Many conflicted adolescents would rather be someone bad than a nobody. Thus the choice of a negative identity is based on roles presented as undesirable or dangerous. If the adolescent feels unable to make a commitment to more positive roles, the negative ones become the most real. These may include the drug dealer, prostitute, or any model that represents failure in the eyes of society.

Negative identity may also include the behavior and attitudes the individual has been punished or made to feel guilty for. Or, there may be a role model for a negative identity—for example, an uncle or a friend who is labeled an alcoholic or a failure in some way.

STRUCTURE

Body

Experience is anchored in the ground-plan of the body. (Erikson, 1963, p. 108)

The role of the bodily organs is especially important in Erikson's early stages. Later in life, the development of physical as well as intellectual skills helps determine whether the individual will achieve a sense of competence and an ability to choose demanding roles in a complex society. For example, healthy children derive a sense of competence as their bodies become larger, stronger, faster, and more capable of learning complex skills.

As a psychosocial theorist, Erikson is aware of the constant interaction of body, psychological processes, and social forces. He acknowledges the classical Freudian view of fundamental biological drives but insists that these drives are also socially modifiable.

Social Relationships

A stage has a new configuration of past and future, a new combination of drive and defense, a new set of capacities fit for a new setting of tasks and opportunities, a new and wider radius of significant encounters. (Erikson, 1964, p. 166)

Erikson's basic epigenetic principle states, "Personality . . . can be said to develop according to steps predetermined in the human organism's readiness to be driven toward, to be aware of, and to interact with a widening radius of significant individuals and institutions" (1968, pp. 92–93).

Social relationships are central in virtually every stage of development. Interaction with one's parents, family, and peers is crucial in the first five stages. The emergence of a sense of identity is strongly affected by the presence of affirming peers. The stage of intimacy brings opportunities for deeper social relationships. Another qualitative change occurs during the stage of generativity, when individuals learn to care for and nurture those who are younger, weaker, and less knowledgeable.

Will

Erikson details the development of will in his discussion of autonomy versus shame and doubt. The development of a healthy and balanced will (and goodwill) continues throughout life.

Traditional psychoanalysis deals primarily with the examination of an individual's conception of reality, focusing on thoughts, emotions, and essentially private behavior. Erikson emphasizes, in addition, the importance of will and action in the world. One of the goals of psychoanalysis is to restore "a productive interplay between psychological reality and historical actuality" (1964, p. 201)—that is, to integrate inner, subjective experiences with external actions and events. According to Erikson, reality refers to "the world of phenomenal experience, perceived with a minimum of distortion." Although distortion and misunderstanding are inevitable, Erikson stresses the need for an understanding of actuality, "the world of participation, shared with other participants" (1964, p. 165).

Reassessing Freud's classic case study of Dora, Erikson points out that although Freud made a brilliant analysis of Dora's personality dynamics and distortions, he failed to consider her powerlessness as a young girl in a middle-class Viennese family. Dora initially saw Freud for three months, when she was 19 years old. She had been propositioned at the age of 16 by Mr. K, a friend of the family. Her father had asked Freud to "bring her to reason." It turned out that Dora's father was having an affair with Mr. K's wife, and he seemed willing to allow Mr. K's advances to his daughter. To further complicate matters, everyone seemed to make Dora a confidante—her father and mother, Mr. K., and Mrs. K.

Dora tried to confront her parents with the situation. Freud saw this as acting out, but Erikson disagreed. To him, Dora was actively searching for honesty and fidelity, qualities that the adult role models in her life sorely lacked.

Successful action requires both social and historical possibilities and will. To see accurately does not guarantee that one can act effectively.

Emotions

As a psychoanalyst, Erikson emphasizes the emotional component of psychological processes. His awareness of the role emotions play is implicit throughout his theories. As a theorist, he focused on incorporating new cognitive, historical, and social findings into a psychoanalytic framework. However, Erikson does not discuss explicitly the emotions as a distinct aspect of psychological processes.

Intellect

Like emotion, the intellect is seen as an essential element in psychological processes. Erikson does not pay specific attention to the role of intellectual capacities. He does point out, however, that the development of intellectual skills is critical in the formation of a sense of competence, if the individual is to master the tasks of a technological society, form a sense of identity, and choose an acceptable vocation and social roles.

Self

For Erikson, a sense of identity includes both the development of ego identity and the flowering of a sense of self:

> The ego, if understood as a central and partially unconscious organizing agency, must at any given stage of life deal with a changing Self. . . . What could consequently be called the *self-identity* emerges from experiences in which temporarily confused selves are successfully reintegrated in an ensemble of roles which also secure social recognition. Identity formation, thus, can be said to have a self-aspect and an ego aspect. (1968, p. 211)

Self-identity results from the integration of our past and present social roles and self-images.

Therapist

Erikson has pointed out that a competent therapist has a strong sense of the patient's potential for growth and development. The therapist's job is to foster that growth rather than impose his or her own future expectations or past experience on the patient. This focus is implicit in the requirement that the practitioner undergo training analysis and in the stress on the role of transference and countertransference in psychoanalysis. *Transference* refers to the positive or negative feelings that patients develop for their therapists. These feelings are often strong, irrational, and rooted in childhood relationships with parents. Conscious understanding of the dynamics of transference can be an extremely valuable part of psychotherapy. *Countertransference* refers to the positive or negative feelings that therapists frequently develop for their patients. Jung had said that every patient who came to him took his life in his own hands. In response, Erikson commented, "This is true, but one must add that he came to *me*, and not to somebody else, and after that he will never be the same—and neither will I" (Erikson in Evans, 1969, p. 103).

EVALUATION

Erikson has been criticized for his vagueness. He is an artist with words rather than a logician. His beautiful and brilliant formulations can appear to dissolve into conceptual sketches rather than develop into linear, logical analysis. For example, Erikson's discussion of identity consists of a diverse collection of ideas that are often more confusing than clarifying. As one reviewer has commented,

> Reading Erikson is like walking in a dense and beautiful forest with a thousand paths leading through it. The very richness of the forest can be confusing. There is so much there. . . . Erikson has never watered down or simplified his writing. Thank God! They [his books] are written with a kind of magnificent obscurity. . . . His work needs to be read and reread; his books need to be outlined and meditated on. They have a lasting quality. (Gross, 1987, p. 3)

On the other hand, Hamachek pointed out that "most of Erikson's conclusions are based on highly personal and subjective interpretations that lack the hard empirical data to support intuitions about their correctness" (1988, p. 36). Hamachek (1988, 1990) attempted to connect each of Erikson's stages to observable behaviors, as a first step in developing the empirical study of Erikson's theory.

Other critics (for example, Appadurai, 1978; Roazen, 1976) raised questions about the universality of Erikson's theories. Can his epigenetic model be applied as successfully to non-Western cultures both past and present? For example, viewing adolescence as a distinct developmental stage is a relatively new phenomenon. Also, issues like autonomy, initiative, and identity may not be central in cultures such as those in India or in tribal societies.

Other questions have been raised about the applicability of Erikson's developmental model even in the West. For example, Erikson proposes that generativity begins with parenthood. That this is not necessarily true is proven by teenage pregnancy, which is a common occurrence in many cultures. Young mothers and fathers, who are generally in the identity stage, may even thrive on the responsibilities of parenthood. Also, Erikson's work has been criticized as being focused primarily on the male, and relatively unclear about the particular issues of female maturation (Gilligan, 1982).

Erikson was limited by psychoanalysis. His tools are those of a clinician, intended for the treatment of unwell patients. Application of these tools to the exploration of the healthy personality is not always satisfactory. This drawback is evident in Erikson's studies of great individuals. In his analysis of Gandhi, for example, Erikson skillfully applies the tools and insights of the psychoanalyst. He does not, however, address seriously the role of Gandhi's spiritual ideals and spiritual discipline. The dynamics of Gandhi's life and thought are seen largely in terms of dysfunction rather than of psychological and spiritual transformation. Gandhi's inner state, refined by years of spiritual disciplines such as fasting and silence, may have been qualitatively different from that of the average patient in therapy. Also, Erikson has been criticized for underestimating the role of Indian culture and the social context of many of the key events in Gandhi's life (Appadurai, 1978).

Erikson's psychoanalytic tools were not always adequate for the tasks he took on. By using these tools, he expanded psychoanalysis while at the same time revealing its limitations. In a sense, Erikson smuggled the concept of the human spirit into psychoanalytic theory. This is one of the secrets of his great appeal. He was also a groundbreaking social scientist, a model interdisciplinarian (Smelser, 1998).

Erikson provides a stimulating, relevant reformulation of psychoanalysis. He successfully brought Freud's compelling system of thought into a new era. Erikson's concern for social and cultural determinants of behavior and his integration of psychology, sociology, and anthropology with the insights of psychoanalysis predict the future of the psychology of personality.

RECENT DEVELOPMENTS: ERIKSON'S INFLUENCE

Erikson's ideas continue to stimulate research and theory today. There are several excellent biographies of Erikson (Coles, 1970; Friedman, 1999) and a first-rate collection of his selected writings (Coles, 2000). Erikson's work has been applied cross-culturally (Arcaya, 1999) and historically (Lifton, 1998). His concept of generativity has been used in a wide variety of research including the study of women in midlife (Peterson, 1998), study of gay men at midlife (Cohler, et al., 1998), and in psychobiographies of the great modern dancer Martha Graham (Lee, 1998) and the noted architect Frank Lloyd Wright (de St. Aubin, 1998).

The Theory Firsthand

EXCERPT FROM *CHILDHOOD AND SOCIETY*

In this passage, Erikson, revealing his keen psychoanalytic skills, provides a real-life example of a young boy in a crisis of role identification.

During the last war a neighbor of mine, a boy of five, underwent a change of personality from a "mother's boy" to a violent, stubborn, and disobedient child. The most disquieting symptom was an urge to set fires.

The boy's parents had separated just before the outbreak of war. The mother and the boy had moved in with some women cousins, and when war began the father had joined the air force. The women cousins frequently expressed their disrespect for the father, and cultivated babyish traits in the boy. Thus, to be a mother's boy threatened to be a stronger identity element than to be a father's son.

The father, however, did well in war; in fact, he became a hero. On the occasion of his first furlough the little boy had the experience of seeing the man he had been warned not to emulate become the much-admired center of the neighborhood's attention. The mother announced that she would drop her divorce plans. The father went back to war and was soon lost over Germany.

After the father's departure and death the affectionate and dependent boy developed more and more disquieting symptoms of destructiveness and defiance, culminating in fire setting. He gave the key to the change himself when, protesting against his mother's whipping, he pointed to a pile of wood he had set afire and exclaimed (in more childish words), "If this were a German city, you would have liked me for it." He thus indicated that in setting fires he fantasied being a bombardier like the father, who had told of his exploits.

We can only guess at the nature of the boy's turmoil. But I believe that we see here the identification of a son with his father, resulting from a suddenly increased conflict at the very close of the Oedipus age. The father, at first successfully replaced by the "good" little boy, suddenly becomes both a newly vitalized ideal and a concrete threat, a competitor for the mother's love. He thus devaluates radically the boy's feminine identifications. In order to save himself from both sexual and social disorientation, the boy must, in the shortest possible time, regroup his identifications; but then the great competitor is killed by the enemy—a fact which increases the guilt for the competitive feeling itself and compromises the boy's new masculine initiative which becomes maladaptive.

A child has quite a number of opportunities to identify himself, more or less experimentally, with habits, traits, occupations, and ideas of real or fictitious people of either sex. Certain crises force him to make radical selections. However, the historical era in which he lives offers only a limited number of socially meaningful models for workable combinations of identification fragments. Their usefulness depends on the way in which they simultaneously meet the requirements of the organism's maturational stage and the ego's habits of synthesis.

To my little neighbor the role of the bombardier may have suggested a possible synthesis of the various elements that comprise a budding identity: his temperament (vigorous); his maturational stage (phallic-urethral-locomotor); his social stage (Oedipal) and his social situation; his capacities (muscular, mechanical); his father's temperament (a great soldier rather than a successful civilian); and a current historical prototype (aggressive hero). Where such synthesis succeeds, a most surprising coagulation of constitutional, temperamental, and learned reactions may produce exuberance of growth and unexpected accomplishment. Where it fails, it must lead to severe conflict, often expressed in unexpected naughtiness or delinquency. For should a child feel that the environment tries to deprive him too radically of all the forms of expression which permit him to develop and to integrate the next step in his identity, he will defend it with the astonishing strength encountered in animals who are suddenly forced to defend their lives. And indeed, in the social jungle of human existence, there is no feeling of being alive without a sense of ego identity. Deprivation of identity can lead to murder.

I would not have dared to speculate on the little bombardier's conflicts had I not seen evidence for a solution in line with our interpretation. When the worst of this boy's dangerous initiative had subsided, he was observed swooping down a hill on a bicycle, endangering, scaring, and yet deftly avoiding other children. They shrieked, laughed, and in a way admired him for it. In watching him, and hearing the strange noises he made, I could not help thinking that he again imagined himself to be an airplane on a bombing mission. But at the same time he gained in playful mastery over his locomotion; he exercised circumspection in his attack, and he became an admired virtuoso on a bicycle....

Our little son of a bombardier illustrates a general point. Psychosocial identity develops out of a gradual integration of all identifications. But here, if anywhere, the whole has a different quality from the sum of its parts. Under favorable circumstances children have the nucleus of a separate identity early in life; often they must defend it even against the necessity of overidentifying with one or both of their parents. These processes are difficult to study in patients, because the neurotic self has, by definition, fallen prey to overidentifications which isolate the small individual both from his budding identity and from his milieu. (Erikson, 1963, pp. 238–241)

CHAPTER HIGHLIGHTS

- Erikson's model of the human life cycle integrates human growth and development from birth to old age, in eight stages.
- Positive and negative outcomes may occur at each stage. Personality development continues throughout life.

- Each successive stage is predicated on the development of the previous one; the process occurs in a manner similar to that of the growth of an embryo.
- The human personality develops according to predetermined steps, or stages, in the growing person's readiness to be aware of, and interact with, a widening social radius. Each stage relates systematically to the others and must develop in the sequence given.
- A specific psychological crisis or developmental task characterizes each stage and must be resolved in order for the individual to continue to the next.
- The strengths and skills essential to each stage are developed and tested in a period of crisis. This process, in turn, allows for the development of new attitudes and skills. Following the successful resolution of each crisis, an increased sense of judgment, inner unity, and capacity to function effectively is available to the individual.
- Erikson's model is distinguished by his focus on the positive attributes, or virtues, acquired at each stage. Characterized by a sense of positive development and potency, these virtues are considered inherent strengths.
- Each stage holds a dynamic ratio between two poles (for example, trust versus mistrust). Both poles are extremes, and the healthy middle ground lies in the space between these two, where elements of each pole are dynamically present.
- The concept of identity brings together theories of cognitive and ego psychologies. Some aspects of identity include a sense of individuality, a sense of continuity and sameness, a sense of synthesis and wholeness, and a sense of social solidarity.
- The development and flowering of a sense of self results in a sense of identity.
- Lack of a healthy sense of identity may result in hostility toward available values and social goals. A conflicted adolescent who feels unable to commit to a positive social role may choose a negative role instead.
- Psychobiography and psychohistory combine the methods of psychoanalysis and history in the study of individual and collective life.

KEY CONCEPTS

Autonomy versus shame and doubt The second stage of development, in which the child interacts with the world in new ways and a sense of autonomy develops with the sense of free choice. The virtue acquired at this stage is will, which develops into the basis for adult acknowledgment of a spirit of justice, manifest in the social institution of the law.

Basic trust versus basic mistrust The first stage of development, in which an infant's sense of trust in self and in the world develops from the quality of primary care. It results in the virtue or strength of hope, which lays the foundation for the development of faith.

Crisis in development The turning point, occurring at each stage of development, in which the skills and strengths of that stage are developed and tested.

Generativity versus stagnation The seventh stage of development, including concerns with creativity and productivity in work and in personal life, for children as well as for ideas, products, and principles. Care is the strength developed at this stage.

Identity A term that includes a sense of individuality, a sense of continuity and sameness, a sense of synthesis and wholeness, and a sense of social solidarity. The concept has both social and psychological aspects.

Identity crisis The loss of ego identity—a state in which the continuity, sameness, and belief in one's social role has diminished or disappeared.

Identity versus identity confusion The fifth stage of development, a time when the adolescent questions past role models and identifications. During this period of transition between childhood and adulthood, the question of "Who am I?" is primary. Fidelity is the basic strength of this stage, as the individual faces the need to commit to a set of values and a career, forming a cornerstone of his or her identity.

Industry versus inferiority The fourth stage of development, involving a shift from focus on play to a sense of work. The virtue of this stage is competence, based on the development of practical skills, general capacities, and a sense of workmanship.

Initiative versus guilt The third stage of development, in which the most basic activity is play. The virtue of this stage, purpose, is rooted in fantasy and play, which form the roots of drama, dance, and ritual in adult life.

Integrity versus despair The eighth stage of development, a time of dealing with ultimate concerns. Development of the ability to see one's life as a whole and an increased sense of perspective. Despair may result if one has not attained some sense of self-acceptance. Wisdom is the strength that develops out of encounters with both despair and integrity, in the light of ultimate concerns.

Intimacy versus isolation The sixth stage of development, in which a sense of adult responsibility develops, along with independence from parents and school. Intimate relationships with others are established. True mutuality with a love partner forms the basis for the critical commitment that generally occurs at this stage. Love is the virtue that is associated with this stage; it manifests itself in true intimacy and mutuality.

Psychobiography The study of a historical figure's life from the perspective of psychoanalysis. This approach differs from a case history, in which the therapist is looking for why the patient developed problems. The life history focuses on understanding how a person managed to make creative contributions, often in spite of complexes, conflicts, and crises.

Psychohistory A study that combines the methods of history and psychoanalysis to examine individual and collective life.

ANNOTATED BIBLIOGRAPHY

Coles, R. (2000). *The Erik Erikson reader*. New York: Norton.

Includes writings from Erikson's entire career and charts the influence of his thinking in the areas of child development, lifelong human development, leadership, and moral growth.

Erikson, E. (1963). *Childhood and society* (2d ed.). New York: Norton.

Erikson's first and most seminal book. It includes his most detailed description of the eight stages of human development, papers on his work with the Sioux and Yurok, and psychobiographies of Hitler and Gorky, which provide a look at the psychological implications of German and Russian culture.

Erikson, E. (1964). *Insight and responsibility*. New York: Norton.

A brilliant set of essays, including a psychobiographical look at Freud, an analysis of psychosocial strengths, psychological reality, and historical actuality, and a discussion of the Golden Rule today.

Erikson, E. (1969). *Gandhi's truth*. New York: Norton.

An epic psychobiography of Gandhi, which provides a model for looking at a great figure in history through psychological eyes. It also serves as a useful example of the limits of psychoanalysis, in its lack of focus on the spiritual and transpersonal aspects of Gandhi's life.

Erikson, E., Erikson, J., & Kivnick, H. (1986). *Vital involvement in old age*. New York: Norton.

A remarkable portrait of the experience of old age, based on interviews with octogenarians who have been studied for over 50 years. A review of the life cycle from the perspective of old age.

Web Sites

http://www.britannica.com/seo/e/erik-h-erikson/

A basic biography of Erik Erikson, with links to additional information.

http://elvers.stjoe.udayton.edu/history/people/Erikson.html

A short biography and detailed summary and discussion of Eriksonian theory.

REFERENCES

Appadurai, A. (1978). Understanding Gandhi. In P. Homans (Ed.), *Childhood and selfhood*. Cranbury, NJ: Associated University Presses.

Arcaya, J. (1999). Hispanic American boys and adolescent males. In A. Horne & M. Kiselica (Eds.), *Handbook of counseling boys and adolescent males*. Thousand Oaks, CA: Sage.

Cohler, B., Hostetler, A., & Boyer, A. (1998). Generativity, social context, and lived experience: Narratives of gay men in middle adulthood. In D. McAdams & E. de St. Aubin (Eds.) *Generativity and adult development*. Washington, DC: American Psychological Association.

Coles, R. (1970). *Erik Erikson: The growth of his work*. Boston: Little, Brown.

Coles, R. (2000). *The Erik Erikson reader*. New York: Norton.

de St. Aubin, E. (1998). Truth against the world: A psychobiological exploration of generativity in the life of Frank Lloyd Wright. In D. McAdams & E. de St. Aubin (Eds.), *Generativity and adult development*. Washington, DC: American Psychological Association.

Erikson, E. (1958). *Young man Luther*. New York: Norton.

Erikson, E. (1963). *Childhood and society* (2d ed.). New York: Norton.

Erikson, E. (1964). *Insight and responsibility*. New York: Norton.

Erikson, E. (1965). *The challenge of youth*. New York: Doubleday Anchor Books.

Erikson, E. (1968). *Identity, youth and crisis*. New York: Norton.

Erikson, E. (1969). *Gandhi's truth*. New York: Norton.

Erikson, E. (1980a). *Identity and the life cycle*. New York: Norton.

Erikson, E. (1982). *The life cycle completed*. New York: Norton.

Erikson, E. (1987). *A way of looking at things: Selected papers from 1930 to 1980*. New York: Norton.

Erikson, E. (1993). The problem of ego identity. In G. Pollock (Ed.), *Pivotal papers on identification*. Madison, CT: International Universities Press.

Erikson, E., & Erikson, J. (1997). *The life cycle completed.* (Extended version). New York: Norton.

Erikson, E., Erikson, J., & Kivnick, H. (1986). *Vital involvement in old age*. New York: Norton.

Evans, R. (1969). *Dialogue with Erik Erikson*. New York: Dutton.

Friedman, L. (1999). *Identity's architect*. New York: Scribner/Simon and Schuster.

Gilligan, C. (1982). *In a different voice*. Cambridge, MA: Harvard University Press.

Gross, F. (1987). *Introducing Erik Erikson: An invitation to his thinking*. Lanham, MD: University Press.

Hamachek, D. (1988). Evaluating self-concept and ego development within Erikson's psychosocial framework: A formulation. *Journal of Counseling and Development, 66,* 354–360.

Hamachek, D. (1990). Evaluating self-concept and ego development in Erikson's last three psychosocial stages. *Journal of Counseling and Development, 68,* 677–683.

Kivnick, H. (1998). Through the life cycle: Psychosocial thoughts on old age. In G. Pollock & S. Greenspan (Eds.), *The course of life,* Vol. 7. Madison, CT: International University Press.

Lee, S. (1998). Generativity and the life course of Martha Graham. In D. McAdams & E. de St. Aubin (Eds.), *Generativity and adult development*. Washington, DC: American Psychological Association.

Lifton, R. (1998). Entering history: Erik Erikson's new psychological landscape. In R. Wallerstein & L. Goldberger (Eds.), *Ideas and identities: The life work of Erik Erikson*. Madison, CT: International Universities Press.

Peterson, B. (1998). Case studies of midlife generativity: Analyzing motivation and realization. In D. McAdams & E. de St. Aubin (Eds.), *Generativity and adult development*. Washington, DC: American Psychological Association.

Roazen, P. (1976). *Erik Erikson: The power and limits of a vision*. New York: Free Press.

Sheehy, G. (1977). *Passages*. New York: Basic Books.

Sheehy, G. (1995). *New passages*. New York: Ballantine.

Smelser, N. (1998). Erik Erikson as social scientist. In R. Wallerstein & L. Goldberger (Eds.), *Ideas and identities: The life work of Erik Erikson*. Madison, CT: International Universities Press.

Weiland, S. (1994). Erik Erikson: Ages, stages, and stories. In D. Shenk & W. Achenbaum (Eds.), *Changing perceptions of aging and the aged*. New York: Springer.

william james
and the psychology
of consciousness

William James saw psychology as bounded by biology on one side and philosophy on the other; it addressed all areas of human experience. James helped introduce psychology to the United States, teaching the first course and establishing the first laboratory. He had already published a fully developed theory of consciousness before Breuer and Freud's (1895) first ideas were in print. After a period of relative obscurity, his many contributions to psychology have reemerged. His interest in inner experiences passed out of fashion as psychology became more involved in psychoanalysis and in the reductionistic orientation of behaviorism. Moreover, the increasing fixation on objective data left little room for James's brilliant and incisive speculations.

Since the 1960s, however, sustained research has explored the nature of consciousness. Researchers concerned with the implications of altered states of consciousness, paranormal phenomena, and intuitive states returned to and expanded on James's original expositions. His ideas are once again being debated as an integral part of the curriculum in education. His theory of emotions has returned to center stage in psychophysical circles, cognitive neuroscience has embraced him, while one of his philosophical contributions—pragmatism—has been gradually and completely absorbed into mainstream thinking.

James's works are free of the kind of petty arguments that currently divide psychological theorists. He was more concerned with clarifying the issues than with developing a unified approach, and he understood that different models were necessary for an understanding of different kinds of data. His explorations defined the field of psychology in the late 19th and early 20th centuries. He anticipated, among other things, Skinner's behaviorism, existential psychology, much of cognitive psychology, Gestalt theory, and the Rogerian self-concept.

James was a self-confessed *moral psychologist* (*moral* meaning "conscience" as well as "consciousness"), a term that has almost vanished from our modern vocabulary. Fully aware that no science was value free, he reminded other teachers that science always must be interpreted by someone and that even their most scientific actions always had ethical and moral implications: If your students believe what you are teaching them and act on these beliefs, only then does your teaching have real consequences. James himself took full responsibility for his actions and worked passionately for the side he advocated:

> I can't bring myself, as so many men seem able to, to blink the evil out of sight, and gloss it over. It's as real as the good, and if it is denied, good must be denied too. It must be accepted and hated, and resisted while there's breath in our bodies. (James in H. James, 1920, Vol. 1, p. 158)

James's major works, *The Principles of Psychology* (1890), *The Will to Believe* (1896), *The Varieties of Religious Experience* (1902), and *Pragmatism* (1907), continue to be studied. The only problem is that psychologists generally focus almost exclusively on James's *Principles of Psychology* and read nothing else after 1890, religious thinkers read only the *Varieties* and do not normally read *The Principles,* and philosophers read only *The Will to Believe* and *Pragmatism,* ignoring the rest. Thus, it is no mystery why the questions James posed remain largely unanswered, even though they are increasingly at the center of current controversies within psychology and philosophy, especially with regard to our understanding of consciousness.

William James is a towering figure in the history of American thought—without doubt the foremost psychologist this country has produced. His depiction of mental life is faithful, vital, subtle. In verve he has no equal. (Allport, 1961, p. xiii)

[James] helped launch psychology as a modern scientific enterprise, and he pioneered in what we would now call the fields of abnormal psychology, parapsychology, and the psychology of religion . . . and as the main spokesperson for the American philosophical movement called pragmatism, . . . a method for testing beliefs in terms of their outcome. (Taylor, 1995, p. 435)

His own model is still probably more encompassing than most of the models we are generating today. It can be grasped in a half-dozen historical and conceptual stages. Between 1861 and 1875 James wrote on consciousness within the context of Darwinian evolutionary theory. Between 1875 and 1890 he established the study of consciousness as a laboratory science in the context of physiological psychology and argued for a psychology of individual differences, despite the whining of the Social Darwinists that the individual was insignificant because it was subservient to the species. In 1890 he focused on a cognitive psychology of consciousness, but by 1896 he had turned his attention to a dynamic psychology of subconscious states. By 1902 he was arguing for the supremacy of mystical states of consciousness over purely discursive ones, and after 1904, while pragmatism was the international rage, he developed a metaphysics called *radical empiricism* to account for pure experience in the immediate moment, before the differentiation between subject and object—a way of accounting for how we both observe and experience consciousness almost simultaneously. His pragmatism dominated the final phase of his intellectual career, despite the fact that radical empiricism remained the core of his metaphysical system, but, in the end, it was presented only as an unfinished arch.

PERSONAL HISTORY

William James was born into a well-to-do New England family on January 11, 1842. In his early years, he traveled with his parents to Newport, New York, Paris, London, Geneva, Bologna, and Bonn. For more than a year he studied painting; then, under pressure from his father turned his attention to the sciences (Lewis, 1991). He entered Harvard through his father's literary connections to the transcendentalists but was unsure what area to pursue. Initially, he studied chemistry, then comparative anatomy. During this time he fell in with the Darwinians around the botanist Asa Gray, and with Chauncey Wright and Charles S. Peirce, and took up the study of consciousness in the context of Darwin's theories. In 1864 he transferred to Harvard's medical school. A year later, in 1865, he took a leave of absence to accompany the naturalist Louis Agassiz on an expedition to the Amazon Basin. The hazards and discomforts of the trip convinced James that he was better suited to thinking and writing about science than engaging in active scientific exploration.

> My coming was a mistake. . . . I am convinced now, for good, that I am cut out for a speculative rather than an active life. . . . I had misgivings to this effect before starting: but I was so filled with enthusiasm, and the romance of the thing seemed so great, that I stifled them. Here on the ground the romance vanishes and the misgivings float up. (In H. James, 1920, Vol. 1, pp. 61–63)

He returned to Harvard for another year but left again to study in Germany and France. He returned to Harvard and only after a series of illnesses finally earned his medical degree in 1869 (Allen, 1970; Feinstein, 1984; Perry, 1935). Upon graduating, he suffered a pronounced depression. He experienced himself as worthless; several times he even considered suicide. One incident during this period had a lasting and profound effect on his life.

> Whilst in this state of philosophic pessimism and general depression of spirits about my prospects, I went one evening into a dressing-room in the twilight to procure some article

that was there; when suddenly there fell upon me without any warning, just as if it came out of the darkness, a horrible fear of my own existence. Simultaneously there arose in my mind the image of an epileptic patient whom I had seen in the asylum, a black-haired youth with greenish skin, entirely idiotic, who used to sit all day on one of the benches, or rather shelves against the wall, with his knees drawn up against his chin, and the coarse gray undershirt, which was his only garment, drawn over them enclosing his entire figure. He sat there like a sort of sculptured Egyptian cat or Peruvian mummy, moving nothing but his black eyes and looking absolutely non-human. This image and my fear entered into a species of combination with each other. *That shape am I,* I felt, potentially. Nothing that I possess can defend me against that fate, if the hour for it should strike for me as it struck for him. There was such a horror of him . . . it was as if something hitherto solid within my breast gave way entirely, and I became a mass of quivering fear. After this the universe was changed for me altogether. I awoke morning after morning with a horrible dread at the pit of my stomach, and with a sense of the insecurity of life that I never knew before, and that I have never felt since. . . . It gradually faded, but for months I was unable to go out into the dark alone.

In general I dreaded to be left alone. I remember wondering how other people could live, how I myself had ever lived, so unconscious of that pit of insecurity beneath the surface of life. My mother in particular, a very cheerful person, seemed to me a perfect paradox in her unconsciousness of danger, which you may well believe I was very careful not to disturb by revelations of my own state of mind. (James, 1902/1958, pp. 135–136)

James's diary and letters recorded the steps in his recovery.

February 1, 1870: Today I about touched bottom, and perceive plainly that I must face the choice with open eyes: shall I *frankly* throw the moral business overboard, as one unsuited to my innate aptitudes, or shall I follow it, and it alone, making everything else merely stuff for it? I will give the latter alternative a fair trial. (In Perry, 1935, Vol. 1, p. 322)

The depression continued, however, until April 30, 1870, when James put a conscious and purposeful end to it. He chose to believe in free will. "My first act of free will shall be to believe in free will. For the remainder of the year, I will voluntarily cultivate the feeling of moral freedom" (in H. James, 1920, Vol. 1, p. 147). James understood that freedom, in its essential nature, was not an arbitrary or a capricious act. It could be neither derived from nor restricted by any other condition. Therefore, to act with freedom was to act for himself—something that, given his upbringing, was never easy to do.

After his recovery, James took a teaching position at Harvard. He taught first in the department of anatomy and physiology; then in 1875, he created and taught the nation's first courses in physiological psychology.

In 1878 he married and began to work on his textbook *The Principles of Psychology,* supposed to be finished in two years, but not finally published until 1890. It was a revolutionary work that placed psychology within the study of the sciences and made James into a national figure. In it James focused primarily on what we would call today a cognitive psychology of consciousness, although he laced his text with tantalizing references to subliminal states.

At the same time, his colorful style of communicating, as well as his concern with moral and practical issues, made him a popular lecturer. Two collections of talks, *The Will to Believe and Other Essays* (1896) and *Talks to Teachers on Psychology and to Students on Some of Life's Ideals* (1899), furthered his growing national reputation. In 1896 he presented a lecture series, "Exceptional Mental States" (Taylor, 1982). His focus on a spectrum of interior states of consciousness from the pathological through the normal to the transcendent helped initiate the field of clinical psychology and empowered

No one could be more disgusted than I at the sight of the book *Principles of Psychology.* No subject is worth being treated of in 1,000 pages! Had I ten years more, I could rewrite it in 500; but as it stands it is this or nothing—a loathsome, distended, tumefied, bloated, dropsical mass testifying to nothing but two facts: 1st, that there is no such thing as a science of psychology, and 2nd, that WJ is an incapable. (James, to his publisher, 1890)

I spent two delightful evenings with William James alone, and I was tremendously impressed by the clearness of his mind and the complete absence of intellectual prejudices. (Jung in Adler & Jaffe, 1978)

the fields of parapsychology and the psychology of religion (Taylor, 1996, 1999, 2000). In 1902 he published *The Varieties of Religious Experience,* which established the primacy of the transcendent experience in transforming personality and which later influenced such movements as clinical pastoral education and Alcoholics Anonymous.

In the last decade of his life, James wrote and lectured on philosophical metaphysics, his best-known idea being *pragmatism.* Pragmatism became an international philosophic movement based on the ideas of Charles S. Peirce, but launched by William James and expanded upon by John Dewey. Pragmatism proposed that truth should be evaluated by its utility and that beliefs should be tested by their practical consequences. This conception was in sharp distinction to alternative philosophies concerned with the absolute nature of truth. But James was in tune with that dominant American point of view, which stresses the practical and the useful and is not swayed exclusively by the theoretical. Contemporary expressions of pragmatism may be heard in such phrases as "Cut to the chase" "What's the bottom line?" "What good is it?" and "Yes, but what is it used for?"

After teaching a semester at Stanford University (interrupted by the great earthquake of 1906), James returned to Harvard. Soon thereafter, he retired but continued to travel, write, and lecture until his death in 1910.

He was twice elected president of the American Psychological Association (1894, 1904) and was active in establishing psychology as a discipline independent of physiology and philosophy. James's definition of psychology in 1890—"the description and explanation of states of consciousness as such" (1892a, p. 1)—set the direction for the discipline until it was displaced first by psychophysics and then psychoanalysis and behaviorism. His lineage lived on, however, in the general form of what came to be called American functional psychology.

> Inborn rationalists and inborn pragmatists will never convert each other. We shall always look on them as spectral and they on us as trashy—irredeemably both! . . . Why not simply express ourselves positively, and trust that the truer view quietly will displace the other. (H. James, 1926, Vol. 2, p. 272)

INTELLECTUAL ANTECEDENTS

James grew up as a member of a remarkable and gifted family. His father, Henry James, a prominent follower of the Swedish scientist-mystic Emanuel Swedenborg, was one of the most controversial writers on politics and religion in the 19th century (Habegger, 1994). Their home was a hotbed of new ideas—from socialism, the antislavery movement, and women's suffrage to high art, low theater, and the ability to distinguish between good and bad writing. The family knew practically everyone worth knowing, and the boys were required to have an opinion about everything.

William James became a passionate and skilled speaker in a family that rewarded and demanded such skills. His brother Henry James Jr., more introspective than William, gained prominence as one of the great masters of modern psychological fiction. The two younger brothers, Garth and Robertson, were farmers, not writers. Their invalid sister Alice developed the diary as her genre. William and Henry had international reputations, were in constant communication, and remained devoted fans and thorough critics of each other's works (Matthiessen, 1980; Taylor, 1992b).

In the years of his own growing professional maturity, William James became familiar with most of the leading philosophers, researchers, writers, and educators of the day. He corresponded with various ones and often exchanged photographs. In general, however, he frequently acknowledged his debt to this or that thinker but did not appear to be a disciple of any. For a more extensive discussion of James's intellectual antecedents, see our **web** site.

MAJOR CONCEPTS

James explored the full range of human psychology, from brain-stem functioning to religious ecstasy, from the perception of space to psychical research (now called ESP). He could argue both sides of a controversy with equal brilliance. There seemed to be no limit to James's curiosity and no theory, however unpopular, that he would not consider (MacLeod, 1969). He pursued most vigorously the task of understanding and explaining the basic units of thought. Fundamental concepts, including the nature of perception, attention, habit, will, and emotion, commanded his attention, as did the larger questions of what is consciousness and how it can be studied scientifically.

For James, personality arises from the continual interplay of instincts, habits, and personal choices. He viewed personal differences, developmental stages, psychopathology, and the rest of personality as arrangements and rearrangements of the basic building blocks supplied by nature and slowly refined by evolution.

Jamesian theory includes contradictions, and James was keenly aware of this state of affairs, knowing full well that what holds for one aspect of his approach may not apply to others. Instead of attempting to create a grand and unified scheme, he indulged in what he called *pluralistic thinking*—that is, holding to more than one theory at a time. James acknowledged psychology as an immature science, lacking sufficient information in its formulation of consistent laws of sensation, perception, or even the nature of consciousness. Thus he was at ease with a multitude of theories, even with those that contradicted his own. In an introduction to a book that questioned his own ideas, James wrote: "I am not convinced of all of Dr. Sidis's positions, but I can cordially recommend this volume to all classes of readers as a treatise both interesting and instructive, and original in a high degree" (Sidis, 1898, p. vi).

In the conclusion to *Psychology: Briefer Course* (1892a), the abridged edition of his famous textbook, he admits to the limits of psychology—limits that still exist today.

> When, then, we talk of "psychology as a natural science," we must not assume that means a sort of psychology that stands at last on solid ground. It means just the reverse; it means a psychology particularly fragile, and into which the waters of metaphysical criticism leak at every joint. A string of raw facts; a little gossip and wrangle about opinions; a little classification and generalization on the mere descriptive level; a strong prejudice that we have states of mind, and that our brain conditions them. This is no science, it is only the hope of a science. (pp. 334–335)

James considered many different, even opposing, ideas to be basic to an understanding of psychology. In this section, the discussion of major concepts is highly selective. The topics include the self, the elements of consciousness, and, finally, how consciousness selects.

The Self

The *self* is that personal continuity that we all recognize each time we awaken. It is more than personal identity; it is the place from which all our mental processes originate and through which all our experiences are filtered. James described several layers of the self, which, like consciousness, he saw, paradoxically, as simultaneously continuous and discrete (Knowles & Sibicky, 1990).

It seems to me that psychology is like physics before Galileo's time—not a single elementary law yet caught a glimpse of. (James, 1890)

The Biological Self.   The *biological self* is our physical, corporal being. It is our hereditary makeup, our physical features, our physiological processes. It is everything to do with our biological functions. It is the vehicle that transports us physically from birth to death, that exists in the physical world. It is this unique heart that is mine; this unique brain, just this hand, just this foot, just this tongue—the physicalness of personal identity that is me and no other person. It can be taken as a subset of the material self.

The Material Self.   In addition to the biological self, the **material self** includes those specific items in the physical world with which we personally identify. It is the total world of objects that we own. The material self encompasses the sum total of our home, possessions, friends, and family.

> In its widest possible sense, however, a man's Self is the sum total of all that he CAN call his, not only his body and his psychic powers, but his clothes and his house, his wife and children, his ancestors and friends, his reputation and works, his lands and horses, and yacht and bank-account. All these things give him the same emotions. If they wax and prosper, he feels triumphant; if they dwindle and die away, he feels cast down,—not necessarily in the same degree for each thing, but in much the same way for all. (James, 1890, Vol. 1, pp. 291–292)

To the extent that a person identifies with an external person or object, it is part of his or her self. Teenagers in gangs, for example, will even kill one another to protect a piece of clothing or a street corner that they see as part of themselves.

A man's social self is the recognition which he gets from his mates. (James, 1890, Vol. 1, p. 293)

The Social Self.   We willingly or unwillingly accept any and all roles. A person may have few or many **social selves.** These may be consistent or inconsistent. But whatever they are, we identify with each in the proper setting. We have, in fact, as many different selves as we have individual relationships, he said. James suggests that the proper course of action is to pick a self that seems admirable and to act like that self in as many situations as possible. "All other selves thereupon become unreal, but the fortunes of this self are real. Its failures are real failures, its triumphs real triumphs" (1890, Vol. 1, p. 310). This phenomenon James called the *selective industry of the mind* (Suls & Marco, 1990). Some researchers have reduced this idea to the distinction between private and public selves (Baumgardner, Kaufman, & Cranford, 1990; Lamphere & Leary, 1990), but that is clearly an oversimplification of James's original observations.

The social self constitutes patterns of personal habit that form the mainstay of our relationships. James viewed it as the shifting, malleable surface of personality, often little more than a set of masks, changed to suit different audiences. He argued that social habits are necessary; they make life orderly. Habit is a cushion; it renders relationships safe and predictable. To James, the constant interplay between cultural conformity and individual expression was beneficial to both.

The Spiritual Self.   The **spiritual self** is the individual's inner and subjective being. It is an active element in all consciousness. According to James, it is "the most enduring and intimate part of the self" (1890, Vol. 1, p. 296). It is not where we experience pleasure or pain but that part of us that pleasure and pain affect. It is the source of effort, attention, and the will.

personal reflection

WHO AM I?

Test James's proposition about the material self. Imagine that someone is ridiculing a person, idea, or thing that matters to you. Are you objective in evaluating the merits of the attack, or do you react as if you yourself were under attack? If someone insults your brother, your parents, your hairstyle, your country, your jacket, or your religion, are you aware of the investment that you have in each? Some confusion between ownership and identification is clarified by understanding this expanded concept of the self.

What James struggled to explain was a "felt" sense that we are more than personalities, and certainly more than the objects we call our own. The spiritual self is of a different order of feeling from the other selves, and while it is hard to define, it can be experienced. One expression of this self is exemplified in religious experiences, which James saw as coming from a region more central than the area of ideas or of intellect. James remained undecided on the reality of a personal soul; however, he was convinced that there is something greater than individual identity. "Out of my experience . . . one fixed conclusion dogmatically emerges. . . . There is a continuum of cosmic consciousness, against which our individuality builds but accidental fences, and into which our several minds plunge as into a mother-sea or reservoir" (James in Murphy & Ballou, 1960, p. 324).

But James also said that while all of our various selves could be unified in the experience of mystical awakening, this unification is never complete. We may be permitted to see the possibility of unity, but its actualization remains the great task of living. Personality integration always stands in relation to the ultimate plurality of selves that make up who we are. Yes, we have the unitive experience, but we also always have the "ever not quite," those few loose strands that never fit into the big picture. It is always easier to get caught up in the vision of the greater whole, but we ignore these anomalies at our peril, for they are what preserves uniqueness between people. "There is very little difference from person to person," James had said, "but what difference there is, is very important." Unity, wholeness, and continuity may be the rule in most personalities, but discontinuity, disassociation, and fragmentary loose ends make diversity both within and between personalities the more pragmatic reality.

> To give up pretensions is as blessed a relief as to get them gratified. . . . How pleasant is the day when we give up striving to be young—or slender! Thank God! we say, those illusions are gone. Everything added to the self is a burden. (James, 1890, Vol. I, pp. 310–311)

Characteristics of Thought

Most of the other theorists in this book are interested primarily in the contents of thought, but James insists that we take one step back and look at the actual nature of thinking. Until we do that, he argues, we will miss the chance to see how the mind itself functions.

Personal Consciousness.   There is no such thing as individual consciousness independent of an owner. Every thought is personal. Therefore, says James, there is only the process of thought as experienced or perceived by an individual. Consciousness always exists in relation to someone; it is not a disembodied or an abstract event. So, in his *Principles of Psychology* (1890) he maintained that to be scientific, we should presume that "the thinker is the thought." Later he would say that multiple personalities, while not ruling out the possibility of actual invasions by another individual, are largely aspects of our own fragmented self (Taylor, 1982). Finally, he would maintain that no such thing exists as consciousness, by which he meant no disembodied consciousness independent of someone's experience somewhere (James, 1904).

Changes in Consciousness.   We can never have exactly the same thought twice. Our consciousness may repeatedly encounter the sight of a certain object, the sound of a specific tone, or the taste of a particular food, but how we perceive these sensations differs with each encounter. What seems upon cursory inspection to be repetitious thought is actually a changing series of thoughts. Each thought within a series is unique, and each is partially determined by previous modifications of the original thought.

> Often we are ourselves struck at the strange differences in our successive views of the same thing. We wonder how we ever could have opined as we did last month about a certain matter. . . . From one year to another we see things in new light. What was unreal has grown real, and what was exciting is insipid. The friends we used to care the world for are shrunken to shadows; the women, once so divine, the stars, the woods, and the waters, how now so dull and common; . . . as for the books, what was there to find so mysteriously significant in Goethe, or in John Mill so full of weight? (James, 1890, Vol. 1, p. 233)

James astutely highlighted a central fact about consciousness: its inevitable changeableness—in fact, the impossibility of its being any other way.

The Continuity of Thought and the Stream of Consciousness.
Observing our thoughts leads us to the seeming paradox that while thoughts continually change, we retain an equally obvious felt sense of personal continuity. James suggested a resolution: each thought affects the one that follows it.

> Each passing wave of consciousness, each passing thought is aware of all that has preceeded in consciousness; each pulse of thought as it dies away transmits its title of ownership of its mental content to the succeeding thought. (in Sidis, 1898, p. 190)

What is present at the moment, conscious or not, is the personality. (Carl Rogers, the Perls, B. F. Skinner, and Zen Buddhism come to different conclusions derived from similar observations.)

Each emerging thought takes part of its force, focus, content, and direction from preceding thoughts.

> Consciousness, then, does not appear to itself chopped up in bits. Such words as "chain" or "train" do not describe it fitly. . . . It is nothing jointed: it flows. A "river" or a "stream" are the metaphors by which it is most naturally described. In talking of it hereafter, let us call it the stream of thought, of consciousness, or of subjective life. (James, 1890, Vol. 1, p. 239)

The **stream of consciousness,** a method of spontaneous writing that attempts to mimic the flow and jumble of thought, arose in part from James's teaching. Gertrude Stein, a major exponent of this genre, as a student at Harvard learned the technique of automatic writing under James, published two studies on the scientific literature on its prevalence, and then went on to develop it as a technique in her own novels.

In consciousness, the stream is continuous. James (as did Freud) based many of his ideas about mental functions on the assumption of continuous thought. We have gaps in feelings, gaps in awareness, but even when there are perceived gaps in

---

The only thing which psychology has a right to postulate at the outset is the fact of thinking itself. (James, 1890, Vol. 1, p. 224)

Within each personal consciousness thought is always changing. (James, 1890, Vol. 1, p. 225)

personal reflection

STREAM OF CONSCIOUSNESS

Try one or all of these stream-of-consciousness exercises. In order to derive the greatest benefit from them, share and discuss your findings with other students.

1. Sit quietly and let your thoughts wander for five minutes. Afterward, write down as many of your thoughts as you can recall.

2. Allow your thoughts to wander for one minute. When the minute is over, recall your thoughts during that minute. Write down, if possible, the whole series. Here is an example of such a series:

   I will do this one-minute exercise:
   pencil to write thoughts down
   my desk has pencils
   bills on my desk
   do I still want to buy fluoridated spring water?
   Yosemite last year
   lakes frozen at the edge in the morning
   my sleeping bag zipper stuck that night, freezing cold

3. Try to control your thoughts for one minute, keeping them on a single track. Write down those thoughts.

Does it seem realistic to consider your consciousness as a stream? When you controlled your thoughts, did they seem actually under your control, or did they continue to "flow," moving from one idea or image to another?

---

consciousness, we experience no accompanying feeling of discontinuity. For example, when you awaken in the morning, you never wonder who is waking up. You feel no need to rush to a mirror to see if it is you. You need no convincing that the consciousness you awoke with is the same as the one you took to sleep.

How Consciousness Selects: The Role of the Fringe, Attention, Habit, and Will. A basic attribute of consciousness for James is its incessant selectivity: "It is always interested more in one part of its object than in another, and welcomes and rejects, or chooses, all the while" (1890, Vol. 1, p. 284). What and how an individual chooses and what determines those choices is the subject matter of much of the rest of psychology.

The Fringe. Almost all contemporary theories of consciousness have taken up the model, proposed by Freud, of the mind unevenly divided between an aware conscious and a complex and less aware unconscious. James independently suggested a different way to explain how it is that thoughts and feelings move continually in and out of awareness. For him, awareness has two aspects: the definite portion and the vague portion, or the *nucleus* and the *fringe* (1890, Vol. 1, pp. 258–261). For James, "consciousness was a field, with a focus and a margin" (Taylor, 1982).

What we attend to is what we are aware of at any particular moment; what is on the fringe is the context, or the web of associations and feelings that give meaning to the content. Some common experiences of the fringe include the following:

■ The feeling of almost knowing. When we say, it's on the "tip of my tongue," we know that we know something but we can't yet express it.

- The feeling of being "on the right track." Research on creative problem-solving groups shows that when a group believes it is moving toward a solution, it is correct much of the time even though almost no elements of the actual solution have surfaced yet (Gordon, 1961; Prince, 1969).
- The intention to act before you know exactly what action you are going to take. Some people report that when dealing with a new situation, they "know" that they will know what to do as it develops.

Instead of imagining your mind as an iceberg, with a tip of consciousness above the surface and the bulk of it below the surface (or unconscious), imagine instead that your consciousness is a lake and that you are in a glass-bottom boat. You see clearly everything in whatever part of the lake you find yourself. The parts close by are the near fringe; all of the lake is potentially available for your inspection.

Long neglected, this model, based initially on subjective observation, has been revived by cognitive psychologists as an alternative model of mental experience (Baars, 1993; Galen & Mangan, 1992; Gopnik, 1993; Mangan, 1993).

> The mind is at every stage a theatre of simultaneous possibilities. Consciousness consists in the comparison of these with each other, the selection of some, and the suppression of the rest. (James, 1890, Vol. 1, p. 288)

Attention.   Philosophers before James (John Locke, David Hume, Robert Hartley, Herbert Spencer, and others) assumed that the mind is initially passive and that experience simply rains upon it. The personality then develops in direct proportion to the amounts of various experiences received. James considered this idea naive and the conclusions patently false. Before experience can be *experienced*, it must be attended to. "My experience is what I agree to attend to. Only those items which I *notice* shape my mind—without selective interest, experience is an utter chaos. Interest alone gives accent and emphasis, light and shade, background and foreground—intelligible perspective, in a word" (1890, Vol. 1, p. 402). Although the capacity to make choices is restricted by conditioned habits, it is still possible—and for James essential—to make real and meaningful decisions from moment to moment.

Intellect and the Sentiment of Rationality.   We have two levels of knowing: knowing through direct experience and knowing through abstract reasoning. James calls the first level **knowledge of acquaintance.** It is sensory, intuitive, poetic, and emotional.

> Mind engenders truth upon reality.... Our minds are not here simply to copy a reality that is already complete. They are here to complete it, to add to its importance by their own remodeling of it, to decant its contents over, so to speak, into a more significant shape. In point of fact, the use of most of our thinking is to help us to change the world. (James in Perry, 1935, Vol. 2, p. 479)

> I know the color blue when I see it, and the flavor of a pear when I taste it; I know an inch when I move my finger through it: a second of time when I feel it pass . . . but about the inner nature of these facts or what makes them what they are, I can say nothing at all. (1890, Vol. 1, p. 221)

In his *Principles* of 1890, James implied the superiority of **knowledge about.** It is intellectual, focused, and relational; it can develop abstractions; it is objective and unemotional.

> When we know about it, we can do more than merely have it; we seem, as we think over its relations, to subject it to a form of *treatment* and *operate* upon it with our thought. . . . Through feelings we become acquainted with things but only with our thoughts do we know about them. (James, 1890, Vol. 1, p. 222)

As his ideas about radical empiricism developed throughout the 1890s, he slowly came to change his mind, eventually giving a higher priority to direct experience, believing that both rational and emotional ways of knowing both occur within the larger field of experience.

Within this large field of experience, different ways of knowing can lead to different social consequences in ways that each work on the other. Why does a person accept one rational idea or theory and reject another? James suggests that it is partly an emotional decision; we accept the one, because it enables us to understand the facts in a more emotionally satisfying way. James describes this emotional satisfaction as "a strong feeling of ease, peace, rest. The feeling of sufficiency of the present moment, of its absoluteness—this absence of all need to explain it, account for it, or justify it— is what I call the **sentiment of rationality**" (1948, pp. 3–4). Before a person will accept a theory (any of the theories expounded in this book, for example), two separate sets of needs must be satisfied. First, the theory must be intellectually palatable, consistent, logical, and so on. Second, it must be emotionally palatable; it must encourage us to think or act in ways that we find personally acceptable and gratifying.

Consider the way we seek advice. If, for instance, you wanted to learn more about the effects of smoking marijuana, who would you go to for such advice? Could you predict the kinds of information and suggestions you would hear from your parents, friends who do not smoke marijuana, friends who do, someone who sells marijuana, a police officer, a psychiatrist, a member of the clergy, or a person working in a college counseling center? You probably could predict the kind and quality of information that each might offer, as well as your willingness to accept the information.

Often we are not consciously aware of this aspect of decision making. We like to believe that we can make decisions based entirely on rational thinking. Yet another critical variable enters into the process: the desire to find facts that resolve our emotional confusion, that make us more comfortable. The sentiment of rationality involves emotionally embracing an idea *before* we can turn to the business of decision making.

Habit. Habits are actions or thoughts that form seemingly automatic responses to a given experience. They differ from instincts in that habits can be created, modified, or eliminated by conscious direction. They are valuable and necessary. "Habit simplifies the movements required to achieve a given result, makes them more accurate and diminishes fatigue" (James, 1890, Vol. 1, p. 112). In this sense, habits are one facet of the acquisition of skills. On the other hand, "habit diminishes the conscious attention with which our acts are performed" (1890, Vol. 1, p. 114). Whether a habitual response is advantageous or not depends on the situation. Withdrawing attention from an action makes the action easier to perform but also makes it resistant to change.

> The fact is that our virtues are habits as much as our vices. All our life, so far as it has definite form, is but a mass of habits—practical, emotional, and intellectual—systematically organized for our weal or woe, and bearing us irresistibly toward our destiny, whatever the latter may be. (James, 1899, p. 33)

James was struck by the complexity of acquired habits as well as by their resistance to extinction. The following is one example:

> Houdin [a stage magician who was the namesake of the famous Houdini] early practiced the art of juggling with balls in the air; and having, after a month's practice, become thorough master of the art of keeping up four balls at once, he placed a book before him, and, while the balls were in the air, accustomed himself to read without hesitation. "This," he [Houdin] says, "will probably seem extraordinary; but . . . though thirty years have elapsed and . . . though I have scarcely once touched the balls during that period, I can still manage to read with ease while keeping three balls up." (1890, Vol. 1, p. 117)

A man who thought he was dead was talking to a friend. Unable to convince him otherwise, the friend finally asked, "Do dead men bleed?" "Of course not," replied the man. The friend took a needle and jabbed it into the man's thumb. It began to bleed. The man looked at his thumb and then turned to his friend. "Hey, dead men do bleed!"

Who can decide offhand which is better, to live or understand life? (James, 1911)

The only things which we commonly see are those which we preperceive. (James, 1890, Vol. 1, p. 444)

Fortunately, we can solve the problem of education without discovering or inventing additional reinforcers. We merely need to make better use of those we have. (Skinner, 1972, p. 173)

Pessimism is essentially a religious disease. (James, 1896)

Habits of Learning. As an educator of students and teachers, James was concerned with the formation of proper habits, for instance, the habit of attending to our actions instead of performing them automatically. He suggested that the systematic training of students to develop the habit of attention was far more important in education than the rote learning still so popular. "Continuity of training is the great means of making the nervous system act infallibly right" (1899, p. 35). Although much of our lives is determined by habit, we still have the ability to choose which habits to cultivate.

A new habit is formed in three stages. First, the individual must have a need or a desire—for example, the desire to exercise regularly or to understand French. Then the individual requires information: methods of learning how to maintain the habit. The person might read books, attend classes, and consciously explore the ways in which others have developed the desired habit. The last stage is simple repetition; the individual consciously does the exercise or actually reads and speaks French until the act becomes usual and *habitual*.

Bad Habits. Most obvious and most prevalent among the obstacles to growth in our daily lives are our own bad habits. They are, by definition, those forces that retard our development and limit our happiness; we even have the bad habit of overlooking or ignoring our other bad habits. Examples might include overweight people who "don't notice" the size of the portions they serve themselves, and poor students who remain steadfastly unaware of the dates papers are due or exams are to be given.

Habitual actions are those we do with a minimum of awareness; habit patterns preclude new learning. Because they restrict our awareness, James stresses, many of our daily routines may actually prevent us from experiencing a sense of well-being. Resistance to changing a habit becomes critical when it prevents new possibilities from becoming part of our lives.

Will. James defined **will** as the combination of attention (focusing consciousness) and effort (overcoming inhibitions, laziness, or distractions). Acts of will cannot be inattentively performed. A distinct concept of these acts and deliberate mental focus must precede them (James, 1899a). According to James, an idea inevitably produces an action unless another idea conflicts with it. "The essential achievement of the will, in short, when it is most 'voluntary,' is to ATTEND to a difficult object and hold it fast before the mind" (1890, Vol. 2, p. 561). Will is, then, the process that holds one choice among alternatives long enough to allow that choice to occur.

> Suppose, for instance, that you are climbing a mountain, and have worked yourself into a position from which the only escape is by a terrible leap. Have faith that you can successfully make it, and your feet are nerved to its accomplishment. But mistrust yourself, and think of all the sweet things you have heard the scientists say of maybes, and you will hesitate so long that, at last, all unstrung and trembling, and launching yourself in a moment of despair, you roll in the abyss. . . . You make one or the other of two possible universes true by your trust or mistrust. (James, 1896, p. 59)

This example is central to James's idea that intention can actually override objective reality and lead to a more favorable outcome than would otherwise be the case.

Strengthening the Will. The development of a strong will was of major concern to James, and it is a concern that continues among psychologists today. James understood that doing what you wish to do is not always easy. He suggested that a simple and readily available method to achieve this end is to perform a useless task every day.

personal reflection

A USELESS TASK

To explore how a useless task might strengthen your will, try this exercise.

Obtain a small box of matches, paper clips, pushpins, or candies. Place the box on a table in front of you. Open the box. Take out the items inside one by one. Then close the box. Open it again. Put the items back into the box, one by one. Close the box. Repeat this cycle for five minutes.

Write down the feelings this exercise engenders. Pay special attention to any reasons you thought of for not completing the task.

If you were to repeat this task over several days, each time you might discover a host of new reasons for quitting. Although you would find the task difficult at first, it would gradually become easier to complete. You also would feel a sense of personal power and self-control.

The reasons you might invent for not doing this exercise represent a partial list of the elements in your own personality that inhibit your will. You have only your will to counter these many (and excellent) reasons. There is no "good reason" to continue the exercise beyond your decision to do so.

> Be systematically heroic in little unnecessary points, do something every day for no other reason than its difficulty, so that, when the hour of dire need draws nigh, it may find you not unnerved and untrained to stand the test. . . . The man who has daily inured himself to habits of concentrated attention, energetic volition, and self denial in unnecessary things will stand like a tower when everything rocks around him, and his softer fellow-mortals are winnowed like chaff in the blast. (1899, p. 38)

The act itself is unimportant; being able to do it, in spite of its being unimportant, is the critical element.

Training the Will. Improving voluntary attention includes training the will. A developed will allows consciousness to attend to ideas, perceptions, and sensations not necessarily pleasant or inviting, and difficult, or even distasteful.

Try, for example, to imagine yourself eating your favorite food. Keep the images and sensations uppermost in your mind for 20 seconds. You will probably find this not too difficult. Now, for 20 seconds, imagine that you are cutting the surface of your thumb with a razor blade. Notice how your attention scoots off in every direction as soon as you are imagining the subjective sensation of pain, the color and wetness of your own blood, and the mixture of fear, fascination, and revulsion. Only an act of will can constrain your instinctual desire to avoid running from the experience.

The Personal Reflection titled A Useless Task illustrates another aspect of the problems associated with training the will: the mind's natural tendency to wander. Unless the individual develops the capacity to learn, the content of the teaching is of little importance.

Surrender of the Will. On rare occasions, the individual, rather than strengthen his or her will, must surrender it, must allow it to be overwhelmed by inner experiences. In his studies of spiritual states, James found that at these moments other aspects of consciousness appear to assume control. Will is necessary to bring "one close to the complete unification aspired after; [however] it seems that the very last step must be left to other forces and performed without the help of its activity" (James, 1902, p. 170). By *complete unification,* James means a state in which all facets of the personality seem to be in harmony with one another and the person perceives the inner

The great thing in all education is to make our nervous system our ally instead of our enemy. It is to fund and capitalize our acquisitions, and live at ease upon the interest of the fund. For this we must make automatic and habitual, as early as possible, as many useful actions as we can, and as carefully guard against the growing into ways that are likely to be disadvantageous. (James, 1899a, p. 34)

world and the external world as unified. *Transcendence of limitations, mystical union,* and *cosmic* or *unitive consciousness* are terms used to describe this transformed state. In it, the personality is reorganized to include more than the will and more than personal identity. It is as if you find yourself part of a larger system, rather than a single, time-bound consciousness. Here, for instance, is the case of Dr. Richard Maurice Bucke, a successful Canadian psychiatrist:

> I had spent the evening in a great city, with two friends, reading and discussing poetry and philosophy. We parted at midnight. I had a long drive in a hansom to my lodging. My mind, deeply under the influence of the ideas, images, and emotions called up by the reading and talk, was calm and peaceful. I was in a state of quiet, almost passive enjoyment, not actually thinking, but letting ideas, images, and emotions flow of themselves, as it were, through my mind. All at once, without warning of any kind, I found myself wrapped in a flame-colored cloud. For an instant I thought of fire, an immense conflagration some-where close by in that great city; the next I knew that the fire was within myself. Directly afterward, there came upon me a sense of exaltation, of immense joyousness accompanied or immediately followed by an intellectual illumination impossible to describe. (Brucke, in James, 1902, p. 399)

Bucke continued to say that he saw immediately that the universe was not dead, but alive and conscious; that we, in fact, possess eternal life right here in the immediate moment; that all men and women are immortal; that the foundation principle of the world is love; and that happiness in the long run is absolutely certain. Finally, he said that the profound and certain truth of that experience, even though it lasted but a few seconds and was gone, never left him again, from that day forward, for the rest of his life.

DYNAMICS: FORCES SUPPORTING AND LIMITING PERSONAL GROWTH

James was convinced that there is an underlying drive in human beings to increase their own well-being. Running through his lectures and papers is the notion that aware-ness can lead to self-control and that controlled awareness will almost always improve the quality of a person's life.

Psychological Growth: Emotion and Pragmatism

James rejected absolutes, such as *God, Truth,* or *Idealism* (and any other capitalized ultimate), in favor of personal experience—especially the individual's discovery of the means to self-improvement. A recurrent theme in his writings is that personal evolu-tion is possible and everyone has an inherent capacity to modify or change his or her attitudes and behaviors. In his lectures on pragmatism (1907), for instance, when he was talking about the relation of the one to the many, he said that each individual's greatest contribution to the larger community was that each should do their level best to actualize their personal potential. In that way, instead of foisting our "undeveloped-ness" onto each other, we assist others toward their own personal growth, simply because they do not have to deal with our shortcomings, but instead can be inspired, themselves, by our unique achievements.

personal reflection

BODY AND EMOTION

James says his theory of emotion is easiest to observe with the "grosser" emotions—love, anger, and fear. You can experience the interplay between physical sensations and feelings as follows:

Part I

1. Allow yourself to become angry. Visualize a person, situation, or political figure you do not like. Let the emotion build: allow your posture to change, your hands to tighten into fists, your teeth to clench, your jaw to come forward and up slightly. Be aware of these or any other physical changes. If you work in pairs, have your partner take notes as to your posture and the way your muscles change.
2. Relax: move around, shake yourself, take a few deep breaths. Let the emotion go.
3. Allow yourself to feel lonely, withdrawn, isolated. (This is probably easier to do lying down.) Curl up your body; draw your knees and head close to your chest. Notice what your hands do.
4. Now, relax as before.

Part 2

Now evoke the same feelings—that is, anger and then loneliness while sitting comfortably and relaxed, without any physical tension. Compare how it feels to experience emotion with or without the attendant physical changes.

Emotions.   According to the *James–Lange theory of emotion,* an emotion depends on feedback from one's own body. The theory was so called because the Danish psychologist Carl Lange published a similar theory at about the same time James did (Koch, 1986). This biological theory of emotion includes a psychological component. James says that we perceive a situation in which an instinctual physical reaction occurs, and then we are aware of an emotion (for example, sadness, joy, surprise). The emotion is based on the recognition of the physical feelings, not of the initial situation.

> Were this bodily commotion suppressed, we should not so much *feel* fear as call the situation fearful; we should not feel surprise, but coldly recognize that the object was indeed astonishing. One enthusiast [James himself] has even gone so far as to say that when we feel sorry it is because we weep, when we feel afraid it is because we run away, and not conversely. (1899a, p. 99)

This interpretation seems contrary to the popular conception. Most of us assume that we perceive a situation, begin to have feelings about it, and then have physical responses—we laugh, cry, grit our teeth, run away, and so on. If James is correct, however, we should expect different emotions to arise from different physical reactions. Evidence that sensory feedback contributes to the awareness of emotions continues to be verified experimentally (Hohman, 1966; Laird, 1974; Laird & Bresler, 1990) as well as clinically (Bandler & Grinder, 1979).

Criticism of the theory centers on the assumption of no clear-cut connection between emotional states and patterns of physiological arousal (Cannon, 1927). According to James, however, "the emotions of different individuals may vary indefinitely," and he quotes Lange: "We have all seen men dumb instead of talkative, with joy. . . . [W]e have seen grief run restlessly about lamenting, instead of sitting bowed down and mute; etc., etc." (1890, Vol. 2, p. 454). Thus, current researchers are finding that

In short, the assumption that the experience of emotion is basically an interpretation of behavior has considerable theoretical agreement and empirical support. (Averill, 1980, p. 161)

emotion does not exist without arousal (Schacter, 1971) and that the pattern of arousal is individual, repeatable, and predictable (Shields & Stern, 1979).

Work by Schacter and Singer (1962) has demonstrated that when subjects fail to understand the real cause for their emotional arousal, they label their feelings to fit the external cues. Rather than rely on internal prompts, they are swayed by social and environmental influences, which may actually conflict with their visceral feelings. So-called misattribution research—in which subjects receive false information about a drug administered to them or a procedure conducted on them—follows James's lead and Schacter's model (Winton, 1990). If subjects are aware of why they are aroused (informed that their feelings result from side effects of a drug, for example), they are less likely to label their own feelings inappropriately. The event *plus* the individual *plus* the setting will determine what emotion is experienced. Our emotions are based on our physical reactions plus our perception of the situation, not on our physical sensations alone.

James's general position also seems to be partially borne out by developments in psychopharmacology. Increasingly, specific emotional responses can be evoked by inhibiting or stimulating physiological processes through the ingestion of certain medications. Groups of drugs are commonly categorized by the changes in moods they produce. The emotional difficulties experienced by mental patients can be controlled or even eliminated through daily doses of these drugs. Clearly, James's insights are at the core of certain research studies of emotion and arousal (Berkowitz, 1990; Blascovich, 1990; Buck, 1990).

Nonattachment to Emotional Feelings.   James contended that a balance between detachment and the expression of feelings serves the organism best. He quotes Hannah Smith:

> Let your emotions come or let them go . . . and make no account of them either way. . . . They really have nothing to do with the matter. They are not the indicators of your spiritual state, but are merely the indicators of your temperament or of your present physical condition. (1899a, p. 100)

Emotional Excitement.   Although detachment is a desirable state, there are advantages to being overwhelmed by feelings. Emotional upset is one means of disrupting long-standing habits; it frees people to try new behaviors or to explore new areas of awareness. James himself experienced and researched psychological states arising from mystical experiences, hypnosis, faith healing, mediumship, psychedelic drugs, alcohol, and personal crisis. He concluded that the precipitating event was not the critical factor; rather, the response the individual made to the arousal formed the basis for change.

Healthy-Mindedness.   James considered a state of healthy-mindedness one where if the individual acted as though things were well, they would be. Idealism was more than a philosophic concept to James; it was an active force. His own return to mental health began with his decision to hold fast to the ideal of free will. James argued that a positive attitude was more than useful; it was necessary. "I do not believe it to be healthy-minded to nurse the notion that ideals are self-sufficient and require no actualization to make us content. . . . Ideals ought to aim at the *transformation of reality*— no less!" (James in H. James, 1920, Vol. 2, p. 270). He also saw it as the vital element, a dividing line between religious experiences, those that tend toward happiness and those that tend toward despair (1902).

While James Taylor waited expectantly for my late-twentieth-century spin on the somewhat arcane James-Cannon debate I suddenly had a big aha!. 'Why it's both! It's not either/or: in fact it's both and neither. It's simulataneous—a two-way street,' I blurted out. (Pert, 1997, p. 137)

Pragmatism. **Pragmatism,** originally developed by William James and Charles Peirce to clarify or eliminate unnecessary considerations about issues in one's life or one's thought, became a school of philosophy in its own right. "Grant an idea or belief to be true, . . . what concrete difference will its being true make in any one's actual life?" (1909, p. v). If no practical differences exist whether an idea is true or false, then, James suggests, further discussion is pointless. From this he proposes a pragmatic, or useful, definition of truth. "True ideas are those we can assimilate, validate, corroborate, and verify. False ideas are those that we cannot" (1907, p. 199). He understands that some truths cannot be assimilated and so on, but he points out that this second class of truths (which he sees as useless) may be cast aside when one is faced with a personal choice or a real decision. Although this point of view may appear obvious, it was roundly criticized at its inception. James writes:

> I fully expect the pragmatist's view of truth to run through the classic stages of a theory's career. First, you know, a new theory is attacked as absurd; then it is admitted to be true, but obvious and insignificant; finally it is seen to be so important that its adversaries claim that they themselves discovered it. (1948, p. 159)

By now, most of us think that pragmatism is part of normal, everyday thinking. We can add a final stage to James's analysis of a "theory's career": eventually the theoretical view becomes so ingrained in the culture that no one is given credit for it.

Obstacles to Growth

Since James was not a therapist, the obstacles he noted are those that all of us have experienced: unexpressed emotions, too much of an emotion, and misunderstandings among people.

Unexpressed Emotions. Long before the rise of modern psychotherapy as well as the encounter movement and 12-step groups, James recognized the need to release emotional energy. He believed that blocked or bottled-up emotion can lead to mental and physical illness. Although the specific emotion doesn't have to be expressed—especially if doing so might hurt the individual or others—some outlet for the arousal should be found. Moreover, he believed that it is as necessary to express noble feelings as to express hostile ones. If one is feeling brave or charitable or compassionate, those feelings ought to be translated into action rather than be allowed to subside.

Errors of Excess. It is common practice to label some personal characteristics as beneficial and others as detrimental. We say that being loving is a virtue, being stingy is a vice. James was convinced that this simple dichotomy was valid only for moderate displays of feeling. For instance, an excess of love becomes possessiveness, an excess of loyalty becomes fanaticism, and an excess of concern becomes sentimentality. Each virtue can diminish a person if allowed to assume its extreme form.

Personal Blindness. In an essay that was a favorite of his, James describes a "certain blindness," in which he discusses the inability of people to understand one another. Our failure to be aware of this **blindness** is a major source of unhappiness. Whenever we presume we can decide for others what is good for them or what they should be taught or what their needs are, we experience a certain kind of blindness.

Jamesian pragmatism influenced the laws of operationalism and complimentarity in physics, the mental testing movement in education, and the development of dynamic methods of psychotherapy in clinical psychology and psychiatry. It also had a major impact in fields as diverse as political science and the psychology of religion. (Taylor, 1995, pp. 3–4)

[James] influenced Bill Wilson, who said he derived the first three of the Twelve Steps from reading James's *Varieties*. (Taylor, 2002, p. 13)

personal reflection

CAN YOU NOURISH YOURSELF?

Test the validity of regenerative phenomena in this exercise. Start by testing one of James's propositions (Taylor, 1981).

James says:

> The way to success is by surrender to passivity, not activity. Relaxation, not intentness should be now the rule. Give up the feeling of responsibility, let go your hold. . . . It is but giving your private convulsive self a rest and finding that a greater self is there. . . . The regenerative phenomena which ensue on the abandonment of effort remain firm facts of human nature. (1890)

Choose a time when you are engaged in long, difficult activity, either intellectual or physical. If you are a coffee drinker or a candy muncher, pick a time when you really want such a stimulant. Instead of having a stimulant, lie flat on the floor for five minutes, breathe slowly and fully. Do not try to do anything; simply allow your muscles to relax, your thoughts to wander, and your breathing to slow down.

After five minutes, get up and check yourself. Are you refreshed? How does this inactivity compare with getting something to eat? Have you experienced James's regenerative phenomena?

Hands off: neither the whole of truth nor the whole of good is revealed to any single observer, although each observer gains a partial superiority of insight from the peculiar position in which he stands! (James in McDermott, 1977, p. 645)

The blindness we have in relation to one another is only a symptom of a more pervasive blindness, a blindness to an inner vision of reality. For James, this vision was not at all mysterious; it was tangible in the immediacy of experience itself. Our blindness prevents us from being aware of the intensity and the perfection of the present moment. Like Whitman and Tolstoy before him, James advocated grasping nature directly, without the filters of habit, manners, or taste. "Wherever it is found, there is the zest, the tingle, the excitement of reality; and there is 'importance' in the only real and positive sense in which importance ever anywhere can be" (1899a, p. 115).

> Life is always worth living, if one has such responsive responsibilities. We are trained to seek the choice, the rare, the exquisite exclusively, and to overlook the common. We are stuffed with abstract conceptions and glib with verbalities and verbosities. . . . [T]he peculiar sources of joy connected with our simpler functions often dry up, and we grow stone-blind and insensible to life's more elementary and general goods and joys. (1899a, p. 126)

Symptoms of our blindness may include the inability to express our feelings, the lack of awareness that leads to errors of excess, and the willing acceptance of habits that restrict consciousness.

STRUCTURE

The Mind Is in the Body

My experience is only what I agree to attend to. (James, 1890, Vol. I, p. 402)

James's own bouts with illness caused him to reexamine continually the relationship between the body and consciousness. He concluded that even the most spiritual person must be concerned with and aware of physical needs, because the body is the initial source of sensation. However, consciousness can transcend any level of physical excitement for a limited period of time. The body, necessary for the origin and maintenance of personality, is subservient to the activities of the mind. For example, intellectual concentration can be so tightly focused "as not only to banish ordinary sensations, but even the severest pain" (James, 1890, Vol. 1, p. 49). We

personal reflection

DAILY EXERCISE

Decide to exercise for one week, 15 to 20 minutes each day. Choose the kind of exercise you will do: running, swimming, riding a bike, or whatever appeals to you. Do it as well as you can.

Observe: Does anything interfere with your carrying out the activity? What do you feel each time you complete the exercise you have set out for yourself? Does your body seem to have its own point of view that is different from your own?

see numerous reports of soldiers in battle who suffer severe wounds but do not notice them until the intensity of the fighting abates. Common also are cases of athletes who break a wrist, a rib, or a collarbone but are unaware of the break while engaged in physical activity. Examining this evidence, James concludes that the focus of attention determines whether external physical sensations will affect conscious activity. The body is an expressive tool of the indwelling consciousness, rather than the source of stimulation itself.

Good physical health, although rare in James's own life, had, for him, its own inner logic "that wells up from every part of the body of a muscularly well-trained human being, and soaks the indwelling soul of him with satisfaction. . . . [It is] an element of spiritual hygiene of supreme significance" (1899a, p. 103). Although James wrote that the body is not more than the place where consciousness dwells, he never lost sight of its importance.

THE ROLE OF THE TEACHER

James was first and foremost a teacher. As such, he understood teachers' problems and was acutely concerned with improving the quality of teaching in the primary grades as much as at the college level. "A professor has two functions: (1) to be learned and distribute bibliographical information; (2) to communicate truth. The 1st function is the essential one, officially considered. The 2nd is the only one I care for" (H. James, 1920, Vol. 2, p. 268). His most widely read books were about education, and he was in constant demand as a lecturer to teachers. In *Talks to Teachers on Psychology and to Students on Some of Life's Ideals* (1899), James applied general psychological principles to the art and practice of instruction. He proposed that children are innately interested in and capable of learning. The task of the teacher, therefore, is to establish a climate that will encourage the natural process of learning. Teaching, therefore, is less a matter of content and more a matter of intent. Teachers should teach behaviors that promote effective learning. "My main desire has been to make them conceive, and if possible, reproduce sympathetically in their imagination, the mental life of the pupil" (1899, p. v).

James was sympathetic to the fact that certain personality defects seemed endemic to the teaching profession.

> Experience has taught me that teachers have less freedom of intellect than any class of people I know. . . . A teacher wrings his very soul out to understand you, and if he does ever understand anything you say, he lies down on it with his whole weight like a cow on a doorstep so that you can neither get out or in with him. He never forgets it or can reconcile anything else you say with it, and carries it to the grave like a scar. (James in Perry, 1935, Vol. 2, p. 131)

It is not a paradox that you live in a world indistinguishable from ours. The background in all of us in this world is our beliefs. That is the world of the permanencies and the immensities, and our relations with it are mostly verbal. We think of its history and structure in verbal terms exclusively. (James, 1908, in a letter to Helen Keller, who was born blind and deaf)

To one who proposed that, in the Medical School, lectures be replaced by the "case system," he said, "I think you are entirely right, but your learned professor would rebel. He much prefers sitting and hearing his own beautiful voice to guiding the stumbling minds of his students." (Perry quoting James, 1935, Vol. 1, p. 444)

The cardinal responsibility of the teacher is to encourage the student to increase his or her capacity for sustained attention. Sustained attention to a single subject or idea is not a natural state for children or adults. Normal consciousness is a series of patterned interruptions; thoughts shift rapidly from one idea to another. Training is necessary to alter this tendency until longer and longer periods of focused attention can be maintained. For the child's own development, the teacher should recognize and inhibit the involuntary lapses of attention. "This reflex and passive character of the attention . . . which makes the child seem to belong less to himself than to every object which happens to catch his notice, is the first thing which the teacher must overcome" (1890, Vol. 1, p. 417).

To aid teachers, James offered several suggestions. First, the content of education must be relevant to student needs or made to appear so. Students should be aware of connections between what they are learning and their own needs, however remote these connections actually are. This approach draws the child's initial interest, fitful though it may be at first. Second, the subject matter may need to be enriched in order to encourage the return of students' drifting attention, because "from an unchanging subject the attention inevitably wanders away" (1899, p. 52).

James rejected punishment as a way of teaching, as B. F. Skinner would 50 years later. Instead of punishing students for being bored, James suggested they be given work that would reengage their interest. He suggested that more class time be devoted to active projects than to passive study. The goal, however, is not just to accomplish tasks but to improve the students' underlying capacity to control and direct their attention. The aim of teaching is to train students in basic learning skills and habits so that they may have the capacity and the motivation to learn whatever they choose to learn.

> Voluntary attention cannot be continuously sustained, it comes in beats. (James, 1899, p. 51)

CURRENT IMPORTANCE AND INFLUENCE

The span of James's interests is unequaled. He was as concerned about the experiences of the saints as he was about the biological substrata of behavior. Only after James's time was psychology divided into specialties, like the lands of a great monarchy divided by the ruler's children into smaller, easier-to-govern portions.

James advocated an active, involved role of psychology-in-the-marketplace for the science he helped to establish. It mattered to him what people did with their lives, and he believed that psychology could and should help them. In many ways, we are still in his debt and in his shadow. The broad spectrum of phenomena he laid out for psychology to investigate is wider than most psychologists have dared put forth. James was what we would call today a *humanistic* psychologist, keenly aware of the moral responsibilities inherent in teaching and counseling others. Humanistic psychologists have claimed him as an early founder in this regard (Taylor, 1991). He was also a *behaviorist,* convinced that behavior was the primary and fundamental source of information. As well, James was a *transpersonal* psychologist, sensitive to the reality of higher states of consciousness and intrigued with the effects those states had upon those who experienced them.

His insistence that we have much to learn from the examination of mental healers, psychics, and visionaries has been validated by contemporary research on altered states of consciousness.

Beyond psychology, James has had a lasting effect on education (particularly through his colleague and friend John Dewey and Dewey's followers) and on philosophy—not only on pragmatism but on phenomenology as well (Edie, 1987). Various James's ideas have come in and out of fashion in academic psychology, but no one (including his most severe critics) ever suggested that the way he portrayed his findings and ideas was anything less than inspiring.

See our web site for more information on James's influence beyond psychology.

Table 7.1 illustrates only part of the historical scholarship that shows James's influence on different fields (Taylor 2004). Much of his influence on mainstream psychology has not been included. James's influence has two areas of special interest for this book: the current study of personality psychology and the contemporary influence of James's psychology of the emotions.

TABLE 7.1 A Spectrum of Fields Influenced by James

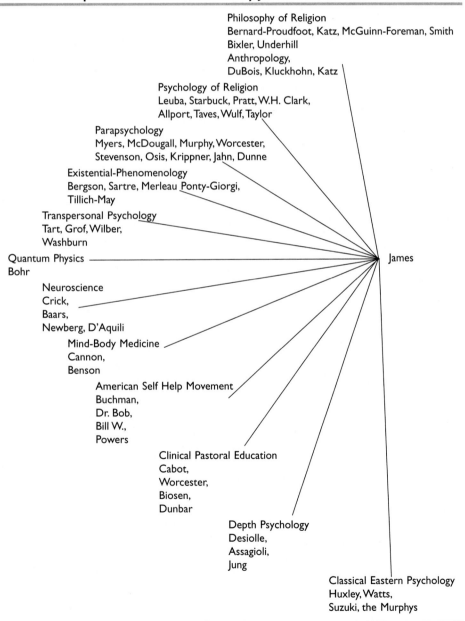

Philosophy of Religion
Bernard-Proudfoot, Katz, McGuinn-Foreman, Smith
Bixler, Underhill
Anthropology,
DuBois, Kluckhohn, Katz

Psychology of Religion
Leuba, Starbuck, Pratt, W.H. Clark,
Allport, Taves, Wulf, Taylor

Parapsychology
Myers, McDougall, Murphy, Worcester,
Stevenson, Osis, Krippner, Jahn, Dunne

Existential-Phenomenology
Bergson, Sartre, Merleau Ponty-Giorgi,
Tillich-May

Transpersonal Psychology
Tart, Grof, Wilber,
Washburn

Quantum Physics
Bohr

Neuroscience
Crick,
Baars,
Newberg, D'Aquili

Mind-Body Medicine
Cannon,
Benson

American Self Help Movement
Buchman,
Dr. Bob,
Bill W.,
Powers

Clinical Pastoral Education
Cabot,
Worcester,
Biosen,
Dunbar

Depth Psychology
Desiolle,
Assagioli,
Jung

Classical Eastern Psychology
Huxley, Watts,
Suzuki, the Murphys

James

James's Continuing Influence in the Field of Personality

Freud was a reader of James but seems to have confined his interest to James's discussion of the instincts in *Principles of Psychology* (Sulloway, 1979). Jung, on the other hand, was profoundly influenced by James's formulation of inward versus outwardly directed individuals, devoting an entire chapter in *Psychological Types* (1922) to an essay on James's ideas on the subject (Taylor, 1992a). Likewise, Roberto Assagioli, founder of psychosynthesis, borrowed heavily from James in defining his own psychology by emphasizing James's references to the growth-oriented dimension of personality (Assiagioli, 1965, 1973). As well, James's ideas played a major role in the psychology of Gordon Allport, Henry A. Murray, and Gardner Murphy, all pioneers in the scientific study of personality in the 1930s and 1940s (Taylor, 1992b). Allport focused on the normal personality, the single case study, and the person-centered approach to psychology.

Murray, a specialist in abnormal psychology, developed the field of "personology," the multivariate assessment of the individual at many levels of complexity by a team of investigators. Murphy, both a personality-social psychologist and a parapsychologist, entered the field because of James's writings. All three were instrumental in helping to launch the humanistic movement in psychology by the 1950s. Maslow included peak experiences in his conception of the self-actualizing personality, and Charles Tart drew analogies with James's emphasis on the mystical experience in *The Varieties of Religious Experience* (1902) (Taylor, 1991). Rollo May was an avid reader of James, as was Paul Tillich, his mentor.

Some conceptions of personality, however, tend to be highly influenced by trait theories (see Chapter 9) that employ paper-and-pencil tests, something James thought quite useless. While the need for a conception of the person has practically disappeared in cognitive neuroscience, James is receiving renewed interest because of his still far-reaching conceptions of consciousness, particularly in the contemporary work of such theorists as Karl Pribram (1969), Barnard Baars (1997), and Francis Crick (1993).

Scientific Study of the Emotions

James's influence on personality psychology has been most obvious in the scientific study of emotions. Since the James-Lange theory was first articulated, the study of emotions has in a sense developed in two quite different streams, one psychophysiological, and the other more cognitive and behavioral. Within the psychophysiological tradition we have the early work of Walter Cannon and Philip Bard, who endeavored to show that, contrary to James's contention that the emotions were visceral, the emotional center of the brain was the hypothalamus (Cannon, 1915). Emotional experience was understood as some combination of electrical and chemical activity largely under the control of the autonomic rather than central nervous system. James had said in 1884 that the emotion was experienced before any formal cognitive labeling. The feeling preceded conscious awareness. Psychophysiologists, such as Elmer and Alyce Green at the Menninger Foundation's Laboratory for the Voluntary Control of Internal States and other investigators in the new field of biofeedback in the 1970s, operated on a similar principle—that, although emotional responses may seem automatic, how we perceive an event still determines our reaction. The key here is that *perceptions* are different from *cognitions*. Perceptions occur immediately and may be largely unconscious; cognitions involve greater intentionality and organizational complexity. James's theory suggests that normally unconscious physiological functions can be triggered by immediate perception but also can be altered if brought under direct conscious control. An example of this might be our breathing, which reflects automatically the emotional changes in each situation. Breathing, however, can also be taken over and controlled by awareness at any time, thus, potentially modifying the course of the emotion.

Another researcher influenced by James has been Candace Pert. **More information about current research on emotions is available on our web site.**

The second stream in the scientific study of the emotions that James heavily influenced is the cognitive and behavioral. Cognitivists acknowledge the work of both James and Cannon, almost always beginning with a comparison of the James-Lange theory versus the Cannon-Bard theory of emotions, but Barbalet (1999) has made a convincing case that most cognitive scientists get the theory completely wrong. Lambie & Marcel (2002) give a useful summary of most of these cognitively oriented theorists. They include Arnold and Glassen (1954), Schacter and Singer (1962), Tomkins (1962), Izard (1977), Mandler (1984), Smith and Ellsworth (1985), Frijida(1986), and Damasio (1994).

> It appears that the tradition of the macro-personality theorists such as Murray and Allport, the humanistic and transpersonal psychologists, and also the psychophysiological researchers tend to support James's interpretation of the emotions. However, while the cognitive and behavioral researchers refer extensively to James they seem to misunderstand even to distort him. (Taylor 2002)

THE PSYCHOLOGY OF CONSCIOUSNESS

James, in laying out the scope of psychology, said that the discipline would consider any and all "mental states" as its data and would investigate their origins and their linkages to physical and physiological data in order to be useful for education, medicine, religion, and any other activity that needs to consider the control of the mind (1892b). He studied a wide range of states of consciousness and, in so doing, did not draw a fixed line between abnormal and normal experience. Portions of his work on altered states, religious states, hypnosis, and paranormal states were ignored. However, as psychology has evolved new methods of investigation, these areas are once again being actively researched. "The study of consciousness . . . is emerging as a field of study because of the ardent interest of people scattered throughout the many arms of psychology and well beyond" (Goleman & Davidson, 1979, p. xvii). Professional associations such as the Biofeedback Research Society and the Association for Transpersonal Psychology publish journals and support new lines of inquiry. Indeed, the entire neuroscience revolution could be said to focus on the biology of consciousness. There has been corresponding popular interest, as articles and best-selling books about consciousness appear regularly. The growing interest in consciousness research across a host of disciplines has not yet yielded any definitive answers. One reason may be that, as Nobel Prize–winner Roger Sperry describes it, there is a dynamic interweaving between the riddle of consciousness and the changing scientific worldview (1995).

A few areas have particular implications for personality theory. Research findings on psychedelic substances, biofeedback, meditation, and hypnosis have challenged some basic assumptions about consciousness and the nature of reality. New methods, new instruments, and a renewed willingness to investigate subjective phenomena are providing a scientific foundation for James's philosophical speculations.

Even after almost a century we cannot yet answer the question of what consciousness is—because it may not be answerable within our usual ways of explanation—but we

> The whole drift of my education goes to persuade me that the world of our present consciousness is only one of many worlds of consciousness that exist, and that those other worlds must contain experiences which have a meaning for our life also; and that although in the main their experiences and those of this world keep discrete, yet the two become continuous at certain points and higher energies filter in. (James, 1902/1958, p. 391)

> As William James, the father of American psychology said a century ago, consciousness is not a thing but a process. (Francis Crick, codiscoverer of the DNA helix)

are learning more about the contents of consciousness and the forms that it takes. Ornstein (1972) argues, as have many others over the centuries, that consciousness can never be understood using an objective approach alone. "There is no way to simply write down the answer, as we might give a textbook definition. The answers must come personally, experientially" (p. ix).

> Altered states of consciousness can be triggered by hypnosis, meditation, psychedelic drugs, deep prayer, sensory deprivation, and the onset of acute psychosis. Sleep deprivation or fasting can induce them. Epileptics and migraine sufferers often experience an altered awareness in the aura that precedes attacks. Hypnotic monotony, as in solo high-altitude jet flight, may bring on an altered state. Electronic stimulation of the brain (ESB), alpha or theta brain-wave training, clairvoyant or telepathic insights, muscle-relaxation training, isolation (as in Antarctica), and photic stimulation (light flicker at certain speeds) may bring on a sharp change in consciousness. (Ferguson, 1973, p. 59)

The research has shifted from how to induce states of consciousness to a better understanding of what can be learned from the experiences themselves. James, with his model that consciousness is a field with a focus and a margin, was already pursuing these lines of investigation 100 years ago.

Psychedelic Research

As a trained physician, William James was tremendously interested in the influence of plant substances on consciousness. There are records of his investigating various mind-altering chemicals as early as age 12. Later in life, as a physician, like so many other doctors, he tried chloroform, nitrous oxide (laughing gas), and chloral hydrate, among other substances. He once ate peyote buttons provided to him by an eminent neurologist charged by the U.S. government to investigate the properties of the cactus, which had been collected from Indians in the Southwest. He also frequented the homes of the natives in the Amazon during his year on Aggasiz's Brazilian expedition in 1865 and drew them in their habit of smoking.

Today we know that most cultures, tribal or civilized, have used herbs, seeds, or plants to alter body chemistry, emotional outlook, and levels of awareness (Bravo & Glob, 1989; McKenna, 1991). James, himself, was deeply impressed by his experiences (Tymoczko, 1996).

> With me, as with every other person of whom I have heard, the keynote of the experience is the tremendously exciting sense of an intense metaphysical illumination. Truth lies open to the view in depth beneath depth of almost blinding evidence. The mind sees all the logical relations of being with an apparent subtlety and instantaneity to which its normal consciousness offers no parallel; only as sobriety returns, the feeling of insights fades, and one is left staring vacantly at a few disjointed words and phrases, as one stares at a cadaverous-looking snow-peak from which the sunset glow has just fled, or at the black cinder left by an extinguished brand. (James, 1969, pp. 359–360)

It appears that some of the distinctions we maintain between ourselves and the outer world are arbitrary and alterable. Our usual perceptions may be partially a function of the state of consciousness we are in. We see a world of many colors, but colors are only a small part of the spectrum that exists. The finding that a person may lose what he or she calls "personal" identity without feeling a loss of identity (now hard to define) leads us back to James, who described the self not as a stable, fixed structure but as a constantly fluctuating field.

When James wrote *The Varieties of Religious Experience* in 1902, he observed that experiencing so-called mystical consciousness was a rare and unpredictable event. The widespread use and continued availability of psychedelics have made experiencing such states—or at least the subjective impression of having experienced such states—more possible. Subjects regularly have what they call religious, spiritual, or transpersonal experiences. Determining the value as well as the validity of these reported experiences, now that they are more common, has become crucial (Bennett, Osburn, & Osburn, 1995; Weil & Rosen, 1993).

This issue is of concern to the religious community as well. Religious conversion, experiences during prayer, visions, and talking in tongues—all these occur during altered states of consciousness. The validity of these experiences provides the foundation for a number of diverse religious doctrines. The discovery and examination of substances used in religious rituals, which have proved to be active psychedelic agents, have revived interest among theologians in the origin and meaning of chemically induced religious experience (Doblin, 1991) as well as the ethics involved in having access to such experiences (Clark, 1985; Smith, 1988). The term *entheogen* (naturally occurring plant substances used to facilitate mystical awakening) has been coined to differentiate such use from psychotherapeutic or recreational use (Jesse, 1997; Ott, 1993).

Consciousness, time, and space appear to interact. Modern physicists and ancient mystics are sounding more and more alike in their attempts to define the known universe (LeShan, 1969). Reports of psychedelic experiences suggest that the nature and genesis of consciousness may be more realistically described by mystics and modern physics than by contemporary psychology (Capra, 1975; Smith, 2000; Zukav, 1979). This view, known as the *physics and consciousness movement,* has widespread appeal throughout the American psychotherapeutic counter-culture, if still not a firm establishment in classical physics.

Research into various states of consciousness (Lukoff & Lu, 1989; Valle & von Eckartsberg, 1981) suggests that any theory of personality that does not take into account altered states is an incomplete portrayal of fundamental human experience. Consciousness may be described as a spectrum (Myers, 1903; Wilber, 1977) in which our normal awareness is only a small segment. This normal awareness—unaltered consciousness—seems to be a special case (Bentov, 1977; Tart, 1975) with its own dynamics and limitations.

Biofeedback Research

James's theory that emotion depends on feedback from one's body has been expanded in a variety of ways through biofeedback research. Biofeedback is an application of the engineering concept of *feedback*—the mechanical principle controlling most equipment that operates automatically. A furnace and its thermostat, for instance, form a self-contained feedback system. *Biofeedback* is a means of monitoring a biological process. For example, when you use your fingers to feel your pulse, you receive feedback concerning your heart rate.

Given immediate feedback, researchers found, subjects could control a wide range of physical parameters that included heart rate, blood pressure, skin temperature, and brain-wave frequency (Barber, Dicara, Kamiya, Shapiro, & Stoyva, 1971–1978). It is safe to say that almost any bodily process that can be monitored can be consciously modified and controlled. The fact that people are unaware of how they control a bodily process does not limit their capacity to do so. People and animals can actually *think* their temperatures up and down, slow down or accelerate their heart rates, or shift from one brain-wave frequency to another.

A monkey has learned to fire a single nerve cell to obtain a reward. At Queen's University in Kingston, Ontario, John Basmajian trained human subjects to discharge a single motor nerve cell, selected from the brain's ten billion cells. Miller's rats [Neal Miller of Rockefeller University] learned to form urine at greater or lesser rates, to redden one ear and blanch the other, and increase or decrease the blood in their intestinal lining. (Ferguson, 1973, pp. 32–33)

Research has spawned a host of clinical applications. Among the conditions that respond to treatment based on biofeedback are tension and migraine headaches, Raynaud's disease (cold hands and feet), asthma, epilepsy, Parkinson's disease, ulcers, bed-wetting, hypertension, and cardiac abnormalities, including fibrillation. Additional experiments, often paired with other relaxation methods, have demonstrated improvements in metastatic cancer (Gruber, Hall, Hersh, & Dubois, 1988), test anxiety (Hurwitz, Kahane, & Mathieson, 1986), rheumatoid arthritis (Lerman, 1987), and posttraumatic stress disorder (Hickling, Sison, & Vanderploeg, 1986), as well as problems ranging from phobia and hysteria to impotence (Clonini & Mattei, 1985). It appears that any physical process that can be brought into sustained awareness can be treated effectively through biofeedback training.

Implications.   The nervous system's capacities have been redefined. Scientists used to believe that along with the consciously controllable voluntary nervous system, humans had an autonomic, or involuntary, nervous system, which they could not consciously control. However, this distinction has all but vanished. Now it is more accurate to speak of the *gross* anatomy and physiology of the central nervous system, which is open to conscious control with little or no training, and the *autonomic* nervous system, which, to a limited degree, is open to conscious control with specialized training.

Images from Eastern religions of apparently incredible feats—yogis resting on beds of nails, saints being buried alive, devotees walking slowly over hot coals—were feats used by adepts to demonstrate the range of human possibilities. Since some of these behaviors can be replicated in the laboratory, it behooves researchers to look again at the implications of such capabilities (Brown, 1974; Karlins & Andrews, 1972; Rama, Ballentine, & Weinstock, 1976). The evidence for "human transformative capacity" (Murphy, 1992) is so extensive that Western science is only now starting to let go of the definitions of mind-body interaction suitable in a far less scientific era.

We may need to redefine what it means to be *in control* (Shapiro, 1994). Physical control may be closely linked to, or may lead to, emotional control. If so, we could find advantages to teaching children or disturbed adults basic biofeedback techniques to increase their awareness and their ability to control their own reactions. Benson, et al. (1971), Kamiya and Kamiya (1981), and Peper and Williams (1981) were among the first to demonstrate positive and lasting results from this training.

James defined will as the combination of attention and volition (wishing). Kimble and Perlmuter (1970) conclude that the will is critical in successful biofeedback training. They note, as well, that the role of attention is important in the willing process. They present an engaging example of what can occur if you wish to do something but do not pay close attention.

ARE YOU PAYING ATTENTION?

QUESTION: What do you call the tree that grows from acorns?
ANSWER: An oak.
QUESTION: What do we call a funny story?
ANSWER: A joke.
QUESTION: The sound made by a frog?
ANSWER: A croak.
QUESTION: The white of an egg?
ANSWER: A . . .

(From Kimble & Perlmuter, 1970, p. 373)

Only if you are attentive will you escape the pattern established in the series, which tends to elicit the incorrect answer *yolk*. You may wish to give the correct answer, but it is the combination of your wish (volition) plus your attention that makes it possible to do what you will. (If you wish to verify this point, try reading these questions to a friend and asking him or her to respond.)

Passive volition is defined as the willingness to let things happen. It refers to the particular state of consciousness that people learn to use in successful biofeedback training. It is attention without effort. A task in biofeedback training might be, for example, to learn to lower the temperature in the right hand. At first, people will "try"; the temperature in their right hands will rise. Then many people will "try not to." This usually results in their temperatures rising as well. Eventually, over the course of training, people learn to stop "trying" and to "allow" their temperatures to fall. Passive volition has not been part of our cultural training. We are brought up to be assertive, to succeed, to resist those forces that oppose us. James's distinctions between passive and active willing turn out to be important ones.

Most theories of personality that seek to treat mental illness specify the genesis of and contributing factors to mental disorders. Biofeedback research has shown an alternative treatment that focuses on "psychological" symptoms and ignores the psychological origins of the symptoms. As Green and Green (1972) suggest, because we can become physically ill in responding to psychological stress, perhaps we can eliminate the illness by learning to control the physiological response.

Perhaps aspects of our personalities can be modified by biofeedback, a form of external, mechanistic, nonpsychological training. Areas usually associated with psychotherapy now targeted for biofeedback include alcoholism, chronic anxiety, drug abuse, learning disabilities, insomnia, obsessive phobic-depressive syndrome, and writer's cramp (O'Regan, 1979). James did the initial research into what was then called *mind cure* nearly a century ago (Meyer, 1980; Taylor, 1996). Biofeedback training is still but one application of James's pioneering investigations.

Meditation

James was familiar with the Asian concept of meditation through his literary and familial connections to the Concord transcendentalists (Taylor, 1978). He later saw demonstrations firsthand when the eccentric Polish philosopher Wincenty Lutoslawski came to visit him in Cambridge and practiced yoga and meditation in the nude on the James family porch, much to the distress of Mrs. James. Swami Vivekananda came to lecture at Harvard in March 1896 and gave numerous demonstrations that James later wrote about in *Talks to Teachers on Psychology,* and the Buddhist monk Anagarika Dharmapala lectured to James's classes on meditation at Harvard in 1904. The scientific study of meditation did not develop in the United States until the 1930s. Today, it is a burgeoning industry with probably 100 new citations added to the experimental literature each year (Murphy, Donovan, & Taylor, 1997).

This research is beginning to demonstrate that numerous physiological behaviors are affected by meditation (Shapiro & Walsh, 1981), especially lowered heart rate, lowered blood pressure, and decreased metabolism from the sitting forms of the discipline (Benson & Wallace, 1972). *Meditation* can be defined as the directing, stilling, quieting, or focusing of one's attention in a systematic manner. It may be practiced either in silence or in the presence of noise, with eyes open or shut, while sitting or standing, and even while walking. There are hundreds of techniques, practices, and systems of meditation. Most of the early laboratory work was done on one system, transcendental meditation (Benson & Wallace, 1971; Kanelakos & Lukas, 1974). Apparently, the data obtained are also valid for other systems (Benson, 1975). Later work draws more heavily from research on Buddhist mindfulness practices (Brown & Engler, 1980; Epstein, 1990; Sweet & Johnson, 1990). Most of the research continues to focus on stress management; fewer studies investigate its utility as a strategy for self-exploration, and fewer still explore its original use as a way for self-liberation in a host of religious traditions.

With the widespread acceptance of meditation, organizations offering training have emerged in many large cities and on most college campuses. Interest in the practical application of meditation in psychotherapy (Carrington, 1978; Delmonte, 1990), and evidence of its utility in the treatment of cancer (Simonton, Mathews-Simonton, & Creighton, 1978) and drug abuse (Benson & Wallace, 1972), ensure its continued use as a therapeutic technique subject to further evaluation.

With the support of the Dalai Lama, interest has surged in researching the psychophysical dimensions of conscious reached by highly trained meditators in various Buddhist triaditions. New tools to measure brain activity, and scientists who are also long-time Buddhist meditators, have helped several either verify or discard theoretical positions. For example, trained meditators claim to be able to hold their attention on a single object for hours or to shift attention rapidly many times in a second. These claims can now be tested. "Training the attention has not been touched by cognitive neurosciences." (Kanwisher in Barinaga, 2003)

Implications. What are the contents of consciousness? James proposed that we consider consciousness as if it were a stream or a river. Research reports indicate that a more complete description might portray consciousness as having multiple streams, all flowing simultaneously. Or, to use another analogy, awareness may move from track to track like a searchlight playing over different tracks in a train depot.

What is in consciousness besides discrete thoughts? Reports from meditators suggest something more than the varied thought forms that float to the surface of the mind. As one explores consciousness, changes occur in the content, structure, and form of thought itself.

Tart (1972) encouraged researchers to consider the need for specialized training to enter and observe these specific states. Just as dentists must have special training to detect tiny irregularities in X rays of the teeth, or astronauts need special training to work in antigravity situations, so should investigators working in *state-specific* science have appropriate training. James's complaint that the insights generated under nitrous oxide "fade out" may reflect his own lack of training, not just the fleeting effects of the gas.

What effects does meditation have on personal values, lifestyle, and motivation? Ram Dass (1974) comments that his previous beliefs, developed while teaching Western motivational psychology, were severely threatened by his experiences in meditation. Some meditation systems he worked with did not even suggest that the so-called basic drives for affiliation, power, or achievement—or even the biologically rooted drives for food, water, or survival—were necessary for personal well-being. From the writings of Ram Dass (1978), Sayadaw (1954), and others, it is evident that models of personality exist that are based on suppositions beyond those considered in Western psychology.

If science proves facts that are different from Buddhist understandings, Buddhism must change. (The Dalai Lama in Begley, 2003)

Of all the hard facts of science, I know of none more solid and fundamental than the fact that if you inhibit thought (and persevere) you come at length to a region of consciousness below or behind thought ... and a realization of an altogether vaster self than that to which we are accustomed. (Edward Carpenter, 1844–1929)

Hypnosis

Little known to most psychologists, James was an expert hypnotist and, at the time, he wrote extensively on the subject and conducted numerous laboratory experiments and demonstrations. Hypnosis had been rehabilitated as a medical tool by Jean Martin Charcot in France in the early 1880s, and James and his colleagues at Harvard used it to investigate both mediums in the trance state and hysterics suffering from psychopathology (Taylor, 1982).

Paradoxically, although hypnosis has been an area of scientific research for more than a hundred years, it is still not a well-defined phenomenon. Some of its applications today include psychotherapy, athletic training, techniques for modulating pain, and even nightclub entertainment. Subjective reality and the responses of the subject to external stimuli are markedly changed in hypnosis. Tart (1970) described the range of effects.

> One of the standard tests we use, for instance, is to tell someone they can't smell and then you hold a bottle of ammonia under their nose and say, "take a good deep breath." They sit there with a blank face if they're a good subject. (It horrifies me every time I see it done, but it works beautifully.) You can induce total analgesia for pain for surgical operations, for instance. You can have people hallucinate. If you tell them there's a polar bear in the corner, they'll see a polar bear in the corner. You can tamper with their memory in certain ways. . . . You can take them back in time so they feel as if they were a child at a certain age level and so forth. (pp. 27–28)

Well-trained subjects have demonstrated unusual physical, emotional, perceptual, and psychic capacities while in a hypnotically induced state. Because hypnotic inductions can lead to a variety of altered states, hypnosis is considered a tool for exploring consciousness, rather than a means of inducing any single state.

Implications.   Who is in control of your consciousness? In stage hypnosis, the hypnotist appears to be in full control and can force subjects to do foolish and embarrassing things. Laboratory research indicates that the relationship is a cooperative one. A subject who trusts the hypnotist will go along with many kinds of suggestions. To some extent, we are all hypnotized by advertising and television. How does this kind of conditioning compare to hypnotic induction? If you do what you are told, are you fully responsible for your act? In dental hypnosis, the patient is taught to move the pain out of the teeth or to "turn off the pain." How is this done? We do not know, but we do know it is successful. If pain is subjective—that is, subject to voluntary control—what does it mean to say, "I am in pain" or even "I am tired" or "I am angry"? This evidence suggests that consciousness *can* be highly selective in what it admits into awareness.

A different approach to pain control, one that you can try for yourself, makes use of the mind's natural tendency to wander. The next time you are in pain—from a burn, insect sting, or a sprained ankle—close your eyes and consciously try to intensify the pain. Concentrate fully on only the pain and the affected part of your body. Experience it as completely as you can. Try to maintain this total absorption for at least 30 seconds. When you relax, the pain will be greatly diminished or gone.

To what extent is our acceptance of painful stimuli partly a result of not understanding alternative ways of dealing with unpleasant sensations?

Within the province of the mind, what I believe to be true is true or becomes true, within the limits to be found experientially and experimentally. These limits are further beliefs to be transcended. (Lilly, 1973)

Identity Loss. In what is labeled *deep* hypnosis (Sherman, 1972; Tart, 1970), personality appears to undergo a series of radical transformations. One by one, aspects of identity seem to be put aside. The sense of time passing, awareness of one's own body, awareness of the room, and awareness of personal identity itself fades away. Although communication continues between subject and experimenter, even that awareness fades until the experimenter is perceived as no more than a distant voice.

> I asked him about his sense of identity at various points. "Who are you? What's your identity?" That sort of thing. He starts out as himself, ego, and then his sense of identity tends to become less distributed through his body and more just his head; just sort of a thinking part. And that becomes a little more so and then that begins a kind of dropping out until his ordinary identity—let's call him John Smith—steadily decreases and as he goes deeper into hypnosis John Smith no longer exists. But there is a change taking place in who he is. He becomes more and more identified with a new identity, and that identity is potential. He's not anybody in particular; he's *potential*. He could be this, he could be that. He's aware of identifying with this flux of potentiality that could evolve into many sorts of things. (Tart, 1970, p. 35)

These results suggest that personality *can be separated* from something more central in our awareness. What or who is responding, if, as the researcher says, "John Smith no longer exists"?

See our **web** site for research and discussion regarding time and space perception.

The Hidden Observer. In hypnosis, one part of the personality may be aware of some of what is going on, while another part is absolutely unaware. The early controversial work in this area by James (1889) languished. He reported on a hypnotic subject whose right hand commented in writing about pinpricks it had been given. When questioned about it, the subject was unaware of the physical sensations and, upon reading the writings of his own hand, dismissed them.

Hilgard (1977, 1978) did a series of similar experiments and reported apparent divided awareness—meaning that two parts of the personality, equally capable and intelligent were unaware of each other. The so-called *hidden observer* was rediscovered by accident.

> We first found the phenomenon in a young man—a blind subject who had achieved hypnotic deafness. He had been unperturbed by noises and by the remarks the students were yelling at him. At one point one of the students said, "How do we know he isn't hearing anything?" So I asked him to raise his finger if he could hear what was being said. The finger went up. Then the subject said, "Would you mind bringing me out so you can tell me what just happened—what caused my finger to lift?"
>
> I then told him that when I placed my hand on his head, I wanted to be in touch with the part of him that had lifted the finger. As soon as I placed my hand on his head, I was able to get from him descriptions of what had been said, how many times I had clapped the wooden blocks together and so on. When I lifted my hand, he reverted to the earlier hypnotic state and said, "The last thing I remember, you told me I would talk to you when you placed your hand on my head. Did I say anything?" (Hilgard, 1977, p. 186)

Do you think a part of you is aware, observing, and yet unknown to most of you? Evidence is growing that the answer is yes (Nadon, D'eon, McConkey, Laurence, & Campbell, 1988; Spanos, Flynn, & Gwynn, 1988). If this is so, then what are the characteristics of that part? What does it know, and how does it affect your behavior?

Multiple Personality

William James subscribed to the idea that we are not a single unitary self, although it may at first appear that way. We are, rather, a multiplicity of selves, some segments connected in larger proportions than others. In cases of psychopathology, we see the disintegration of personality into its most primitive fragments; in unitive consciousness of the mystic experience, all appears as One—that single, unitary vision of totality—the universe and ourselves appear fused together in a seamless web. But with regard to both psychopathology and transcendence, James said, there is always the "ever not quite"—those loose strands that never fit neatly into a complete package or give the total explanation of who we are.

James, himself, was an early pioneer in the development of personality theory, studying cases of *multiple personality,* examining the variety of states of consciousness it is possible for the normal person to experience, and even positing a growth-oriented dimension to personal development, if we would just appeal to it. His views are most specifically worked out in his chapter on "Multiple Personality" in his 1896 Lowell lectures, "Exceptional Mental States" (Taylor, 1982), and in his definition of personality for Johnson's *Universal Cyclopedia,* published between 1895 and 1898 (James, 1895; Taylor, 1996).

In brief, James subscribed to the spectrum of consciousness first articulated by F. W. H. Myers, the British psychical researcher. Myers said that waking consciousness was only one state out of many, existing approximately midway between states of psychopathology and transcendence. Summarizing advances in experimental psychopathology in Europe and England, Myers maintained that trauma caused indigestible fragments of experience to break off from the waking state, fall into the subconscious, and float around, acting according to laws of their own. He called this **"the reality of the buried idea."** Every time similar traumatic experiences occurred and additional fragments split away, they were appropriated by these floating complexes in the subconscious. Eventually, these complexes could break through into waking consciousness in disguised form and appear as a symptom—fainting, paralysis, loss of voice or hearing—the typical symptoms of hysteria, or they could gather enough energetic power from their additional subconscious fragments to burst forth into the field of waking consciousness and appear as full-fledged but separate personalities in their own right. This was the origin, James said, following the ideas of not only Myers but also Pierre Janet and Morton Prince of multiple personality.

Today, ample experimental evidence suggests that some people seem to have more than one personality; that is to say, they have inside them many personalities, each with a different name, storehouse of memories, and way of thinking and behaving. Even age and gender can differ among the personalities. Extreme cases have been fully reported by the people "themselves" (Casey, 1991; Chase, 1987); clients with multiple personalities have been described by their therapists (Mayer, 1990; Schoenewolf, 1991) or by objective researchers (Keyes, 1981; Schreiber, 1974). In addition, there exists a large body of clinical data (Ross, 1989) and psychophysiological research (Coons, 1988; Miller & Triggiano, 1992; Putnam, 1984) detailing the phenomenon.

Apparently, when the human psyche is subjected to severe stress, such as sexual abuse in childhood or war-related terror, or as Freud said, to long-term, chronic, and unresolvable conflict, the personality can split. One portion retains the feelings and memories of the traumatic event, while other portions do not. These splits do not seem to fuse back together but maintain a separate existence, developing along separate lines, often having different skills, even knowing different languages (Keyes, 1981). Moreover, laboratory testing has shown that multiple personalities can differ in their reactions to medications, blood pressure readings, allergic reactions, even different eyeglass prescriptions (Miller, Blackburn, Scholes, & White, 1991).

Such data stretch the term *personality* far beyond its current limits.

Implications. An unquestioned assumption posits that all the conditions we class as "abnormal" or pathological are extreme variations of normal behavior. For example, paranoia is excessive vigilance, exemplified in extreme distrust of the unfamiliar; hysteria is an excess of emotional excitement; and so forth. If this assumption is applied to the study of multiple personality, corroborating James, it suggests a normal capacity for multiplicity within each of us.

If we look at common internal events, this idea becomes more convincing. Have you ever quarreled with yourself? Who is on the other side of the argument? Have you gone to sleep with a problem, only to find upon awakening that you have a solution? What does it mean when we say, "I don't know what got into me" or "I cannot imagine how I could have said or done that"?

The reports of individuals with severe drug or alcohol problems often suggest that one part of them wants desperately to stop the habit, while another part is not at all willing to do so. If their behavior is evidence of multiplicity, then what can be done to ensure, for example, that the part of the person who does the drinking is present during therapy?

Multiplicity may not be a pathology at all but a survival-linked characteristic, a way to function successfully under extreme conditions. This approach to multiple personality could alter some goals of psychotherapy as well as other kinds of personal education (Dawson, 1990). The evidence that disturbed multiples have exceptional capacities to heal themselves might shed light on ways to expand human capabilities, as Murphy (1992) suggests.

The existence of multiple personalities graphically raises the issue that our examination of other areas of research has raised. The question "Who am I?" has answers that may be far more complex and far less obvious than we have hitherto thought possible.

EVALUATION

All of the areas discussed in this section describe research findings that do not fit the existing paradigm of conventional personality theory. Each one shows clearly that the simplistic notion of a personality limited to the physical world and to the boundaries of the physical body is not an accurate representation of our possibilities. Either the data must be disproved or invalidated—which seems highly unlikely—or personality theory must enlarge its scope to take in these thought-provoking findings. Just as we saw that Freud's generalizing his ideas about male behavior to include women was in error, so may other theorists and researchers in this book be overstating their case when they define the scope and capacities of human personality.

The Theory Firsthand

EXCERPT FROM *TALKS TO TEACHERS* AND *THE VARIETIES OF RELIGIOUS EXPERIENCE*

The wide range of James's interests has led us to include two excerpts. The first is part of a lecture to teachers. It is James at his most moral and most pragmatic. The second, an excerpt from The Varieties of Religious Experience *(1902), illustrates James's transpersonal concerns.*

It is very important that teachers should realize the importance of habit, and psychology helps us greatly at this point. We speak, it is true, of good habits and of bad habits; but, when people use the word "habit," in the majority of instances it is a bad habit which they have in mind. They talk of the smoking-habit and the swearing-habit and the drinking-habit, but not of the abstention-habit or the moderation-habit or the courage-habit.... I believe that we are subject to the law of habit in consequence of the fact that we have bodies. The plasticity of the living matter of our nervous system, in short, is the reason why we do a thing with difficulty the first time, but soon do it more and more easily, and finally, with sufficient practice, do it semi-mechanically, or with hardly any consciousness at all. Our nervous systems have (in Dr. Carpenter's words) grown to the way in which they have been exercised, just as a sheet of paper or a coat, once creased or folded, tends to fall forever afterward into the same identical folds.

Habit is thus a second nature, or rather, as the Duke of Wellington said, it is "ten times nature,"—at any rate as regards its importance in adult life; for the acquired habits of our training have by that time inhibited or strangled most of the natural impulsive tendencies which were originally there. Ninety-nine hundredths or, possibly, nine hundred and ninety-nine thousandths of our activity is purely automatic and habitual, from our rising in the morning to our lying down each night. Our dressing and undressing, our eating and drinking, our greetings and partings, our hat-raisings and giving way for ladies to precede, nay, even most of the forms of our common speech, are things of a type so fixed by repetition as almost to be classed as reflex actions. To each sort of impression we have an automatic, ready-made response. My very words to you now are an example of what I mean; for having already lectured upon habit and printed a chapter about it in a book, and read the latter when in print, I find my tongue inevitably falling into its old phrases and repeating almost literally what I said before.

So far as we are thus mere bundles of habit, we are stereotyped creatures, imitators and copiers of our past selves. And since this, under any circumstances, is what we always tend to become, it follows first of all that the teacher's prime concern should be to ingrain into the pupil that assortment of habits that shall be most useful to him throughout life. Education is for behavior, and habits are the stuff of which behavior consists....

There is no more miserable human being than one in whom nothing is habitual but indecision, and for whom the lighting of every cigar, the drinking of every cup, the time of rising and going to bed every day, and the beginning of every bit of work are subjects of express volitional deliberation. Full half the time of such a man goes to the deciding or regretting of matters which ought to be so ingrained in him as practically not to exist for his consciousness at all. If there be such daily duties not yet ingrained in any one of my hearers, let him begin this very hour to set the matter right....

...Seize the very first possible opportunity to act on every resolution you make, and on every emotional prompting you may experience in the direction of the habits you aspire to gain. It is not in the moment of their forming, but in the moment of their producing motor effects, that resolves and aspirations communicate the new "set" to the brain.

No matter how full a reservoir of maxims one may possess, and no matter how good one's sentiments may be, if one has not taken advantage of every concrete opportunity to act, one's character may remain entirely unaffected for the better. With good intentions, hell proverbially is paved.... When a resolve or a fine glow of feeling is allowed to evaporate without bearing practical fruit, it is worse than a chance lost: it works so as positively to hinder future resolutions and emotions from taking the normal path of discharge. There is no more contemptible type of human character than that of the nerveless sentimentalist and dreamer, who spends his life in a weltering sea of sensibility, but never does a concrete manly deed. (1899, pp. 33–36)

The following selection includes portions of the final lecture James gave on religious experiences. These lectures, among the first psychological overviews of the effects of spiritual experiences on consciousness and behavior, did not take a stand on whether this or that belief was right or wrong, moral or immoral. After having given, in his preceding lectures, hundreds of examples, their effects, and his analysis of them, James attempts, here, to generalize his findings and suggest what they might mean.

Summing up in the broadest possible way the characteristics of the religious life, as we have found them, it includes the following beliefs:

1. That the visible world is part of a more spiritual universe from which it draws its chief significance;
2. That union or harmonious relation with that higher universe is our true end;
3. That prayer or inner communion with the spirit thereof—be that spirit "God" or "law"—is a process wherein work is really done, and spiritual energy flows in and produces effects, psychological or material, within the phenomenal world.

Religion includes also the following psychological characteristics:

4. A new zest which adds itself like a gift to life, and takes the form either of lyrical enchantment or of appeal to earnestness and heroism.
5. An assurance of safety and a temper of peace, and, in relation to others, a preponderance of loving affections. . . .

We must next pass beyond the point of view of merely subjective utility, and make inquiry into the intellectual content itself.

First, is there, under all the discrepancies of the creeds, a common nucleus to which they bear their testimony unanimously?

And second, ought we to consider the testimony true?

I will take up the first question first, and answer it immediately in the affirmative. The warring gods and formulas of the various religions do indeed cancel each other, but there is a certain uniform deliverance in which religions all appear to meet. It consists of two parts:

1. An uneasiness; and
2. Its solution.

1. The uneasiness, reduced to its simplest terms, is a sense that there is something wrong about us as we naturally stand.
2. The solution is a sense that we are saved from the wrongness by making proper connection with the higher powers.

In those more developed minds which alone we are studying, the wrongness takes a moral character, and the salvation takes a mystical tinge. I think we shall keep well within the limits of what is common to all such minds if we formulate the essence of their religious experience in terms like these:

The individual, so far as he suffers from his wrongness and criticizes it, is to that extent consciously beyond it, and in at least possible touch with something higher, if anything higher exists. Along with the wrong part there is thus a better part of him, even though it may be but a most helpless germ. With which part he should identify his real being is by no means obvious at this stage; but when stage 2 (the stage of solution or salvation) arrives, the man Identifies his real being with the germinal higher part of himself; and does so in the following way. He becomes conscious that this higher part is conterminous and continuous with a MORE of the same quality, which is operative in the universe outside of him, and which he can keep in working with, and in a fashion get on board and save himself when all his lower being has gone to pieces in the wreck.

It seems to me that all the phenomena are accurately describable in these very simple general terms. They allow for the divided self and the struggle; they involve the change of personal centre and the surrender of the lower self; they express the appearance of exteriority of the helping power and yet account for our sense of union with it; and they fully justify our feelings of security and joy. There is probably no autobiographic document, among all those which I have quoted, to which the description will not well apply. One need only add such specific details as will adapt it to various theologies and various personal temperaments, and one will then have the various experiences reconstructed in their individual forms.

So far, however, as this analysis goes, the experiences are only psychological phenomena. They possess, it is true, enormous biological worth. Spiritual strength really increases in the subject when he has them, a new life opens for him, and they seem to him a place of conflux where the forces of two universes meet; and yet this may be nothing but his subjective way of feeling things, a mood of his own fancy, in spite of the effects produced. I now turn to my second question: What is the objective "truth" of their content?

The part of the content concerning which the question of truth most pertinently arises is that "MORE of the same quality" with which our own higher self appears in the experience to come into harmonious working relation. Is such a "more" merely our own notion, or does it really exist? If so, in what shape does it exist? Does it act, as well as exist? And in what form should we conceive of that "union" with it of which religious geniuses are so convinced?

It is in answering these questions that the various theologies perform their theoretic work, and that their divergencies most come to light. They all agree that the "more" really exists; though some of them hold it to exist in the shape of a personal god or gods, while others are satisfied to conceive it as a stream of ideal tendency embedded in the eternal structure of the world. They all agree, moreover, that it acts as well as exists, and that something really is effected for the better when you throw your life into its hands. It is when they treat of the experience of "union" with it that their speculative differences appear most clearly. Over this point pantheism and theism, nature and second birth, works and grace and karma, immortality and reincarnation, rationalism and mysticism, carry on inveterate disputes. (1902/1958, pp. 367–369, 383–385)

CHAPTER HIGHLIGHTS

- James defined psychology as "the description and explanation of states of consciousness as such." The field of psychology was defined by his explorations and findings.
- Concerned more with clarifying issues than with developing a unified approach, James understood that different models were useful in understanding different kinds of data.
- The personal continuity recognized each time one awakens is the self. It has several layers, the biological, the material, the social, and the spiritual. Like consciousness, it is simultaneously continuous and discrete.
- There is no individual consciousness independent of an owner. Every thought is part of a personal consciousness. Consciousness always exists in relation to some person. The same exact thought can never occur twice.
- Thought is continuous, within each personal consciousness. Each thought emerges from a stream of consciousness, taking part of its force, content, focus, and direction from preceding thoughts.
- Consciousness is selective. Attention and habit are major variables in what an individual chooses and what determines the choice.
- Awareness has two aspects, a definite portion and a vague portion, a nucleus and a fringe. What we are aware of at any given moment is what we attend to. What is on the fringe comprises the web of feelings and associations that give meaning to the content.
- Consciousness was a field, with a focus and a margin.
- James rejected the notion that the mind is passive and that experience simply rains upon it. He believed that before something can be experienced, it must be attended to. Experience is utter chaos without selective interest, or attention.
- Habits are actions or thoughts that are seemingly automatic responses. They diminish the conscious attention the individual needs to pay to his or her actions. Withdrawing attention from an action makes it resistant to change, although easier to perform.
- Bad habits are the most obvious and prevalent obstacles to growth in daily life. New possibilities are prevented through resistance to changing a habit.
- Will is the combination of effort (overcoming distractions, inhibitions, or laziness) and attention (focusing consciousness). Will is necessary to bring the individual close to the transformed state of mystical union and cosmic or unitive consciousness.
- Human beings have an underlying drive to increase their own well-being.
- An emotion depends on feedback from one's body. Developments in psychopharmacology partially support this general position.
- The organism is best served by a balance between expression of feelings and detachment. An attitude of healthy-mindedness is necessary. No less than a transformation of reality is the proper aim of one's ideals.
- Pragmatism: If no practical differences exist whether an idea is true or false, then further discussion of it is pointless.

- Unexpressed emotions, errors of excess, and what James termed a "certain blindness" are obstacles to growth. Blocked or bottled-up emotion, positive or negative, can lead to mental and physical illness.
- The cardinal responsibility of the teacher is to encourage students to increase their capacity for sustained attention. Training is necessary to maintain longer and longer periods of focused attention.
- The psychology that James introduced addressed all areas of human experience bounded on one side by mysticism and by biology on the other. He did not separate abnormal, normal, or transcendent experience in his study of a wide range of states of consciousness. He saw them all as part of a single continuum.
- Basic assumptions about consciousness and the nature of reality are questioned by research with biofeedback, psychedelic drugs, hypnosis, and meditation. Current research on subjective phenomena parallels the work of James on altered states, religious states, paranormal states, and hypnosis.
- James described the self as an experience of many selves in a constantly fluctuating field. This seems congruent with the finding that a person may lose what is termed personal identity without feeling a loss of actual identity.
- Any theory of personality that fails to take into account altered states of consciousness is an incomplete description of fundamental human experience.
- The part of consciousness holding our unaltered awareness is but a small part, and a special case with its own limitations and rules.
- Biofeedback research has found that emotion depends on feedback from one's body.
- The distinction between passive and active willing turns out to be crucial in biofeedback training. Passive volition, the willingness to let things happen, is the particular state of consciousness that people learn to use.
- Meditation is the practice of stilling, focusing, and sustaining attention. It is useful in the treatment of some mental and physical conditions. It is also a tool to explore the structure of thought.
- Specific states of consciousness are accessible through specialized training.
- Rather than a means for inducing any single state, hypnosis is increasingly considered to be a tool for exploring consciousness.

KEY CONCEPTS

Blindness The presumption that we can judge for others what is good for them, what their needs are, or what they should be taught. It is a symptom of a more pervasive blindness to a vision of an inner reality, that in turn prevents us from being aware of the perfection and the intensity of the present moment. Symptoms may include errors of excess, the inability to express our feelings, and the willing acceptance of consciousness-restricting habits.

Biological self Our physical being; everything that has to do with our heredity, our physical health or illness, and our physical functions.

Knowledge about For James, the higher level of knowing through abstract reasoning. It is focused, intellectual, and relational; it can develop abstractions. It is unemotional and objective.

Knowledge of acquaintance Sensory, emotional, intuitive, and poetic awareness. It is what James terms knowing through direct experience.

Material self The layer of the self that includes those elements with which we personally identify—not only our bodies but also our possessions, home, friends, and family. An external person or object an individual identifies with may be considered part of his or her material self.

Passive volition The willingness to let things happen. The term refers to the state of consciousness that people learn to use in successful biofeedback training; it is attention without effort.

The reality of the buried idea The theory that traumatic experiences, which cannot be successfully integrated into waking consciousness, may sometimes split off from the waking state and float around in the subconscious, acting according to laws of their own.

Pragmatism The theory that truth is always tested by its consequences. Also the first uniquely American philosophy to have international consequences, developed first by James and Peirce and later by philosophers such as John Dewey, to clarify or eliminate unnecessary considerations about issues in one's life or thought. If no practical differences exist whether an idea is true or false, then further discussion is pointless. From this, true ideas become those that can be verified, corroborated, validated, and assimilated.

Sentiment of rationality The emotional state of wishing to believe that we are being rational. The desire to find facts that make us more comfortable or that resolve our emotional confusion. The sentiment enters into the decision-making process as much as the exercise of rational thinking does.

Social self The possibility that we have as many social selves as we have relationships, since we reveal a different part of who we are to everyone we meet, and no two relationships are ever the same.

Spiritual self That simultaneously highest, deepest, and most all-encompassing dimension of personality. The active element in all consciousness, the individual's inner and subjective being. It is also the place from which the decisions of the will emanate and the source of attention and effort.

Stream of consciousness In literature, a form of writing that attempts to mimic the jumble and flow of thought; also known as stream of thought. In consciousness, the stream is continuous. Gaps occur in awareness and in feelings, but with no accompanying feeling of discontinuity.

Will The combination of attention (focusing consciousness) and effort (overcoming laziness, inhibitions, or distractions). It is also the process that holds one choice among the alternatives long enough for that choice to take place.

ANNOTATED BIBLIOGRAPHY

Allen, G. W. (1970). *William James: A biography*. New York: Viking.

  Still the best chronological biography yet written. The author has also published biographies on Walt Whitman and Ralph Waldo Emerson.

Donnelly, M. (Ed.). (1992). *Reinterpreting the legacy of William James*. Washington, DC: American Psychological Association.

  By evaluating the effects James has had on their specializations, 23 scholars demonstrate the continuing force of James's ideas on their own. The first article makes the case for a uniquely American Jamesean tradition in psychology, including after James, the major personality theorists of the 1930s and 1940s, as well as the founders of humanistic and transpersonal psychology in the 1960s.

Feinstein, H. (1984). *Becoming William James*. Ithaca, NY: Cornell University Press.

  An unusual biography that deals primarily with the histories of James's grandfather and great-grandfather and their influence on James during his formative years, written by an MD psychoanalyst who returned to college to earn a PhD in history before he helped to take over the field of family systems theory.

James, W. (1902). *The varieties of religious experience*. Various editions.

  James's lectures on the psychology of religion and religious experience, using a phenomenological method that he called the *documents humaine*—the living human documents, meaning first-person accounts of lived experience. The work is a full introduction to the more general psychology of altered states of consciousness, although most of the many examples come specifically from religious literature. An annotated version, published by Harvard, is for scholars.

James, W. (1961). *Psychology: Briefer course*. New York: Harper & Row. With an introduction by Gordon W. Allport.

  A cut-and-paste version of the two-volume *Principles of Psychology* (1890) that became a standard textbook in American colleges and universities for the subsequent 20 years. James's students immediately dubbed the two-volume *Principles* "James" and *Briefer Course* "the Jimmy." The 1961 edition has the outdated chapters on the nervous system excised from the beginning.

James, W. (1962). *Talks to teachers on psychology and to students on some of life's ideals*. New York: Dover.

  A popular exposition applying the content of *The Principles* (1890) to the topic of educational psychology for teachers. Full of sensible advice about the way to cultivate and train young minds. James himself said that his accompanying *Talks to Students,* despite the fact they were delivered to popular, public audiences, contained essays that revealed the center of his philosophic vision.

McDermott, J. J. (Ed.). (1977). *The writings of William James: A comprehensive edition*. Chicago: University of Chicago Press.

  The best single-volume collection of James's writings. A good introduction, with ample selections from his psychological and philosophical writings. It contains the most complete annotated bibliography of James's writing currently in print, although it has been superceded by a much more complete collection—the Harvard edition of James's writings, Burkhardt, Bowers, and Skrupskelis's *Critical Edition Collected Works of William James*. (1975–1988).

Myers, G. (1986). *William James, his life and thought*. New Haven, CT: Yale University Press.

  James was not systematic in his thinking and changed his positions over the course of his life. To try to remedy this, Myers has interpreted James according to normative philosophy, sanitizing all of James's ideas to make them more palatable to the rationalists.

Perry, R. B. (1935). *The thought and character of William James* (2 vols.). Boston: Little, Brown. Abridged, Cambridge, MA: Harvard University Press, 1948.

  Abridged version of the two-volume masterpiece that won Perry the Pulitzer prize.

Taylor, E. I. (1982). *William James on exceptional mental states: Reconstruction of the unpublished 1896 Lowell lectures.* New York: Scribner's.

> Historical reconstruction using James's archival notes, books he checked out of the college library, and annotations from James's personal book collection of his unpublished 1896 Lowell Lectures, "Exceptional Mental States." The first four lectures show the workings of a dynamic theory of the subconscious, and the second four show the pathological working of the subconscious in the social sphere.

Taylor, E. I. (1996). *William James on consciousness beyond the margin.* Princeton, NJ: Princeton University Press.

> This work is an exposition of James's psychology after the 1890s, which included major advances in experimental psychopathology, psychical research, and the psychology of religion. These developments overlapped with the historical evolution of James's doctrine of radical empiricism, meant as a critique of experimental psychology and science generally and also as the basis for a modern science of consciousness.

Web Sites

William James
http://www.emory.edu/EDUCATION/mfp/james.html.

> This site is an adventure not only in every aspect of James you might imagine and more, but also a look at how fine a job a **web** site can do in making it easy and inviting to go deeply into a topic. If you open no other site mentioned in this book, go to this one. It also links to every other site about James you can envision.

Psychedelics
http://www.psychedelic-library.org/
http://www.erowide.org

> The two most comprehensive resources for the literature of psychedelic drugs. Research reports, philosophical essays, articles, and complete-text books are available both for professional research and for general interest.

http://www.maps.org/

> "The Multidisciplinary Association for Psychedelic Studies (MAPS) is a membership-based nonprofit research and educational organization. They assist scientists to design, fund, obtain approval for and report on studies into the healing and spiritual potentials of MDMA, psychedelic drugs and marijuana." Reports of ongoing research worldwide.

http://www.csp.org/chrestomathy/a_chrestomathy.html

> An ongoing review of books that comment on psychedelic or enthoegenic (spiritual) uses. An easy entrance to the literature.

Biofeedback
http://www.biofeedback.net/eeg.html

> The biofeedback network. Organizations, journals, advertisements. look for this line and try it: "See & hear Dr. Miller's brain on EEG!"

Meditation
http://www.questia.com/Index.jsp?CRID=meditation&OFFID=se1&KEY=meditation_research.

> Most **web** sites offer to teach you or to convert you. This one at least just offers you a good way to look over the research literature.

Hypnosis
http://www.asch.net/

> The **web** site for the American Society of Clinical Hypnosis.

Multiple Personality
http://www.astraeasweb.net/plural/

> A curious and compelling site. It links to many personal multiple sites, a full list of books in the area, plus sharply opinionated reviews. Whatever you think about this way of looking at personality, this site will shake up any certainty.

REFERENCES

Adler, G., & Jaffe, A. (1978). *Letters of C. G. Jung* (Vol. 1). Princeton, NJ: Princeton University Press.

Allen, G. (1970). *William James, a biography.* New York: Viking Press.

Allport, G. (Ed.). (1961). *William James: Psychology, the briefer course.* New York: Harper & Row.

Arnold, M. B., & Gassen, S. J. (1954). Feelings and emotions as dynamic factors in personality integration. In Arnold, A. B., & Gasson (Eds.), *The human person* (pp. 293–313). New York: Ronald Press.

Assagioli, R. (1965). *Psychosynthesis.* New York: Hobbs, Dorman.

Assagioli, R. (1973). *The Act of Will.* New York: Penguin.

Averill, J. R. (1980). Autonomic response patterns during sadness and mirth. *Psychophysiology,* 99–214.

Baars, B. (1993). Putting the focus on the fringe: Three empirical cases. *Conscious and Cognition,* 2(2), 126–136.

Baars Barnard. (1997). *In the theater of consciousness: The workspace of the mind.* New York: Oxford University Press, 1997.

Bandler, R., & Grinder, J. (1979). *Frogs into princes: Neurolinguistic programming.* Moab, UT: Real People Press.

Barbalet, J. M. (1999). William James' theory of emotions: Filling in the picture. *Journal for the Theory of Social Behavior,* 29(3), 0021–8308. HTML full text PSYCHINFO.

Barber, T. X., Dicara, L., Kamiya, J., Shapiro, D., & Stoyva, J. (Eds.). (1971, 1972, 1973, 1974, 1975–1976, 1976–1977, 1977–1978). *Biofeedback and self-control: An Aldine annual.* Chicago: Aldine.

Barinaga, Marcia. Buddhism and Neuroscience: Studying the well-trained mind. *Science, 302,* (5642), October 3, 2003, p. 44–46.

Baumgardner, A., Kaufman, C., & Cranford, J. (1990). To be noticed favorably: Links between private self and public self. *Personality and Social Psychology Bulletin, 16*(4), 705–716.

Begley, Sharon. Dalai Lama and MIT together investigate value of meditation. *Wall Street Journal,* September 21, 2003, p. D1.

Bennett, C., Osburn, L., & Osburn, J. (1995). *Green gold, the tree of life: Marijuana in magic and religion.* Frazier Park, CA: Access Unlimited.

Benson, H. (1975). *The relaxation response.* New York: Morrow.

Benson, H., Shapiro, D., Tursky, B., & Schwartz, G. E. (1971). Decreased systolic blood pressure through operant conditioning techniques in patients with essential hypertension. *Science, 173,* 740–742.

Benson, H., & Wallace, R. K. (1972). *Decreased drug abuse with transcendental meditation: A study of 1,862 subjects.* Proceedings of Drug Abuse, International Symposium for Physicians (pp. 369–376). Philadelphia: Lea & Ferbinger.

Bentov, I. (1977). *Stalking the wild pendulum.* New York: Dutton.

Berkowitz, L. (1990). On the formation and regulation of anger and aggression: A cognitive-neo-associationistic analysis. American Psychological Association: Distinguished scientific award for the applications of psychology address. *American Psychologist, 45*(4), 494–503.

Blascovich, J. (1990). Individual differences in physiological arousal and perception of arousal: Missing links in Jamesian notions of arousal-based behaviors. *Personality and Social Psychology Bulletin, 16*(4), 665–675.

Bravo, G., & Glob, C. (1989). Shamans, sacraments, and psychiatrists. *Journal of Psychoactive Drugs, 21*(1), 123–128.

Breuer, J., & Freud, S. (1895). Studies in hysteria. In J. Strachy (Ed. and Trans.), *The standard edition of the complete psychological works of Sigmund Freud* (Vol. 2). London: Hogarth Press, 1953–1966.

Brown, B. (1974). *New mind, new body.* New York: Harper & Row.

Brown, D. P., & Engler, J. (1980). The stages of mindfulness meditation: A validation study. *Journal of Transpersonal Psychology, 12*(2), 143–192.

Buck, R. (1990). William James, the nature of knowledge, and current issues in emotion, cognition, and communication. *Personality and Social Psychology Bulletin, 16*(4), 612–625.

Cannon, W. B. (1915). *Bodily changes in pain, hunger, fear, and rage: An account of recent researches into the function of emotional excitement.* New York, London: Appleton.

Cannon, W. B. (1927). The James–Lange theory of emotions: A critical examination and an alternative theory. *American Journal of Psychology, 39,* 106–124.

Capra, F. (1975). *The tao of physics.* New York: Bantam Books.

Carrington, P. (1978). The uses of meditation in psychotherapy. In A. Sugarman & R. Tarter (Eds.), *Expanding dimensions of consciousness.* New York: Springer-Verlag.

Casey, J., with Wilson, L. (1991). *The flock.* New York: Knopf.

Chase, T. (the troops of). (1987). *When rabbit howls.* New York: Dutton.

Clark, W. (1985). Ethics and LSD. *Journal of Psychoactive Drugs, 17*(4), 229–234.

Clonini, L., & Mattei, D. (1985). Biofeedback and cognitive-behavioral therapy. *Medicini-Psicosomatica, 30*(2), 151–161.

Coons, P. (1988). Psychophysiologic aspects of multiple personality disorder: A review. *Dissociation Progress in the Dissociative Disorders, 1*(1), 47–53.

Crick, F., & Koch, C. (1993). *Mind and brain: Readings from* Scientific American *magazine.* New York: Freeman/Times Books/Holt. pp. 125–136.

Damasio, A. (1994). *Descarte's error.* London: Macmillan.

Dawson, P. (1990). Understanding and cooperation among alter and host personalities. *American Journal of Occupational Therapy, 44*(11), 994–997.

Delmonte, M. (1990). The relevance of meditation to clinical practice: An overview. *Applied Psychology: An International Review, 39*(3), 331–354.

Doblin, R. (1991). Panke's "Good Friday experiment": A long-term follow-up and methodological critique. *Journal of Transpersonal Psychology, 23*(1), 1–28.

Epstein, M. (1990). Beyond the oceanic feeling: Psychoanalytic study of Buddhist meditation. *International Review of Psychoanalysis, 17*(2), 159–166.

Feinstein, H. (1984). *Becoming William James.* Ithaca, NY: Cornell University Press.

Ferguson, M. (1973). *The brain revolution.* New York: Taplinger.

Frijida, N. H. (1986). *The emotions.* Cambridge, England: Cambridge University Press.

Galen, D., & Mangan, B. (1992). *Two-part structure of consciousness: Application of William James' forgotten concept, "The Fringe."* Presented at International Neuropsychological Society, San Diego.

Goleman, D., & Davidson, R. (1979). *Consciousness: Brain, states of awareness, and mysticism.* New York: Harper & Row.

Gopnik, A. (1993). The psychopsychology of the fringe. *Conscious and Cognition, 2*(2), 109–112.

Gordon, W. (1961). *Synectics: The development of creative capacity.* New York: Harpers.

Green, E., & Green, A. (1972). How to make use of the field of mind theory. In *The dimensions of healing.* Los Altos, CA: Academy of Parapsychology and Medicine.

Gruber, B., Hall, N., Hersh, S., & Dubois, P. (1988). Immune system and psychological changes in metastatic cancer patients using relaxation and guided imagery: A pilot study. *Scandinavian Journal of Behavior Therapy, 17*(1), 25–46.

Habegger, A. (1994). *The Father: A life of Henry James, Sr.* New York: Farrar, Straus, & Giroux.

Hickling, E., Sison, G., & Vanderploeg, R. (1986). Treatment of post-traumatic stress disorder with relaxation and biofeedback training. *Biofeedback and Self-Regulation, 11*(2), 125–134.

Hilgard, E. (1977). *Divided consciousness.* New York: Wiley.

Hilgard, E. (1978). New approaches to hypnosis. *Brain Mind Bulletin, 3*(7), 3.

Hohman, G. W. (1966). Some effects of spinal cord lesions on experienced emotional feelings. *Psychophysiology, 3,* 143–156.

Hurwitz, L., Kahane, J., & Mathieson, C. (1986). The effects of EMG biofeedback and progressive muscle relaxation on the reduction of test anxiety. *Educational and Psychological Research, 6*(4), 291–298.

Izard, C. E. (1977). *Human emotions.* New York: Plenum.

James, H. (Ed.). (1920). *The letters of William James* (2 vols.). Boston: Little, Brown.

James, W. (1889). *Automatic writing.* Proceedings of the American Society for Psychical Research, *199,* 548–564.

James, W. (1890). *The principles of psychology* (2 vols.). New York: Henry Holt. Unaltered republication, New York: Dover, 1950.

James, W. (1892a). *Psychology: Briefer course.* New York: Henry Holt. New edition, New York: Harper & Row, 1961.

James, W. (1892b). A plea for psychology as a "natural science." *Philosophical Review, 1,* 146–153.

James, W. (1895). Person and personality. In Johnson's *Universal Cyclopedia.* New York: Appleton.

James, W. (1896). *The will to believe and other essays in popular philosophy.* New York: Henry Holt.

James, W. (1899). *Talks to teachers on psychology and to students on some of life's ideals.* New York: Henry Holt. Unaltered republication, New York: Dover, 1962.

James, W. (1902). *The varieties of religious experience.* New York: Longmans, Green.

James, W. (1904). Does consciousness exist? *Journal of Philosophy, Psychology, and Scientific Methods, 1,* 477–491.

James, W. (1907). *Pragmatism: A new name for some old ways of thinking.* New York and London: Longmans, Green.

James, W. (1908). Personal letter to Helen Keller. Helen Keller Archives, American Foundation for the Blind.

James, W. (1909). *The meaning of truth.* New York: Longmans, Green.

James, W. (1948). *Essays in pragmatism.* Alburey Castell (Ed.). New York: Hafner Press.

James, W. (1969). Subjective effects of nitrous oxide. In C. Tart (Ed.), *Altered states of consciousness* (pp. 359–362). New York: Wiley.

Jesse, R. (1997). Testimony of the Council on Spiritual Practices (R. Forte, Ed.). In *Entheogens and the future of religion* (pp. 7–14). San Francisco: CSP Press.

Kamiya, J., & Kamiya, J. (1981). Biofeedback. In A. Hastings, J. Fadiman, & J. Gordon (Eds.), *Health for the whole person* (pp. 115–130). New York: Pocket Books.

Kanelakos, D., & Lukas, J. (1974). *The psychobiology of transcendental meditation: A literature review.* Menlo Park, CA: Benjamin.

Karlins, M., & Andrews, L. (1972). *Biofeedback: Turning on the power of your mind.* Philadelphia: Lippincott.

Keyes, D. (1981). *The minds of Billy Milligan.* New York: Random House.

Kimble, G. A., & Perlmuter, L. C. (1970). The problem of volition. *Psychological Record, 77,* 361–384.

Knowles, E., & Sibicky, M. (1990). Continuity and diversity in the stream of selves: Metaphorical resolutions of William James's one-in-many-selves paradox. *Personality and Social Psychology Bulletin, 16*(4), 676–687.

Laird, J. (1974). Self-attribution of emotion: The effect of expressive behavior on the quality of emotional experience. *Journal of Personality and Social Psychology, 29,* 475–486.

Laird, J., & Bresler, C. (1990). William James and the mechanisms of emotional experience. *Personality and Social Psychology Bulletin, 16*(4), 636–651.

Lambie, A., & Marcel, A. J. (2002). Consciousness and the varieties of emotion experience. *Psychological Review,* 0033-295X, 109:2, Database: psyARTICLES.

Lamphere, R., & Leary, M. (1990). Private and public self-processes: A return to James's constituents of the self. *Personality and Social Psychology Bulletin, 16*(4), 717–725.

Lerman, C. (1987). Rheumatoid arthritis: Psychological factors in the etiology, course, and treatment. *Clinical Psychology Review, 7*(4), 413–425.

LeShan, L. (1969). Physicists and mystics: Similarities in world view. *Journal of Transpersonal Psychology, 1,* 1–20.

Lewis, R. (1991). *The James: A family narrative.* New York: Farrar, Straus, & Giroux.

Lilly, J. C. (1973). *The center of the cyclone.* New York: Bantam Books.

Lukoff, D., & Lu, F. (1989). Transpersonal psychology research review. Topic: Computerized databases, specialized collections. *Journal of Transpersonal Psychology, 21*(2), 211–223.

MacLeod, R. B. (Ed.). (1969). *William James: Unfinished business.* Washington, DC: American Psychological Association.

Mandler, G. (1984). *Mind and body: Psychology of emotion and stress.* New York: Norton.

Mangan, B. (1993). Taking phenomenology seriously: The "fringe" and its implications for cognitive research. *Conscious and Cognition, 2*(2), 89–106.

Matthiessen, T. H. (1980). *The James family.* New York: Random House.

Mayer, R. (1990). *Through divided minds.* New York: Avon.

McDermott, J. J. (Ed.). (1977). *The writings of William James: A comprehensive edition.* Chicago: University of Chicago Press.

McKenna, T. (1991). *The archaic revival.* San Francisco: Harper San Francisco.

Meyer, D. (1980). *The positive thinkers.* New York: Pantheon Press.

Miller, S., Blackburn, T., Scholes, G., & White, G. (1991). Optical differences in multiple personality disorder: A second look. *Journal of Nervous and Mental Diseases, 179*(3), 132–135.

Miller, S., & Triggiano, P. (1992). The psychophysiological investigation of multiple personality disorder: Review and update. *American Journal of Clinical Hypnosis, 35*(1), 47–61.

Murphy, G., & Ballou, R. (Eds.). (1960). *William James on psychical research.* New York: Viking Press.

Murphy, M. (1992). *The future of the body: Explorations into the further evolution of human nature.* Los Angeles: Tarcher.

Murphy, M., Donovan, S., & Taylor, E. I. (Ed.). *The physical and psychological effects of meditation: A review of contemporary research with a comprehensive bibliography, 1931–1996,* 2nd ed. Sausalito, CA: Institute of Noetic Sciences, 1997.

Nadon, R., D'eon, J., McConkey, K., Laurence, J., & Campbell, P. (1988). Posthypnotic amnesia, the hidden observer effect, and duality during hypnotic age regression. *International Journal of Clinical and Experimental Hypnosis, 36*(1), 19–37.

O'Regan, B. (1979). Biofeedback: The growth of a technique. *Institute of Noetic Sciences Newsletter, 7*(1), 10.

Ornstein, R. (1972). *The psychology of consciousness.* San Francisco: Freeman; New York: Viking Press.

Ott, J. (1993). *Pharmacotheon.* Kennewick, WA: Natural Products.

Peper, E., & Williams, E. A. (1981). Autogenic therapy. In A. Hastings, J. Fadiman, & J. Gordon (Eds.), *Health for the whole person* (pp. 131–138). New York: Pocket Books.

Perry, R. B. (1935). *The thought and character of William James* (2 vols.). Boston: Little, Brown.

Pert, Candace. (1997). *Molecules of Emotion: Why you feel the way you feel.* New York: Scribner.

Pribram, K. (1969). *Mood, states and mind: Selected readings.* Baltimore: Penguin Books.

Prince, G. (1969). *The practice of creativity.* Cambridge, MA: Synectics.

Putnam, F. (1984). The psychophysiologic investigation of multiple personality. *Psychiatric Clinics of North America, 7*(1), 31–39.

Rama S., Ballentine, R., & Weinstock, A. (1976). *Yoga and psychotherapy.* Glenview, IL: Himalayan Institute.

Ram Dass. (1974). *The only dance there is.* New York: Doubleday.

Ram Dass. (1978). *Journey of awakening: A meditator's guidebook.* New York: Doubleday.

Ross, C. (1989). *Multiple personality disorder: Diagnosis, clinical features, and treatment.* New York: Wiley.

Sayadaw, M. (1954). *Satipatthana Vipassana meditation.* Original edition in Burmese. English edition, n.d. San Francisco: Unity Press.

Schacter, S. (1971). *Emotion, obesity, and crime.* New York: Academic Press.

Schacter, S., & Singer, J. (1962). Cognitive, social and physiological determinants of emotional states. *Psychological Review, 69,* 379–399.

Schmitt, F. O. (1984). Molecular regulators of brain function: A new view, *Neuroscience, 13*(4), 991–1001.

Schoenewolf, G. (1991). *Jennifer and her selves.* New York: Fine.

Schreiber, F. (1974). *Sibyl.* New York: Warner.

Shapiro, D. (1994). Exploring the content and context of meditation. *Journal of Humanistic Psychology, 34*(4), 101–135.

Shapiro, D., & Walsh, R. (Eds.). (1981). *The science of meditation: Research, theory, and experience.* New York: Aldine.

Sherman, S. E. (1972). Brief report: Continuing research on "very deep hypnosis." *Journal of Transpersonal Psychology, 4,* 87–92.

Shields, S., & Stern, R. (1979). Emotion: The perception of bodily change. In P. Pliner, K. Blankstein, & I. Spigel (Eds.), *Perception of emotion in self and others* (pp. 85–106). New York: Plenum Press.

Sidis, B. (1898). *The psychology of suggestion.* New York: Appleton-Century-Crofts. (Preface by William James.)

Simonton, C., Mathews-Simonton, S., & Creighton, J. (1978). *Getting well again.* Los Angeles: Tarcher.

Skinner, B. F. (1972). *Cumulative record: A selection of papers* (3rd ed.). New York: Appleton-Century-Crofts.

Smith C. A., & Ellsworth, P. C. (1985). Patterns of appraisal in emotion. *Journal of Personality and Social Psychology, 48,* 813–838.

Smith, E. (1988). Evolving ethics in psychedelic drug taking. *Journal of Drug Issues, 18*(2), 201–214.

Smith, H. (2000). *Cleaning the doors of perception.* San Francisco, Council on Spiritual Practices.

Spanos, N., Flynn, D., & Gwynn, M. (1988). Contextual demands, negative hallucinations, and hidden observer responding: Three hidden observers observed. *British Journal of Experimental and Clinical Hypnosis, 5*(1), 5–10.

Sulloway, Frank. (1979). *Freud: Biologist of the Mind: Beyond the psychoanalytic legend.* New York: Basic Books.

Suls, J., & Marco, C. (1990). William James, the self, and the selective industry of the mind. *Personality and Social Psychology Bulletin, 16*(4), 688–698.

Sweet, M., & Johnson, C. (1990). Enhancing empathy: The interpersonal implications of a Buddhist meditation technique. *Psychotherapy, 27*(1), 19–29.

Tart, C. (1970). Transpersonal potentialities of deep hypnosis. *Journal of Transpersonal Psychology, 2,* 27–40.

Tart, C. (1971). Scientific foundations for the study of altered states of consciousness. *Journal of Transpersonal Psychology, 3,* 93–124. (Shorter version in *Science,* 1972, 176, 1203–1210.)

Tart, C. (1975). *States of consciousness.* New York: Dutton.

Taylor, E. (1981). The evolution of William James' definition of consciousness. *ReVISION, 4*(2), 40–47.

Taylor, E. (1982). *William James on exceptional mental states: Reconstruction of the 1896 Lowell lectures.* New York: Scribner's.

Taylor, E. (1991). William James and the humanistic tradition. *Journal of Humanistic Psychology, 31*(1).

Taylor, E. (1999). The future of psychology belongs to your work: William James and Sigmund Freud. *Journal of the American Psychological Society, 10*(6), 465–469.

Taylor, E. (2000). Psychotherapeutics and the problematic origins of clinical psychology in America. *The American Psychologist, 55*(9), 180–190.

Taylor, E. (2004). *William James and the Spiritual Roots of American Pragmatism.* Lectures delivered in honor of the centenary of James's *Varieties of Religious Experience* (1902) for the Swedenborg Society at Harvard University, Oct, 2001–June, 2002. In preparation. By permission.

Taylor, E. I. (1978). Psychology of Religion and Asian Studies: The William James legacy. *Journal of Transpersonal Psychology, 10*(1), 66–79.

Taylor, E. I. William James and Carl Jung. (1992a). In Papadopoulos, R. K. (Ed.), *Carl Gustav Jung: Critical assessments*. London: New York: Routledge, 1992.

Taylor, E. I. (1992b). The case for a uniquely American Jamesian tradition in psychology. In Margaret Donnelly (Ed.), *Reinterpreting the Legacy of William James* (APA Centennial William James Lectures) (pp. 3–28). Washington, D.C.: American Psychological Association.

Taylor, E. I. (1995). *Studia Swedenborgiana 9*(2), pp. 1–20.

Taylor, E. I. (1996). *William James on consciousness beyond the margin*. Princeton, NJ: Princeton University Press.

Taylor, E. I. (2002). William James and Depth Psychology. *Journal of Consciousness Studies 9*(9–10), 11–36.

Taylor, E. I. (2004). *William James and the Spiritual Roots of American Pragmatism*. Lectures delivered in honor of the centenary of James's *Varieties of Religious Experience* (1902) for the Swedenborg Society at Harward University, Oct, 2001–June, 2002. In preparation. By permission.

Tomkins, S. (1962). *Affect, imagery, consciousness*. Vol. 1, The positive affects. New York: Springer.

Tymoczko, D. (1996). The nitrous oxide philosopher. *The Atlantic Monthly, 277*(5), 93–101.

Valle, R., & von Eckartsberg, R. (1981). *The metaphors of consciousness*. New York: Plenum Press.

Weil, A., & Rosen, W. (1993). *From chocolate to morphine*. Boston: Houghton Mifflin.

Wilber, K. (1977). *The spectrum of consciousness*. Wheaton, IL: Theosophical.

Wilber, K. (1981). *Up from Eden*. New York: Doubleday.

Winton, W. (1990). Jamesian aspects of misattribution research. *Personality and Social Psychology Bulletin, 16*(4), 652–664.

Zukav, G. (1979). *The dancing Wu Li masters*. New York: Morrow.

b. f. skinner and
radical behaviorism

B. F. Skinner was for many years the most famous psychologist in the United States. The effects of his work reached far beyond the confines of professional psychology. His distaste for and distrust of mental, subjective, intervening, or what he called "fictional" explanations led him to focus on observable behavior and to formulate ways of observing, measuring, predicting, and understanding the behavior of people and animals.

No theorist since Freud has been by turns so lauded, quoted, misquoted, attacked, and supported. Yet Skinner delighted in confronting his critics and debating major thinkers who opposed his positions (Catania & Harnad, 1988; Skinner, 1972d, 1977b; Wann, 1964). His great personal charm and his willingness to speculate on the implications of his position, bolstered by his absolute, unshakable faith in his fundamental assumptions, helped to make Skinner a pivotal figure in contemporary psychology.

Freud wrote that his detractors, by the emotional intensity of their criticisms, unwittingly proved the very propositions of psychoanalytic theory they so vehemently opposed. Similarly, Skinner thought his critics displayed the nonscientific and inaccurate ways of thinking that his work attempted to correct. Both men, while vigorously criticized, were also acclaimed for developing and defending alternative visions of human nature.

In a survey of department chairmen at American universities . . . Skinner was chosen overwhelmingly as the most influential figure in modern psychology. (*New York Times Magazine,* 1984)

PERSONAL HISTORY

B. F. Skinner was born in 1904 and reared in Susquehanna, Pennsylvania, a small town in the northeastern part of the state. His father practiced law. As a boy, he was encouraged to be controlled, constrained, and tidy, and to "do the right thing." Skinner wrote that his home was "warm and stable. I lived in the house I was born in until I went to college" (1976a, p. 387). His boyhood fascination with mechanical inventions foreshadowed his later concern with modifying observable behavior.

> Some of the things I built had a bearing on human behavior. I was not allowed to smoke, so I made a gadget incorporating an atomizer bulb through which I could "smoke" cigarettes and blow smoke rings hygienically. (There might be a demand for it today.) At one time my mother started a campaign to teach me to hang up my pajamas. Every morning while I was eating breakfast, she would go up to my room, discover that my pajamas were not hung up, and call to me to come up immediately. She continued this for weeks. When the aversive stimulation grew unbearable, I constructed a mechanical device that solved my problem. A special hook in the closet of my room was connected by a string-and-pulley system to a sign hanging above the door to the room. When my pajamas were in place on the hook, the sign was held high above the door out of the way. When the pajamas were off the hook, the sign hung squarely in the middle of the doorframe. It read: "Hang up your pajamas"! (1967a, p. 396)

After completing his bachelor's degree with honors in English literature at Hamilton College, in Clinton, New York—a program that sustained and enriched his interest in literature and the arts—he returned home and attempted to become a writer.

> I built a small study in the attic and set to work. The results were disastrous. I fretted away my time. I read aimlessly, built model ships, played the piano, listened to the newly invented radio, contributed to the humorous column of a local paper but wrote almost nothing else, and thought about seeing a psychiatrist. (1967a, p. 394)

He finally terminated this experiment and went to New York City, where he lived in Greenwich Village for six months "self-consciously seeking an alternative culture"

(Bjork, 1993, p. 72). He spent the summer of 1928 in Europe. His adventures there included flying in the open cockpit of a plane in the rain, spending a shabby evening with a prostitute, and pursuing a round of ordinary touring with his parents. On his return, he began studying psychology at Harvard Graduate School. He generalized his personal failure as a writer into a lifelong distrust of the literary method of observation.

> I had failed as a writer because I had nothing important to say, but I could not accept that explanation. It was literature which must be at fault. . . . A writer might portray human behavior accurately, but he did not therefore understand it. I was to remain interested in human behavior, but the literary method had failed me; I would turn to the scientific. (1967a, p. 395)

During graduate school he worked diligently but not as hard as he liked to recall. In an early autobiographical essay (1967a, pp. 397–398), he wrote

> I would rise at six, study until breakfast, go to classes, laboratories, and libraries with no more than fifteen minutes unscheduled during the day, study until exactly nine o'clock at night and go to bed. I saw no movies or plays, seldom went to concerts, had scarcely any dates and read nothing but psychology and physiology.

I'm taking it easy my first semester. . . . After January I expect to settle down and solve the riddle of the universe. Harvard is fine. (Skinner, 1979a)

Much later he amended his description of his graduate years, recalling a normal blend of classes, activities, friends, dull papers, incomplete work, and dating (1979a).

After receiving his doctorate, he worked for five years at Harvard Medical School, researching animal nervous systems. In 1936 Skinner accepted a position at the University of Minnesota, teaching introductory and experimental psychology.

In 1938 he published *The Behavior of Organisms,* which described his own experiments in modifying the behavior of animals under laboratory conditions. This book established Skinner as an important learning theorist and laid the foundation for subsequent publications.

After nine years at Minnesota, he left to chair the psychology department at Indiana University. Three years later, he moved to Harvard, where he remained throughout semiretirement and until his death. After he stopped teaching, he continued to write. Later publications include a three-volume autobiography (Skinner, 1976b, 1979a, 1984a), one popular book about the problems of old age (Skinner & Vaughan, 1985), philosophical papers (Skinner, 1986, 1990b), and several essays that criticize general psychology, which he believed had lost its way (Skinner, 1987a, 1989, 1990a).

While pursuing his animal research studies, Skinner had the time and the creative capacity to apply his ingenuity in other ways. In 1945 he invented the air crib, a device that catapulted him into national prominence. It was a glassed-in, temperature-controlled crib with a bottom made of absorbent cloth (Skinner, 1945). In it a child could move freely without cumbersome diapers, pants, or other clothes. The absorbent bottom was easily replaced as the child soiled it. A rush of interest followed the crib's first appearance. However, the fact that the child was glassed in ran counter to many people's beliefs about child rearing and never became popular.

Ever the scientist, Skinner reflected on his concerns that led to the crib's invention:

My experience with American industry has been very sad. Nobody ever took up the air crib properly. (Skinner in Goodell, 1977)

> I must confess also to an ulterior motive. If, as many people have claimed, the first year is extraordinarily important in the determination of character and personality, then by all means let us control the conditions of that year as far as possible in order to discover the important variables. (1979a, p. 290)

He also designed a musical toilet seat for his child, but it was never actually manufactured (Skinner, 1989).

In 1948 Skinner published *Walden Two,* a novel describing a utopian community based on behaviorist learning principles. It was Skinner's initial effort to generalize his laboratory findings to human situations. Despite slow sales in its first years, the book became increasingly popular and controversial, and, to date, has sold close to three million copies. Skinner found writing the novel a remarkable experience. "I wrote my utopia in seven weeks. I would dash off a fair version of a short chapter in a single morning. I wrote directly on the typewriter . . . and I revised sparingly. . . . I wrote some parts with an emotional intensity that I have never experienced at any other time" (1979a, pp. 297–298). "It was pretty obviously a venture in self-therapy, in which I was struggling to reconcile two aspects of my own behavior represented by Burris and Frazier [the two major characters]" (1967a, p. 403).[1] A series of books by Skinner successively defined his ideological stance as his work moved further and further from its experimental beginnings. These include *Science and Human Behavior* (1953), *Cumulative Record* (1959, 1961, 1972a), *The Technology of Teaching* (1968), *Beyond Freedom and Dignity* (1971), *About Behaviorism* (1974), and *Reflections on Behaviorism and Society* (1978a). Among his more personal books are *Particulars of My Life* (1976b), *The Shaping of a Behaviorist* (1979a), *Notebooks* (1980), and *A Matter of Consequences* (1984a).

His willingness to appear in the media (Skinner, 1977a, 1978b, 1979b) kept his ideas before the general public. He wrote throughout his life, finishing the revisions for his last published paper (1990b) the day before his death at age 86.

> I really wrote *Walden Two* for the sake of feminine liberation but very few women liked it. (Skinner in Goodell, 1977)

> Behaviorism is a formulation which makes possible an effective experimental approach to human behavior. . . . It may need to be clarified, but it does not need to be argued. I have no doubt of the eventual triumph of the position. (Skinner, 1967a, pp. 409–410)

INTELLECTUAL ANTECEDENTS

Skinner acknowledged that he was deeply influenced by his early reading of the English scientist-philosopher Francis Bacon (1561–1626). "Three Baconian principles have characterized my professional life."

1. "I have studied nature not books"
2. "Nature to be commanded must be obeyed"
3. "A better world was possible, but it would not come about by accident. It must be planned and built, and with the help of science" (1984a, pp. 406–412).

Skinner says of himself, "I have . . . asked questions of the organism rather than of those who have studied the organism" (1967a, p. 409). Skinner stressed careful laboratory experimentation and the accumulation of measurable behavioral data. When we consider the possible richness of human personality, his approach is austere; yet it has led to a theory that in turn began a series of revolutions in both experimental and clinical psychology.

Darwinism and the Canon of Parsimony

The idea that animal studies could shed light on human behavior arose as an indirect result of Darwin's research and the subsequent development of evolutionary theories. Many psychologists, including Skinner, assumed that humans are essentially no different from other animals. While this extreme position has become less and less

---

[1]Skinner's first name was Burrhus; his middle name was Frederic.

acceptable, it is at the heart of Skinner's application of animal research to an understanding of human beings.

The first researchers of animal behaviors were interested in discovering the reasoning capacities of animals. In effect, they tried to raise the status of animals to that of thinking beings. The examinations of *higher* thought processes in animals were not supported, however, by the ideas of two prominent psychologists, Lloyd Morgan and Edward Thorndike. Morgan proposed a **canon of parsimony,** which states that given two explanations, a scientist should always accept the simpler one. Thorndike's research demonstrated that although animals seemed to display reasoning, their behaviors could be more parsimoniously explained as the result of noncognitive processes (Skinner, 1964). Consequently, research emphasis shifted. Also, researchers began to speculate that human behavior could be understood, in parsimonious terms, by ignoring the little-understood complexities of consciousness.

> After the horror of atheism, there is nothing that leads weak minds further astray from the paths of virtue than the idea that the minds of other animals resemble our own, and that, therefore, we have no greater right to future life than have gnats and ants. (René Descartes, 1649, "A Treatise on the Passions of the Soul")

Watson

American John B. Watson (1878–1958), the first avowed behaviorist, defined **behaviorism** as follows:

> Psychology as the behaviorist views it is a purely objective branch of natural science. Its theoretical goal is the prediction and control of behavior. Introspection forms no essential part of its methods. . . . The behaviorist, in his efforts to get a unitary scheme of animal response, recognizes no dividing line between man and brute. (1913, p. 158)

> The time seems to have come when psychology must discard all references to consciousness. (Watson, 1913, p. 163)

Watson argued against such a thing as consciousness, declaring that all learning is dependent upon the external environment and that all human activity is conditioned and conditionable. Skinner was attracted to the broad philosophical outlines of his work (Watson, 1928a) but not by his more extreme suggestions. For example, one of Watson's most widely read books on child rearing contains the following advice: "Never hug and kiss them [children], never let them sit on your lap. If you must, kiss them once on the forehead when they say good-night. Shake hands with them in the morning" (1928b, pp. 81–82).

Skinner criticized Watson for his denial of genetic characteristics as well as for his tendency to generalize without the support of concrete data.

> It is a mistake to suppose that there are internal stimuli. (Skinner in Evans, 1968, p. 21)

> His new science was also, so to speak, born prematurely. Very few scientific facts about behavior—particularly human behavior—were available. . . . He needed more factual support than he could find, and it is not surprising that much of what he said seemed oversimplified and naive. (Skinner, 1974, p. 6)

More surprising was Watson's fascination with Freud's work, despite his determined rejection of Freud's central idea of the unconscious. "In popular articles and books Watson 'explained' [reinterpreted] psychoanalytic concepts within the framework of behaviorism" (Rilling, 2000 p. 301).

Pavlov

Ivan Pavlov (1849–1936), a Russian physiologist, did the first important modern work in the area of behavioral conditioning (1927). His research demonstrated that autonomic functions could be conditioned. He showed that salivation could be evoked by a stimulus other than food, such as a ringing bell. Pavlov was not merely observing and predicting the behaviors he was studying; he could produce them on command. While other animal experimenters were content with using statistical analysis to predict the likelihood that a behavior would occur, Skinner was fascinated with the step beyond prediction—control. Pavlov's work pointed Skinner toward tightly controlled laboratory experiments on animals. By restricting an animal's environment, Skinner found, he could achieve almost perfectly replicable results. Individual differences could be effectively controlled, and laws of behavior valid for any member of a species might be discovered. Skinner's contention was that in this way, psychological research could eventually be elevated from a probabilistic science to an exact one.

Philosophy of Science

I often say that when you can measure what you are speaking about, and express it in numbers, you know something about it; but when you cannot express it in numbers, your knowledge is of a meager and unsatisfactory kind . . . but you have scarcely, in your thoughts, advanced to the stage of Science. (Lord Kelvin, 1824–1907)

Skinner was impressed with the ideas of philosophers of science, including Percy Bridgman, Ernst Mach, and Jules Henri Poincaré. They created new models of explanatory thinking that did not depend on any metaphysical substructures. To Skinner, behaviorism "is not the science of human behavior; it is the philosophy of that science" (1974, p. 3). Behaviorism allows questions to be clearly formulated for which answers can be found. For example, only when biology left metaphysics behind, dismissing its concern with "vital fluids" and other unmeasurable, unprovable, and unpredictable notions, could it become an experimental science.

Skinner's position, he contended, was essentially nontheoretical (1950, 1956; Sagal, 1981). He worked from observable data alone. However, his impact on psychology and society arose from extrapolations of his data into theories reaching far beyond the confines of animal research.

MAJOR CONCEPTS

Skinner did not develop his theory from close observations of either children or adults; many of his formulations emerged instead from the animal laboratory. This is one reason why his major concepts differ significantly from those of other theorists considered in this book.

Scientific Analysis of Behavior

A scientific analysis of behavior must, I believe, assume that a person's behavior is controlled by his genetic and environmental histories rather than by the person himself as an initiating, creative agent. (Skinner, 1974, p. 189)

Behavior, no matter how complex, can be investigated, like any other observable phenomena.

> Science is a disposition to deal with the facts rather than what someone has said about them. . . . It is a search for order, for uniformities, for lawful relations among the events in nature. It begins, as we all begin, by observing single episodes, but it quickly passes on the general rule, to scientific law. (Skinner, 1953, pp. 12–13)

The goal is to look at a behavior and its **contingencies** (from a Latin word meaning "to touch on all sides"). For Skinner, these include the antecedents of the behavior, the response to it, and the consequences or results of the response. Behavior, for Skinner, is anything an organism can be observed doing (Skinner, 1938, p. 6). A complete analysis of the behavior would also consider the genetic endowment of the organism and previous behaviors related to those being studied.

The scientific analysis of behavior begins by isolating the parts of a complex event so that the individual items can be better understood. Skinner's experimental research follows this analytic procedure, restricting itself to conditions amenable to rigorous scientific analysis. The results of his experiments can be verified independently, and his conclusions checked against the recorded data.

Freud and the psychodynamic theorists were equally interested in the developmental history of the individual as the basis for later behavior. Skinner, on the other hand, advocated a more extreme position, stating that it is behavior, and behavior alone, that can be studied. Behavior, as distinct from an inner life, can be fully described; that is, it is observable and perceivable with measuring instruments.

Personality

Skinner argues that if you base your definition of the self on observable behavior, you need not discuss the inner working of the self or the personality at all.

Personality, therefore, in the sense of a separate self, has no place in a scientific analysis of behavior. Personality, as defined by Skinner, is a *collection of behavior patterns*. Different situations evoke different response patterns. An individual response is based solely on previous experiences and genetic history. To look for "mental or psychic states," says Skinner, is to look in the wrong place. "By emphasizing an inner life as an object of study, [Freud] put science back fifty years" (Skinner, 1953, in Skinner, 1984c, p. 56).

Buddhism—to the surprise of most behaviorists—also concludes that because there is no observable individual self, the self does not exist. Buddhists do not believe in an entity called personality, but in overlapping behaviors and sensations, all of which are impermanent. Skinner and the Buddhists developed their ideas based on the assumption of no ego, no self, no personality, except as characterized by a collection of behaviors. Both theories emphasize that a proper understanding of the causes of behavior eliminates confusion and misunderstanding. The theories, however, diverge widely in their explanation of the causes. (See in Chapter 14, "Selflessness," on p. 407.)

Explanatory Fictions

Explanatory fictions (Skinner's term) are terms nonbehaviorists employ to describe behavior. Skinner believed that people use these concepts when they do not understand the behavior involved or are unaware of the pattern of reinforcements that preceded or followed the behavior. Examples of explanatory fictions for Skinner include *freedom, autonomous man, dignity,* and *creativity.* According to behaviorism, using such terms as explanations for behavior is simply incorrect. Skinner believed that this type of explanation is actually harmful: it gives a misleading appearance of being satisfactory and thus might preclude the search for more objective variables.

> Unfortunately, references to feelings and states of mind have an emotional appeal that behavioral alternatives usually lack. Here is an example, "If the world is to be saved, people must learn to be noble without being cruel, to be filled with faith, yet open to truth, to be inspired by great purposes without hating those who thwart them." This is an "inspiring" sentence. . . . But what does it inspire us to do? (Skinner, 1987a)

When I can do what I want to do, there is my liberty for me, but I can't help wanting what I do want. (Voltaire, 1694–1778)

Skinner's argument, that language glosses over or prevents real observation, is a constant theme.

If there is freedom, it is to be found in the randomness of variations. (Skinner, 1990a, p. 1208)

Freedom.   *Freedom* is a label that we attach to behavior when we are unaware of the causes for the behavior. One example may clarify Skinner's meaning. A series of studies conducted by Milton Erickson (1939) demonstrated that through hypnosis, subjects could evoke various kinds of psychopathological symptoms. While a subject was in a trance, Erickson would make posthypnotic suggestions. In most cases, the subjects later carried out the suggestion and developed the symptom. In no case did the subject recall, when asked, that the suggestion had been given under hypnosis. Whenever subjects were asked what were the reasons for their unusual behaviors, they would invent (and apparently believe) a host of explanations. If one listened to the subject's comments, one would conclude that all of the subjects were acting out of their own *free will.* The subjects were convinced that their behaviors were the result of their own decisions. But the observers, knowing that the subjects had no recall of the preceding events, were equally convinced that free will was not the full explanation.

There is no subjugation so perfect as that which keeps the appearance of freedom. (Jean-Jacques Rousseau, 1712–1778)

Skinner suggests that the feeling of freedom is not really freedom; furthermore, he believes that the most repressive forms of control are those that reinforce the feeling of freedom, such as the voters' "freedom" to choose between candidates whose positions are extremely similar. These repressive tactics restrict and control action in subtle ways not easily discernible by the people being controlled.

The objection to inner states is not that they do not exist, but that they are not relevant in a functional analysis. (Skinner, 1953, p. 35)

Autonomous Man.   **Autonomous man** is an explanatory fiction Skinner described as an *indwelling agent,* an inner person who is moved by vague inner forces independent of the behavioral contingencies. To be autonomous is to initiate "uncaused" behavior, behavior that does not arise from prior behaviors and is not attributable to external events. Skinner found no evidence that such an autonomous being exists, and he was distressed that so many people believed in the idea.

Intelligent people no longer believe that men are possessed by demons, . . . but human behavior is still commonly attributed to indwelling agents. (Skinner, 1971, p. 5)

Skinner's research demonstrated that if one plots certain kinds of learning experiences, the shape of the resulting curve (and the rate of the learning) is the same for pigeons, rats, monkeys, cats, dogs, and human children (Skinner, 1956). This parallelism between animal and human learning underlies Skinner's analysis of human behavior. From his first book, *The Behavior of Organisms* (1938), he performed experiments that postulate no major distinction between humans and other species. In that book he states, "I may say that the only differences I expect to see revealed between the behavior of rat and man (aside from enormous differences of complexity) lie in the field of verbal behavior" (p. 442). Fifty years later, he had not changed his opinion. "There is no place in a scientific analysis of behavior for a mind or self" (1990a, p. 1209).

Dignity.   *Dignity* (or credit or praise) is another explanatory fiction.

> The amount of credit a person receives is related in a curious way to the visibility of the causes of his behavior. We withhold credit when the causes are conspicuous. . . . [W]e do not give credit for coughing, sneezing, or vomiting even though the result may be valuable. For the same reason, we do not give much credit for behavior which is under conspicuous aversive control even though it may be useful. (Skinner, 1971, p. 42)

Rights and duties, like a moral or ethical sense, are examples of hypothetical internalized environmental sanctions. Skinner, 1975, p. 48)

In other words, we often praise an individual for behavior when the circumstances or the additional contingencies are unknown. By way of contrast, for example, we do not praise acts of charity if we know they are done only to lower income taxes. We do not praise a confession of a crime if the confession came out only under extreme pressure. We do not censure a person whose acts inadvertently cause others damage. Skinner suggests that if we would admit our ignorance, we would withhold both praise and censure.

Creativity.   With a certain amount of puckish delight, Skinner dismisses the last stronghold of the indwelling agent: the poetic or creative act. It is for Skinner still another example of using a metaphysical label to hide the fact that we do not know the specific causes of given behaviors.

Skinner derides the opinions of creative artists who maintain that their works are spontaneous or arise from sources beyond the artist's life experience. Evidence from hypnosis and from the vast body of literature on the effectiveness of propaganda and advertising, as well as the findings of psychotherapy, all shows that an individual is often unaware of what lies behind his or her own behavior. Skinner asks the question "Does the poet create, originate, initiate the thing called a poem, or is his behavior merely the product of his genetic and environmental histories?" (1972c, p. 34). His conclusion is that creative activity is no different from other behaviors except that the behavioral elements preceding it and determining it are more obscure. He sides with Samuel Butler, who noted that "a poet writes a poem as a hen lays an egg, and both of them feel better afterwards."

Will.   Skinner considers the notion of will confusing and unrealistic. For him, will, free will, and willpower are nothing more than explanatory fictions. Skinner assumes that no action is free. "When we recognize this, we are likely to drop the notion of responsibility altogether and with it the doctrine of free will as an inner causal agent" (1953, p. 116).

Other researchers, however, have shown that people who believe that external forces are responsible for their actions feel less in control of their behavior than people who feel personally responsible for their actions. Davison and Valins (1969) found that "if a person realizes that his behavior change is totally dependent upon an external reward or punishment, there is no reason for the new behavior to persist once the environmental contingencies change" (p. 33).

Lefcourt reviewed studies in which subjects were tested both when they operated under the belief that they could control outcomes and when they could not control them. These studies suggest that depriving animals or people of the "illusion" of freedom has negative behavioral effects. "The sense of control, the illusion that one can exercise personal choice, has a definite and positive role in sustaining life. The illusion of freedom is not to be easily dismissed without anticipating undesirable consequences" (1973, pp. 425–426).

Skinner's investigation of will has drawn more criticism than any other aspect of his work. Considerable research has been conducted on what is now called the *locus of control*, or "Who do I think is in charge—me or my environment?" The data favors the position that the individual's belief in the possibility of directing his or her behavior matters (Lefcourt, 1980). Even prominent behaviorists such as Mahoney and Thoresen (1974) talk about self-control and a sense of freedom as the core of successful behavioral manipulation.

Self.   Skinner considers the term *self* an explanatory fiction.

If we cannot show what is responsible for a man's behavior, we say that he himself is responsible for it. The precursors of physical science once followed the same practice, but the

---

I have never been able to understand why he [poet I. A. Richards] feels that Coleridge made an important contribution to our understanding of human behavior, and he has never been able to understand why I feel the same way about pigeons. (Skinner, 1972c, p. 34)

To say that the "central pathology of our day is a failure of will, which brought psychoanalysis into being," seems more profound than to say that in the world of our day very little behavior is positively reinforced and much is punished and that psychoanalysis came into being to arrange better contingencies. (Skinner, 1974, p. 163)

What is controversial about Skinner is not so much his view that man is a very superior machine but his views as to what runs the machine. . . . Skinner dismisses all the baggage of consciousness, all feelings, all motives, all intentions as, at best, by-products. (Cohen, 1977)

There is no place in the scientific position for a self as a true originator or initiator of action. (Skinner, 1974, p. 225)

> wind is no longer blown by Aeolus, nor is the rain cast down by Jupiter Pluvius. . . . The practice resolves our anxiety with respect to unexplained phenomena and is perpetuated because it does so. . . . A concept of self is not essential in an analysis of behavior. (1953, pp. 283, 285)

It may be difficult to follow this line of reasoning, because something in you says, No! I have a self. Skinner would reply that you have been conditioned to have such a response. But where, then, is this self that you say exists? (See Chapter 14, Zen and the Buddhist Tradition, for a different way to consider the same issue.)

Conditioning and Reinforcement

A better understanding of the patterns that change behaviors or keep them stable is one of Skinner's major contributions.

Respondent Behavior.   **Respondent behavior** is reflexive behavior. An organism responds automatically to a stimulus. Your knee jerks when the patellar tendon is struck; your body begins to perspire as the outside temperature increases; the pupil in your eye contracts when exposed to a bright light. Pavlov discovered that certain respondent behaviors can be conditioned. In his classic experiment, he conditioned the salivation response in dogs by pairing a bell with the arrival of food. Dogs naturally salivate at the sight or smell of food. After Pavlov had accompanied the presentation of food with the ringing of a bell, the dogs would salivate to the sound of the bell alone. The dogs were conditioned to respond to a stimulus that previously had evoked no response. Like Pavlov's dogs, we can be conditioned to salivate when we enter a restaurant or hear a dinner bell. Respondent conditioning is readily learned and exhibited. Advertisers who link an attractive person with a product are seeking to form an association and elicit a certain response. They hope that through the pairing, consumers will respond positively to the product.

> Operant conditioning is not pulling strings to make a person dance; it is arranging a world in which a person does things that affect that world, which in turn affects him. (Skinner, 1972b, p. 69)

Operant Conditioning.   Operant behaviors are behaviors that occur spontaneously. "Operant behavior is strengthened or weakened by the events that *follow* the response. Whereas respondent behavior is controlled by its antecedents, operant behavior is controlled by its consequences" (Reese, 1966, p. 3). The conditioning that takes place depends on what occurs after the behavior has been completed. Skinner became fascinated by operant behaviors, because he could see that they can be linked to far more complex behaviors than is true of respondent behaviors. Skinner concluded that almost any naturally occurring behavior in an animal or in a human can be trained to occur more often, more strongly, or in any chosen direction.

The following example illustrates some facets of operant conditioning: I am attempting to teach my daughter to swim. She enjoys the water but is unwilling or afraid to get her head or face wet or to blow bubbles underwater. This has hindered her progress considerably. I have agreed to give her a piece of candy if she wets her face. Once she can freely wet her face, I will give her a piece of candy but only if she ducks her whole head. After she is able to do that, she will get a piece of candy only for blowing bubbles underwater. Stage by stage, she will modify her behaviors, rewarded, or *reinforced,* by the candies, leading to her learning how to swim.

Operant conditioning is the process of shaping and maintaining a particular behavior by its consequences. Therefore, it takes into account not only what is presented before the response but what happens after the response. I condition my daughter's

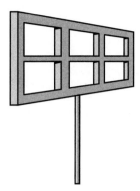

FIGURE 8.1 "Ames" Illusion
This is not a rectangle at an angle. It is a trapezoid looked at straight on. Seeing a rectangle is a conditioned, not an innate, response.

behavior by giving her a piece of candy after she performs certain acts. I use the candy to reinforce certain of her behaviors in the water. "When a bit of behavior is followed by a certain kind of consequence, it is more likely to occur again, and a consequence having this effect is called a reinforcer" (Skinner, 1971, p. 25).

Extensive research on the variables that affect operant conditioning have led to the following conclusions:

1. Conditioning can and does take place without awareness. Numerous demonstrations illustrate that what we perceive depends, in large measure, on our past perceptions, which have been partially conditioned. For example, the way we perceive the optical illusions used by Ames (1951) was considered a function of the physiology of vision. (See Figure 8.1.) However, when illusions like the "rectangle" in the figure were shown to people from cultures in which the dwellings and windows do not contain right angles, they did not see the illusion. Perception, in part, is culturally conditioned. A summary of research concludes that conditioning can take place "in human beings . . . in the state of sleep, and in the waking state while the subject is entirely unaware of the fact that he is learning to respond to a conditioned stimulus" (Berelson & Steiner, 1964, p. 138).

2. Conditioning is maintained in spite of awareness. It is disconcerting to realize that you can be conditioned even when you know that the process is happening and you may be resisting it. One experimenter trained subjects to lift a finger at the sound of a tone paired with a shock to the finger. The subjects continued to raise their fingers even after they had been told that the shock had been turned off. They continued to raise their fingers even when asked by the experimenter not to do so. Only after the electrodes had been removed from their fingers could they control their own recently conditioned responses (Lindley & Moyer, 1961).

3. Conditioning is less effective when the subject is aware but uncooperative (Goldfried & Merbaum, 1973). Efficient conditioning is a collaboration. Conditioning is inherently unstable when it is not undertaken with full cooperation. The following story illustrates what can happen when cooperation is not obtained:

> A half dozen aging alcoholics in a midwestern veterans hospital were given an alcohol treatment. [They were administered a drug that induced vomiting anytime they drank alcohol. Eventually, the men were conditioned so that drinking alcohol without taking the drug caused vomiting.] The men were thoroughly conditioned, and just the thought of drinking made them shake.

personal reflection

OBSERVING AND MODIFYING BEHAVIOR

Observing behavior and recording what you observe is the cornerstone of behavior modification. Try this exercise in observing and modifying your own behavior. Use tally sheets or graph paper to record your observations.

Keep a record of the time you spend working on each of your courses. A simple bar graph, marked off in hours, with different bars for each subject would be appropriate. Keep records for a week to establish a baseline. Then decide which class you need to spend more study time on.

For the next week, each time you study for that class, give yourself positive reinforcement; read a chapter of a novel, eat some candy, spend time with a friend, make a phone call, or do whatever appeals to you. Make sure the reinforcement is something that you really enjoy. Keep a record of the reinforcers and when you gave them to yourself.

Do you find the amount of time you are spending on the course increasing? What are the possible causes for this increase?

One afternoon, the old men started talking about their new lives and each discovered that the others hated it. They decided they would rather be in danger of being drunkards again than be terrified of the bottle.

So they plotted an evening to escape. They sneaked out to a bar, crowded together on their barstools, and through their sweating, shaking, and vomiting, they bolstered and chided one another to down drink after drink. They downed enough so their fears left them. (Hilts, 1973)

When I was a Freudian somebody would say, "I've been thinking about my mother's vagina," and I'd write down "mother's vagina" you know, and pretty soon I've got the patient reinforced so that every time I pick up my pencil he gets a flash ... [H]e's winning my attention and love ... [and] pretty soon he's talking about his mother's vagina 15 minutes of the hour. And then I think, "Ah, we're getting some place." (Ram Dass, 1970, p. 114)

Reinforcement.   A **reinforcer** is any stimulus that follows the occurrence of a response and increases or maintains the probability of that response. In the example of the child learning to swim, candy was the reinforcer offered after she successfully exhibited a specific behavior.

Reinforcers may be either positive or negative.

A *positive reinforcer* strengthens any behavior that *produces* it: a glass of water is positively reinforcing when we are thirsty, and if we then draw and drink a glass of water, we are more likely to do so again on similar occasions. A *negative reinforcer* strengthens any behavior that *reduces* or *terminates* it: when we take off a shoe that is pinching, the reduction in pressure is negatively reinforcing, and we are more likely to do so again when a shoe pinches. (Skinner, 1974, p. 46)

Negative reinforcers are aversive: they are stimuli a person or an animal turns away from or tries to avoid.

Positive and negative consequences regulate or control behaviors. This is the core of Skinner's position; he proposes that all behavior is shaped by a combination of positive and negative reinforcers. Moreover, he asserts, it is possible to explain the occurrence of any behavior if one has sufficient knowledge of the prior reinforcers.

Skinner conducted his original research on animals; the reinforcers he used included food, water, and electric shocks. The connection between the reinforcers and the animals' needs was straightforward. For example, a hungry animal learned to do a task, such as open a hatch or push a lever, and was rewarded with food. The reinforcements are more difficult to perceive when one investigates more complex or abstract situations. What reinforcers lead to overeating? What reinforces a person who volunteers for a life-threatening job? What keeps students doing coursework when they have no interest in the subject?

Primary reinforcers are events or stimuli that are innately reinforcing. They are unlearned, present at birth, and related to physical needs and survival. Examples are air, water, food, and shelter. *Secondary* reinforcers are neutral stimuli that become associated with primary reinforcers so that they eventually function as reinforcers. Money is one example of a secondary reinforcer; it has no intrinsic value, but money or the promise of money is one of the most widely used and effective reinforcers.

Money is an effective secondary reinforcer for more than humans. It has been shown that chimpanzees can learn to work for tokens. They have been trained to spend the tokens in vending machines that dispense bananas and other rewards. When they were denied access to the machines for a time, they would continue to work, hoarding their tokens until the machines were once again available.

Schedules of Reinforcement.   How often or how regularly a new behavior is reinforced affects how quickly the behavior is learned and how long or how often it will be repeated (Ferster & Skinner, 1957). *Continuous* reinforcement will increase the speed at which a new behavior is learned. *Intermittent* or *partial* reinforcement will produce more stable behavior—that is, behavior that will continue to be produced even after the reinforcement stops or appears rarely. Thus researchers have found that to change or maintain behaviors, the scheduling is as important as the reinforcement itself (Kimble, 1961). A slot machine, for example, works on an intermittent reinforcement schedule. It rewards the player only now and then but often enough so that the act of playing the machine is hard to extinguish. Changing working conditions are still improved by the skillful application of schedules of reinforcement, for example the work of Mawhinney and Fellows (1999) with groups of telemarketers.

Reinforcing a correct response improves learning. It is more effective than punishment (aversive control), because reinforcement selectively directs behavior toward a predetermined goal. The use of reinforcement is a highly focused and effective strategy for shaping and controlling desired behaviors.

Behavioral Control.   While many psychologists are concerned with predicting behavior, Skinner is interested in the control of behavior.

> We are all controlled by the world in which we live. . . . The question is this: Are we to be controlled by accident, by tyrants, or by ourselves in effective cultural design?
>
> The danger of the misuse of power is possibly greater than ever. It is not allayed by disguising the facts. We cannot make wise decisions if we continue to pretend that human behavior is not controlled, or if we refuse to engage in control when valuable results might be forthcoming. Such measures weaken only ourselves, leaving the strength of science to others. The first step in a defense against tyranny is the fullest possible exposure of controlling techniques. . . .
>
> It is not time for self-deception, emotional indulgence, or the assumption of attitudes which are no longer useful. Man is facing a difficult test. He must keep his head now, or he must start again—a long way back. (Skinner, 1955, pp. 56–57)

Therefore, if one can make changes in the environment, one can begin to control behavior.

What Supports or Impedes Personal Growth?

Growth for Skinner means the ability to minimize adverse conditions and to increase the beneficial control of our environment. By clarifying our thinking, we can make better use of the available tools for predicting, maintaining, and controlling our own behavior.

Ignorance.   Skinner defines *ignorance* as lack of knowledge about what causes a given behavior. The first step in overcoming ignorance is to acknowledge it; the second is to change the behaviors that have maintained the ignorance. One way to eliminate ignorance is to stop using nondescriptive, mental terms. In the following example, Skinner illustrates how an individual's portrayal of behavior can reveal the way that person views the causes of the behavior being observed:

> A hungry pigeon was conditioned to turn around in a clockwise direction by reinforcing successive approximations with food. Students who had watched the demonstration were asked to write an account of what they had seen. Their responses included the following: (1) The organism was conditioned to *expect* reinforcement for the right kind of behavior. (2) The pigeon walked around, *hoping* that something would bring the food back again. (3) The pigeon *observed* that a certain behavior seemed to produce a particular result. (4) The pigeon *felt* that food would be given it because of its action; and (5) the bird came to *associate* his action with the click of the food-dispenser. The observed facts could be stated respectively as follows: (1) The organism was reinforced *when* it emitted a given kind of behavior. (2) The pigeon walked around *until* the food container again appeared. (3) A certain behavior *produced* a particular result. (4) Food was given to the pigeon when it acted in a given way; and (5) the click of the food-dispenser *was temporarily related* to the bird's action. These statements describe the contingencies of reinforcement. The expressions "expect," "hope," "observe," "feel," and "associate" go beyond them to identify effects on the pigeon. The effect actually observed was clear enough; the pigeon turned more skillfully and more frequently; but that was not the effect reported by the students. (Skinner in Wann, 1964, pp. 90–91)

This example is one of many Skinner has used to show people how their determination to think in "fictions" prevents them from being in touch with the actual, vital, and concrete world.

Functional Analysis.   **Functional analysis** is an examination of cause-and-effect relationships. It treats every aspect of behavior as a *function* of a condition that can be described in physical terms. Thus the behavior and its causes can be defined without explanatory fictions.

> When we see a man moving about a room, opening drawers, looking under magazines, and so on, we may describe his behavior in fully objective terms. "Now he is in a certain part of the room; he has grasped a book between the thumb and forefinger of his right hand; he is lifting the book and bending his head so that any object under the book can be seen." We may also interpret his behavior or "read a meaning into it" by saying "he is looking for something" or, more specifically, that "he is looking for his glasses." What we have added is not a further description of his behavior but an inference about some of the variables responsible for it. This is so even if we ask what he is doing and he says, "I am looking for my glasses." This is not a further description of his behavior but of the variables of which his behavior is a function; it is equivalent to "I have lost my glasses,"

"I shall stop what I am doing when I find my glasses," or "When I have done this in the past, I have found my glasses." (Skinner in Fabun, 1968, p. 18)

Precise descriptions of behavior help us make accurate predictions of future behaviors and improve the analysis of the reinforcements that led to the behavior. Behavior is neither random nor arbitrary but is a purposeful process we can describe by considering the environment in which the behavior is embedded.

Skinner says that explanations that depend on terms such as *will, imagination, intelligence,* or *freedom* are not functional. They obscure rather than clarify the causes of behavior because they do not truly describe what is occurring.

Punishment.   Punishment provides no information about how to do something correctly. It neither meets the demands of the person inflicting the punishment nor benefits the person receiving it. Thus it inhibits personal growth. People who make mistakes want to learn how to correct their error or how to come to the correct solution next time. Often, when students have tests returned to them, they learn which answers they got wrong. No further explanation is given; the correct solutions are not forthcoming. In such situations, people may feel actually prevented from learning. Skinner, although often misunderstood, is solidly against punishment in families, in schools, and in social institutions—not on moral grounds but on practical ones.

Punishment does not work—that is to say, punished behaviors usually do not go away. Unless new learning is available, the punished responses will return, often disguised or coupled with new behaviors. The new behaviors may be attempts to avoid further punishment, or they may be retaliation against the person who administered the original punishment. The more a teacher uses punishment, the more discipline problems he or she will have. The effects of a prison term illustrate the ineffectiveness of punishment. Prison life punishes inmates for their prior behaviors but rarely teaches the individuals more socially acceptable ways to satisfy their needs. Prisoners who have not learned behaviors to replace those that landed them in jail will, once released—and exposed to the same environment and subject to the same temptations—probably repeat those behaviors. The high proportion of criminals returning to prison underscores the accuracy of these observations.

A related problem is that punishment selectively reinforces and encourages the punisher.

Thus, a slave driver induces a slave to work by whipping him when he stops; by resuming work the slave escapes from the whipping (and incidentally reinforces the slave driver's behavior in using the whip). A parent nags a child until the child performs a task; by performing the task the child escapes nagging (and reinforces the parent's behavior). The blackmailer threatens exposure unless the victim pays; by paying the victim escapes from the threat (and reinforces the practice). A teacher threatens corporal punishment or failure until his students pay attention; by paying attention the students escape from the threat of punishment (and reinforce the teacher for threatening it). In one form or another intentional aversive control is the pattern of most social coordination—in ethics, religion, government, economics, education, psychotherapy, and family life. (Skinner, 1971, p. 26)

Skinner concluded that although punishment may be used briefly to suppress a behavior that is highly undesirable or could cause injury or death, a far more useful

personal reflection

PUNISHMENT VERSUS REINFORCEMENT

Part 1. Punishment

Write down a behavior of your own that you wish to modify. You might choose coming to class late, writing letters during class, eating too much, going to sleep late, or being rude. If you are married, if you live with someone, or if you have a roommate, you can each pick a habit and help each other.

Punish yourself or have your partner punish you each time the behavior occurs. The punishment might be an insult ("Hey, piggy, you're overeating again"), forfeiture of a treat, or another deprivation. An easy punishment is to fine yourself money each time the behavior occurs. The accumulated fines can be given to charity. (A variation of this is to give the fines to your partner so that he or she is rewarded every time you are punished. This will make your partner more alert.) After a week, review your progress.

Part 2. Positive Reinforcement

Now choose a behavior that you would like to perform more often, such as exercising.

Begin to reinforce yourself every time you perform the desired behavior. Give yourself, or have your partner give you, small gifts: praise, gold stars, or some other reward. Being noticed is among the most effective rewards, so be sure that both you and your partner note the desired behavior when it occurs.

After a week, review your behavior pattern. Have there been any changes? How do you feel about this way of modifying your behavior? Consider the different effects punishment and reward reinforcement could have in your life.

approach is to establish a situation in which a new, competing, and more beneficial behavior can be learned and reinforced.

STRUCTURE

Body

In a system based solely on observable data, the role of the body is of primary importance. However, one need not know neuroanatomy or the physiological processes to predict how people will behave. In fact, Skinner considers personality an explanatory fiction, therefore, all that exists is the body.

In spite of this, the body never interested Skinner. He treats a person as an unopened, but certainly not empty, box. "Rather than hypothesize the needs that may propel a particular activity, they try to discover the events that strengthen its future likelihood, and that maintain or change it. Thus they search for the conditions that regulate behavior rather than hypothesize need states inside the person" (Mischel, 1976, p. 62). Thus Skinner and later behaviorists emphasize the inputs and outputs, because, in their terms, these are the only observable elements.

Relationships and the Psychology of Women

Skinner's interest lay in the forces that shape and control individuals from outside themselves. Therefore for Skinner, social behavior is neither special nor distinct from other behavior. Social behavior is simply a series of interactions between two or more people.

Relationships.   Skinner devotes considerable attention to verbal behavior (1957) and to the importance of the verbal community's role in shaping behavior, especially early language development and other behavior in children. For Skinner, verbal behavior includes speaking, reading, writing: any activity that uses words. The **verbal community** is defined as the people who respond to the verbal behavior of others in the same community. For example, a child listens to parents, siblings, other children, and teachers. He or she responds by changing or maintaining various behaviors. This is common sense, even when expressed in behavioral terms; but Skinner goes on to say that there are *no other relevant variables* for behavior beyond a person's history, genetic endowment, and events in the immediate environment. This remains an active research area with its own journal and disagreements (Knapp, 1998).

The reinforcements you receive in a social situation depend partly on your behavior and partly on how others react to your behavior. In a conversation you say something you receive feedback. The feedback you receive, however, is based not only on what you said but also on how the other person behaved after hearing it. For example, you say something as a joke. The other person takes it seriously and becomes upset. You modify your behavior and add, "I was only kidding." Thus we modify our behaviors in interpersonal relationships as much on the basis of others' reactions as on our own perceptions. This is the verbal community in action.

Although Skinner, writing as a psychologist, did not discuss social relationships, his characters in *Walden Two* discuss them at length. Frazier, the designer of the utopian community, describes the place of the conventional family.

> The significant history of our times is the story of the growing weakness of the family. . . . A community must solve the problem of the family by revising certain established practices. That's absolutely inevitable. The family is an ancient form of community, and the customs and habits which have been set up to perpetuate it are out of place in a society which isn't based on blood ties. Walden Two replaces the family, not only as an economic unit, but to some extent as a social and psychological unit as well. What survives is an experimental question. (1948, p. 138)

The Psychology of Women.   Skinner, in keeping with his atheoretical outlook, did not describe a psychology of women per se. According to Skinner, "a self is a repertoire of behavior appropriate to a given set of contingencies. . . . The identity conferred upon a self arises from the contingencies responsible for the behavior" (Skinner, 1971, pp. 189–190). Thus a woman's identity is unique and different from a man's identity only insofar as the contingencies responsible for women and men's behaviors differ. To the extent, then, that a society indeed offers different contingencies to men than it does to women (in terms, say, of roles and behaviors reinforced as culturally appropriate), the "psychologies" of men and women will differ. In the society that Skinner has envisioned in *Walden Two,* for example, the contingencies determining behavior are in fact quite different from those prevalent in contemporary Western society, and conceptions of femininity and masculinity differ accordingly. Skinner did not distinguish, for instance, between jobs on the basis of sexual stereotypes but suggests that individuals will find jobs and develop skills best suited to them and the general needs of the group.

personal reflection

MODIFYING SOMEONE ELSE'S BEHAVIOR

Many experiments have established that verbal behavior can be conditioned by selectively rewarding types of words or phrases (Berelson & Steiner, 1964). You can experiment with rewarding certain verbal behaviors by simply nodding your head or saying "mmm-hmmm" or "yeah."

Try this exercise. In conversations, indicate agreement by nodding every time a particular behavior is expressed (for example, the use of long, complex words, swear words, or emotional statements). Notice if the number of such expressions increases as you continue to reinforce them.

The "emotions" are excellent examples of the fictional causes to which we commonly attribute behavior. (Skinner, 1953, p. 160)

Emotions

"But the emotions are—fun!" said Barbara. "Life wouldn't be worth living without them."

"Some of them yes," said Frazier. "The productive and strengthening emotions—joy and love. But sorrow and hate—and the high voltage emotions of anger, fear, and rage—are out of proportion with the needs of modern life, and they are wasteful and dangerous." (Skinner in *Walden Two,* 1948, p. 102)

James and others were on the right track. . . . We both strike and feel angry for a common reason, and that reason lies in the environment. (Skinner, 1975, p. 43)

Skinner advocates an essentially descriptive approach to emotions. Instead of treating emotions as vague inner states, he suggests that we learn to observe associated behaviors. "We define an emotion—insofar as we wish to do so—as a particular state of strength or weakness in one or more responses" (1953, p. 166). He points out also that even a well-defined emotion like anger will include different behaviors on different occasions, even with the same individual.

> When the man in the street says that someone is afraid or angry or in love, he is generally talking about predispositions to act in certain ways. The "angry" man shows an increased probability of striking, insulting, or otherwise inflicting injury and a lowered probability of aiding, favoring, comforting, or making love. The man "in love" shows an increased tendency to aid, favor, be with, and caress and a lowered tendency to injure in any way. "In fear" a man tends to reduce or avoid contact with specific stimuli—as by running away, hiding, or covering his eyes and ears; at the same time he is less likely to advance toward such stimuli or into unfamiliar territory. These are useful facts, and something like the layman's mode of classification has a place in a scientific analysis. (1953, p. 162)

Skinner believes that current difficulties in understanding, predicting, and controlling emotional behaviors could be reduced by observing behavioral patterns, not by referring to unknown internal states.

Thinking and Knowing

Descriptions of thinking, for Skinner, are as unreliable and vague as descriptions of emotional states.

> "Thinking" often means "behaving weakly," where the weakness may be due, for example, to defective stimulus control. Shown an object with which we are not very familiar, we may say, "I think it is a kind of wrench," where "I think" is clearly opposed to "I know." We report a low probability for a different reason when we say, "I think I shall go," rather than "I shall go" or "I know I shall go."
>
> There are more important uses of the term. Watching a chess game, we may wonder "what a player is thinking of" when he makes a move. We may mean that we wonder what he will do next. In other words, we wonder about his incipient or inchoate behavior. To say, "He was thinking of moving his rook," is perhaps to say, "He was on the point of moving it." Usually, however, the term refers to completed behavior which occurs on a scale so small that it cannot be detected by others. (Skinner, 1974, p. 103)

personal reflection

MODIFYING A PROFESSOR'S BEHAVIOR

This is a popular stunt designed by behavioral psychology students. Try it. Choose as your subject a professor who ambles about during lectures. The experimenters in this study will be comprised of as many of the class members as agree to participate. Experimenters can begin by reinforcing the professor's walking toward one side of the room. This can be done as follows: As the professor turns or moves to one side of the classroom, the experimenters should lean forward, write notes diligently, and appear to pay close attention to what he or she is saying. When the professor moves to the other side of the classroom, experimenters should relax and become much less attentive.

Many classes have found that after several lectures, they can keep their professors in a corner for most of the class. You might do well to restrict this exercise to professors of psychology, so that when it is explained to them, they will not misunderstand your intentions but will reinforce you with behavioristic goodwill.

Skinner defines knowledge as a *repertoire of behaviors*. "A man 'knows his table of integrals' in the sense that under suitable circumstances he will recite it, make corresponding substitutions in the course of a calculation, and so on. He 'knows his history' in the sense of possessing another highly complex repertoire" (1953, pp. 408–409).

Knowledge is the behavior displayed when a particular stimulus is applied. Other theorists tend to consider behaviors such as naming the major character in *Hamlet* or explaining the influence of German silver-mine production on medieval European history as "signs" or evidence of knowledge; Skinner regards these behaviors as knowledge itself. Another way he defines knowledge is the probability of skilled behavior. To say that a person "knows how to read" means, to Skinner, that the occasions upon which reading is reinforced tend to produce the behavioral repertoire called reading. Skinner believes that conventional ways of teaching suffer without the tools of behavioristic analysis. His concern moved him to devise learning situations and devices that accelerate the pace and enlarge the scope of established learning.

> But if a behavioristic interpretation of thinking is not all we should like to have, it must be remembered that mental or cognitive explanations are not explanations at all. (Skinner, 1974, p. 103)

Self-knowledge

Skinner does explore the repertoire of behaviors known as *self-knowledge*. In so doing, he describes cases in which self-knowledge is lacking. "A man may not know that *he has done something* . . . may not know that *he is doing something* . . . may not know that *he tends to*, or *is going to, do something* . . . may not recognize the variables of which his behavior is a function" (Skinner, 1958, pp. 288–289). These cases are of intense interest to nonbehaviorists because they are said to be manifestations of various internal states (for example, complexes, habit patterns, repressions, or phobias). Skinner labels these incidents simply as behaviors that lack positive reinforcement for noticing or remembering them. "The crucial thing is not whether the behavior which a man fails to report is actually observable by him, but whether he has ever been given any reason to observe it" (Skinner, 1953, p. 289). In other words, it is not what has happened to you that counts but whether you were given a reward for noticing.

Therapy

Skinner views therapy as a controlling agency of almost unlimited power. Because the therapist is designated as a highly likely source of relief, any promised or actual relief becomes positively reinforcing, increasing the therapist's influence.

personal reflection

DESENSITIZATION

This exercise is not intended to show you how a therapist would actually work. It is a way for you to experience some of the dynamics that occur when you focus on a single item of behavior.

One procedure behavior therapists use is desensitization, a method that gradually decreases a person's sensitivity to a disturbing stimulus.

Part 1. Identify a Symptom

Think of a fear you have had for some time, perhaps a phobia (phobias are the easiest to work with). Fears of snakes, worms, blood, or heights are good examples. If you cannot think of or are unwilling to consider a phobia, choose a negative emotional reaction you have to a given situation. For example, you may become anxious every time a police car drives behind you, you may feel defensive whenever someone mentions your religion, or you may panic just before you begin an exam. Look for a response that seems repetitive and disturbing.

Part 2. Relaxation

Sit in a comfortable chair or lie down. Let your whole body relax. Concentrate on one part of your body after another, telling it to relax and noticing the relaxation. Let your toes relax, your feet, your ankles, knees, legs, and so forth. This will take a few minutes. Practice this progressive relaxation a few times. If you cannot tell whether or not a part of your body has relaxed, tense the muscles in that area and then relax them.

Part 3. Desensitization

After completing the relaxation exercise in Part 2, while you are relaxed, think of something that has a distant relationship to the phobia or habit you are working with. If you have a fear of snakes, think of reading about a small, harmless snake that is found only in a distant country. If you have a fear of police officers, think about a clown dressed like a police officer, giving away balloons at a circus.

Try to maintain an image in your mind related to the anxiety-provoking stimulus, while you stay physically relaxed. If you start feeling tense ("Yuck, a snake!"), stop concentrating on the image and focus on relaxing, going back to the relaxation exercise until you are once again relaxed. Repeat this procedure until you can hold the image in your mind while still remaining fully relaxed.

All the following steps build on one another. Think of an image or situation that is a little more vivid, and closer to the real object or situation of fear. Visualize or imagine it while you maintain a state of relaxation. Then visualize an image that is closer still to the actual one, as you continue to be relaxed. For a snake phobia, for example, the remaining successive steps in the desensitization process could include actually reading about snakes, then looking at pictures of snakes, followed by having a snake in a cage across the room from you, then having a snake in the same cage next to you, and finally holding the snake in your hand.

Do not skip steps. Do not go to a later image or situation until you are relaxed in all the earlier ones.

Skinner's theory includes no *self*. Therefore, therapy cannot aim to make the client feel better, be better adjusted, or achieve insight or self-understanding. From the behaviorist's position, therapy must try to modify the shape or order of behaviors—that is, prevent undesirable behaviors from recurring and have desirable behaviors occur more often.

Operating from this premise, behavior therapists have successfully treated problems including some not readily improved by psychodynamic therapies. An extensive review of behavior therapies (Rachman & Wilson, 1980) described several well-designed studies with generally favorable results. These studies explore such areas as sexual dysfunction, sexual deviance, marital conflict, psychotic disorders, and addictive disorders, including alcoholism, smoking, and obesity.

Despite differing approaches to behavior therapy, it is generally accepted that a behavior therapist is primarily interested in actual behaviors, not in inner states or historical antecedents. According to behaviorists, *the symptom is the disease,* not a manifestation of an underlying illness. The symptom—such as a facial tic, premature ejaculation, chronic drinking, or a fear of crowds—is dealt with directly. Symptoms do not provide an entrée to an investigation of early memories or of the patient's existential perspective.

The patient sees the therapist as a nonthreatening audience, which is also true of the psychodynamic therapies. In behavior-therapy terms, the client is therefore free to express previously unexpressed behaviors, such as weeping, hostile feelings, or sexual fantasies. However, the behavior therapist is intent upon withholding reinforcement in the face of these expressions. The therapist is interested in teaching, training, and rewarding behaviors that can effectively compete with and eliminate uncomfortable or disabling behaviors. For example, progressive relaxation may be taught as a means to lessen specific anxiety reactions, or assertiveness training may help a patient overcome timid behaviors.

The following statements describe the special nature of behavior therapy, as well as what it shares with other forms of therapy.

1. Behavior therapy helps people respond to life situations the way they would like to respond. This includes increasing the frequency and/or range of a person's desired behaviors, thoughts, and feelings; and decreasing or eliminating unwanted behaviors, thoughts, and feelings.
2. Behavior therapy does not try to modify an emotional core of attitudes or feelings within the personality.
3. Behavior therapy takes the posture that a positive therapeutic relationship is a necessary, but not sufficient, condition for effective psychotherapy.
4. In behavior therapy, the complaints of the client are accepted as the primary focus of psychotherapy—not as symptoms for some underlying problem.
5. In behavior therapy, the client and the therapist come to an explicit understanding of the problem presented in terms of the actual behavior (for example, actions, thoughts, feelings) of the client. They decide mutually on specific therapeutic goals, stated in such a way that both client and therapist know when these goals have been attained. (Jacks, 1973)

Beyond Behaviorism

B. F. Skinner's position, often described as "radical behaviorism," is at the core of behavior therapies; however, significant liberalization of his position has allowed behavior therapies to become the fastest-growing and most eclectic group of therapies in the English-speaking world.

While it is historically correct to credit Skinner with the founding of cognitive psychology, it is an honor that appalled him (Skinner, 1978c). In a review of the first century of psychological science, Anastasi (1992) says, "The cognitive revolution has not overthrown behaviorism; it has greatly expanded and enriched the kinds of learning investigated." Skinner—who found cognitive psychology a hotbed of murky thinking, revived mentalism, and explanatory fictions—argued passionately that almost all the descriptive words used by cognitive psychologists meant nothing, described nothing, and retarded rather than advanced psychological science (1989).

In spite of Skinner's pronouncements, most people, including behaviorists, persist in their belief that thinking, although not easily measured, must be examined nonetheless. The task of the cognitive behavior therapist is to modify behaviors and emotional expressions, but to do so *while* considering the patient's thoughts.

Other major research areas that Skinner and his followers pioneered are examined on our **web site** in these sections: Applied Behavior Analysis, From Programmed Learning to Computer Games, and Augmented Learning.

EVALUATION

Skinner's behaviorism has been applied to create new modes of therapy and instruction. The impact of his ideas has led to modifications of programs in universities, jails, mental hospitals, clinics, and primary schools. Several experimental communities attempted to make the visions of *Walden Two* a reality (Ishaq, 1991; Kinkade, 1973; Roberts, 1971).

As Skinner extended his interests into the workplace, the classroom, and the home, he attracted admirers as well as critics. His treatment of freedom, creativity, and the self, and his unswerving belief in a world dominated by external forces, were chilling and compelling. In 1984 Skinner allowed six of his seminal papers to be sent to a group of professionals who had a stake in behavioral psychology. One hundred seventy-four of them responded. Their detailed comments dissected every facet of Skinner's ideas: ideological, experimental, and philosophical. Skinner then wrote a response to each and every commentator.

These critiques of Skinner's papers, along with his replies, filled an entire issue of *Behavioral and Brain Sciences* (1984). Skinner's response to almost all of his critics was that they were either misinformed, misaligned, or just plain wrong. Having discovered that the more he stood his ground, the more his ideas attracted serious attention, he chose to stand firm on all of his positions, even those that dated back more than 30 years. In his final summation, Skinner writes, "In my experience, the skepticism of psychologists and philosophers about the adequacy of behaviorism is an inverse function of the extent they understand it" (1984b, p. 723).

In his last years, Skinner continued undaunted. In a radio interview conducted a few months before his death, he remarked, with amusement, "I will die before my critics can come at me for this last work" (NPR, 1990). While his statement was literally true, shortly after his death a triple-length volume of the *American Psychologist,* the only magazine sent to all members of the American Psychology Association, was devoted to "Reflections on B. F. Skinner and Psychology." Almost every article lauded Skinner's contribution to various fields of psychology. One even pointed out how his critics, by misrepresenting him, had confused many other psychologists as well as the general public (Todd & Morris, 1992).

In his determination to render life more understandable, Skinner proposed a view of human nature that is inherently appealing in its compactness, its directness, and its dismissal of all metaphysical speculation. Firmly rooted in the methodology of modern science, it offers the hope of understanding ourselves without recourse to intuition or divine intervention.

Skinner presented himself as a psychologist whose basic ideas originated in laboratory findings with rats and pigeons. However, with the writing of *Walden Two,* he made a "critical transition, from laboratory scientist . . . to outspoken public advocate for a behavioristic science of human behavior" (Elms, 1981, p. 478). Skinner's

I think the main objection to behaviorism is that people are in love with the mental apparatus. If you say that doesn't really exist, that it's a fiction and let's get back to the facts, then they have to give up their first love. (Skinner, 1967b, p. 69)

Of all contemporary psychologists, B. F. Skinner is perhaps the most honored and the most maligned, the most widely recognized and the most misrepresented, the most cited and the most misunderstood. (Catania, 1984, p. 473)

I am a radical behaviorist simply in the sense that I find no place in the formulation for anything which is mental. (Skinner, 1964, p. 106)

own thrust for the past 30 years was best stated in his own words: "I am proceeding on the assumption that nothing less than a vast improvement in our understanding of human behavior will prevent the destruction of our way of life or of mankind" (1975, p. 42).

Just as Freud's suggestion that we are immoral and driven by lust and greed scandalized a generation of Victorians, Skinner's assertions that we are amoral and are pushed and turned by our external environment has disturbed a generation brought up to admire and value self-generated choices and personal independence.

In a late paper titled "What Is Wrong with Daily Life in the Western World?" (1986), he cites the alienation of many individuals from their work. He points to examples of people helping those who would rather help themselves, controlling others by punishment instead of by reinforcements, and "reinforcing looking, listening, reading, gambling and so on while strengthening very few other behaviors" (p. 568). He suggested that the solution to these quality-of-life issues is to apply what we already know, what has already worked—the extensions and applications of behavioral research. He insisted that differences should be resolved on the basis of actual evidence, not abstract speculations. By forcing the argument back to science and away from purely emotional discussions, Skinner forged a systematic approach to understanding human behavior that continues to exert considerable influence on current cultural practices and beliefs.

The Theory Firsthand

EXCERPT FROM "HUMANISM AND BEHAVIORISM"[2]

There seem to be two ways of knowing, or knowing about, another person. One is associated with existentialism, phenomenology, and structuralism. It is a matter of knowing what a person is, or what he is like, or what he is coming to be or becoming. We try to know another person in this sense as we know ourselves. We share his feelings through sympathy or empathy. Through intuition we discover his attitudes, intentions, and other states of mind. We communicate with him in the etymological sense of making ideas and feelings common to both of us. We do so more effectively if we have established good interpersonal relations. This is a passive, contemplative kind of knowing: If we want to predict what a person does or is likely to do, we assume that he, like us, will behave according to what he is; his behavior, like ours, will be an expression of his feelings, state of mind, intentions, attitudes, and so on.

The other way of knowing is a matter of what a person does. We can usually observe this as directly as any other phenomenon in the world; no special kind of knowing is needed. We explain why a person behaves as he does by turning to the environment rather than to inner states or activities. The environment was effective during the evolution of the species, and we call the result the human genetic endowment. A member of the species is exposed to another part of that environment during his lifetime, and from it he acquires a repertoire of behavior which converts an organism with a genetic endowment into a person. By analyzing these effects of the environment, we move toward the prediction and control of behavior.

But can this formulation of what a person does neglect any available information about what he is? There are gaps in time and space between behavior and the environmental events to which it is attributed, and it is natural to try to fill them with an account of the intervening state of the organism. We do this when we summarize a long evolutionary history by speaking of genetic endowment. Should we not do the same for a personal history? An omniscient physiologist should be able to tell us, for example, how a person is changed when a bit of his behavior is reinforced, and what he thus becomes should explain why he subsequently behaves in a different way. We argue in such a manner, for example, with respect to immunization. We begin with the fact that vaccination makes it less likely that a person will contract a disease at a later date. We say that he becomes immune, and we speak of a state of immunity, which we then proceed to

He sought a parsimonious, elegant, and useful path to a science of psychology. Most of his efforts were steps in the right direction. (Gilbert & Gilbert, 1991)

examine. An omniscient physiologist should be able to do the same for comparable states in the field of behavior. He should also be able to change behavior by changing the organism directly rather than by changing the environment. Is the existentialist, phenomenologist, or structuralist not directing his attention precisely to such a mediating state?

A thoroughgoing dualist would say no, because for him what a person observes through introspection and what a physiologist observes with his special techniques are in different universes. It is at this point that a behavioristic analysis of self-knowledge becomes most important and, unfortunately, is most likely to be misunderstood. Each of us possesses a small part of the universe within his own skin. It is not for that reason different from the rest of the universe, but it is a private possession: We have ways of knowing about it that are denied to others. It is a mistake, however, to conclude that the intimacy we thus enjoy means a special kind of understanding. We are, of course, stimulated directly by our own bodies. The so-called interoceptive nervous system responds to conditions important in deprivation and emotion. The proprioceptive system is involved in posture and movement, and without it we would scarcely behave in a coordinated way. These two systems, together with the exteroceptive nervous system, are essential to effective behavior. But knowing is more than responding to stimuli. A child responds to the colors of things before he "knows his colors." Knowing requires special contingencies of reinforcement that must be arranged by other people, and the contingencies involving private events are never very precise because other people are not effectively in contact with them. In spite of the intimacy of our own bodies, we know them less accurately than we know the world around us. And there are, of course, other reasons why we know the private world of others even less precisely.

The important issues, however, are not precision but subject matter. Just what can be known when we "know ourselves"? The three nervous systems just mentioned have evolved under practical contingencies of survival, most of them nonsocial. (Social contingencies important for survival must have arisen in such fields as sexual and maternal behavior.) They were presumably the only systems available when people began to "know themselves" as the result of answering questions about their behavior. In answering such questions as "Do you see that?" or "Did you hear that?" or "What is that?" a person learns to observe his own responses to stimuli. In answering such questions as "Are you hungry?" or "Are you afraid?" he learns to observe states of his body related to deprivation and emotional arousal. In answering such questions as "Are you going to go?" or "Do you intend to go?" or "Do you feel like going?" or "Are you inclined to go?" he learns to observe the strength or probability of his behavior.

Do I mean to say that Plato never discovered the mind? Or that Aquinas, Descartes, Locke, and Kant were preoccupied with incidental, often irrelevant by-products of human behavior? Or that the mental laws of physiological psychologists like Wundt, or the stream of consciousness of William James, or the mental apparatus of Sigmund Freud have no useful place in the understanding of human behavior? Yes, I do. And I put the matter strongly because, if we are to solve the problems that face us in the world today, this concern for mental life must no longer divert our attention from the environmental conditions of which human behavior is a function. . . .

Better forms of government are not to be found in better rulers, better educational practices in better teachers, better economic systems in more enlightened management, or better therapy in more compassionate therapists. Neither are they to be found in better citizens, students, workers, or patients. The age-old mistake is to look for salvation in the character of autonomous men and women rather than in the social environments that have appeared in the evolution of cultures and that can now be explicitly designed.

CHAPTER HIGHLIGHTS

- Skinner believed that only behavior can be studied. Distinct from an inner life, behavior is observable, measurable, and perceivable with data-collecting instrumentation. If observable behavior is the basis for defining the self, then to discuss the inner working of the personality or the self becomes unnecessary.
- He formulated distinct ways of observing, measuring, predicting, and understanding behavior. His distrust for subjective, mental, intervening, or fictional explanations led him to base his ideas on the observable behavior of animals and people.
- Skinner spoke of studying the organism itself. His propositions rest upon the accumulation of measurable behavioral data and careful laboratory experimentation.

- Although Skinner worked from observable data alone, contending that his position was a nontheoretical one, his impact on society and psychology grew from extrapolation of his data into theories stretching far beyond the boundaries of animal research.
- Rather than considering individuals as creating, initiating agents, Skinner held that genetic and environmental histories control a person's behavior.
- Future events are assumed to be predictable, given observation of past events.
- Explanatory fictions are employed when people do not understand the behavior involved, or when the pattern of reinforcements that preceded or followed the behavior is unknown. According to Skinner, it is incorrect to use any of these terms to explain behavior: *freedom, dignity, autonomous man, will,* or *creativity.*
- Skinner concluded that almost any naturally occurring behavior in a human or in an animal can be trained to occur more often and more strongly in any chosen direction.
- Research on the variables that affect operant conditioning indicates that conditioning can take place without awareness, that conditioning is maintained in spite of awareness, and that conditioning is most effective when the subject is aware and cooperative.
- Positive and negative consequences control or regulate behaviors. If one has sufficient knowledge of the prior reinforcers, it is possible to explain the occurrence of any behavior.
- How quickly a behavior is learned, and how often it will be repeated, depend on how regularly and how often the behavior is reinforced. The speed at which new behavior is learned is increased by continuous reinforcement.
- Learning is improved when a correct response is reinforced. Because reinforcement selectively directs behavior toward a predetermined goal, it is more effective than aversive control, or punishment.
- One can begin to control behavior if one can make changes in the environment. Controlling one's behavior means freedom.
- For Skinner, personal growth refers to the capacity to increase the beneficial control of our environment and to minimize adverse conditions. Functional analysis is useful in framing behavior as a cause-and-effect relationship.
- Skinner considers personality, as the term is normally used, to be an explanatory fiction. Mind and body are not separate.
- Rather than treat emotions as vague inner states, Skinner suggests that a descriptive approach be used. Individuals should learn to observe associated behaviors.
- The symptom is the disease, according to behaviorists, not a manifestation of an underlying illness, and it is to be dealt with directly.
- Derived from his animal experiments, Skinner's most original achievement was the development of programmed learning. His research showed that when people are given instant and accurate feedback on their progress, they learn more quickly.

KEY CONCEPTS

Autonomous man An explanatory fiction, in this case described as an inner person or indwelling agent, who is moved by vague inner forces independent of the behavioral contingencies.

Behaviorism The philosophy of the science of human behavior.

Canon of parsimony A formulation proposed by Lloyd Morgan. It states that given two explanations, a scientist should always accept the simpler one.

Contingencies The antecedents of the behavior, the response to it, and the results or consequences of the response. Contingencies include an organism's genetic endowment and previous behaviors.

Explanatory fictions Terms nonbehaviorists use to describe behavior. For Skinner, examples include freedom, dignity, autonomous man, and creativity. To use any of these terms as explanation for behavior is simply incorrect, according to behaviorists.

Functional analysis An examination of cause-and-effect relationships. Each aspect of behavior is treated as a function of a condition that can be described in physical terms. Explanations that depend on terms such as *will, intelligence, imagination,* or *freedom* obscure the causes of behavior, as they do not describe what is actually occurring.

Reinforcer Any stimulus that follows the occurrence of a response and maintains or increases the probability of that response. A positive reinforcer strengthens any behavior that produces it. A negative reinforcer strengthens any behavior that reduces or terminates it. Primary reinforcers are stimuli or events that are innately reinforcing (air, water, food, shelter). Secondary reinforcers are neutral stimuli that come to function as reinforcers through association with primary reinforcers (money is one example).

Respondent behavior Reflexive behavior in which an organism responds automatically to a stimulus.

Verbal community The people who respond to the verbal behavior of others. Verbal behavior is any activity that uses words—reading, speaking, or writing.

ANNOTATED BIBLIOGRAPHY

Bjork, D. (1993). *B. F. Skinner: A life*. New York: Basic Books.

> Far superior to Skinner's own tedious biography, Bjork's work helps the reader see how Skinner's ideas arose from his upbringing. His radical stance is depicted as an extension of his early social and personal isolation.

Catania, C., & Harnad, S. (Eds.). (1988). *The selection of behavior: The operant behaviorism of B. F. Skinner. Comments and consequences*. New York: Cambridge University Press.

> Six of his seminal papers and comments on each from various authors, as well as Skinner's replies. More than most people would ever want to know about the pros and cons of his basic ideas.

Lattal, K. (1992). Reflections on B. F. Skinner and Psychology. *American Psychologist, 47*(11), 1269–1533.

> A full range of generally positive detailed and often highly technical articles on Skinner's impact on psychology.

Nye, R. (1979). *What Is B. F. Skinner really saying?* Upper Saddle River, NJ: Prentice Hall.

> A well-written summary of Skinner's ideas, presented without much recourse to Skinnerian jargon.

Skinner, B. F. (1948, 1976). *Walden two*. New York: Macmillan.

> A novel about a full-blown utopian community designed and managed by a behaviorist. No plot to speak of, but all facets of the culture are fully described and discussed, from child rearing to work schedules to planned leisure.

Skinner, B. F. (1953). *Science and human behavior*. New York: Macmillan.

> The most complete exposition of Skinner's basic ideas.

Skinner, B. F. (1971). *Beyond freedom and dignity*. New York: Knopf.

> An examination of contemporary culture, especially its failure to apply behavioral analysis to personal understanding. A powerful, popular book on the folly of thinking the way most of us still do.

Skinner, B. F. (1972). *Cumulative record: A selection of papers* (3rd ed.). New York: Appleton-Century-Crofts.

> Skinner's choice of what he considered his most important papers; covers areas not included in this chapter.

Skinner, B. F. (1974). *About behaviorism*. New York: Knopf.

> A direct answer to Skinner's critics. It explores popular misconceptions about behaviorism. This scaled-down version of *Science and Human Behavior* is written for the general public.

Web Sites

http://www.bfskinner.org

> Site of the B. F. Skinner Foundation, established in 1987 to publish significant literary and scientific works in the analysis of behavior and to educate both professionals and the public about the science of behavior. The site contains information about the activities of the foundation, a brief autobiography of B. F. Skinner (1904–1990), books by Skinner, and an extensive bibliography of Skinner's publications published between 1930 and 1993.

REFERENCES

Ames, A., Jr. (1951). Visual perception and the rotating trapezoidal window. *Psychological Monographs, 65*, 324.

Anastasi, A. (1992). A century of psychological science. *American Psychologist, 47*(7), 842.

Behavioral and Brain Sciences. (1984). The canonical papers of B. F. Skinner, 7(4). (Later reprinted: Catania, C., & Harnad, S. [Eds.], [1988]. *The selection of behavior: The operant behaviorism of B. F. Skinner. Comments and consequences*. New York: Cambridge University Press.)

Berelson, B., & Steiner, G. A. (1964). *Human behavior: An inventory of scientific findings*. New York: Harcourt Brace Jovanovich.

Bjork, D. (1993). *B. F. Skinner: A life*. New York: Basic Books.

Catania, C. (1984). The operant behaviorism of B. F. Skinner. *Behavioral and Brain Sciences, 7*, 473–475.

Cohen, D. (1977). *Psychologists on psychology*. New York: Taplinger.

Davison, G., & Valins, S. (1969). Maintenance of self-attributed and drug-attributed behavior change. *Journal of Personality and Social Psychology, 11*, 25–33.

Elms, A. (1981). Skinner's dark year and Walden two. *American Psychologist, 36*(5), 470–479.

Erickson, M. H. (1939). Experimental demonstrations of the psychopathology of everyday life. *Psychoanalytic Quarterly, 8,* 338–353.

Evans, R. (1968). *B. F. Skinner: The man and his ideas.* New York: Dutton. (Edited dialogues with Skinner.)

Fabun, D. (1968). On motivation. *Kaiser Aluminum News, 26*(2).

Ferster, C. B., & Skinner, B. F. (1957). *Schedules of reinforcement.* New York: Appleton-Century-Crofts.

Goldfried, M. R., & Merbaum, M. (Eds.). (1973). *Behavior change through self-control.* New York: Holt, Rinehart and Winston.

Goodell, R. (1977). B. F. Skinner: High risk, high gain. In *The visible scientists* (pp. 106–119). Boston: Little, Brown.

Hall, C., & Lindzey, G. (1978). *Theories of personality* (3rd ed). New York: Wiley.

Hilts, P. J. (1973, May 3). Pros and cons of behaviorism. *San Francisco Chronicle.* (Originally printed in the *Washington Post.*)

Ishaq, W. (Ed.). (1991). *Human behavior in today's world.* New York: Praeger.

Jacks, R. N. (1973). *What therapies work with today's college students: Behavior therapy.* Paper presented at the annual meeting of the American Psychiatric Association, Honolulu, Hawaii.

Kimble, G. A. (1961). *Hilgard and Marquis' conditioning and learning.* New York: Appleton-Century-Crofts.

Kinkade, K. (1973). *A Walden two experiment: The first five years of Twin Oaks Community.* New York: Morrow. (Excerpts published in *Psychology Today,* 1973, *6*[8], 35–41, 90–93; *6*[9], 71–82.)

Knapp, T. (1998). Current status and future directions of operant research on verbal behavior. Baselines. *Analysis of Verbal Behavior, 15,* 121–123.

Lefcourt, H. M. (1973). The function of the illusions of control and freedom. *American Psychologist, 28,* 417–426.

Lefcourt, H. M. (1980). Locus of control and coping with life's events. In E. Staub (Ed.), *Personality: Basic aspects and current research* (pp. 201–235). Upper Saddle River, NJ: Prentice Hall.

Lindley, R., II, & Moyer, K. E. (1961). Effects of instructions on the extinction of conditioned finger-withdrawal response. *Journal of Experimental Psychology, 61,* 82–88.

Mahoney, M. (Ed.). (1981). *Cognitive Therapy and Research, 5*(1).

Mahoney, M., & Thoresen, C. E. (1974). *Self control: Power to the person.* Monterey, CA: Brooks/Cole.

Mawhinney, T. C., & Fellows, C. K. (1999). Positive contingencies versus quotas: Telemarketers exert countercontrol. *Journal of Organizational Behavior Management, 19*(2), 35–57.

Mischel, W. (1976). *Introduction to personality.* New York: Holt, Rinehart and Winston.

National Public Radio. (1990, July 27). *All things considered.* Interview with B. F. Skinner.

Pavlov, I. P. (1927). *Conditioned reflexes.* London: Oxford University Press.

Rachman, S. J., & Wilson, G. T. (1980). *The effects of psychological therapy* (2d ed). Elmsford, NY: Pergamon Press.

Ram Dass, B. (1970). Baba Ram Dass lecture at the Menninger Clinic. *Journal of Transpersonal Psychology, 2,* 91–140.

Reese, E. P. (1966). The analysis of human operant behavior. In J. Vernon (Ed.), *General psychology: A self-selection textbook.* Dubuque, IA: Brown.

Rilling, M. (2000). John Watson's paradoxical struggle to explain Freud. *American Psychologist 55*(3), 301–312.

Roberts, R. E. (1971). *The new communes: Coming together in America.* Upper Saddle River NJ: Prentice Hall.

Sagal, P. (1981). *Skinner's philosophy.* Waltham, MA: University Press of America.

Skinner, B. F. (1938). *The behavior of organisms: An experimental analysis.* New York: Appleton-Century-Crofts.

Skinner, B. F. (1945, October). Baby in a box. *Ladies Home Journal.* (Also in *Cumulative record: A selection of papers* [3rd ed]. New York: Appleton-Century-Crofts, 1972, pp. 567–573.)

Skinner, B. F. (1948). *Walden two.* New York: Macmillan.

Skinner, B. F. (1950). Are theories of learning necessary? *Psychological Review, 57,* 193–216.

Skinner, B. F. (1953). *Science and human behavior.* New York: Macmillan.

Skinner, B. F. (1955). Freedom and the control of men. *American Scholar, 25,* 47–65.

Skinner, B. F. (1956). A case history in scientific method. *American Psychologist, 11,* 211–233.

Skinner, B. F. (1957). *Verbal behavior.* New York: Appleton-Century-Crofts.

Skinner, B. F. (1958). Teaching machines. *Science, 128,* 969–977.

Skinner, B. F. (1959). *Cumulative record.* New York: Appleton-Century-Crofts.

Skinner, B. F. (1961). *Cumulative record* (2nd ed). New York: Appleton-Century-Crofts.

Skinner, B. F. (1964). Behaviorism at fifty. In W. T. Wann (Ed.), *Behaviorism and phenomenology: Contrasting bases for modern psychology* (pp. 79–108). Chicago: University of Chicago Press.

Skinner, B. F. (1967a). Autobiography. In E. G. Boring & G. Lindzey (Eds.), *History of psychology in autobiography* (Vol. 5) (pp. 387–413). New York: Appleton-CenturyCrofts.

Skinner, B. F. (1967b). An interview with Mr. Behaviorist: B. F. Skinner. *Psychology Today, 1*(5), 20–25, 68–71.

Skinner, B. F. (1968). *The technology of teaching.* New York: Appleton-Century-Crofts.

Skinner, B. F. (1971). *Beyond freedom and dignity.* New York: Knopf.

Skinner, B. F. (1972a). *Cumulative record: A selection of papers* (3rd ed). New York: Appleton-Century-Crofts.

Skinner, B. F. (1972b). Interview with E. Hall. *Psychology Today, 6*(6), 65–72, 130.

Skinner, B. F. (1972c, July 15). On "having" a poem. *Saturday Review,* pp. 32–35. (Also in *Cumulative record: A selection of papers* [3rd ed]. New York: Appleton-Century-Crofts, 1972.)

Skinner, B. F. (1972d). "I have been misunderstood. . . ." An interview with B. F. Skinner. *Center Magazine, 5*(2), 63–65.

Skinner, B. F. (1974). *About behaviorism.* New York: Knopf.

Skinner, B. F. (1975). The steep and thorny way to a science of behavior. *American Psychologist, 30,* 42–49.

Skinner, B. F. (1976a). *Walden two.* New York: Macmillan.

Skinner, B. F. (1976b). *Particulars of my life.* New York: Knopf.

Skinner, B. F. (1977a). A conversation with B. F. Skinner. *Harvard Magazine, 79*(8), 53–58.

Skinner, B. F. (1977b). Hernstein and the evolution of behaviorism. *American Psychologist, 32,* 1006–1016.

Skinner, B. F. (1978a). *Reflections on behaviorism and society.* Upper Saddle River, NJ: Prentice Hall.

Skinner, B. F. (1978b). Why don't we use the behavioral sciences? *Human Nature, 1*(3), 86–92.

Skinner, B. F. (1978c). *Why I am not a cognitive psychologist. Reflections on behaviorism and society.* Upper Saddle River, NJ: Prentice Hall.

Skinner, B. F. (1979a). *The shaping of a behaviorist.* New York: Knopf.

Skinner, B. F. (1979b). Interview. *Omni, 1*(12), 76–80.

Skinner, B. F. (1980). *Notebooks* (Robert Epstein, Ed.). Upper Saddle River, NJ: Prentice Hall.

Skinner, B. F. (1984a). *A matter of consequences.* New York: New York University Press.

Skinner, B. F. (1984b). Reply to Harnad's article, "What are the scope and limits of radical behaviorist theory?" *Behavioral and Brain Sciences, 7,* 721–724.

Skinner, B. F. (1986). What is wrong with daily life in the Western world? *American Psychologist, 41*(5), 568–574.

Skinner, B. F. (1987a). Whatever happened to psychology as the science of behavior? *American Psychologist, 42*(8), 780–786.

Skinner, B. F. (1989). The origins of cognitive thought. *American Psychologist, 44*(1), 13–18.

Skinner, B. F. (1990a). Can psychology be a science of mind? *American Psychologist, 45*(11), 1206–1210.

Skinner, B. F. (1990b). To know the future. In C. Fadiman (Ed.), *Living philosophies* (pp. 193–199). New York: Doubleday.

Skinner, B. F., & Vaughan, M. E. (1985). *Enjoy old age: Living fully in your later years.* New York: Warner Books.

Todd, J., & Morris, E. (1992). Case histories in the great power of steady misrepresentation. *American Psychologist, 47*(11), 1441–1453.

Wann, W. T. (Ed.). (1964). *Behaviorism and phenomenology: Contrasting bases for modern psychology.* Chicago: University of Chicago Press.

Watson, J. B. (1913). Psychology as the behaviorist views it. *Psychological Review, 20,* 158–177.

Watson, J. B. (1928a). *The ways of behaviorism.* New York: Harper & Row.

Watson, J. B. (1928b). *Psychological care of infant and child.* New York: Norton.

cognitive psychology
and its applications

This chapter has a format unlike those of other chapters. It is an examination of several specific applications of cognitive psychology rather than a description of a full theory of personality.

Since the 1970s, cognitive psychology has risen to prominence as a field of study and therapeutic applications. It is vitally concerned with the core elements of consciousness, just as William James was when he created the discipline known as psychology. Cognitive psychology is not, strictly speaking, a theory of personality. Nor does it form a single, coherent system but rather comprises a variety of theories and therapeutic applications of diverse aims and methods. Two areas in cognitive psychology are especially relevant to an understanding of human personality. One entails the mapping of the structure of the intellect, the other involves developing therapeutic techniques to modify the impact of the intellect and thinking on human emotional life and well-being.

RESEARCHING HUMAN COGNITION

All cognitive psychologists share a concern for the principles and mechanisms that govern the phenomena of **human cognition.** Cognition comprises mental processes such as perceiving, thinking, remembering, evaluating, planning, and organizing (Anderson, 1985; Honeck, Case, & Firment, 1991; Mayer, 1981; Miller, Galanter, & Pribram, 1960; Neisser, 1967).

Rather than attend to the uniqueness and variations of the human personality, cognitive psychologists searched for the principles common to all human cognitive processes. And their search took a decisive turn when a computer scientist and a psychologist offered a joint proposal that the human mind could be viewed as an *information-processing system,* much like the computer (Newell, Shaw, & Simon, 1958; Newell & Simon, 1961, 1972). Computer simulation, using a computer to imitate or represent a real-life process, came to be used by many psychologists for testing their hypotheses about how humans perceive, think, remember, or use language (Anderson & Bower, 1973; Johnson-Laird, 1977; Lachman, Lachman, & Butterfield, 1979; Quillian, 1969). But the use of computer models has also had its detractors (Dreyfus, 1972; Gunderson, 1971; Neisser, 1976b; Weizenbaum, 1976). They consider it impossible for a computer to duplicate all the subtlety and complexity of human consciousness.

Not all cognitive research has been devoted to the investigation of the primary mental processes. The differences in the way individuals perceive, think about, organize, and evaluate their experience has continued to be a topic of interest among cognitive theorists. These theorists have asked questions like, "Are people pessimistic in their thinking because they feel sad, or do they feel sad because they think pessimistically?" Lively debates over the primacy of cognition versus emotion added momentum to the cognitive movement in the 1960s and 1970s (Lazarus, 1982, 1984, 1991a; Leventhal & Scherer, 1987; Scheff, 1985; Zajonc, 1980, 1984) and generated research on how people cope with stress (e.g., Horowitz, 1979; Lazarus, 1966, 1991b; Lazarus & Folkman, 1984). Debates also focused on how cognitive processes develop in infancy and childhood (e.g., Harris, 1989; Izard, 1978, 1984; Stein & Levine, 1987; Stenberg & Campos, 1990; Stroufe, 1984) as well as on life-span development extending to adulthood and old age (Labouvie-Vief, Hakim-Larson, DeVoe, & Schoeberlein, 1989).

A significant development during recent decades has been the proliferation of cognitive approaches and techniques in psychotherapy. Beginning with Aaron Beck's (1961, 1967, 1976, 1991) pioneering work in the understanding and treatment of depression from a cognitive perspective, techniques have been devised for the treatment of diverse disorders, including marital or couples problems (Beck, 1988), anxiety disorders, phobias (Beck & Emery with Greenberg, 1985), and schizophrenia (Perris, 1988).

These developments in cognitive theory do not constitute a comprehensive theory of personality. Work in cognitive psychology focuses on specific functions, such as perception, thinking, memory, and language. But these functions point to phenomena unique to the human species and inseparable from the human personality. Indeed, cognitive theory and the advances in cognitive therapy techniques contain within them powerful explanations of what it means to be human and thus have implications for human personality.

COMPUTER MODELS AND HUMAN INFORMATION PROCESSING

The similarities between computers and human minds are so compelling that one could be viewed as the mirror of the other. But which is the mirror and which the thing being mirrored? And does the mirror tell all? The relationship between computers and minds is beset with thorny philosophical questions. The notion that minds are really machines, or that the computer adequately mirrors the mind, has inspired much theory and research in cognitive psychology. Not surprisingly, however, this notion has its critics as well.

Minds and Machines.   A. M. Turing (1912–1954) was a British mathematician, logician, and pioneering computer scientist. He invented the prototype for the modern digital computer, the Turing machine. "Can machines think?" he asked. His bold response was that indeed they can. They imitate or *simulate* human thinking so well that the distinction between genuine and imitation becomes meaningless (Turing, 1950/1991).

In 1958, psychologist Allen Newell and computer scientist Herbert A. Simon proposed that human cognition can be viewed as an information-processing system and that the behavior of this system can be described "by a well-specified program, defined in terms of elementary information processes" (Lachman, Lachman, & Butterfield, 1979, p. 98). The analogy between the human mind and the computer proposed by Newell and Simon spurred a wealth of research and theoretic formulations based on computer models. According to these models, humans, like computers, *encode* symbolic *input, recode* it, make decisions about it and store some of it in memory, and, finally, *decode* and give back the symbolic *output* (Lachman, Lachman, & Butterfield, 1979).

For many information-processing psychologists, the computer came to serve two functions. First, it provided a model that inspired theories about how people talk, think, remember, and recognize. Second, it was a tool by which these theories could be tested. For example, Quillian (1969) expressed his theory of language comprehension in a simulation program called the Teachable Language Comprehender (TLC). This program related "input" assertions to information previously stored in its memory and came up

I believe that in about fifty years' time it will be possible to programme computers, with a storage capacity of about 10^9, to make them play the imitation game so well that an average interrogator will not have more than [a] 70 percent chance of making the right identification after five minutes of questioning. The original question, "Can machines think?" I believe to be too meaningless to deserve discussion. (Turing, 1950/1991)

with a meaningful and relevant "output." The performance of TLC was limited to certain kinds of phrases and sentences. Nevertheless, it was a beginning that held promise of the exciting developments to come in understanding how human language and thinking work.

Since then, sophisticated programs have been created that can "learn," "recognize" things, reorganize knowledge, even make analogies (Waldrop, 1985). Among the most successful programs are those that "specialize" in particular areas of knowledge, such as medical diagnoses or master chess strategies, not to mention the games of skill played on millions of home computers.

Criticisms of Computer Modeling.   Numerous areas of technology and the entertainment field have benefited from computer modeling. Few would argue this point. Whether computers have brought us any closer to unraveling the mysteries of the human mind, however, remains a controversial question. Even if computers in some sense "think," do they really think as we do? When it comes to knowing who and what we are, few researchers agree with Turing (1950/1991) that simulation, no matter how good, is the same as the real thing.

Critics of the computer models point to the contextually determined nature of human responses. For human beings, the horizons of the context are always fuzzy, whereas computers do not deal well with fuzziness. Much of the empirical research with human subjects has occurred under highly artificial laboratory conditions that bypass this problem. But the research also suffers from a lack of "ecological validity" (Neisser, 1976a); that is, it has little relevance to human experience and cognitive performance in real-life situations. Another feature of human cognition that seems difficult—some say impossible—for the computer to replicate is the experience of insight, the "aha!" experience, which comes as a jolt of recognition when we suddenly see how to tackle a problem in a wholly different, far superior way. The insight occurs as if by a "leap" rather than by logically ordered steps. The mind seems truly magical, its processes not mechanically reproducible by a computer!

To these criticisms, the advocates of computer modeling maintain that the mind is not so magical, just hidden from our conscious awareness (Waldrop, 1985). Perhaps, as Freud said, nothing happens by accident in the mind. Perhaps every leap of insight is determined by strictly mechanistic laws operating within the unconscious. And the computer may be able to show what we cannot see—the trudging steps that actually make up the leaps of intuition. That is, the computer may really be able to structurally approximate human cognitive processes.

To this day, the issue of mind versus machine has not been settled. Some psychologists and computer scientists believe that it is only a matter of time before we fully unravel the machinations of the human mind, whereas others are convinced that no machine can ever have the last word on the human mind. The relationship between mind and machine appears to be such that no single solution seems possible—at least not one that would satisfy everyone. Kelly's notion of reflexivity suggests why this is so. The computer model proposes to account for how humans construe their worlds. But the computer model itself is a construct. In other words, creating computer models of the mind is a reflexive endeavor in which the mind seeks to create its own construction processes. Perhaps it could be said that the designing of computer models of the mind is a genuine attempt by human beings to test our machine-making abilities. Thus we are likening the machine to the mind. On the other hand, when empirical researchers isolate their human subjects from their real-life environments and have them

We also happen to believe that, given the present state of psychological theories, almost any program able to perform some task previously limited to humans will represent an advance in the psychological theory of that performance. (Quillian, 1969, p. 459)

But none of this gets at the soul-disturbing essence of the question. If a machine can be made to think, then perhaps we are machines. (Waldrop, 1985, p. 31)

personal reflection

MINDS AND MACHINES

Here are some questions to ponder about minds and machines.

A machine is designed for a particular purpose. Cars are designed for the purpose of transportation. Computers are designed for various purposes having to do with handling information. Machines serve (more or less effectively) the purposes of their designers.

If the human mind is like a computer, was it, like the computer, created for a purpose? Who designed it?

If the human mind was not created for a purpose and has no designer, in what sense is it like a machine?

Do any machines create their own purpose and design?

If the human mind's purpose is the survival of the organism, does the purpose of survival originate inside or outside the mind?

respond in artificial experimental conditions that simulate the circumstance of the computer, then it is a case of molding the mind to fit the machine. We have come full circle!

Breaking Out of the Mind-Machine Circle. A way out of the circle has been suggested by Varela, Thompson, and Rosch (1991). These researchers propose that cognition and cognitive science (which they see as being itself a cognitive endeavor) are *enactive;* the very act of theorizing or data gathering about the mind changes the mind. Coming up with a computer model enacts a different cognitive process and outcome than, for example, contemplating the meaning of a painting. In a remarkable parallel with Kelly's notions of construing and reflexivity, these researchers suggest that *enactment* is an open, self-modifying process in which "cognition is not the representation of a pregiven world by a pregiven mind but is rather the enactment of a world and a mind on the basis of a history of the various actions that a being in the world performs" (Varela, Thompson, & Rosch, 1991, p. 9).

When seen as enactive, cognitive science and its object, the human mind, perform an intricate dance together, each modifying the other. This intimate partnership is quite unlike the detached objectivity cognitive research usually maintains toward its object. Varela and colleagues (1991) note that scientists in general and cognitive psychologists in particular have a deep distrust of human experience and tend to dismiss it as subjective, unreliable, and arbitrary—in a word, as *mindless*. Varela, Thompson, and Rosch urge a restoration of faith in human experience and the inclusion of *mindful* experience as an equal partner in research. The education of a cognitive scientist and his or her research subject should include training not just in the theories and research methods of the field but also in mindful observation of their own mental states. Varela and colleagues call for a closing of the gap between science and experience by reclaiming human experience as a source of valid knowledge (Puhakka, 1993).

Computers and the computer modeling of mind have evolved hand in hand. As computers have become more complex and capable of operations we previously thought only the human mind could perform, they seem to yield better models of the mind. Out of this dialectical dance between mind and machine, the machine has emerged as an intriguing metaphor for the human mind. When cognition is viewed as enactive, mind modifies machine, and machine alters mind, in an endless, reflexive, open spiral.

ALBERT BANDURA AND SOCIAL COGNITIVE THEORY

Albert Bandura is one of the best known psychologists alive today. He was born in 1925 in a small town in Canada, and received his undergraduate degree in psychology from the University of British Columbia. Then Bandura enrolled at the University of Iowa, which was a major center of behaviorism and learning theory.

Bandura received his doctorate in 1952 and, after finishing a clinical internship, began teaching at Stanford University where he has remained throughout his career. In 1973 Bandura was elected president of the American Psychological Association. He received the APA Distinguished Scientific Contribution Award in 1980 for "innovative experiements on a host of topics including moral development, observational learning, fear acquisition, treatment strategies, self-control . . . and cognitive regulation of behavior. . . . [His] warmth, and humane example have inspired his many students. . . . (*American Psychologist,* 1981, p. 27).

For Bandura, the terms *cognitive* and *social* are closely related. Bandura has stressed that people learn as much from observing the behavior of others as they learn from their own experience. Through various cognitive processes we remember and evaluate what we have observed in others. For example, when we see someone else receive a reward for their behavior we naturally think, "If I act the same, I will probably receive a reward also."

Although he was surrounded by behaviorists, Bandura did not become a traditional behaviorist himself. Behaviorists have generally preferred animal research. Bandura has studied human subjects and emphasized our human capacities for symbolic thought. People develop complex cognitive structures through language and symbols and form hypotheses about the possible effects of their behavior (Bandura, 1999a).

> At the time of my graduate training, the entire field of psychology was behaviorally oriented with an almost exclusive focus on the phenomenon of learning. But I never really fit in the behavioral orthodoxy. At the time, virtually all of the theorizing and research centered on learning through the effects of reinforcing outcomes. In my first major program of research, I argued against the primacy of conditioning in favor of observation learning in which people neither emit responses nor receive reinforcements during the process of learning. . . . I conceptualized observational learning as mediated through perceptual and cognitive processes. (Bandura in Monte & Sollod, 2003, p. 559)

Major Concepts

Reciprocal Determinism.   Personality theorists often debate whether inner or outer forces control our behavior. Some insist environmental factors are the most important. Others claim control of behavior comes from within. In contrast, Bandura focuses on the interaction of behavior, internal dynamics, and external factors. Bandura coined the term **reciprocal determinism** for the effects on our behavior of both our cognitive processes and the external social and physical environment.

Nurture shapes nature. (Albert Bandura[1])

Bandura later developed the concept of **triadic reciprocality** to refer to the interaction among behavior, environment, and internal factors such as awareness and cognition (see Figure 9.1). Bandura asserts that "people . . . function as contributors to their own motivation, behavior, and development within a network of reciprocally interacting influences" (Bandura, 1989a, p. 6).

[1]Bandura sidebar quotes are taken from www.emory.edu/EDUCATION/mfp/banquotes.

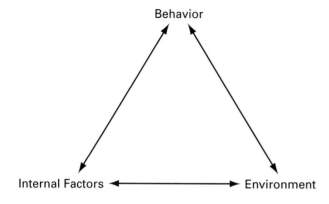

Behavior

Internal Factors ⟷ Environment

FIGURE 9.1 Bandura's Triadic Reciprocality

Triadic reciprocality rests on several powerful assumptions. One assumption is that behavior affects internal factors. For example, continued success at a certain activity brings confidence in your abilities in that area. Bandura (2001a) also claims behavior can affect our neurobiological functions. If we continue to read, write, and talk about a particular topic, we develop a "neurological network" for handling information about that topic that makes it easier to learn more about the topic.

Internal factors are also affected by the environment. For example, women who live together in a dormitory often come to match their menstrual cycles (Matlin & Foley, 1997). In addition, behavior affects the environment, just as irrigation brings water and abundant crops to deserts.

Internal events, such as thoughts and feelings, influence both our behavior and the environment. Our belief that our behavior in a certain task will not succeed makes it far more likely we will fail (Bandura, 1989a). Beliefs about the environment may have important environmental consequences. If we place little value on our forests, we will allow the forests to disappear.

Observational Learning.   In contrast to traditional behaviorists, Bandura has argued that much significant learning occurs through observation. According to Skinnerian theory, responses must first occur and then be reinforced. Other behavioral theories also stress that learning comes from reinforcing behavior. In contrast, Bandura showed that significant learning often occurs when subjects simply observe models as they perform various behaviors.

Bandura has called this **observational (or vicarious) learning.** This kind of learning occurs "as a function of observing the behavior of others and its reinforcing consequences, without the modeled responses being overtly performed by the view during the exposure period (Bandura, 1965, p. 3). We receive vicarious reinforcement whenever we observe someone receiving rewards for their behavior.

In a classic study of observational learning (Bandura, Ross, & Ross, 1963), preschool children watched a film in which an adult hit and kicked a large inflated "Bobo" doll. The adult also shouted phrases like "Pow, right in the nose!" while hitting the doll. When the children were allowed to play with the doll themselves, the experimental group was twice as aggressive as a control group that had not seen the model attack the doll. The researchers found the same increase in aggression with a model shown on television and also with a cartoon character.

To study the effects of parental **modeling,** Bandura also compared the parents of highly aggressive children and more inhibited children (Bandura & Walters, 1963).

People who hold a low view of themselves will credit their achievements to external factors rather than to their own capabilities. (Albert Bandura)

If you've seen one redwood, you've seen them all. (Attributed to Ronald Reagan, then governor of California)

The parents of the inhibited children proved were inhibited and the parents of the aggressive children proved more aggressive.

Characteristics of the Modeling Situation.
Bandura (1977, 1986) found that three factors influence observational learning:

1. The characteristic of the models
2. The characteristics of the observers
3. The rewards associated with the behaviors

First, Bandura found that people are more influenced by a model who is similar to them than by someone who is significantly different. In the Bobo-doll studies, for example, children were more aggressive after exposure to a live model than a cartoon character.

We are more likely to imitate a model of our same sex and age. Status and prestige also add to the model's influence. For example, one research study found pedestrians are more likely to cross the street against a red light if they see a well-dressed person crossing than if they see one poorly dressed crossing. We can see one direct application of this line of reasoning in advertisements that use either well-known figures or highly attractive models to influence us to use a particular product.

Second, observer attributes are also important. Those low in self-confidence and self-esteem are more likely to imitate a model than are those high in self-confidence and self-esteem. Also, the more we have been rewarded for imitating a model, the more likely we are to be influenced by the model's behavior.

Third, if we see a model is rewarded for a certain behavior, we are more likely to imitate that behavior. In the Bobo-doll study, one group of children saw the model receive praise and a soda and candy. Another group watched the model receive criticism and physical punishment for the same behavior. The children who observed the reward displayed more aggression than the children who saw the punishment.

We are more affected by the behavior of models than we realize. For example, suicide rates rise after the suicide of a celebrity (Phillips, 1974). Murder rates increased more than 12 percent for a three-day period after a televised boxing championship match; this increase remained constant over a fifteen-year period (Phillips, 1983).

> We are more heavily invested in the theories of failure than we are in the theories of success. (Albert Bandura)

Conditions for Observational Learning.
Bandura believed that successful observational learning is based on five conditions:

1. *Pay attention to the model.* We don't retain everything we observe. For observation learning to occur, we must pay sufficient attention and perceive the model's behavior accurately enough to allow us to recall and imitate the model's behavior.
2. *Remember what we observed.* Memory is not a passive process. We reflect on what we have observed and tend to remember whatever we consider useful or important. We must retain essential elements of the model's behavior in order to repeat it later.
3. *Reproduce what we have learned.* Focused attention and prior knowledge of the modeled behavior help us understand, remember, and imitate the modeled behavior. Without prior knowledge, we are far less likely to understand and remember complex behaviors. For example, someone with no knowledge of physics is unlikely to retain anything from an advanced physics lecture.

   According to Bandura we use two representational systems: imaginal and verbal. The *imaginal representational system* is composed of vivid, retrievable images formed while observing a model. The *verbal representational system* consists of the words an observer uses to describe observed behavior.

4. *Be motivated to perform the activity observed.*   When do people turn their observations into behavior? We are more likely to carefully observe and imitate behavior associated with positive outcomes than we are behavior with neutral or negative outcomes. This is strongest when we perceive a model's behavior leads to reward and expect our reproduction of that behavior to produce a similar reward.

   Bandura (1994b) indicates that motivation can come from three sources. First, we observe a model receiving reward for a particular behavior. Second, the model (a parent or teacher, for example) rewards our attempts to reproduce their behavior. Third, and perhaps most important, we reward ourselves for our performance; we "pat ourselves on the back."

5. *Practice.*   Production of any complex behavior requires practice. When we learn to drive a car, for example, we may begin by watching parents and others driving and take classes on the rules and regulations regarding driving. No matter how much preparation we have made, our initial attempts to drive are inevitably awkward. We need practice and feedback on our behavior to learn to brake and steer smoothly.

Bandura's approach to observational learning is well summarized in an old Chinese proverb: "I hear and I forget, I see and I remember, I do and I understand."

Applied Research.   Bandura's work has inspired a variety of applied research studies. Modeling techniques have been used to affect subjects' ability to tolerate pain (Symbaluk, Heth, Cameron, & Pierce, 1997), to decrease anxiety, including fear of hospitalization and surgery (Melamed & Siegel, 1975), and to lower text anxiety (Sarason, 1975).

Bandura has applied modeling to reduce phobias (Bandura, Grusec, & Menlove, 1967). Children who were afraid of dogs observed another child with a dog. As the children watched (from a distance), the model moved closer to the dog. After petting the dog while it was in a playpen the model went into the pen and played with the dog. Simply observing this reduced the children's fear considerably. In another study, adults with snake phobias watched a film in which children and adults made increasingly closer contact with a snake (Bandura, Blanchard, & Ritter, 1969). The models moved from handling plastic snakes to touching live snakes to letting a snake crawl over their bodies. The phobic adults could stop the film whenever it became too frightening. Their phobias gradually diminished. Such a considerable body of research on the use of modeling to reduce phobias and anxiety dramatically illustrates the power and effectiveness of observational learning (Bandura, 1997).

Self-Efficacy.   Most of us remember the children's book *The Little Engine That Could* and the brave little engine that struggled up the mountain, saying, "I think I can. I think I can. I think I can." Bandura called this belief in oneself **self-efficacy.**

Self-efficacy is defined as "people's beliefs in their capabilities to produce desired effects by their own actions" (Bandura, 1997, p. vii). Self-efficacy theory holds that these beliefs are among the most important factors in our behavior.

Self-efficacy is a judgment about whether or not your skills and capacities can lead you to success in a particular task. It is not a belief about what you *will* do, but a belief about what you *can* do. Self-efficacy is not self-esteem. Self-esteem is built on your judgments about yourself; self-efficacy applies to your expectations of success in a particular activity.

A strong sense of self-efficacy, a belief we can succeed in spite of obstacles, leads to greater patience and perseverance and a higher level of performance. Confident people treat difficulties as challenges instead of threats. They have less fear of failure, higher aspirations, and greater problem-solving abilities.

By sticking it out through tough times, people emerge from adversity with a stronger sense of efficacy. (Albert Bandura)

If self-efficacy is lacking, people tend to behave ineffectually, even though they know what to do. (Albert Bandura)

On the other hand, a weak sense of self-efficacy creates feelings of helplessness and a belief that efforts are likely to result in failure rather than success. Small difficulties often cause such people to give up. Lack of a sense of self-efficacy can damage motivation, lower goals, and even affect our health. Research on self-efficacy has demonstrated its influence on an extraordinary range of behaviors, from daily social interaction to psychopathology. Bandura (1997) has studied the effects of self-efficacy in three major areas: how we cope with threat, how our intellectual interests develop, and the effects of self-efficacy on physical and psychological health.

Self-efficacy develops from five sources (Maddux, 2002):

1. *Successful performance.*   Success based on our own efforts is the most powerful source of a sense of self-efficacy (Bandura, 1977, 1997).
2. *Vicarious experiences of success.*   Observation of others' behaviors and the consequences of those behaviors. This helps us form expectancies about our own behaviors and their consequences. Observing others' successes helps develop a sense of self-efficacy to the extent we believe we are similar to those we have observed (Bandura, 1997).
3. *Internal success images.*   Imaging can strengthen our sense of self-efficacy. Most effective are images of success based on real or invented experiences similar to an anticipated situation.
4. *Verbal persuasion.*   Others' positive opinions of us can enhance our sense of self-efficacy. Although this source is less effective than the first three, it is probably the most common. Parents, teachers, coaches, and friends frequently encourage us verbally. They basically give us the message that we can succeed at a certain behavior. Realistic verbal persuasion is most successful. For example, it is more effective to encourage a C student to work harder and get Bs than to tell the student he or she can be a straight-A student.
5. *Physiological and emotional arousal.*   Our emotional and physiological states influence our sense of self-efficacy. Everyone has experienced the association of success and positive emotions and also the connection between failure and negative emotions. When we are worried or depressed, our sense of self-efficacy is likely to sink. When we are cheerful and optimistic, our self-efficacy beliefs are likely to rise. Paradoxically, in sports and other physical activities, our sense of self-efficacy may rise as we experience pain and fatigue, because these physiological states have been associated with past success (Bandura, 1986, 1997).

Persons who have a strong sense of efficacy deploy their attention and effort to the demands of the situation and are spurred by obstacles to greater effort. (Albert Bandura)

Bandura found that the sense of self-efficacy can be enhanced by the following practical methods:

1. Provide people with success experiences by setting for them difficult but achievable goals.
2. Observe models performing successfully.
3. Supply verbal encouragement that the person can perform successfully.
4. Use diet, stress reduction, and exercise to control physiological arousal and thus increase stamina, strength, and relaxation under pressure.

Bandura has applied the above principles to enhance self-efficacy in a variety of situations, including learning to play a musical instrument, relating to others of the opposite sex, developing computer skills, quitting smoking, and conquering phobias.

Health treatments are more successful for people with high self-efficacy (O'Leary, 1985). A high sense of self-efficacy relates to success in overcoming substance abuse and eating disorders (Bandura, 1997; DiClemente, Fairhurst, & Piotrowski, 1995). A sense of self-efficacy also enhances our physiological response to stress, including strengthening the immune system (O'Leary & Brown, 1995). On the other hand, a low sense of self-efficacy is related to depression, and increases susceptibility to infection and hastens the progression of disease (Bandura, 1997).

Bandura (1977) examined the ways schools instill a sense of self-efficacy in students. In high-achieving schools, the administration is more concerned with education than rule enforcement, and teachers set high standards and high expectations for their students. In low-achieving schools, administrations act more as disciplinarians and less as educators, and teachers had low academic expectations.

Bandura argues that therapy will succeed to the extent it increases the sense of self-efficacy. He claims, "treatments that are most effective are built on an empowerment model. If you really want to help people, you provide them with the competencies, build a strong self-belief, and create opportunities for them to exercise those competencies" (Bandura in Evans, 1989, p. 16).

> Self-belief does not necessarily ensure success, but self-disbelief assuredly spawns failure. (Albert Bandura)

Researchers differ on the definition of self-efficacy. Some see self-efficacy as a general trait, describing a wide variety of behaviors (for example, Shelton, 1990). Bandura tends to measure self-efficacy beliefs for particular areas of behavior. For example, one person may have a high sense of academic self-efficacy, but a low sense of self-efficacy in sports. If we look more closely, that same person may have a high sense of self-efficacy in, say, history and literature, and a much lower sense in math and science.

Self-efficacy supports setting challenging goals and enhances our goal-directed activities, inspiring greater persistence in the face of inevitable setbacks and difficulties (Wood & Bandura, 1989). A sense of self-efficacy also influences our effectiveness and efficiency in problem and decision making activities (Hepner & Lee, 2002). Bandura suggests that groups can develop a sense of *collective efficacy* once members believe the group can accomplish worthwhile goals (Evans, 1989).

> People not only gain understanding through reflection, they evaluate and alter their own thinking. (Albert Bandura)

The Self.

Bandura sees the **self** as a set of cognitive processes and structures "for perceiving, evaluating, and regulating behavior, not a psychic agent that controls action" (Bandura, 1978, p. 344). One aspect of the self is self-efficacy, and another is *self-regulation*. We receive reinforcement for our behavior from others and from the environment; we also set personal standards for our behavior and reward ourselves when we meet those standards.

For example, a good saleswoman carefully observes and judges her own work. She asks herself questions such as "Have I spoken with enough clients this week?" "Have I done the best job possible in presenting both the pros and cons of choosing my product over others?" "Did I make an effective presentation?" If the saleswoman concludes she has been doing an excellent job, she might decide to take the rest of the afternoon off as a reward. This is the kind of self-regulation that enhances performance (Bandura, 1991).

Goal setting is an important aspect of self-regulation. In a study of goal setting, Bandura (2000b, 2001a) measured four groups of subjects. The first group set goals and received feedback regarding their progress. A second group just set goals and a third group just received feedback. A control group neither set goals nor received feedback. The first group showed significantly higher effort, and the other three were roughly equal in low goal-oriented activity. Bandura also found it is more effective to set specific goals that can be broken down into clear sub-goals.

> Self-appraisals are influenced by evaluative reactions of others. (Albert Bandura)

Moral Disengagement.

Sometimes individuals fail in self-regulation concerning moral and ethical behavior. Bandura (1978) calls this **moral disengagement** and points out, "Over the years, much cruelty has been perpetrated by decent, moral people in the name of religious principles, righteous ideology and social order" (1977, p. 156). Bandura also has observed, "People do not ordinarily engage in reprehensible conduct until they have justified to themselves the morality of their actions" (Bandura, 1999c, p. 194). He has listed a series of self-exonerative cognitive activities that enable people to engage in moral disengagement. These activities are highly similar to the ego defense mechanisms described in psychoanalysis (see Chapter 1). They have the acronym 3-D GAMBLE.

> **Dehumanization** is a cognitive process that reduces some people to less than human status. This is often done through derogatory racist or sexist labels.
> **Displacement** means blaming others for one's own actions. For example, soldiers may claim, "I was only obeying orders."
> **Diffusion of responsibility** is spreading responsibility for behavior to others. For example, when a group of spectators fails to help someone in trouble, people may say they were waiting for someone else to act first.
> **Gradualistic moral disengagement** occurs when people move step by step toward immoral behavior. Training young soldiers or terrorists to kill is a gradual process that may take months.
> **Advantageous comparison** makes immoral actions seem righteous by comparing them with more flagrant inhumanities. For example, Hitler responded to criticism of his mistreatment of the Jews by referring to the subjugation of Native Americans and the British oppression of Indians.
> **Moral justification** makes immoral behavior acceptable because it serves worthy purposes. For example, Hitler justified his aggressive policies in the name.
> **BLaming victims** for their own fate. For example, rapists often blame their victims: "She wore sexy clothing."
> **Euphemistic labeling** uses labels designed to make unforgivable behavior innocuous or even praiseworthy. In Vietnam, for example, destruction of crops and forests was called "defoliation." Killings were labeled "body counts."

AARON BECK AND COGNITIVE THERAPY

Cognitive therapy focuses on the effect of cognition on human emotions. Its theoretical roots are largely derived from common sense and naturalistic introspective observation of the human mind at work, typically in psychotherapeutic settings. Practical in its concern, cognitive therapy aims at modifying and regulating the negative effects of certain cognitive processes on a person's emotional well-being. One of the major approaches to psychotherapy today, cognitive therapy owes its basic theory and therapeutic techniques to the pioneering work of Aaron Beck.

Beck's Discovery. Aaron Beck trained as a psychoanalyst and, for several years, practiced psychoanalysis in the traditional way by having patients verbalize their *free associations,* communicating whatever came to mind. One day, however, something happened that changed his approach. A patient in the course of free-associating had been criticizing Beck angrily. After a pause, Beck (1976) asked the patient what he was feeling, and the patient responded, "I feel very guilty." This was not unusual. But the patient then spontaneously added that while he had been expressing angry criticisms of his analyst, self-critical thoughts had been occurring simultaneously in his mind. Thus a second thought stream had been running parallel to the thoughts of anger and hostility he had reported during his free association. The patient described this second stream as follows: "I said the wrong thing. . . . I shouldn't have said that. . . . I'm wrong to criticize him. . . . I'm bad. . . . [H]e won't like me" (p. 31).

This second stream of thought provided the link between the patient's expression of anger and feelings of guilt. The patient was feeling guilty because he had been criticizing himself for being angry with his analyst. Perhaps analogous to Freud's *preconscious,* this kind of stream has to do with what people say to themselves rather than what they might say in a conversation with another person. It seems to be a self-monitoring system operating alongside the thoughts and feelings being expressed in a conversation. The thoughts that have to do with the self-monitoring tend to arise quickly and automatically, as if by reflex (Beck, 1991). They are usually followed by an unpleasant emotion. Sometimes patients, either spontaneously or with the prompting of the therapist, express this emotion, but they almost never report the automatic thoughts that precede the emotion. In fact, they are typically only dimly, if at all, aware of them.

Automatic thoughts supply a running commentary on much of what people do or experience. These thoughts are present in the experiences of healthy as well as emotionally troubled people. The difference has to do with the kind of messages the thoughts contain and how much they interfere with a person's life. For example, depressed people talk to themselves in highly critical tones, blaming themselves for every mishap, expecting the worst, and feeling that they deserve whatever misfortune befalls them, because they are worthless anyway. Severely depressed people tend to talk to themselves more loudly. For them, the negative thoughts are not merely whispers on the periphery of consciousness but are loud, repetitive screams that can consume much energy and distract the person from other activities.

Automatic thinking and unpleasant physical or emotional symptoms combine to form vicious cycles that maintain and exaggerate the symptoms, resulting sometimes in full-blown emotional disorders. Beck gives an example of a person who is suffering from symptoms of anxiety, including heart palpitation, sweating, and dizziness. The patient's thoughts of dying lead to increased anxiety, as manifested by the physiological symptoms; these symptoms then are interpreted as signs of imminent death (1976, p. 99).

Cognitive Therapy and Common Sense. The discovery of automatic thoughts marked a shift in Beck's approach to therapy as well as in his view of the human personality. The meanings of these thoughts "did not usually revolve around esoteric themes such as castration anxiety or psychosocial fixations, as might be suggested by classical psychoanalytic theory, but were related to vital social issues such as success or failure, acceptance or rejection, respect or disdain" (Beck, 1991, p. 369).

An important feature of automatic thoughts is their accessibility to the patient's own awareness, which allows introspection. Even though they are difficult to notice at first, these thoughts can, with training, be brought into conscious awareness, as Beck discovered. Therefore, the source as well as the solution to emotional problems lies within the sphere of the person's own awareness, within the reach of his or her cognition.

This is the principle underlying Beck's cognitive approach to therapy. At the heart of this approach is respect for human beings' capabilities to heal themselves and a celebration of common sense, which embodies the wisdom by which people have, through generations, exercised these capabilities. Beck calls attention to the everyday feats of our cognitive capabilities:

> If it were not for man's ability to filter and attach appropriate labels to the blizzard of external stimuli so efficiently, his world would be chaotic, and he would be bounced from

The way a person monitors and instructs himself, praises and criticizes himself, interprets events and makes predictions not only illuminates normal behavior, but sheds light on the inner workings of the emotional disorders. (Beck, 1976, p. 38)

one crisis to another. Moreover, if he were not able to monitor his highly developed imagination, he would be floating in and out of a twilight zone unable to distinguish between the reality of a situation and the images and personal meanings that it triggers. In his interpersonal relations, he is generally able to select the subtle cues that allow him to separate his adversaries from his friends. He makes the delicate adjustments in his own behavior that help him to maintain diplomatic relationships with people whom he dislikes or who dislike him. He is generally able to penetrate the social masks of other people, to differentiate sincere from insincere messages, to distinguish friendly mocking from veiled antagonism. He tunes into the significant communications in a vast babble of noises so that he can organize and modulate his own responses. These psychological operations seem to work automatically without evidence of much cognition, deliberation, or reflection. (Beck, 1976, pp. 11–12)

This is a powerful expression of Beck's faith in the basic human capacity for healing and wholeness. His celebration of our natural competence in mental health is reminiscent of Kelly's **man-the-scientist** (Chapter 10). Both have an appreciation of the capacities of the human mind that incline them to respect the common person and to view the gap between the expert (scientist or therapist), who knows, and the layperson, who presumably doesn't, as being much narrower and more easily bridged than is typically believed. Beck and his followers have freely shared their discoveries with therapists as well as with the general population.

Cognitive Techniques for Therapy and Self-Help.   A variety of techniques that focus on specific problems and require relatively short-term therapy have evolved out of Beck's approach (Beck, Rush, Shaw, & Emery, 1979; Emery, 1981; McMullin, 1986). Their aim is to modify the negative or self-defeating automatic thought processes or perceptions that seem to perpetuate the symptoms of emotional disorders. Either directly or indirectly, these techniques challenge, dispute, or restructure the clients' perception or understanding of themselves and their life situations.

In cognitive therapy, the therapist and the client form a collaborative, almost collegial relationship. The therapist does not presume to know the client's thoughts or feelings but invites the client to explore and critically examine them autonomously. In cognitive therapy, clients are in charge of their problems; they have direct access to the patterns of perception and thinking that intensify maladaptive feelings and behaviors, and they are capable of changing these patterns.

Not surprisingly, cognitive therapy has inspired a wealth of self-help literature. In fact, most of the popular literature on how to assert yourself, boost your self-esteem, deal with your anger, get rid of your depression, save your marriage or relationship, or simply feel good is based on the work of cognitive therapists (Burns, 1980; Ellis & Harper, 1975; McMullin & Casey, 1975).

The individual who has perhaps done the most to popularize the methods of cognitive therapy is Albert Ellis (1962, 1971, 1974). His forceful tactics of confrontation and persuasion have won him followers among therapists as well as laypeople. Ellis's approach is known as *rational-emotive therapy (RET)*. Based on the notion that irrational beliefs cause emotional suffering and behavioral problems, RET uses logic and rational argument to expose and attack the irrationality of the thoughts that maintain the undesirable emotions and behavior. Though more confrontative than other cognitive therapies, Ellis's approach shares the commonsense logic of all cognitive methods.

personal reflection

PATTERNS OF NEGATIVE THINKING

Try this experience to reach a better understanding of your patterns of negative thinking. When you are feeling anxious, depressed, upset, or just a little blue, observe the thoughts that spontaneously arise and fade away. Let the thoughts come and go without judging, suppressing, or trying to change them in any way. Simply monitor them for a few minutes.

Take a sheet of paper and divide it into the following three columns: Automatic Thoughts, Cognitive Distortions, and Rational Response. In the Automatic Thoughts column, list the thoughts or recurrent themes as they occur. Then go over your list, and, in the second column, identify the distortions in each thought listed in the first column. In the third column, for each thought, write a rational substitute using accurate, neutral descriptions.

The next time you feel similarly anxious, depressed, or upset about something, try extinguishing any distorted thoughts by first monitoring them and then substituting the rational thoughts for them.

The **logic of the cognitive approach** can be simply stated in terms of the following four principles (Burns, 1980, pp. 3–4): (1) When people are depressed or anxious, they think in an illogical, negative manner and inadvertently act in a self-defeating way. (2) With a little effort, people learn to rid themselves of harmful thought patterns. (3) As their painful symptoms are eliminated, they become happy and productive again and will respect themselves. (4) These aims are generally accomplished within a relatively brief period of time, using straightforward methods.

The first step is to become aware of one's automatic thoughts and identify any patterns of distortion. Burns (1980, pp. 40–41) describes the following ten types of distortions that commonly occur in the thinking of depressed people:

1. *All-or-Nothing Thinking.*   Seeing things in black-and-white categories. For example, falling short of perfection means total failure.
2. *Overgeneralization.*   Seeing one negative event as a confirming instance of a never-ending pattern of defeat.
3. *Mental Filter.*   Dwelling on a single negative detail exclusively until negativity colors all of an experience.
4. *Disqualifying the Positive.*   Insisting that positive experiences do not count, for whatever reason, thereby maintaining a negative belief in the face of evidence to the contrary.
5. *Jumping to Conclusions.*   Drawing negative conclusions even without definite facts to support them. This happens, for example, when a person arbitrarily concludes that another person is reacting negatively to him or her without bothering to find out whether it is true. Or a person so anticipates that things will turn out badly that he or she becomes convinced that they will.
6. *Magnification (Catastrophizing) or Minimization.*   Exaggerating the importance of things (for example, one's own slipups) or belittling their importance (for example, one's own desirable qualities).
7. *Emotional Reasoning.*   Assuming that one's negative emotions necessarily reflect the way things are: "I feel it, therefore it must be true."
8. *"Should" Statements.*   Trying to motivate oneself with "shoulds" and "shouldn'ts," as if one cannot act unless using psychological self-force. Feelings of guilt can result when the "shoulds" are directed toward oneself; directed toward others, one can feel anger, frustration, and resentment.
9. *Labeling and Mislabeling.*   Using negative appellations when referring to an error, instead of describing what happened. For example, rather than stating, "I lost the key," one attaches a negative label to oneself: "I am a loser." If someone else's behavior rubs

one the wrong way, a negative label might be attached to this person, for example, "He is a louse." Mislabeling involves describing an event with emotionally loaded language that does not ring true.

10. *Personalization.* Seeing oneself as the cause of an external event for which, in fact, one is not primarily responsible.

Once the distortions are discovered and correctly identified in a person's habitual, automatic thinking, the thoughts may be modified by substituting rational, realistic ideas for the distorting ones. For example, a person who was let down by a friend may hold on to the thought, "I am a real sucker and a complete fool." This reaction is an example of mislabeling and also of all-or-nothing thinking. Rational, realistic thoughts that more accurately describes what is going on might be, "I made a mistake in trusting this friend" and "I don't always know when I should or shouldn't trust a person, but with more experience I will learn to make that discrimination better." Cognitive therapists believe that with concentration and hard work the client, with the help of the therapist, can extinguish the automatic thoughts and their distortions. Rational, accurate thoughts can be substituted to create and maintain a happier, healthier way of living.

EVALUATION

Cognitive psychology tells us that human consciousness can be described as a machine, its operations precise and automatic and fully determined by rules and environmental input. The computer modeling of mind brings up challenging and perhaps ultimately unanswerable questions. If consciousness is a machine that operates in a wholly mechanistic fashion, then one might rightly ask, "Who controls the machine?" Cognitive therapists share a basic optimism in asserting that people can take control of their own mental processes much more than had seemed possible. According to these therapists, negative, self-defeating patterns of thinking and acting can be changed to bring about a happier, more fulfilling life. Cognitive psychology has gained mainstream acceptance. Nowhere is this more apparent than in the numerous self-help programs that proliferate outside the confines of academia. It may be that the work described here is having greater impact on the culture than any psychology since Freud, whose works shattered late Victorian rational complacency and led to an explosion of interest and alternative ways to explore consciousnes and understand one's self.

The Theory Firsthand

EXCERPT FROM COGNITIVE THERAPY AND THE EMOTIONAL DISORDERS

The following excerpt is by Aaron Beck (1976).

Let us conjecture, for the moment, that a person's consciousness contains elements that are responsible for the emotional upsets and blurred thinking that lead him to seek help. Moreover, let us suppose that the patient has at his disposal various rational techniques he can use, with proper instruction, to deal with these disturbing elements in his consciousness. If these suppositions are correct, then emotional disorder may be approached from an entirely different route: *Man has the key to understanding and solving his psychological disturbance within the scope of his own awareness.* . . .

The cognitive approach brings the understanding and treatment of the emotional disorders closer to a patient's everyday experiences. The patient can regard his disturbance as related to the kinds of misunderstandings he has experienced numerous times during his life. Moreover, he has undoubtedly had previous successes in correcting misinterpretations, either through acquiring more adequate information or by recognizing the logical fallacy of his misunderstandings. The cognitive approach makes sense to a patient because it is somehow related to his previous learning experiences and can stimulate confidence in his capacity to learn how to deal effectively with present misconceptions that are producing painful symptoms. Furthermore, by bringing emotional disorders within the purview of everyday experience and applying familiar problem-solving techniques, the therapist can immediately form a bridge to the patient. (pp. 3–4)

EXCERPT FROM *THE EMBODIED MIND: COGNITIVE SCIENCE AND HUMAN EXPERIENCE*

The following excerpt is by Varela, Thompson, & Rosch (1991).

"We began . . . with a reflection on the fundamental circularity in scientific method that would be noted by a philosophically inclined cognitive scientist. From the standpoint of enactive cognitive science, this circularity is central; it is an epistemological necessity. . . . The basic assumption, then, is that to every form of behavior and experience we can ascribe specific brain structures (however roughly). And, conversely, changes in brain structure manifest themselves in behavioral and experiential alterations. . . . Yet upon reflection we cannot avoid as a matter of consistency the logical implication that by this same view any such scientific description, either of biological or mental phenomena, must itself be a product of the structure of our own cognitive system.

When we ignore the fundamental circularity of our situation, this double face of cognitive science gives rise to two extremes: we suppose either that our human self-understanding is simply false and hence will eventually be replaced by a mature cognitive science, or we suppose that there can be no science of the human life-world because science must always presuppose it. . . . Unless we move beyond these oppositions, the rift between science and experience in our society will deepen. Neither extreme is workable for a pluralistic society that must embrace both science and the actuality of human experience. To deny the truth of our own experience in the scientific study of ourselves is not only unsatisfactory; it is to render the scientific study of ourselves without a subject matter. But to suppose that science cannot contribute to an understanding of our experience may be to abandon, within the modern context, the task of self-understanding. Experience and scientific understanding are like two legs without which we cannot walk. (pp. 9–14)

CHAPTER HIGHLIGHTS

- Cognitive psychology encompasses diverse approaches that share a concern with how consciousness, or the human mind, works. Mapping the structure of the intellect, and then applying the maps to improve therapy, are two aspects especially relevant to the study of personality.
- Cognitive psychologists look for principles that may be common to all human cognitive processes, rather than the variations and uniqueness of the human personality.
- Computer simulation has been useful in the investigation of various hypotheses about how humans think, perceive, remember, and use language.
- Though the benefits of computer modeling are evident in technology and entertainment, questions remain about how computer processes relate to mental processes. Critics of computer modeling point to the process of insight, the experience of "aha!" as one not mechanically reproducible. Advocates suggest that perhaps strictly mechanistic laws operating in the unconscious make up the leaps of intuition.
- Aaron Beck suggested that unpleasant emotional or physical symptoms combine with automatic thinking to form vicious cycles that exaggerate and maintain the symptoms. Full-blown emotional disorders are sometimes the result.
- Underlying Beck's cognitive approach is the notion that the source and the solution to one's emotional problems lie within the sphere of one's own awareness, within the reach of one's cognition. It has at its heart a deep respect for the self-healing capabilities of humans, as well as a celebration of common sense.
- Short-term therapeutic strategies, evolved out of Beck's work, aim at modifying the self-defeating or negative automatic thought perceptions or processes that seem to perpetuate the symptoms of emotional disorders.

■ The work of Albert Ellis, known as rational-emotive therapy, is based on the proposition that irrational beliefs cause emotional suffering and behavioral problems. Rational argument and logic are used to expose and attack the irrationality of beliefs that maintain undesirable behavior and emotions.

KEY CONCEPTS

Automatic thoughts In Beck's model, a running commentary on much of what people do or experience. They are present in the experience of healthy people as well as troubled people. Having to do with self-monitoring, they tend to arise on their own, as if by reflex, and are usually followed by an unpleasant emotion.

Human cognition Phenomena that comprise the processes of thinking, perceiving, remembering, evaluating, planning, and organizing, to name a few. The principles and mechanisms that govern these phenomena are of underlying concern to all cognitive psychologists.

Logic of the cognitive approach The commonsense basis of Ellis's and other cognitive therapies. The logic can be expressed in four principles: (1) When people are anxious or depressed, they inadvertently act in a self-defeating way and think in a negative, illogical manner. (2) People can learn to rid themselves of harmful thought patterns, with a little effort. (3) They will become happy and productive again and will respect themselves as their painful symptoms are eliminated. (4) These aims, which employ straightforward methods, are usually accomplished in a fairly brief period of time.

Man-the-scientist The notion that scientists are also people, who construe, or interpret, their hypotheses about the individuals they are investigating in the same way that ordinary people construe their environment. This concept is of interest and relevance to psychological inquiry, rather than a problem.

Modeling Imitation of the behavior of significant others.

Moral disengagement For Bandura, this is a failure in self-regulation concerning our moral and ethical behavior.

Observational (or vicarious) learning Learning that occurs as a result of observing the behavior of others.

Reciprocal determinism Bandura's term for the interaction of cognitive processes and the external social and physical environment.

Self Bandura defines the self as the cognitive processes and structures we use to observe and regulate our own behavior.

Self-efficacy The beliefs we hold about our own capacity to perform a task or accomplish a goal.

Triadic reciprocity Bandura's theory of interaction among behavior, internal factors, and the environment.

ANNOTATED BIBLIOGRAPHY

Beck, A. T. (1972). *Depression: Causes and treatment.* Philadelphia: University of Pennsylvania Press. (Originally published, 1967, as *Depression: Clinical, experimental, and theoretical aspects.*)

Presents the cognitive perspective and reviews research on the treatment of depression.

Beck, A. T. (1976). *Cognitive therapy and the emotional disorders.* New York: International Universities Press.

A clear and readable interpretation of various psychological disorders from the cognitive perspective. Also describes the principles of cognitive therapy for their treatment.

Lachman, R., Lachman, J. L., & Butterfield, E. (1979). *Cognitive psychology and information processing.* Hillsdale, NJ: Erlbaum.

This book offers a comprehensive view of the information-processing paradigm in cognitive psychology.

Varela, F. J., Thompson, E., & Rosch, E. (1991). *The embodied mind: Cognitive science and human experience.* Cambridge, MA: MIT Press.

Critical of the view that human cognition can be represented by a computer or any other model, the authors propose that cognition creates and is influenced by its own models.

Web Sites

http://www.ke.shinshu-u.ac.jp/psych/index.html

Resources for psychology and cognitive sciences on the Internet maintained by Department of Kansei Engineering, Faculty of Textile Science and Technology, Shinshu University, Nagano, Japan.

http://www-psych.stanford.edu/cogsci/

Cognitive and psychological sciences on the Internet
An index to Internet resources relevant to research in cognitive science and psychology.

http://www.learninginfo.com

Site of a company that sells cognitive development, skills, and therapy. Cool opening diagram.

http://129.7.160.115/inst5931/COGNTIVE.PSY

This cognitive psychology review is for a course in technology and learning at the University of Houston Clear Lake. Suggests that cognitive psychology is far broader than we have defined it in this book. One of numerous cognitive course overviews from various universities posted on the **Web**.

REFERENCES

American Psychologist. (1981). Award for distinguished contributions to Albert Bandura *38*, 27–42.

Anderson, J. R. (1985). *Cognitive psychology and its implications.* New York: Freeman.

Anderson, J. R., & Bower, G. H. (1973). *Human associative memory.* Washington, DC: Winston.

Bandura, A. (1965). Vicarious processes: A case of no-trial learning. In. L. Berkowitz (Ed.), *Advances in experimental social psychology* (Vol. 2, pp. 1–55). New York: Academic Press.

Bandura, A. (1977). *Social learning theory.* Upper Saddle River, NJ: Prentice Hall.

Bandura, A. (1978). The self system in reciprocal determinism. *American Psychologist, 33,* 334–358.

Bandura, A. (1986). *Social foundations of thought and action: A social cognitive theory.* Upper Saddle River, NJ: Prentice Hall.

Bandura, A. (1989a). Social cognitive theory. In *Annals of Child Development* (Vol. 6, pp. 1–60). New York: Jai Press.

Bandura, A. (1991). Social cognitive theory of self-regulation. *Organizational Behavior and Human Decision Processes, 50,* 248–287.

Bandura, A. (1994b). Self-efficacy. In V. S. Ramachaudran (Ed.), *Encyclopedia of Human Behavior* (Vol. 4, pp. 71–81). New York: Academic Press.

Bandura, A. (1997). *Self-efficacy: The exercise of control.* New York: Freeman.

Bandura, A. (1999a). Social cognitive theory of personality. In L. Pervin & O. John (Eds.), *Handbook of personality* (2nd ed., pp. 154–196). New York: Guilford.

Bandura, A. (1999c). Moral disengagement in the perpetration of inhumanities. *Personality and Social Psychology Review, 3,* 193–209.

Bandura, A. (2000b). Cultivate self-efficacy for personal and organizational effectiveness. In E. A. Lock (Ed.), *Handbook of Princples of Organization Behavior* (pp. 120–136). Oxford, UK: Blackwell.

Bandura, A. (2001a). Social cognitive theory: An agentic perspective. *Annual Review of Psychology, 52,* 1–23.

Bandura, A., Blanchard, E. B., & Ritter, B. (1969). The relative efficacy of desensitization and modeling approaches for inducing behavioral, affective, and attitudinal changes. *Journal of Personal and Social Psychology, 13,* 173–199.

Bandura, A., Grusec, J. E., & Menlove, F. L. (1967). Vicarious extinction of avoidance behavior through symbolic modeling. *Journal of Personality and Social Psychology, 5,* 16–22.

Bandura, A., Ross, D., & Ross, S. A. (1963). Imitation of film-mediated aggressive models. *Journal of Abnormal and Social Psychology, 66,* 3–11.

Bandura, A., & Walters, R. (1963). *Social learning and personality development.* New York: Holt, Rinehart and Winston.

Beck, A. T. (1961). A systematic investigation of depression. *Comprehensive Psychiatry, 2,* 163–170.

Beck, A. T. (1967). *Depression: Clinical, experimental, and theoretical aspects.* New York: Harper & Row.

Beck, A. T. (1976). *Cognitive therapy and the emotional disorders.* New York: International Universities Press.

Beck, A. T. (1988). *Love is never enough.* New York: Harper & Row.

Beck, A. T. (1991). Cognitive therapy: A 30-year retrospective. *American Psychologist, 46*(4), 368–374.

Beck, A., & Emery, G., with Greenberg, R. (1985). *Anxiety disorders and phobias.* New York: Basic Books.

Beck, A., Rush, A. J., Shaw, B. F., & Emery, G. (1979). *Cognitive therapy of depression.* New York: Guilford Press.

Burns, D. D. (1980). *Feeling good: The new mood therapy.* New York: New American Library.

DiClemente, C. C., Fairhurst, S. K., & Piotrowski, N. A. (1995). Self-efficacy and addictive behaviors. In J. E. Maddux (Ed.), *Self-efficacy, adaptation, and adjustment: Theory, research, and application* (pp. 109–142). New York: Plenum.

Dreyfus, H. L. (1972). *What computers can't do.* New York: Harper & Row.

Ellis, A. (1962). *Reason and emotion in psychotherapy.* New York: Lyle Stuart.

Ellis, A. (1971). *Growth through reason: Verbatim cases of rational-emotive therapy.* Hollywood, CA: Wilshire Books.

Ellis, A. (1974). *Techniques for disputing irrational beliefs (DIB's).* New York: Institute for Rational Living.

Ellis, A., & Harper, R. A. (1975). *A new guide to rational living.* Hollywood, CA: Wilshire Books.

Emery, G. (1981). *A new beginning.* New York: Simon & Schuster.

Evans, R. I. (1989). *Albert Bandura: The man and his ideas—A dialogue.* New York: Praeger.

Gunderson, K. (1971). *Mentality and machines.* Garden City, NY: Doubleday.

Harris, P. L. (1989). *Children and emotion: The development of psychological understanding.* Oxford, England: Blackwell.

Heppner, P. P., & Lee, D. (2002). Problem-solving appraisal and psychological adjustment. In C. R. Snyder & S. J. Lopez (Eds.)., *Handbook of positive psychology* (pp. 288–298). New York: Oxford University Press.

Honeck, R. P., Case, T. J., & Firment, M. J. (Eds.), (1991). *Introductory readings in cognitive psychology.* Guilford, CT: Dushkin.

Horowitz, M. J. (1979). *Stress response syndromes.* New York: Jason Aronson.

Izard, C. E. (1978). On the ontogenesis of emotion and emotion-cognition relationships in infancy. In M. Lewis & L. Rosenblum (Eds.), *The development of affect* (pp. 389–413). New York: Plenum Press.

Izard, C. E. (1984). Emotion-cognition relationships in human development. In C. E. Izard, J. Kagan, & R. B. Zajonc (Eds.), *Emotions, cognition and behavior* (pp. 17–37). New York: Cambridge University Press.

Johnson-Laird, P. N. (1977). Procedural semantics. *Cognition, 5,* 189–214.

Labouvie-Vief, G., Hakim-Larson, J., DeVoe, M., & Schoeberlein, S. (1989). Emotions and self-regulation: A life-span view. *Human Development, 32,* 279–299.

Lachman, R., Lachman, J. L., & Butterfield, E. C. (1979). *Cognitive psychology and human information processing.* Hillsdale, NJ: Erlbaum.

Lazarus, R. S. (1966). *Psychological stress and the coping process.* New York: McGraw-Hill.

Lazarus, R. S. (1982). Thoughts on the relations between emotion and cognition. *American Psychologist, 37,* 1019–1024.

Lazarus, R. S. (1984). On the primacy of cognition. *American Psychologist, 39,* 124–129.

Lazarus, R. S. (1991a). Cognition and motivation in emotion. *American Psychologist, 46*(4), 352–367.

Lazarus, R. S. (1991b). *Emotion and adaptation.* New York: Oxford University Press.

Lazarus, R., & Folkman, S. (1984). *Stress, appraisal and coping.* New York: Springer.

Leventhal, H., & Scherer, K. (1987). The relationship of emotion to cognition: A functional approach to a semantic controversy. *Cognition and Emotion, 1,* 3–28.

Maddux, J. E. (2002). Self-efficacy. In C. R. Snyder & S. J. Lopez (Eds.), *Handbook of positive psychology* (pp. 277–287). New York: Oxford University Press.

Matlin, M. W., & Foley, H. J. (1997). *Sensation and perception.* Boston: Allyn & Bacon.

Mayer, R. E. (1981). *The promise of cognitive psychology.* San Francisco: Freeman.

McMullin, R. E. (1986). *Handbook of cognitive therapy techniques.* New York: Norton.

McMullin, R. E., & Casey, B. (1975). *Talk sense to yourself: A guide to cognitive restructuring therapy.* New York: Institute for Rational Emotive Therapy.

Melamed, B. G., & Siegel, L. J. (1975). Reduction of anxiety in children facing hospitalization and surgery by use of filmed modeling. *Journal of Consulting and Clinical Psychology, 43,* 511–521.

Miller, G. A., Galanter, E., & Pribram, C. (1960). *Plans and the structure of behavior.* New York: Henry Holt.

Monte, C., & Sollod, R. (2003). *Beneath the mask.* New York: Wiley.

Neisser, U. (1967). *Cognitive psychology.* New York: Appleton-Century-Crofts.

Neisser, U. (1976a). *Cognition and reality.* San Francisco: Freeman.

Neisser, U. (1976b). General, academic, and artificial intelligence. In L. B. Resnick (Ed.), *The nature of intelligence.* Hillsdale, NJ: Erlbaum.

Newell, A., Shaw, J. C., & Simon, H. (1958). Elements of a theory of human problem solving. *Psychological Review, 65,* 151–166.

Newell, A., & Simon, H. (1961). The simulation of human thought. In W. Dennis (Ed.), *Current trends in psychological theory.* Pittsburgh, PA: University of Pittsburgh Press.

Newell, A., & Simon, H. (1972). *Human problem solving.* Upper Saddle River, NJ: Prentice Hall.

O'Leary, A. (1985). Self-efficacy and health. *Behavior Research and Therapy, 23,* 437–452.

O'Leary, A., & Brown, S. (1995). Self-efficacy and the physiological stress response. In J. E. Maddux (Ed.), *Self-efficacy, adaptation, and adjustment: Theory, research, and application* (pp. 227–248). New York: Plenum.

Perris, C. (1988). *Cognitive therapy with schizophrenics.* New York: Guilford Press.

Phillips, D. P. (1974). The influence of suggestion on suicide: Substantive and theoretical implications of the Werther effect. *American Sociological Review, 39,* 340–354.

Phillips, D. P. (1983). The impact of mass media violence on U.S. homicides. *American Sociological Review, 48,* 560–568.

Puhakka, K. (1993). Review of Varela, F. J., Thompson, E., & Rosch, E. (1991). The embodied mind: Cognitive science and human experience. *The Humanistic Psychologist, 21*(2), 235–246.

Quillian, M. R. (1969). The teachable language comprehender: A simulation program and theory of language. *Communications of the ACM, 12,* 459–476.

Sarason, I. (1975). Test anxiety and the self-disclosing coping model. *Journal of Consulting and Clinical Psychology, 43,* 148–153.

Scheff, T. J. (1985). The primacy of affect. *American Psychologist, 40,* 849–850.

Shelton, S. H. (1990). Developing the construct of general self-efficacy. *Psychological Reports, 66,* 987–994.

Stein, N., & Levine, L. (1987). Thinking about feelings: The development and organization of emotional knowledge. In R. E. Snow & M. Farr (Eds.), *Aptitude, learning and instruction* (Vol. 3, Cognition, conation, and affect, pp. 165–197). Hillsdale, NJ: Erlbaum.

Stenberg, C. R., & Campos, J. J. (1990). The development of anger expressions in infancy. In N. Stein, B. Leventhal, & T. Trabasso (Eds.), *Psychological and biological approaches to emotion* (pp. 247–282). Hillsdale, NJ: Erlbaum.

Stroufe, L. A. (1984). The organization of emotional development. In K. R. Scherer & P. Ekman (Eds.), *Approaches to emotion* (pp. 109–128). Hillsdale, NJ: Erlbaum.

Symbaluk, D. G., Heth, C. D., Cameron, J., & Pierce, W. D. (1997). Social modeling, monetary incentives, and pain endurance: The role of self-efficacy in pain perception. *Personality and Social Psychology Bulletin, 23,* 258–269.

Turing, A. M. (1950). Computing machinery and intelligence. *Mind, 59,* 236. In R. P. Honeck, T. J. Case, & M. J. Firment (Eds.), *Introductory readings in cognitive psychology* (pp. 15–24). Guilford, CT: Dushkin.

Varela, F. J., Thompson, E., & Rosch, E. (1991). *The embodied mind: Cognitive science and human experience.* Cambridge, MA: MIT Press.

Waldrop, M. M. (1985, March). Machinations of thought. *Science, 85,* 38–45.

Weizenbaum, J. (1976). *Computer power and human reason: From judgment to calculation.* San Francisco: Freeman.

Wood, R., & Bandura, A. (1989). Impact of conceptions of ability on self-regulatory mechanisms and complex decision making. *Journal of Personality and Social Psychology, 56,* 407–415.

Zajonc, R. B. (1980). Feeling and thinking: Preferences need no inferences. *American Psychologist, 35,* 151–175.

Zajonc, R. B. (1984). On the primacy of affect. *American Psychologist, 39,* 117–123.

george kelly and personal construct psychology

Franz R. Epting, Larry M. Leitner,
Jonathan D. Raskin

INTRODUCTION

Personal construct theory approaches understanding others by attempting to step inside their world and speculate how the world might appear from that vantage point. If, for example, you find yourself disagreeing with another person, George Kelly might advise you to stop for a moment and tell the other person that you will state the issues of disagreement from their point of view to their satisfaction if they will agree to do the same for you. This will involve you in a subjective and personal way with the other person and offer you both an opportunity to understand each other more completely, even if you find no quick solution or basis for agreement. The terms you use to understand each other or to describe yourself and your own position are called **personal constructs** or **personal constructions,** and they are formed out of your own private meanings and the meaning you adopt from your social world. Much of this chapter will be concerned with describing how we grasp our own and others' personal constructions and how systems of personal constructions work.

Rather than specify a set of basic needs or provide specific contents that make up the person, personal construct theory lets every person provide the content of his or her life and relies on the theory only to describe ways of understanding how this specific content takes form. Many texts that describe construct theory make much of Kelly's (1955) early metaphor of "man(person)-the-scientist" in order to understand Kelly's way of describing the *form* of personal constructions. This metaphor pictures people acting as scientists in that they formulate hypotheses about the world in the form of personal constructions and then test these notions, much as a scientist would, to gain predictive certainty and control over events. Perhaps this was Kelly's attempt to strike a familiar chord with his more cognitive and behavioral colleagues. Hinkle (1970, p. 91) reports Kelly, musing over current affairs in psychology, saying, "American psychologists have seemed like such a sorry lot; imagine being that cut off from an understanding of the wonder of people and the truth of human relationships! I wondered in writing construct theory if I could devise a way to help them discover people and yet still feel scientifically respectable in doing that."

In using this metaphor Kelly pointed out that people like scientists, and, furthermore, scientists are human, too. This view describes important aspects of the theory, but it fails to describe the heart of the theory as Kelly did in his later work. In fact he states that if he had it to do over, he would write the theory more honestly. He started this project in his unfinished book *The Human Feeling* (Fransella, 1995, p. 16). Some of the completed chapters appeared after his death in Maher's (1969) collected papers of George Kelly. The overreliance on the man(person)-as-scientist metaphor in representing Kelly's work has led some textbooks to classify his work as a cognitive theory or as a theory that bridges between the cognitive approach and a more humanistic approach. We argue here, however, that he fits more centrally within the humanistic theories of Rogers, Maslow, and others (Epting & Leitner, 1994; Leitner & Epting, 2001). In fact he was one of the key presenters at the Old Saybrook Conference, where humanistic psychology was founded in the United States (Taylor, 2000). Kelly, however, wrote a different kind of humanistic theory, which posits a foundation for his theory emphasizing self-invention (Butt, Burr, & Epting, 1997). This contrasts with Maslow who posited a hierarchy of specific needs emphasizing self-discovery (Maslow, 1987). In addition, Kelly was concerned with specific operations to make his concepts observable.

His solid footing in humanistic psychology develops through his central formulation that people constantly reinvent themselves. Kelly saw reality as soft, full of invitation, creativity, and renewal. *Personal construct theory* is basically a psychology of understanding subjects' point of view and helping them decide what choices to make in light of their present position. Because people construct the meaning of their lives early in life, they often are unaware, later, of the many ways they can change and reorient themselves to the world. Reality is not as hard as we think once we find ways to free it up a bit. People can reconstrue reality. They need not paint themselves into a corner, a discovery that often proves greatly liberating. Kelly proposes a view of people in the process of constant change and sees difficulties arising when that change is arrested. He created a truly humanistic theory of action designed to carry the person into a constantly changing world and offering up both challenges and possibilities for growth.

PERSONAL HISTORY

George Alexander Kelly, an only child, was born April 28, 1905, on a farm near Perth, Kansas, a small town south of Wichita. Both of Kelly's parents were educated and knowledgeable about the larger world around them (Fransella, 1995, p. 5). His mother, born on Barbados in the West Indies, was the daughter of an adventuresome sea captain who moved his family to many different locations. His father, a Presbyterian minister, abandoned the ministry soon after his marriage and moved to the Kansas farm.

Kelly's elementary education consisted of a combination of classroom work and home schooling when no local school was available. From the age of 13, Kelly lived away from home most of the time and attended four different high schools without actually receiving a diploma from any of them. In 1925, after three years at Friends University, he transferred to Park College in Parkville, Missouri, where he received his baccalaureate. He majored in physics and mathematics, which was to set him up for an engineering career, but instead, fascinated by social issues, he entered a University of Kansas master's degree program in educational sociology. In 1927, he began applying for teaching positions before completing his thesis. Finding nothing, he moved to Minneapolis and secured three night-school jobs: one for the American Bankers Association, another a speech class for labor organizers, and an Americanization class for prospective citizens.

Kelly also was enrolled in the University of Minnesota's programs in sociology and biometrics but, unable to pay his fees, had to withdraw. Nevertheless, at age 22 he completed his University of Kansas master's thesis, "One Thousand Workers and Their Leisure." In the winter of 1927–28 he finally found a job at Sheldon Junior College in Sheldon, Iowa, teaching psychology and speech and coaching the dramatics group. In 1929, he successfully applied for a foreign-exchange fellowship at the University of Edinburgh. While in Scotland, he completed his bachelor of education with a thesis on the prediction of teaching success. When he returned to the United States, he entered his first psychology graduate program at the University of Iowa. Nine months later, he was awarded a PhD.

Two days after graduation, Kelly married Gladys Thompson. He secured an assistant professor position in psychology at Fort Hay State University in Kansas, where he stayed for the next 12 years.

His early publications concerned mainly practical issues in the application of psychology to school systems and clinical populations. He was concerned that good use be made of psychological knowledge. Teaching psychology as well as speech and drama, he began to question his use of Freudian interpretations, finding that any number of plausible alternative interpretations worked equally well. He then began to experiment with the therapeutic use of dramaturgical role plays. He wrote his unpublished psychology textbook, "Understandable Psychology," and later his *Handbook of Clinical Practice* (Kelly, 1936), both of which served to solidify his emerging psychology of action.

As the world began to prepare for war, Kelly was put in charge of the university's flight training program established by the Civil Aeronautics Administration. He even taught himself to fly. In 1943, he was commissioned in the U.S. Naval Reserve and stationed in Washington, DC, in the Bureau of Medicine and Surgery. After the war, Kelly accepted an associate professor position at the University of Maryland. The next year, he was appointed professor and director of clinical psychology at the Ohio State University in Columbus, Ohio. He remained there for twenty years and published his major work while in that position.

At age 50, Kelly published his major two-volume work, *The Psychology of Personal Constructs, Volume One: A Theory of Personality* and *The Psychology of Personal Constructs, Volume Two: Clinical Diagnosis and Psychotherapy* (Kelly, 1955). His own time was spent seeing clients at no charge, writing theoretical papers, delivering around the world invited papers designed to explain and extend his theory, and devoting himself to the professional development of clinical psychology. He served as president of both the clinical and consulting divisions of the American Psychological Association and president of the American Board of Examiners in Professional Psychology. In 1965, he took a position at Brandeis University. However, in early March he went into the hospital for a relatively routine operation. Unexpected complications developed, and he died soon after.

INTELLECTUAL ANTECEDENTS

Pragmatism and John Dewey

The pragmatic philosophy and psychology of John Dewey (1859–1952) exerted the strongest single influence on the development of personal construct theory. This is particularly true during the early stages in the theory's development. In fact, Kelly (1955, p. 154) states, "Dewey, whose philosophy and psychology can be read between many of the lines of the psychology of personal constructs, envisioned the universe as an ongoing affair which had to be anticipated to be understood."

Pragmatism, said to be America's only original contribution to world philosophy, grows out of the concern with the practical significance of things. It is concerned with an idea's usefulness in furthering some practical end.

Heavily influenced by both William James and Charles Peirce, Dewey wanted to apply his ideas to the education of children in such a way that children see the practical implications of what they are learning. This ties directly to Kelly's intention to create a psychology of action and use. Both John Novak (1983) and Bill Warren (1998) have attempted to carefully examine this linkage to Dewey and to emphasize similarities between Kelly and Dewey in the way they view human experience as anticipatory in nature and human inquiry as an experiment carried out in the world, and the way they use hypothetical thinking in the context of the scientific attitude.

Existential-Phenomenological Psychology

Both Butt (1997) and Holland (1970) have argued convincingly that personal construct theory is a variety of existential phenomenology, despite Kelly's repeated protest that his theory could not be subsumed by any other position. Unlike Rogers and Maslow, Kelly rejected the vocabulary of the existentialists but embraced their principles in a clear way. Butt (1997, p. 21) asserts that Kelly imported his existentialism through his thoroughgoing embrace of pragmatism. For example, Kelly clearly asserts that *existence* precedes *essence.* Sartre considered this the defining feature of existentialism:

> It means that, first of all, man exists, turns up, appears on the scene, and, only afterwards, defined [sic] himself. If man, as the existentialist conceives him, is indefinable, it is because at first, he is nothing. Only afterwards will he be something, because he himself will have made what he will be. (1995, pp. 35–36)

This principle is directly reflected in Kelly's affirmation of self-invention and process and his refusal to posit any psychological content, set of drives, stages of development, or inevitable conflicts.

Korzybski and Moreno

Kelly is deeply indebted to the semantic theory of Alfred Korzybski and to Jacob Moreno's invention of psychodrama as a therapeutic medium. Kelly (1955, p. 260) makes direct references to these two men when presenting his own fixed-role therapy. Kelly was most taken with Korzybski's (1933) classic negation of the Aristotelian laws of logic in his book *Science and Sanity,* and his assertion that it is more useful to start helping people by encouraging them to change the labels and names they use to conceive of objects in the world rather than begin by trying to change the external world directly. For Korzybski (1933, 1943), "Suffering and unhappiness result from a disturbance in the relationship between something in the world and its semantic, linguistic referents in the person" (Stewart & Barry, 1991). Kelly combined this idea with Moreno's (1923, 1937) idea of helping people by involving them in a personal play about their own lives that is cast by a director and then performed on a formal stage. Kelly was most impressed by Moreno's use of spontaneous improvisation and self-presentation. Kelly's notion was to encourage people to enact a new role in order to see the world differently, thereby opening the possibility of taking brave new actions.

In Kelly's words, "Men change things by changing themselves first, and they accomplish their objectives, if at all, only by paying the price of altering themselves—as some have found to their sorrow and others to their salvation" (Kelly, 1970a, p. 16).

MAJOR CONCEPTS[1]
Constructive Alternativism: A Philosophical Position

Personal construct theory takes the position that each theory of personality and psychotherapy must explicate the philosophical assumptions made in building that theory. This basic philosophical position for personal construct theory is known as **constructive alternativism,** which Kelly succinctly stated in the following way:

> Like other theories, the psychology of personal constructs is the implementation of a philosophical assumption. In this case the assumption is that whatever nature may be, or

What is so special about a psychologist? He experiments? Who doesn't? He enacts his questions? Don't we all? His inquiries produce more questions than answers: Who has ever found it to be otherwise? (Kelly, 1969a, p. 15)

[1]The material in this section is adapted from Epting (1984, pp. 23–54).

howsoever the quest for truth will turn out in the end, the events we face today are subject to as great a variety of constructions as our wits will enable us to contrive. This is not to say that one construction is as good as any other, nor is it to deny that at some infinite point in time human vision will behold reality out to the utmost reaches of existence. But it does remind us that all our present perceptions are open to question and reconsideration, and it does broadly suggest that even the most obvious occurrences of everyday life might appear utterly transformed if we were inventive enough to construe them differently. (Kelly, 1970a, p. 1)

Although there exists a real world external to our perceptions of it, we, as individuals, come to know that world by placing our own interpretation upon it. The world does not automatically and directly reveal itself to us; we must strike up a relationship with it. Only through the relationship we form with the world do we gain the knowledge we need to progress. We are responsible for the type of knowledge we have of the world in which we live. Kelly characterized this aspect of his philosophical foundation as a position of epistemological responsibility (Kelly, 1969b). Another reason for adopting this active approach to knowledge is the fact that Kelly considered the world itself "in process." It is constantly changing so that an adequate understanding of the world requires a continual reinterpretation of it. Knowledge of the world cannot be collected, stored up, and built upon like so many secure building stones. An adequate understanding requires constant change.

[W]e saw no need for a closet full of motives to explain the fact that man was active rather than inert; there was no sense in assuming he was inert in the first place.... Result: no catalogue of motives to clutter up our system and, we hope, a much more coherent psychological theory about living man. (Kelly, 1969b, p. 89)

Personal construct theory involves the additional assumption that knowledge of the world is unitary, and over the long haul we will know what things are really like. At some point in the far distant future, it will eventually be clear which conception of the world we should accept, which conception is veridical, or genuine. At the present time, however, it may be a much better strategy to entertain various interpretations (constructive alternatives) in order to see what advantage each might demonstrate. In addition, adopting an expanded time frame may have advantages over viewing the person from moment to moment or within the confines of any single situation.

Personal Construct Systems: Basic Characteristics

Included in this discussion are what Kelly termed his *fundamental position,* and his concepts of construction and dichotomy. We present this material together because it contains the defining attributes of the basic system of constructs and is the bedrock upon which the total theory rests. It is a statement of the "givens" one starts from in order to understand the nature of persons from this point of view. This basic material is stated in the following way. First, Kelly took the *fundamental position*[2] in developing construct theory that we understand ourselves and others by becoming aware of what we anticipate will happen in our lives. Second, we anticipate things, thereby offering a *construction* of them, by looking for something similar, yet a little different, from what we already know. Third, the nature of this understanding happens in a binary way best described as a *dichotomy*.

These statements of the theory give information about what the person is and how we are to approach an understanding of this person. First, we are to understand

---

[2]Kelly described the overall structure of his theory as a fundamental postulate and 12 corollaries. A complete list and their definitions are available on the **web** section for this chapter. Unfortunately, Kelly's definitions are formal and sometimes difficult to understand. Therefore we have chosen to explain each of his major ideas without quoting him in the text.

the person as an organized whole. The person cannot, then, be examined in part functions such as memory, cognition, perception, emotion, sensations, learning, and so on; nor can we see the person simply as a part of a social group. Rather, we recognize the person in his or her own right as the focus of study, an individual to be understood in his or her own terms. The unit of analysis is the **personal construct,** and we consider the person as if he or she were structured psychologically as a system of personal constructs. Using the concept of a personal construct, the clinician approaches the person according to the meaning dimensions the person imposes upon the world in order to make the world interpretable. For the most part, the therapist is concerned with the system of meaning the person uses to understand interpersonal relations—the person's way of viewing his or her relationship to a parent, a spouse, a friend or neighbor, an employer, and so on. Another way of characterizing this approach is to say that the concern is with the person's worldview, particularly in the area of interpersonal relations.

This understanding of the person's worldview applies to both the client and the professional psychologist. The theory is designed to be a *reflexive* theory: The way the client is explained can likewise explain the therapist as he or she creates this explanation. Any explanation applied to the client must likewise be applied to the person who offers the explanation. This thesis has been discussed at length by Oliver and Landfield (1962).

These constructs and systems of constructs operate in specifiable ways. The emphasis is placed on the process nature of the psychological life of the person. The person is seen as constantly changing and moving in one direction or another. Furthermore, this movement is regulated—it forms a pattern, it is channelized. This process or change operates within a finite realm. The construct system of a given person at a given time is limited by definite parameters. We see the person as an imaginative but limited system of constructs, rather than as simply trailing off into an infinite, nebulous conglomerate of construct dimensions. At any given moment, the person is understandable as a system of more or less definite size. This, however, says nothing about what the person may become in the future. Some people may develop extensive and extraordinary personal systems.

As a matter of fact, construct systems orient toward the future. The person anticipates what is coming next and takes what has gone before and uses the present moment to grasp what is coming the next moment, day, or year. The person attempts to use the past to capture the familiar in the new events and, at the same time, add to them the unique qualities they deserve. The process involves forecasting events in such a way that offers some prediction concerning what things are and the form they should take. This process is described as *construing a replication.* The person listens for familiar themes to repeat themselves and then uses this to grasp the nature of the world as he or she passes into the future.

For example, we might consider a particular woman, "Anne," who is assumed to possess dimensions of meaning (personal constructs) that she uses to understand the other people in her life and her relationships to them. One thing she understands (at some level of awareness) is how she relates to and what she thinks and feels about the men currently in her life. Let us suppose that for the most part she sees them as having definite opinions concerning almost everything. She finds this reassuring at times and a bit disquieting or even irritating at other times. Then she meets a new fellow. Anthony, as a man, comes in a rather familiar package—she anticipates that he is likely to have definite opinions. These personal constructs do more than simply describe; they are predictions about how things are likely to be. In this case, however, Anthony does not seem to structure his life according to his opinions. He has opinions, but he uses his opinions in a way different from the other men in her life. For the present, Anne might keep seeing him as a man who rejects being treated as an exact duplicate of the other men in her life. This is the stuff of which new constructs are made. She may now realize that Anthony is a man of values who does not have to express these values as dogmatic opinions.

Another example, which illustrates simply the application of an existing construct dimension, is that of "John" who seems to recognize a theme unnoticed before in an older friend. He might say to himself, *the qualities here put me in mind of the way I felt in the presence of my sister. Yes, it is similar to the compassion and kind of affection I used to receive from her.* There is then a searching (at some level of awareness) for what contrasts with this quality, which sets the limits on the total construct dimension and completes its meaning. John might say that this compassionate quality contrasts with the uncaring and neglecting impression conveyed by his uncle who always seemed to be interested only in how clever people could be. This contrasting quality of the dimension is used to locate a total set of elements (other people) in the person's life, some related to likenesses and others to contrasts. These construct dimensions are used to locate the elements as we use compass points to locate objects in relative terms, that is, only in relation to one another. In John's case, the old friend's compassion fixes him in relationship to the sister, which in turn contrasts with the uncle. That same uncle might, indeed, appear the compassionate person in relation to other people John has recently met.

These construct dimensions are *bipolar* (have two poles and are dichotomous); in other words, they are not continuous, not unipolar. The relationship between the two poles is that of a contrast; one pole is the opposite of the other. The dichotomous nature of the construct is, however, difficult to understand. Kelly's position is that all psychological dimensions, which may be experienced as continuous, can be broken down to their ultimate dichotomous form. Nevertheless, a great deal of research has used construct dimensions in the continuous form (Bannister and Mair, 1968; Fransella & Bannister, 1977; Epting, 1984).

Organizational Structure of Construct Systems.   Up to this point we have been talking as if personal constructs were separate units. Now we will be concerned with how personal constructs, as single units, relate to one another. First, the principle of *ordination* states that constructs are organized in a hierarchical fashion. Second, the concept of *fragmentation* states that the total construct system contains a certain amount of internal contradiction. Third, the term *range* states that constructs cover only a limited amount of material. Finally, the concept of *modulation* concerns itself with how **permeable** constructs are open to modification.

A full discussion of ordination, fragmentation, range, and modulation, as Kelly defines and uses them in laying out his theory, is available at the **web** site for this textbook.

Process and Function of Construct Systems

Even though construct systems have a definite form (structure) they are always in the process of changing. This process is built directly into the construct's structure. Kelly strongly opposed the traditional concept of motivation, implying that external forces are either pushing or pulling some static structure.

Instead, the person is understood psychologically through his or her own set of personal constructs, which are constantly in motion. Both the person and his or her environment are seen as constantly moving and changing. For the person who is seen as constantly "in process," the problem of psychological importance is to understand the direction in which he or she moves. These "motivational" concerns are stated in the following ways: First, Kelly's motion of *choice* means choosing, within one's own constructions, that alternative which offers the best way for us either to extend our understanding of a matter further or to defining more carefully the matter before us. Second, Kelly's idea of *experience* involves one's ability to continuously reinterpret (reconstrue) the events so that life continues to have currency in an ever-changing world .

Because choice has traditionally been considered as the central statement of motivational concerns within personal construct theory, this is where our discussion begins. The concept of choice focuses on the person's direction of movement. This is put forth in terms of the choices that experientially exist for the person. In this theory, the person is always seen as needing to make choices, but these choices are seen as orderly, understandable, and predictable when the person's own point of view is taken into consideration. The person's choices are the choices that exist between the poles of the constructs. For example, a relevant dimension in dealing with a certain person might be the meaning dimension of "sensitive to feelings," which in bipolar form might be stated as "sensitive to feelings of others" versus "insensitive." Let us suppose further that these two dimensions are held in place by the superordinate construct of "concerns of the heart" versus "intellectual power."

This is to say, the choice made is in the direction where the person sees the best opportunity for the most complete understanding of his or her world at the moment. This can be either in the direction of a more comprehensive view of the situation or in the direction of a more detailed knowledge of the matter. The choice is made in the direction that seems to provide the greater possibility for his or her total growth and development as he or she understands it. This principle governs the direction of movement in the system. This is a far cry from saying that the choice is directed by the hedonic principle of pleasure versus pain, or even that it is based on validation or invalidation of the hypothesis. Personal construct theory, however, sees distinct advantages in using the validation versus invalidation concept for other purposes that we will explain later.

Returning to our example, let us say our client has chosen the "concerns of the heart" pole of the construct "concerns of the heart" versus "intellectual power." The client thus indicates that his or her best opportunities can be realized by moving in this direction. The client might be saying that something central to values is to be dealt with rather than the ability to put forth a logical argument. With this decision made, the relevant question concerns the dichotomy of "sensitive to feelings" versus "insensitive to feelings." The client then takes the "insensitive to feelings" alternative because it implies the greater possibility for understanding the other person at this time. Perhaps the other person has just humiliated someone by turning a clever phrase. This choice offers, at the moment, the best understanding of the other person.

We are addressing only the issue of choice itself. This choice is, of course, structured by the particular construct dimension the person has available and the final decision point is between the two poles of a particular construct dimension. This does not imply, necessarily, that any of this choosing is accomplished at a high level of awareness. The choice itself is governed by the possibilities that the choice holds for the person. Kelly insists that this holds even in the case of self-inflicted death. One particular

> Ultimately a man sets the measure of his own freedom and his own bondage by the level at which he chooses to establish his convictions. The man who orders his life in terms of many special and inflexible convictions about temporary matters makes himself the victim of circumstances. (Kelly, 1955a, p. 16)

kind of suicide makes this clear—the type illustrated by Socrates (Kelly, 1961). Socrates's choice was between renouncing all his teaching or drinking the hemlock to end his physical life. Socrates chose the hemlock in order to provide for the possibility of continuing his real life, his teaching. Choice is taken in the direction of where the person sees his or her greatest possibilities. This points to the essentially psychological nature of this theory. Personal decisions are the initial steps in a person having impact in the world. Kelly says of this:

> . . . man makes decisions which initially affect himself, and which affect other objects only subsequently—and then only if he manages to take some effective action. . . . Men change things by changing themselves first, and they accomplish their objectives, if at all, only by paying the price of altering themselves—as some have found to their sorrow and others to their salvation. The choices that men make are choices of their own acts, and the alternatives are distinguished by their own constructs. The results of the choices, however, may range all the way from nothing to catastrophe, on the one hand, or to consummation, on the other. (1969b, p. 16)

The other main aspect of motivational concerns in personal construct theory relates to the accumulation of experience. The emphasis is on the person's active interpretation of events rather than on the nature of the events themselves. The events of life, according to Kelly, are necessarily ordered on a time dimension. It is the task of the individual to constantly seek out the repetitive themes in the flow of new events. At first, new events are only dimly perceived. There follows a search for similarity to other known events that can serve to establish a repetitive theme that can, in turn, be contrasted with other events. Here, one has the emergence of a new construct that results in the person's ability to build an enriched system for living. The person uses his or her knowledge to tentatively explain something new. This groping with uncertainty characterizes personal construct theory. It could be called a theory of the unknown (Kelly, 1977).

The term *experience* focuses on the person being confronted with the validation and invalidation of his or her construct system. The idea is that "confirmation may lead to reconstruing quite as much as disconfirmation—perhaps even more. A confirmation gives one an anchorage in some areas of his life, leaving him free to set afoot adventuresome explorations nearby, as, for example, in the case of a child whose security at home emboldens him to be the first to explore what lies in the neighbor's yard. . . . A succession of such investments and dislodgments constitutes the human experience" (Kelly, 1969b, p. 18).

The unit of experience is seen as a cycle of five phases: anticipation, investment, encounter, confirmation or disconfirmation, and constructive revision. It presents a model for how Kelly represented the psychotherapeutic enterprise, fully described in the **web** section of this chapter. It is sufficient, for the present, simply to point to the fact that the person must first anticipate events and then invest himself or herself in a personal way in order for the system to progress. Encountering events entails commitment to the outcome because an investment has taken place. At that point, the person is open to validation or invalidation in such a way that constructive revision takes place. To shortcut this complete cycle of experience is to prevent the person from benefiting from living a life enriched by true variability in the construct system. Kelly described a school official who had had 13 years of experience but made so little use of his experiences that he in effect had only one year of experience repeated thirteen times.

Individual Differences and Interpersonal Relations

This portion of the basic theory deals with the nature of the relationships that exist among people. The nature of the social process is approached in terms of how one gains a truly psychological understanding of social relationships. Personal construct theory approaches social concerns from the person's own unique system of personal constructs. These concerns are as follows. First, the concept of *individuality* means that each person has unique construct systems. Second, the principle of *commonality* states that people are psychologically similar to one another if they interpret (construe) their life experiences the same way. Third, the concern with *sociality* involves us with the lives of others most productively by taking the trouble of understanding the other person from their own point of view. We are said then to be in a *role* relationship with that other person.

The concern with individuality presents the thesis that each person has aspects of his or her construct system identical with those of no other person. In addition to differences among people in the content of their construct dimensions, differences arise in the ways these constructs are combined into their system of constructs. This thesis is particularly important for the therapist, who must see each client as unique. Despite similarities between one person and another, many aspects of each person must be dealt with as his or her unique content and organization of constructs dictate. This places the demand on therapists to build new constructs of their own in order to deal with each new client.

A rough analogy drawn in the literature on uniqueness is the meteorologist who must understand the general principles of weather systems but who must become particularly concerned with a single hurricane that is named and tracked as an individual system. This same concern is reflected in Gordon Allport's work with the morphogenic analysis of particular individuals (Allport, 1962). The individuality part of this theory is concerned with how a particular person goes about structuring his or her life.

Contrast individuality with commonality, which emphasizes the psychological similarity that occurs among different people. As might be expected, the similarity pertains to the construct system rather than to the similarity of the events with which a person has had to deal in his or her life. This principle implies that two people may have quite similar life circumstances, but if their interpretations of these circumstances are quite different, then one will find two quite psychologically dissimilar people. On the other hand, two people may encounter quite different external events in life but may interpret them in the same way and thus produce psychological similarity.

How this statement of commonality goes beyond even construct similarity must be explained. For two people to be considered psychologically similar they must not only be able to predict the same things on the basis of similar construct dimensions, but they must also be similar in how they produced the predictions. Kelly states, "We are interested, not only in the similarities in what people predict, but also in the similarities in their manner of arriving at their predictions" (Kelly, 1955, p. 94). Kelly had another way of stating the principle of psychological similarity: "I wanted it to be clear that the construction would have to cover the experience itself, as well as the external events with which experience was ostensibly concerned. At the end of an experiential cycle, one has a revised construction of the events he originally sought to anticipate as well as a construction of the process by which he reached his new conclusions about them. In launching his next venture, whatever its concern might be, he will have reason to take account of the effectiveness of the experiential procedures he employed in his last" (Kelly, 1969b, p. 21).

What must be similar is the final conclusion people draw concerning what has happened to them, what that means to their life, and what questions it leads them to ask next. The psychological similarity is the similarity in what it leads people to pursue from this present moment in life onward. The nature of this similarity is important to recognize because it may lead to conclusions different from those of an analysis based only on past exposures to situations. This is perhaps best illustrated by the psychological similarity of two persons despite their contrasting cultural backgrounds. People from Bali, Chad, Russia, and the United States may all be quite similar if they have structured their different experiences in the same or similar ways. The emphasis is on *the way the person has structured his or her experiences*. As expressed by Kelly, " . . . the psychological similarity between the processes of two persons depends upon the similarity of their constructions of their personal experiences, as well as upon the similarity in their conclusions about external events" (Kelly, 1969b, p. 21). It does not matter that persons might have used different pathways in their construct system in order to arrive at a prediction. It does matter, however, that they make the same thing from the way these conclusions were reached, as well as reaching the same conclusions, as such.

We end our discussion of the basic theory with an examination of sociality. This concern reaches beyond the question of commonality to the issue of interpersonal relations, or how people relate to one another. Personal construct theory holds two orientations that stand in contrast to each other. On the one hand, we have relationships with others based on the ability of one person to predict and perhaps control the relationship with the other. The intention here is to accurately predict the other person's behavior. This orientation is seen as a limiting human condition, one where the other matters not as a "person" but only as a behavior-emitting machine. In certain situations, such as in a large shopping center, this might even be appropriate. On entering a department store one simply needs an accurate understanding of the traffic flow to avoid being crushed by the opposing line of shoppers. The point is that at times people might best be regarded as behavior machines so that prediction and control are appropriate for understanding the situation. On the other hand, certain qualities of interpersonal relationships transcend the purely behavioristic orientation, and we regard the other as a person in his or her own right. Described as establishing a role relationship with the other person, this requires that the one person construes the behavior of the other and attempts to construe the way the other person is experiencing his or her own world. The concept of sociality focuses on this process. The person attempts to subsume the construction processes of the other. Within this orientation to interpersonal relationships, how we act in relation to others is based on our understanding of what the other person is actually like. This does not mean that by understanding the other we would automatically agree with them. We might even decide to oppose what we see in the other, but this opposition reflects a role relationship with the other. We are not opposing a behavior-emitting robot, but another person who in some respect we credit with personhood similar to our own in some ways, but perhaps quite different in other ways. It is posited that such a role relationship creates a more compassionate relationship with others, even with others whom we oppose. This is offering a purely psychological definition of the term *role*. A role depends on one person's psychological activity, the activity of undertaking an understanding of the other's outlook.

Sociality is an important concept for the psychotherapist because the role relationship forms the cornerstone for building the psychotherapeutic relationship. To be effective, the therapist must establish a role relationship with the client. Thus, the counselor must base his or her understanding of the client on the understanding gained through attempting to subsume the client's construction processes. It must be added that the client might return the compliment and construe the therapist's constructions at the same time. The one does not preclude the other.

Transitional Constructions

Transitional constructions deal with the person as he or she changes. These issues are concerned with things people feel intensely. It is as if the person has strong feelings when he or she is most alive and is undergoing a particular transition in life. The human emotions are seen as particular kinds of transitions in the personal construct system.

The first of these concerns is **anxiety,** one of the most frequently addressed topics in any psychological investigation of the human condition. Anxiety, as a transition term, refers to the person undergoing a significant personal change. It is defined as follows:

> *Anxiety is the recognition that the events with which one is confronted lie outside the range of convenience of one's construct system.* (Kelly, 1955/1991a, p. 495/365)

The most obvious quality of anxiety is, of course, the strong feeling component of pain, confusion, bewilderment, and sometimes panic. This feeling state is seen as the reaction you have when your construct system sketches in only enough of the outline of the problem that you can perceive your available set of constructs as inadequate to handle the situation. This requires recognition of the problem, otherwise you would simply not perceive the situation and therefore be unaffected by it.

Anything that reduces the range of convenience of the construct system could generate anxiety by increasing the probability that any given event would then be inadequately handled. One would further expect that a less-elaborate system, having fewer constructs, would increase the likelihood of producing anxiety. A person can become anxious when presented with unfamiliar issues. For example, having to answer questions about mathematics could make the person unschooled in such matters extremely anxious.

While anxiety is painful, it can also have its beneficial components. The anxiety you feel is often part of the creative quest for new information. By jumping on the road to discovery you are likely to often confront problems that lie mostly outside your present construct system.

> " . . . anxiety, per se, is not to be classified as either good or bad. It represents the awareness that one's construction system does not apply to the events at hand. It is, therefore, a precondition for making revisions". (Kelly, 1955/1991, p. 498/367)

A human condition sometimes confused with anxiety is **threat,** defined as follows:

> *Threat is the awareness of an imminent comprehensive change in one's core structures.* (Kelly, 1955/1991, p. 489/361)

In threat, unlike anxiety, people recognize the life events being dealt with all too clearly. As the person recognizes the material, the implications for profoundly changing the person become obvious. People feel threatened in situations that promise to change them significantly. One of Kelly's examples is one's impending death. It is perceived as unavoidable and has the power of radically altering what the person now takes himself or herself to be.

Closely related to threat is the concept of **fear,** which is defined as follows:

> *Fear is the awareness of an imminent incidental change in one's core structures.* (Kelly, 1955/1991, p. 533/364)

Fear differs from threat in that the implied change is incidental rather than comprehensive; not as much of the core structure is involved. We fear what we know less about because we may not clearly see how profoundly it can change us. If we know little about radiation poisoning it will *frighten* us. As we gain more knowledge about this matter and how it can affect our present life and the lives of future generations, it is more likely to *threaten* us. Even a change that may affect only a small area of our lives can frighten us.

Another component of transitional emotional experience in people's lives is described in the personal construct definition of **guilt:**

> *Perception of one's apparent dislodgment from his core role structure constitutes the experience of guilt.* (Kelly, 1955/1991, p. 502/370)

With this concept, often approached from an external-social perspective, it is important to note that in construct theory guilt is dealt with as an emotional condition defined solely from the point of view of the person—from the inside out. Guilt occurs when people find that what they are doing is discrepant from what they take themselves to be. The core role structure involves those constructs the person uses to interact with others. These constructs also serve to maintain that person's sense of integrity and identity. Defined in this way, the person feels guilty when he or she slips out of this role or is dislodged from this structure. People feel guilt when they steal only if they do not see themselves as thieves. If stealing is not discrepant from the core role structure, then no guilt will occur. If you have not formed a clear role relationship with others, then you can feel little guilt.

Defined in this way, guilt has little to do with violation of social norms as seen from an external perspective. The concern instead is with the way the person has structured core role relationships. To lessen the self-narrowing effects of guilt, the personal construct therapist concentrates on the nature of a self-structure that can begin to understand the nature of the dislodgment and that might guide the person in this transitional experience. When one feels guilt, as with the other issues described in this section, some personal change is indicated.

Yet another concern, in this area of transition, is with the forward movement of the person. This concern is reflected in the definition of **aggressiveness:**

> *Aggressiveness is the active elaboration of one's perceptual field.* (Kelly, 1955/1991, p. 508/374)

The type of transition indicated here is seen by the person who actively pursues the choice points that his or her own personal construct system offers. A kind of spontaneous quality to aggression enables the person to investigate more fully what implications his or her system has for what can be done. The people around such a person might feel threatened because the person might involve them in a rapid-fire line of action that would alter them in some profound way. Aggression is likely to occur in areas of anxiety where the person is attempting to build a structure to handle events presently outside his or her realm of understanding. For the most part, aggression is treated as a constructive enterprise that might well be identified with a person's assertive qualities. The aggressive qualities are, in fact, the assertive building of the construct system. Some more negative qualities commonly identified with aggression are seen as **hostility**—defined as follows:

> *Hostility is the continued effort to extort validational evidence in favor of a type of social prediction which has already proved itself a failure.* (Kelly, 1955/1991, p. 510/375)

Hostility is not to be confused with aggression, which is simply the active (spontaneous) elaboration of the system. In hostility, the person may be passionately angry or methodically cool, calm, and collected. Anger or its lack is a less important dimension than the fact that part of the person's world is beginning to crumble (become invalidated), and the person believes it necessary to insist that supporting evidence be produced. For example, a husband might be being hostile when he insists that his wife overtly express her love when, in fact, the two no longer have a loving relationship. The core of the hostile person is involved in this enterprise. From this perspective, one can see that a hostile person may be fighting for his or her whole world. This compassionate picture of the hostile person is missed in many views of our understandings of hostility. For the person, the job focuses on the question of what is being invalidated and what makes this invalidation impossible for the person to bear just now.

McCoy (1977) has attempted to add to this transitional conception of emotional experiences by offering definitions of bewilderment, doubt, love, happiness, satisfaction, complacency, sadness, self-confidence, shame, contempt or disgust, contentment, startle or surprise, and anger. Consult her work for a valuable discussion of these additional terms. One example is her definition of love. "Love: Awareness of validation of one's core structure. . . . In short, in love one sees oneself completed by the loved person and core structures are validated" (McCoy, 1977, p. 109).

This is a kind of affirmation of oneself as a total being. "Completion of the person" is implied in this definition. Epting (1977) offered a slightly different definition: "Love is a process of validation and invalidation which leads to the best elaboration of ourselves as complete persons."

This definition covers not only the love found in confirmation and support as in a validation, but also covers the love that serves to invalidate those things about us unworthy of us. The loving act is not always supportive, but it is always in a direction intended to complete us as a person. This love also places us on the edge of our construct systems and enables us to become truly experimental with our lives.

Kelly's own concise description of the major concepts described here are found on the **web** site for this textbook "The Theory's Assumptive Structure."

Cycles of Experience

This last section of transitional constructions pertains to the *cycles of experience* involving action and creativity. Presented first is the cycle pertaining to the person's ability to take effective action in life:

> *The C-P-C cycle is a sequence of construction involving, in succession,* circumspection, preemption, *and* control, *and leading to a choice precipitating the person into a particular situation.* (Kelly, 1955/1991a, p. 515/379)

Any therapy must undertake to understand human action, otherwise the person is left at best with only a better understanding of life with no way of putting that understanding into practice. This sequence begins with *circumspection,* which is the matter of employing constructs in a propositional way. The matter at hand is construed in many different ways at once—various interpretations of the life situation are offered. Then comes the *preemption,* when one of these alternative dimensions of meaning is selected for special consideration. Failing to select one dimension, at least momentarily, makes action impossible; the person would be constantly considering alternatives. Life at that point presents itself as a choice between the poles of a single dimension. In this way, the person exercises personal *control* in his or her system by making the choice and taking action. This choice is made of course in the direction of elaborating the total system. This cycle offers an understanding of human action by attending to the weights placed on different parts of the cycle. On the one hand, you have the contemplative person who accomplishes little because each alternative is so appealing that no one choice is made. On the other hand, one finds the person who might be described as an "action-type," who perhaps leaps all too quickly into a decision that leads to a specific act. In fact, *impulsivity* is defined in the following way:

> *The characteristic feature of impulsivity is that the period of circumspection which normally precedes decision is unduly shortened.* (Kelly, 1955/1991a, p. 526/387)

This means that in some circumstances the person attempts to find a sudden solution to a problem. One might expect this to occur when the person feels anxious or guilty or threatened. An understanding of this cycle perhaps helps define the problem of impulsivity and offers productive solutions.

The second major cycle is that of *creativity:*

> *The creativity cycle is one which starts with loosened construction and terminates with tightened and validated construction.* (Kelly, 1955/1991a, p. 565/388)

The creativity process is then a matter of loosening and tightening. The planning of psychotherapy is largely centered around this tightening and loosening dimension. Thus, the process of psychotherapy is seen mainly as a creative enterprise where the therapist attempts to aid the client to become more inventive with his or her life. The creativity cycle addresses the question of how one creates new meaning dimensions so that the system can be elaborated to cover truly new material. The term *creativity* covers processes used to account for something fresh and new being introduced into the system.

The answer to that problem lies in the direction of allowing the client to loosen the present meaning system so that new material has a chance to be recognized in hazy form. In this loosened phase the person is usually reluctant to verbalize what is taking place. These approximations to new conceptualizations are then progressively brought into a tightened structure—a structure that will allow testable formulations to be made and permit validation. Creativity, then, involves both loosening and tightening. In order that new meaning may emerge, the counselor must aid the client to undertake both and to see both as valuable aspects of his or her personality.

See our **web site** for sections on dynamics, diagnosis, therapy, and additional aspects of the theory (ordination, fragmentation, range, and modulation).

EVALUATION

Criticism of Kelly's theory has generally focused on the perception of personal construct psychology as too formal a system, one that emphasizes logic and scientific thinking over affect and experience. This perception probably results from Kelly's (1955a, 1955b) stodgy writing style in *The Psychology of Personal Constructs*. This heavy style was an unfortunate side effect of Kelly's effort to market his theory to fellow psychologists in 1955; the strategy may have been effective in 1955, but the mere mention of postulates and corollaries likely scares off many current psychologists. Kelly was aware of this problem and was working on a new, less mathematical-sounding formulation of his ideas at the time of his death. If one can see past the format in which Kelly presented personal construct theory, its exciting emphasis on the central role of human meaning making in psychological life becomes more evident.

Kelly (1970b) took great pride that people from a variety of psychological orientations claimed his theory was consistent with their work. However, he was reluctant to have personal construct theory closely identified with any particular psychological perspective. As a result, psychologists have generally not known what to make of personal construct psychology. Most often it is categorized as a cognitive theory and in many undergraduate personality textbooks is discussed along with the works of Aaron Beck and Albert Ellis. Kelly may be identified as much, if not more, with a humanistic perspective.

In recent years, Kelly's work has become more readily associated with constructivism, an array of approaches to psychology that emphasize the central role human beings play in constructing and living according to their own psychological meanings. Like personal construct psychology, constructivist approaches are often conceived of as they pertain to the clinical realm of psychotherapy (Ecker & Hulley, 1996; Eron & Lund, 1996; Hoyt, 1998; Neimeyer & Mahoney; 1995; Neimeyer & Raskin, 2000; White & Epston, 1990). However, evidence indicates that constructivism is infiltrating psychology more generally (Botella, 1995; Bruner, 1990; Gergen, 1985; Guidano, 1991; Mahoney, 1991; Sexton & Griffin, 1997). Constructivism's emphasis on how the individual creates meanings and then lives by them is quite consistent with Kelly's idea of constructive alternativism. Traditionally, personal construct psychologists have worked together in a small but tightly knit community of scholars. Some personal construct psychologists worry about Kelly's theory becoming watered down as it becomes one among many competing constructivist approaches (Fransella, 1995). Despite these concerns, in recent years many personal construct psychologists have begun incorporating other constructivist approaches as well as narrative and social constructionist themes into their work. In fact, in 1994 the *International Journal of Personal Construct Psychology* changed its name to the *Journal of Constructivist Psychology* in order to reflect the wider move toward meaning-based approaches to psychology that Kelly's theory trail-blazed.

CHAPTER HIGHLIGHTS

- Individuals have a system of mental constructs that make up their personalities.
- These constructs are arranged in a hierarchy from higher, or superordinate to lower, or subordinate. The hierarchy helps people avoid chaos by sorting the important things from the trivial.
- These constructs also regulate how the person handles different situations.

■ Constructs influence how the person formulates new concepts of the world. Permeable constructs allow new information to enter that enables the construct system to change. This allows people to see implications for their actions.

Inconsistencies may arise between constructs. Certain contradictions in the person's life may be important to their creative abilities. A loose overall structure is sufficient to hold the person together psychologically.

KEY CONCEPTS

Aggressiveness When one actively puts one's constructs to the test, one is being aggressive. Aggression is an excellent way to extend, revise, and elaborate one's constructs.

Anxiety Occurs when one's constructs do not apply to the events at hand.

Behavior as an experiment Closely related to Kelly's metaphor of the person-as-scientist; the idea is that we test the viability of our personal constructs by engaging in behavior. The results of our behavior either confirm or disconfirm our constructions. This, in turn, leads us to either revise or maintain our present ways of construing.

Constructive alternativism The philosophical starting point of personal construct psychology, which states that there are an infinite number of ways to construe events and that people need only entertain new possibilities in order to construe the world in new ways.

Fear Results when there is an imminent change in one's peripheral constructs.

Guilt When one does things that are discrepant with their view of themselves and against their personal moral code.

Hostility Occurs when one tries to force events to fit with one's constructs, even though those same events seem to disconfirm one's constructs.

Individual corollary The person's own construction of events.

Loose versus tight construing A loose construct makes varying predictions, while a tight construct makes reliable predictions. If a construct is too loose, predictions cannot be made with any reliability. If a construct is too tight, it does not allow for creativity or alternative outcomes.

Permeability The degree to which the construct system allows new information to enter that will enable the construct system to change.

Personal constructs Bipolar dimensions of meaning that people apply to the world in order to meaningfully anticipate coming events. A construct is bipolar, consisting of something and its perceived opposite. "Happy-responsible," "strong-vulnerable," and "afraid-talkative" are all examples of bipolar constructs. Each person's constructs are hierarchically organized.

Threat Results with an imminent comprehensive change to one's core constructs.

ANNOTATED BIBLIOGRAPHY

Burr, V. (1995). *An introduction to social constructionism.* London: Routledge & Kegan Paul.

> This clear and easy-to-read book does an excellent job of introducing newcomers to the basic tenets of social constructionism.

Burr, V., & Butt, T. (1992). *Invitation to personal construct psychology.* London: Whurr.

> Cleverly introduces personal construct psychology to readers by encouraging them to apply Kelly's theory to everyday experiences.

Ecker, B., & Hulley, L. (1996). *Depth-oriented brief psychotherapy.* San Francisco: Jossey-Bass.

> Presents a modern constructivist psychotherapy that emphasizes the importance of unconsciously held positions (constructions) and how these positions are accessed and dealt with therapeutically.

Epting, F. R. (1984). *Personal construct counseling and psychotherapy.* New York: Wiley.

> Contains a clear and thorough overview of personal construct psychology and its therapeutic applications.

Eron, J. B., & Lund, T. W. (1996). *Narrative solutions in brief therapy.* New York: Guilford.

> Outlines a more recent constructivist approach to psychotherapy that, while not directly based on personal construct psychology, owes a lot to the meaning-based approaches of Kelly and Rogers.

Faidley, A. J., & Leitner, L. M. (1993). *Assessing experience in psychotherapy: Personal construct alternatives.* Westport, CT: Praeger.

> Provides a sophisticated overview of personal-construct–based assessment and therapy, including extensive and rich case material.

Fransella, F. (1995). *George Kelly*. London: Sage.

The first chapter presents a detailed biography of Kelly's life, with recollections from his students and colleagues; the remainder of the book provides a nice introduction to personal construct psychology and its applications.

Gergen, K. J. (1991). *The saturated self: Dilemmas of identity in contemporary life*. New York: Basic Books.

This trade book provides an engaging overview of Gergen's ideas about personal identities in the postmodern world.

Journal of Constructivist Psychology (1988–present).

Formerly the *International Journal of Personal Construct Psychology;* publishes theoretical and empirical articles pertaining to personal construct psychology and other constructivist approaches.

Kelly, G. A. (1963). *A theory of personality*. New York: Norton.

This paperback book contains the first three chapters of the first volume of Kelly's *The Psychology of Personal Constructs;* a readily available and inexpensive alternative to tackling the two-volume set.

Kelly, G. A. (1991a). *The psychology of personal constructs: Vol. 1. A theory of personality*. London: Routledge & Kegan Paul. (Original work published 1955.)

This volume provides an outline of Kelly's basic theory, written in Kelly's inimitable style. In addition to the basic theory, detailed discussions of the Rep Grid and fixed-role therapy are included.

Kelly, G. A. (1991b). *The psychology of personal constructs: Vol. 2. Clinical diagnosis and psychotherapy*. London: Routledge & Kegan Paul. (Original work published 1955.)

Volume 2 addresses applied aspects of personal construct psychology, especially those with therapeutic implications. Transitive diagnosis and disorders of construction, among other clinical applications, are delineated.

Maher, B. (Ed.) (1969). *Clinical psychology and personality: The selected papers of George Kelly*. New York: John Wiley.

The papers in this collection were written later in Kelly's career, from 1957 on. They possess a less formal and more accessible style than *The Psychology of Personal Constructs;* providing a less cognitive-seeming view of personal construct psychology.

Neimeyer, R. A., & Mahoney, M. J. (Eds.). (1995). Constructivism in psychotherapy. Washington, DC: American Psychological Association.

These essays provide a broad array of constructivist approaches to psychotherapy, some of which are rooted in Kelly's work.

Neimeyer, R. A., & Neimeyer, G. J. (Eds.). (1990–2000). *Advances in personal construct psychology*. (Vols. 1–5). Greenwich, CT: JAI Press.

This ongoing book series presents new developments in personal construct psychology and constructivism.

Neimeyer, R. A., & Raskin, J. D. (Eds.). (2000). *Constructions of disorder: Meaning-making frameworks for psychotherapy*. Washington, DC: American Psychological Association.

Uses case material to introduce constructivist perspectives on disorder and psychotherapy that do not rely on *DSM-IV* diagnostic categories.

Web Sites

http://repgrid.com/pcp/

A major site for personal construct psychology. The site strives to find and display links to all other related sites, worldwide. Easy to use.

http://www.brint.com/PCT.htm

For therapists and serious researchers.

http://ksi.cpsc.ucalgary.ca/PCP/Kelly.html

A short biography and a full bibliography of Kelly's work and subsequent work.

http://www.oikos.org/kelen.htm

A cheerful site featuring a lovely set of quotations by Kelly and a list of articles about him.

REFERENCES

Allport, G. W. (1962). The general and the unique in psychological science. *Journal of Personality, 30,* 405–422.

Bannister, D., & Mair, J. M. M. (1968). *The evaluation of personal constructs*. New York & London: Academic Press.

Botella, L. (1995). Personal construct theory, constructivism, and postmodern thought. In R. A. Neimeyer & G. J. Neimeyer (Eds.), *Advances in personal construct psychology* (Vol. 3, pp. 3–35). Greenwich, CT: JAI Press.

Bruner, J. (1990). *Acts of meaning*. Cambridge, MA: Harvard University Press.

Butt, T. (1997). The existentialism of George Kelly. *Journal of the Society for Existential Analysis, 8,* 20–32.

Butt, T., Burr, V., & Epting, F. R. (1997). Core construing: Self-discovery or self-invention? In G. Neimeyer & R. Neimeyer (Eds.), *Advances in personal construct psychology,* Vol. 4. Greenwich, CT: JAI Press.

Ecker, B., & Hulley, L. (1996). *Depth-oriented brief therapy*. San Francisco: Jossey-Bass.

Epting, F. R. (1977). *The loving experience and the creation of love*. Paper presented at the Southeastern Psychological Association, Hollywood, FL.

Epting, F. R. (1984). *Personal construct counseling and psychotherapy*. New York: Wiley.

Epting, F. R., & Leitner, L. M. (1994). Humanistic psychology and personal construct theory. In F. Wertz (Ed.), *The humanistic movement: Recovering the person in psychology* (pp. 129–145). Lake Worth, FL: Gardner Press.

Eron, J. B., & Lund, T. W. (1996). *Narrative solutions in brief therapy*. New York: Guilford.

Fransella, F. (1995). *George Kelly*. London: Sage.

Fransella, F., & Bannister, D. (1977). *A manual for repertory grid technique*. London: Academic.

Gergen, K. J. (1985). The social constructionist movement in modern psychology. *American Psychologist, 40,* 266–275.

Gergen, K. J. (1994). *Realities and relationships*. Cambridge, MA: Harvard University Press.

Guidano, V. F. (1991). *The self in process*. New York: Guilford.

Hinkle, D. N. (1970). The game of personal constructs. In D. Bannister (Ed.), *Perspectives in personal construct theory*. London: Academic Press.

Holland, R. (1970). George Kelly: Constructive innocent and reluctant existentialist. In D. Bannister (Ed.), *Perspectives in personal construct theory*. London: Academic Press.

Honos-Webb, L. J., & Leitner, L. M. (in press). How DSM diagnoses damage: A client speaks. *Journal of Humanistic Psychology.*

Hoyt, M. F. (1998). *The handbook of constructive therapies: Innovative approaches from leading practitioners*. San Francisco: Jossey-Bass.

Kelly, G. A. (1936). *Handbook of clinical practice*. Unpublished manuscript. Fort Hays State University.

Kelly, G. A. (1955/1991a). *The psychology of personal constructs: Vol. 1: A theory of personality*. London: Routledge & Kegan Paul. (Original work published 1955.)

Kelly, G. A. (1955/1991b). *The psychology of personal constructs: Vol. 2: Clinical diagnosis and psychotherapy*. London: Routledge & Kegan Paul. (Original work published 1955.)

Kelly, G. A. (1961). Theory and therapy in suicide: The personal construct point of view. In N. Farberow & E. Schneidman (Eds.), *The cry for help* (pp. 255–280). New York: McGraw-Hill.

Kelly, G. A. (1969a). Humanistic methodology in psychological research. In B. Maher (Ed.), *Clinical psychology and personality: The selected papers of George Kelly* (pp. 133–146). New York: Wiley.

Kelly, G. A. (1969b). Man's construction of his alternatives. In B. Maher (Ed.), *Clinical psychology and personality: The selected papers of George Kelly* (pp. 66–93). New York: Wiley.

Kelly, G. A. (1970a). A brief introduction to personal construct theory. In D. Bannister (Ed.), *Perspectives in personal construct theory* (pp. 1–29). London: Academic Press.

Kelly, G. A. (1970b). Behavior in an experiment. In D. Bannister (Ed.), *Perspectives in personal construct theory* (pp. 255–270). London: Academic Press.

Kelly, G. A. (1977). The psychology of the unknown. In D. Bannister (Ed.), *New perspectives in personal construct theory* (pp. 1–19). London: Academic Press.

Korzybski, A. (1933). *Science and sanity: An introduction to non-Aristotelian systems and general semantics*. Lakeville, CT: Institute of General Semantics.

Korzybski, A. (1943). General semantics, psychiatry, psychotherapy and prevention. In M. Kendig (Ed.), *Papers from the second American Conference on General Semantics: Non-Aristotelian methodology (applied) for sanity in our time*. Lakeville, CT: Institute of General Semantics.

Leitner, L. M., & Epting, F. R. (2001). Constructivist approaches to therapy. In K. J. Schneider, J. F. T. Bugental, & J. Fraser Pierson (Eds.), *The handbook of humanistic psychology: Leading edges in theory, research, and practice*. (421–431) Thousand Oaks, CA: Sage.

Maher, B. (Ed.) (1969). *Clinical psychology and personality: The selected papers of George Kelly*. New York: Wiley.

Mahoney, M. J. (1991). *Human change processes*. New York: Basic Books.

Maslow, A. (1987). *Motivation and personality* (3rd ed.). New York: Harper & Row.

McCoy, M. M. (1977). A reconstruction of emotion. In D. Bannister (Ed.), *New perspectives in personal construct theory*. London: Academic Press.

Moreno, J. L. (1923). *Spontaneity theater*. Potsdam: Kiepenheuer Verlag.

Moreno, J. L. (1937). Inter-personal therapy and the psychopathology of interpersonal relations. *Sociometry: A Journal of Inter-Personal Relations, 1,* 9–76.

Neimeyer, R. A., & Raskin, J. D. (Eds.). (2000). *Constructions of disorders: Meaning-making frameworks for psychotherapy*. Washington, DC: American Psychological Association.

Novak, J. M. (1983). Personal construct theory and other perceptual pedagogies. In J. R. Adams-Webber & J. C. Mancuso (Eds.), *Applications of personal construct theory*. New York: Academic Press.

Oliver, D. W., & Landfield, A. W. (1962). Reflexivity: An unfaced issue in psychology. *Journal of Individual Psychology, 18,* 114–124.

Sartre, J. -P. (1991). Humanism and existentialism. In W. Baskin (Ed.), *Essays in existentialism* (pp. 31–62). New York: Citadel Press.

Sexton, T. L., & Griffin, B. L. (1997). *Constructivist thinking in counseling practice, research, and training*. New York: Teachers College Press.

Stewart, A. E., & Barry, J. R. (1991). Origins of George Kelly's constructivism in the work of Korzybski & Moreno. *International Journal of Personal Construct Psychology, 4,* 121–136.

Taylor, E. (2000). "What is man, psychologist, that thou are so unmindful of him?" Henry A. Murray on the historical relation between classical personality theory, and Humanistic psychology. *Journal of Humanistic Psychology. 40*(3) 29–42.

Warren, B. (1998). *Philosophical dimensions of personal construct psychology*. London & New York: Routledge & Kegan Paul.

White, M., & Epston, D. (1990). *Narrative means to therapeutic ends*. New York: Norton.

carl rogers and the person-centered perspective

Carl Rogers has had an indelible influence on psychology and psychotherapy as well as education. He created and fostered client-centered therapy, pioneered the encounter-group movement, was one of the founders of humanistic psychology, and was the pivotal member of the first person-centered groups working to resolve international political conflicts.

Throughout his working life, while his interests grew to include not only individual psychotherapy and group therapy but also educational, social, and governmental systems, Rogers's philosophical viewpoint remained consistently optimistic and humanitarian.

> I have little sympathy with the rather prevalent concept that man is basically irrational, and thus his impulses, if not controlled, would lead to destruction of others and self. Man's behavior is exquisitely rational, moving with subtle and ordered complexity toward the goals his organism is endeavoring to achieve. (1969, p. 29)

It will have been evident that one implication of the view I have been presenting is that the basic nature of the human being, when functioning freely, is constructive and trustworthy. (Rogers, 1969, p. 290)

Unwilling to be limited by the popularity and acceptance of his earlier works, Rogers continued to modify his ideas. He encouraged others to test his assertions and discouraged the formation of a "Rogerian school," which would only mimic or repeat his discoveries.

> What started for me in the 30's as a changing but supposedly well-accepted way of working therapeutically with individuals, was clumsily articulated as my own view in the early 1940's. . . . One might say that a "technique" of counseling became a practice of psychotherapy. This in turn brought into being a theory of therapy and of personality. The theory supplied the hypotheses which opened a whole new field of research. Out of this grew an approach to all interpersonal relationships. Now it reaches into education as a way of facilitating learning at all levels. It is a way of conducting intensive group experiences, and has influenced the theory of group dynamics. (1970)

Through the 1970s and early 1980s, Rogers's interest shifted away from therapy with clients to an international involvement in team building and large-scale community development. He also became more aware of and tolerant of spiritual and mystical experiences. His belief in the power of individuals to help themselves continues to influence counselors, psychologists, and other professionals worldwide (Caspary, 1991; Macy, 1987). In 2002, at a symposium to honor his hundredth birthday, people noted Rogers's contributions to psychotherapy, education, pastoral counseling, paraprofessional counseling, expressive arts, conflict resolution, organizational development, community programs, cross-cultural work, politics, and peace making.

PERSONAL HISTORY

Carl Rogers, the fourth of six children, was born on January 8, 1902, in Oak Park, Illinois, into a prosperous and strict fundamentalist Protestant home. His childhood was restricted by the beliefs and attitudes of his parents and by his own interpretation of their ideas:

> I think the attitudes toward persons outside our large family can be summed up schematically in this way: Other persons behave in dubious ways which we do not approve in our family. Many of them play cards, go to movies, smoke, dance, drink, and engage in other activities—some unmentionable. So the best thing to do is be tolerant of them, since they may not know better, and to keep away from any close communication with them and live your life with the family. (1973a, p. 3)

Rogers was an introspective child and a gifted student who loved books. But he was neither aggressive nor athletic and experienced childhood as lonely. "Anything I would today regard as a close and communicative interpersonal relationship was completely lacking during that period" (1973a, p. 4). To further protect their children from the "corrupting influences of the city and suburbs" (Kirschenbaum, 1980, p. 10), Rogers's parents moved to a farm near Glen Ellyn, Illinois, during his high school years. He maintained an excellent academic record and developed a strong interest in science.

> I realized by now that I was peculiar, a loner, with very little place or opportunity for a place in the world of persons. I was socially incompetent in any but superficial contacts. My fantasies during this period were definitely bizarre, and probably would be classed as schizoid by a diagnostician, but fortunately I never came in contact with a psychologist. (1973a, p. 4)

However, when he went on to college at the University of Wisconsin, he found the time meaningful and rewarding. "For the first time in my life outside of my family I found real closeness and intimacy" (1967, p. 349). In his sophomore year he began to study for the ministry. The following year, 1922, he went to China to attend a World Student Christian Federation conference in Peking. Subsequently, he went on a speaking tour through western China and other countries in Asia. The trip mellowed his fundamentalist religious attitudes and gave him his first opportunity to develop psychological independence. "From the date of this trip, my goals, values, aims, and philosophy have been my own and very divergent from the views which my parents held and which I had held up to this point" (1967, p. 351).

In 1924, he married Helen Elliott, whom he had known since grammar school. Both families discouraged Rogers from returning to school after he and Helen were married, but Rogers asserted himself and decided to continue his education. The couple moved to New York City, where Rogers began graduate studies at Union Theological Seminary. He later chose to finish his work in psychology at Teachers College, Columbia University. This shift was prompted in part by a student-directed seminar that gave him the opportunity to examine his rising doubts about his religious commitment. Later, in a psychology course, he was pleasantly surprised to discover that a person interested in counseling could earn a living *outside* the church, working closely with individuals who needed help.

His first job was in Rochester, New York, in a child guidance center, working with children referred by various social agencies. "I wasn't connected with a university, no one was looking over my shoulder from any particular treatment orientation. . . . [The agencies] didn't give a damn how you proceeded but hoped you could be of some assistance" (1970, pp. 514–515). From 1928 to 1939, while he was in Rochester, Rogers's understanding of the process of psychotherapy changed. He eventually exchanged a formal, directive approach for what he would later call *client-centered* therapy.

While in Rochester, Rogers wrote *The Clinical Treatment of the Problem Child* (1939). The book was well received and led to his being offered a full professorship at Ohio State University. Rogers has said that by starting at the top, he escaped the pressures and tensions that exist on the lower rungs of the academic ladder—pressures that stifle innovation and creativity.

At Ohio State, Rogers made the first recordings of actual therapy sessions. It was considered unthinkable to record, and therefore to scrutinize, psychoanalytic sessions. However, as Rogers was not part of that therapeutic community, he was not caught up

It began to occur to me that unless I had a need to demonstrate my own cleverness and learning, I would be better to rely upon the client for the direction of movement in the process. (Rogers, 1967, p. 359)

in its subculture. The findings, combined with his teaching, prompted Rogers to write a formal examination of the therapeutic relationship, *Counseling and Psychotherapy* (1942).

Although the widespread success of the book was almost immediate, it was not reviewed by any major psychiatric or psychological publication. Furthermore, while his classes were enormously popular with students, Rogers was "an outcast in his own department at Ohio State, relegated to a small office, assigned to courses at odd hours and given little cooperation" (Kirschenbaum, 1995, p. 19).

In 1945, the University of Chicago offered him the chance to establish a new counseling center based on his ideas. He served as its director until 1957. Rogers's growing emphasis on trust was reflected in the democratic decision-making policies of the center. If patients could be trusted to direct their own therapy, certainly staff members could be trusted to administer their own working environment.

In 1951, Rogers published *Client-Centered Therapy*. It contained his first formal theory of therapy, his theory of personality, and some of the research that reinforced his conclusions. In it, he suggested that the major directing force in the therapeutic relationship should be the client, not the therapist. This reversal of the usual relationship was revolutionary and attracted considerable criticism. Client-centered therapy questioned one of the most basic, unchallenged assumptions of the therapeutic relationship—that the therapist is all knowing and the patient is unaware. The general implications of this position, beyond therapy, were spelled out in *On Becoming a Person* (1961).

Rogers's experience in Chicago was exciting and satisfying. He also suffered a personal setback that, ironically, caused a positive change in his professional outlook. While working closely with an extremely disturbed client, Rogers became enmeshed in her pathology. Close to a breakdown himself, he literally fled the center, took a three-month vacation, and finally returned to enter therapy with one of his colleagues. After the therapy, Rogers's own interactions with clients became increasingly free and spontaneous.

Rogers went to the University of Wisconsin at Madison in 1957, with a joint appointment in psychiatry and psychology. Rogers found himself in growing conflict with the psychology department. He believed that his freedom to teach and his students' freedom to learn were being restricted. "I'm pretty good at living and letting live, but when they wouldn't let my students live, that became a dissatisfying experience" (1970, p. 528).

Rogers's rising indignation was captured in the paper "Current Assumptions in Graduate Education: A Passionate Statement" (1969). Although rejected by *The American Psychologist* for publication, it enjoyed a wide distribution through the graduate student underground before it was eventually printed. "The theme of my statement is that we are doing an unintelligent, ineffectual and wasteful job of preparing psychologists, to the detriment of our discipline and society" (1969, p. 170). Implicit assumptions that Rogers attacked included the following:

- The student cannot be trusted to pursue his own scientific and professional learning.
- Evaluation is education; education is evaluation.
- Presentation equals learning: What is presented in the lecture is what the student learns.
- The truths of psychology are known.
- Creative scientists develop from passive learners. (1969, pp. 169–187)

Not surprisingly, Rogers left his tenured professorship in 1963 and moved to the newly founded Western Behavioral Science Institute in La Jolla, California. A few years later, he helped establish the Center for the Studies of the Person, a loosely structured collection of people in the helping professions.

I have often been grateful that by the time I was in dire need of personal help, I had trained therapists who were persons in their own right, not dependent upon me, yet able to offer me the kind of help I needed. (Rogers, 1967, p. 367)

His growing popularity among educators had become so important that he wrote a book to clarify the kinds of educational settings he was advocating and was actively engaged in establishing. *Freedom to Learn* (1969) and *Freedom to Learn for the 80's* (1983) contain his clearest statements on the nature of human beings.

His work with encounter groups stems from his years in California, where he was free to experiment, invent, and test his ideas without the interference of social institutions or academia. His encounter research is summed up in *Carl Rogers on Encounter Groups* (1970).

One of his moves away from psychotherapy took the form of exploring the changing trends and values in normal marriages. His naturalistic study *Becoming Partners: Marriage and Its Alternatives* (1972) is an examination of the advantages and disadvantages of different patterns of relationship.

After splitting his interests for several years, Rogers finally combined his group work and his efforts in educational innovation. Along with some members of the Center for the Studies of the Person, he ran ongoing, intensive groups for the faculty and students of a Jesuit training college and a Catholic school system (elementary through college). He also did extensive consultations for the Louisville, Kentucky, school system (Rogers, 1974b, 1975a, 1975b).

Emboldened by successful results, Rogers moved away from the client-centered relationships that had been the focus of most of his career. He looked instead to *person-centered* situations, with their revolutionary implications for every sort of political and social system. His own internal revolution and resulting conclusions are described in *Carl Rogers on Personal Power* (1978a).

In an article written when he was 85 years old, Rogers noted his pleasure with the growing impact of his work. "Two documents arriving yesterday constitute a small sample. One mentions finding 165 published papers on the person-centered group approach between 1970 and 1986. The shocker is that these 165 articles are those published and written in *Japan!* The other tells of a large conference in Brazil devoted to the client-centered/person-centered approach" (1987b, p. 150).

Until his death in 1987, at the age of 85, he remained at the Center for the Studies of the Person. In the last decade of his life, he applied his ideas specifically to political situations and led successful workshops in conflict resolution and citizen diplomacy in South Africa, Austria, and the former Soviet Union (Macy, 1987; Rogers, 1986b, 1987a; Swenson, 1987).

Rogers became interested in altered states of consciousness, that is, "inner space—the realm of the psychological powers and the psychic capabilities of the human person" (1980b, p. 12). He also became more open and expressive in his relationships. He said of these shifts, "I am no longer simply talking about psychotherapy, but about a point of view, a philosophy, an approach to life, a way of being in which growth—of a person, a group, or a community—is part of the goal" (1980a, p. ix).

Rogers summarizes his own position by quoting Lao-tze, a Chinese philosopher of the sixth century BC, believed to be a contemporary of Confucius.

> If I keep from meddling with people, they take care of themselves,
> If I keep from commanding people, they behave themselves,
> If I keep from preaching at people, they improve themselves,
> If I keep from imposing on people, they become themselves. (1973a, p. 13)

On the day of his death, a letter arrived informing him that he had been nominated for the Nobel Peace Prize, a remarkable ending to his long career (Dreher, 1995).

What do I mean by a person-centered approach? It expresses the primary theme of my whole professional life, as that theme has become clarified through experience, interaction with others, and research. I smile as I think of the various labels I have given to this theme during the course of my career—nondirective counseling, client-centered therapy, student-centered teaching, group-centered leadership. (Rogers, 1980a, p. 114)

The work we've done in South Africa is probably the most dramatic of all because the situation is so full of tension and is so critical. (Rogers, in Rogers & Russell, 2002, p. 216)

Our experiences, it is clear, involve the transcendent, the indescribable, the spiritual. I am compelled to believe that I, like many others, have underestimated the importance of this mystical, spiritual dimension. (Rogers, 1984)

INTELLECTUAL ANTECEDENTS

There has never been any one outstanding person in my learning . . . so as I went on there was no one I had to rebel against or leave behind. (Rogers, 1970, p. 502)

Rogers's theory of personality developed primarily from his own clinical experiences, and he believed that he retained his objectivity by avoiding close identification with any particular school or tradition. Nevertheless, he was deeply influenced by his Protestant upbringing and by his exposure to the ideas of Dewey and William Kilpatrick, the leader of the progressive education movement and one of Rogers's college teachers (Sollad, 1978).

Rogers seemed unaware of these influences and described himself as both forgetful and "ahistorical" (Rogers, 1978b). He said of himself

> I have never really *belonged* to any professional group. I have been educated by or had close working relationships with psychologists, psychoanalysts, psychiatrists, psychiatric social workers, social caseworkers, educators, and religious workers, yet I have never felt that I really belonged, in any total or committed sense, to any one of these groups. . . . Lest one think I have been a complete nomad professionally I should add that the only groups to which I have ever *really* belonged have been close-knit, congenial task forces which I have organized or helped organize. (1967, p. 375)

Protestant Thought

In sharp contrast to Freud's "almost rabbinical" quality of psychoanalysis, where both patient and therapist trust the trained reasoning and discernment of the therapist, the Protestant ethic has a strong emphasis on a person working out her or his own situation, trusting intuition to guide the process. The minister is more likely to be seen as a wise listener who helps a person get in touch with their own feelings than a director or formal guide.

Dewey and Kilpatrick

Sollad (1978) argues that "the parallels between progressive education and client-centered therapy . . . reach to the very definitions of a person" (p. 97). He quotes passages from Kilpatrick that seem to parallel the central ideas later expressed by Rogers.

Rogers, in a letter to Sollad, agrees with these corrections to his own intellectual biography and adds that the Asian influences also began far earlier than he had recognized. He had explored Taoist ideas that including allowing, not forcing, internal growth as far back as his missionary trip to China in 1922, "It is quite possible that these ideas were taken in but did not seem real to me until I had experienced them myself" (1978b).

He acknowledged that his own thinking had been supported early on by the example of Otto Rank, an early Freudian who had left the strict psychoanalytic camp by then, as well as by later work with a Rankian-trained social worker (Kramer, 1995; Rogers & Haigh, 1983; deCarvelho, 1999). He also noted that Adler's work with children contrasted markedly from the elaborate Freudian procedures employed at the time (Watts, 1998). This stark contrast affected his own orientation (Rogers in Ansbacher, 1990).

Rogers's students at the University of Chicago suggested that his emerging position seemed to echo the ideas of Martin Buber and Søren Kierkegaard. Indeed, these thinkers were a source of support and helped to confirm his brand of existential

Neither the Bible nor the Prophets—neither Freud nor research— . . . can take precedence over my own direct experience. (Rogers, 1961, p. 24)

philosophy. Well into his career, Rogers discovered parallels to his own work in Eastern sources, notably Zen Buddhism and the works of Lao-tze. Although Rogers's work clearly was affected by others, his contribution to our understanding of human nature is original and very much his own.

MAJOR CONCEPTS

Fundamental to all of Rogers's work is the assumption that people define themselves through observing and evaluating their own experiences. His basic premise is that people's realities are private affairs and can be known only by the individuals themselves. In his major theoretical work, Rogers (1959) defines the concepts at the core of his theory of personality, therapy, and personal relationships. These primary constructs are the framework upon which people build and modify their images of themselves.

The Field of Experience

There is a **field of experience** unique to each individual. This field contains "all that is going on within the envelope of the organism at any given moment which is potentially available to awareness" (1959, p. 197). It includes events, perceptions, and sensations of which a person is unaware but could recognize if he or she focused on these inputs. It is a private, personal world that may or may not correspond to observed, objective reality.

This field of experience is selective, subjective, and incomplete (Van Belle, 1980). It is bounded by psychological limitations (what we are willing to be aware of) and biological limitations (what we are able to be aware of). Our attention, while theoretically open to any experience, focuses on immediate concerns to the exclusion of almost everything else. When we are hungry, our field of experience is completely filled with thoughts of food. When we are lonely, our singular focus is how to relieve the loneliness. This field of experience is our actual world, even if it may not be the actual world perceived by anyone else.

The Self as a Process

Within the field of experience is the self. The self is an unstable, changing entity. Observed at any moment, however, it appears firm and predictable because we freeze a section of experience in order to observe it. Rogers concluded that "we were not dealing with an entity of slow accretion, of step by step learning. . . . [T]he product was clearly a gestalt, a configuration in which the alteration of one minor aspect could completely alter the whole pattern" (1959, p. 201). The self is an organized, consistent gestalt, constantly forming and reforming as situations change.

In other words, the self cannot be captured as if by still photography. Because it is a changing, fluid entity, "stills" would reveal nothing of its unstable nature.

Many use the word *self* to point to that part of the personal identity that is stable and unchanging. Rogers's meaning of the word is almost the opposite. Rogers's self is a *process*, a system, that by definition is shifting. This difference, this emphasis on change and flexibility, is the linchpin of his theory. From the notion of fluidity, Rogers formulated the belief that not only are people capable of growth and personal development but that such positive change is a natural and expected progression. The self

Words and symbols bear to the world of reality the same relationship as a map to the territory which it represents. . . . We live by a perceptual "map" which is never reality itself. (Rogers, 1951, p. 485)

or self-concept, then, is a person's understanding of himself or herself, based on past experience, present inputs, and future expectancies (Evans, 1975).

The Ideal Self

The **ideal self** is "the self-concept which the individual would most like to possess, upon which he places the highest value for himself" (Rogers, 1959, p. 200). The ideal self is a model toward which a person can strive. Like the self, it is a shifting structure, constantly undergoing redefinition. If one's ideal self differs significantly from the actual self, the person may be uncomfortable, dissatisfied, and experience neurotic difficulties. To see oneself accurately and to be comfortable with oneself is a sign of mental health. Conversely, to the extent that the ideal self is grossly different from one's actual behavior and values, it may inhibit one's capacity to develop.

An excerpt from a case history may clarify this point. A student was planning to drop out of college. The best student in his junior high and the top student in high school, he had been doing extremely well in college. He was leaving because he had received a C in a course. His image of always being the best was endangered. The only plan of action he could envision was to escape, to leave the academic world, to deny the discrepancy between his actual performance and his ideal vision of himself. He said that he would work toward being the "best" in some other way.

He left school, traveled around the world, and held a host of odd jobs for several years. When he returned he could consider the possibility that it *might* not be necessary to be the best from the beginning, but he still had great difficulty exploring any activity that carried a potential for failure.

The ideal self can become an obstacle to personal health when it differs greatly from the real self. People who suffer from such a discrepancy often are unwilling to see the difference between ideals and acts. For example, some parents say they will "do anything" for their children but actually resent their obligations and fail to fulfill the promise they make. The result is a confused child.

personal reflection

SELF VERSUS IDEAL SELF

To explore the discrepancy between your ideal self and your real self, try this exercise. Write down a list of your faults or weaknesses. Use full sentences. Here are some examples:

> "I'm 10 pounds overweight."
> "I'm selfish, especially with my books."
> "I will never understand mathematical concepts."

Rewrite the same statements as discrepancies between your real self and your ideal self. For example:

> "My ideal self weighs 10 pounds less than I do."
> "My ideal self is generous, lending or even giving books to friends who ask for them."
> "My ideal self is a good mathematician, not a professional but able to learn easily and to remember concepts."

Evaluate these statements. Are any of your aspirations unrealistic? Should you modify some of the goals assumed in your ideal-self description? If so, why?

Self-Actualizing Tendency

The **self-actualizing tendency** is a part of human nature. Moreover, this urge is not limited to human beings but is part of the process of all living things: it is the urge evident in all organic and human life—to expand, extend, become autonomous, develop, mature. It is the tendency to express and activate all the capacities of the organism to the extent that such activation enhances the organism or the self (Rogers, 1961, p. 35).

Rogers concludes that in each of us lies an inherent drive toward being as competent and capable as we are biologically able to be. As a plant grows to become a healthy plant, as a seed contains within it the push to become a tree, so a person is impelled to become a whole, complete, and self-actualized person. Although Rogers did not include any religious or spiritual dimensions in his formulations, others have expanded his theories to include transcendental experiences (Campbell & McMahon, 1974; Fuller, 1982). Late in his life, Rogers acknowledged that he found "definitely appealing the view of Arthur Koestler that individual consciousness is but a fragment of a cosmic consciousness" (1980a, p. 88).

The drive toward health is not an overwhelming force that sweeps aside obstacles; it is easily blunted, distorted, twisted, and repressed. Rogers sees it as the dominant motivating force in a person who is "functioning freely," who is not crippled by past events or current beliefs. Abraham Maslow came to similar conclusions; he called this tendency a small, weak internal voice, one that is easily muffled. The assumption that growth is possible, and central to the purpose of the organism, is crucial to Rogers's thought.

> It should be noted that this basic actualizing tendency is *the only motive* which is postulated in this theoretical system. . . . The self, for example, is an important construct in our theory, but the self does not "do" anything. It is only one expression of the general tendency of the organism to behave in those ways which maintain and enhance itself. (Rogers, 1959, p. 196)

For Rogers, the tendency toward self-actualization is more than simply another motive among many; it is the primarily motivational drive.

Personal Power

As Rogers turned his attention away from strictly therapeutic concerns, he began to consider the problems of individuals in political and social contexts. The person-centered approach in society that he calls **personal power** is concerned with "*the locus of decision-making power:* who makes the decisions which, consciously or unconsciously, regulate or control the thoughts, feelings, or behavior of others or oneself. . . . In sum it is the process of gaining, using, sharing or relinquishing power, control, decision making" (1978, pp. 4–5). Rogers assumed that each of us, if given the opportunity, has an enormous capacity to use our personal power correctly and beneficially. "The individual has within himself vast resources for self-understanding, for altering his self-concept, his attitudes, and his self-directed behavior" (1978, p. 7). This drive toward self-development is impeded by placing people under others' control. This domination, when overt—as in a dictatorship—is often resisted.

What concerns Rogers are the more subtle and accepted kinds of domination. In particular, he singles out therapists who control and manipulate patients, teachers who control and manipulate students, government bodies that control and manipulate various segments of the population, and businesses that control and manipulate their employees. He predicts that without these agreed-upon restrictions of personal power, individuals and groups would collaborate in finding solutions to their problems—solutions that do not require the domination of the many by the few. This development in his work, from the intimacy of the therapeutic situation to the rough-and-tumble interactions of political, social, and community organizations, has been described as radical and revolutionary. He suggests not a change in the kinds of control (one government for another) but a gradual restructuring of organizations to fully take into account the personal power of the members (Rogers, 1978).

Congruence and Incongruence

Rather than label people as adjusted or maladjusted, sick or well, normal or abnormal, Rogers looks at their capacity to perceive the reality of their situation. He defines the term **congruence** as the degree of accuracy between experience, communication, and awareness. A high degree of congruence means that communication (what one is expressing), experience (what is occurring), and awareness (what one is noticing) are all nearly equal. One's observations and those of an external observer would be consistent in a situation that has high congruence.

Small children exhibit high congruence. They express their feelings so readily and completely that experience, communication, and awareness are much the same for them. A child who is hungry is all hungry, right now! When children are loving or angry, they express these emotions fully and completely. This may account for the rapidity with which children flow from one emotional state to another. Full expression of their feelings prevents the accumulation of the kind of emotional baggage that adults often carry with them into new encounters. Congruence is accurately described by the Zen Buddhist saying: "When I am hungry, I eat; when I am tired, I sit; when I am sleepy, I lie down."

Incongruence occurs when differences emerge between awareness, experience, and communication. For example, people exhibit incongruence when they appear angry (fists clenched, voices raised, cursing) but insist otherwise, even when pressed. Incongruence is also evident in people who say they are having a wonderful time yet act bored, lonely, or ill at ease. Incongruence, more generally, is the inability to perceive accurately, the inability or unwillingness to communicate accurately, or both.

Incongruence between awareness and experience is called *repression* or *denial*. The person simply is unaware of what he or she is doing. Most psychotherapy works on this aspect of incongruence, helping people become more aware of their actions, thoughts, and attitudes as these behaviors affect the clients themselves and others.

When incongruence manifests as a discrepancy between awareness and communication, a person does not express what he or she is actually feeling, thinking, or experiencing. A person who exhibits this kind of incongruence may be perceived by others as *deceitful, inauthentic,* or *dishonest*. Often these behaviors become the focus of discussions in group therapy or encounter settings. A person who behaves in a deceitful or dishonest fashion may appear malicious, but trainers and therapists report that the lack of social congruence—the apparent unwillingness to communicate—actually shows a lack of self-control and a lack of personal awareness, rather than a mean-spirited nature. Fears or old habits of concealment that are difficult to overcome prevent the person from expressing real emotions and perceptions. Also, the person may have difficulty understanding what others want, or cannot express his or her perceptions in such a way that others understand (Bandler & Grinder, 1975).

The more the therapist is able to listen acceptantly to what is going on within himself, and the more he is able to be the complexity of his feelings, without fear, the higher the degree of his congruence. (Rogers, 1961, p. 61)

personal reflection

CONGRUENCE

This reflection can help you become aware of the nature of the self as Rogers describes it. It can clarify your ideas about your own congruence. The list of adjectives in Table 11.1 (p. 322) is a sample of personality characteristics.

Part 1

1. Real Self: Check those adjectives that apply to you. These characteristics reflect what you know yourself to be, whether or not anyone else may characterize you as such.
2. How Others See Me: Check only those that you think others who know you would attribute to you.
3. Ideal Self: Check off those attributes that describe you at your best.

Remember that this last column is your ideal self, not some plaster saint. (Note: None of us are any of these adjectives all the time. For example, you do not have to be perpetually cheerful in order to select this adjective. If you think you are usually cheerful, then check it.)

Part 2

Circle the adjectives where there is inconsistency across the columns. These represent possible areas of incongruence in your life. Whether you circle many or only a few is not of great importance. Few people are completely congruent.

From this point on, the exercise is up to you. You can work in small groups to discuss your internal discrepancies. You can write about them for personal use or as a class assignment.

Incongruence may be experienced as tension, anxiety, or, in more extreme circumstances, disorientation and confusion. Mental-hospital patients who do not know where they are or what time of day it is, or even who they are, are exhibiting high incongruence. The discrepancy between their external reality and subjective experience has become so great that they can no longer function without protection.

Most of the symptoms described in the psychopathology literature can be understood in terms of incongruence. The important issue for Rogers was that incongruence demands resolution; he considered the type of incongruence a person exhibits less relevant. Conflicting feelings, ideas, or concerns are not in themselves symptomatic of incongruence. They are, in fact, normal and healthy. Incongruence occurs when a person is *unaware* of these conflicts, does not understand them, and therefore cannot begin to resolve or balance them.

We can observe incongruence in remarks such as, "I can't come to any decisions," "I don't know what I want," and "I never seem to be able to stick to anything." When one is unable to sort out the different inputs one receives, confusion can result. Consider the case of a client who reports, "My mother tells me I have to take care of her; it's the least I can do. My girlfriend tells me to stand up for myself, not to be pushed around. I think I'm pretty good to Mother, a lot better than she deserves. Sometimes I hate her, sometimes I love her. Sometimes she's good to be with, at other times she belittles me."

Recognizing that we have different and even opposing feelings is healthy and challenging. We behave differently at different times. This is neither unusual nor unhealthy; but inability to recognize, cope, or admit to our conflicting feelings indicate incongruence.

TABLE 11.1 Self, Social Self, and Ideal Self

ADJECTIVE	1 REAL SELF	2 HOW OTHERS SEE ME	3 IDEAL SELF
cheerful			
persistent			
noisy			
responsible			
absent-minded			
restless			
demanding			
snobbish			
frank			
honest			
excitable			
immature			
courageous			
self-pitying			
ambitious			
calm			
individualistic			
serious			
friendly			
mature			
artistic			
intelligent			
humorous			
idealistic			
understanding			
warm			
relaxed			
sensitive			
sexy			
active			
lovable			
selfish			
shrewd			
affectionate			
opinionated			

Source: From Rogers, 1952a, p.

DYNAMICS

Psychological Growth

Positive forces toward health and growth are natural and inherent in the organism. Based on his own clinical experience, Rogers concluded that individuals have the capacity to experience and to become aware of their own maladjustments. That is, one can experience the incongruence between one's self-concept and one's actual experiences. This capacity is coupled with the ability to modify one's self-concept so that it becomes, in fact, in line with reality. Thus, Rogers postulates a natural movement away from conflict and toward resolution. He sees adjustment as a process in which new learning and new experiences are accurately assimilated. "The central hypothesis of this approach can be briefly stated. It is that the individual has within him or herself vast resources for self-understanding, for altering his or her self-concept, attitudes, and self-directed behavior" (Rogers, 1984).

Rogers is convinced that these tendencies toward health are facilitated by interpersonal relationships in which at least one member is free enough from incongruence to be in touch with his or her own self-correcting center. Self-acceptance is a prerequisite to an easier and more genuine acceptance of others. In turn, being accepted by another leads to a greater willingness to accept oneself. The last necessary element is **empathic understanding** (Rogers, 1984), the ability to accurately sense the feelings of others. This self-correcting and self-enhancing cycle helps people overcome obstacles and facilitates psychological growth.

Obstacles to Growth

Obstacles arise in childhood and are inherent in the normal stages of development. Lessons that are beneficial at one age can become detrimental at a later stage. Freud described situations in which childhood lessons were carried on into adult life as neurotic fixations. Rogers does not dwell on specific details but describes potential patterns of restrictions that can occur as a child grows up.

Conditions of Worth.   As the infant begins to have an awareness of self, he or she develops a need for love or positive regard. "This need is universal in human beings, and in the individual is pervasive and persistent. Whether it is an inherent or learned need is irrelevant to the theory" (Rogers, 1959, p. 223). Because children do not separate their actions from who they are, they often react to approval for an action as if it were approval for *themselves*. Similarly, they react to being punished for an action as if they were being disapproved of in general.

So important is love to an infant that "he comes to be guided in his behavior not by the degree to which an experience maintains or enhances the organism, but by the likelihood of receiving maternal love" (1959, p. 225). The child starts to act in ways that win love or approval, whether or not the behaviors are healthy. Children may act against their own self-interests, coming to view themselves in terms originally designed to please or placate others. Theoretically, this state of affairs might not develop if the child is accepted unconditionally, and provided that the adult accepts the child's negative feelings but rejects the accompanying behaviors. In such an ideal setting, the child would never be pressured to disown or deny unattractive but genuine parts of his or her personality.

> This, as we see it, is the basic estrangement in man. He has not been true to himself, to his natural organismic valuing of experience, but for the sake of preserving the positive regard of others has now come to falsify some of the values he experiences and to perceiving them in terms based only on their value to others. Yet this has not been a conscious choice, but a natural—and tragic—development in infancy. (1959, p. 226)

Behaviors or attitudes that deny some aspect of the self are called **conditions of worth.** Such conditions are considered necessary for a sense of worth and to obtain love. Conditions of worth inhibit not only behavior but also maturation and awareness; they lead to incongruence and eventually to less personal awareness.

These conditions become the basic obstacles to accurate perception and realistic thinking. They are selective blinders and filters a child uses to help ensure a supply of love from parents and others. As children, we learn that certain conditions, attitudes, or actions are essential to our remaining worthy of love. To the extent that these attitudes and actions are contrived, they are areas of personal incongruence. In the extreme, conditions of worth are characterized by the belief that "I must be loved or respected by everyone I come in contact with." Conditions of worth create a discrepancy between the self and the self-concept.

I feel warmed and fulfilled when I can let in the fact, or permit myself to feel that someone cares for, accepts, admires, or prizes me.... [I]t has been very difficult for me to do this. (Rogers, 1980a, p. 19)

If you have been told, for example, "You must love your new baby sister or Mommy and Daddy won't love you," the message is that you must deny or repress any genuinely negative feelings you have for your sister. Only if you manage to hide your ill will, your desire to hurt her, and your normal jealousy will your mother and father continue to love you. If you admit such feelings, you risk the loss of your parents' love. A solution (which creates a condition of worth) is to deny such feelings whenever they occur, blocking them from your awareness. This means that the feelings, because they must come to the surface in some form, will likely find an inappropriate outlet of expression. You may begin responding in such ways as, "I really do love my little sister; I hug her until she screams," or "My foot slipped under hers. That's why she tripped," or the universal "She started it!"

This author can still recall the enormous joy that my older brother exhibited when he was given an opportunity to hit me for something I had done. My mother and I were stunned by his violence. In recalling the incident, my brother remembers that he was not particularly angry with me, but he understood that this was a rare occasion and wanted to unload as much accumulated ill will as possible while he had permission. Admitting such feelings and expressing them as they occur is healthier, says Rogers, than denying or disowning them.

The Growth of the False Self-Image. As the child matures, the problem may persist. In order to support the false self-image, a person continues to distort experiences—the greater the distortion, the greater the chance for mistakes and the creation of additional problems. The behaviors, errors, and confusion that accumulate are manifestations of the initial distortions.

The situation feeds back on itself. Each experience of incongruence between the self and reality leads to increased imbalance, which in turn leads to increased defensiveness, shutting off experiences and creating new occasions for incongruence.

Sometimes the defensive maneuvers fail. The person becomes aware of the obvious discrepancies between behaviors and beliefs. The results may be panic, chronic anxiety, withdrawal, or even psychosis. Rogers has observed that psychotic behavior often seems to be the acting out of a previously denied aspect of an individual's experience. Perry (1974) corroborates this, presenting evidence that the psychotic episode is a desperate attempt by the personality to rebalance itself and allow satisfaction of frustrated internal needs. Client-centered therapy strives to establish an atmosphere in which detrimental conditions of worth can be set aside, thus allowing the healthy forces, which Rogers sees as inherent, to regain their original dominance.

STRUCTURE

Body

Despite evidence that Roger's person-centered work focuses on physical feelings (Fernald, 2000), Rogers gives no special attention to the role of the body. As he points out, "My background [referring to his strict upbringing] is not such as to make me particularly free in this respect" (1970, p. 58). Even in his own encounter settings, he did not promote or facilitate physical contact or work directly with physical gestures until much later in his life.

Social Relationships

Rogers considered relationships fundamental. Early relationships can be congruent and supportive, or they can create conditions of worth and personality constriction. Later relationships can restore congruence or diminish it. Interactions with others are crucial to developing awareness and the capacity for high congruence. While his ideas resonate with many conclusions reached by the feminist scholars at the Stone Center (see Chapter 5), his acceptance of the client's frame of reference raises concerns within the feminist therapeutic community.

Relationships Are Necessary to Discover the Self.   Rogers believes that relationships enable an individual to directly discover, uncover, experience, or encounter his or her actual self. *Our personalities become visible to us primarily through relating to others.* In therapy, in encounter situations, and in daily interactions, the feedback from others offers us opportunities to experience ourselves.

For Rogers, relationships offer the best opportunity to be fully functioning, to be in harmony with the self, others, and the environment. Through relationships, the basic needs of the individual can be fulfilled. The desire for fulfillment motivates people to invest incredible amounts of energy in relationships, even in those that may appear unhealthy or unfulfilling.

Marriage.   Marriage is a special relationship; it is potentially long term, it is intensive, and it carries with it the possibility of sustained growth and development.

Rogers believes that marriage follows the same general laws that hold true for encounter groups, therapy, and other relationships. Better marriages occur between partners who are congruent themselves, have fewer impeding conditions of worth, and are capable of genuine acceptance of others. When marriage is used to sustain incongruence or to reinforce existing defensive tendencies, it is less fulfilling and less likely to endure.

Rogers's conclusions about any long-term, intimate relationship, including marriage, rest on four basic elements: ongoing commitment, expression of feelings, avoidance of specific roles, and the capacity to share one's inner life. He summarizes each element as a pledge, an agreed-upon ideal for a continuing, beneficial, and meaningful relationship.

Dedication of Commitment.   Each member of a marriage should view "a partnership as a continuing process, not a contract. The work that is done is for personal as well as mutual satisfaction." Rogers suggests "We each commit ourselves to working together on the changing process of our present relationship, because that relationship is currently enriching our love and our life and we wish it to grow" (1972, p. 201). A relationship is work; it is work for separate as well as common goals.

> I would like to propose . . . that the major barrier to mutual interpersonal communication is our very natural tendency to judge, to evaluate, to approve or disapprove, the statement of the other person, or the other group. (Rogers, 1952a)

> All our troubles, says somebody wise, come upon us because we cannot be alone. And that is all very well. We must all be able to be alone. Otherwise we are just victims. But when we are able to be alone, then we realize that the only thing to do is to start a new relationship with another—or even the same—human being. That people should all be stuck up apart, like so many telegraph poles, is nonsense. (D. H. Lawrence, 1960, pp. 114–115)

Communication—the Expression of Feelings.   Rogers insists on full and open communication. "I will risk myself by endeavoring to communicate any persistent feeling, positive or negative, to my partner—to the full depth that I understand it in myself—as a living part of me. Then I will risk further by trying to understand, with all the empathy I can bring to bear, his or her response, whether it is accusatory and critical or sharing and self-revealing" (1972, p. 204). Communication has two equally important phases: the first is to express the emotion; the second is to remain open and experience the other's response.

Rogers is not simply advocating the acting out of feelings. He is suggesting that one must be concerned about how one's feelings affect one's partner. And one must be equally concerned about the feelings themselves. This is far more difficult than simply "letting off steam" or being "open and honest." Both partners must be willing to accept the real risks involved: rejection, misunderstandings, hurt feelings, and retribution.

Nonacceptance of Roles.   Numerous problems develop from trying to fulfill the expectations of others instead of our own. "We will live by our own choices, the deepest organismic sensings of which we are capable, but we will not be shaped by the wishes, the rules, the roles which others are all too eager to thrust upon us" (1972, p. 260). Rogers reports that many couples suffer severe strain attempting to live up to inappropriate images that their parents and society have thrust upon them. A marriage laced with too many unrealistic expectations and images is inherently unstable and potentially unrewarding.

Becoming a Separate Self.   This commitment represents a profound attempt to discover and accept one's total nature. It is the most challenging of the commitments, a dedication to removing masks as soon as and as often as they are created.

> Perhaps I can discover and come closer to more of what I really am deep inside—feeling sometimes angry or terrified, sometimes loving and caring, occasionally beautiful and strong or wild and awful—without hiding these feelings from myself. Perhaps I can come to prize myself as the richly varied person I am. Perhaps I can openly be more of this person. If so, I can live by my own experienced values, even though I am aware of all of society's codes. Then I can let myself be all this complexity of feelings and meaning and values with my partner—be free enough to give of love and anger and tenderness as they exist in me. Possibly then I can be a real member of a partnership, because I am on the road to being a real person. And I am hopeful that I can encourage my partner to follow his or her own road to a unique personhood, which I would love to share. (1972, p. 209)

These suggestions are difficult for the best of couples to maintain, but if held to they support an excellent long-term relationship.

Emotions

The healthy individual is aware of his or her emotions, expressed or not. Feelings denied expression distort perception of and reactions to the experience that triggered them.

For example, one might feel anxiety without knowing why. The initial cause of the anxiety was *not admitted to awareness,* because it was perceived as threatening to the self-image. The unconscious reaction (McCleary & Lazarus, 1949) alerts the organism to possible danger and causes psychophysiological changes. These defensive reactions are one way the organism maintains incongruent beliefs and behaviors.

Is not marriage an open question when it is alleged, from the beginning of the world, that such as are in the institution wish to get out, and such as are out wish to get in? (Ralph Waldo Emerson, 1803–1882)

Never go to bed mad. Stay up and fight. (Phyllis Diller)

Yet, if we are truly aware, we can hear the "silent screams" of denied feelings echoing off of every classroom wall and university corridor. And if we are sensitive enough, we can hear the creative thoughts and ideas that often emerge during and from the open expression of our feelings. (Rogers, 1973b, p. 385)

A person can act on these beliefs but be unaware of why he or she is acting. For instance, a man might become uncomfortable at seeing overt homosexual affection. His self-report would include the discomfort but not the cause. He cannot admit his own unresolved sexual identity, or (perhaps) hopes and fears concerning his own sexuality. Distorting his perceptions, he may in turn react with open hostility to homosexuals, treating them as an external threat instead of admitting his internal conflict.

Intellect

Rogers values intellect as a tool that may serve effectively in integrating one's experience. He is skeptical, however, of educational systems that overemphasize intellectual skills and undervalue the emotional and intuitive aspects of full human functioning.

In particular, Rogers finds graduate training in many fields excessively demanding, demeaning, and depressing. The pressure to churn out limited and unoriginal work, coupled with the passive and dependent roles forced on graduate students, effectively stifles or retards their creative and productive capabilities. He quotes Albert Einstein as a student: "This coercion had such a deterring effect [upon me] that, after I had passed the final examination, I found the consideration of any problem distasteful for me for an entire year" (1969, p. 177).

If intellect, like other freely operating functions, tends to direct the organism toward more congruent awareness, then forcing the intellect into specified channels may not be beneficial. Rogers contends that people are better off deciding what to do for themselves, with support from others, than doing what others decide for them.

> We all know the effects on children of compulsory spinach and compulsory rhubarb. It's the same with compulsory learning. They say, "It's spinach and the hell with it." (Rogers, 1969)

Knowing

Rogers describes three ways psychologically mature people have of knowing, of determining what is real. These are subjective knowing, objective knowing, and interpersonal knowing.

Most important is **subjective knowing**—the knowledge of whether one loves, hates, is disdainful of, or enjoys a person, an experience, or an event. You improve the quality of subjective knowing by recognizing your inner emotional processes. By paying attention to "gut" feelings, to inner indications, a person perceives that one course of action feels better than another. The capacity to know enough allows a person to act without verifiable evidence. In science, for example, such ability enables one to follow hunches in solving specific problems. Research in creative problem solving indicates that a person "knows" that he or she is on the right track long before discovering what the solution will include (Gordon, 1961; Fadiman, 1993).

> Who can bring into being this whole person? From my experience I would say the least likely are university faculty members. Their traditionalism and smugness approach the incredible. (Rogers, 1973b, p. 385)

Objective knowing is a way of testing hypotheses, speculations, and conjectures against external frames of reference. In psychology, reference points may include observations of behavior, test results, questionnaires, or the judgments of other psychologists. Sensing the value of sharing of information with colleagues depends on the notion that people trained in a given discipline will apply similar methods of judgment to a given event. Expert opinion may be objective, but it may also be a collective misperception. Any group of experts can exhibit rigidity and defensiveness when asked to consider data that contradict axiomatic aspects of their own training. It is Rogers's experience that theologians, communist dialecticians, and psychoanalysts exemplify this tendency.

It has been considered slightly obscene to admit that psychologists feel, have hunches, or passionately pursue unformulated directions. (Rogers, 1964)

Do not judge another man's road until you have walked a mile in his moccasins. (Pueblo Indian saying)

Rogers is hardly alone in questioning the validity of so-called objective knowledge, especially in attempting to understand someone else's experience. Polanyi (1958), a philosopher of science, has clarified the different uses and limitations of personal, or subjective, knowledge and public, or objective, knowledge. Both types of knowledge are helpful in describing and understanding various kinds of experiences. According to Tart (1971, 1975), different types of training are necessary for the sake of simply perceiving, not to mention evaluating, different kinds of subjective experiences.

The third form of knowledge, **interpersonal knowing** or *phenomenological knowing,* is at the core of Rogerian psychotherapy. It is the practice of empathic understanding: penetrating the private, unique, subjective world of the other to understand the other's views. The goal is not merely to be objectively correct, not just to see if someone else agrees or disagrees with one's point of view, but *to comprehend the other's experience as the other experiences it.* Empathic knowing is tested by asking the other person if he or she has been understood. One might say, for example: "You seem depressed this morning, are you?" "It seems to me that you are telling the group that you need their help." "I wonder if you are too tired to finish this right now." The capacity to truly know another's reality is the foundation for forming genuine relationships.

THE FULLY FUNCTIONING PERSON

While textbook writers generally class Rogers as a "self" theorist (Hall & Lindzey, 1978; Krasner & Ullman, 1973), Rogers is, in fact, more concerned with perception, awareness, and experience than with the hypothetical construct, the "self." As we have already described Rogers's definition of the self, we can now turn to a description of the **fully functioning person:** a person who is completely aware of his or her ongoing self.

> "The fully functioning person" is synonymous with optimal psychological adjustment, optimal psychological maturity, complete congruence, complete openness to experience. . . . Since some of these terms sound somewhat static, as though such a person "had arrived," it should be pointed out that all the characteristics of such a person are *process* characteristics. The fully functioning person would be a person-in-process, a person continually changing. (Rogers, 1959, p. 235)

The fully functioning person has several distinct characteristics, the first of which is an *openness to experience.* There is little or no use of the early warning signals that restrict awareness. The person is continually moving away from defensiveness and toward direct experience. "He is more open to his feelings of fear and discouragement and pain. He is also more open to his feelings of courage, and tenderness, and awe. . . . He is more able fully to live the experiences of his organism rather than shutting them out of awareness" (Rogers 1961, p. 188).

A second characteristic is *living in the present*—fully realizing each moment. This ongoing, direct engagement with reality allows "the self and personality [to] emerge *from* experience, rather than experience being translated or twisted to fit a preconceived self-structure" (1961, pp. 188–189). An individual is capable of restructuring his or her responses as experience allows or suggests new possibilities.

A final characteristic is *trusting in one's inner urgings and intuitive judgments,* an ever-increasing trust in one's capacity to make decisions. A person who takes in and utilizes data is more likely to value his or her capacity to summarize those data and respond. This activity involves not only the intellect but the whole person. Rogers suggests that the fully functioning person will make mistakes through incorrect information, not incorrect processing or misperceptions.

This self-trust is similar to the behavior of a cat held upside down and dropped to the ground from a significant height. The cat does not reflect on who dropped it from such a height, what the motives might have been, or what is likely to occur in the future. The cat does not consider wind velocity, angular momentum, or the rate of descent, yet on some level takes these factors into account—as can be assumed from the cat's success in responding. The animal responds to the immediate situation, the most pressing problem by turning in midair and landing upright, instantly adjusting its posture to cope with the next event.

"The person who offers the most hope in our crazy world today, which could be wiped out, is the individual who is most fully aware—most fully aware of what is going on within himself" (Rogers in Kirschenbaum & Henderson, 1989, p. 189). Thus, fully functioning persons are free to respond and free to experience their response to situations. They represent the essence of what Rogers calls "living the good life." Such individuals continually further their self-actualization (1959).

> The good life is a *process*, not a state of being. It is a direction, not a destination. (Rogers, 1961, p. 186)

PERSON-CENTERED THERAPY

Rogers was a practicing therapist through most of his professional career. His theory of personality arises from and is integral to his methods and ideas about therapy. Rogers's theory of therapy went through numerous developmental phases and shifts in emphases, yet a few fundamental principles that Rogers first articulated in 1940 he found still valid 30 years later. His approach focused on the individual's drive toward growth, health, and adjustment. Therapy was a way to free the client to resume his or her normal development. It emphasized feeling more than intellect, and the immediate life situation more than the past. Finally, it saw the therapeutic relationship as a growth experience (1970).

Rogers initially used the word *client* and later the word *person* rather than the traditional term *patient*. A patient is usually defined as someone who is ill, needs help, and seeks treatment by trained professionals, whereas a client desires a service but feels unable to perform that service alone. Clients, although they may have problems, are inherently capable of understanding their own situation. An equality of relating is implied in the person-centered model that is not present in the doctor–patient relationship.

The therapy assists a person in unlocking his or her own dilemma with minimum intervention. Rogers defined *psychotherapy* as "the releasing of an already existing capacity in a potentially competent individual, not the expert manipulation of a more or less passive personality" (1959, p. 221). The therapy is called person-centered because the person does whatever directing is necessary. Rogers insisted that "expert interventions" of any sort are ultimately detrimental to a person's growth.

The Client-Centered, or Person-Centered, Therapist

The client holds the keys to recovery, but the therapist should have certain personal qualities, in addition to professional tools, that aid the client in learning how to use

The individual has within him the capacity, at least latent, to understand the factors in his life that cause him unhappiness and pain, and to reorganize himself in such a way as to overcome those factors. (Rogers, 1952b)

these keys. "These powers will become effective if the therapist can establish with the client a relationship sufficiently warm, accepting and understanding" (Rogers, 1952b, p. 66). By understanding, Rogers meant "the willingness and ability to understand the client's thoughts, feelings, and struggles from the client's point of view; the ability to see completely through the client's eyes and his frame of reference" (1950, p. 443). In order to work with clients, therapists must be authentic and genuine. Therapists must avoid playing a role—especially that of a therapist—when they are with clients.

> [This] involves the willingness to be and to express in my words and my behavior, the various feelings and attitudes which exist in me. This means that I need to be aware of my own feelings, in so far as possible, rather than presenting an outward facade of one attitude, while actually holding another. (1961, p. 33)

For more on person-centered therapy, see our web site.

GROUP WORK

Because Rogers asserted that people, not experts, have inherent therapeutic skills, it was perhaps inevitable that he would eventually become involved in working with groups. When he moved to California, he devoted time to participating in, establishing, and evaluating this form of group experience.

History

Apart from group therapy, the encounter group has a history that predates its popularity during the 1950s and 1960s. Within the American Protestant tradition and, to a lesser extent, within Hassidic Judaism, group experiences have been engineered to alter people's attitudes toward themselves and to change the way they interact with others. Techniques have included working in small peer groups, insisting on honesty and disclosure, focusing on the here and now, and maintaining a warm, supportive atmosphere (Ogden, 1972).

Modern encounter groups originated in Connecticut in 1946 with a training program for community leaders. This program included evening meetings for the trainers and observers to evaluate the day's events. Participants came to listen and eventually to take part in these extra sessions. The trainers realized that giving feedback to participants enhanced everyone's experience. Some trainers of the Connecticut groups joined with others to establish National Training Laboratories (NTL) in 1947. NTL helped expand and further develop the T-group (training group) as a tool in government and industry. Participation in these groups gave people experience in observing their own functioning and in learning how to respond to direct feedback about themselves.

A striking feature of the T-group experiences was that a few weeks of working with peers in a relatively supportive setting could lead to major personality changes previously associated with long-term psychotherapy. In a review of 106 studies, Gibb (1971) concluded that "the evidence is strong that intensive group training experiences have therapeutic effects." For more on encounter-style groups, see our **web** site.

Conflict Resolution: The International Workshops

In the last decade of his life, Rogers decided to apply his ideas about the healing power of open communication to national and international groups separated by race, ethnic orientation, war, or long-simmering hatred. He demonstrated that methods designed to aid individuals in personal growth could, with skilled facilitation, be applied to divided peoples, by improving communication, developing real trust, and encouraging them to work together despite their opposing cultures or ideologies.

The groups thus facilitated by Rogers and other staff members of the Center for the Study of the Person included Catholics and Protestants in Northern Ireland, blacks and whites in South Africa, and members of warring nations throughout Central America. He also worked with thousands of Russians in the former Soviet Union, where his person-centered techniques were even shown on national television. These international workshops, unlike the formlessly structured traditional encounter groups, were organized around specific political rather than personal agendas.

The results were encouraging. In every group, inevitably, the level of rhetoric declined and trust increased. Afterward, participants reported major shifts in their thinking about those whom they had been against. Many formed new groups, applying the same format to other political and social settings (O'Hara, 1989; Rogers, 1986b, 1987a; Swenson, 1987).

Rogers considered the therapeutic principles demonstrated by clinicians and academic journals invaluable in individual practice and used these concepts to make a positive and distinct contribution to world peace and international understanding (Caspary, 1991). His emphasis on the centrality of relationships harmonized with certain non-Western cultures where one's identity is not rooted in the "egotistical self but in the ecological self," the self in community (Korbei, 1998).

> Even imperfect attempts to create a climate of freedom and acceptance and understanding seem to liberate a person to move toward social goals. (Rogers in a dialogue with Paul Tillich, in Kirschenbaum & Henderson, 1989, p. 68)

EVALUATION

During a conversation in 1966, Rogers described his status:

> I don't have very much standing in psychology itself, and I couldn't care less. But in education and industry and group dynamics and social work and the philosophy of science and pastoral psychology and theology and other fields my ideas have penetrated and influenced in ways I never would have dreamt. (1970, p. 507)

By the time of his death, his work was accepted worldwide (Macy, 1987). In fact, he had established an extensive network for client-centered therapy in Japan (Hayashi, Kuno, Osawa, Shimizu, & Suetake, 1992; Saji & Linaga, 1983). More recently, his influence in Japan has included ongoing community groups and corporate training (Ikemi & Kubota, 1996; Murayama & Nakata, 1996). His work is spreading in Europe as well (Thorne & Lambers, 1998). His work continues to spread. ". . . Most of his influence at this point is in Europe, England, Russia, Japan, Mexico and Argentina" (N. Rogers, 2003).

Critics of Rogers's positive view of the human condition worry that he is glossing over the dark side of humanity. To base therapy and learning on the innate capacity of a person for self-actualization has been called "hopelessly naive" (Ellis,

> Rogers revolutionized the field of psychotherapy by demonstrating that each person has self-direction implicitly and that utilizing these implicit understandings in therapy was so much more valuable than the diagnostic and therapeutic interpretations imposed onto the client by the therapist. (Doi and Ikemi, 2003, p. 81)

1959; Thorne, 1957). Various writers argue that Rogers did not take into account the ingrained patterns of psychopathology.

> Whether human nature, unspoiled by society, is as satisfactory as this viewpoint leads us to believe is certainly questionable. And it will be difficult either to confirm or to disconfirm this proposition, on empirical grounds. . . . The emphasis on self-actualization . . . suffers, in our opinion, from the vagueness of its concepts, the looseness of its language, and the inadequacy of the evidence related to its major contentions. (Coffer & Appley, 1964, pp. 691–692)

Others suggest that self-actualization is neither an innate characteristic nor a learned desire in human development but derives from a more primary drive, the need for stimulation (Butler & Rice, 1963). At the heart of these criticisms is a distrust of Rogers's steadfast optimism. His unbending belief in the innate goodness of human beings does not echo the experience of those who deride his work. People who do not believe in essential human goodness rarely see it exhibited. Maslow saw human goodness as easily muffled by personal and cultural pressures. And Rollo May says, "The Rogerian agenda hides the power drives of the therapist and not judging is not real." Walt Anderson insists, "Not judging, not manipulating. This was not taking into account full humanness" (Arons & Harri, 1992). Nevertheless, a careful and impartial reading of the results of Rogers's conflict resolution work suggests that treating people as he treated them leads to the results he predicted.

Reading the emotional as well as the sensible critics of Rogers, one tends to conclude that either they have seen different kinds of patients or they simply do not accept Rogers's ideas that others can be trusted to find their own way (Rogers & Skinner, 1956). Karl Menninger feels that Rogers's insistence on the indwelling thrust toward health is an expression of, at best, a half truth. "Many patients whom we see seem to have committed themselves, consciously or unconsciously, to stagnation or slow spiritual death" (Menninger, 1963, p. 398).

The argument continues with neither side referring to data or research anymore, but obviously relying on their individual experience. Thus Quinn (1993) is of the opinion that "the practice of psychotherapy in the person-centered approach overemphasizes empathy and caring to the detriment of genuineness and this fault is grounded in an overly optimistic belief" (p. 7). Let us allow Rogers, in an article discovered and published after his death, the last word of the argument.

> I would not want to be misunderstood on this. I do not have a Pollyanna view of human nature. I am quite aware that out of defensiveness and inner fear individuals can and do behave in ways which are horribly destructive, immature, regressive, antisocial, hurtful. Yet, one of the most refreshing and invigorating parts of my experience is to work with such individuals and to discover the strongly positive directional tendencies which exist in them, as in all of us, at the deepest levels. (Rogers, 1995, p. 21)

The newest wave of criticism of Rogers's thinking (and the same criticism might be leveled at almost all other theorists in this book) is that it assumes that the separate person is inherently more healthy than the person imbedded in either family, tribe, clan, or village (MacDougall, 2002). It does, and because Rogers's works are constantly gaining in importance and are more widely read each year; and his popularity within

You [Rollo May] never seemed to care whether the evil impulses in man are genetic and inherent or whether they are acquired at birth. . . . For me their origin makes a great deal of difference. (Rogers, 1982b)

and beyond clinical psychology continues to increase, it should be seen as a realistic limit to its universality.

Although clearly an oversimplification, it can be said that just as Freud's ideas met a growing need to understand aspects of human nature, so too do Rogers's ideas, only his fulfill a particularly American need. Rogers's philosophy "fits snugly into the American democratic tradition. The client is treated as an equal who has within him the power to 'cure' himself with no need to lean heavily on the wisdom of an authority or expert" (Harper, 1959, p. 83). Rogers's close alignment to the American world view has facilitated the widespread acceptance of his ideas, his ways of doing therapy, and his affirmation of the individual's capacity and desire to be whole.

His therapeutic orientation continues to be a subject for intense debate (Bozarth, 2002; Kahn, 1999, 2002; Merry & Brodley, 2002; Sommerbeck, 2002). His intense focus on the person is well expressed in a series of his statements. They are the summation of "the thousands of hours I have spent working intimately with people in personal distress" (Rogers, 1961, p. 16). The following are some of his conclusions:

1. In my relationships with persons, I have found that it does not help in the long run to act as though I am something that I am not.
2. I find that I am more effective when I can listen acceptantly to myself, and can be myself.
3. I have found it of enormous value when I can permit myself to understand another person.
4. I have found it enriching to open channels whereby others can communicate their feelings, their private perceptual worlds, to me.
5. I have found it highly rewarding when I can accept another person.
6. The more I am open to the realities in me and in the other person the less do I find myself wishing to rush in to "fix things."
7. I can trust my experience. (pp. 16–22)

His work in conflict resolution led to a set of similar axioms, a few of which Rogers stated as follows:

I am most satisfied politically:

■ When every person is helped to become aware of his or her own power and strength.
■ When group members learn that the sharing of power is more satisfying than endeavoring to use power to control others.
■ When each person enforces the group decisions through self-control of his or her behavior.
■ When every member of the group is aware of the consequences of a decision, on its members and the external world. (1984)

Rogers concludes his list by saying, "I'm sure many of you regard this list as hopelessly idealistic. But in my experience, especially when a facilitative climate is provided for a group, the members choose to move in somewhat the ways that I have described." Rogers remained convinced of humanity's ultimate goodness from his first years doing therapy with disturbed families to his last years working with disturbed nations. Whether he was right or misguided is not to be decided by scholarship but by one's personal observations and experience.

This new world will be more human and humane. It will explore and develop the richness and capacities of the human mind and spirit. It will produce individuals who are more integrated and whole. It will be a world that prizes the individual person—the greatest of our resources. (Rogers, 1980a, p. 356)

With the best of leaders
When the work is done
The Task is accomplished
The people all say
"We did it ourselves"
(Lao-tze in the *Tao Te Ching*. Carried by Rogers in his wallet)

The Theory Firsthand

EXCERPT FROM "ROGERS'S IDEAS"[1]

This selection illustrates Rogers's ideas about client-centered therapy.

The theoretical concepts that have been defined and the brief, formal statements of the process and outcomes of client-centered psychotherapy are astonishingly well illustrated in a letter written to the author by a young woman named Susan who has been in therapy with an individual who has obviously created the conditions for a therapeutic climate. The letter appears below, followed by an explanation of the way the theoretical statements have operated in her case.

Dear Dr. Rogers: I have just read your book, *On Becoming a Person,* and it left a great impression on me. I just happened to find it one day and started reading. It's kind of a coincidence because right now I need something to help me find me. Let me explain.... [She tells of her present educational situation and some of her tentative plans for preparing herself for a helping vocation.] I do not feel that I can do much for others until I find me....

I think that I began to lose me when I was in high school. I always wanted to go into work that would be of help to people but my family resisted, and I thought they must be right. Things went along smoothly for everyone else for four or five years until about two years ago, I met a guy who I thought was ideal. Then nearly a year ago I took a good look at us, and realized I was everything that he wanted me to be and nothing that I was. I have always been emotional and I have had many feelings. I could never sort them out and identify them. My fiancé would tell me that I was just mad or just happy and I would say okay and leave it at that. Then when I took this good look at us I realized that I was angry because I wasn't following my true emotions.

I backed out of the relationship gracefully and tried to find out where all the pieces were that I had lost. After a few months of searching had gone by I found that there were many more pieces than I knew what to do with and I couldn't seem to separate them. I began seeing a psychologist and am presently seeing him. He has helped me to find parts of me that I was not aware of. Some parts are bad by our society's standards but I have found them to be very good for me. I have felt more threatened and confused since going to him but I have also felt more relief and more sure of myself.

I remember one night in particular. I had been in for my regular appointment with the psychologist that day and I had come home feeling angry. I was angry because I wanted to talk about something but I couldn't identify what it was. By 8 o'clock that night I was so upset I was frightened. I called him and he told me to come to his office as soon as I could. I got there and cried for at least an hour and then the words came. I still don't know all of what I was saying. All I know is that *so much hurt* and *anger* came out of me that *I never really knew existed.* I went home and it seemed that an *alien* had taken over and I was hallucinating like some of the patients I have seen in a state hospital. I continued to feel this way until one night I was sitting and thinking and I realized that this alien was the *me* that I had been trying to find.

I have noticed since that night that people no longer seem so strange to me. Now it is beginning to seem that life is just starting for me. I am alone right now but I am not frightened and I don't have to be doing something. I like meeting me and making friends with my thoughts and feelings. Because of this I have learned to enjoy other people. One older man in particular—who is very ill—makes me feel very much alive. He accepts everyone. He told me the other day that I have changed very much. According to him, I have begun to open up and love. I think that I have always loved people and I told him so. He said, "Were they aware of it?" I don't suppose I have expressed my love any more than I did my anger and hurt.

Among other things, I am finding out that I never had too much self-respect. And now that I am learning to really like me I am finally finding peace within myself. Thanks for your part in this.

The Linkage to Theory

By summarizing some of the key portions of Susan's letter, the relationship between her statements and the theoretical ones will be evident. "I was losing me. I needed something to help find *me.*" As she looks back, she realizes that she felt a vague discrepancy between the life she was experiencing and the person she believed herself to be. This kind of vague awareness of discrepancy or incongruence is a real resource for the person who becomes aware of it and attends to it. She also gives clues as to some of the reasons for her loss of contact with her own experiencing.

[1]From *Comprehensive Textbook of Psychiatry* by A. M. Freedman, H. I. Kaplan, & B. J. Sadock, 1975, Baltimore: Williams & Wilkins. Copyright 1975 by Williams & Wilkins. Reprinted by permission.

"My inner reactions meant to me that I wanted to do a certain type of work, but my family showed me that was not their meaning." This certainly suggests the way in which her false self-concept has been built. Undoubtedly, the process began in childhood or she would not have accepted the family's judgment now. A child experiences something in his organism—a feeling of fear, or anger, or jealousy, or love, or, as in this case, a sense of choice, only to be told by parents that this is not what he is experiencing. Out of this grows the construct "Parents are wiser than I and know me better than I know myself." Also, there grows an increasing distrust in one's own experiencing and a growing incongruence between self and experiencing. In this case, Susan distrusts her inward feeling that she knows the work she wants to do and accepts the judgment of her family as right and sound. . . .

"Things went along smoothly for everyone else." This is a marvelously revealing statement. She has become a very satisfactory person for those whom she is trying to please. This false concept of self that they have unwittingly built up is just what they want. . . .

"I left me behind and tried to be the person my boyfriend wanted." Once more, she has denied to her awareness (not consciously) the experiencing of her own organism, and is simply trying to be the self desired by her lover. It is the same process all over. . . .

"Finally, something in me rebelled and I tried to find me again. But I couldn't, without help." Why did she at last rebel against the manner in which she had given herself away? This rebelling indicates the strength of the tendency toward actualization. Although suppressed and distorted for so long, it has reasserted itself. . . . She was fortunate in finding a counselor who evidently created a real and personal relationship, fulfilling the conditions of therapy.

"Now I am discovering *my* experiences—some of them bad, according to society, parents and boyfriend—but all constructive as far as I am concerned." She is now reclaiming as her own the right to evaluate her own experiences. The "locus of evaluation" now resides in herself, not in others. It is through exploring her own experiencing that she determines the meaning of the evidence being provided within her. When she says, "some parts are bad by society's standards but I have found them good for me," she might be referring to any of several feelings—her rebellion against her parents, against her boyfriend, her sexual feelings, her anger and bitterness, or other aspects of herself. At least as she trusts her own valuing of her experience, she finds that it is of worth and significance to her.

"An important turning point came when I was frightened and upset by unknown feelings within me." When aspects of experiencing have been denied to awareness, they may, in a therapeutic climate, come close to the surface of awareness with resulting strong anxiety or fright. . . .

"I cried for at least an hour." Without yet knowing what she is experiencing, she is somehow preparing herself to come in contact with these feelings and meanings which are so foreign to her concept of self.

"When the denied experiences broke through the dam, they turned out to be deep hurts and anger of which I had been *absolutely* unaware." Individuals are able completely to deny experiencings that are highly threatening to the concept of self. Yet, in a safe and nonthreatening relationship, they may be released. Here, for the first time in her life, Susan is experiencing all the pent-up feelings of pain and rage that have been boiling under the facade of her false self. To experience something *fully* is not an intellectual process; in fact, Susan cannot even remember clearly what she said, but she did feel, in the immediate moment, emotions that for years had been denied to her awareness.

"I thought I was insane and that some foreign person had taken over in me." To find that "I am a person full of hurt, anger and rebellion," when formerly she had thought, "I am a person who always pleases others, who doesn't even know what her feelings are," is a very drastic shift in the concept of self. Small wonder that she felt this was an alien, a frightening someone she had never known.

"Only gradually did I recognize that this alien was the real *me*." What she has discovered is that the submissive, malleable self by which she had been living, the self that tried to please others and was guided by their evaluations, attitudes, and expectations is no longer her self. This new self is a hurt, angry self, feeling good about parts of herself, which others disapprove, experiencing many things, from wild hallucinatory thoughts to loving feelings. . . . Her self is becoming much more firmly rooted in her own organismic processes. Her concept of herself is beginning to be rooted in the spontaneously felt meanings of her experiencing. She is becoming a more congruent, a more integrated, person.

"I like meeting me and making friends with my thoughts and feelings." Here is the dawning self-respect, self-acceptance, and self-confidence of which she has been deprived for so long. She is even feeling some affection for herself. Now that she is much more acceptant of herself, she will be able to give herself more freely to others and to be more genuinely interested in others.

"I have begun to open up and love." She will find that as she is more expressive of her love she can also be more expressive of her anger and hurt, her likes and dislikes, her "wild" thoughts and feelings, which later may well turn out to be creative impulses. She is in the process of changing from a person with a false facade, a false self-concept, to a more healthy personality with a self that is much more congruent with experiencing, a self that can change as her experience changes.

"I am finally finding peace within myself." She has discovered a peaceful harmony in being a whole and congruent person—but she will be mistaken if she thinks this is a permanent reaction. Instead, if she is really open to her experience, she will find other hidden aspects of herself that she has denied to awareness, and each such discovery will give her uneasy and anxious moments or days until they are assimilated into a revised and changing picture of herself.

CHAPTER HIGHLIGHTS

- Rogers's philosophical viewpoint remained humanitarian and optimistic, as his interests evolved from individual psychotherapy and group therapy, to work in social, educational, and governmental systems.
- In client-centered therapy, the client should be the major directing force in the therapeutic relationship, not the therapist. Rogers moved from a client-centered to a person-centered approach, influenced in part by his experiences in different educational settings. He saw that his work had broad implications for many kinds of social and political systems.
- People define themselves through observing and evaluating their own experiences. Realities are private affairs and can be known only by the individuals themselves.
- The self is a fluid process rather than unchanging and stable. Rogers believed that people are capable of growth and personal development, and that positive change is a natural and expected progression.
- To the extent that the ideal self varies from the actual or real self, it hampers personal health and development. A person may become dissatisfied, uncomfortable, and even experience neurotic difficulties if the discrepancy is too great.
- A tendency toward greater health or "self-actualization" is part of human nature. It is a major motivating factor in individuals who are not hampered by past difficulties or current restrictive beliefs.
- The terms *congruence* and *incongruence* refer to the degree of accuracy between communication, experience, and awareness. An external observer's observations and one's own observations would be consistent in a situation of high congruence. Most of the symptoms described in the literature on psychopathology may be better understood in terms of incongruence.
- Once an individual becomes aware of incongruence between self-concept and experience, there follows a natural movement to resolve the discrepancy.
- Rogers considers the need for positive regard, or for love, universal. Conditions of worth are basic obstacles to realistic thinking and accurate perception. They create a discrepancy between the self-concept and the self.
- Four basic elements provide the foundation for beneficial and meaningful relationships: ongoing commitment, expression of feelings, avoidance of specific roles, and the capacity to share one's inner life.
- Whether or not they are expressed, a healthy individual is aware of her or his emotions. When they are not brought into awareness, perception of and reactions to the experience that prompted them may be distorted.
- A person-in-process, one continually changing, is a fully functioning person. Free to respond and free to experience his or her response to situations, such a person would be engaged in ongoing self-actualization.
- Person-centered therapy contains an implied equality of relating not found in the conventional doctor–patient relationship. The person in therapy does whatever directing is necessary to unlock his or her own dilemma, with minimum intervention.
- Therapy, for Rogers, is a relationship that depends in part on the mental health of the therapist to nurture the growth of mental health in the client.
- Basic theoretical concepts used in individual therapy can be applied to group work. As members work together both emotional intensity and tolerance for emotional intensity will increase.

■ Rogers applied his ideas about the healing power of open communication in group work to national and international settings; he used these sessions to seek conflict resolution on a national and international level.

KEY CONCEPTS

Conditions of worth Behaviors or attitudes that deny some aspect of the self. The individual sees these conditions as necessary to obtain love and to gain a sense of worth. Behavior, maturation, and awareness are inhibited by these self-imposed restrictions. They lead to incongruence, and eventually to rigidity of one's personality.

Congruence The degree of accuracy between communication, experience, and awareness. If what one is expressing (communication), what is occurring (experience), and what one is noticing (awareness) are all nearly equal, there is a high degree of congruence.

Empathic understanding The ability to accurately sense the feelings of others. A necessary element in the self-correcting and self-enhancing cycle to help people overcome obstacles and facilitate psychological growth.

Field of experience An entity, unique to each individual, that contains all that is occurring and is available to awareness. The field may or may not correspond to observed, objective reality. A personal, private world, it is subjective, selective, and incomplete.

Fully functioning person An individual who is completely aware of his or her ongoing self. The person has several distinct characteristics: an openness to experience, living in the present, and trusting in one's intuitive judgments and inner urgings. Trust in one's capacity to make decisions involves the whole person, not just one's intellect.

Ideal self The self-concept that the individual would most like to possess. Like the self, it is constantly being redefined. It may function as a model to strive toward but may also inhibit the capacity to develop, if it is significantly at odds with one's actual values and behavior.

Incongruence The unwillingness or inability to communicate accurately, or the inability to perceive accurately, or both. It occurs when differences emerge between experience, communication, and awareness.

Interpersonal knowing In Rogerian psychotherapy, the practice of empathic understanding. The goal is to comprehend the other's experience as the other experiences it, rather than to be objectively correct.

Objective knowing Knowledge in the public domain. It is a way of testing speculations, hypotheses, and conjectures against external frames of reference.

Personal power The person-centered approach found in society at large. It is concerned with the locus of decision-making power and control.

Self-actualizing tendency A part of the process of all living things. In humans, it is the drive to activate and express all the capacities of the organism. Self-actualization is the only motive postulated in Rogers's system.

Subjective knowing The knowledge of whether one hates, loves, enjoys, or is disdainful of a person, event, or experience. Such awareness may be improved by recognizing one's private, or "gut," feelings. It is the capacity to know enough to act on hunches, or to follow one's intuition, without verifiable evidence.

Unconditional positive regard Caring that demands no personal gratification and is not possessive. It invites the person to be what he or she actually is, regardless of what that may be. It is not a positive evaluation that can restrict behaviors by punishing some and rewarding others.

ANNOTATED BIBLIOGRAPHY

Kirschenbaum, H., & Henderson, V. (Eds.). (1989). *The Carl Rogers reader*. Boston: Houghton Mifflin.

An excellent selection of Rogers's most important writing. Includes personal papers as well as excerpts from his more influential books. If you read only one Rogers book, this should be your choice.

Lietaer, G. (2002). Sixty years of client-centered/experiential psychotherapy and counseling: bibliographical survey of books 1940–2000. *Journal of Humanistic Psychology, 42*(2), 97–131.

As extensive a list as anyone would ever need.

Raskin, N. J., & Rogers, C. (1989). Person-centered therapy. In R. Corsini & D. Wedding (Eds.), *Current psychotherapies* (4th ed.) (pp. 155–194). Itasca, IL: F. E. Peacock.

Finished after Rogers's death, it is a substantial, well-written summary of his ideas as they relate to psychotherapy.

Rogers, C. R. (1951). *Client-centered therapy: Its current practice, implications and theory*. Boston: Houghton Mifflin.

The core volume for what is called Rogerian therapy. Rogers himself saw some of the material here as too rigid. Still a useful and important book.

Rogers, C. R. (1959). A theory of therapy, personality, and interpersonal relationships, as developed in the client-centered framework. In S. Koch (Ed.), *Psychology, the study of a science. Vol. 3: Formulations of the person and the social context* (pp. 184–225). New York: McGraw-Hill.

The only time Rogers laid out his work in a formal, detailed, and organized theory. He succeeds, but this essay remains one of his least-read works. The obscurity is undeserved. If you stick with Rogers, eventually you will want to read this.

Rogers, C. R. (1961). *On becoming a person: A therapist's view of psychotherapy.* Boston: Houghton Mifflin.

A personal, practical, and extensive consideration of the major themes in Rogers's work. A book that remains lucid and useful to those in the people-helping professions.

Rogers, C. R. (1969). *Freedom to learn.* Columbus, OH: Merrill.

A set of challenges to educators. According to Rogers, most teaching is set up to discourage learning and encourage anxiety and maladjustment. More strident than his gentler, therapy-oriented volumes.

Rogers, C. R. (1970). *Carl Rogers on encounter groups.* New York: Harper & Row.

A sensible discussion of the ups and downs of the encounter group. Most of the discussion is drawn from groups that Rogers has run or observed, so the material is both representative and explicit. Probably the best introduction to this form of interpersonal gathering in print. Not sensational and not critical.

Rogers, C. R. (1972). *Becoming partners: Marriage and its alternatives.* New York: Dell (Delacorte Press).

Rogers interviews couples who have taken varying approaches to marriage. He points out the strengths and weaknesses of the relationships. Mainly reporting, he calls attention to those forces that lead to successful or unsuccessful long-term relationships. Useful.

Rogers, C. R. (1978). *Carl Rogers on personal power.* New York: Dell.

The first book in which Rogers considers the wide social implications in his work. It is subtitled accurately: "Inner strength and its revolutionary impact. The extension of ideas developed in therapy to educational and political systems."

Rogers, C. R. (1980). *A way of being.* Boston: Houghton Mifflin.

A collection of essays and speeches that serves as a small autobiography and illustrates Rogers's growing realization of the social impact of his work beyond psychology. Moving and optimistic, this is his most intimate and gentle book.

Rogers, C. R. (1983). *Freedom to learn for the 80's.* Columbus, OH: Merrill.

A revision and expansion of the earlier edition. He spends considerable time describing his own work in classrooms, facilitating "responsible freedom."

Rogers, C. R., & Russell, D. (2002). *Carl Rogers, the quiet revolutionary: An oral history.* Roseville, CA: Penmartin.

A virtual autobiography, but more fun. The most informative and informal book on Rogers and by Rogers. His side of the story.

Rogers, C. R., & Stevens, B. (1967). *Person to person.* Walnut Creek, CA: Real Peoples Press (New York: Pocket Books, 1971).

A collection of articles, mostly by Rogers, with fascinating commentaries on them by Barry Stevens.

Rogers, N. (2002). *Carl Rogers: A daughter's tribute.* (DVD) mindgardenmedia.com

A new format for biography. Excerpts from his books, photos taken throughout his life, full bibliography, and marvelous video clips. A combination of family album and scholarly retrospective.

Web Sites

http://psy1.clarion.edu/jms/syll.html

Not only a Rogers site but a good model of what a faculty member can do with a site. It is person centered (in a very Rogerian sense) and contains what students and other faculty need to know. The professor teaches behaviorism, Rogers, and Gestalt—an unusually wide span of interests.

http://www.nrogers.com/carlrogers.html

Best overall Rogers site. It is kept up by Natalie Rogers, Carl's daughter. She is a gifted therapist who runs programs in expressive arts therapy. Links to all the other Rogers sites, books, and an undated list of new books based on Rogers and his work. Invaluable for anyone doing serious additional work on Rogers.

REFERENCES

Ansbacher, H. (1990). Alfred Adler's influence on the three leading cofounders of humanistic psychology. *Journal of Humanistic Psychology, 30*(4), 45–53.

Arons, M., & Harri, C. (1992). *Conversations with the founders.* Manuscript submitted for publication.

Bandler, R., & Grinder, J. (1975). *The structure of magic* (Vols. 1, 2). Palo Alto, CA: Science and Behavior.

Bozarth, J. (2002). Nondirectivity in the person-centered approach: Critique of Kahn's critique. *Journal of Humanistic Psychology, 42*(2), 78–83.

Butler, J. M., & Rice, L. N. (1963). Audience, self-actualization, and drive theory. In J. M. Wepman & R. W. Heine (Eds.), *Concepts of personality* (pp. 79–110). Chicago: Aldine.

Campbell, P., & McMahon, E. (1974). Religious type experiences in the context of humanistic and transpersonal psychology. *Journal of Transpersonal Psychology, 6,* 11–17.

Caspary, W. (1991). Carl Rogers—values, persons and politics: The dialectic of individual and community. *Journal of Humanistic Psychology, 31*(4), 8–31.

Coffer, C. N., & Appley, M. (1964). *Motivation: Theory and research.* New York: Wiley.

DeCarvalho, R. (1999). Otto Rank, the Rankian Circle in Philadelphia and the origins of Carl Rogers' Person-Centered Therapy. *History of Psychology, 2*(2), 132–148.

Doi, A., & Ikemi, A. (2003). How getting in touch with feelings happens: The process of referencing. *Journal of Humanistic Psychology, 43*(4), 87–101.

Dreher, D. (1995). Toward a person-centered politics: John Vasconcellos. In M. M. Suhd (Ed.), *Carl Rogers and other notables he influenced* (pp. 339–372). Palo Alto, CA: Science and Behavior.

Ellis, A. (1959). Requisite conditions for basic personality change. *Journal of Consulting Psychology, 23,* 538–540.

Evans, R. I. (Ed.). (1975). *Carl Rogers: The man and his ideas.* New York: Dutton.

Fadiman, J. (1993). *Unlimit your life.* Berkeley, CA: Celestial Arts.

Fernald, P. (2000). Carl Rogers: Body Centered Counselor. *Journal of Counseling and Development, 78,* 172–179.

Freedman, A. M., Kaplan, H. I., & Sadock, B. J. (1975). *Comprehensive textbook of psychiatry.* Baltimore: Williams & Wilkins.

Fuller, R. (1982). Carl Rogers, religion, and the role of psychology in American culture. *Journal of Humanistic Psychology, 22*(4), 21–32.

Gibb, J. R. (1971). The effects of human relations training. In A. E. Bergin & S. L. Garfield (Eds.), *Handbook of psychotherapy and behavior change* (pp. 2114–2176). New York: Wiley.

Gordon, W. (1961). *Synectics.* New York: Harper & Row.

Hall, C., & Lindzey, G. (1978). *Theories of personality* (3rd ed.). New York: Wiley.

Harper, R. A. (1959). *Psychoanalysis and psychotherapy.* Upper Saddle River, NJ: Prentice Hall.

Hayashi, S., Kuno, T., Osawa, M., Shimizu, M., & Suetake, Y. (1992). The client-centered therapy and person-centered approach in Japan: Historical development, current status and perspectives. *Journal of Humanistic Psychology, 32*(2), 115–136.

Ikemi, A., & Kubota, S. (1996). Humanistic psychology in Japanese corporations: Listening and the small steps of change. *Journal of Humanistic Psychology, 36*(1), 104–121.

Kahn, E. (1999). A critique of nondirectivity in the person-centered approach. *Journal of Humanistic Psychology, 39*(4), 94–110.

Kahn, E. (2002). A way to help people by holding theory lightly: A response to Bozarth, Merry, Brodley, & Sommerbeck. *Journal of Humanistic Psychology, 42*(2), 88–96.

Kirschenbaum, H. (1980). *On becoming Carl Rogers.* New York: Dell (Delacorte Press).

Kirschenbaum, H. (1995). Carl Rogers. In M. M. Suhd (Ed.), *Carl Rogers and other notables he influenced* (pp. 1–104). Palo Alto, CA: Science and Behavior.

Kirschenbaum, H., & Henderson, V. (Eds.). (1989). *The Carl Rogers reader.* Boston: Houghton Mifflin.

Korbei, L. (1998). Client-centered psychotherapy: the individual and socialization process. In N. Madu & P. Baguma (Eds.), *In quest for psychotherapy for modern Africa Sovenga,* South Africa, UNIN Press, 100–104.

Kramer, R. (1995). The birth of client-centered therapy: Carl Rogers, Otto Rank, and "the beyond." *Journal of Humanistic Psychology, 35*(4), 54–110.

Krasner, L., & Ullman, L. (1973). *Behavior influence and personality: The social matrix of human action.* New York: Holt, Rinehart and Winston.

Lawrence, D. H. (1960). *The ladybird together with the captain's doll.* London: Harborough.

Lieberman, M. A., Miles, M. B., & Yalom, I. D. (1973). *Encounter groups: First facts.* New York: Basic Books.

MacDougall, C. (2002). Roger's person-centered approach: consideration for use in multicultural counseling. *Journal of Humanistic Psychology, 42*(2), 44–65.

Macy, F. (1987). The legacy of Carl Rogers in the U.S.S.R. *Journal of Humanistic Psychology, 27*(3), 305–308.

McCleary, R. A., & Lazarus, R. S. (1949). Autonomic discrimination without awareness. *Journal of Personality, 19,* 171–179.

Menninger, K. (1963). *The vital balance: The life process in mental health and illness.* New York: Viking Press.

Merry, T., & Brodley, B. The nondirective attitude in client-centered therapy: A response to Kahn. *Journal of Humanistic Psychology, 42*(2), 66–77.

Murayama, S., & Nakata, Y. (1996). Fukuoka human relations community: A network approach to developing human potential. *Journal of Humanistic Psychology, 36*(1), 91–103.

Ogden, T. (1972). The new pietism. *Journal of Humanistic Psychology, 12,* 24–41. (Also appears in *The intensive group experience: The new pietism.* Philadelphia: Westminster Press, 1972.)

O'Hara, M. (1989). Person-centered approach as conscientização: The works of Carl Rogers and Paulo Friere. *Journal of Humanistic Psychology, 29*(1), 11–35.

Perry, J. W. (1974). *The far side of madness.* Upper Saddle River, NJ: Prentice Hall.

Polanyi, M. (1958). *Personal knowledge.* Chicago: University of Chicago Press.

Quinn, R. (1993). Confronting Carl Rogers: A developmental-interactional approach to person-centered therapy. *Journal of Humanistic Psychology, 33*(1), 6–23.

Quinn, R. (1959). *The study of man.* Chicago: University of Chicago Press.

Rogers, C. R. (1939). *The clinical treatment of the problem child.* Boston: Houghton Mifflin.

Rogers, C. R. (1942). *Counseling and psychotherapy.* Boston: Houghton Mifflin.

Rogers, C. R. (1950). A current formulation of client-centered therapy. *Social Service Review, 24,* 440–451.

Rogers, C. R. (1951). *Client-centered therapy: Its current practice, implications and theory.* Boston: Houghton Mifflin.

Rogers, C. R. (1952a). Communication: Its blocking and its facilitation. *Northwestern University Information, 20*(25).

Rogers, C. R. (1952b). Client-centered psychotherapy. *Scientific American, 187*(5), 66–74.

Rogers, C. R. (1959). A theory of therapy, personality, and interpersonal relationships, as developed in the client-centered framework. In S. Koch (Ed.), *Psychology, the study of a science. Vol. 3: Formulations of the person and the social context* (pp. 184–256). New York: McGraw-Hill.

Rogers, C. R. (1961). *On becoming a person: A therapist's view of psychotherapy*. Boston: Houghton Mifflin.

Rogers, C. R. (1964). Towards a science of the person. In T. W. Wann (Ed.), *Behaviorism and phenomenology: Contrasting bases for modern psychology* (pp. 109–133). Chicago: University of Chicago Press.

Rogers, C. R. (1967). Carl Rogers. In E. Boring & G. Lindzey (Eds.), *History of psychology in autobiography* (Vol. 5). New York: Appleton-Century-Crofts.

Rogers, C. R. (1969). *Freedom to learn*. Columbus, OH: Merrill.

Rogers, C. R. (1970). *Carl Rogers on encounter groups*. New York: Harper & Row.

Rogers, C. R. (1972). *Becoming partners: Marriage and its alternatives*. New York: Dell (Delacorte Press).

Rogers, C. R. (1973a). My philosophy of interpersonal relationships and how it grew. *Journal of Humanistic Psychology, 13*, 3–16.

Rogers, C. R. (1973b). Some new challenges. *The American Psychologist, 28*, 379–387.

Rogers, C. R. (1974b). The project at Immaculate Heart: An experiment in self-directed change. *Education, 95*(2), 172–189.

Rogers, C. R. (1975a). Empathic: An unappreciated way of being. *The Counseling Psychologist: Carl Rogers on Empathy* (special topic), *5*(2), 2–10.

Rogers, C. R. (1975b). The emerging person: A new revolution. In R. I. Evans (Ed.), *Carl Rogers: The man and his ideas*. New York: Dutton.

Rogers, C. R. (1978a). *Carl Rogers on personal power*. New York: Dell.

Rogers, C. R. (1978b). Letters to Sollad, D. Unpublished.

Rogers, C. R. (1980a). *A way of being*. Boston: Houghton Mifflin.

Rogers, C. R. (1980b). Growing old—or older and growing. *Journal of Humanistic Psychology, 20*(4), 5–16.

Rogers, C. R. (1982b). Reply to Rollo May's letter to Carl Rogers. *Journal of Humanistic Psychology, 22*(4), 85–89.

Rogers, C. R. (1983). *Freedom to learn for the 80's*. Columbus, OH: Merrill.

Rogers, C. R. (1984). *A client-centered, person-centered approach to therapy*. Unpublished manuscript.

Rogers, C. R. (1986a). Client-centered therapy. In I. L. Kutash & A. Wolf (Eds.), *Psychotherapists casebook: Therapy and technique in practice* (pp. 197–208). San Francisco: Jossey-Bass.

Rogers, C. R. (1986b). The Rust workshop. *Journal of Humanistic Psychology, 26*(3), 23–45.

Rogers, C. R. (1987a). Inside the world of the Soviet professional. *Journal of Humanistic Psychology, 27*(3), 277–304.

Rogers, C. R. (1987b). On reaching 85. *Person Centered Review, 2*(2), 150–152.

Rogers, C. R. (1995). What understanding and acceptance mean to me. *Journal of Humanistic Psychology, 35*(4), 7–22.

Rogers, C. R., & Haigh, G. I. (1983). Walk softly through life. *Voices: The Art and Science of Psychotherapy, 18*, 6–14.

Rogers, C. R., & Russell, D. (2002). *Carl Rogers: The quiet revolutionary, an oral history*. Roseville, CA: Penmarin.

Rogers, C. R., & Skinner, B. F. (1956). Some issues concerning the control of human behavior. *Science, 124*, 1057–1066.

Rogers, N. (2003). Personal communication to author.

Saji, M., & Linaga, K. (1983). *Client chushin rycho [Client-centered therapy]*. Tokyo: Yuhikaku.

Smith, M. B. (1990). Humanistic psychology. *Journal of Humanistic Psychology, 30*(4), 6–21.

Sollad, D. (1978). Letters to Carl Rogers. Unpublished.

Sommerbeck, L. (2002). Person-centered or eclectic? A response to Kahn. *Journal of Humanistic Psychology, 42*(2), 84–87.

Swenson, G. (1987). When personal and political processes meet: The Rust workshop. *Journal of Humanistic Psychology, 27*(3), 309–333.

Tart, C. T. (1971). Scientific foundations for the study of altered states of consciousness. *Journal of Transpersonal Psychology, 3*, 93–124.

Tart, C. T. (1975). Some assumptions of orthodox, Western psychology. In C. T. Tart (Ed.), *Transpersonal psychologies* (pp. 59–112). New York: Harper & Row.

Thorne, F. C. (1957). Critique of recent developments in personality counseling therapy. *Journal of Clinical Psychology, 13*, 234–244.

Van Belle, H. A. (1980). *Basic intent and the therapeutic approach of Carl Rogers*. Toronto, Canada: Wedge Foundation.

Watts, R. (1998). The remarkable parallel between Rogers's core conditions and Adler's social interest. *Journal of Individual Psychology, 54*(1), 4–9.

chapter 12

Abraham Maslow
and transpersonal psychology

Abraham Maslow believed that an accurate and viable theory of personality must include not only the depths but also the heights that each individual is capable of attaining. He is one of the founders of humanistic psychology and transpersonal psychology, two major new fields that evolved as alternatives to behaviorism and psychoanalysis. The concepts of Skinner, Freud and their followers have tended to ignore or to explain away the cultural, social, and individual achievements of humanity, including creativity, love, altruism, and mysticism. These were among Maslow's greatest interests.

> Abraham Maslow has done more to change our view of human nature and human possibilities than has any other American psychologist of the past fifty years. His influence, both direct and indirect, continues to grow, especially in the fields of health, education, and management theory, and in the personal and social lives of millions of Americans. (Leonard, 1983, p. 326)

Maslow was a pioneer, interested in exploring new issues and new fields. His work is a collection of thoughts, opinions, and hypotheses rather than a fully developed theoretical system. More a theorist than a research scientist, Maslow rarely came up with final answers. His genius was in formulating significant questions—questions that many social scientists today consider critical.

PERSONAL HISTORY

Abraham Maslow was born in Brooklyn, New York, in 1908, of Russian Jewish immigrant parents. His father, a barrel maker by trade, had moved to the United States from Russia as a young man. He later sent for the woman who would be his wife. In his youth, Abe was extraordinarily shy and highly neurotic. A bright, unhappy, and lonely boy, he was so convinced he was ugly he would ride deserted subway cars to spare others the sight of him.

Maslow entered the City College of New York at the age of 18. His father wanted Abe to become a lawyer, but the son could not stand the thought of law school. When his father asked what he intended to do instead, Abe said he wanted to go on studying "everything."

As a teenager, Maslow fell in love with his first cousin and found excuses to spend time with her family, often gazing lovestruck at her but not daring to touch her. At the age of 19, when he finally embraced his cousin, he experienced his first kiss. Maslow later described this moment as one of the *peak experiences* of his life. Her acceptance of him, instead of the rejection he had feared, was a tremendous boost to his shaky self-esteem. A year later they were married; she was 19 and he was 20. Marriage and his immersion in psychology represented a period of renewal in Maslow's life.

In his first year in college, Maslow discovered music and drama. He fell in love with both, a love that would remain with him throughout his life. Maslow transferred to the University of Wisconsin, where his interest focused on psychology. He was captured by J. B. Watson's vision of behaviorism as a powerful tool for affecting human life. Maslow trained in the experimental method at Wisconsin and worked in the psychology laboratory there, conducting research using rats and other animals. He received his bachelor's degree in 1930 and his doctorate in 1934 at age 26.

After graduation, Maslow returned to New York to work with Edward Thorndike, an eminent Columbia University psychologist. Thorndike was particularly impressed with Maslow's performance on the intelligence test that Thorndike developed. Maslow scored 195 on the test, the second-highest IQ score thus far recorded. Eighteen months later, Maslow found a teaching job at Brooklyn College, where he remained for 14 years. New York at that time was a stimulating intellectual center, attracting many of the finest scholars who had fled Nazi persecution. Maslow studied with several psychotherapists, including Alfred Adler, Erich Fromm, and Karen Horney. He was most strongly influenced by Max Wertheimer, one of the founders of Gestalt psychology, and by Ruth Benedict, a brilliant cultural anthropologist.

Maslow's involvement in the practical applications of psychology dates back to the beginning of his career. Even as a behaviorist graduate student, Maslow was convinced that Freud was right in his emphasis on sexuality. Maslow chose for his dissertation research the relationship between dominance and sexual behavior among primates. After leaving Wisconsin, he began an extensive investigation of human sexual behavior. Maslow believed that any advance in our understanding of sexual functioning would lead to improvements in human adjustment.

During World War II, when he realized the insignificance of psychology's contribution to reducing international conflict, Maslow's work shifted from experimental psychology to social and personality psychology. He wanted to devote himself to "discovering a psychology for the peace table" (Hall, 1968, p. 54).

> Human nature is not nearly as bad as it has been thought to be. (Maslow, 1968, p. 4)

In addition to his professional work, Maslow became involved with the family barrel-manufacturing business during a prolonged illness. His interest in business and in applied psychology eventually resulted in *Eupsychian Management* (1965), a compilation of thoughts and articles related to management and industrial psychology. For years, an out-of-print classic, it has been recently republished as *Maslow on Management* (Maslow, 1999). He wrote these pieces during the summer that he spent as visiting fellow at a small electronics plant in Del Mar, California.

In 1951, Maslow accepted a position near Boston, at Brandeis University, which had just been established, and remained there until 1968. He was chair of the first psychology department and was instrumental in the development of the university as a whole.

Throughout his career, Maslow's pioneering work was generally dismissed as unscientific and considered outside the mainstream of psychology. His colleagues liked him, though, and his ideas gradually became better appreciated. Much to his own surprise, Maslow was elected president of the American Psychological Association in 1967 and served for one year.

Maslow considered the labels applied to the various schools of psychology highly limiting. "We shouldn't have to say humanistic psychology. The adjective should be unnecessary. Don't think of me as being antibehavioristic. I'm antidoctrinaire. . . . I'm against anything that closes doors and cuts off possibilities" (Maslow in Hall, 1968, p. 57).

> I am a Freudian, I am behavioristic, I am humanistic. (Maslow, 1971, p. 144)

In January 1969, Maslow left Brandeis to accept a fellowship that allowed him to write full time. In June 1970, at the age of 62, he died of a heart attack.

INTELLECTUAL ANTECEDENTS

The most important influences on Maslow's thinking were psychoanalysis, social anthropology, Gestalt psychology, and the work of the neurophysiologist Kurt Goldstein.

Psychoanalysis

To oversimplify the matter somewhat, it is as if Freud supplied to us the sick half of psychology and we must now fill it out with the healthy half. (Maslow, 1968, p. 5)

In the 1950s, when clinical psychology was a relatively new field, Maslow believed that psychoanalysis provided the best system for analyzing psychopathology and also the best form of psychotherapy available. However, he found the psychoanalytic system unsatisfactory as a general psychology applicable to all of human thought and behavior.

> The picture of man it presents is a lopsided, distorted puffing up of his weaknesses and shortcomings that purports then to describe him fully. . . . Practically all the activities that man prides himself on, and that give meaning, richness, and value to his life, are either omitted or pathologized by Freud. (Maslow in Goble, 1971, p. 244)

Psychoanalytic theory significantly influenced Maslow's life and thought. Freud's sophisticated description of the neurotic and maladaptive aspects of human behavior inspired Maslow to develop a scientifically grounded psychology relevant to the full range of human behavior. Maslow's own personal analysis profoundly affected him and demonstrated the substantial differences that exist between intellectual knowledge and actual, gut-level experience.

Social Anthropology

As a student at Wisconsin, Maslow seriously studied the work of social anthropologists such as Bronislaw Malinowski, Margaret Mead, Ruth Benedict, and Ralph Linton. In New York he studied with leading figures in the field of culture and personality, in which psychoanalytic theories are applied to the examination of behavior in other cultures. In addition, Maslow was fascinated by William Sumner's book *Folkways* (1940). According to Sumner, human behavior is largely determined by cultural patterns and prescriptions. Maslow was so inspired by Sumner that he vowed to devote himself to the same areas of study.

Gestalt Psychology

Maslow was also a serious student of Gestalt psychology, which investigates perception, cognition, and other sophisticated human activities in terms of complex, whole systems. He admired Max Wertheimer, whose work on productive thinking is closely related to Maslow's writings on cognition and to his work on creativity. For Maslow, as for Gestalt psychologists, an essential element in effective reasoning and creative problem solving is the ability to perceive and think in terms of wholes or patterns rather than isolated parts.

Kurt Goldstein

Another important influence on Maslow's thinking was the work of Kurt Goldstein, a neurophysiologist who emphasized the unity of the organism—what happens in any part affects the entire system. Maslow's work on self-actualization was inspired partly by Goldstein, who was the first to use the term. Maslow dedicated *Toward a Psychology of Being* (1968) to Goldstein. In the preface, he stated:

> If I had to express in a single sentence what Humanistic Psychology has meant for me, I would say that it is an integration of Goldstein (and Gestalt Psychology) with Freud (and

the various psychodynamic psychologies), the whole joined with the scientific spirit that I was taught by my teachers at the University of Wisconsin. (1968, p. v)

A neurophysiologist whose main focus was brain-damaged patients, Goldstein viewed self-actualization as a fundamental process in every organism, a process that may have negative as well as positive effects on the individual. In Goldstein's view, every organism has one primary drive: "[The] organism is governed by the tendency to actualize, as much as possible, its individual capacities, its 'nature,' in the world" (1939, p. 196).

Goldstein argued that tension release is a strong drive but only in sick organisms. A healthy organism's primary goal is "the *formation* of a certain level of tension, namely, that which makes possible further ordered activity" (1939, pp. 195–196). A drive such as hunger is a special case of self-actualization, in which the organism seeks tension reduction to return to optimal condition for further expression of its capacities. However, only in an extreme situation does such a drive become overwhelming. A normal organism, Goldstein asserts, can temporarily put off food, sex, sleep, and so forth, if other motives, such as curiosity or playfulness, are present.

According to Goldstein, successful coping with the environment often involves uncertainty and shock. In fact, the healthy self-actualizing organism invites such shock by venturing into new situations in order to utilize its capacities. For Goldstein (and for Maslow also), self-actualization does not rid the individual of problems and difficulties; on the contrary, growth may bring a certain amount of pain and suffering. Goldstein wrote that an organism's capacities determine its needs. For instance, the possession of a digestive system makes eating a necessity; muscles require movement. A bird needs to fly, just as an artist needs to create, despite the fact that the act may require painful struggle and great effort.

> Capacities clamor to be used, and cease their clamor only when they are used sufficiently. (Maslow, 1968, p. 152)

MAJOR CONCEPTS

The most influential part of Maslow's theory was his model of the hierarchy of needs, which includes the full range of human motivations. His most important concept was self-actualization, the highest level of human need. Maslow also investigated peak experiences, special moments in each individual's life. He distinguished between two basic kinds of psychology, *deficiency psychology* and *being psychology*, and pioneered in the development of the latter. Maslow was also deeply interested in the social implications of his theory, especially with *eupsychia*, his term for a Utopian society, and synergy, or cooperation within a society.

Hierarchy of Needs

Most of what psychology has learned about human motivation has come from the analysis of patients in therapy, and this troubled Maslow. Although we have learned a great deal from these patients, their psychological drives clearly do not reflect the motivations of the population at large. In his theory of the **hierarchy of needs** (see Figure 12.1), Maslow accomplished an intellectual tour de force. He managed to integrate in a single model the approaches of the major schools of psychology—behaviorism, psychoanalysis and its offshoots, and humanistic and transpersonal psychology. He illustrated that no one approach is better or more valid than another. Each has its own place and its own relevance.

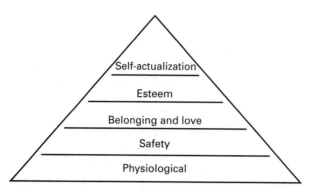

FIGURE 12.1 Maslow's Hierarchy of Needs

Maslow defined neurosis and psychological maladjustment as *deficiency diseases;* that is, they are caused by deprivation of certain basic needs, just as the absence of certain vitamins causes illness. The best examples of basic needs are the physiological ones, such as hunger, thirst, and sleep. Deprivation clearly leads to illness, sooner or later, and the satisfaction of these needs is the only treatment. Basic needs are found in all individuals. The amount and kind of satisfaction varies among societies, but basic needs (such as hunger) can never be ignored.

Physiological needs include the need for food, drink, oxygen, sleep, and sex. Many people in our culture can satisfy these needs without difficulty. However, if biological needs are not adequately met, the individual becomes almost completely devoted to fulfilling them. Maslow argues that a person who is literally dying of thirst has no great interest in satisfying any other needs. But once this particular overwhelming need is met, it becomes less important, allowing other drives to surface.

Certain **psychological needs** must also be satisfied in order to maintain health. Maslow includes the following as basic psychological needs: the need for safety, security, and stability; the need for love and a sense of belonging; and the need for self-respect and esteem. In addition, every individual has growth needs: a need to develop one's potentials and capabilities and a need for self-actualization.

By *safety needs,* Maslow means the individual's need to live in a relatively stable, safe, predictable environment. We have a basic need for structure, order, and limits. People need freedom from fear, anxiety, and chaos. As with physiological needs, most people take a smoothly running, stable, protective society for granted. In modern Western society, the need for safety usually becomes dominant only in real emergencies, such as natural disasters, epidemics, and riots.

All people have *belonging and love needs.* We are motivated to seek close relationships with others and to feel part of various groups, such as family and groups of peers. These needs, Maslow wrote, are increasingly frustrated in our highly mobile, individualistic society. Further, the frustration of these needs is most often found at the core of psychological maladjustment.

Maslow (1987) described two kinds of *esteem needs.* First is a desire for competence and individual achievement. Second, we need respect from others—status, fame, appreciation, and recognition. When these needs are unmet, the individual tends to feel inferior, weak, or helpless. In Maslow's view, the esteem needs were stressed by Adler and relatively neglected by Freud, but awareness of their importance has been

Living at the higher need level means greater biological efficiency, greater longevity, less disease, better sleep, appetite, etc. (Maslow, 1948)

growing. Healthy self-esteem comes from personal effort resulting in achievement and deserved respect from others.

Even if all these needs are satisfied, Maslow points out, individuals still feel frustrated or incomplete unless they experience *self-actualization*—full use of their talents and capacities. The form that this need takes varies widely from person to person. Each of us has different motivations and capacities. To one person, becoming an excellent parent may be a source of self-actualization; another may feel impelled to achieve as an athlete, painter, or inventor.

According to Maslow, more basic needs must be fulfilled before less critical needs are met. For example, both physiological and love needs are essential to the individual; however, when one is starving, the need for love is not a major factor in behavior. On the other hand, Maslow argues, even when frustrated in love, we still need to eat (romantic novels to the contrary).

> It is quite true that man lives by bread alone—when there is no bread. But what happens to man's desires when there is plenty of bread and when his belly is chronically filled? *At once other (and higher) needs emerge,* and these, rather than physiological hungers, dominate their organism. And when these in turn are satisfied, again new (and still higher) needs emerge, and so on. (Maslow, 1987, p. 17)

> Man's higher nature rests upon man's lower nature, needing it as a foundation and collapsing without this foundation. That is, for the mass of mankind, man's higher nature is inconceivable without a satisfied lower nature as a base. (Maslow, 1968, p. 173)

Self-actualization

Maslow loosely defined **self-actualization** as "the full use and exploitation of talents, capacities, potentialities, etc." (1970, p. 150). Self-actualization is not a static state. It is an ongoing process in which one's capacities are fully, creatively, and joyfully utilized. "I think of the self-actualizing man not as an ordinary man with something added, but rather as the ordinary man with nothing taken away. The average man is a full human being with dampened and inhibited powers and capacities" (Maslow in Lowry, 1973b, p. 91).

Most commonly, self-actualizing people see life clearly. They are less emotional and more objective, less likely to allow hopes, fears, or ego defenses to distort their observations. Maslow found that all self-actualizing people are dedicated to a vocation or a cause. Two requirements for growth are commitment to something greater than oneself and success at one's chosen tasks. Major characteristics of self-actualizing people include creativity, spontaneity, courage, and hard work.

Maslow deliberately studied only those who were relatively free of neurosis and emotional disturbance. He found that his psychologically healthy subjects were independent and self-accepting; they had few self-conflicts and were able to enjoy both play and work. Although only one of Maslow's subjects belonged to an orthodox religious faith, virtually all believed in a life that could be called spiritual. The self-actualizing subjects, Maslow found, took pleasure in life, despite pain, sorrow, and disappointment. They had more interests and less fear, anxiety, boredom, or sense of purposelessness. Whereas most other people had only occasional moments of joy, triumph, or peak experience, self-actualizing individuals seemed to love life in general.

> *There are no perfect human beings!* Persons can be found who are good, very good indeed, in fact, great. There do in fact exist creators, seers, sages, saints, shakers and movers. This can certainly give us hope for the future of the species even if they are uncommon and do not come by the dozen. And yet these very same people can at times be boring, irritating, petulant, selfish, angry, or depressed. To avoid disillusionment with human nature, we must first give up our illusions about it. (Maslow, 1970, p. 176)

One of Maslow's main points is that we are always desiring something and rarely reach a state of complete satisfaction, one without any goals or desires. His need hierarchy is an attempt to predict what kinds of desires will arise once the old ones are sufficiently satisfied and no longer dominate behavior. Many individual exceptions occur, especially in a culture such as ours, in which most basic needs are partially satisfied and still serve to motivate without becoming overwhelming. Maslow developed his hierarchy as part of a general theory of motivation, not as a precise predictor of individual behavior.

Metamotivation.   **Metamotivation** refers to behavior inspired by growth needs and values. According to Maslow, this kind of motivation is most common among self-actualizing people, who are by definition already gratified in their lower needs. Metamotivation often takes the form of devotion to ideals or goals, to something "outside oneself." Frustration of *metaneeds* brings about *metapathologies*—a lack of values, meaningfulness, or fulfillment in life. Maslow argues that a sense of identity, success in a career, and commitment to a value system are as essential to one's psychological well-being as are security, love, and self-esteem.

Grumbles and Metagrumbles.   Maslow's system includes different levels of complaints that correspond to the levels of frustrated needs. In a factory situation, for example, low-level *grumbles* might be responses to unsafe working conditions, authoritarian supervisors, or a lack of job security. These complaints address deprivations of basic needs for physical safety and security. Complaints of a higher level might be inadequate recognition of accomplishments, loss of prestige, or lack of group solidarity—that is, complaints based on threats to belonging needs or esteem needs.

Metagrumbles speak to the frustration of metaneeds, such as perfection, justice, beauty, and truth. This level of grumbling is a good indication that everything else is going fairly smoothly. When people complain about the unaesthetic nature of their surroundings, for example, it probably means that their more basic needs have been relatively well satisfied.

Maslow assumes that we should never expect an end to complaints; we should only hope to move to higher levels of complaint. When grumblers are frustrated over the imperfection of the world, the lack of justice, and so on, it is a positive sign: despite a high degree of basic satisfaction, people are striving for still greater improvement and growth. In fact, Maslow suggests, a good measure of the enlightenment of a community is the percentage of metagrumblers among its members.

Research on Self-actualization.   Maslow's investigations of self-actualization were first stimulated by his desire to understand more completely two inspiring teachers, Ruth Benedict and Max Wertheimer. Although Benedict and Wertheimer were dissimilar personalities and were concerned with different fields of study, Maslow believed they enjoyed a level of fulfillment in their professional and private lives that he had rarely seen in others. In Benedict and Wertheimer, Maslow saw two eminent scientists who were also deeply fulfilled, creative human beings. He began a private research project to discover what made them so special, and he kept a notebook filled with whatever data he could accumulate about their personal lives, attitudes, values, and so forth. Maslow's comparison of Benedict and Wertheimer set the stage for his lifelong study of self-actualization.

Maslow argued that it was more accurate to generalize about human nature from studying the best examples he could find than from cataloging the problems and faults of average or neurotic individuals.

Growth is theoretically possible only because the "higher" tastes are better than the "lower" and because the "lower" satisfaction becomes boring. (Maslow, 1971, p. 147)

To have committees . . . heatedly coming in and complaining that rose gardens in the parks are not sufficiently cared for . . . is in itself a wonderful thing because it indicates the height of life at which the complainers are living. (Maslow, 1965, p. 240)

Self-actualizing people are, without one single exception, involved in a cause outside their own skin, in something outside of themselves. (Maslow, 1971, p. 43)

Certainly a visitor from Mars descending upon a colony of birth-injured cripples, dwarfs, hunchbacks, etc., could not deduce what they *should* have been. But then let us study not cripples, but the closest approach we can get to whole, healthy men. In them we find qualitative differences, a different system of motivation, emotion, value, thinking, and perceiving. In a certain sense, only the saints are mankind. (Maslow in Lowry, 1973a, p. 90)

By studying the best and healthiest men and women, researchers can explore the limits of human potential. In order to determine how fast human beings can run, for example, one should work with the finest athletes and track performers available. It would make no sense to test an average sample from the general population. Similarly, Maslow argued, to study psychological health and maturity, we should investigate the most mature, creative, and well-integrated people.

In looking for subjects for a study of "good human beings," Maslow found only one clearly usable subject among 3,000 undergraduates. Two criteria for including people in his initial study had been established. First, all subjects had to be relatively free of neurosis or other major personal problems. Second, all those studied had to be making the best possible use of their talents and capabilities.

In his research, Maslow was finally forced to rely on personal acquaintances as well as public figures. This group consisted of 18 individuals: 9 contemporaries and 9 historical figures, including Abraham Lincoln, Thomas Jefferson, Albert Einstein, Eleanor Roosevelt, Jane Addams, William James, Albert Schweitzer, Aldous Huxley, and Baruch Spinoza. It is noteworthy that Maslow's list includes intellectual giants and social reformers but no spiritual teachers or mystics; his interest in transpersonal psychology emerged later in his career. Obviously, Maslow's bias toward active, successful,

Eleanor Roosevelt

intellectual personalities as the "best" people has strongly affected his writing on self-actualization. Another psychologist, who valued introverted, artistic, and spiritual qualities in people, would have formulated a different theory.

Maslow lists the following characteristics of self-actualizers (1970, pp. 153–172):

1. more efficient perception of reality and more comfortable relations with it
2. acceptance (self, others, nature)
3. spontaneity; simplicity; naturalness
4. problem centering [as opposed to being ego-centered]
5. the quality of detachment; the need for privacy
6. autonomy; independence of culture and environment
7. continued freshness of appreciation
8. mystic and peak experiences
9. *Gemeinschaftsgefühl* [a feeling of kinship with others]
10. deeper and more profound interpersonal relations
11. the democratic character structure
12. discrimination between means and ends, between good and evil
13. philosophical, unhostile sense of humor
14. self-actualizing creativeness
15. resistance to enculturation; the transcendence of any particular culture

Maslow pointed out that the self-actualizers he studied were not perfect or even free of major faults. Their strong commitment to their chosen career and values may even lead self-actualizers to be ruthless at times in pursuing their goals; their work may take precedence over others' feelings or needs. In addition, self-actualizers can carry their independence to extremes. Self-actualizers also share many of the problems of average people: guilt, anxiety, sadness, conflict, and so on.

Self-actualization Theory. In his last book, *The Farther Reaches of Human Nature* (1971), Maslow describes eight ways in which individuals self-actualize, or eight behaviors leading to self-actualization. It is not a neat, clean, logically tight discussion, but it represents the culmination of Maslow's thinking on self-actualization.

1. Concentration. "First, self-actualization means experiencing fully, vividly, selflessly, with full concentration and total absorption" (Maslow, 1971, p. 45). Usually, we are relatively unaware of what is going on within or around us. (Most eyewitnesses recount different versions of the same occurrence, for example.) However, we have all had moments of heightened awareness and intense involvement, moments that Maslow would call self-actualizing.

2. Growth Choices. If we think of life as a series of choices, then self-actualization is the process of making each decision a choice for growth. We often have to choose between growth and safety, between progressing and regressing. Each choice has its positive and its negative aspects. To choose safety is to remain with the known and the familiar but to risk becoming stultified and stale. To choose growth is to open oneself to new and challenging experiences but to risk the unknown and possible failure.

3. Self-awareness. In the process of self-actualizing we become more aware of our inner nature and act in accordance with it. This means we decide for ourselves whether we like certain films, books, or ideas, regardless of others' opinions.

I very soon had to come to the conclusion that great talent was not only more or less independent of goodness or health of character but also that we know little about it. (Maslow, 1968, p. 135)

One cannot choose wisely for a life unless he dares to listen to himself, his own self, at each moment in life. (Maslow, 1971, p. 47)

personal reflection

SELF-ACTUALIZATION

Think of four or five self-actualizing people you have known personally or have heard about. What do these people have in common? What are some of their outstanding qualities? Are they different from your own personal heroes and heroines, or are they the same people? In what ways do these people bear out Maslow's theories? In what ways does each differ from Maslow's model of self-actualization?

4. Honesty. Honesty and taking responsibility for one's actions are essential elements in self-actualizing. Rather than pose and give answers that are calculated to please another or to make ourselves look good, we can look within for the answers. Each time we do so, we get in touch with our inner selves.

5. Judgment. The first four steps help us develop the capacity for "better life choices." We learn to trust our own judgment and our own inner feelings and to act accordingly. Maslow believes that following our instincts leads to more accurate judgments about what is constitutionally right for each of us—better choices in art, music, and food, as well as in major life decisions, such as marriage and a career.

6. Self-development. Self-actualization is also a continual process of developing one's potentialities. It means using one's abilities and intelligence and "working to

> [Self-actualization] is not an absence of problems but a moving from transitional or unreal problems to real problems. (Maslow, 1968, p. 115)

Albert Einstein

do well the thing that one wants to do" (Maslow, 1971, p. 48). Great talent or intelligence is not the same as self-actualization; many gifted people fail to use their abilities fully, while others, with perhaps only average talents, accomplish a great deal.

Self-actualization is not a *thing* that someone either has or does not have. It is a never-ending process of making real one's potential. It refers to a way of continually living, working, and relating to the world rather than to a single accomplishment.

7. Peak Experiences. "Peak experiences are transient moments of self-actualization" (Maslow, 1971, p. 48). We are more whole, more integrated, more aware of ourselves and of the world during peak moments. At such times we think, act, and feel most clearly and accurately. We are more loving and accepting of others, have less inner conflict and anxiety, and are better able to put our energies to constructive use. Some people enjoy more peak experiences than others, particularly those Maslow called transcending self-actualizers. *(See the following sections: "Peak Experiences" and "Transcendence and Self-actualization.")*

8. Lack of Ego Defenses. A further step in self-actualization is to recognize our ego defenses and to be able to drop them when appropriate. To do so, we must become more aware of the ways in which we distort our images of ourselves and of the external world—through repression, projection, and other defenses.

Peak Experiences

The term *peak experiences* is a generalization for the best moments of the human being, for the happiest moments of life, for experiences of ecstasy, rapture, bliss, of the greatest joy. (Maslow, 1971, p. 105)

Peak experiences are especially joyous and exciting moments in the life of every individual. Maslow notes that peak experiences are often inspired by intense feelings of love, exposure to great art or music, or the overwhelming beauty of nature. "All peak experiences may be fruitfully understood as completions-of-the-act . . . or as the Gestalt psychologists' closure, or on the paradigm of the Reichian type of complete orgasm, or as total discharge, catharsis, culmination, climax, consummation, emptying or finishing" (Maslow, 1968, p. 111).

Virtually everyone has peak experiences, although we often take them for granted. One's reactions while watching a vivid sunset or listening to a moving piece of music are examples of peak experiences. According to Maslow, peak experiences tend to be triggered by intense, inspiring occurrences: "It looks as if any experience of real excellence, of real perfection . . . tends to produce a peak experience" (1971, p. 175). These experiences may also be triggered by tragic events. Recovering from depression or a serious illness, or confronting death, can initiate extreme moments of love and joy. The lives of most people are filled with long periods of relative inattentiveness, lack of involvement, or even boredom. By contrast, peak experiences, understood in the broadest sense, are those moments when we become deeply involved, excited by, and absorbed in the world.

The most powerful peak experiences are relatively rare. For Maslow, the highest peaks include "feelings of limitless horizons opening up to the vision, the feeling of being simultaneously more powerful and also more helpless than one ever was before, the feeling of great ecstasy and wonder and awe, the loss of placing in time and space" (1970, p. 164). They have been portrayed by poets as moments of ecstasy; by the religious, as deep mystical experiences.

Plateau Experiences. A peak experience is a "high" that may last a few minutes or several hours, but rarely longer. Maslow also discusses a more stable and long-lasting kind of experience that he refers to as a **plateau experience**. The plateau

personal reflection

YOUR OWN PEAK EXPERIENCES

Try to clearly recall one peak experience in your life—a joyous, happy, blissful moment that stands out in your memory. Take a moment to relive the experience. Now consider the following questions.

1. What brought about this experience? Was anything unique about the situation that triggered it?
2. How did you feel at the time? Was this feeling different from your usual experience—emotionally, physically, or intellectually?
3. Did you seem different to yourself? Did the world about you appear different?
4. How long did the experience last? How did you feel afterward?
5. Did the experience have any lasting effects (on your outlook or your relations with others, for example)?
6. How does your own experience compare with Maslow's theories concerning peak experiences and human nature?

To gain a clearer sense of peak experiences, compare experiences with classmates. Look for differences as well as similarities. Are the differences the result of dissimilar situations or perhaps of variations in personality or background? What do the similarities imply about Maslow's ideas or about human potential in general?

experience represents a new and more profound way of viewing and experiencing the world. It involves a fundamental change in attitude, a change that affects one's entire point of view and creates a new appreciation and intensified awareness of the world. Maslow experienced this himself late in life, after his first heart attack. His intensified consciousness of life and sense of death's imminence caused him to see the world in a wholly new way. (For a more complete description in Maslow's own words, *see "The Theory Firsthand"* in this chapter.)

Transcending Self-actualization.   Maslow found that some self-actualizing individuals tend to have many peak experiences, whereas other people have them rarely, if ever. He came to distinguish between self-actualizers who are psychologically healthy, productive human beings, with little or no experience of transcendence, and those for whom transcendence is important or even central. The first group is generally pragmatic in orientation. "Such persons live in the world, coming to fulfillment in it. They master it, lead it, use it for good purposes, as (healthy) politicians or practical people do" (1971, p. 281).

Transcending self-actualizers are more often aware of the sacredness of all things, the transcendent dimension of life, in the midst of daily activities. Their peak or mystical experiences are often valued as the most important aspects of their lives. They tend to think more holistically than "merely healthy" self-actualizers; they are better able to transcend the categories of past, present, and future, and good and evil, and to perceive a unity behind the apparent complexity and contradictions of life. They are more likely to be innovators and original thinkers than systematizers of the ideas of others. As their knowledge develops, so does their sense of humility and ignorance, and they may come to regard the universe with increasing awe.

Because transcenders generally regard themselves as the carriers of their talents and abilities, they are less ego-involved in their work. A transcender is honestly

At the highest levels of development of humaneness, knowledge is positively rather than negatively correlated with a sense of mystery, awe, humility, ultimate ignorance, reverence, and a sense of oblation. (Maslow, 1971, p. 290)

able to say, "I am the best person for this job, and therefore I should have it"; or, on the other hand, to admit, "You are the best one for this job, and you should take it from me."

Not everyone who has had a mystical experience is a transcending self-actualizer. Many who have had such experiences have not developed the psychological health and the productiveness Maslow considered to be essential aspects of self-actualization. Maslow also found as many transcenders among business executives, managers, teachers, and politicians as among poets, musicians, ministers, and the like, for whom transcendence is almost assumed.

Eupsychia

There is a kind of a feedback between the Good Society and the Good Person. They need each other. (Maslow, 1971, p. 19)

Maslow coined the term **eupsychia** (yu-sí-kē-a) to refer to ideal, human-oriented societies and communities. He preferred it to *utopia,* which Maslow considered overused and whose definition suggests impracticality and ungrounded idealism. The development of an ideal society by psychologically healthy, self-actualizing individuals was quite possible, he believed. All members of the community would be engaged in seeking personal development and fulfillment in their work and in their personal lives.

But even an ideal society will not necessarily *produce* self-actualizing individuals.

> A teacher or a culture doesn't create a human being. It doesn't implant within him the ability to love, or to be curious, or to philosophize, or to symbolize, or to be creative. Rather it permits, or fosters, or encourages, or helps what exists in embryo to become real and actual. (Maslow, 1968, p. 161)

Maslow preferred eupsychian, or enlightened, management practices to authoritarian business management. Authoritarian managers assume that workers and management have basically different, mutually incompatible goals—that workers want to earn as much as possible with minimal effort and therefore must be closely watched.

Enlightened managers, however, assume that employees *want* to be creative and productive and that they should be supported and encouraged rather than restricted and controlled. The enlightened approach works best with stable, psychologically healthy employees. Some hostile, suspicious people might function more effectively in an authoritarian structure and might take unfair advantage of greater freedom. Because eupsychian management works only with people who both enjoy and can handle responsibility and self-direction, Maslow suggested that eupsychian communities be composed of self-actualizing people.

Synergy

The term **synergy** was originally used by Maslow's teacher Ruth Benedict (1970) to refer to the degree of interpersonal cooperation and harmony within a society. *Synergy* means cooperation (from the Greek word for "work together"). *Synergy* also refers to a combined action of elements resulting in a total effect that is greater than all the elements taken independently.

As an anthropologist, Benedict observed that people in some societies are clearly happier, healthier, and more efficient than in others. Some groups have beliefs and customs that are basically harmonious and satisfying to their members, whereas other groups have traditions that promote suspicion, fear, and anxiety.

Under conditions of low social synergy, the success of one member brings about loss or failure for another. For example, if each hunter shares the daily catch with only the immediate family, hunting is likely to become strongly competitive. Hunters who improve their techniques or discover a new source of game may try to hide their achievements from others.

High social synergy maximizes cooperation. The cultural belief system reinforces cooperation and positive feelings between individuals, and helps minimize conflict and discord. An example would be a hunting society similar to the one just described, but with a single important difference—communal sharing of the catch. Under these conditions, each hunter benefits from the success of the others.

Maslow also writes of synergy in individuals. Identification with others tends to promote high individual synergy. If the success of another is a source of genuine satisfaction to the individual, then help is freely and generously offered. In a sense, both selfish and altruistic motives are merged. In aiding another, the individual is also seeking his or her own satisfaction.

Synergy can also be found within the individual as unity between thought and action. To force oneself to act indicates some conflict of motives. Ideally, individuals do what they should do because they *want* to do so. The best medicine is taken not only because it is effective but also because it tastes good.

DYNAMICS

Psychological Growth

The pursuit of self-actualization cannot begin until the individual is free of the domination of the lower needs, such as needs for security and esteem. According to Maslow, early frustration of a need may fixate the individual at that level of functioning. For instance, those who were unpopular as children may crave attention, recognition, and praise from others throughout their lives.

> As the person becomes integrated, so does his world. As he feels good, so does the world look good. (Maslow, 1971, p. 165)

The pursuit of satisfaction of higher needs is in itself one index of psychological health. Maslow argues that fulfillment of higher needs is intrinsically more satisfying and that metamotivation is an indication that the individual has progressed beyond a deficiency level of functioning.

Self-actualization represents a long-term commitment to growth and to the development of capabilities to their fullest. Self-actualizing work involves the choice of worthwhile, creative goals. Maslow writes that self-actualizing individuals are attracted to the most challenging and intriguing problems, to questions that demand their best and most creative efforts. They are willing to cope with uncertainty and ambiguity and prefer challenges to easy solutions.

Obstacles to Growth

In Maslow's view, growth motivation is less basic than the drive to satisfy physiological needs and needs for security, esteem, and so on. The process of self-actualization can be limited by (1) negative influences from past experience and resulting unproductive habits; (2) social influence and group pressure that often operate against our own taste and judgment; and (3) inner defenses that keep us out of touch with ourselves. Because self-actualization tops the need hierarchy, it is the weakest need and is easily inhibited by frustration of more fundamental needs. Also,

> There are two sets of forces pulling at the individual, not just one. In addition to the pressures forward toward health, there are also fearful-regressive pressures backward, toward sickness and weakness. (Maslow, 1968, p. 164)

most people avoid self-knowledge, which is at the heart of the process of self-actualization, and are afraid of the changes in self-esteem and self-image that self-knowledge brings.

Poor Habits. Poor habits often inhibit growth. Maslow included in these addiction to drugs or alcohol, poor diet, and other behaviors that adversely affect health and efficiency. A destructive environment or rigid, authoritarian education can easily lead to unproductive habits based on a deficiency orientation. Also, any deep-seated habit tends to interfere with psychological growth because it diminishes the flexibility and openness necessary to operate effectively in a variety of situations.

Group pressure and social propaganda also tend to limit the individual. They act to reduce autonomy and stifle independent judgment; the individual is pressured to substitute external, societal standards for his or her own taste or judgment. A society may inculcate a biased view of human nature as seen, for example, in the Western belief that most human instincts are essentially sinful and must be controlled or subjugated. Maslow argued that this negative attitude often frustrates growth and that the opposite is in fact true; our instincts are essentially good and impulses toward growth are the major sources of human motivation.

Ego Defenses. Maslow considered ego defenses internal obstacles to growth. The first step in dealing with ego defenses is to recognize them and to see clearly how they operate. Then the individual should attempt to minimize distortions created by the defenses. Maslow adds two new defense mechanisms—*desacralization* and the *Jonah complex*—to the traditional psychoanalytic listing of projection, repression, denial, and the like.

Desacralization. **Desacralization** refers to the act of impoverishing one's life by the refusal to treat anything with deep seriousness and concern. Today, few cultural or religious symbols receive the care and respect they once enjoyed; consequently, they have lost their power to thrill, inspire, or even motivate us. Maslow often referred to modern values concerning sex as an example of desacralization. Although a more casual attitude toward sex may lessen frustration and trauma, Maslow believed that sexual experience has lost the power it once had to inspire artists, writers, and lovers.

The Jonah Complex. The **Jonah complex** refers to the refusal to realize one's full capabilities. Just as old Testament Jonah attempted to avoid the responsibilities of becoming a prophet, many people avoid responsibility because they actually fear using their capacities to the fullest. They prefer the security of undemanding goals over ambitious ones that require them to fully extend themselves. This attitude is not uncommon among students who "get by," utilizing only a fraction of their talents and abilities. In the past, many women were taught that a successful career was somehow incongruent with femininity or that intellectual achievement might make them less attractive to men. (See, for example, Horner, 1972.)

This "fear of greatness" may be the largest barrier to self-actualization. Living fully is more than many of us feel we can bear. At times of deepest joy and ecstasy, people often say, "It's too much," or, "I can't stand it." The root of the Jonah complex lies in the fear of letting go of a limited but manageable existence, the fear of losing control, being torn apart, or disintegrating.

Though, in principle, self-actualization is easy, in practice it rarely happens (by my criteria, certainly in less than 1% of the adult population). (Maslow, 1968, p. 204)

STRUCTURE

Body

Maslow does not discuss in detail the body's role in self-actualization. He assumes that once physiological needs are met, the individual is free to deal with needs further up in the hierarchy. However, he writes that the body must receive its due. "Asceticism, self-denial, deliberate rejection of the demands of the organism, at least in the West, tend to produce a diminished, stunted, or crippled organism, and even in the East, bring self-actualization to only a very few, exceptionally strong individuals" (1968, p. 199).

Maslow mentions the intense stimulation of the physical senses in peak experiences, which are often triggered by natural beauty, art, music, or sex. He also indicates that training in dance, art, and other physical forms of expression can provide an important supplement to traditional, cognitively oriented education. Physical and sense-oriented systems of instruction require the kind of active, participatory learning important in all types of education.

Social Relationships

According to Maslow, love and esteem are basic needs fulfilled only in relationship. He deplored the failure of most psychology textbooks even to mention the word *love*, as if psychologists considered love unreal, something that must be reduced to concepts like libido projection or sexual reinforcement.

> The fact is that people are good, if only their fundamental wishes [for affection and security] are satisfied.... Give people affection and security, and they will give affection and be secure in their feelings and behavior. (Maslow in Lowry, 1973b, p. 18)

Will

Will is a vital ingredient in the long-term process of self-actualization. Maslow found that self-actualizing individuals strive hard to attain their chosen goals. "Self-actualization means working to do well the thing that one wants to do. To become a second-rate physician is not a good path to self-actualization. One wants to be first-rate or as good as he can be" (Maslow, 1971, p. 48). His faith in the essential health and goodness of human nature led Maslow to place little emphasis on willpower's role in the process of overcoming unacceptable instincts or impulses. Maslow saw healthy individuals as relatively free from internal conflict, except perhaps for bad habits that must be broken. Will can be employed to develop their abilities still further and to attain ambitious, long-range goals.

Emotions

Positive emotions, Maslow maintained, play a role in self-actualization. He encouraged other psychologists to begin serious research on happiness, calmness, joy, and to investigate fun, games, and play. He believed that negative emotions, tension, and conflict drain energy and inhibit effective functioning.

> If you deliberately plan to be less than you are capable of being, then I warn you that you'll be deeply unhappy for the rest of your life. (Maslow, 1971, p. 36)

For Maslow, maturity includes "being able to give oneself over completely to an emotion, not only of love but also of anger, fascination" (1966, p. 38). Maslow goes on to point out that our fear of deep emotions leads us to desacralize much of life or to use intellectualization as a defense against feeling. Orthodox science, he believed, has mistakenly taken "cool" perceiving and detached thinking as the best means for discovering scientific truth. This limited approach has tended to banish, from scientific study, experiences of wonder, awe, ecstasy, and other forms of transcendence.

We begin life filled with joy and creativity.

Intellect

Maslow emphasized the need for holistic thinking, which deals with systems of relationships and wholes rather than with individual parts. He found that peak experiences often contain striking examples of thinking that break through the usual dichotomies with which we experience reality. During peak experiences, individuals have often reported seeing past, present, and future as one, life and death as part of a single process, and good and evil within the same whole.

Holistic thinking also appears in creative individuals who break with the past and look beyond conventional categories in investigating possible new relationships. This kind of thinking requires freedom, openness, and an ability to cope with inconsistency and uncertainty. Although such ambiguity can be threatening to some, it is part of the essential joy of creative problem solving for self-actualizers.

Maslow (1970) has written that creative people are **problem centered** rather than **means centered.** Problem-centered people focus primarily on the demands and requirements of the desired goals. Means-centered individuals, on the other hand, often become so concerned with technique or methodology that they may do intensely detailed work in trivial areas. Problem centering stands in contrast to ego centering, in which individuals see what they wish rather than what actually is.

Self

Self-actualizing people, those who have come to a high level of maturation, health, and self-fulfillment, have so much to teach us that sometimes they seem almost like a different breed of human beings. (Maslow, 1968, p. 71)

Maslow defines the *self* as an individual's inner core or inherent nature—one's tastes, values, and goals. Understanding one's inner nature and acting in accordance with it is essential to actualizing the self.

Maslow approaches understanding the self by studying those individuals most in tune with their own natures, those who provide the best examples of self-expression or self-actualization. However, he does not discuss the self as a specific structure within the personality.

Therapist

For Maslow, as for Rogers, psychotherapy is effective primarily because it involves an intimate and trusting relationship with another human being. Along with Adler, Maslow

What happens?

believed that a good therapist is like an older brother or sister, someone who offers care and love. But more than this, Maslow proposed the model of the Taoist helper, a person who offers assistance without interference. A familiar example is a good coach who works with the athlete's natural style to strengthen and improve his or her style. A skillful coach does not try to force all athletes into the same mold. Good parents are like Taoist helpers when they resist doing everything for their child. The child develops best by means of guidance, not interference.

Although Maslow underwent psychoanalysis for several years and received informal training in psychotherapy, his interests always revolved around research and writing rather than the actual practice of psychotherapy. Maslow (1987) did make an important distinction between what he called *basic needs therapy,* designed to help people meet primary needs such as safety, belonging, love, and respect, and *insight therapy,* which is a profound, long-term process of growth in self-understanding.

Maslow viewed therapy as a way of satisfying the frustrated basic needs for love and esteem in virtually everyone who seeks psychological help. He argued (1970) that warm human relationships can provide much of the same support found in therapy.

Good therapists should love and care for the being or essence of the people they work with. Maslow (1971) wrote that those who seek to change or manipulate others lack this essential attitude. For example, he argued that a true dog lover would never crop the animal's ears or tail, and one who really loves flowers would not cut or twist them to make fancy floral arrangements.

It has been pointed out that a therapist can repeat the same mistakes for 40 years and then call it "rich clinical experience." (Maslow, 1968, p. 87)

RECENT DEVELOPMENTS: MASLOW'S INFLUENCE

Although Maslow did little in the way of formal research, his work has inspired dedicated investigators. Shostrom (1963) developed the Personal Orientation Inventory (POI) as a measure of self-actualization. A significant body of research has been conducted using this instrument (Gray, 1986; Kelly & Chovan, 1985; Rychman, 1985). Maslow's concept of peak experience has also sparked research (Wilson & Spencer, 1990; see Mathes, et al., 1982, for a literature review). Case studies of self-actualizing individuals have confirmed Maslow's theory and also related self-actualization to Dabrowski's (1967) theory of emotional development (Piechowski, 1978, 1990; Piechowski & Tyska, 1982; Brennan & Piechowski, 1991). Content validation has further clarified Maslow's original formulation of self-actualization (Leclerc, et al., 1998).

Maslow's work continues to have an impact on the study of religion (Fuller, 1994), education (Kunc, 1992), and business (Schott, 1992). His long-out-of-print classic on business, *Eupsychian Management,* has been reprinted as *Maslow on Management* (Maslow, 1998a). Other major works (Maslow, 1994, 1998b) have been reprinted as well. A new biography details Maslow's life and summarizes his thinking (Hoffman, 1999).

EVALUATION

I am a new breed—a theoretical psychologist parallel to . . . theoretical biologists. . . . I think of myself as a scientist rather than an essayist or philosopher. I feel myself very bound to and by the facts that I am trying to perceive, not to create. (Maslow in *International Study Project,* 1972, p. 63)

Maslow's great strength lies in his concern for the areas of human functioning that most other theorists have almost completely ignored. He is one of few psychologists who have seriously investigated the positive dimensions of human experience.

His major contributions might be summarized in the following three central ideas:

1. Human beings have an innate tendency to move toward higher levels of health, creativity, insight, and self-fulfillment.
2. Neurosis is basically a blockage of the innate tendency toward self-actualization.
3. Business efficiency and personal growth are not incompatible. In fact, the process of self-actualization brings each individual to greater efficiency, creativity, and productivity.

Maslow's experimental work was mostly inconclusive; *exploratory* might be a better term to describe it, and he was the first to acknowledge this:

It's just that I haven't got the time to do careful experiments myself. They take too long, in view of the years that I have left and the extent of what I want to do. So I myself do only "quick-and-dirty" little pilot explorations, mostly with a few subjects only, inadequate to publish but enough to convince myself that they are probably true and will be confirmed one day. Quick little commando raids, guerrilla attacks. (Maslow in *International Study Project,* 1972, pp. 66–67)

Maslow never sought to experimentally "prove" or verify his ideas. His research was more a way of clarifying and adding detail to his theories. Even so, Maslow sometimes seems like a philosopher who remains aloof from the possible contradictions of new facts or experiences. He was generally clear on what he wanted to demonstrate in his research, but he rarely seemed to find new data to alter his preconceived ideas. For example, Maslow always stressed the importance of positive triggers for peak experiences: experiences of love, beauty, great music, and so on. His writings tend to ignore negative triggers, despite the fact that many people report their most intense peak experiences as preceded by negative emotions (fear and depression, for instance) that then transcend and transform into highly positive states. (See, for example, William James's *The Varieties of Religious Experience*, 1943.) Maslow's investigations seldom uncovered this kind of new information.

Maslow's greatest value is as a psychological theorist who has stressed the positive dimensions of human experience—particularly the tremendous potential in all men and women. Maslow has been an inspiration for virtually all humanistic and transpersonal psychologists. In his book on Maslow and modern psychology, Colin Wilson writes

> Maslow was the first person to create a truly comprehensive psychology stretching, so to speak, from the basement to the attic. He accepted Freud's clinical method without accepting his philosophy. . . . The "transcendent" urges—aesthetic, creative, religious—are as basic and permanent a part of human nature as dominance or sexuality. If they are less obviously "universal," this is only because fewer human beings reach the point at which they take over. Maslow's achievement is enormous. Like all original thinkers, he has opened up a new way of seeing the universe. (1972, pp. 181–184)

Maslow has been called "the greatest American psychologist since William James" (*Journal of Transpersonal Psychology*, 1970). Although many might consider this praise somewhat exaggerated, no one can deny Maslow's central importance as an original thinker and a pioneer in human potential psychology.

TRANSPERSONAL PSYCHOLOGY

Maslow added transpersonal psychology to the first three forces in Western psychology—behaviorism, psychoanalysis, and humanistic psychology. For Maslow, behaviorism and psychoanalysis were too limited in scope to form the basis of a complete psychology of human nature. Psychoanalysis is derived largely from studies of psychopathology. Behaviorism has attempted to reduce the complexities of human nature to simpler principles but has failed to address fully such issues as values, consciousness, and love.

In the early 1960s, humanistic psychology emerged from the work of Maslow, Rogers, and other theorists concerned with psychological health and effective functioning. Many humanistic psychologists have used Maslow's theories, especially his work on self-actualization, as the framework for their writing and research.

In 1968, Maslow called attention to the limitations of the humanistic model. In exploring the farthest reaches of human nature, he found possibilities beyond self-actualization. When peak experiences are especially powerful, the sense of self dissolves into an awareness of a greater unity. The term *self-actualization* did not seem to fit these experiences.

Transpersonal psychology contributes to the more traditional concerns of the discipline an acknowledgment of the spiritual aspect of human experience. This level of experience has been described primarily in religious literature, in unscientific and often theologically biased language. A major task of transpersonal psychology is to provide a scientific language and a scientific framework for this material.

In the late 1960s, Abraham Maslow and Anthony Sutich, a psychotherapist and founder of the *Journal of Humanistic Psychology*, decided that "transpersonal" would be the most appropriate term for this new branch of psychology, and in 1969

> The human being needs a framework of values, a philosophy of life . . . to live by and understand by, in about the same sense that he needs sunlight, calcium or love. (Maslow, 1968, p. 206)

Sutich launched the *Journal of Transpersonal Psychology*. In 1971, the *Association for Transpersonal Psychology,* the first formal association dedicated to transpersonal studies, was founded. Maslow introduced the new field as follows:

> I should say also that I consider Humanistic, Third Force Psychology to be transitional, a preparation for a still "higher" Fourth Psychology, transpersonal, transhuman, centered in the cosmos rather than in human needs and interest, going beyond humanness, identity, self-actualization and the like. . . . We need something "bigger than we are" to be awed by and to commit ourselves to in a new, naturalistic, empirical, non-churchly sense, perhaps as Thoreau and Whitman, William James and John Dewey did. (Maslow, 1968, pp. iii–iv)

One basic tenet of transpersonal psychology is that in each individual resides a deeper or true self experienced in transcendent states of consciousness. Distinct from the personality and the personal ego, it is the source of inner wisdom, health, and harmony.

Webster's Tenth New Collegiate Dictionary defines *transpersonal* as "extending or going beyond the personal or individual." The term refers to an extension of identity beyond both individuality and personality. One premise of transpersonal psychology is that we do not know the full range of human potential. The sense of a vast potential for growth within the individual provides a context for transpersonal psychology. Collections of basic essays and articles on transpersonal psychology include Ornstein (1973), Tart (1969, 1975), Walsh and Shapiro (1983), Walsh and Vaughan (1980, 1993). Frager (1989) and Valle (1989) have provided overviews of the field.

Approaches to Transpersonal Psychology

Without the transcendent and the transpersonal, we get sick, violent and nihilistic, or else hopeless and apathetic. (Maslow, 1968, p. iv)

Major contributors to the field of transpersonal psychology differ in their approaches and interests. The following is a series of excerpts that reflect these varying approaches.

One of the earliest formal definitions of the new discipline was published in the first issue of the *Journal of Transpersonal Psychology:*

> Transpersonal (or "fourth force") Psychology is the title given to an emerging force in the psychology field by a group of psychologists and professional men and women from other fields who are interested in those *ultimate* human capacities and potentialities that have no systematic place in positivistic or behavioristic theory ("first force"), classical psychoanalytic theory ("second force"), or humanistic psychology ("third force"). (Sutich, 1969, p. 15)

For some, transpersonal psychology is particularly important because it includes the psychological wisdom of other cultures and traditions:

> Transpersonal psychology is bringing together the insights of the individualistic psychologies of the West with the spiritual psychologies of the East and Middle East. The realization that our own training has been limited and that Western ideas are not the center of the psychological universe is disturbing at first. The feeling passes when one becomes aware of the amazing amount of work that has already been accomplished, but which awaits validation with the scientific and experimental tools of Western psychology, to be fully realized. (Fadiman, 1980, p. 181)

Many other transpersonal psychologists have sought to integrate insights and concepts from Asian sources (see, for example, Frager, 1989; Walsh, 1989; as well as

personal reflection

TRANSPERSONAL EXPERIENCE

Think of a time when your experience went beyond your usual sense of self or identity. It may have been an active time of peak performance, a powerful experience of great beauty, or a deeply spiritual shift in consciousness. How did the experience affect you? Did it have a lasting impact on your life in some ways? What did you learn from it?

Chapters 13 to 16 in this book). Asian psychologies generally focus more on spiritual levels of experience and much less on the pathological. They include maps of states of consciousness, discussions of developmental levels, and stages that extend beyond traditional psychological formulations. Walsh (1989) summarizes the literature on Eastern meditation and related practices as psychotherapeutic. Another approach emphasizes transpersonal psychology's inclusion of experiences ignored or explained away in other fields of psychology:

> Transpersonal experiences may be defined as experiences in which the sense of identity or self extends beyond *(trans)* the individual or personal to encompass wider aspects of humankind, life, *psyche,* and cosmos. . . . Transpersonal psychology is the psychological study of transpersonal experiences and their correlates [which include daily lives, creativity, or spirituality inspired by such experiences]. (Walsh & Vaughan, 1993, p. 3)

In a survey of forty definitions of the field (Lajoie & Shapiro, 1992), the authors synthesized the following: "Transpersonal psychology is concerned with the study of humanity's highest potential and with the recognition, understanding, and realization of unitive, spiritual, and transcendent experiences."

Transpersonal research is a rapidly growing field. Anderson and Braud (1998) provide extensive coverage of a wide variety of qualitative approaches to research without ignoring quantitative methods. They illustrate ways of empirically studying extraordinary human experience, including ultimate values and meanings, peak experiences, transcendence, and higher awareness. Hart, et al. (2000) explore various ways of knowing, both ourselves and the world, in a collection of essays by respected thinkers in transpersonal psychology. Scotton, et al. (1996) have surveyed the roots of transpersonal psychology in William James and Carl Jung, and in shamanism, Christian, Jewish, and Eastern mysticism. They also include the latest research on meditation and parapsychology, and present case studies illustrating work with spiritual emergencies.

Washburn (1995) has analyzed the structure and development of consciousness. He grounds the notion of ego transcendence in the psychoanalytic theory of ego development (Washburn, 1999).

The Perennial Model

The underlying concept of human nature in transpersonal psychology is not a new one. It has always existed in human culture. It has been called the "perennial philosophy" (Huxley, 1944), the "perennial religion" (Smith, 1976), and the "perennial psychology" (Wilber, 1977). What is new is the task of bringing together ideas from many different traditions and cultures to form a modern psychological language and scientific framework. (See, for example, Vaughan, 1995.)

Not all transpersonal psychologists or scholars of religion agree with the assumption of a perennial tradition underlying the diverse forms of religion. At the other extreme is the position that denies *any* fundamental and neutral mystical experience subsequently interpreted by each mystic. The mystical experience itself is shaped by the mystic's tradition and cannot meaningfully be taken out of its cultural and religious context. (See, for example, Katz, 1978.)

The perennial model includes the following four basic premises (Valle, 1989):

1. A transcendent reality or unity binds together all (apparently separate) phenomena.
2. The ego or individual self is but a reflection of a greater, transpersonal ("beyond the personal") self or oneness. We come from and are grounded in that self. However, we have become estranged from our origins and we need to return to them in order to become fully healthy and whole human beings.
3. The fact that individuals can directly experience this reality or greater self is at the core of the spiritual dimensions of life.
4. This experience involves a qualitative shift in experiencing oneself and the larger world. It is a powerful, self-validating experience.

Another transpersonal theorist, Ralph Metzner (1986), has collected descriptions of transpersonal growth, or the transformation of human consciousness. These portrayals include such key metaphors as the transforming of a caterpillar into a butterfly; awakening from a dream to reality; moving from captivity to liberation; going from darkness to light; being purified by inner fire; going from fragmentation to wholeness; journeying to a place of vision and power; returning to the source; and dying and being reborn.

A New Paradigm

It should be clear by now that transpersonal psychology is based on premises radically different from those of other approaches to psychology. It is what Thomas Kuhn (1962) called a *new paradigm.*

Kuhn defined *paradigm* as a set of values and beliefs shared by the members of a scientific community. In any given community, both theory and research will conform to these fundamental beliefs and values. Critical progress in science, Kuhn points out, often comes from a paradigm shift. Unfortunately, initial resistance to the new paradigm is almost inevitable. Advocates of the new paradigm are frequently accused of using unscientific methods or studying unscientific problems.

Tart (1975) has given a detailed analysis of the ways in which the paradigm of transpersonal psychology differs from that of traditional psychology. These include the following:

1. *Old:* Physics is the ultimate science, the study of the real world. Dreams, emotions, and human experience in general are all derivative.
   New: Psychological reality is just as real as physical reality. And modern theoretical physics indicates that the two are not so far apart.
2. *Old:* The individual exists in relative isolation from the surrounding environment. We are each essentially independent creatures. (And so we can seek to control the world as if we are not part of it.)
   New: All forms of life share a deep level of psychological/spiritual connection. Each individual is a cosmic creature, deeply embedded in the cosmos.

3. *Old:* Our ordinary state of consciousness is the best, most rational, most adaptive way the mind can be organized. All other states are inferior or pathological. Even "creative states" are suspect, often seen as bordering on the pathological (for example, "regression").

    New: Higher orders of feeling, awareness, and even rationality are possible. What we call waking consciousness is really more like "waking sleep," in which we use but a small fraction of our awareness or capacities.

4. *Old:* Seeking altered states of consciousness is a sign of pathology or immaturity.

    New: Seeking to experience different states of consciousness is a natural aspect of healthy human growth.

5. *Old:* The basic development of personality is complete by adulthood, except for neurotics, people with traumatic childhoods, and the like.

    New: Ordinary adults exhibit only a rudimentary level of maturity. The basic "healthy" adult personality is merely a foundation for spiritual work and the development of a far deeper level of wisdom and maturity.

In various spiritual traditions, authorities point out, our usual state of consciousness is not only limited—it is also dreamlike and illusory. From this perspective, psychotherapies that deal only with personality dynamics are superficial palliatives, just as giving candy to a sick friend is comforting though ineffective as treatment.

The Work of Ken Wilber

Ken Wilber is an important transpersonal theorist. In his first major work, *The Spectrum of Consciousness* (1977), Wilber integrates a vast array of Eastern and Western thought into a single model. According to Wilber, growth is the healing of a series of dichotomies within the individual. First is the split between conscious and unconscious, or persona and shadow. Next is the division between mind and body. Following this is the separation of organism and environment. The final stage is the attainment of unity with the universe. Each level of consciousness, Wilber argues, has its own issues, problems, and appropriate forms of therapy or spiritual practice.

Wilber (1980) has also written about human growth and development in terms of two fundamental processes. First is the *outward arc,* the process of personal, ego development. The second process is the *inward arc,* the process of transpersonal, spiritual development, from self-consciousness to *superconsciousness.*

> The story of the Outward Arc is the story of the Hero—the story of the terrible battle to break free of the sleep in the subconscious. . . . The story of the Outward Arc is also the story of the ego, for the ego *is* the Hero. . . . But the Outward Arc, the move from subconsciousness to self-consciousness, is only half of the story of the evolution of consciousness. . . . Beyond the self-conscious ego, according to mystic-sages, lies the path of return and the psychology of eternity—the Inward Arc. (Wilber, 1980, p. 4)

In the outward arc, we begin with what Wilber calls the *membership self,* as we acquire language and become socialized in a particular culture. Next comes the stage of the *mental egoic self,* in which we assume a positive self-concept and a healthy, balanced ego. The final stage of the outward arc is the *integrated self,* the stage of self-actualization, generally the highest level of human development identified in Western psychology.

The inner arc begins with the *low-subtle self,* which includes highly developed intuition and various kinds of extrasensory perceptions. The next stage, the *high-subtle self,*

	Inner	Outer
Individual	subjective experience	behavior
Collective	culture	social systems

FIGURE 12.2 Wilbur's Four-Quadrant Model

has been described by the world's great mystics as the experience of bliss and visions of divine realms. The final stages are the *low-causal self* and the *high-causal self,* portrayed in mystical literature as the highest levels of illumination and spiritual attainment.

Wilber (1995, 1996) views the course of evolution as the ongoing manifestation of Spirit. In the higher stages of spiritual development, Spirit becomes conscious of itself.

Wilber (2000b) has refined his stage theory. Each stage is seen as a wave of consciousness, and each wave "transcends and includes" its predecessors. He has also developed a four-quadrant model (Wilber, 1996, 2000a, b) that provides a powerful metatheory that encompasses most conceivable approaches to human experience and behavior. The variables that generate the four quadrants shown in Figure 12.2 are Individual and Collective, and Inner and Outer.

The upper right quadrant is the individual viewed objectively and includes physiology and also behavior (the traditional domains of academic psychology). The upper left quadrant is the individual's *subjective* experience, and includes thoughts, feelings, values, and consciousness. The lower left quadrant includes those patterns in consciousness shared by members of a particular culture or subculture. The lower right quadrant includes the *objective* correlate of cultural patterns. Wilber calls these "intersubjective realities" the social system, which includes social institutions, patterns of communication, and economic and political structures.

The Work of Stanislav Grof

Another important transpersonal theorist is Stanislav Grof, a European psychiatrist who has written extensively on psychedelic research and altered states of consciousness. The mind, Grof (1993) says, can be compared to a hologram. One piece of a hologram retains all the information of the original whole. Grof argues that although we are separate individuals, our minds contain universal patterns and truths in addition to our personal experience.

Grof (1975, 1993) has described the major characteristics of psychedelic experience. They include transcendence of space and time; transcendence of distinctions between matter, energy, and consciousness; and transcendence of the separation between the individual and the external world.

Grof (1975) has broken down psychedelic experiences into four categories: abstract, psychodynamic, perinatal, and transpersonal.

1. Abstract experiences, which are primarily sensory, include the extraordinarily vivid perception of colors or sounds.

2. Psychodynamic experiences, in which emotionally charged memories are relived, also include symbolic experiences similar to dream images.

3. Perinatal experiences deal with birth and death. Grof discusses four stages of the birth process. The first begins from the time before labor, the developing child resting comfortably in the womb. This stage is associated with a sense of limitlessness and with symbols such as the ocean. The second stage, the onset of labor, is associated with anxiety and threat, a sense of being trapped. During the third stage, the fetus moves through the birth canal. This stage is symbolized by struggle for survival, crushing pressure, and a sense of suffocation. The fourth stage is birth itself, the struggle that finally ends in relief and relaxation. It may include visions of light and beauty, a sense of liberation or salvation, or the experience of death and rebirth.

4. Transpersonal experiences include the sense of consciousness expanding beyond ego boundaries and beyond space and time. Among other experiences are extrasensory perception, visions of archetypal images, ancestral memories, memories of prior incarnations, or the sense of merging completely with others.

Grof has argued that these four levels are closely interrelated. He has observed that work with psychodynamic memories tends to lead to perinatal and then transpersonal experiences. Conversely, those who have had profound spiritual or transpersonal experiences find it easier to work with psychological issues.

Grof (1988) has developed the techniques of *holotropic breathwork,* which enable individuals to enter states of consciousness similar to psychedelic experiences. Many individuals have reported breathwork experiences that replicate his LSD studies. He has summarized the literature on nonordinary states of consciousness (Grof, 1998) and has provided a systematic and comprehensive overview of his forty years of research on consciousness (Grof, 2000).

The Work of Michael Washburn

In his book *The Ego and the Dynamic Ground,* Michael Washburn provides a transpersonal theory of psychological development. Washburn presumes "the ego, as ordinarily constituted, can be transcended and that a higher, trans-egoic plane or stage of life is possible" (Washburn, 1995, p. v). This higher stage occurs when the ego is rooted in its *dynamic ground,* the psychological locus of the divine. Washburn indentifies three major stages in human development:

1. **Pre-egoic:** from infancy to early childhood. The ego is weak and undeveloped and dominated by the dynamic ground.
2. **Egoic:** in late childhood through middle adulthood. The ego makes psychological growth possible by dissociating from the dynamic ground through repression.
3. **Trans-egoic:** later adulthood. In later adulthood a developed and mature ego becomes integrated with the dynamic ground.

Washburn has included elements of thought from both Freud and Jung. His development process is similar to Jung's individuation. With Freud, Washburn considers repression and regression major elements in development. However, where Freud discussed repression in the service of the ego, Washburn focuses on repression in the service of transcendence.

Progress through Washburn's three stages is nonlinear. The individual continues to repress or deny the dynamic ground and return to the dynamic ground. This cycle continues until final integration is reached.

Psychosynthesis

If humanistic science may be said to have any goals beyond sheer fascination with the human mystery and enjoyment of it, these would be to release the individual from external control and to make him less predictable to the observer . . . even though perhaps more predictable to himself. (Maslow, 1966, p. 40)

Another important transpersonal pioneer is Roberto Assagioli (1971). Assagioli, an Italian psychiatrist who studied with both Freud and Jung, developed the system called *psychosynthesis.*

> The fact that we have spoken of the ordinary self and the profounder Self, must not be taken to mean that there are two separate and independent 'I's, two beings in us. The Self in reality is one. What we call the ordinary self is that small part of the deeper Self that the waking consciousness is able to assimilate in a given moment. . . . It is a reflection of what can become ever more clear and vivid; and it can perhaps someday succeed in uniting itself with its source. (Assagioli in Hardy, 1987, p. 31)

Assagioli distinguishes two levels of work in psychosynthesis: personal and transpersonal. *Personal psychosynthesis* focuses on the integration of the personality around the personal self. *Transpersonal psychosynthesis* involves alignment of the personality with the transpersonal self. Assagioli points out that the self at the personality level is basically a reflection of the transpersonal self.

Psychosynthesis has been applied to healing our deepest, primal wounding (Firman & Gila, 1997). Modern psychosynthesis practitioners have integrated psychosynthesis with developmental, personality, and clinical theory and research (Firman & Gila, 2000).

Evaluation of Transpersonal Psychology

The transpersonal realm of human experience was once the exclusive domain of the priest, shaman, or spiritual teacher. Today, the transpersonal is very much the concern of psychology. When we deal with such human questions as values, meaning, and purpose, we inevitably raise issues of a spiritual, transpersonal nature.

Carl Jung has argued that only through the transformation of consciousness can we change and grow.

> All the greatest and most important problems of life are fundamentally insoluble. . . . They can never be solved, but only outgrown. This "outgrowing" proved on further investigation to require a new level of consciousness. Some higher or wider interest appeared on the patient's horizon. (Jung in Jacoby, 1959, p. 302)

As a field, transpersonal psychology is devoted to the study and explication of this process of growth and the investigation of these new levels of consciousness.

The Theory Firsthand

EXCERPT FROM "THE PLATEAU EXPERIENCE"

The following quotation, from the Journal of Transpersonal Psychology, *is taken from a discussion between Maslow and several other psychologists.*

I found that as I got older, my peak experiences became less intense and also became less frequent. In discussing this matter with other people who are getting older, I received this same sort of reaction. My impression is that this may have to do with the aging process. It makes sense because to some extent, I've learned that I've become somewhat afraid of peak experiences because I wonder if my body can stand them. A peak experience can produce great turmoil in the autonomic nervous system; it may be that a decrease in peak experiences is nature's way of protecting the body....

As these poignant and emotional discharges died down in me, something else happened which has come into my consciousness which is a very precious thing. A sort of precipitation occurred of what might be called the sedimentation or the fallout from illuminations, insights, and other life experiences that were very important—tragic experiences included. The result has been a kind of unitive consciousness which has certain advantages and certain disadvantages over the peak experiences. I can define this unitive consciousness very simply for me as the simultaneous perception of the sacred and the ordinary, or the miraculous and the rather constant or easy-without-effort sort of thing.

I now perceive under the aspect of eternity and become mythic, poetic, and symbolic about ordinary things. This is the Zen experience, you know. There is nothing excepted and nothing special, but one lives in a world of miracles all the time. There is a paradox because it is miraculous and yet it doesn't produce an autonomic burst.

This type of consciousness has certain elements in common with peak experience—awe, mystery, surprise, and esthetic shock. These elements are present, but are constant rather than climactic. It certainly is a temptation to use as kind of a model, a paradigm for the peaking experience, the sexual orgasm, which is a mounting up to a peak and a climax, and then a drop in the completion and its ending. Well, this other type of experience must have another model. The words that I would use to describe this kind of experience would be "a high plateau." It is to live at a constantly high level in the sense of illumination or awakening or in Zen, in the easy or miraculous, in the nothing special. It is to take rather casually the poignancy and the preciousness and the beauty of things, but not to make a big deal out of it because it's happening every hour, you know, all the time.

This type of experience has the advantage, in the first place, that it's more voluntary than peak experience. For example, to enter deeply into this type of consciousness, I can go to an art museum or a meadow rather than into a subway. In the plateau experiences, you're not as surprised because they are more volitional than peak experiences. Further, I think you can teach plateau experiences; you could hold classes in miraculousness.

Another aspect I have noticed is that it's possible to sit and look at something miraculous for an hour and enjoy every second of it. On the other hand, you can't have an hour-long orgasm. In this sense, the plateau type of experience is better. It has a great advantage, so to speak, over the climactic, the orgasm, the peak. The descending into a valley, and living on the high plateau doesn't imply this. It is much more casual.

There are some other aspects of this experience. There tends to be more serenity rather than an emotionality. Our tendency is to regard the emotional person as an explosive type. However, calmness must also be brought into one's psychology. We need the serene as well as the poignantly emotional....

The important point that emerges from these plateau experiences is that they're essentially cognitive. As a matter of fact, almost by definition, they represent a witnessing of the world. The plateau experience is a witnessing of reality. It involves seeing the symbolic, or the mythic, the poetic, the transcendent, the miraculous, the unbelievable, all of which I think are part of the real world instead of existing only in the eyes of the beholder.

There is a sense of certainty about plateau experience. It feels very, very good to be able to see the world as miraculous and not merely in the concrete, not reduced only to the behavioral, not limited only to the here and now. You know, if you get stuck in the here and now, that's a reduction.

Well, it's very easy to get sloppy with your words and you can go on about the beauty of the world, but the fact is that these plateau experiences are described quite well in many literatures. This is not the standard description of the acute mystical experience, but the way in which the world looks if the mystic experience really takes. If your mystical experience changes your life, you go about your business as the great mystics did. For example, the great saints could have mystical revelations, but also could run a monastery. You can run a grocery store and pay the bills, but still carry on this sense of witnessing the world in the way you did in the great moments of mystic perception. (Maslow in Krippner, 1972, pp. 112–115)

CHAPTER HIGHLIGHTS

■ A theory of personality, to be considered viable and accurate, ought to include the heights as well as the depths that an individual might reach. One should investigate the most creative, mature, and well-integrated people to study the upper reaches of psychological health and maturity.

- In the hierarchy of needs, physiological urges (hunger, sleep, sex, etc.) must be met before psychological needs. Basic psychological needs are safety (stability, order), love (belonging), esteem (self-respect, recognition), and self-actualization (development of capacities). Needs emerge from and build on the needs before.
- The hierarchy of needs model suggests that behaviorism, psychoanalysis, humanistic psychology, and transpersonal psychology each have their place and their relevance; no one approach is better than another.
- Deprivation of basic needs (including the need for self-actualization as well as physiological needs) can cause neurosis and maladjustment. The satisfaction of those needs is the only treatment.
- People still feel frustrated, even if all their other needs are met, unless they utilize their talents and capacities and experience self-actualization.
- Self-actualizing people are dedicated to a cause or a vocation, without exception. Commitment to something greater than oneself and to doing well one's chosen tasks, are two requirements for growth. Major characteristics of self-actualizing people are hard work, courage, creativity, and spontaneity.
- Maslow identified eight behaviors that lead to self-actualization: concentration, growth choices, self-awareness, honesty, judgment, self-development, peak experiences, and lack of ego defenses.
- Being psychology tends to be most applicable to self-actualizers, and peak experiences are generally related to this realm as well. In deficiency cognition, objects are seen only as need fulfillers; in being cognition, perceptions are less likely to be distorted by wants or needs.
- Until the individual is free of the domination of the lower needs, such as for security and esteem, the pursuit of self-actualization cannot begin. The pursuit of higher needs is itself one index of psychological health.
- Growth motivation is less basic than physiological drives or psychological needs for security, esteem, and so forth. Self-actualization may be hindered by negative influences from past experience and resulting poor habits, social pressure and group influence, and inner defenses that keep the individual out of touch with his or her inner self.
- Ego defenses are internal obstacles to growth. To become aware of them and to see clearly how they operate is the first step in dealing with them. It is important, as well, to minimize the distortions they create. Maslow has added desacralization and the Jonah complex to the traditional psychoanalytic listing of defenses.
- Maslow recognized possibilities beyond self-actualization. When peak experiences are especially powerful, the sense of self dissolves into an awareness of a greater unity.
- The field of transpersonal psychology acknowledges the importance of the transcendent aspects of human experience. Maslow called this level of awareness the fourth force in Western psychology—after behaviorism, psychoanalysis, and humanistic psychology.

KEY CONCEPTS

Desacralization The act of impoverishing one's life by the refusal to treat anything with deep concern and seriousness. It may result from a fear of deep emotion.

Eupsychia Ideal, human-oriented communities and societies, composed of psychologically healthy, self-actualizing individuals.

Hierarchy of needs A model of human drives that suggests that basic physiological needs must be met before basic psychological needs can be addressed. Each level of need emerges from the one before. At the top are needs for growth and self-actualization.

Jonah complex The refusal to realize one's full capabilities. It is rooted in the fear of letting go of a familiar but limited existence, of being torn apart, disintegrating, or losing control. The complex may be a major obstacle to self-actualization.

Means centered A characteristic of individuals who become disproportionately engaged in the techniques or methodology of a project or process, often losing sight of the goals.

Metagrumbles Level of complaints that correspond to the frustration of metaneeds, such as justice, perfection, beauty, truth. These grumbles usually indicate that more basic needs are reasonably well satisfied.

Metamotivation Behavior inspired by growth values and needs. It occurs most commonly among self-actualizing people.

Peak experiences Those exciting, joyous moments when individuals become deeply involved and absorbed in the world. Such experiences are often inspired by intense feelings of love, by the beauty of nature, or by exposure to great art and music.

Physiological needs In Maslow's hierarchy of needs, the most basic human wants. Biological needs for oxygen, food, drink, sleep, and sex are included here.

Plateau experiences A fundamental change in attitude that affects one's entire point of view and creates an intensified awareness and a new appreciation of the world. More stable and longer lasting than a peak experience, it represents a new, more profound way of experiencing and viewing the world.

Problem centered One of the characteristics of creative people, in which the focus is on the requirements of the desired goals. This approach contrasts with ego centering, in which individuals see what they wish rather than what actually is.

Psychological needs In Maslow's hierarchy, the human drives that cannot be satisfied until the physiological needs are met. Psychological needs include (in this order) safety and security, belonging and love, self-esteem and respect, and self-actualization.

Self-actualization In Maslow's system, an ongoing process in which one's capacities are creatively, joyfully, and fully utilized. It is a way of continually working, living, and relating to the world.

Synergy The combined action of elements that results in a total effect greater than the sum of all the elements taken independently. The word also refers to cooperation among individuals.

ANNOTATED BIBLIOGRAPHY

Maslow, A. H. (1968). *Toward a psychology of being* (2nd ed.). New York: Van Nostrand.

> Maslow's most popular and widely available book. It includes material on deficiency versus being, growth psychology, creativity, and values.

Maslow, A. H. (1971). *The farther reaches of human nature.* New York: Viking Press.

> In many ways, Maslow's best book. A collection of articles on psychological health, creativeness, values, education, society, metamotivation, and transcendence. Includes a complete bibliography of Maslow's writings.

Maslow, A. H. (1987). *Motivation and personality* (3rd ed.). New York: Harper & Row.

> A psychology textbook that provides a more technical treatment of Maslow's work, including motivation theory, the needs hierarchy, and self-actualization.

Web Sites

www.maslow.com/

> A complete guide to publications by and about Maslow, including audiovisual material and unpublished papers and letters.

www.maslow.org/

> Includes articles on Maslow's ideas, biographical sketches, and related resources in humanistic and transpersonal psychology.

www.sagemagic.com/

> SAGE is an acronym for Self-Actualization Growth Education. This site is dedicated to help you work on your own self-actualization and personal development. It includes counseling, life-skills coaching, support groups, and tools for solving life problems.

REFERENCES

Anderson, R., & Braud, W. (Eds.). (1998) *Transpersonal research methods in the social sciences.* Thousand Oaks, CA: Sage.

Assagioli, R. (1971). *Psychosynthesis.* New York: Viking Press.

Benedict, R. (1970). Synergy: Patterns of the good culture. *American Anthropologist, 72,* 320–333.

Brennan, T., & Piechowski, M. (1991). A developmental framework for self-actualization. *Journal of Humanistic Psychology, 31,* 43–64.

Dabrowski, K. (1967). *Personality shaping through positive disintegration.* Boston: Little, Brown.

Fadiman, J. (1980). The transpersonal stance. In R. Walsh & F. Vaughan (Eds.), *Beyond ego.* Los Angeles: Tarcher.

Firman, J., & Gila, A. (1997). *The primal wound.* Albany: SUNY Press.

Firman, J., & Gila, A. (2000). *Psychosynthesis: An essential text.* Palo Alto, CA. Psychosynthesis Palo Alto (461 Hawthorne Av.; Palo Alto, CA 94301).

Frager, R. (1989). Transpersonal psychology: Promise and prospects. In R. Valle & S. Halling (Eds.), *Existential-phenomenological perspectives in psychology.* New York: Plenum Press.

Fuller, A. (1994). *Psychology and religion.* Lanham, MD: Littlefield Adams.

Goble, F. (1971). *The third force: The psychology of Abraham Maslow.* New York: Pocket Books.

Goldstein, K. (1939). *The organism.* New York: American Book.

Gray, S. W. (1986). The relationship between self-actualization and leisure satisfaction. *Psychology, 23,* 6–12.

Grof, S. (1975). *Realms of the human unconscious*. New York: Viking Press.

Grof, S. (1988). *Adventures of self-discovery*. New York: State University of New York Press.

Grof, S., with H. Bennett. (1993). *The holotropic mind*. New York: HarperCollins.

Grof, S. (1998). *The cosmic game*. Albany: SUNY Press.

Grof, S. (2000). *The psychology of the future*. Albany: SUNY Press.

Hall, M. (1968). A conversation with Abraham Maslow. *Psychology Today, 2*(2), 34–37, 54–57.

Hardy, J. (1987). *A psychology with a soul: Psychosynthesis in evolutionary context*. New York: Routledge & Kegan Paul.

Hart, T., Nelson, P., & Puhakka, K. (Eds.). (2000). *Transpersonal knowing: Exploring the horizon of consciousness*. Albany: SUNY Press.

Hoffman, E. (1999). *The right to be human*. New York: McGraw-Hill.

Horner, M. (1972). The motive to avoid success and changing aspirations of college women. In J. Bardwick (Ed.), *Readings on the psychology of women* (pp. 62–67). New York: Harper & Row.

Huxley, A. (1944). *The perennial philosophy*. New York: Harper & Row.

International Study Project. (1972). *Abraham H. Maslow: A memorial volume*. Monterey, CA: Brooks/Cole.

Jacoby, J. (1959). *Complex, archetype, symbol in the psychology of C. G. Jung*. New York: Pantheon.

James, W. (1943). *The varieties of religious experience*. New York: Random House (Modern Library).

Journal of Transpersonal Psychology Editorial Staff. (1970). An appreciation. *Journal of Transpersonal Psychology, 2*(2), iv.

Katz, S. T. (1978). Language, epistemology and mysticism. In S. T. Katz (Ed.), *Mysticism and philosophical analysis*. New York: Oxford University Press.

Kelly, R. B., & Chovan, W. (1985). Yet another empirical test of the relationship between self-actualization and moral judgement. *Psychological Reports, 56*, 201–202.

Krippner, S. (Ed.). (1972). The plateau experience: A. H. Maslow and others. *Journal of Transpersonal Psychology, 4*, 107–120.

Kuhn, T. (1962). *The structure of scientific revolutions*. Chicago: University of Chicago Press.

Kunc, N. (1992). The need to belong. In R. Villa, J. Thousand, W. Stainback, & S. Stainback (Eds.), *Restructuring for caring and effective education*. Baltimore: Paul H. Brookes.

Lajoie, D., & Shapiro, S. (1992). Definitions of transpersonal psychology: The first twenty-three years. *Journal of Transpersonal Psychology, 24*, 79–98.

Leclerc, G., Lefrancois, M., Dube, M., Hebert, R., & Gaulin, P. (1998). The self-actualization concept: A content validation. *Journal of Social Behavior and Personality, 13*, 69–84.

Leonard, G. (1983, December). Abraham Maslow and the new self. *Esquire,* pp. 326–336.

Maslow, A. (1948). Higher and lower needs. *Journal of Psychology, 25*, 433–436.

Maslow, A. (1965). *Eupsychian management: A journal*. Homewood, IL: Irwin.

Maslow, A. (1966). *The psychology of science: A reconnaissance*. New York: Harper & Row.

Maslow, A. (1968). *Toward a psychology of being* (2nd ed.). New York: Van Nostrand.

Maslow, A. (1970). *Motivation and personality* (rev. ed.). New York: Harper & Row.

Maslow, A. (1971). *The farther reaches of human nature*. New York: Viking Press.

Maslow, A. (1987). *Motivation and personality* (3rd ed.). New York: Harper & Row.

Maslow, A. (1994). *Religion, values and peak experiences*. New York: Viking Press.

Maslow, A. (1998a). *Maslow on management*. New York: Wiley.

Maslow, A. (1998b). *Toward a psychology of being*. New York: Wiley.

Maslow, A. H., with Chiang, H. (1969). *The healthy personality: Readings*. New York: Van Nostrand.

Mathes, E., Zevon, M., Roter, P., & Joerger, S. (1982). Peak experience tendencies. *Journal of Humanistic Psychology, 22*, 92–108.

Metzner, R. (1986). *Opening to inner light*. Los Angeles: Tarcher.

Ornstein, R. (1973). *The nature of human consciousness*. New York: Viking Press.

Piechowski, M. (1978). Self-actualization as a developmental structure: A profile of Antoine de Saint-Exupéry. *Genetic Psychology Monographs, 97*, 181–242.

Piechowski, M. (1990). Inner growth and transformation in the life of Eleanor Roosevelt. *Advanced Developmental Journal, 2*, 35–53.

Piechowsky, M., & Tyska, C. (1982). Self-actualization profile of Eleanor Roosevelt, a presumed nontranscender. *Genetic Psychology Monographs, 105*, 95–153.

Rychman, R. M. (1985). Physical self-efficacy and actualization. *Journal of Research in Personality, 19*, 288–298.

Schott, R. (1992). Abraham Maslow, humanistic psychology, and organization leadership. *Journal of Humanistic Psychology, 32*, 106–120.

Scotton, B., Chinen, A., & Battista, J. (Eds.). (1996). *Textbook of transpersonal psychiatry and psychology*. New York: Basic Books.

Shostrom, E. (1963). *Personal orientation inventory*. San Diego, CA: Edits.

Smith, H. (1976). *Forgotten truth*. New York: Harper & Row.

Sumner, W. (1940). *Folkways*. New York: New American Library.

Sutich, A. (1969). Some considerations regarding transpersonal psychology. *Journal of Transpersonal Psychology, 1*, 11–20.

Tart, C. (Ed.). (1969). *Altered states of consciousness*. New York: Wiley.

Tart, C. (Ed.). (1975). *Transpersonal psychologies*. New York: Harper & Row.

Valle, R. (1989). The emergence of transpersonal psychology. In R. Valle & S. Halling (Eds.), *Existential-phenomenological perspectives in psychology*. New York: Plenum Press.

Vaughan, F. (1995). *Shadows of the sacred.* Wheaton, IL: Theosophical Publishing.

Walsh, R. (1989). Asian psychotherapies. In R. Corsini & D. Wedding (Eds.), *Current psychotherapies* (4th ed.). Itasca, IL: F. E. Peacock.

Walsh, R., & Shapiro, D. (Eds.). (1983). *Beyond health and normality: Explorations of exceptional psychological well being.* New York: Van Nostrand Reinhold.

Walsh, R., & Vaughan, F. (Eds.). (1980). *Beyond ego: Transpersonal dimensions in psychology.* Los Angeles: Tarcher.

Walsh, R., & Vaughan, F. (Eds.). (1993). *Paths beyond ego: The transpersonal vision.* Los Angeles: Tarcher.

Washburn, M. (1995). *The ego and the dynamic ground.* Albany: SUNY Press.

Washburn, M. (1999). *Transpersonal psychology in psychoanalytic perspective.* Albany: SUNY Press.

Wilber, K. (1977). *The spectrum of consciousness.* Wheaton, IL: Theosophical Publishing.

Wilber, K. (1980). *The Atman project.* Wheaton, IL: Quest.

Wilber, K. (1995). *Sex, ecology, spirituality: The spirit of evolution.* Boston: Shambhala.

Wilber, K. (1996). *A brief history of everything.* Boston: Shambhala.

Wilber, K. (2000a). *A theory of everything.* Boston: Shambhala.

Wilber, K. (2000b). *Integral psychology.* Boston: Shambhala.

Wilson, C. (1972). *New pathways in psychology: Maslow and the post-Freudian revolution.* New York: Mentor.

Wilson, S., & Spencer, R. (1990). Intense personal experiences. *Journal of Clinical Psychology, 46,* 565–573.

yoga and
the hindu tradition

Yoga has two aspects. First, it encompasses virtually all the mystical and ascetic practices of India, including meditation, physical discipline, and devotional chanting. Second, Yoga is a specific school of Indian philosophy systematized in the Yoga sutras of Patanjali and first mentioned in India's ancient, 3,000-year-old Vedas, the world's oldest recorded literature. The roots of Yoga practice undoubtedly go even farther back to Indian prehistory.

Yoga is a Sanskrit word meaning "to join" or "to unite." The goal of Yoga practice is self-realization, which occurs when consciousness is turned within and united with its source, the Self. *Yoga* also means "method." It embraces both the goal of union and the wide variety of yogic techniques meant to accomplish this end. In this sense, Yoga is the technology of self-realization or ecstasy.

In its broadest sense, Yoga embraces all systematic disciplines designed to promote self-realization by calming the mind and focusing consciousness on the Self, the immortal, unchanging essence in each individual. Later in this chapter we will compare Yoga psychology with Jung's concept of individuation and Rogers' and Maslow's concepts of self-actualization.

HISTORY

The roots of Yoga are ancient, going back before 2500 BC, to the pre-Hindu culture of India. Yoga is an integral part of the rich and complex Hindu tradition, which encompasses hundreds of different traditions and sacred texts. These are all based on the Vedas.

> Lead me from the unreal to the real. From darkness lead me to light. From death lead me to immortality. (Brihadaranyaka Upanishad, I:iii, 28)

The Bhagavad-Gita

The *Bhagavad-Gita* (Mascaro, 1962) is the first and also the most popular work on Yoga. It is a part of the great Indian epic of the second century BC called *Mahabharata*, a magnificent collection of mythology, religion, ethics, and customs. It is about 100,000 stanzas long, almost eight times the length of the *Iliad* and the *Odyssey* combined. Yoga and related philosophies are discussed in the epic.

Metaphorically, the *Bhagavad-Gita* is a dialogue between Arjuna (the ego) and Krishna (the Self). Arjuna is a warrior, and Krishna, his charioteer, is an incarnation of God and a great spiritual teacher. Krishna discusses duty and the Yoga of action. He teaches Arjuna the importance of devotion, self-control, meditation, and other yogic practices, to serve as an example for others. As charioteer, Krishna symbolizes the *guru*, or spiritual teacher, who can guide students with the problems and conflicts they encounter in the process of spiritual development. However, the teacher, like the charioteer, cannot fight the students' battles for them.

> He who works not for an earthly reward, but does the work to be done ... he is a Yogi. (*Bhagavad-Gita*, VI:1)[1]

MAJOR CONCEPTS
Three Principles of Creation

Nature *(Prakriti)* has three primary constituents, or principles, the three *gunas: tamas* (inertia), *rajas* (activity), and *sattva* (clarity or light). These three principles function together to generate all activity. All the various manifestations of Nature (matter, thought, and so forth) are composed of different combinations of the three gunas.

[1]Quotes from the Bhagavad-Gita are taken from Mascaro (1962), Prabhavananda & Isherwood (1951), and Feuerstein (1989).

personal reflection

AUSTERITIES

General Principles

The simplest, most direct, and most difficult practice of austerity is to give up satisfying one of your desires—for example, if you desire food, then you should fast. If you love to sleep, make do with less. Giving up small pleasures and comforts can be an important self-discipline. If you usually get up at 8:00 AM, try getting up at 6:00 or 7:00 every morning. If you like sleeping on a soft, comfortable bed, start sleeping on a thin mattress on the floor.

There are important cautions in this kind of practice. Austerities may have the side effect of strengthening pride and egotism. Pride in your accomplishments, pride in suffering, or masochistic enjoyment of austerities for their own sake are all indications of ego involvement. Another thing to avoid is excessive austerity. This is also a demonstration of ego and may actually cause you mental or physical harm.

Fasting

Short periods of fasting are an excellent practice of austerity. You can begin simply by deliberately missing one or two meals. A one-day fast is not too difficult for anyone in good health. Drink plenty of water and drink orange juice if you feel the need for additional nourishment. Fasting for one day a week is an excellent practice. When you fast, you are confronted with the need to overcome temptation and to set your will against the desire for food.

Silence

Silence is another traditional practice. Try remaining silent for a few hours at home or around friends to whom you have explained your practice. Or spend a day in silence. Carry paper and pencil with you to communicate in writing if necessary. Observe yourself and others, as well as your reactions to conversations. Try to overcome your need to communicate actively. Learn just to be, in silence.

In the process of creating a statue, for example, tamas can be seen in the untouched, inert stone. Rajas is the act of carving, and sattva is the image in the sculptor's imagination. All three are essential. Pure tamas alone is inert, dead matter. Pure rajas is energy without direction or goal. Pure sattva is a plan that remains unrealized.

Every individual balances these three qualities, although most people are dominated by one of them. Sattva is considered the most spiritual. One of the goals of Yoga practice is to increase the sattvic element in the individual, which supports the process of Self-realization. Virtually everything can be classified in terms of the gunas. Rich or heavy foods are tamasic, because they are difficult to digest and cause laziness or sleepiness. Spicy, hot foods are rajasic, since they lead to activity, strong emotions, or nervousness. Fresh fruit and vegetables are sattvic and promote calmness. Certain places, such as mountains and the ocean shore, are sattvic and thus suitable for spiritual practice.

The three gunas are always found together, like three strands of intertwined rope. In the average person, rajas and tamas dominate, with relatively little highly developed awareness, or sattva. Emotions *(rajas)* and bodily drives *(tamas)* distort the focus and clarity of pure sattvic experience. The goal of yoga practice is to decrease rajas and tamas, and increase and intensify sattvic awareness.

Consciousness

The mind is like a miraculous rubber band that can be expanded to infinity without breaking. (Yogananda, 1968a)

In Yoga terminology, mind, or consciousness *(chitta)*, embraces all thought processes. Patanjali defines Yoga as "controlling the activities of the mind." This stops the incessant "chatter" of mental activity and brings about a state of deep calm and inner peace.

Yoga includes the complete focusing of attention on whatever object is contemplated. The final goal is to focus attention on the Self. When mental processes, or waves of consciousness, are active, the Self is obscured, like a bright light suspended in churning water.

All Yoga practices work toward one end: to quiet the waves of consciousness and calm the mind. Some schools of Yoga focus on control of the body and others on breathing techniques; still others teach meditation practices. In a sense, all Yoga techniques and practices are preliminary exercises designed to still the mind. Once mind and body are calm and disciplined, awareness of the Self can emerge.

Karma

Karma means action and also its results. Karma is based on the principle that every activity brings with it certain consequences, and every individual's life is influenced by past actions. This influence occurs in part through the creation of subconscious tendencies, in the sequence shown in Figure 13.1.

In order to avoid the formation of new subconscious tendencies or the strengthening of old ones, the yogi refrains from "acting out." In other words, anger tendencies are strengthened by angry thoughts and feelings and reinforced further by angry speech and actions. The yogic ideal is not suppression of unacceptable tendencies but transmutation of negative action and thought into positive action and thought. One effective way of dealing with strong emotions is to look calmly and deeply at their roots. Inner awareness can transform subsequent thoughts and feelings. Through self-discipline, right action, and Yoga practice, the individual gradually changes his or her consciousness, transmuting old habits and thought patterns. The yogi learns to substitute positive, constructive actions for old, destructive habits. Long-term, positive change in actions results in positive alterations in subconscious tendencies, followed by transformation of consciousness. (See Figure 13.1.)

> Before you act, you have freedom, but after you act, the effect of that action will follow you whether you want it to or not. That is the law of *karma*. You are a free agent, but when you perform a certain act, you will reap the results of that act. (Yogananda, 1968b)

Subconscious Tendencies

Control of the waves of consciousness is possible only when we diminish the subconscious tendencies. Such tendencies *(samskaras)* shape mental activity. These subconscious patterns are created by past actions and experiences, from this life and from past lives. Tendencies are built up by the continued action of thought waves or waves of consciousness. For example, anger waves of consciousness gradually create anger tendencies, which predispose the individual to angry reactions.

The goal of Yoga is *complete* reformation of consciousness. Otherwise, the subconscious tendencies will seek to actualize themselves, sprouting suddenly like dormant seeds. Through meditation, self-analysis, and other powerful inner disciplines, we

> You cannot achieve emancipation unless you have burned the seeds of past actions in the fires of wisdom and meditation. (Yogananda, 1968a, p. 110)

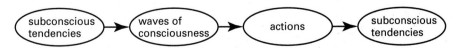

FIGURE 13.1 Karma and Its Effects

may "roast" such seeds, destroy their potential for further activity; that is, through fundamental inner change we can grow free of the influence of the past.

In this theory of the subconscious tendencies, Yoga anticipated by many centuries the modern notion of the unconscious. Further, Yoga has gone beyond the insights and goals of most schools of psychotherapy in developing techniques for complete transformation of the unconscious.

Schools of Yoga

Several major schools of Yoga emerged in India, each suiting a particular personality. For example, *Karma-yoga*, the Yoga of action, is especially appropriate for those who possess a strong will or those who need to develop their will as their next stage of growth; it is also chosen by those who hold service to others as a central ideal. *Jnana-yoga*, the Yoga of knowledge, benefits those with keen minds and provides an essential discipline for those who need to develop discrimination. *Bhakti-yoga*, the Yoga of devotion, is ideal for those with a strongly emotional nature. *Hatha-yoga* is for individuals with strong self-discipline and interest in developing physical mastery. *Kundalini-yoga* generally involves meditative techniques most suited to those with potential for subtle awareness of inner processes. *Raja-yoga* fits those with the potential for deep concentration and mental control.

> My own temperament is principally devotional. It was disconcerting at first to find that my *guru*, saturated with *jnana* but seemingly dry of *bhakti*, expressed himself chiefly in terms of cold spiritual mathematics. But, as I attuned myself to his nature, I discovered no diminution but rather an increase in my devotional approach to God. A Self-realized master is fully able to guide his various disciples along the natural lines of their essential bias. (Yogananda, 1972, p. 145)

A sophisticated teacher may prescribe a particular form of Yoga practice that builds on a disciple's strengths or assign a specific practice that calls forth underdeveloped attributes. Less-sophisticated teachers will simply assign their own favorite practices, without considering individual differences.

> Everything we do, physical or mental, is karma, and it leaves its marks on us. (Vivekananda, 1978b, pp. 3–4)

The Yoga of Action (Karma-yoga). Karma-yoga teaches us to act selflessly, without attachment to gain or loss, success or failure. The karma-yogi seeks to serve other people and act according to high ideals. Learning to overcome one's selfishness, laziness, and pride demands considerable discipline. Swami Vivekananda writes:

> This is the one central idea in the *Gita:* Work incessantly, but be not attached to it. . . . God is unattached because He loves; that real love makes us unattached. . . . To attain this nonattachment is almost a life work. But as soon as we have reached this point we have attained the goal of love and become free. (1978b, pp. 38, 45–46)

Karma-yoga can be an important discipline for all people and places—for those who live in secluded caves in the Himalayas as well as for those who have jobs and families. As long as we are alive, we must act. We all can learn to act well.

The practitioner of karma-yoga need not believe in a particular religious doctrine, or even in God or Spirit. The karma-yogi is transformed by developing selflessness through service rather than through ostensible religious discipline.

The Yoga of Knowledge (Jnana-yoga).

Jnana-yoga, the Yoga of knowledge, is a discipline of rigorous self-analysis, a path for those endowed with a clear, refined intellect. It is basically a path of discrimination. The jnana-yogi seeks to understand the forces of delusion and bondage and to counter or avoid the influences of passion, sense attachment, and identification with the body.

This yogi is a true philosopher, a sage who wants to go beyond the superficial, fleeting things of this world.

> Not even the teaching of thousands of books will satisfy him. Not even all the sciences will satisfy him; at the best, they only bring this little world before him. . . . His very soul wants to go beyond all that into the very heart of Being, by seeing Reality as It is; by realizing It, by being It, by becoming one with that Universal Being. (Vivekananda, 1976, p. 395)

Ramana Maharshi (1879–1950) is regarded by many as India's greatest modern sage and exemplar of jnana-yoga. He taught his followers a technique called *Self-inquiry* for regaining identification with the Self. It is a method of continuously inquiring "Who am I?" and looking beyond the body, the thoughts, and emotions for the source of consciousness. Some of the flavor of this approach can be seen in Maharshi's responses to questions.

> "How is one to realize the Self?"
> "Whose Self? Find out."
> "Mine; but, who am I?"
> "It is you who must find out."
> "I don't know."
> "Just think over the question, Who is it that says: 'I don't know'?"
> "Who is the 'I' in your statement? What is not known? Why was I born?"
> "Who was born? The answer is the same to all your questions."
> "However much I may try, I do not seem to catch the I [italics added]. It is not even clearly discernible."
> "Who is it that says that the 'I' is not discernible? Are there two 'I's in you, that one is not discernible to the other?"
> (Osbourne, 1962, pp. 121–122)

Ramana Maharshi saw self-realization as the task of removing delusional understanding, not as a matter of acquiring something new. "Once the false notion 'I am the body' or 'I am not realized' has been removed, Supreme Consciousness or the Self alone remains and in people's present state of knowledge they call this 'Realization.' But the truth is that Realization is eternal and already exists, here and now" (Osbourne, 1962, p. 23 [see also Figure 13.2]).

The individual seeks the Self by discarding, through intelligent discrimination, all that is not the Self, all that is limiting, perishable, or illusory.

The Yoga of Devotion (Bhakti-yoga).

Bhakti-yoga is a way of reforming one's personality through the development of love and devotion. Its proponents argue that this simple path is most suitable to the modern era, in which few people have the time and discipline to pursue fully the other traditional paths of Yoga.

Followers of bhakti-yoga use deep devotion to concentrate the mind and transform the personality. It is easier for most people to love God personified in human form than to love abstract Spirit or consciousness. The practice of devotional Yoga is closer to traditional religion than any other form of Yoga. It includes ritual worship,

Offer all thy works to God, throw off selfish bonds, and do thy work. No sin can then stain thee, even as waters do not stain the leaf of the lotus. (*Bhagavad-Gita*, V:10)

Self-scrutiny, relentless observance of one's thoughts, is a stark and shattering experience. It pulverizes the stoutest ego. But, true self-analysis mathematically operates to produce seers. (Yogananda, 1972, p. 51)

By steady and continuous investigation into the nature of the mind, the mind is transformed into that to which "I" refers; and that is in fact the Self. (Ramana Maharshi in Osbourne, 1962, p. 113)

If you must be mad, be it not for the things of the world. Be mad with the love of God. (Ramakrishna, 1965, p. 187)

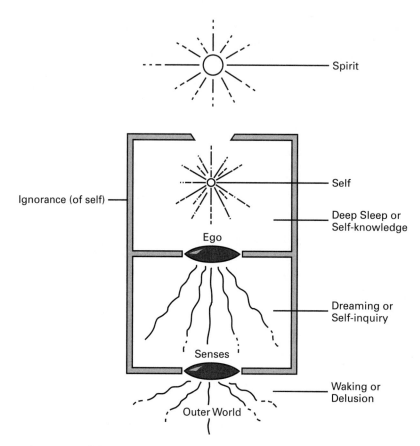

Spirit

Ignorance (of self)

Self

Deep Sleep or
Self-knowledge

Ego

Dreaming or
Self-inquiry

Senses

Waking or
Delusion

Outer World

FIGURE 13.2 A Jnana-yoga Model of the Self and Consciousness
Source: Adapted from Osbourne, 1969, pp. 23–24.

chanting, and the worship of God. The great incarnations of God, such as Rama and Krishna, are a common focus of devotion in parts of India, and the goddess Kali, or the Divine Mother, in others.

Long sessions of spiritual chanting typically form an important part of traditional Indian religious practice as well as a basic bhakti-yoga practice. A spiritual chant is "a song born out of the depths of true devotion to God and continuously chanted, audibly or mentally, until response is consciously received from Him in the form of boundless joy" (Yogananda, 1963, p. xiii). Chants are often simple and repetitive, inspiring concentration on one aspect of the Divine. Chanting practices can also help channel emotions, develop single-pointed concentration, and energize mind and body.

The Yoga of the Body (Hatha-yoga). The practices of **hatha-yoga** are designed to purify and strengthen the body for advanced meditation and higher states of consciousness. Enlightenment is a whole-body event. Through hatha-yoga, the yogi seeks to manifest the infinite self in the finite body-mind.

The body is seen as a vehicle for vital energies, or *pranas*. Hatha-yoga disciplines strengthen these energies and bring control of them, enhancing physical, mental, and spiritual activity. Certain postures are intended to keep the body limber, exercise the

Hatha-yoga is a system of health and hygiene involving both body and mind. It aims at the whole man for his full development and self-realization. It takes into account not only the proper growth, strength and tone of the different muscles of the body but also the efficiency and function of the basic factors of constitutional health, namely, the inner organs and the glands. (Majumdar, 1964, p. 99)

personal reflection

THE CORPSE POSE

This pose is designed for deep relaxation. It is practiced when the yogi has completed a series of postures or when he or she desires to relax. It is best to practice on a thick carpet or pad.

Lie on your back with your arms resting on the floor, palms up. Close your eyes and consciously relax every part of your body, starting with the feet. Feel your body sinking into the floor as you relax. Imagine that you have abandoned your body completely so that it lies perfectly limp, detached from your mind. Observe your body as if you were outside of it. Observe your breath as it flows in and out, without any attempt to control it. After some time, gradually lengthen your breathing and make it rhythmical. Practice 10 to 20 minutes.

spine, stimulate various nerves and organs, and increase breathing capacity. According to Yoga physiology, all functions require vital energy. The more available energy, the healthier and more effective the individual.

Practice of Yoga **asanas,** or postures, is only part of hatha-yoga. In fact, most hatha-yoga taught in the United States is more a form of gymnastics for physical health than a complete system of Yoga. In addition to postures, classical hatha-yoga includes celibacy, vegetarian diet, breathing and concentration exercises, and techniques for washing and cleansing the nasal passages and the entire alimentary canal, from the throat to the intestines. These disciplines form an integrated psychospiritual technology whose purpose is to move the practitioner toward self-realization.

The first principle behind the practice of Yoga postures is to accustom the body to a given pose and then gradually lengthen the time in that posture. Various postures take pressure off parts of the body and intensify pressure in others, increase blood flow to certain body parts, and stretch or compress organs. Combinations of postures can provide balanced stimulation for the entire body. Many people in India practice routines of 15 to 20 postures daily. A given posture may have several variations, each designed to exercise different muscles or different organs. It is best to study hatha-yoga under a qualified teacher who can correct major mistakes and also individualize instruction to a person's specific build and other physical characteristics.

Each of the classic asanas has many levels of significance. Physical benefits include flexibility, strength, balance, and stimulation of the endocrine and other organ systems. Each posture also has psychological and spiritual benefits. Swami Radha's *Hatha Yoga: The Hidden Language* (1987) explains these various levels of significance for the most common postures.

Through hatha-yoga practice, one may develop great mental and physical abilities. However, without additional mental and spiritual discipline, these abilities may simply feed the ego. One authority commented that the followers of hatha-yoga he had met "had great powers, strong healthy bodies and immense vanity . . . some more worldly than average worldly men" (Purohit, 1938, p. 30). One of the authors met a yogi of this type in India. The yogi had been a subject of considerable scientific research, demonstrating extraordinary control over his brain waves, heartbeat, and other bodily functions. At a major Yoga conference, the man insisted on challenging all the other yogis present to demonstrate "scientifically" their mastery of Yoga and to determine, by physical measurement, who was the "greatest yogi."

Young woman practicing a yoga posture

It is not your passing inspirations or brilliant ideas so much as your everyday mental habits that control your life. (Yogananda, 1968b)

The Yoga of Sacred Chanting (Mantra-yoga).   A **mantra** is a sacred phrase or syllable, charged with psychospiritual power. In **mantra-yoga,** these sacred sounds are used to attain a one-pointed meditative state and to transform the individual's consciousness. According to Indian metaphysics, the universe is in constant vibration. Correct repetition of a mantra will attune the individual to that cosmic vibration.

The most important mantra in Vedic chanting was *om,* which is said to be the basic level of vibration in the universe. *Om* is still the most widely recognized and most frequently used mantra in India.

Traditionally, the disciple receives a mantra during an initiation ritual. Some authorities claim that the only real and effective mantras are sounds received in this way. For yogis who have not received initiation, *om* and other sacred sounds are not truly mantras; therefore, repeating them will be ineffective (Feuerstein, 1989).

The Yoga of Subtle Energy (Kundalini-yoga).   *Kundalini* means "she who is coiled." According to Yoga physiology, a subtle energy known as kundalini lies coiled at the base of the spine. All energies of mind and body are manifestations of kundalini energy, which can be consciously controlled by an accomplished yogi.

This energy is generally latent. It begins to awaken and flow freely as a result of the disciplines of **kundalini-yoga,** including meditation, visualization, breathing exercises, and the purification techniques of hatha-yoga. Once fully active, kundalini energy rises through all levels of consciousness, leading to major physical, psychological, and spiritual changes in the individual. The psychiatrist Lee Sanella (1987) has developed a neurophysiological model that explains the kundalini process as a transformation of the electromagnetic fields of the body. Jung has discussed in detail the relationship between kundalini yoga, the chakras, and his approach to psychology

personal reflection

MEDITATION EXERCISES

Heartbeat

Sit with spine erect and body relaxed. Close your eyes and sink your mind into the depths of your heart. Become aware of your heart bubbling with life-giving blood, and keep your attention on your heart until you feel its rhythmic beat. With every heartbeat, feel the pulse of infinite life throbbing through you. Picture that same all-pervading life flowing through all other human beings and in billions of other creatures. Open your heart, body, mind, and feelings to receive more fully that universal life.

Expanding Love

Sit erect with eyes closed. Expand your realm of love beyond longheld limits of your love for the body and identification with your body. With the love you have given to the body, love all those who love you. With the expanded love of all those who love you, love all those who are close to you. With the love for yourself and for your own, love those who are strangers. Extend your love to those who do not love you, as well as to those who do. Bathe all beings in your selfless love. See your family, friends, all people, all beings in the sea of your love.

Peace

Sit erect, with eyes closed. Look inwardly between the eyebrows at a shoreless lake of peace. Observe the waves of peace expanding, spreading from the eyebrows to the forehead, from the forehead to the heart, and on to every cell in your body. As you watch, the lake of peace deepens and overflows your body, inundating the vast territory of your mind. The flood of peace flows over the boundaries of your mind and moves on in infinite directions. (Adapted from Yogananda, 1967)

(Shamdasani, 1996). In a classic account of kundalini awakening, Gopi Krishna (1971) writes

> Suddenly, with a roar like that of a waterfall, I felt a stream of liquid light entering my brain through the spinal cord.
>
> Entirely unprepared for such a development, I was completely taken by surprise, but regaining self-control instantaneously, I remained sitting in the same posture, keeping my mind on the point of concentration. The illumination grew brighter and brighter, the roaring louder, I experienced a rocking sensation and then felt myself slipping out of my body, entirely enveloped in a halo of light. (pp. 12–13)

Research has shown that kundalini awakening occurs spontaneously in a surprising number of individuals. Some have engaged in meditation or other Yoga practices, and others have not (Greenwell, 1990; Kieffer, 1996; Ramaswami, 1989).

The Three Energy Channels.   Three energy channels run along the spine through seven consciousness centers called **chakras.** The central channel is the *sushumna,* which is also the path for the ascending kundalini. To the left lies *ida,* and to the right lies the *pingala* channel. They are represented by the moon and the sun. These two channels wind around the sushumna in a helical pattern. (See Figure 13.3.)

Most people's **prana,** or vital energy, flows primarily in ida and pingala, as their attention is externalized. Through meditation and other inwardly focused disciplines, the yogi brings more and more energy into sushumna. This stimulates the dormant kundalini energy, which then rushes upward through the sushumna channel, leading to a

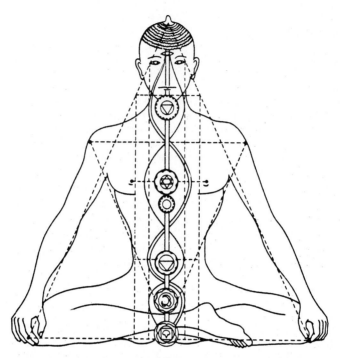

FIGURE 13.3 The Centers of Consciousness in the Body
Source: From Danielou, 1955, p. ii.

state of *samadhi,* or illumination. Stimulating the kundalini energy with prana is like bombarding an atomic nucleus with high-energy particles in order to trigger a nuclear reaction (Feuerstein, 1989).

As kundalini reaches the higher chakras, it produces various degrees of illumination. Each chakra is associated with different physical and spiritual attributes; some are related to various senses and elements, and some to other qualities, such as form or color.

The Seven Chakras[2]

1. First chakra *(Muladhara)* is located at the base of the spinal column. It is associated with the element earth, inertia, the birth of sound, the lower limbs, the mantra *lam,* the elephant (symbolizing strength), and the sense of smell. It is portrayed as a deep-red, four-petaled lotus. It is the location of the dormant kundalini.

2. Second chakra *(Svadisthana)* is situated several inches above the first center. It is associated with the element water, the color white, the hands, the mantra *vam,* a crocodile-like animal (fertility), and the sense of taste. It is pictured as a crimson, six-petaled lotus.

3. Third chakra *(Manipura)* is located at the level of the navel. It is related to the element fire, the sun, the anus, the mantra *ram* (fiery energy), and the sense of sight. It is depicted as a bright yellow lotus of ten petals.

4. Fourth chakra *(Anahata)* is located at the level of the heart. The name of this chakra comes from its association with transcendental sound, which is "unstruck." It is associated with the color red, the element air, the penis, the mantra *yam,* a

[2]The descriptions of the chakras are taken from Eliade (1969) and Feuerstein (1989).

black antelope (swiftness), and the sense of touch. It is drawn as a blue lotus of twelve petals.

5. Fifth chakra *(Vishuddha)* is located in the region of the throat. It is associated with the element ether, the color white, the mouth and skin, the mantra *ham,* a snow-white elephant (pure strength), and the sense of hearing.

6. Sixth chakra *(Ajna)* is situated in the brain, midway between the eyes. It is the seat of cognitive faculties, the mantra *om,* the subtle senses, and the sense of individuality. It is represented by a downward pointing triangle and a pale gray, two-petaled lotus.

7. Seventh chakra *(Sahasrara)* is located at the top of the head. It is a body-transcending center where consciousness connects to the human form. It is represented by a thousand-petaled lotus. The seventh center includes the brain. When the brain is stimulated and energized by kundalini, the individual experiences a tremendous change in consciousness, an experience of bright illumination, or *samadhi,* "the blossoming of the thousand-petaled lotus."

Ram Dass, a noted psychologist who became a yogi, explains that the chakras can be considered a personality system, a system of personality typologies.

For most people in the Western universe, in fact most people in the world, almost all of the energy is located either in the first, second, or third chakras. The first chakra can be characterized crudely as being connected with survival and survival of the individual as a separate being. . . . It's a survival-of-the-fittest-type model. It's a Darwinian assumption about the motivations of beings. When you're at that chakra your motivation is to protect yourself as a separate being, your separateness. . . . [Then] you've got your security under control and now you start to go into sensual gratification and sexual desires and reproduction [the second chakra]. You can't be busy reproducing if you're protecting your life, but the minute your life's protected a little bit, then you can concern yourself with the next matter, which is reproducing the species. So the second chakra is primarily concerned with sexual actions, reactions, and so on—at the reproduction level. Procreative. Sex.

The third chakra is like Wall Street and Washington and London. It's primarily connected with power, with mastery, with ego control. Most of the world that we think of is connected with those particular centers. All the energy's located there. People justify their lives in terms of reproduction or sexual gratification, sensual gratification, or power or mastery. And it's interesting that pretty much any act we know of in the Western world can be done in the service of any one of those energies. So that a man can build a huge dynamic industry and we can say, "Aha, phallic," meaning second chakra. Or a person can seduce many women in order to have mastery and power over them and we say, "Aha, concerned with power and mastery," meaning third chakra. Doing sex in the service of third chakra. . . .

Freud is the absolutely unequaled spokesman and master of second-chakra preoccupation, that is, of those beings who were primarily involved in second chakra. So he could say quite honestly, because it is true at the second chakra, that religion is sublimated sex. . . . Adler is primarily concerned with third chakra. Jung is primarily concerned with fourth chakra [the heart chakra]. . . . So that to the extent that you have "uncooked seeds" of the second chakra and you have a Freudian analyst, he's going to help you cook those seeds. He's not going to do much about where you're stuck in the third chakra, particularly. And he hasn't much to say about the fourth chakra, which is what Jung pointed out about Freud. (Ram Dass, 1974, pp. 29–30)

The Classical Yoga of Patanjali (Raja-yoga).   **Raja-yoga,** or royal yoga, emphasizes the development of mental control as the most effective and efficient

personal reflection

BREATHING EXERCISES: OBSERVING THE BREATH

Sit on a chair or on the floor, with your back straight and your body relaxed. Close your eyes. Exhale and then inhale calmly and deeply for as long as is comfortable without straining. Observe your breath flowing in and out, as if you were on the seashore observing the ocean waves. With each intake of breath, feel that you are breathing in fresh energy and vitality with the oxygen. With each outtake of breath, feel that you are breathing out tiredness, fatigue, and negativity as you expel carbon dioxide. Feel the fresh, vitalizing energy permeating your mind and body as you continue to do the exercise. Then, sit quietly with your mind peaceful and calm.

discipline. Patanjali's raja-yoga has been called "psychological Yoga." Some consider it a combination of all the schools of Yoga. Some see raja-yoga as one of the major Yoga schools, and others recognize Patanjali's work as the source of all of classical Yoga (Feuerstein, 1996).

Patanjali systematized this path in eight limbs of Yoga: (1) abstentions, (2) observances, (3) postures, (4) vital energy control, (5) interiorization, (6) concentration, (7) meditation, and (8) illumination. They can be thought of as successive levels of achievement, each limb building upon the one that precedes it. The eight limbs are closely interrelated branches of a single discipline; therefore, improvement in one branch tends to benefit the others.

The **abstentions** and **observances** are the moral code that serves as the foundation for Yoga practice. Abstentions include nonviolence, truthfulness, nonstealing, chastity, and nongreed. The observances are purity, austerity, contentment, study, and devotion. The abstentions and observances—the yogic equivalent of the Ten Commandments and the principles of right action found in all religions—are not an arbitrary system of morality. They are followed for practical reasons, to strengthen the effectiveness of the rest of Yoga practice. If a yogi lacks a calm and disciplined daily life, the concentration and peace gained from Yoga practice soon dissipate, like water carried in a pail riddled with holes.

It is impossible to progress without developing abstentions and observances. However, we cannot expect to master them at first. Nonviolence and truthfulness, for example, are profound disciplines.

Abstentions and observances have great depth. They are not simply representations of conventional morality; they are practical principles that bring a harmony to life consistent with the consciousness for which Yoga aims. Purification of mind and body also prepares the entire system to handle the higher "voltage," the greater power of the full flow of spiritual energy in samadhi.

Posture refers to the ability to remain still, in a single position, for long periods of time. The essence of posture is the stilling of both body and mind. Patanjali writes that "posture implies steadiness and comfort. It requires relaxation and meditation on the Immovable" (*Yoga Sutras,* II:46–47).[3] In India, students of Yoga attempt to increase gradually the time they can sit in a given posture. The student masters a posture upon being able to hold that pose for three hours without stirring.

A master bestows the divine experience of cosmic consciousness when his disciple, by meditation, has strengthened his mind to a degree where the vast vistas would not overwhelm him. (Yogananda, 1972, pp. 169–170)

---

[3]Quotes from the *Yoga Sutras* of Patanjali are taken from Purohit (1938).

personal reflection

CONCENTRATION

Try this simple exercise in concentration: Look at the second hand of your watch or a clock while simultaneously remaining aware of your breathing. See how long it takes before your mind begins to wander.

Few people can focus their concentration for even a short period of time. Like any other skill, this one improves with practice. (Adapted from Tart, 1986)

Control of vital energy is the unique, fundamental aspect of Yoga. The original Sanskrit term *pranayama* is often mistranslated as "breath control." Breathing exercises can slow the metabolism and free vital energy; however, they are only an indirect means of controlling vital energy. The breath is just one manifestation of *prana,* the vital force that sustains all life.

The goal of complete mastery over vital energy can be attained through various Yoga practices. Accomplished yogis have demonstrated this mastery by stopping their heartbeat or their breathing at will, and in the past yogis have buried themselves alive for days or weeks. (See, for example, Yogananda, 1972.) Modern physiological studies have confirmed the ability of practicing yogis to control their heart rates and achieve breathlessness. (For a detailed bibliography of research on Yoga and various forms of meditation, see Timmons & Kamiya, 1970; Timmons & Kanellakos, 1974.)

Interiorization refers to the shutting off of the senses. Vital energy is withdrawn from the sense organs, and the yogi is no longer distracted by the ceaseless bombardment of outer stimuli. The yogi becomes increasingly alive within his or her own mind.

Achievement of interiorization has been verified by Indian scientists who found that brain waves of meditating yogis are unaffected by outside stimuli (Anand, Chhina, & Singh, 1961). Patanjali defines interiorization as "the restoration of sense to the original purity of mind, by renouncing its objects" (*Yoga Sutras,* II:54).

When we sit still, the outward rush of consciousness begins to subside. We learn then to slow down our breathing and to quiet our minds. During interiorization, consciousness stops flowing out through our senses into the world. We become aware of the source within as the energy flow turns back to the brain and consciousness.

Concentration is "attention fixed upon an object" (*Yoga Sutras,* III:1). There are two aspects of concentration: the *withdrawal* of the attention from objects of distraction and the *focusing* of attention upon one thing at a time. Concentration is a relaxed state, not a struggle or forcing of attention. Some development of interiorization must precede the practice of concentration. When all five senses are active, it is like trying to concentrate with five telephones constantly ringing. External sensations bring thoughts that in turn produce an endless series of memories and speculations. The sound of a car prompts us to think, "Oh, there is a car going by." Then we think about cars we once owned, cars we would like to buy, and so forth.

Meditation is a term used loosely in the West. In yogic terminology, meditation is a highly advanced practice in which only a single thought, the object of meditation alone, remains in the consciousness of the meditator. As concentration develops and becomes deeper and more prolonged, we achieve a natural state of meditation. In

Yogi doing yogic breathing exercise

meditation, the mind is fully concentrated, completely focused on the object of meditation. (See Figure 13.4.)

Illumination *(samadhi)* is, in a sense, the essence of Yoga practice. It is the state that defines Yoga, and only those who have attained illumination can be regarded as true yogis. All others are students of Yoga. *Samadhi* has also been translated as "ecstasy" (Feuerstein, 1989). According to Patanjali, illumination is a state in which "union as union disappears, only the meaning of the object on which the attention is fixed being present" (*Yoga Sutras,* III:3).

Self-realization can occur once the mind is totally calm and concentrated, reflecting the qualities of the Self within. As the Self is infinite, illumination is not a final or static state. Illumination includes a variety of states of consciousness. The contents in the field of consciousness become more and more subtle as meditation deepens.

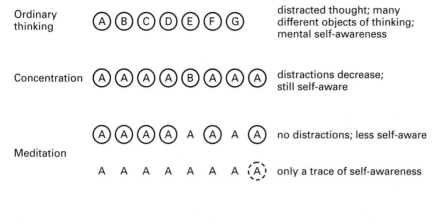

FIGURE 13.4 **Thought Processes in Yoga Practice.** The circles indicate self-awareness.
Source: Adapted from Taimni, 1961, p. 284.

Eventually, there exists only consciousness of deep joy or peace, and, finally, all that remains is consciousness of the Self. (See Figure 13.5).

Illumination without content defies description, as the field of consciousness contains nothing to which words refer. Those who have reached this stage are said to have become totally free of the influences of karma and of their subconscious tendencies.

DYNAMICS

Psychological Growth

The yogic way of life best known in the West is that of ascetic renunciation, including celibacy, poverty, and "giving up" the world to devote oneself completely to the disciplines of Yoga. In India, another ideal path of spiritual growth balances a life of worldly service and responsibilities plus the practice of spiritual discipline.

The Vedas describe various types of ascetics and sages. The ascetics, who practiced austerities and other yogic disciplines, were most likely the forerunners of the wandering yogic ascetics of modern India. The ancient *rishis,* or sages, on the other hand, emphasized the importance of sacrifices and hymns and were more a part of the Indian social order. (For a fuller discussion, see Feuerstein & Miller, 1972.)

Four Stages of Life. The classical, idealized Indian life cycle of the sage has four stages: *student, householder, forest dweller,* and *renunciant* (Smith, 1987). According to traditional Indian conceptions, each stage should last 25 years, as the normal life span was said to be 100 years in past ages.

Many classical Indian works emphasize that an individual must pass through all four stages to achieve self-realization. Each stage has its own duties, and each provides certain essential lessons and experiences.

During the first stage, the **student** serves as an apprentice, living with a teacher and the teacher's family. In addition to the acquisition of occupational skills, traditional

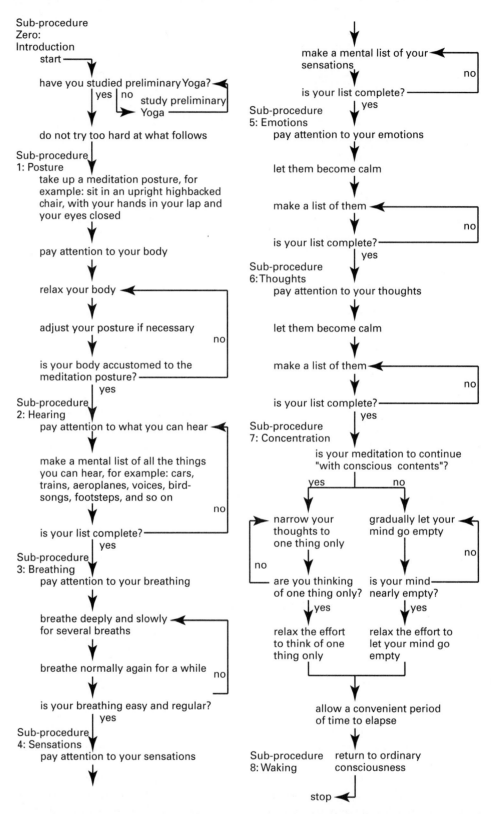

FIGURE 13.5 The Flow of Meditation. Instructions in the "Program for Patanjali," formalized by John H. Clark of Manchester University in a flow chart of the type prepared for computers. *Source:* Adapted from Clark, 1970.

Indian education is devoted to character building through emotional and spiritual discipline. The goal is to become a mature individual, fully equipped to live a harmonious and productive life, rather than remain a slave to one's moods, habits, and drives.

At the completion of this stage, the apprentice returns home and, after marrying, enters the stage of the **householder.** The duties of the householder include carrying on the family business and rearing a family. The householder seeks satisfaction in family pleasures, in achieving vocational success, and in serving the community as an active, responsible citizen. As a result of the character training received during the first stage, the householder can lead a balanced, self-controlled life. He or she has disciplined desires for sex, fame, and wealth and can enjoy the pleasures and duties of the householder in a moderate way.

The third stage is that of the **forest dweller.** It refers to gradual retirement from family and occupational affairs. When a husband and wife are over 50 years of age, their children have become old enough to assume the family responsibilities. The older couple might retire to a small, secluded cottage in the forest or remain in the family house after withdrawing from all duties and affairs. They remain available to the rest of the family, consulting with and advising their children when needed.

The individual's last quarter century is devoted to the fourth stage, *renunciation.* Entrance into this stage is marked by a ritual closely resembling funeral rites. The individual, or **renunciant,** is now officially dead to all social obligations and personal ties, and free to pursue self-realization without external demands or restrictions.

> If you run after the world the world will run from you. If you run from the world, it will run after you. (Hari Dass, 1973)

Self-realization.   The details of spiritual development vary with different branches of Yoga. For the karma-yogi, growth involves the development of self-discipline, willpower, and selfless service. For the bhakti-yogi, growth is most closely related to increase in devotion to God. For the jnana-yogi, growth is the development of powers of discrimination and self-analysis. In various other schools of Yoga, growth brings the ability to meditate, to withdraw one's attention from the world and the senses, and to focus, with increasing concentration, on some aspect of Self or Spirit.

The diverse branches of Yoga share certain fundamental principles. The path of Yoga is basically the process of turning the consciousness away from the activities of the external world back to the source of consciousness—the Self. The karma-yogi seeks to act with self-awareness without becoming overinvolved in the action itself or in the possible results of the action. The bhakti-yogi endeavors to keep the mind devotionally focused on a person or representation that symbolizes an aspect of Spirit or Self. The jnana-yogi seeks the Self by bringing the mind hack to the roots of thought and rejecting all that is not Self.

Ramakrishna, the great devotional yogi, wrote

> The secret is that the union with God (Yoga) can never happen unless the mind is rendered absolutely calm, whatever be the "path" you follow for God realization. The mind is always under the control of the Yogi, and not the Yogi under the control of his mind. (1965, p. 186)

As we mentioned, *Yoga* literally means "union," union with the Self, or illumination. One classic commentary by Vyasa (in Taimni, 1961) on Patanjali's *Yoga Sutras* states that Yoga is illumination. All the various paths and disciplines included in Yoga share the fundamental goal of illumination and self-realization.

> The wise man beholds all beings in the Self, and the Self in all beings. (*Isa Upanishad*, 6)

Obstacles to Growth

Patanjali lists five major *afflictions,* or causes of suffering: *ignorance, egoism, desire, aversion,* and *fear* (*Yoga Sutras,* II:3). The afflictions are gradually weakened by Yoga disciplines, especially austerity and self-control, scriptural study, and devotion. The yogi gradually strengthens subconscious tendencies that oppose the afflictions, weakening their influence. Afflictions have two aspects: gross and subtle. In their gross forms, the afflictions are actual thought waves (of fear, desires, and so forth). In their finer aspects, the afflictions are subconscious tendencies (*toward* fear, desire, and so forth), and these tendencies remain until the attainment of illumination.

Ignorance. **Ignorance** is the major obstacle to growth. The basis for all suffering is ignorance of our true identity. "Ignorance is the cause, the others are the effects. . . . Ignorance thinks of the perishable as imperishable, of the pure as impure, of the painful as pleasurable, of the non-Self as Self" (*Yoga Sutras,* II:4–5).

Concern with the external world and with continually active senses inhibits self-awareness. Ignorance is mistaking the effect for the cause, that is, attributing the qualities of the Self to the world by treating the world as the source of experience and remaining unaware of the Self as the ultimate cause.

Egoism. **Egoism** results from the identification of the Self with the body and the thoughts. "Egoism is the identification of the Seer with the limitations of the eye" (Yoga Sutras, II:6). Identification with the body leads to fear, desire, and a sense of limitation, and identification with the thoughts leads to restlessness and emotionality.

Desire and Aversion. Patanjali defines **desire** and **aversion** simply and elegantly: "Desire is longing for pleasure. Aversion is recoiling from pain" (*Yoga Sutras,* II:7–8). These afflictions tie the individual to the constant change and fluctuation of the external world, and they make deep calmness or peace impossible. One major aim of Yoga discipline is to overcome our tremendous sensitivity to pain, pleasure, success, failure, and other changes in the outer world. The yogi seeks freedom from the domination of the world, learning to be in control of physical, mental, and emotional reactions rather than being controlled by them.

Desire and aversion bring about attachment to whatever increases pleasure or reduces pain. **Attachment** arises from the feeling that we must have something for our own pleasure or fulfillment. Its stress on overcoming attachment does not mean, however, that Yoga is a negative, joyless self-discipline. The idea of **nonattachment** is to enjoy whatever one receives, while being ready to give it up without a sense of loss or sorrow.

A young disciple studying nonattachment was shocked to find his guru relishing a meal of exotic, imported fruits and nuts. His teacher seemed to be deeply attached to the food he was eating, instead of being properly unconcerned with what he ate. The master explained that nonattachment does not require us to give up the experience of good food or other pleasures; rather, it is the full enjoyment of what one has and the lack of regret when those pleasures are no longer available. One who has mastered nonattachment enjoys the present without trying to change it by wishing for more pleasure or less pain.

Fear. **Fear** is the fifth affliction. "Fear is constant natural terror of death, that is rooted even in the minds of the learned" (*Yoga Sutras,* II:9). In his commentary on the *Yoga Sutras,* Purohit writes: "Fear of death is constant in the mind, and as desire

> Satisfying the sensory desires cannot satisfy you, because you are not the senses. They are only your servants, not your Self. (Yogananda, 1968a, p. 60)

> The knowing Self is not born; It does not die. It has not sprung from anything; nothing has sprung from It. Birthless, eternal, everlasting, and ancient, It is not killed when the body is killed. (*Katha Upanishad,* I:ii, 18)

and aversion are the result of some experience in the past, so is the fear of death the result of dying in the past" (1938, p. 48). Fear stems from identification with the perishable body instead of the imperishable Self.

STRUCTURE

Body

Schools of Yoga regard the body in different ways. These attitudes range from outright rejection of the body, because it is seen as the source of desires and attachments, to an appreciation of the body as the main vehicle for spiritual growth.

The *Bhagavad-Gita* counsels that "Yoga is a harmony. Not for him who eats too much, or for him who eats too little; not for him who sleeps too little, or for him who sleeps too much" (VI:16). Most Yoga disciplines advocate a moderate approach to the body, neither indulgent nor unduly ascetic.

Social Relationships

Traditionally, Yoga has been associated with isolation from the world, living in a secluded cave or *ashram*. However, the *Bhagavad-Gita* teaches that each individual has his or her duty in this world, and this obligation must be carried out fully whether it entails renunciation or service to others within society. "And do thy duty, even if it be humble, rather than another's, even if it be great. To die in one's duty is life: to live in another's is death" (*Bhagavad-Gita*, III:35).

Religious devotion can also be learned through social relationships. In the West, we have tended to view God solely as a cosmic father figure, but, in India, the Divine has many faces: parent, child, friend, guru, or beloved. By experiencing love and devotion in one's relations with family and friends, the individual learns to expand and spiritualize these feelings.

Those who have attained self-realization understand that their social existence and behavior before realization were largely products of sociocultural conditioning. After achieving realization, they are in society but not of society. They truly have free choice. Realized yogis are free to fit conventional patterns of behavior or to behave according to other standards. Their newfound freedom comes from being grounded in Self, grounded in a conscious sense of the peaceful, transcendental center of Being (Chaudhuri, 1975).

> Learn to see God in all persons, of whatever race or creed. You will know what divine love is when you begin to feel your oneness with every human being, not before. (Yogananda, 1968b)

Will. The earliest forms of Yoga involved severe asceticism and tremendous will. The concept of **tapas,** ascetic discipline or austerity, still remains central to much of Yoga practice today. *Austerity* refers to the disciplining of mind and body, as the individual goes beyond comfortable limits and overcomes tendencies of self-indulgence and restlessness. Fasting, holding the body motionless in asana, and meditation practice are among the most popular austerities in Yoga today. One Yoga master summarized the attitude of disciplined will: "Daily renewed sense yearnings sap your inner peace. . . . Roam in the world as a lion of self-control; don't let the frogs of sense weakness kick you around!" (Sri Yukteswar in Yogananda, 1972, p. 149). Exercise of will also provides Yoga students with the direct experience of confronting laziness, resistance to discipline, and similar personality traits.

> True freedom consists in performing all actions in accordance with right judgments and choice of will, not in being compelled by habits. (Yogananda, 1968b)

The man who sees Brahman [God] abides in Brahman; his reason is steady, gone is his delusion. When pleasure comes he is not shaken, and when pain comes he trembles not. (*Bhagavad-Gita*, V:20)

Emotions. One approach to the emotions is to direct their energy to spiritual growth.

> So long as these passions [of anger, lust, and so forth] are directed towards the world and its objects, they behave like enemies. But when they are directed towards God, they become the best friends of man, for then they lead him into God. The lust for the things of the world must be changed into the hankering for God, the anger that man feels in relation to his fellow man should be turned towards God for not revealing Himself to him. One should deal with all the passions in the same manner. These passions cannot be eradicated but can be educated. (Ramakrishna, 1965, p. 138)

Patanjali distinguishes between painful and nonpainful waves of consciousness (*Yoga Sutras*, I:5). Painful waves are thoughts and emotions that increase ignorance, confusion, or attachment. They do not always seem unpleasant (as in pride, for example). Nonpainful waves lead to greater freedom and knowledge. The greatest obstacles to peace are painful waves of consciousness such as anger, desire, and fear. These can be countered by nonpainful waves such as love, generosity, and courage. Cultivation of nonpainful waves creates positive subconscious tendencies that counteract the negative tendencies. However, the goal of Yoga is eventually to transcend even the positive emotions (Prabhavananda & Isherwood, 1953). It may seem unnatural to transcend feelings of love and joy, but even the most positive experiences tend to bind us to the world of the senses. We must go beyond that to experience the Self.

Intellect

Do not confuse understanding with a larger vocabulary. . . . Sacred writings are beneficial in stimulating desire for inward realization, if one stanza at a time is slowly assimilated. Otherwise, continual intellectual study may result in vanity, false satisfaction, and undigested knowledge. (Yogananda, 1972)

Intellectual development in Yoga is not a matter of acquiring new information but of attaining understanding through experience. In ancient India, disciples studied sacred texts by carefully digesting one stanza at a time.

> Dabru Ballav [a renowned teacher] had gathered his disciples around him in the sylvan solitudes. The *holy Bhagavad-Gita* was open before them. Steadfastly they looked at one passage for half an hour, then closed their eyes. Another half hour slipped away. The master gave a brief comment. Motionless, they meditated again for an hour. Finally the guru spoke.
> "Do you now understand the stanza?"
> "Yes, sir." One in the group ventured this assertion.
> "No, not fully. Seek the spiritual vitality that has given these words the power to rejuvenate India century after century." Another hour passed in silence. (Yogananda, 1972, p. 136)

Mind is a mirror in which the light of the soul reflects. (Hari Dass, 1986, p. 31)

Scholars who study scriptures without attempting to put them into practice remain trapped in sterile intellectualism. "They consider philosophy to be a gentle setting-up exercise. Their elevated thoughts are carefully unrelated either to the crudity of outward action or to any scourging inner discipline" (Yogananda, 1972, p. 152). Through Yoga practice, the individual develops self-awareness and increased understanding. By discipline and experience, the yogi transforms knowledge into wisdom.

Self

According to Yoga psychology, the **Self** is the core of human consciousness. It is transcendent, changeless, and unlike anything else in this world. The Self is the fundamental ground of our consciousness or awareness, and is completely distinct from our ordinary consciousness, with its turmoil of thoughts and emotions. We become more aware of the Self as we cease to identify with our overactive, constantly changing mind and body.

One yoga authority emphasizes that our own efforts can only take us so far, ". . . there is nothing anyone can do to 'acquire the Self.' On the contrary, Self-realization must be a matter of the Self disclosing itself of its own accord. This means Self-realization is dependent on grace" (Feuerstein, 1989, p 150).

Teacher

The word **guru** comes from the Sanskrit root "to uplift." Many teachers in India are called gurus; the name connotes a spiritual teacher, one who can raise the student's consciousness. (In India, teachers of music, dance, and other traditional skills do more than instruct students in technique; they are considered masters of disciplines that affect one's whole life and character.) In Yoga, a guru is considered essential for several reasons. The techniques taught are complex and subtle and cannot be learned from books. Also, the teacher must adapt many techniques to the specific physical and mental makeup of the student.

The guru is a disciplinarian who pushes the student beyond self-imposed limitations. As one who has been through the discipline already, the guru knows from experience the extent of human capacity. Thus the guru demands that students exert themselves to the limits of their capabilities. In addition, students are inspired by their teacher's living example to realize their highest potential.

The guru also fosters the student's emotional and psychological development. The teacher is like a mirror, exposing student faults and limitations but remaining conscious of the essential purity and perfection of the Self behind such limitations. This kind of discipline can be administered only by someone who is relatively free of ego and strong personal biases or blind spots, which would distort the guru's reactions to the student.

The guru's most important attribute is spiritual consciousness. A teacher who has realized the Self transmits a sense of inner peace and bliss. One yogi describes this as follows: "If I entered the hermitage in a worried or indifferent frame of mind, my attitude imperceptibly changed. A healing calm descended at the mere sight of my guru. Each day with him was a new experience in joy, peace, and wisdom" (Yogananda, 1972, pp. 137–138).

Vivekananda points out that the guru teaches from his or her state of being:

> If a man wants to teach me something of dynamics, of chemistry, or any other physical science, he may be anything he likes, because what the physical sciences require is merely an intellectual equipment; but in the spiritual sciences it is impossible from first to last that there can be any spiritual light in the soul that is impure. . . . Hence with the teacher of religion we must see first what he is, and then what he says. He must be perfectly pure, and then alone comes the value of his words, because he is only then the true "transmitter." What can he transmit, if he has not spiritual power in himself? . . . The function of the teacher is indeed an affair of the transference of something, and not one of mere stimulation of the existing intellectual or other faculties in the taught. Something real and appreciable as an influence comes from the teacher and goes to the taught. Therefore, the teacher must be pure. . . .
>
> The teacher must not teach with any ulterior selfish motive—for money, name, or fame—his work must be simply out of love, out of pure love for mankind at large. The

only medium through which spiritual force can be transmitted is love. . . . God is love, and only he who has known God as love, can be a teacher of godliness and God to man. (Vivekananda, 1978a, pp. 32–33)

Initiation.   Many authorities maintain that initiation is a crucial element in Yoga practice. According to Kularnava-Tantra, self-realization is impossible without initiation, and there can be no real initiation without a qualified teacher initiated into a lineage himself or herself (Feuerstein, 1989).

Initiation is primarily a form of spiritual transmission. Through this transmission the disciple is transformed physically, mentally, and spiritually. Initiation creates a special bond between teacher and disciple. The disciple enters the teacher's spiritual lineage, a chain that may go back unbroken for centuries.

One of the later Yoga texts, the *Kularnava-Tantra*, classifies six different types of yoga teachers, according to basic function (Feuerstein, 1989). A teacher generally is a composite of several of these: (1) the *Impeller* motivates and inspires the prospective disciple, leading him or her to initiation; (2) the *Indicator* prescribes the most appropriate form of spiritual practice and discipline; (3) the *Explainer* interprets and clarifies the spiritual process and its goal; (4) the *Revealer* clarifies the details of the process; (5) the *Teacher* supervises the disciple's spiritual discipline; and (6) the *Illuminator* kindles in the disciple mental and spiritual understanding.

One great danger in the role of the yoga teacher is ego inflation. Feuerstein, a scholar of Yoga, points out that although enlightened yogis may live out of the identity of the Self, their personalities remain intact (1993). He suggests that integration of the personality is a necessary complement to transcendence for any guru.

A guru is not a magician who transforms students without any effort on their part. Gurus are instructors of subtle truths and practices; as in any learning situation, students' achievements are in proportion to their effort, ability, and receptivity:

The conditions for the taught are purity, a real thirst after knowledge, and perseverance. . . . Purity in thought, speech, and act is absolutely necessary for anyone to be religious. As to the thirst after knowledge, it is an old law that we all get whatever we want. None of us can get anything other than what we fix our hearts on. . . . The success may sometimes come immediately, but we must be ready to wait patiently even for what may look like an infinite length of time. The student who sets out with such a spirit of perseverance will surely find success in realization at last. (Vivekananda, 1978a, pp. 28–29)

The Yoga model of the guru–disciple relationship is an example of deep love and respect for a model teacher. A real yoga teacher becomes a powerful force for change and inner growth. Unfortunately, an ego-driven teacher can take tremendous advantage of loyal students.

EVALUATION

Most schools of Yoga focus on inner experience at the expense of outward interests, and this emphasis may not appeal to everyone. The attitude that worldly, sensory experiences distract from the Self within, if improperly exercised, can lead to a retreat from life's problems and a certain kind of passivity. Also, the doctrine of karma, depending on how one approaches it, can mean the passive acceptance of one's lot in life. Although Yoga does include the discipline of action, most branches tend to emphasize inner peace at the expense of outward activity.

Yoga, as practiced in the West, often seems more a system for health and mental concentration than a complete spiritual discipline. Without mental and emotional discipline, or without practice of the moral precepts of Yoga, the postures, breathing exercises, or concentration techniques can result in unbalanced development. They may even reinforce pride and egotism.

People generally enter psychotherapy because they are functioning inadequately or are suffering mentally or physically. Yoga traditionally begins with normal, healthy individuals and aims not to restore normality or improve worldly function, but to completely transform the individual (Feuerstein, 1972).

The major emphasis in Yoga lies in the practical effectiveness of the techniques. Experience, rather than theoretical knowledge, is at the heart of Yoga. The various disciplines can suit virtually any individual, whether active, intellectual, or emotional in disposition. No other system contains so many different methods for self-development. Yoga includes seven central practices common to Buddhism, Sufism, and other contemplative disciplines (Walsh, 1999). These are ethics, emotional development, spiritualized motivation, attention and awareness training, wisdom development, and the practice of altruism and service.

> Success is immediate where effort is intense. (*Yoga Sutras* 1:21)

The Theory Firsthand

EXCERPT FROM *RADHA: DIARY OF A WOMAN'S SEARCH*

The following passage describes experiences of Swami Radha with her guru Swami Sivananda, one of the greatest Yoga masters in India in the twentieth century.

How wonderful it is when one can gather all the rays of spiritual love and tenderness from his voice, undisturbed by the loud voices of other people, when one can read unspoken words of understanding in his eyes. On the spiritual path it seems that the struggles and suffering are tremendous in proportion to the success. Motherly and fatherly guidance is needed from one who knows about the tribulations that have to be faced. In ordinary life, the world, especially the business world, is very impersonal. Even within a family one can be left with feelings of loneliness, longing for love and acceptance. On the spiritual path this loneliness does not seem to diminish. Slowly I begin to have more of a grasp of Sivananda's wisdom. All Gurudev's gifts and attention are meant to implant in students feelings of affection, of being wanted as his devotee. It often appears that the weaker the student, the more attention is given, since each receives exactly what is needed. From some he demands a great deal, sometimes the seemingly impossible. This is determined individually by what he senses in each devotee. I have noticed that occasionally he will speak directly, at other times just hint. It has also happened that he will give the answer before the question is asked. . . .

With my hands full of new books I stood outside Master's office. He was only a few steps from me with a group of people. Suddenly he called my name:

"Radha! Let—it—drop!"

It appeared to me that he was looking at my left hand. For a moment I hesitated, but then dropped all the books I held in that hand. But he repeated:

"Radha! Let—it—drop!"

It flashed through my mind. IT—the EGO! Not the books.

I walked over to him and touched his feet—for the first time. . . .

[That evening] "When you go back to the West," he said, "do not work any more for money!"

"But Gurudev, how shall I live?"

"God will look after you. Nobody else than God has looked after you till now!"

"America and Canada are very money conscious. Nobody would understand, if I start living on alms."

"Why, you are afraid! When you came to India, were you not afraid of tigers, cobras, cheetahs? God has protected you here. He will protect you anywhere."

Master could not see my point. I made another attempt. "There are very few people who are really interested in yoga and Vedanta. If they have to look after me, I will soon be a great burden to them. And I am healthy, why should I not work?"

"Because," Master interrupted my word flow, "you cannot tell people to live on faith in God Alone, if you don't do it yourself. You must try to be in every way an example."

How right he is! Because he himself is such an example, he has conquered my heart and convinced my mind. But I? I have not the courage to make such an experiment.

"Radha! There is still too much pride—hidden!" He hit the sore spot. No use in arguing. He is perfectly right. How can I ever hope to get out of this whole thing!

(Radha, 1981, pp. 68–69, 168–169)

CHAPTER HIGHLIGHTS

- The roots of Yoga are anchored in India's pre-Hindu culture. First mentioned in the ancient Vedas, Yoga was systematized by Patanjali as a specific school of philosophy.
- The most popular work on Yoga is the *Bhagavad-Gita,* itself part of the great Indian epic *Mahabharata.* In the *Bhagavad-Gita,* Krishna (the Self, or guru) guides Arjuna (the ego).
- Classical Yoga refers to the work of Patanjali, which emphasizes the necessity of experiencing ecstatic states of consciousness *(samadhi).*
- The ideal of Yoga is to seek joy from its source—the Self. In its broadest sense, Yoga encompasses all religious and systematic practices designed to promote self-realization through calming the mind and focusing consciousness on the Self.
- Control of the waves of consciousness is possible when the subconscious tendencies *(samskaras)* are diminished.
- In India, the guru's most important attribute is spiritual consciousness. Six functions of a guru include the Impeller, the Indicator, the Explainer, the Revealer, the Teacher, and the Illuminator.
- Initiation is a crucial facet of Yoga practice. Primarily a form of spiritual transmission, it establishes a special bond between guru and disciple, as the disciple enters the guru's lineage.
- Major schools of Yoga have developed to suit different personalities: karma-yoga (the Yoga of action), jnana-yoga (the Yoga of knowledge), bhakti-yoga (the Yoga of devotion), hatha-yoga (the Yoga of the body), mantra-yoga (the Yoga of sound), kundalini-yoga (the Yoga of energy), and raja-yoga (the royal Yoga of mind and body).
- Patanjali outlined the eight limbs of Yoga: abstentions, observances, postures, vital energy control, interiorization, concentration, meditation, and illumination.
- The idealized Indian life cycle included four stages: student, householder, forest dweller, and renunciant.
- Ignorance, egoism, desire, aversion, and fear are the major causes of suffering, or afflictions, according to Patanjali.
- Patanjali distinguishes between painful and nonpainful waves of consciousness. Thoughts and emotions that increase ignorance, attachment, or confusion are painful. Nonpainful waves, such as love, courage, and generosity, lead to greater freedom and knowledge.
- Attaining understanding through experience is considered an essential complement to intellectual development in Yoga. What one studies must be put into practice to escape sterile intellectualism.

KEY CONCEPTS

Abstentions Part of the moral code that serves as the foundation of Yoga practice, and the first of Pantanjali's eight limbs of Yoga. Abstentions include nongreed, nonstealing, chastity, truthfulness, and nonviolence.

Asanas Postures in hatha-yoga that have accompanying levels of psychological and spiritual significance. The physical benefits include strength, balance, flexibility, and stimulation of the endocrine and other organ systems.

Attachment The feeling that we must possess things for our own pleasure or fulfillment. One of the five obstacles to growth, it is prompted by desire and aversion.

Aversion In Patanjali's words, "recoiling from pain." As an obstacle to growth, it reinforces the individual's tie to the outer world.

Bhakti-yoga The Yoga of devotion. It is a way, through love and devotion, of transforming one's personality. Closer to traditional religions than any other form of Yoga, it includes ritual worship, chanting, and the worship of God.

Chakras Seven centers of consciousness that lie along the spine. Each chakra associates with particular spiritual and physical attributes; some relate to various forms, colors, senses, or elements.

Concentration The state in which attention is fixed on an object, and the sixth of Patanjali's eight limbs of Yoga. It has two aspects: the focusing of attention on one thing at a time and the withdrawal of the attention from objects of distraction. Some degree of interiorization must precede the practice of concentration.

Control of vital energy The unique and fundamental aspect of Yoga, and the fourth of Patanjali's eight limbs of Yoga. The goal is complete mastery over vital energy, or prana. Control can be attained through various Yoga practices, including breathing exercises.

Desire According to Patanjali, the "longing for pleasure." One of the five obstacles to growth, desire links the individual to the outside world and thus makes calmness impossible.

Egoism The state that results from identification with the body (which leads to a sense of limitation, desire, and fear) and with the thoughts (which leads to emotionality and restlessness). Egoism is one of the five obstacles to growth.

Fear The natural terror of death that results from identification with the impermanent body instead of the imperishable Self. Fear is one of the five obstacles to growth.

Forest dweller Third stage in the idealized life cycle, in which an older couple may withdraw to the forest or to a secluded setting, retiring from active involvement in family and occupational affairs.

Hatha-yoga The Yoga of the body. The practices are designed to strengthen and purify the body for advanced meditation and higher states of consciousness, and to help manifest the infinite Self in the finite body-mind.

Householder Second stage in the idealized life cycle, in which the individual returns home after completion of apprenticeship. The duties include marrying, carrying on the family business, and rearing a family. Satisfaction is sought in vocational success, family pleasures, and service to the community, while living a self-controlled life.

Ignorance The state of remaining unaware of the Self as the ultimate cause. The individual treats the world as the source of experience instead of the Self. Ignorance is the major obstacle to growth, and the basis for all suffering.

Illumination The essence of Yoga practice, and the eighth of Patanjali's eight limbs of Yoga. Known in Sanskrit as *samadhi*, it includes a variety of states of consciousness. Realization of the Self occurs once the mind is totally calm and concentrated, reflecting the qualities of the Self within.

Interiorization The process of shutting off the senses, and Patanjali's fifth limb of Yoga. As vital energy is withdrawn from sense organs, the ceaseless bombardment of outer stimuli is no longer a distraction.

Jnana-yoga The Yoga of knowledge. It is basically a path of discrimination and a discipline of rigorous self-analysis. The jnana-yogi seeks to avoid or counter the influences of passion, sense attachment, and identification with the body, as well as to understand the forces of bondage and delusion.

Karma Action, and also its results. Karma stems from the principle that every person's life is influenced by past actions, and every activity brings with it certain consequences.

Karma-yoga The Yoga of action. It teaches disciples to act selflessly, without attachment to loss or gain, failure or success. The karma-yogi, who seeks to act on high ideals and to serve other people, is transformed by developing selflessness through service rather than through individual religious discipline.

Kundalini-yoga The Yoga of energy. The goal is to awaken the kundalini energy, which lies coiled at the base of the spine. Disciplines of meditation, breathing exercises, visualization, and the purification techniques of hatha-yoga may prompt its flow. When awakened, the energy rises through all the chakras, or centers of consciousness, leading to major psychological, physical, and spiritual changes in the individual.

Mantra A sacred phrase or syllable, charged with psychospiritual power. Traditionally, the disciple receives a mantra during an initiation ceremony. *Om* is the most recognized and widely used mantra in India.

Mantra-yoga The Yoga of sound. Focused repetition of a mantra leads to one-pointed meditation and will attune the individual to the cosmic vibration of the universe.

Meditation A highly advanced practice in which a single thought alone remains in the consciousness of the meditator. Meditation is the seventh of Patanjali's eight limbs of Yoga.

Nonattachment The idea that one is to enjoy whatever one receives and be ready to give it up without a sense of sorrow or loss.

Observances Part of the moral code that serves as the foundation for Yoga practice, and the second of Patanjali's eight limbs of Yoga. The observances are contentment, austerity, purity, study, and devotion.

Posture The ability to remain still and relaxed, for long periods of time. It is the third of Patanjali's eight limbs of Yoga. The term refers also to the practice of hatha-yoga asanas, or postures.

Prana Vital energy of the body. It is strengthened and brought into control through breathing practices, meditation, and other yoga disciplines.

Raja-yoga Royal Yoga, or "psychological Yoga." Its eight limbs are outlined in the Yoga Sutras of Patanjali.

Renunciant Fourth stage in the idealized life cycle. The individual's last quarter century, it is a time to pursue self-realization.

Self The unchanging, immortal manifestation of Spirit in the individual. Like a wave, it is a form that the ocean of Spirit takes on for a time.

Self-realization The process of turning consciousness away from the external world and back to the Self, the source of consciousness.

Student First stage in the idealized life cycle. The goal is to acquire skills and to experience emotional and spiritual discipline as an apprentice.

Tapas The concept of ascetic discipline or austerity. Still central to Yoga today, the practice includes fasting and long periods of motionless posture and meditation.

Yoga A Sanskrit word meaning "to join" or "to unite." It also means "method," and may be considered the technology of self-realization.

ANNOTATED BIBLIOGRAPHY

Eliade, M. (1969). *Yoga: Immortality and freedom*. Princeton, NJ: Princeton University Press.

Scholarly treatment of the many diverse Yoga traditions.

Mascaro, J. (Trans.). (1962). *The Bhagavad Gita*. Baltimore: Penguin Books.

A good, easily obtainable translation.

Prabhavananda, Swami, & Isherwood, C. (Trans.). (1951). *The song of God: Bhagavad Gita*. New York: New American Library (Mentor Books).

Readable and easily obtainable.

Prabhavananda, Swami, & Isherwood, C. (Trans.). (1953). *How to know God: The Yoga aphorisms of Patanjali*. New York: New American Library.

Excellent, easily obtainable, but a somewhat Westernized translation of the *Yoga Sutras*.

Purohit, Swami (Trans.). (1938). *Aphorisms of Yoga by Bhagwan Shree Patanjali*. London: Faber.

Best translation and commentary in English.

Radha, Swami. (1978). *Kundalini: Yoga for the West*. Spokane, WA: Timeless Books.

By far the most detailed and psychologically sophisticated treatment of kundalini-yoga, the chakras, and the images and symbols of Yoga.

Ram Dass, Baba. (1970). *Be here now*. San Cristobal, NM: Lama Foundation.

A modern, "hip" interpretation of Yoga. The work includes meditation techniques and other disciplines a discussion of the transformation of Richard Alpert into Baba Ram Dass; a spiritual reading list; and an inspiring interpretation of Indian philosophy and Yoga through integrated text and pictures.

Taimni, I. K. (1961). *The science of Yoga*. Wheaton, IL: Quest.

Solid and scholarly translation of the *Yoga Sutras*, with extensive commentary.

Vishnudevananda, Swami. (1960). *The complete illustrated book of Yoga*. New York: Pocket Books.

A fine, practical hatha-yoga paperback.

Yogananda, Paramahansa. (1972). *The autobiography of a yogi*. Los Angeles: Self-realization Fellowship.

A classic account of yogis and Yoga training in India. Excellent introduction of the Indian tradition.

Web Sites

Hindu Religious Beliefs and Practices
aol.beliefnet.com

This site includes highly informative sections on all the world's major religious traditions, including Hinduism, Buddhism, and Islam.

Yoga Information
www.yogajournal.com/

Includes a directory of yoga classes, retreats and teachers, information on hatha-yoga postures, and discussions on yoga philosophy and practice.

REFERENCES

Anand, B., Chhina, G., & Singh, B. (1961). Some aspects of electroencephalographic studies in yogis. *Electroencephalography and Clinical Neurology, 13,* 452–456.

Chaudhuri, H. (1975). Yoga psychology. In C. Tart (Ed.), *Transpersonal psychologies*. New York: Harper & Row.

Clark, J. H. (1970, July 23). Program for Patanjali. New Society.

Danielou, A. (1955). *Yoga: The method of re-integration*. New Hyde Park, NY: University Books.

Eliade, M. (1969). *Yoga: Immortality and freedom*. Princeton, NJ: Princeton University Press.

Feuerstein, G. (1989). *Yoga: The technology of ecstacy*. Los Angeles: Tarcher.

Feuerstein, G. (1993). The shadow of the enlightened guru. In Walsh, R., & Vaughan, F. (1993) *Paths beyond ego*. Los Angeles: Tarcher.

Feuerstein, G. (1996). *The philosophy of classical yoga*. Rochester, VT: Inner Traditions.

Feuerstein, G., & Miller, J. (1972). *Yoga and beyond*. New York: Schocken Books.

Greenwell, B. (1990). *Energies of transformation: A guide to the kundalini process*. Cupertino, CA: Shakti River Press.

Hari Dass. (1973). *The yellow book*. San Cristobal, NM: Lama Foundation.

Hari Dass. (1986). *Fire without fuel*. Santa Cruz, CA: Sri Rama Publishing.

Kieffer, G. (Ed.). (1996). *Empowering human evolution*. New York: Paragon.

Krishna, G. (1971). *Kundalini: The evolutionary energy in man*. London: Robinson & Watkins.

Majumdar, S. (1964). *Introduction to Yoga principles and practices*. New Hyde Park, NY: University Books.

Mascaro, J. (Trans.). (1962). *The Bhagavad Gita*. Baltimore: Penguin Books.

Nikhilananda, Swami. (1948). *Ramakrishna: Prophet of new India*. New York: Harper & Row.

Nikhilananda, Swami. (1964). *The Upanishads*. New York: Harper & Row.

Osbourne, A. (1962). *The teachings of Ramana Maharshi*. London: Rider.

Osbourne, A. (1970). *Ramana Maharshi and the path of self-knowledge*. New York: Weiser.

Osbourne, A. (Ed.). (1969). *The collected works of Ramana Maharshi*. London: Rider.

Prabhavananda, Swami, & Isherwood, C. (Trans.). (1951). *The song of God: Bhagavad Gita*. New York: New American Library (Mentor Books).

Prabhavananda, Swami, & Isherwood, C. (1953). *How to know God: The Yoga aphorisms of Patanjali*. New York: New American Library.

Purohit, Swami (Trans.). (1938). *Aphorisms of Yoga by Bhagwan Shree Patanjali*. London: Faber.

Purohit, Swami, & Yeats, W. B. (Trans.). (1965). *The Geeta: The gospel of Lord Shri Krishna*. London: Faber.

Radha, Swami. (1981). *Radha: Diary of a woman's search*. Porthill, ID: Timeless Books.

Radha, Swami. (1987). *Hatha Yoga: The hidden language*. Porthill, ID: Timeless Books.

Ram Dass. (1974). *The only dance there is*. New York: Doubleday.

Ramakrishna. (1965). *Sayings of Sri Ramakrishna*. Madras, India: Sri Ramakrishna Math.

Ramaswami, S. (1989). Yoga and healing. In A. Sheikh & K. Sheikh (Eds.), *Eastern and Western approaches to healing*. New York: Wiley.

Sanella, L. (1987). *The kundalini experience: Psychosis or transcendence?* Lower Lake, CA: Integral Publishing.

Shamdasani, S. (Ed.). (1996). *The psychology of kundalini yoga: Notes of the seminar given in 1932 by C. G. Jung*. Princeton, NJ: Princeton University Press.

Smith, H. (1987). *The religions of man*. New York: HarperCollins.

Taimni, I. K. (1961). *The science of Yoga*. Wheaton, IL: Quest.

Tart, C. (1986). *Waking up: Overcoming obstacles to human potential*. Boston: New Science Library.

Timmons, B., & Kamiya, J. (1970). The psychology and physiology of meditation and related phenomena: A bibliography. *Journal of Transpersonal Psychology, 2,* 41–59.

Timmons, B., & Kanellakos, D. (1974). The psychology and physiology of meditation and related phenomena: Bibliography II. *Journal of Transpersonal Psychology, 4,* 32–38.

Vivekananda, Swami. (1976). *Jnana-yoga*. Calcutta: Advaita Ashrama.

Vivekananda, Swami. (1978a). *Bhakti-yoga*. Calcutta: Advaita Ashrama.

Vivekananda, Swami. (1978b). *Karma-yoga*. Calcutta: Advaita Ashrama.

Walsh, R. (1999). Asian contemplative disciplines: Common practices, clinical applications, and research findings. *Journal of Transpersonal Psychology, 31,* 83–107.

Yogananda, Paramahansa. (1963). *Cosmic chants*. Los Angeles: Self-Realization Fellowship.

Yogananda, Paramahansa. (1967). *Metaphysical meditations*. Los Angeles: Self-Realization Fellowship.

Yogananda, Paramahansa. (1968a). *Sayings of Yogananda*. Los Angeles: Self-Realization Fellowship.

Yogananda, Paramahansa. (1968b). *Spiritual diary*. Los Angeles: Self-Realization Fellowship.

Yogananda, Paramahansa. (1972). *The autobiography of a yogi*. Los Angeles: Self-Realization Fellowship.

chapter 14

zen and
the buddhist tradition

When asked how one should evaluate religious teachings and spiritual teachers, the Buddha replied:

> You who follow me, consider this carefully. Keep an eye open, seekers of truth. Weigh rumor, custom, and hearsay. Don't let anyone's excellence in the Scriptures mislead you. Logic and argument, supply of elaborate reasons, approval of considered opinion, plausibility of ideas, respect for the leader who guides you—beware of too much trust in them. Only when you know, and are sure that you know—this is not good, this is erroneous, this is censured by the intelligent, this will lead to loss and grief—only when you know, should you reject or accept it. *(The Dhammapada, Lal, 1967, p. 17)*

In Zen Buddhism, the primary concern is to lead others to a direct, personal understanding of Truth. The Buddha's teachings emphasize experience over theology or abstract philosophy. Zen is a school of Buddhism that stresses meditation and spiritual practice. As the Zen philosopher D. T. Suzuki has written, "The basic idea of Zen is to come in touch with the inner workings of our being, and to do this in the most direct way possible, without resorting to anything external or super-added" (1964, p. 44). In its broadest sense, Zen provides a practical, experiential approach to spirituality applicable to all religions.

Buddhist psychology distinguishes between the ordinary conscious mind and the deeper Mind:

> To live a spiritual life is to learn and to practice the Way-mind. The Way is the universal path that is complete serenity and tranquillity. It is called Mind. This Mind is not ordinary mind. Mind, as serenity and tranquillity, is the original nature of human consciousness. . . .
>
> In the study of psychology, one tries to understand the basis of consciousness, which is called the unconscious. . . . Psychology tries to understand this unconscious level, and to take things from it. When you try to take things from it, this is nothing but the functioning of ego-consciousness. . . . But whatever the ego can pick up and look at is only the surface of Way-mind. Buddhism is to learn serenity and tranquillity directly, and to practice it. (Katagiri, 1988, p. 13)

Scholars who have compared Buddhist and Western psychological theories include Katz (1983) and Molino (1998). Ramaswami and Sheikh (1989) summarize Buddhist psychology:

> The psychology of Buddhism rests on the notions of the absence of a separate self, impermanence of all things, and the fact of sorrow. Human beings suffer because of self-delusion, striving to possess that which inevitably must crumble, and because of desire. The Buddha did not stop with a mere diagnosis. He proclaimed that the cure is to reach a higher state of being, wherein self-knowledge has eradicated delusion, attachment, and desire. (p. 120)

There is no final doctrine or dogma because there can be no absolute truths, nor even an absolute Buddha, in the face of impermanence. Buddhist teachings orient to human realities. They aim at eliminating the sense of dissatisfaction and inadequacy caused by a limited, selfish ego. In the passage quoted at the beginning of this chapter, the Buddha is reported to have told his disciples not to follow any teachings in response to a particular teacher's reputation or skill with words but to rely on their own judgment and experience. The final criterion for Zen is experience. Teaching and discipline that aid people in becoming more mature, more responsible, and more complete human beings are considered good Buddhism.

HISTORY

Remember thou must go alone;
The Buddhas do but point the
way. (Shakyamuni Buddha)

Buddhism is based on the teachings of Siddhartha Gautama, the Buddha. The term *Buddha* is a title, not a proper name. It means "one who is awake," one who has attained full humanness. According to Buddhist doctrine, many other Buddhas came before Gautama and there are Buddhas still to come. The Buddha never claimed to be more than a man whose realization, attainments, and achievements were the result of his purely human capacities. He developed himself into a completely mature human being, which is such a rare achievement that we tend to look on it as superhuman or divinely inspired. The central attitude in Buddhism is that every individual possesses this *Buddha-nature,* the capacity for developing into a complete human being and becoming a Buddha.

According to the legends of the Buddha's life, he was born as Prince Gautama. Gautama was born about 563 BC, a prince in the Shakya kingdom in northern India (today part of Nepal). At age 16, he was married to a beautiful princess and lived in his palace surrounded by comfort and luxury. When Gautama was in his late twenties, he had occasion to slip out of his palatial prison and abruptly confronted the reality of life and human suffering.

First, Gautama encountered an old man worn down by a life of toil and hardship. On his second trip, he saw a man afflicted with a serious illness. On his third trip, Gautama watched a corpse being carried in a sorrowful funeral procession. Finally, Gautama met a religious ascetic engaged in the traditional Indian pursuit of spiritual discipline. Gautama realized that sickness, old age, and death are unavoidable endings even to the happiest and most prosperous life.

The inevitability of human suffering became the central focus of Gautama's search. His present way of life, he realized, could not provide an answer to the problem of suffering, and he decided to leave his family and palace to seek a solution through spiritual discipline.

Planners make canals, archers
shoot arrows, craftsmen fashion
woodwork, the wise man molds
himself. (*The Dhammapada,* Lal,
1967)

At the age of 29, soon after the birth of his only son, Gautama left his kingdom and studied for six years with many teachers, including two famous Yoga teachers, engaging in severe ascetic practices. Finally, weakened by a long fast, Gautama realized that mortification of the body would never bring about enlightenment, and he accepted food for strength to continue with his spiritual efforts. He then sat beneath a Bodhi tree and resolved that he would not eat or leave his seat until he reached enlightenment, even if he died in the attempt. From Gautama's experience came the Buddhist conception of the *Middle Way:* seeking a healthy and useful discipline without either extreme of complete sense indulgence or self-torture. After deep and prolonged meditation, Gautama underwent a profound inner transformation that altered his perspective on life. His approach to the questions of sickness, old age, and death changed because he changed. At age 35, he became the Buddha.

The Buddha decided to share his understanding with others, and he taught for 45 years, walking from town to town in India with an ever-growing band of followers. He died in 483 BC, at the age of 80.

For many centuries, Buddhism flourished in India and spread gradually throughout Asia. Between AD 1000 and 1200, Buddhism mostly died out in India through the growing weakness of Indian Buddhism, the revival of Hinduism, and persecution by Mughal rulers. The practice is expanding again in India today.

Buddhism currently has two major traditions. The *Theravada* or *Hinayana* tradition is found primarily in Southeast Asia, in Sri Lanka, Burma, and Thailand. The *Mahayana* tradition has flourished mainly in Tibet, China, Korea, and Japan. The Mahayana tradition, which began as a liberal movement within Theravadan

Buddhism, is less strict in interpreting the traditional monastic disciplinary rules, less exclusive with regard to householders, and more willing to adopt later additions to the Buddhist scriptures. The Mahayanists have also placed high value on compassion, as opposed to the Theravada emphasis on self-discipline. Originally, these two great traditions were seen as alternative personal interpretations within Buddhism. Adherents of the Mahayana and Theravadan approaches originally lived together in the same monasteries, obeying the same basic rules.

Zen is a major school of the Mahayana tradition. Traced back all the way to the Buddha, Zen is said to have been brought to China in the sixth century AD by Bodhidharma, an Indian Buddhist monk, who emphasized contemplation and personal discipline over religious ritual. Under the influence of a series of great Chinese masters, Zen gradually developed as an independent school of Buddhism, with its own monasteries, monastic rules, and organization. By AD 1000, Zen had become the second most popular school of Buddhism in China.

Man's inability to control and discipline his mind is responsible for all his problems. (Dalai Lama)

The Dalai Lama

In the twelfth and thirteenth centuries, two Japanese monks, Eisai and Dogen, traveled to China to study Buddhism. When they returned to Japan, these monks established temples, taught prominent disciples, and founded the two great sects of Japanese Zen Buddhism, Soto and Rinzai. According to Master Eisai (1141–1215), who introduced Rinzai Zen in Japan, enlightenment could be achieved through the use of Zen "riddles," or *koan*. Master Dogen (1200–1253), the founder of Japanese Soto Zen, stressed two major points: no gap exists between daily practice and enlightenment, and the right (correct) daily behavior is Buddhism itself.

Just as most chapters in this text examine the work of a particular theorist, this chapter focuses primarily on Zen Buddhism, one of many Buddhist traditions and schools. We will summarize Buddhist concepts and psychology from a Soto Zen perspective.

Basically, there is only one Buddhism. Different teachers and different schools interpret the fundamental truths of Buddhism to fit their own cultures and societies. In "Recent Developments," we outline the major contributions of two other schools of Buddhism prominent in the United States: Theravadan and Tibetan Buddhism. More information on Buddhist history is available on our **web** site.

MAJOR CONCEPTS

At the heart of Buddhist thought are three major characteristics of existence: impermanence, lack of an imperishable Self or soul, and dissatisfaction as an essential attribute of this world. Stemming from these three characteristics are the basic principles of Buddhism—the Four Noble Truths and the Eightfold Path. Zen Buddhism is based on the practice of meditation as a means of directly experiencing the principles and truths of Buddhism—that is, the experience of "enlightenment." Two Buddhist conceptions of the ideal human being are the arhat and the bodhisattva.

The Three Characteristics of Existence

Impermanence.   Everything is constantly changing; **impermanence** characterizes all things. Certainly nothing physical lasts forever. Trees, buildings, the sun, moon, stars—all have a finite existence; furthermore, all are in flux at any given moment.

Impermanence also applies to thoughts and ideas. The concept of impermanence implies no final authority or permanent truth, only a level of understanding suitable for a certain time and place. Because conditions change, what seems true at one time inevitably becomes false or inappropriate at others. Therefore, Buddhism cannot be said to have a fixed doctrine. To understand the concept of impermanence is to realize that nothing ever fully becomes Buddha, that even Buddha, or truth, is subject to change and can still progress. In other words, everything is an ever-changing manifestation of the same reality that is also Buddha.

The Buddhists point out that the primary feature of the universe is change. However, human beings have a strong tendency to conceive of the world as static, to see *things* instead of fluid and constantly changing *processes*. These processes are both ever-changing and also interdependent.

Perhaps the best illustration of the Buddhist concept of **interdependence** comes from Thich Nhat Hanh, a Vietnamese Zen master.

Time flies quicker than an arrow and life passes with greater transience than dew. However skillful you may be, how can you ever recall a single day of the past? (Dogen in Kennett, 1976)

If you are a poet, you will see clearly that there is a cloud floating in this sheet of paper. Without a cloud, there will be no rain; without rain, the trees cannot grow; and without trees, we cannot make paper. The cloud is essential for the paper to exist. . . .

If we look into this sheet of paper even more deeply, we can see the sunshine in it. If the sunshine is not there, the forest cannot grow. In fact, nothing can grow. . . . And if we continue to look, we can see the logger who cut the tree and brought it to the mill to be transformed into paper. And we see the wheat. We know that the logger cannot exist without his daily bread, and therefore the wheat that became his bread is also in this sheet of paper. And the logger's father and mother are in it too. . . .

So we can say that everything is in here with this sheet of paper. . . . Everything co-exists with this sheet of paper. . . . You cannot just *be* by yourself alone. . . . This sheet of paper is, because everything else is. (1988, pp. 3–4)

To realize that everything coexists and is in constant flux is to experience the world in a radically different way.

Selflessness.   Various religions have taught that the Self, or soul, is unchanging and imperishable. The Buddhist notion of impermanence, however, applies to our innermost self as well.

The concept of **selflessness** holds that no immortal soul or eternal, unchanging self exists in each individual. The individual is seen as a collection of elements, all of which are impermanent and constantly changing. According to the Buddha, the individual is made up of five basic factors: body, perception, sensation, consciousness, and mental activities (that is, ideas, intentions, and so on). The term *I* is merely a useful linguistic device to refer to an ever-changing collection of traits that comprise the individual.

In other words, our bodies and our personalities are composed of mortal, constantly changing processes. The individual is not something other than the pattern formed by the temporary interaction of these component processes. When the parts perish, so does the individual. No aspect of ourselves goes on forever, although the consequences of our thoughts and action may continue. All things—not only human beings—lack a separate, undying self, including trees, mountains, plants, and animals. First, they cannot exist except in terms of interdependence or coexistence with all things. Second, all things are composites, or temporary collections of processes.

Dissatisfaction.   **Dissatisfaction,** or suffering, is the third characteristic of existence. The concept of dissatisfaction embraces birth, death, decay, sorrow, pain, grief, despair, and existence itself. Suffering comes not from the world around us but from ourselves. It lies in the limited ego—the relative consciousness—of each individual. Buddhist teachings are designed to help us transcend our limited sense of self. Only through self-transformation can we experience a sense of real satisfaction with ourselves and with the world.

The principle of dissatisfaction has been incorrectly interpreted to mean only that suffering is an inescapable part of existence. The Buddha taught that the source of suffering lies within the individual and optimistically concluded that something can be done about humankind's basic dissatisfaction.

The Four Noble Truths

Gautama searched for a way to overcome the suffering and limitation he saw as an inevitable part of human life. "In what was probably the most important psychological

We are what we think, having become what we thought. (*The Dhammapada*, Lal, 1967)

discovery of all time, the Buddha realized the universality of suffering, its cause, its cure, and the way to attain such liberation" (Mosig, 1990, p. 53). He formulated this diagnosis and prescription as the *Four Noble Truths*.

The Existence of Dissatisfaction. The first Truth is the existence of dissatisfaction. Given the inner state of the average individual, dissatisfaction, or suffering, is inescapable. The Buddha used understanding dissatisfaction as the means to liberate himself. When we recognize our own suffering, or dissatisfaction, the Buddha in us will look at it, discover what has brought it about, and prescribe a course of action that can transform it into peace, joy, and liberation (Hanh, 1998).

Craving as the Root of Dissatisfaction. The second Truth is that dissatisfaction is the result of craving or desire. Most people are caught up in attachment to the positive and pleasurable, and aversion toward the negative and painful. Craving creates an unstable frame of mind in which the present is never completely satisfactory. If our desires are unsatisfied, we are driven by a need to change the present. If satisfied, we fear change, which brings about a renewal of frustration and dissatisfaction. Because all things pass, the enjoyment of fulfilled desires is tempered by the realization that our pleasure is only temporary. Therefore, we always wish things to be other than what they are. The stronger the craving, the more intense is our dissatisfaction, because we know that fulfillment will not last.

Like the spider woven in its own web is the man gripped by his craving. (*The Dhammapada*, Lal, 1967)

Elimination of Craving. The third Truth is that the elimination of craving brings the extinction of suffering. According to Buddhist doctrine, it is possible to learn to accept the world as it is without experiencing dissatisfaction. To eliminate craving does not mean to extinguish all desires. If your happiness depends on the fulfillment of certain wants, or you are controlled by your desires, then they have become unhealthy cravings and should be reined in. Healthy desires—like those for food and sleep—are necessary for survival. Desires also help boost our awareness. If all our wants are immediately satisfied, we can easily slip into a passive, unthinking state of complacency. Acceptance refers to an even-minded attitude of enjoying fulfilled desires without lamenting the inevitable periods when all our dreams don't come true. We learn to accept things as they are. Then, by acting appropriately, in the present, we can work to make things better without becoming attached to any results.

Also, we can ask ourselves "What nourishes joy in me and in others? Do I nourish joy in myself and others enough?" Dissatisfaction will cease if we learn to enjoy the precious gifts we have—hearing, sight, health, and life itself (Hanh, 1998).

The Eightfold Path. The fourth Truth regards the way to eliminate craving and dissatisfaction: the Eightfold Path, or the Middle Way. Most people seek the highest possible degree of sense gratification. Others tend toward the other extreme, self-mortification. The Buddhist ideal is moderation.

> Avoid these two extremes, monks. Which two? On the one hand, low, vulgar, ignoble, and useless indulgence in passion and luxury; on the other, painful, ignoble, and useless practice of self-torture and mortification. Take the Middle Path advised by the Buddha, for it leads to insight and peace, wisdom and enlightenment. (*The Dhammapada*, Lal, 1967, p. 22)

The Eightfold Path consists of right speech, right action, right livelihood, right effort, right mindfulness, right concentration, right thought, and right understanding. The basic principle is that certain ways of thinking and acting tend to harm others and to injure or limit oneself.

The three essentials in Buddhist training are ethical conduct, mental discipline, and wisdom. The Eightfold Path falls under these three categories. Ethical conduct is built on the fundamental Buddhist teachings of universal love and compassion for all living beings. Ethical conduct includes right speech, right action, and right livelihood.

Right speech means abstention from (1) lies; (2) gossip, slander, or any talk that might bring about disunity and disharmony; (3) harsh, rude, or abusive language; and (4) useless and foolish chatter and gossip. We should instead speak the truth and use words that are friendly, pleasant, gentle, and useful. We should not speak carelessly but should consider what is appropriate for the time and place. If we cannot say something useful, the ideal is to keep "noble silence."

Right action means moral, honorable, and peaceful conduct. To achieve this, we should abstain from (1) destruction of life, (2) stealing, (3) dishonest actions, (4) illegitimate sexual intercourse, and (5) drugs or alcohol (which cloud the mind). Also, we should help others lead a peaceful and honorable life.

We can attain *right livelihood* if we abstain from making a living by any means that brings harm to anyone or anything, such as dealing in weapons, intoxicating drinks, drugs, or poisons; killing animals; or cheating. The ideal is to earn a living that is honorable and harmful to no one.

Mental discipline includes right effort, right mindfulness, and right concentration. *Right effort* refers to using our will to (1) prevent unwholesome states of mind from arising, (2) get rid of such states if they do arise, (3) facilitate and produce good and wholesome states of mind, and (4) develop and bring to perfection those good, wholesome states already present.

Right mindfulness means to be aware of and attentive to (1) the functions of the body, (2) sensations or feelings, (3) the activities of the mind, and (4) specific ideas, thoughts, and conceptions. Various types of meditation—including concentration on breathing, on sensations, and on mental activities—have been developed in different schools of Buddhism and promote right mindfulness.

Buddhist psychology distinguishes between generalized activities of the mind and its specific contents. Concerning the activities of the mind, one is to become aware of whether one's mind is given to hatred, delusion, lust, distraction, or any other negative impulses. In focusing on specific ideas and concepts, one learns how they appear and disappear, how they were developed, how they were suppressed, and so on. *Right concentration* refers to the development of mental focus, which helps us accomplish the other aspects of the path.

Wisdom is made up of right thought and right understanding. *Right thought* includes selfless detachment, love, and nonviolence. *Right understanding* is the understanding of things as they are, which is accomplished by working deeply with the Four Noble Truths. Buddhist psychology recognizes two levels of understanding. The first is knowledge, accumulated memory, and an intellectual grasp of the subject. The second is deep understanding, in which a thing is seen clearly, undistorted by name and label. This type of awareness is possible only when the mind is freed from impurities and is fully developed through meditation.

Do not sell the wine of delusion. But there is nothing to be deluded about. If we realize this there is enlightenment itself. (Diamond Sutra in Kennett, 1976)

If we think we hear, we no longer listen.
If we think we see, we no longer look.
If we think we know, we no longer search. (Buddhist saying)

Meditation

Zen comes from the Sanskrit word *dyhāna,* meaning "meditation" (which evolved to *ch'an* in Chinese and *zen* in Japanese). Meditation is a central discipline in Zen. There are two major styles of Zen meditation, or **zazen** (literally "seated zen"). One can simply sit, with concentrated awareness, or one can focus on a koan.

Meditation on a Koan.   A **koan** is a question or exercise impossible to solve by mere thinking or logic. Koans are used today in the Rinzai school of Zen to test students and to force them to go beyond the limits of thought and to contact their deeper, enlightened mind.

Many koans are found in dialogues between Zen student and Zen master. Others are taken from questions posed by a Zen master to stimulate or awaken the student's understanding. The koans vividly and immediately illustrate an aspect of the Zen master's deep understanding of Buddhism. They tend to be paradoxical and beyond logic, forcing the questioner to go beyond the inherent limitations of his or her accustomed categories of experience. One of the most famous koans is known as *Mu:*

> A monk in all seriousness asked Joshu: "Has a dog Buddha-nature or not?" Joshu retorted, "*Mu!*"

The monk was deeply concerned with the Buddhist teaching that all sentient beings have Buddha-nature. (In China at that time, the dog was considered unclean, the lowest of the animals, and the monk was questioning seriously if such a low creature could be said to have the Buddha-nature.)

Joshu's answer might be translated as "nothing!" or read merely as an exclamation. It is not a simple yes-or-no answer. Joshu does not fall into the trap of accepting his questioner's assumption of a particular thing called Buddha-nature that can be possessed. *Mu* is a vigorous denial of dualistic thinking, a window through which the student can first glimpse Joshu's nondualistic perspective. Another Zen teacher comments, "It is clear, then, that Mu has nothing to do with the existence or nonexistence of Buddha-nature but is itself Buddha-nature" (Kapleau, 1965, p. 76).

In meditating on this koan, the individual should not indulge in intellectual speculation on the question and answer, or on their implications. The aim of the koan is to lead Zen students to see their own ignorance, to entice them to go beyond abstract conceptualizing, and to search for truth within themselves. Koan study is always done under the guidance of a qualified teacher with whom the student has regular interviews. One Zen master gave the following instructions to students working on this koan:

> Let all of you become one mass of doubt and questioning. Concentrate on and penetrate fully into Mu. To penetrate into Mu means to achieve absolute unity with it. How can you achieve this unity? By holding to Mu tenaciously day and night! . . . Focus your mind on it constantly. Do not construe Mu as nothingness and do not conceive it in terms of existence or nonexistence. You must not, in other words, think of Mu as a problem involving the existence or nonexistence of Buddha-nature. Then what do you do? You stop speculating and concentrate wholly on Mu—just Mu! (Kapleau, 1965, p. 79)

For a Zen monk the primary prerequisite for improvement is the practice of concentrated zazen. Without arguing about who is clever and who inept, who is wise and who foolish, just do zazen. You will then naturally improve. (Dogen in Kennett, 1976)

All you have to do is cease from erudition, withdraw within and reflect upon yourself. Should you be able to cast off body and mind naturally, the Buddha Mind will immediately manifest itself. (Evening Service in Kennett, 1976)

As a smith removes flaws in silver, a wise man removes flaws in himself, slowly, one by one, carefully. (*The Dhammapada*, Lal, 1967)

"Just Sitting."   The Soto approach to meditation can be thought of as "just sitting," without a koan or other exercise to occupy the mind. The meditator strives to maintain a state of concentrated awareness, in which he or she is neither tense nor relaxed but totally alert. The attitude is like that of someone seated by the roadside watching traffic. The meditator observes the thoughts going by, without getting caught up in them and thus forgetting to remain an aware observer.

Zazen is an expression of faith. "Those who do not have faith will not accept zazen, however much they are taught. If you don't trust this silence and the vastness of existence, if you do not soak yourself in this realm, how can you trust yourself?" (Katagiri, 1988, p. 43).

Visions and similar experiences should not result if zazen is properly performed. Generally, these experiences are the result of tensions that accumulate from sitting improperly in meditation or from daydreamlike states that arise at a certain point in one's meditation. These *makyo,* or illusions, are considered valueless in one's personal growth. They are at best distractions and at worst a source of pride, egotism, and delusion. One Zen teacher has pointed out that "to see a beautiful vision of a Bodhisattva does not mean that you are any nearer becoming one yourself, any more than a dream of being a millionaire means that you are any richer when you awake" (Kapleau, 1965, pp. 40–41).

> Zazen practice is the direct expression of our true nature. Strictly speaking, for a human being, there is no other practice than this practice, there is no other way of life than this way of life. (Suzuki, 1970, p. 23)

Meditation is an important discipline for developing an inner peace and calm and for learning to concentrate and stay balanced. Practicing zazen is like taking a shower. It cleanses the mind regularly, as a shower cleanses the body.

> In Buddhist meditation we do not struggle for the kind of enlightenment that will happen five or ten years from now. We practice so that each moment of our life becomes real life. And, therefore, when we meditate, we sit for sitting; we don't sit for something else. If we sit for twenty minutes, these twenty minutes should bring us joy, life. (Hanh, 1988, p. 53)

In the Soto school of Zen, students learn that the most important aspect of training concerns their daily lives and that each must learn to deal with his or her own personal koan, the riddle of daily life, as it manifests itself.

A personal koan has no final solution. The problem can be handled only by altering one's point of view, a process that results from changing one's personality. The problem doesn't change, but one's attitude toward it and the way one copes with it do. The individual never solves a koan but learns to respond to it at a higher level. For instance, Gautama began his religious quest in the hope of solving the koan of sickness, old age, and death. Even after he became the Buddha, these problems remained. The Buddha did not become immortal or ageless; however, his new level of understanding transcended his previous personal concern with these issues.

Some people's personal koan involves a sense of inadequacy, a feeling of not being enough, not knowing enough, not being able to achieve enough. Others' central koan revolves around a sense of complacency, a feeling that no further advancement or self-examination leading to personal change is needed.

It is important to remember that the practice of meditation is an end in itself, not merely a technique to achieve something. To understand this chapter as more than a collection of words and ideas, you must *experience Zen.* To do this, you must sit (as described in the Personal Reflection "Zazen"). We cannot emphasize too strongly the importance of this kind of direct experience.

personal reflection

ZAZEN

Try this exercise to learn something about Zen as well as about the way your mind works.

First, it is essential that your sitting posture be correct. You should be able to sit comfortably with a straight back, without becoming tense. By "straight back," Zen teachers mean that the spine should curve naturally just below the middle back.

If you wish, you may sit in a chair. Find a chair with a seat that is as flat as possible. A small, flat cushion is optional. Sit forward on the front third of the chair, with your feet flat on the floor. The lower legs should be more or less at right angles to the floor.

If you are going to sit on the floor, use a small, firm cushion to raise the buttocks. (Meditation cushions are often available at local Zen centers.) It is better to sit on a rug or blanket than on the bare floor. Sit on the edge of the cushion only, with just the tip of the bottom of the spine resting on the cushion. For most long-legged Westerners, it is more comfortable to sit Burmese style, your left foot tucked into the juncture of the right thigh and pelvis and your right leg placed immediately in front of your left leg and parallel to it. Both legs are flat on the ground, the knees resting on the ground. Knees and tailbone form a triangle.

The head should be straight, bent neither forward nor backward. The chin is tucked in. Your head should feel comfortable and almost weightless when it is positioned properly. Place your left hand over your right in your lap, with the thumbs lightly touching, and the palms up.

Sit facing a wall far enough away (about 6 feet) so that you can comfortably focus your eyes on the wall. Keep your eyes lowered to a comfortable place on the wall. Do not close them completely.

Sway gently from side to side, backward and forward, to find the most comfortable erect posture. Lift up your rib cage slightly to take the pressure off your lower back and to allow your spine to curve naturally. Take two or three slow, deep breaths before you begin to concentrate.

Now comes the part that is easiest to describe and hardest to do. Just sit. Do not try to do anything. But do not try not to do anything, either. Just sit with a positive mental attitude. Try this practice at least five to ten minutes each day for a week. It will teach you something about Zen and also about the nature of your mind.

More explicit instructions regarding mental activity during meditation have been given by Kennett:

> Now don't deliberately try to think and don't deliberately try not to think; in other words, thoughts are going to come into your head; you can either play with them or you can just sit there and look at them as they pass straight through your head and out the other side. That is what you need to do—just continue to sit; don't bother with the thoughts, don't be highjacked by them and don't try to push them away—both are wrong. . . .
>
> I have often given the likeness of sitting under a bridge watching the traffic go by. You do have to watch the thoughts that travel back and forth, but not be bothered by them in any way. If you do get caught by a thought—and in the beginning it is quite likely—then OK. Right. So you got caught by a thought. Come back to the beginning again and start your meditation over. It's no good sitting there and saying, "Oh, now there, I got caught by another thought," because you will get caught over the annoyance about the other thought, and so it builds up and you never get back to the quiet within. If you get caught in that way, just come back and start again. (1974, pp. 16–17)

Mindfulness.   Zen master Thich Nhat Hanh eloquently describes the practice of mindfulness in daily life:

> You've got to practice meditation when you walk, stand, lie down, sit, and work, while washing your hands, washing the dishes, sweeping the floor, drinking tea, talking to friends, or whatever you are doing: While washing the dishes, you might be thinking

personal reflection

MEDITATION AND ACTIVITY

You can learn something about applying a meditative attitude to your daily activities by doing this exercise.

Meditation can be seen primarily as a way of developing calmness and a sense of centered awareness by learning not to get caught up in your thoughts and emotions. Once you begin to understand this meditative attitude as you sit quietly, you can extend this feeling to your outward activities as well.

Begin with an hour of daily meditative activity. First, sit quietly for five to fifteen minutes, then tell yourself that you are going to remain self-aware, an observer of your thoughts, emotions, and activity for the next hour. If something does pull you off center, stop what you are doing and try to regain that sense of calmness and awareness. Initially, try this practice in silence. For most of us, talking becomes a distraction almost immediately.

It is easiest to begin with an hour of quiet physical work—gardening, cooking, and so forth. Intellectual activity is more difficult and conversation still more so. As you extend this practice to more of your daily life, you can observe where you are the most sensitive and easily disturbed. Make a list of these situations and consider what the list tells you.

about the tea afterwards, and so try to get them out of the way as quickly as possible in order to sit and drink tea. But that means that you are incapable of living during the time you are washing the dishes. When you are washing the dishes, washing the dishes must be the most important thing in your life. . . .

While washing the dishes one should only be washing the dishes, which means that while washing the dishes one should be completely aware of the fact that one is washing the dishes. At first glance, that might seem a little silly: why put so much stress on a simple thing? But that's precisely the point. The fact that I am standing there and washing these bowls is a wondrous reality. I'm being completely myself, following my breath, conscious of my presence, and conscious of my thoughts and actions. There's no way I can be tossed around mindlessly like a bottle slapped here and there on the waves. (1976, pp. 3–4, 23–24)

Meditation and mindfulness go together. Meditation can bring a level of inner calm and heightened awareness into our daily lives. Mindfulness prepares us to sit and meditate with calm awareness.

Enlightenment

The term **enlightenment** tends to be misleading because it seems to refer to some state that one can attain permanently; this notion would, of course, violate the Buddhist concept of impermanence. One Buddhist term related to enlightenment is *nirvana*. Nirvana, a state of mind in which all cravings and desires have become extinguished, is achieved through self-discipline, meditation, and realization of impermanence and selflessness. Nirvana also means extinction, in particular, extinction of all concepts and notions. Our concepts of things prevent us from really touching them. Meditation helps us remove concepts (Hanh, 1998).

One Japanese word frequently used in Zen is *satori*, which literally means "intuitive understanding." Another term is *kensho,* which means "to see into one's own nature." Both terms refer to the individual's firsthand experience of the truth of

While you are doing zazen neither despise nor cherish the thoughts that arise; only search your own mind [or heart for] the very source of these thoughts. (Zen Master Bassui)

Buddhist teachings. The experience is not static; it is a progressive, ever-changing, dynamic state of being, much like Maslow's concept of self-actualizing.

John Daido Loori, an American Zen teacher, has pointed out that the story of the ugly duckling, from a Hans Christian Andersen tale, provides a good example of the experience of kensho. The ugly duckling suffered because he was different from the other ducks. When he realized that he was a beautiful swan, he became overjoyed. Yet nothing had really changed. He had always been a perfect, complete swan. He simply *realized* his true nature and became liberated from the delusion of his imperfection. Realizing the perfection of our real Buddha-nature is much the same process.

> Enlightenment is perfect peace and harmony. If you think enlightenment is something you can get, then it appears right in front of you and you rush to get it; but the more we rush to get it, the more enlightenment eludes us. We try with greater effort, and finally we become a frantic screaming warrior. Then we become exhausted. . . . But enlightenment is completely beyond enlightenment or not-enlightenment. It is just perfect peace and harmony. (Katagiri, 1988, p. 128)

Enlightenment is not some good feeling, or some particular state of mind. The state of mind that exists when you sit in the right posture is, in itself, enlightenment. (Suzuki, 1970, p. 28)

Arhat and Bodhisattva

The Theravada and Mahayana traditions contain different conceptions of the nature of the ideal human being. The Theravada ideal is the *Arhat,* one who has completely cut off all the limitations of attachment to family, possessions, and comfort to become perfectly free of this world. *Arhat* literally means "one who has slain the enemy," or one who has overcome all passions in the process of intensive spiritual discipline. The Arhat, basically an unworldly ascetic, has achieved liberation from pride, selfishness, hate, and greed and has developed wisdom and compassion.

One Buddhist text describes the Arhat:

> He exerted himself, he strove and struggled, and thus he realized that this circle of "Birth-and-Death" . . . is in constant flux. He rejected all the conditions of existence which are brought about by a compound of conditions, since it is their nature to decay and crumble away, to change and to be destroyed. He abandoned all the "defilements" and won Arhatship. . . . Gold and a clod of earth were the same to him. The sky and the palm of his hand to his mind the same. (In Conze, 1959a, p. 94)

The Arhat seeks nirvana, or emancipation from suffering through elimination of craving. The individual who is so transformed experiences nirvana as absolute truth or ultimate reality, a state beyond this world of ever-changing phenomena.

The Mahayana ideal is the *Bodhisattva,* literally "enlightenment-being." The Bodhisattva is a deeply compassionate being who has vowed to remain in the world until all others have been delivered from suffering.

Let others gain Enlightenment; I shall not enter Nirvana until the last blade of grass has entered Buddhahood. (Bodhisattva vow in Conze, 1959b)

In truly understanding the principle of selflessness, the Bodhisattva realizes that he or she is part of all other sentient beings and that until all beings are freed from suffering, he or she can never attain complete liberation. The Bodhisattva vows not to enter nirvana until every sentient being, every blade of grass is enlightened.

> As many beings as there are in the universe of beings . . . egg-born, born from a womb, moisture-born, or miraculously born; with or without form; with perception, without perception, or with neither perception nor no-perception as far as any conceivable form of beings is conceived; all these I must lead to Nirvana. (Diamond Sutra in Conze, 1959b, p. 164)

personal reflection

WALKING MEDITATION

Meditation is not just sitting still. This exercise gives you a chance to practice meditative mindfulness in motion.

All of our physical experiences can become opportunities for mindfulness practice. Walking is a particularly good practice for maintaining awareness in our daily life.

Walk slowly in a natural setting, in a garden or along a river. Breathe normally and easily. Begin to coordinate your breathing with your footsteps. Then lengthen your exhalation by one step, without forcing your breath. See if your inhalation also naturally increases.

After 10 breaths, again lengthen your exhalation by one step. After 20 breaths, return to normal breathing. Five minutes later you can lengthen your breath again. Always return to normal if you feel the least bit tired. The point is to maintain your awareness. Any count will do as the act of counting breaths keeps you in the present. (Adapted from Hanh, 1976)

Compassion is the great virtue of the Bodhisattva, the result of truly feeling the sufferings of all others as one's own. From the Mahayana point of view, this attitude is enlightenment. In the experience of enlightenment, the world is not transcended, but the selfish ego is.

The Bodhisattva path means abandoning the world, but not the beings in it. The path of the Arhat emphasizes the quest for inner perfection and abandonment of the world, without the stress on service. The attitude of the Arhat is that those who desire to help others must first improve themselves. Someone who is lost in delusion is not effective in helping or teaching others; therefore self-development must naturally come first.

These two ideals can be seen as complementary rather than contradictory. The Arhat model focuses on self-discipline, whereas the Bodhisattva ideal emphasizes service to others; both are essential ingredients in inner growth and development.

> Better than a thousand vacuous speeches is one sane word leading to peace. (*The Dhammapada*, Lal, 1967)

DYNAMICS

One traditional way of illustrating psychospiritual growth in Zen has been through a series of ox-herding pictures. This rich group of images provides vivid examples of states of awareness beyond those usually discussed in Western psychology. Classic Zen texts also discuss the obstacles on the path, particularly the "three fires" of greed, hate, and delusion, and also the problem of pride or egotism.

Psychological Growth

Zen masters have often discussed their students' development in terms of the ox-herding pictures, which provide clear and graphic illustrations of Zen thinking.

One teacher outlined the major points of this series in counseling an advanced Zen student:

> If you continue with zazen, you will reach the point of grasping the Ox, i.e., the fourth stage. Right now you do not, so to speak, "own" your realization. Beyond the stage of grasping the Ox is the stage of taming it, followed by riding it, which is a state of awareness

> The mind is restless. To control it is good. A disciplined mind is the road to Nirvana. (*The Dhammapada*, Lal, 1967)

in which enlightenment and ego are seen as one and the same. Next, the seventh stage, is that of forgetting the Ox; the eighth, that of forgetting the Ox as well as oneself; the ninth, the grade of grand enlightenment, which penetrates to the very bottom and where one no longer differentiates enlightenment from non-enlightenment. The last, the tenth, is the stage in which . . . one moves, as himself, among ordinary people, helping them wherever possible, free from all attachment to enlightenment. (Kapleau, 1965, p. 231)

The ox is a symbol of the Buddha-nature, and the events entailed in finding the ox refer to the internal search and inner development of the Zen student. Spiegelman and Miyuki (1985), two Jungian analysts, provide an excellent and sensitive explanation of these pictures in terms of the individuation process. (See Figures 14.1 through 14.10.)

FIGURE 14.1 Seeking the Ox. This picture represents the beginning of the spiritual quest. The man is now aware of spiritual possibilities and potentials. Having become a spiritual seeker, he has become focused on spiritual attainment. The search itself creates a new obstacle, that of seeking outside oneself for what is within. Those who are searching must eventually come to believe that they can "find" the Buddha-nature within themselves. Kakuan, the Zen master who first drew this series, added commentaries to each picture:

> The Ox has never really gone astray, so why search for it? Having turned his back on his True-nature, the man cannot see it. Because of his defilements he has lost sight of the Ox. Suddenly he finds himself confronted by a maze of crisscrossing roads. Greed for worldly gain and dread of loss spring up like searing flames, ideas of right and wrong dart out like daggers. (Kakuan in Kapleau, 1965, p. 302)

FIGURE 14.2 Finding the Tracks. The seeker has begun to study Buddhism seriously. Study of various scriptures and accounts of the lives of Buddhist sages brings an intellectual understanding of basic Buddhist truths, although the student has not yet experienced these truths firsthand.

> He is unable to distinguish good from evil, truth from falsity. He has not actually entered the gate, but sees in a tentative way the tracks of the Ox. (Kakuan in Kapleau, 1965, p. 303)

Obstacles to Growth

In Buddhism, the primary obstacles to growth are basically psychological. We each possess three tendencies that function as major roadblocks: greed, hate, and delusion. Another serious obstacle is pride.

Greed, Hate, and Delusion.   Among these "three fires" of Buddhism, some individuals are dominated by greed, others by hate, and still others by delusion. Virtually every personality contains a mixture of all three qualities, with one predominating, although the balance can change, depending on the circumstances. Certain situations will awaken an individual's greed, whereas others will stimulate tendencies toward anger or delusion.

FIGURE 14.3 First Glimpse of the Ox. The sight of the Ox is the first direct experience of the seeker's own Buddha-nature. The encounter with the Ox is not a result of study or abstract contemplation but direct experience. This first glimpse is for but a moment; it is a realization that comes and goes. Further discipline is required to expand and stabilize this experience.

> If he will but listen intently to everyday sounds, he will come to realization and at that instant see the very Source. The ... senses are no different from this true Source. In every activity the Source is manifestly present. It is analogous to the salt in water or the binder in paint. (Kakuan in Kapleau, 1965, p. 304)

Greed is a major problem for most people. We tend to want more than we have or need—more money, more food, more pleasure. Generally, children are the most obviously greedy. It is often virtually impossible to satisfy their cravings, as one piece of candy only stimulates the desire for another. The Buddhist scriptures have described those dominated by greed as given to vanity, discontent, craftiness, and love of rich, sweet food and fine clothes (Conze, 1959b).

Hate-dominated people have sharp tempers and are quick to anger. For them, life is a continual round of fighting with enemies, getting back at others for real and imagined injuries, and defending themselves against possible attack. Those in whom hate predominates tend to hold grudges, belittle others, and suffer from arrogance, envy, and stinginess (Conze, 1959b).

Delusion refers to a general state of confusion, lack of awareness, and vacillation. Those in whom delusion is strongest find it difficult to make up their minds or to commit to anything. Their reactions and opinions are not their own but are

FIGURE 14.4 Catching the Ox. Now the Zen student must make certain that Buddhist self-discipline permeates the whole of daily life. The goal is to extend the awareness of one's Buddha-nature to all activities and to manifest that awareness in all circumstances. The Ox here illustrates the raw energy and power of the Buddha-nature. Because of the overwhelming pressures of the outside world, the Ox is hard to keep under control. If disciplined practice is abandoned now, this power and energy may dissipate.

> Today he encountered the Ox, which had long been cavorting in the wild fields, and actually grasped it. For so long a time has it reveled in these surroundings that breaking it of its old habits is not easy. It continues to yearn for sweet-scented grasses, it is still stubborn and unbridled. If he would tame it completely, the man must use his whip. (Kakuan in Kapleau, 1965, p. 305)

borrowed from others. Those dominated by delusion tend to do everything inattentively and sloppily. Their behavior is characterized by laziness, obstinacy, confusion, worry, and excitability (Conze, 1959b).

At their worst, these tendencies can blossom into what Westerners call *neurosis* or *psychosis*. However, according to Buddhist thinking, even a psychosis is but a temporary intensification of one of these tendencies. It is viewed as a transient state, as are all mental and physical conditions.

One can overcome all three obstacles. Greed can be turned into compassion, hate into love, and delusion into wisdom. Self-discipline and the discipline of following the Buddha's precepts offer the opportunity for the individual to confront and control his or her greed. The Buddhist teachings, with their emphasis on compassion and respect for others, provide a way to overcome hate. The realization that

One man on the battlefield conquers an army of a thousand men. Another conquers himself—and he is greater. (*The Dhammapada,* Lal, 1967)

FIGURE 14.5 Taming the Ox. An effortless intimacy or friendship with the Ox is now established. The sense of struggle is gone. This is the stage of precise and perfect training. Every act, every thought begins to reflect the true self. The individual ceaselessly works to manifest Buddhism at all times, without a single interruption. Remaining traces of illusion alone now distinguish between the seeker and the Ox.

> He must hold the nose-rope tight and not allow the Ox to roam, lest off to muddy haunts it should stray. Properly tended, it becomes clean and gentle. Untethered, it willingly follows its master. (Kakuan in Kapleau, 1965, p. 306)

all things *are* the Buddha is the antidote for the problem of delusion. Everything merits our deepest care and attention, because everything is a manifestation of the Buddha-nature.

Pride. **Pride** can be another major obstacle to growth. It can result in a lack of respect for one's teacher and create distortions of the teachings. A Zen teacher will attempt to lead students to see and acknowledge their own pride and egotism. One of the Zen patriarchs points out, "Should the teaching you hear from a Zen master go against your own opinion, he is probably a good Zen master; if there is no clash of opinions in the beginning, it is a bad sign" (Dogen in Kennett, 1976, p. 111).

Pride can enter at virtually any point in training, even after kensho. Normally, the direct kensho experience confirms the student's understanding of Buddhism, and the student's convictions about the validity of Buddhist teachings become

To see the self is not to be pleased with the self; not to be pleased with the self is to want to do something about the self; and to want to do something about the self is to study Buddhism. (Dogen in Kennett, 1976)

FIGURE 14.6 Riding the Ox Home. The struggle is over. The student has now become the sage. Although the Ox is still seen as separate, the relation between man and Ox is so intimate that he can ride it effortlessly without needing to pay the slightest attention to where it is going. Life has become simple, natural, and spontaneous. Formal external training is no longer essential once one has become firmly anchored in awareness of the Buddha-nature. The discipline once seen as a burden is now embraced as a source of real freedom and satisfaction.

> "Gain" and "loss" no longer affect him. He hums the rustic tune of the woodsman and plays the simple songs of the village children. Astride the Ox's back, he gazes serenely at the clouds above. His head does not turn [toward temptation]. Try though one may to upset him, he remains undisturbed. (Kakuan in Kapleau, 1965, p. 307)

unshakable. However, at this stage, many students believe that they have learned everything, that they understand Buddhism fully and no longer need a teacher. A good teacher will insist that, at this point, the student continues with regular duties and training in order to ensure that pride and ambition do not distort the initial deep understanding of Buddhism. Delusion is difficult to overcome if it develops at this stage, because the student's convictions are now firmly rooted in actual experience. If training continues, students can conquer the inevitable pride and sense of holiness, or what some Zen masters have called the "smell of enlightenment" or "the stench of Zen." (See the commentary on Figure 14.8.) The student must be reminded of the doctrine of impermanence and the fact that training in Buddhism is endless.

FIGURE 14.7 Ox Forgotten, Self Alone. The seeker has returned home and the Ox is forgotten. The distinction between religious and worldly categories disappears, as everything is seen to possess the Buddha-nature. Training and discipline have become indistinguishable from daily life. The state of meditation is as normal now as walking or breathing and is no longer associated with any sense of motivation or separation from the goal. Everything is sacred, and there is no distinction between enlightenment and ignorance.

> In the Dharma [Teaching] there is no two-ness. The Ox is his Primal-nature: this he has now recognized. A trap is no longer needed when a rabbit has been caught, a net becomes useless when a fish has been snared. Like gold which has been separated from dross, like the moon which has broken through the clouds, one ray of luminous Light shines eternally. (Kakuan in Kapleau, 1965, p. 308)

STRUCTURE

Body

The Buddhist concept of the Middle Way is of central importance in one's attitude toward the body. It involves neither full indulgence of all one's desires nor extreme asceticism or self-mortification. The mealtime ceremonial recited in Zen temples affirms this:

> The first bite is to discard all evil;
> The second bite is so that we may train in perfection;
> The third bite is to help all beings;
> We pray that all may be enlightened.

Both your life and your body deserve love and respect, for it is by their agency that Truth is practiced and the Buddha's power exhibited. (Dogen in Kennett, 1976)

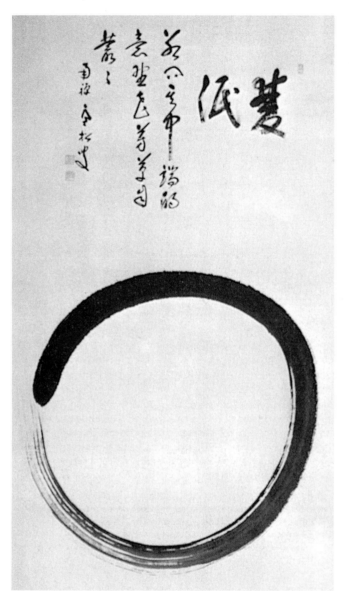

FIGURE 14.8 Both Ox and Self Forgotten. This image refers to the experience of the void, the essential nothingness of all creation. The individual nature and the Buddha-nature were transcended in the previous stage, and now enlightenment itself is transcended. The perfect circle, made by the single brush stroke of the Zen master, is left open. Because the circle is not closed, further growth is possible. The process of enlightenment can go on without becoming frozen or static.

> All delusive feelings have perished and ideas of holiness too have vanished. He lingers not in "Buddha," and he passes quickly on through "not Buddha." Even the thousand eyes [of the Buddhas and patriarchs] can discern in him no specific quality. If hundreds of birds were now to strew flowers about his room, he could not but feel ashamed of himself. (Kakuan in Kapleau, 1965, p. 309)[1]

We must think deeply of the ways and means by which this food has come.
We must consider our merit when accepting it.
We must protect ourselves from error by excluding greed from our minds.
We will eat lest we become lean and die.
We accept this food so that we may become enlightened.
(Mealtime Ceremonial in Kennett, 1976, pp. 236–237)

---

[1]There is a legend of a Chinese Zen master who was so holy that the birds came to offer him flowers as he sat meditating in his mountain retreat. After he became fully enlightened, the birds ceased their offerings, because he no longer gave off any aura, even of devotion and holiness.

FIGURE 14.9 Returning to the Source. If the eighth stage is thought of as the static aspect of absolute truth, the ninth stage may be said to bring a new dynamic appreciation of the world. Nature is not merely void or sacred, it is. If seen clearly, any aspect of the world can serve as a perfect mirror to show us ourselves. There is still a subtle duality here between the manifestation of truth in nature and its manifestation in deluded, suffering humankind. This level must eventually deepen to include our return to human civilization.

> He observes the waxing and waning of life in the world while abiding unassertively in a state of unshakable serenity. This [waxing and waning] is no phantom or illusion [it comes from the Source]. Why then is there need to strive for anything? The waters are blue, the mountains are green. Alone with himself, he observes things endlessly changing. (Kakuan in Kapleau, 1965, p. 310)

In a commentary on the Zen approach to meals, one Zen master wrote

> If you can chant the Buddhist teachings while having a meal you are very lucky. . . . If you have breakfast to offer your body and mind to the Buddha, to the universe, how lucky you are. Offering your body and mind to the Buddha is offering your body and mind to emptiness, or in other words, to the pure sense of human action. (Katagiri, 1988, p. 9)

Hyakujo, the founder of Zen monastic life, always worked with his monks at manual labor, even when he was in his eighties. Although his students tried to restrain him from working as hard as they did, he insisted, saying, "I have accumulated no merit to deserve service from others; if I do not work, I have no right to take my meals" (Ogata, 1959, p. 43).

The body is a vehicle for service to others and for one's pursuit of truth. It should be cared for with this understanding.

FIGURE 14.10 Entering the City with Bliss-Bestowing Hands. This is the final stage, the stage of the Bodhisattva who is free to associate with and help all other beings without limitation. The city refers to the secular world, in contrast to the secluded Zen temple or contemplation retreat. The Bodhisattva is shown with a big belly and a gourd of wine slung over his shoulder. He is willing to share all the amusements and activities of the world, not because of personal desires or attachments but in order to teach others.

> The gate of his cottage is closed and even the wisest cannot find him. His mental panorama [concepts, opinions, and so forth] has finally disappeared. He goes his own way, making no attempt to follow the steps of earlier stages. Carrying a [wine] gourd, he strolls into the market; leaning on his staff, he returns home. He leads innkeepers and fishmongers in the Way of the Buddha. (Kakuan in Kapleau, 1965, p. 311)

The Zen master, who realizes that everything is Buddha, can now return to the activities of the early stages with a different perspective.

Social Relationships

A common misconception found within all meditative disciplines is *quietism,* or withdrawal from the world in order not to disturb one's meditative peace. Buddhist teaching stresses responsibility, the opposite of withdrawal.

Meditation is never an end in itself. One may devote periods of time to meditative practice, while understanding the need to work and eventually to help others. Because everyone has (or rather is) the Buddha-nature, we should ideally look on all other human beings as the Buddha and say to ourselves, "Here comes the Buddha. How can I help him or her?" The Buddha is not beyond this world of suffering, not

Cease from evil, do only good, do good for others. (The Three Pure Precepts in Kennett, 1976)

personal reflection

MINDFUL HOUSECLEANING

More challenging than sitting or walking is practicing mindfulness while working. Perhaps the greatest challenge is to remain mindful while doing chores we dislike. When we do not want to do something, the tendency is to do it badly and halfheartedly. We tend to daydream or to rush through the distasteful experience. Cleaning house is an unpleasant chore for many of us.

Now take a chore like housecleaning and make it an experience in mindfulness. Divide your work into stages, such as putting things away, dusting, sweeping the floors. Allow yourself plenty of time for each stage. Move slowly, about three times more slowly than usual. Focus your attention completely on each task. For example, when putting a book back on the shelf, look at the book, be aware of what book it is, know that you are in the process of putting it back in a specific place on the bookshelf. Avoid any abrupt or rushed movement. Remain aware of your breath, especially when your thoughts wander. (Adapted from Hanh, 1976)

beyond the need for help and compassion. Nor is being Buddha a permanent state (because in Buddhism nothing is seen as permanent).

A liar with a shaven head does not make a monk. (The Dhammapada, Lal, 1967)

Social interactions offer crucial opportunities for practicing Buddhist ideals and principles. Someone who is inebriated can be treated as a drunken Buddha—not permitted to disturb others but treated respectfully. Similarly, one who behaves with wrong or evil intent can be seen as a baby Buddha. The individual needs to be taught, but is never punished for the sake of revenge or cast out as evil or worthless. For if this person is cast out, so too is the Buddha. In addition, social relationships allow the individual to practice the calm awareness developed in meditation.

Will

Dogen writes, "It is by means of the will that we understand the will" (in Kennett, 1976, p. 170). Will develops through the exercise of the will. To grasp the will is to make a real commitment to your training and to take responsibility for your own actions, realizing that no one else can do your training for you.

> It is not easy for anyone, however, to cast away the chain of ignorance and discrimination all at once. A very strong will is required, and one has to search single-heartedly for his True Self, within himself. Here hard training is needed in Zen, and it never resorts to an easygoing, instant means. (Shibayama, 1970, p. 31)

There is only one thing, to train hard, for this is true enlightenment. (Evening Service in Kennett, 1976, p. 290)

One basic Buddhist principle is that daily life and activity should be brought into harmony with ideals and values. Training oneself is not merely a means to an end, but training is an end in itself. Dogen writes:

> It is heretical to believe that training and enlightenment are separable, for in Buddhism the two are one and the same. . . . [A]s this is so, the teacher tells his disciples never to search for enlightenment outside of training since the latter mirrors enlightenment. Since training is already enlightenment, enlightenment is unending; since enlightenment is already training, there can be no beginning whatsoever to training. (In Kennett, 1976, p. 121)

A contemporary Zen teacher cautioned one of his disciples: "Your enlightenment is such that you can easily lose sight of it if you become lazy and forgo further practice. Furthermore, though you have attained enlightenment you remain the same old you—nothing has been added, you have become no grander" (Kapleau, 1965, p. 231).

Training is an ongoing process, because the realization of Buddhist principles has no end. Someone who stops and remains satisfied with an initial enlightening experience will soon be left with nothing but a beautiful memory.

Emotions

An important goal of Buddhist training is to learn to control one's emotions rather than be controlled by them. Most emotions are good, but few people experience their emotions properly or appropriately. They become angry or outraged over trivial matters, suppress their feelings, and carry the emotion into situations far removed from the source of anger.

Through training, the Zen student gradually develops a state of meditative awareness in all daily activities. As the student becomes more aware of emotional reactions to various situations, the emotions tend to lose their hold. One Zen teacher commented that if one does show anger, the display should be like a small explosion or a thunderclap; the anger is then fully experienced and can be dropped completely afterward (Suzuki, n.d.).

The ideal Buddhist emotional state is compassion, which can be thought of as transcended emotion, a feeling of unity with all other beings, the fruit of the experience of nonduality.

Intellect

The study of Buddhist scriptures and the intellectual understanding of Buddhist teachings are important first steps in Buddhist training, as mentioned in the commentaries to the ox-herding pictures. However, reliance on the intellect alone can become a hindrance to true awareness. Ananda, the most clever and most learned of Buddha's disciples, took almost five times longer than the others to reach enlightenment. After the Buddha's passing, the other disciples went to Ananda, whose memory was so prodigious that he could recite, word for word, all the talks of the Buddha. But his love of argument, his pride in his learning, and his attachment to his teacher stood in the way of his enlightenment.

Pure intellect and abstract reasoning are useful. But intellect and reasoning alone do not enable us to comprehend ourselves and the world around us. The intellect is essentially powerless when it comes to satisfying our deepest needs. "It is not the object of Zen to look illogical for its own sake, but to make people know that logical consistency is not final, and that there is a certain transcendental statement that cannot be obtained by mere intellectual cleverness" (Suzuki, 1964, p. 67).

Although erudition alone is not particularly helpful, intellectual understanding plus the actual practice of that understanding is essential. Ideally, intellectual understanding deepens and becomes clarified through meditation and training in daily life, in accordance with Buddhist principles. For instance, one who reads about the concept of compassion without actually serving others knows compassion only as a shallow abstraction. Buddhist teachings are meant to be living truths, actively expressed in people's lives.

O Buddha, going, going, going on beyond, and always going on beyond, always becoming Buddha. (The Scripture of Great Wisdom in Kennett, 1976, p. 224)

Earth penetrates heaven whenever Zazen is truly done. (Dogen in Kennett, 1976, p. 140)

Self

Buddhist thought distinguishes between the lesser self and the greater self. The lesser self is the ego, the consciousness of one's mind and body. The lesser self remains focused on the limitations of the individual, a sense of separateness between the individual and the rest of the world. This level of consciousness must be transcended in order to develop a sense of unity with other beings and with nature.

The lesser self is created, in part, by one's sense of inadequacy. That is, the more insecure, or inadequate, we feel, the greater the extent of our ego. As we become whole, integrated individuals, our lesser selves naturally diminish in strength. We never lose our egos; however, the mature person is in control of the ego, not run by it.

It is possible to identify oneself with one's greater self, which is as large as the entire universe, embracing all beings and all creation. This level of understanding is an essential element in the experience of enlightenment.

Identification with the greater self does not mean that the lesser self must be done away with. Training brings about transcendence of the lesser self so that one is no longer dominated by it. Nirvana is not annihilation of the ego, or lesser self, but transcendence of ego orientation. In Buddhist art, the Bodhisattva Monju is depicted sitting on a ferocious beast. Monju is sitting in serene meditation, although the beast is awake, with its fierce eyes open wide. The beast represents the ego, a useful tool that is not to be killed, although it must be watched and firmly sat upon.

The Zen analysis of the nature of the self has been compared with Western psychological theories (Claxton & Ageha, 1981) and with Horney's concept of the real self (Morvay, 1999).

> To study the Buddha Way is to study the self, to study the self is to forget the self, to forget the self is to be enlightened by the ten thousand things. (Dogen in Maezumi, 1978)

Teacher

A true Buddhist teacher is one who lives by Buddhist principles. Whenever a teacher fails to live up to this ideal, he or she must be ready to acknowledge it. The pupils approach their teacher as the ideal example to follow, as the living Buddha. However, genuine Zen teachers are aware of their limitations and try not to cut themselves off from their pupils by placing themselves on a pedestal. Disciples must see their teacher's humanness and shortcomings yet recognize the Buddha in the teacher in spite of his or her faults.

Originally, Buddhist temples held no statues of the Buddha, only the footprints of the Buddha. This was a reminder to the student of the principle "Thou must go alone, the Buddhas only point the way." Moreover, after seeing a concrete image, students may believe that a teacher should look like a Buddha and that only those who resemble the image are teachers. Buddhist images are symbols of mental qualities such as wisdom or compassion. Rather than icons to be worshipped, they are meant to remind us of qualities that reside within ourselves. More information on the role of the Buddhist teacher can be found on our **web site.**

> When you meet a Zen master who teaches the Truth, do not consider his caste, his appearance, shortcomings or behavior. Bow before him out of respect for his great wisdom and do nothing whatsoever to worry him. (Dogen in Kennett, 1976)

Evaluation

One exciting and intriguing aspect of Buddhism is that it fosters a sense of a vital dialectic, the simultaneous appreciation of the real and the ideal and the recognition of the tension between the two. Besides aspiring to the ideals of Buddhism, students acknowledge the limitations of actuality. The individual must understand and live by this notion: "I am Buddha, and I am not Buddha, and I am Buddha" (Kennett-roshi, personal communication). This dialectic approach manifests itself in virtually all aspects of Buddhist life and thought. It provides a creative tension, at once a way to cope with present limitations and to move toward the ideal.

To say flatly that "such and such is true" is to ignore the principle of impermanence. This kind of statement is misleading at best, but the opposite statement is equally misleading. It is better to say, "It is so, and it is not so, and it is so." Virtually every statement and every situation can be better understood by applying this dialectic.

The Buddhist dialectic also applies to the role of the teacher. As mentioned earlier, the ideal Buddhist teacher recognizes his or her own limitations and acknowledges these limitations to the students. This is a major point of contrast to the Indian Yoga tradition, in which the guru tends to be venerated as the perfect embodiment of all divine virtues and characteristics.

However much anyone might theoretically come to approximate these divine ideals, there is no denying the fact that all religious teachers are merely human. They all have foibles and imperfections. Attempting to maintain a role of holy perfection before one's disciples inevitably leads to a certain amount of posing and hypocrisy. Unless teachers acknowledge their limitations, they are likely to become egotistical and defensive about their slightest faults or mistakes.

Disciples who view their teacher as perfection itself avoid accepting responsibility for their own development, because they can make no connection between their own imperfections and the ostensible perfection of the master. Therefore, rather than continue the hard work of training and self-discipline, students convince themselves that their teacher is a "master" who can accomplish all kinds of things they cannot. Thus they need not even make the effort.

There is great depth in the Zen notion that training is enlightenment. The trainee who maintains this attitude avoids getting caught in the trap of working for an unattainable ideal. To strive continually for a future goal or reward may mean that one is never fully involved in the present. If the path is not in harmony with the goal, how can one ever reach the goal?

This issue is made clear in a well-known Zen story about Baso, a monk who was making great efforts in meditation.

> Nangaku, his teacher, asked: "Worthy one, what are you trying to attain by sitting?"
>
> Baso replied: "I am trying to become a Buddha."
>
> Then Nangaku picked up a piece of roof tile and began grinding it on a rock in front of him.
>
> "What are you doing, Master?" asked Baso.
>
> "I am polishing it to make a mirror," said Nangaku.
>
> "How could polishing a tile make a mirror?"
>
> "How could sitting in zazen [meditation] make a Buddha?"
>
> Baso asked: "What should I do, then?"
>
> Nangaku replied: "If you were driving a cart and it didn't move, would you whip the cart or whip the ox?"
>
> Baso made no reply.
>
> Nangaku continued: "Are you training yourself in zazen? Are you striving to become a sitting Buddha? If you are training yourself in zazen, [let me tell you that] zazen is neither sitting nor lying. If you are training yourself to become a sitting Buddha, Buddha has no one form. The Dharma [Teaching], which has no fixed abode, allows of no distinctions. If you try to become a sitting Buddha, this is no less than killing the Buddha. If you cling to the sitting form you will not attain the essential truth." (In Kapleau, 1965, p. 21)

Dogen has pointed out that "since Buddhist trainees do almost nothing for themselves, how is it possible that they should do anything for the sake of fame and gain? Only for the sake of Buddhism must one train in Buddhism" (in Kennett, 1976, p. 107).

In Zen, Buddhist practice and daily life are not separate; they are seen as one and the same. Practical, unspectacular experience is stressed, and the esoteric and miraculous are downplayed. A Zen master once said, "My miracle is that when I feel hungry I eat, and when I feel thirsty I drink" (Reps, n.d., p. 68). Life is to be lived with full awareness by accepting and fulfilling the requirements of daily life. The Zen master Joshu was once asked for instruction by a new monk.

> Joshu: "Have you breakfasted yet?"
> Monk: "I have had my breakfast."
> Joshu: "Then wash out your bowl."

The monk suddenly understood the true nature of Zen.

A number of scholars have compared Buddhist and Western psychological theories (Katz, 1983; Molino, 1998). Ramaswami and Sheikh (1989) summarize Buddhist psychology:

> The psychology of Buddhism rests on the notions of the absence of a separate self, impermanence of all things, and the fact of sorrow. Human beings suffer because of self-delusion, striving to possess that which inevitably must crumble, and because of desire. The Buddha did not stop with a mere diagnosis. He proclaimed that the cure is to reach a higher state of being, wherein self-knowledge has eradicated delusion, attachment, and desire. (p. 120)

There is no final doctrine or dogma because there can be no absolute truths, nor even an absolute Buddha, in the face of impermanence. Buddhist teachings are oriented to human realities. They are aimed at eliminating the sense of dissatisfaction and inadequacy caused by a limited, selfish ego. In the passage quoted at the beginning of this chapter, the Buddha is reported to have told his disciples not to follow any teachings in response to a particular teacher's reputation or skill with words but to rely on their own judgment and experience. The final criterion for Zen is experience. Teaching and discipline that aid people in becoming more mature, more responsible, and more complete human beings are considered to be good Buddhism.

RECENT DEVELOPMENTS: THE INFLUENCE OF BUDDHISM

Buddhist thinking has had a significant influence on different areas of psychology. Meditation may provide many of the benefits of psychotherapy. Carrington and Ephron (1975) and Engler (1986, 1993) have explored ways in which psychoanalysis and meditation techniques can interact effectively. Erich Fromm (1970) believed that the goals of Zen and psychoanalysis are the same. They include insight into self, liberation from the tyranny of the unconscious, and knowledge of reality. Fromm also pointed out that Zen and psychoanalysis share the principle that knowledge leads to transformation. Zen meditation has been found to be a valuable adjunct to therapy (Boorstein, 1988; Claxton, 1986; Fuld, 1991; Kornfield, 1988), and Eastern systems of psychotherapy inspired by Zen have enjoyed growing popularity in the West (Reynolds, 1980, 1984,

1993). Benoit (1990) and Manne-Lewis (1986) have examined in detail the psychology of transformation in Zen. Soeng (1991) has interpreted Buddhist scriptures in light of modern quantum physics.

Gestalt therapy and Buddhism also share basic principles. Both stress the importance of mindful living in the present. For both, awareness is a primary tool for change. Rather than the unconscious, Perls (1969) argued that the conscious mind is our enemy. Similarly, the Buddha pointed out that the conscious mind clings to cravings and to the false idea of a separate self.

Psychologists have begun to synthesize the insights of meditation and cognitive psychology (Brown & Engler, 1986; Goleman, 1988; Shapiro, 1980; Shapiro & Walsh, 1984). Empirical research has demonstrated significant neurological and physiological effects of Zen meditation (Fromm, 1992; Hirai, 1989; Murphy & Donovan, 1988). Zazen and other Eastern meditative disciplines have been related to better health and ability to cope with stress and tension (Claxton, 1986; Dalai Lama, et al., 1991; Kabat-Zinn, 1990, 1994; Shen-Yen, 1987).

Two other schools of Buddhism have become popular and influential in the United States—Tibetan Buddhism and Theravadan Buddhism. Tibetan Buddhist teachers have emigrated to the West and founded successful Buddhist centers, trained large numbers of students, and written important books. One of the best-known teachers, the late Chogyam Trungpa, established the Naropa Institute in Boulder, Colorado. His books (1975, 1988) have influenced many people interested in Tibetan Buddhism.

The most famous Tibetan teacher is, of course, the Dalai Lama (1991, 1993), who made world headlines when he received the Nobel Peace Prize in 1989. Other important Tibetan Buddhist works include Evans-Wentz (1951, 1954, 1958, 1960) and Lama Govinda (1960).

Numerous works explore Theravadan Buddhism. Daniel Goleman, a well-known transpersonal psychologist, has written about meditation and states of consciousness in the Theravadan tradition (Goleman, 1988; Goleman & Davidson, 1979). Another important figure is Jack Kornfield (1987, 1993), who is both a transpersonal psychologist and a Buddhist meditation teacher. One of the basic Theravadan Buddhist practices, *vipassana,* or "insight meditation," has become widespread (Dhammadudhi, 1968; Goldstein, 1976; Sayadaw, 1972).

Buddhism has grown substantially in the United States since the 1970s. It has been accepted more readily than other Eastern ways of life, because it has been viewed more as a psychology than as a religion. One Zen master has cautioned, however, that Buddhism as a psychology is limited and that Buddhism must be taught and practiced religiously:

> In a sense, Buddhism as a psychology is still part of human culture, influencing, but not exactly penetrating American life. In order to penetrate American life, Buddhism must be accepted as a religion, and zazen must be practiced as an end in itself. . . . In the nineteenth century, Western people didn't accept Buddhism as a religion because it didn't seem to have prayer; it was not what is called revealed religion. . . . Though Buddhism doesn't seem to have prayer, it does have *dhyana.* Dhyana means zazen (meditation), and dhyana is exactly the same as prayer. Shakyamuni Buddha says Dharma is a light you can depend on, the self is a light you can depend on, but this self is really the self based on the Dharma . . . or the Truth itself. So, Buddhism is not a revealed religion, but an awakened religion—it is awakening to the self or to the Truth. (Katagiri, 1988, p. 98)

The literature on Zen Buddhism in English continues to grow. Thich Nhat Hanh's work (1976, 1987, 1988, 1992, 1993, 1996) has had wide influence, as has Katagiri (1988) and Deshimaru (1985, 1987, 1991).

The Theory Firsthand

EXCERPT FROM *THE WILD, WHITE GOOSE*

The following excerpts are taken from the diary—called The Wild, White Goose—*of Jiyu-Kennett (1977), a British woman who studied for many years at a major Zen training temple in Japan. She founded a Zen training temple, Shasta Abbey, in Mount Shasta, California, and wrote several excellent books on Zen.*

11th. Rev. January

Rev. Hajime called me into his room early this evening so that we could get on with the translation for as long a time as possible before the bell [rang] for bed....

"Shakyamuni[2] Buddha and I are one, as all Buddhists with both him and me, and not merely all Buddhists but all people and all things both animate and inanimate. And none of us have anything to do with Shakyamuni Buddha." I paused for a moment, so that he could thoroughly digest what I had written, then I continued. "Shakyamuni Buddha is of no importance at all at the present time and Shakyamuni Buddha lives forever in me."

He was silent, simply looking deeply into my eyes; then he spoke softly. "You should ask Zenji Sama for the Transmission," he said.

[Kennett:] "If Transmission is what I think it is I do not understand you. As I know of it, Transmission is received when all training is finished and the master wishes to give his seal of approval to a disciple before he goes out to teach. I am anything but ready for that."

[Hajime:] "That is a popular misconception. Admittedly it is the giving of the seals of the master to someone whom he knows has understood his Own Nature but they are only given when the master is certain that the disciple concerned regards his training as just beginning every minute of his life and not when he thinks of it as being over. In other words, not when he thinks of himself as being enlightened and having nothing more to do. Understand the *'gyate, gyate'* of the Hannyashingyo as 'going, going,' not 'gone, gone.'"

[Kennett:] "Doesn't one have to have had some great *kensho* [enlightenment] before such a thing takes place? All that happened to me in October was that I realised that there was nothing more I could do but train myself constantly every day of my life and that I was the worst trainee in existence...."

16th. January

...There is no part of me that can ever be chopped off. There is no emotion, no feeling, no thought, no word, no deed that does not come out of the Buddha Mind. I said this to [Reverend Hajime] and went on, "Then the sex act is part of the Buddha Nature and expresses the Buddha Nature at every turn, for it is, of itself, clean. What we have done is made it dirty with our own guilts and misuse."

"You are correct."

"Eating and going to the toilet and washing clothes and scrubbing the floor are all part of the 'with' for they are all expressions of the Buddha Nature." I stopped, amazed at myself.

"Go on," he said.

"...and the sun and the moon and the stars and the earth; and the digging of the earth and the flowing water; these too are all expressions of the Buddha Nature, and the tongue I use to speak these words, and the food I eat, and the differences in the tastes; 'by comparing them you can—Yes! that's what the scripture means. 'By comparing them you can distinguish one from other,'—and yet they're all the same thing; they're all expressions of the Buddha Nature and there is no way in which they can be separated off from it; and there is no way in which one can separate off any person or being or any living thing...."

"...This is the reason why it is so difficult to keep the Precepts and why the Truth can't be given to us until we have kept them and learned to make them our blood and bones. We don't want to know that we can be evil so where is there any need for Precepts? Thus, no-one can enter into the Truths of Buddhism

[2]In Sanskrit, *Shakyamuni* means "wise man of the Shakyas." It is one of the terms frequently used to refer to the Buddha, Siddhartha Gautama, a prince of the Shakya clan.

until he has made the commitment of becoming a priest otherwise he could use the knowledge of his own indestructibility for all sorts of evil purposes. He would know his own true freedom and wouldn't care two hoots what he got up to with other people."

"That is completely right. You have understood the 'with' at last. You see, from now on you can carry on from there and there will be no difficulty in understanding, and you will know that you must hold everyone and everything as the 'with' aspect of the Buddha Mind and recognise that, whatever aspect of the Buddha Mind it shows, the Precepts must always hold it within themselves."

"Then making the Precepts part of my blood and bones means that the Precepts will eventually fall away because I will be their actual embodiment."

"Haven't you realised that, in your case, the early moral form of them already has? You have gone on beyond morality."

"I thought they had but ... oh dear, there goes the bell. We'd better go to service. Can we continue this later?"

"To-morrow. I have to go out this evening."

We bowed to each other, the first time he had bowed to me fully, and I left the room.

CHAPTER HIGHLIGHTS

- Every individual has the capacity to become a Buddha, to develop into a fully mature and complete human being.
- The official life story of the Buddha may be taken as a parable of Buddhist principles and ideals. Born a prince, Gautama came to realize that even in the happiest and most prosperous life, one would encounter sickness, old age, and death.
- At the heart of Gautama's spiritual search was the problem of the inevitability of human suffering.
- Through the Buddha's own experience in religious self-discipline came the concept of the Middle Way, that of seeking a useful and healthy self-control without either extreme—of self-torture or complete indulgence in the senses.
- There are three major characteristics of existence: impermanence, selflessness, and dissatisfaction.
- Basic principles of the Four Noble Truths are these: (1) the existence of dissatisfaction is inescapable; (2) dissatisfaction is a result of desire or craving; (3) elimination of craving brings the extinction of suffering; (4) the way to eliminate craving is the Eightfold Path.
- The Eightfold Path includes right speech, right action, right livelihood, right effort, right mindfulness, right concentration, right thought, and right understanding.
- Zen has two major meditation practices. One can either simply sit with concentrated awareness or one can focus on a koan, a Zen paradox.
- The Rinzai school of Zen emphasizes achievement of enlightenment through the use of koans. The Soto school emphasizes two major points: there is no gap between daily practice and enlightenment, and right (correct) behavior is Buddhism itself.
- In the Soto school, the riddle of daily life as it is manifested for each individual is considered one's personal koan, and is the most important aspect of one's training.
- Not merely a technique to achieve something, meditation is a complete practice in itself.
- The terms *satori*, "intuitive understanding," and *kensho*, "to see into one's own nature," have often been used in Zen for enlightenment. Both terms refer to the experience of the truth of Buddhist teachings as a dynamic state of being, rather than as a static state that one can attain permanently.
- The Arhat is one who has become free of the world and its attachments to family, possessions, and comfort. The quest is for spiritual perfection and abandonment of the world; the focus is on self-development.
- The Bodhisattva is one who has vowed to remain in the world until all sentient beings have been delivered from suffering. Feeling the suffering of others as one's own results in compassion for all beings. The ideal emphasizes service to others.
- The world is not transcended in enlightenment, but the selfish ego is.

- A series of ten ox-herding pictures illustrates the path of spiritual growth in the Zen tradition. The Buddha-nature is symbolized by the ox, and the internal search and spiritual development of the Zen student is reflected in the process of finding the ox.
- Greed, hate, and delusion are seen as the major sources of suffering, or the "three fires" of Buddhism. The individual possesses a mixture of all three qualities, in a balance that changes with circumstances.
- Buddhism fosters the simultaneous appreciation of the real and the ideal, and it recognizes the tension between the two. This dialectic provides a creative tension, a way both to address present limitations and to move toward the ideal.

KEY CONCEPTS

Delusion A general state of vacillation, confusion, and lack of awareness. One dominated by this trait displays worry, confusion, obstinacy, excitability, and laziness. Delusion can be turned into wisdom through the realization that everything contains the Buddha-nature and therefore merits our deepest care and attention. Delusion is one of the "three fires," or obstacles to growth.

Dissatisfaction The belief that suffering, or dissatisfaction, comes not from the outer world but from the limited ego of each individual. The person can experience a sense of satisfaction only through self-transformation. Dissatisfaction, which encompasses birth, death, decay, pain, and existence itself, is one of the fundamental Buddhist concepts.

Enlightenment A dynamic, progressive state of mind that requires self-discipline, meditation, and realization of selflessness. It can bring about an experience of the truth of Buddha's teachings. Another approach is that "it is just perfect peace and harmony."

Greed The desire to possess more than we have or need. It is a major problem for most people. Those in whom greed predominates are discontented, crafty, vain, and extremely fond of sweet, rich foods and fine clothes. Greed can be turned into compassion through self-discipline and obedience to the precepts. Greed is one of the "three fires," or obstacles to growth.

Hate A state in which individuals display quick anger and sharp tempers. Those dominated by hate tend to belittle others, hold grudges, and suffer from envy, arrogance, and stingi-ness. Hate can be turned into love by following the Buddhist teachings that emphasize respect for others and compassion. Hate is one of the "three fires," or obstacles to growth.

Impermanence The idea that nothing is everlasting, that everything is constantly in flux. The result, according to Buddhism, is no final authority or permanent truth. Impermanence is one of the three basic tenets of existence, in Buddhist thought.

Interdependence The Buddhist characterization of the world as fluid, interconnected processes. The concept of interdependence is in contrast to the human tendency to see the world as static and segmented.

Koan A question or exercise that cannot be solved by thinking or logic. Zen riddles paradoxically force one to go beyond logic and the inherent limitations of the way in which one has categorized experience up to that point. The aim of a koan is to entice Zen students to go beyond abstract conceptualizing, to see their own ignorance, and to search for truth within themselves.

Pride A state that may create a distortion of teachings, or lead to a lack of respect for one's teacher. To counter pride, students may need to be reminded that impermanence is a fact of existence or that training in Buddhism is endless. Pride can be an obstacle to growth.

Selflessness The concept of no individual eternal self or immortal soul. Impermanence applies to one's innermost self as well.

Zazen Zen meditation. It has been described as "just sitting."

ANNOTATED BIBLIOGRAPHY

Conze, E. (1959a). *Buddhism: Its essence and development*. New York: Harper & Row.

Survey of the major Buddhist traditions.

Conze, E. (Trans.). (1959b). *Buddhist scriptures*. Baltimore: Penguin Books.

Good collection of various Buddhist texts.

Kapleau, P. (Ed.). (1965). *The three pillars of Zen*. Boston: Beacon Press.

Includes lectures on training and meditation by a contemporary Zen teacher and first person accounts of Zen training experiences.

Kennett, J. (1976). *Zen is eternal life*. Berkeley, CA: Dharma.

Includes an excellent introduction to Zen Buddhist thought, two newly translated classic Zen works, and the major Zen scriptures and ceremonials. For the serious Zen student.

Kennett, J. (1977). *How to grow a lotus blossom, or how a Zen Buddhist prepares for death*. Mount Shasta, CA: Shasta Abbey.

An account of the mystical experiences of a Zen teacher, including past-life experiences and the deep transformation of mind and body.

Lal, P. (Trans.). (1967). *The Dhammapada*. New York: Farrar, Straus & Giroux.

> Fine translation of a major Buddhist scripture.

Reps, P. (Ed.). (n.d.). *Zen flesh Zen bones*. New York: Doubleday (Anchor Books).

> A marvelous collection of Zen stories and koans.

Web Sites

Zen guide
www.zenguide.com/

> An excellent on-line introduction to Zen including a guide to Zen history and concepts. Also includes a discussion section for sharing thoughts and questions, and a guide to locating Buddhist temples and organizations.

Zen virtual library
www.ciolek.com/WWWVL-Zen.html

> A part of the Buddhist Studies Virtual Library, it includes general resources on Zen, koan study pages, listings of Zen newsletters, journals, and organizations. Also provides links to 190 Zen sites worldwide and a Zen on-line bookstore.

Zen and Psychology
www.geocities.com/Athens/parthenon/6469/main/html

> "As Zen replaces the Id." Provides links and book listings on psychology and religion, psychology and Eastern religion, and psychology and Zen. Also includes information on research on meditation, East–West issues in psychology.

REFERENCES

Benoit, H. (1990). *Zen and the psychology of transformation*. Rochester, VT: Inner Traditions.

Boorstein, S. (1988). Tandem paths: Spiritual practices and psychotherapy. *Inquiring Mind, 5,* 11.

Brown, D., & Engler, J. (1986). The stages of mindfulness meditation. In K. Wilber, J. Engler, & D. Brown (Eds.), *Transformations of consciousness*. Boston: Shambhala.

Carrington, P., & Ephron, H. (1975). Meditation and psychoanalysis. *Journal of the American Academy of Psychoanalysis, 3,* 43–57.

Claxton, G. (Ed.). (1986). *Beyond therapy: The impact of Eastern religion on psychological theory and practicex*. London: Wisdom Publications.

Claxton, G., & Ageha, A. (1981). *Wholly human: Western and Eastern visions of the self and its perfection*. Boston: Routledge & Kegan Paul.

Conze, E. (1959a). *Buddhism: Its essence and development*. New York: Harper & Row.

Conze, E. (Trans.). (1959b). *Buddhist scriptures*. Baltimore: Penguin Books.

Dalai Lama. (1993). The Nobel Peace Prize lecture. In R. Walsh & F. Vaughan (Eds.), *Paths beyond ego*. Los Angeles: Tarcher.

Dalai Lama, et al. (1991). *Mind science*. Boston: Wisdom.

Deshimaru, T. (1985). *Questions to a Zen master*. New York: Dutton.

Deshimaru, T. (1987). *The ring of the way: Testament of a Zen master*. New York: Dutton.

Deshimaru, T. (1991). *The Zen way to martial arts*. New York: Arcana.

Dhammadudhi, S. (1968). *Insight meditation*. London: Committee for the Advancement of Buddhism.

Engler, J. (1986). Therapeutic aims in psychotherapy and meditation. In K. Wilber, J. Engler, & D. Brown (Eds.), *Transformations of consciousness*. Boston: Shambhala.

Engler, J. (1993). Becoming somebody and nobody: Psychoanalysis and Buddhism. In R. Walsh & F. Vaughan (Eds.), *Paths beyond ego*. Los Angeles: Tarcher.

Evans-Wentz, W. (1951). *Tibet's great yogi: Milarepa*. New York: Oxford University Press.

Evans-Wentz, W. (1954). *The Tibetan book of the great liberation*. New York: Oxford University Press.

Evans-Wentz, W. (1958). *Tibetan Yoga*. New York: Oxford University Press.

Evans-Wentz, W. (1960). *The Tibetan book of the dead*. New York: Oxford University Press.

Fromm, E. (1970). Psychoanalysis and Zen Buddhism. In D. T. Suzuki, E. Fromm, & R. de Marino (Eds.), *Zen Buddhism and psychoanalysis*. New York: Harper & Row.

Fromm, G. (1992). Neurophysiological speculations on Zen enlightenment. *Journal of Mind and Behavior, 13,* 163–170.

Fuld, P. (1991, Fall/Winter). Zen and the work of a psychotherapist. *The Ten Directions,* pp. 40–41.

Goldstein, J. (1976). *The experience of insight*. Santa Cruz, CA: Unity Press.

Goleman, D. (1988). *The meditative mind*. Los Angeles: Tarcher.

Goleman, D., & Davidson, R. (1979). *Consciousness: Brain states of awareness and mysticism*. New York: Harper & Row.

Govinda, A. (1960). *Foundations of Tibetan mysticism*. New York: Weiser.

Hanh, Thich Nhat. (1976). *The miracle of mindfulness*. Boston: Beacon Press.

Hanh, Thich Nhat. (1987). *Being peace*. Berkeley, CA: Parallax Press.

Hanh, Thich Nhat. (1988). *The heart of understanding*. Berkeley, CA: Parallax Press.

Hanh, Thich Nhat. (1992). *Touching peace*. Berkeley, CA: Parallax Press.

Hanh, Thich Nhat. (1993). *The blossoming of a lotus*. Boston: Beacon Press.

Hanh, Thich Nhat. (1996). *Cultivating the mind of love.* Berkeley, CA: Parallax Press.

Hanh, Thich Nhat. (1998). *The heart of the Buddha's teaching.* Berkeley, CA: Parallax Press.

Hirai, T. (1989). *Zen meditation and psychotherapy.* New York: Japan Publications.

Kabat-Zinn, J. (1990). *Full catastrophe living.* New York: Delacorte.

Kabat-Zinn, J. (1994). *Wherever you go there you are.* New York: Hyperion.

Kapleau, P. (Ed.). (1965). *The three pillars of Zen.* Boston: Beacon Press.

Katagiri, D. (1988). *Returning to silence: Zen practice in daily life.* Boston: Shambhala.

Katz, N. H. (Ed.). *Buddhist and Western psychology.* Boulder, CO: Prajna Press.

Kennett, J. (1974). How to sit. *Journal of the Zen Mission Society, 5*(1), 12–21.

Kennett, J. (1976). *Zen is eternal life.* Berkeley, CA: Dharma.

Kennett, J. (1977). *The wild white goose* (Vol. 1). Mount Shasta, CA: Shasta Abbey.

Kornfield, J. (1987). *Seeking the heart of wisdom.* New York: Shambhala.

Kornfield, J. (1988). Meditation and psychotherapy: A plea for integration. *Inquiring Mind, 5,* 10–11.

Kornfield, J. (1993). *A path with heart.* New York: Bantam.

Lal, P. (Trans.). (1967). *The Dhammapada.* New York: Farrar, Straus & Giroux.

Maezumi, T. (1978). *The way of everyday life.* Los Angeles: Center.

Manne-Lewis, J. (1986). Buddhist psychology: A paradigm for the psychology of enlightenment. In G. Claxton (Ed.), *Beyond therapy.* London: Wisdom.

Molino, A. (Ed.). (1998). *The couch and the tree: Dialogues in psychoanalysis and Buddhism.* New York: North Point Press.

Morvay, Z. (1999). Horney, Zen, and the real self. *American Journal of Psychoanalysis, 59,* 25–35.

Mosig, Y. (1990, Spring). Wisdom and compassion: What the Buddha taught. *Platte Valley Review,* 51–62.

Murphy, M., & Donovan, S. (1988). *The physical and psychological effects of meditation.* San Rafael, CA: Esalen Institute.

Ogata, S. (1959). *Zen for the West.* London: Rider.

Perls, F. (1969). *Gestalt therapy verbatim.* Lafayette, CA: Real People Press.

Ramaswami, S., & Sheikh, A. (1989). Buddhist psychology: Implications for healing. In A. Sheikh & K. Sheikh (Eds.), *Eastern and Western approaches to healing.* New York: Wiley.

Reps, P. (Ed.). (n.d.). *Zen flesh Zen bones.* New York: Doubleday (Anchor Books).

Reynolds, D. (1980). *The quiet therapies.* Honolulu: University of Hawaii.

Reynolds, D. (1984). *Playing ball on running water.* New York: Morrow.

Reynolds, D. (1993). *Plunging through the clouds.* Albany: State University of New York.

Sayadaw, M. (1972). *Practical insight meditation.* Santa Cruz, CA: Unity Press.

Shapiro, D. (1980). *Meditation: Self-regulation strategy and altered states of consciousness.* New York: Aldine.

Shapiro, D., & Walsh, R. (Eds.). (1984). *Meditation: Classic and contemporary perspectives.* New York: Aldine.

Shen-Yen. (1987). *The advantages one may derive from Zen meditation.* Elmhurst, NY: Dharma Drum.

Shibayama, Z. (1970). *A flower does not talk.* Tokyo: Tuttle.

Soeng Mu, S. (1991). *Heart sutra: Ancient Buddhist wisdom in the light of quantum reality.* Cumberland, RI: Primary Point.

Spiegelman, J., & Miyuki, M. (1985). *Buddhism and Jungian psychology.* Phoenix, AZ: Falcon Press.

Suzuki, D. T. (1964). *An introduction to Zen Buddhism.* New York: Grove Press.

Suzuki, S. (1970). *Zen mind, beginner's mind.* New York: Weatherhill.

Suzuki, S. (n.d.). *Teachings and disciplines of Zen.* (Lecture). San Rafael, CA: Big Sur Recordings.

Trungpa, C. (1975). *Cutting through spiritual materialism.* Berkeley, CA: Shambhala.

Trungpa, C. (1988). *Shambhala: The sacred path of the warrior.* Boston: Shambhala.

sufism and
the islamic tradition

> Know, O beloved, that man was not created in jest or at random, but marvelously made and for some great end. (Al-Ghazzali, 1964a, p. 17)

The Sufis explore the depth and breadth of human experience by beginning with the understanding that we are all underdeveloped. They view human development in an evolutionary perspective: we evolved from an inorganic state to vegetable, animal, and human states, and we can continue to evolve to higher spiritual states. However, we are caught by contradictory forces (much as Freud and others have described). We have a fundamental drive toward further evolution, but this is countered by our animal instincts, drives, and selfish motives. Most people do not even recognize this inner conflict. They escape through drugs or alcohol, or through television and other entertainments designed to keep themselves distracted. One Sufi master described the process of spiritual rebirth in Sufism, thus: "Sufism consists of two steps: taking one step out of one's self and taking another step into God." (Arasteh, 1980, p. 50)

Sufism practice varies widely. Its mystical practices have developed for more than a thousand years from the experiences of hundreds of Sufi masters. Over the centuries, Sufi practices have adapted to cultures and societies in Arabia, Iran, India, China, Indonesia, Africa, Europe, and elsewhere.

The term *Sufi* has several root meanings in Arabic, including "purity" and "wool." All Sufis seek outer and inner purity. The early Sufis wore rough, patched woolen cloaks instead of fancier clothing. Another meaning, "row," developed from a group of devoted Muslims sat in a row in front of the Prophet Muhammed's house in Medina. They accompanied him whenever they could, and it is said that this group received esoteric instruction from the Prophet and were the first Sufis.

Several terms apply to those who practice Sufism. Besides Sufi, they are called *dervishes,* a Persian word related to the Persian word for "door." A dervish stands at the threshold between the material and spiritual worlds, constantly seeking to enter more fully the spiritual realm. A third term is *fakir,* from the Arabic root for "poverty," referring to the simple lifestyle practiced by the Sufis. Many early Sufis were wandering mendicants who relied on charity for food and shelter. Another meaning is "inner poverty," or lack of attachment to material possessions.

In psychology, it is both fashionable and realistic to admit how little we know and how much more research we need before we can understand human behavior. Sufism, on the other hand, explicitly asserts that we have teachers who know what is important—that is, they know how to teach their students to reawaken themselves to their natural state, to become real human beings. The objective of the Sufis is not to explain all of behavior; the task is to transmit what **al-Ghazzali** called *useful knowledge:* the knowledge that can help us to understand ourselves, our personality, and its limitations, and to experience the divine spark that lies within us.

There is no single, systematic approach to Sufi teachings, nor can all teachings be communicated in words. The wisdom of Sufism appears in various forms, including stories, poetry, rituals, exercises, readings and study, shrines, ritual movements, and prayer.

Psychiatrists A. R. Arasteh and Anees Sheikh are also serious students of Sufism. They outline the following basic principles in Sufi practice (1989, p. 148):

1. There are as many ways to reach truth (or God) as there are individuals. All ways involve transformation of the ego and service to Creation.

The Sufis are those who have preferred God to everything, so that God has preferred them to everything. Dhu-l-Nun[1]

[1]James Fadiman and Robert Frager. 1997. *Essential Sufism*. San Francisco: HarperSanFrancisco. p. 36.

2. We can live in harmony with others only if we develop an inner sense of justice. This occurs only when we have reduced our selfishness and arrogance.
3. Love is one of the underlying principles of morality. Love springs from self-work and expresses itself in service to others.
4. The cardinal truth is self-knowledge. Knowledge of self ripens into knowledge of God.

HISTORY

Historians usually describe Sufism as the mystical core of Islam and date its appearance to the seventh century AD, within 100 years after Islam emerged as a major religious force. Sufism is most prominent in the Middle East and in countries that embrace Islam, but its ideas, practices, and teachers are found in India, Europe, and the Americas (Shah, 1964). Indeed, Sufis are scattered among virtually all nations of the world. As with any genuine mystical tradition, Sufism has changed form to fit the cultures and societies in which it has been practiced. Because Sufism has flourished in more cultures than any other spiritual tradition, it has become associated with a greater variety of outward forms.

Islam

Islam, the Arabic word for "peace" or "surrender," has three basic meanings: (1) the submission of all of creation to its Creator; (2) the submission of human beings to God's message as revealed through all the great prophets; and (3) the submission of Muhammad's followers to God's guidance as revealed through him. Muhammad had his initial revelation in AD 610. The Muslim era dates from 622, the year Muhammad fled from Mecca to the city of Medina. Islam is described in the Koran, Islam's holy book, as the original monotheistic religion revealed, in constant succession, to such teachers as Abraham, Moses, and Jesus.

> Sufism is not different from the mysticism of all religions. . . . A river passes through many countries and each claims it for its own. But there is only one river. (Ozak, 1987, p. 1)

In one sense, Islam provides an exoteric, or outward, set of practices that supports the inner practices of Sufism. "Sufism without Islam is like a candle burning in the open without a lantern. There are winds which may blow that candle out. But if you have a lantern with glass protecting the flame, the candle will continue to burn safely" (Ozak, 1987, p. 63). Islam provides a way of life that stresses honesty, charity, service, and other virtues forming a solid foundation for spiritual practice. For more on Islam, see our **web** site.

MAJOR CONCEPTS

Sufism has been portrayed as a way of knowledge and also as a way of love. As with all mysticism, it is also a way of experiencing spiritual states beyond our limited, waking state. Those who have experienced such states describe them as a deeper knowing, a connection with ultimate truth.

Four Stages of Sufi Practice

Ibn 'Arabi has described four stages of practice and understanding in Sufism—*sharia* (exoteric religious law), *tariqa* (the mystical path), *haqiqa* (truth), and *marifa* (gnosis) (Ozak, 1988). The last three build upon the first stage.

First is the **sharia,** the basic foundation for the next three stages. The sharia consists of teachings of morality and ethics found in all religions. It provides guidance for us to live properly in this world. Trying to follow Sufism without following the sharia is like trying to build a house on a foundation of sand. No mysticism can flourish without an ordered life built on solid moral and ethical principles. In Arabic, *sharia* means "road." It is a clear track, a well-traveled route that anyone can follow.

Second is the **tariqa,** which refers to the practice of Sufism. Tariqa is the trackless path in the desert that the Bedouin would follow from oasis to oasis. This path is not clearly marked, nor is it even a visible road. To find your way in the trackless desert, you must know the area intimately, or have a guide who knows the destination and is familiar with the local landmarks. As the sharia refers to the outer practice of religion, the tariqa refers to the inner practice of Sufism. The guide you need in order to find your way is the Sufi teacher, or sheikh. The sharia makes our outsides clean and attractive; the tariqa makes us clean and pure from within. Each of these supports the other.

Third is **haqiqa,** or truth. Haqiqa refers to personal understanding of the inner meanings of sharia and tariqa practices and guidance. Without this understanding, we are fated to follow blindly, to imitate mechanically those who know, those who have attained the station of haqiqa. The attainment of haqiqa confirms and solidifies the practice of the first two stages. Before haqiqa all practice is imitation.

Fourth is **marifa,** or gnosis, a deep level of inner knowing, beyond haqiqa. It is the knowledge of Reality, attained by few—the Messengers, the Prophets, and the great sages and saints.

Ibn 'Arabi also explained these four stages as follows: Sharia connotes "yours and mine." That is, the sharia guarantees individual rights and ethical relations between people. At the stage of *tariqa,* "mine is yours and yours is mine." Sufis are expected to treat each other as brothers and sisters—to open their homes, their hearts, and their purses to each other. *Haqiqa* connotes "no mine and no yours." The individual realizes that all things come from God, that we are only caretakers of all that we "possess." We are expected to use the resources God has given us to benefit God's creation. Those who attain haqiqa have gone beyond attachment to possessions, beyond attachment to externals in general, including fame and position. Those who reach *marifa,* experience "no me and no you." The Prophets and saints have realized all is God, and nothing is separate from God.

The first stage represents the outer form of any practice, what one actually *does.* In many traditions, students are simply told what to do, without any significant explanation of why. As a result, their practice tends to be shallow and mechanical. The second stage includes the inner meaning and the function of the practice. A Sufi teacher once explained, "Anyone can learn the outer forms of prayer in a short time, but Sufi practice aims at developing a heart that can pray."

The third stage represents the *experience* developed in practice, an experience which may take years to deepen. This experience brings a deeper level of life and meaning to the practice. The fourth stage involves full understanding of a practice, because the individual has become transformed and has reached a state of knowledge and wisdom.

In Sufism, what is lawful at one level of understanding may not be lawful at another. For example, the sharia requires only the *outer* practices of fasting. However, according to the tariqa, an essential reason for fasting is to develop self-discipline and to control the insatiable ego. A fast that engenders pride in the one fasting is perfectly lawful in the sharia but would be considered a failure in the tariqa.

personal reflection

THE KEY AND THE LIGHT

Throughout this chapter we will make use of teaching stories—stories told by Sufi teachers for more than entertainment. Here is one famous story and some ways to work with it (adapted from Ornstein, 1972).

> A man is looking at Nasrudin, who is searching for something on the ground.
> "What have you lost, Mulla?" the man asked.
> "My key," said the Mulla.
> So they both went down on their knees and looked for it. After a time the man asked, "Where exactly did you drop it?"
> "In my own house."
> "Then why are you looking here?"
> "There is more light here than inside my own house."

The joke is popular in American vaudeville, as well as in Sufism. If you begin to work with it, it can be more than a joke, more than a story about a simpleton.

Read the story a few times. Now imagine that you are searching desperately for something. Consider the following questions:

1. What are you looking for? (Allow an answer, no matter how unusual, to form in your mind.) Where are you looking? Is there a lot of light there? What kinds of associations do these questions evoke? How do you feel now?
2. Now think about a key. What is a key for? What is the key to your life right now? (Again, take your time in allowing an answer, an image, or an idea to form.)
3. Now say to yourself, "I have lost my key." What does this statement evoke in you?
4. Now think, "My key is in my own house." What are your thoughts and feelings?
5. Then put the whole story together: "I am looking for my key—which I really know is in my own house—in places where I know the key is not, but where there is more light." Spend a little more time with the story.

In addition to the personal associations called up by the story, here is another. . . . Two areas of the mind are opposed, the light, or "day," and the dark, or "night." The key is inside the house, in the dark, unexplored area of our house, of the mind, of science. We are normally attracted and a bit dazzled by the light of the day, by which it is generally easier to find objects. But what we are looking for may simply not be there, and often we may have to grope inelegantly in the dark areas to find it. Once we find what we are looking for in the dark, we can bring it into the light and create a synthesis of both areas of the mind. (Ornstein, 1972, pp. 174–175)

Paths of Sufism

Sufism has no single path. As the Prophet said, "There are as many paths to God as there are souls." The most common disciplines of Sufism include devotion, service, remembrance, and community. These disciplines are interconnected; each one supports the others.

Devotion. Sufism has been called the "path of the heart." Great Sufi poets have written eloquently of the soul's love and longing for God, the Beloved. A Sufi master described this love as follows:

> The eyes of the dervish who is a true lover see nought but God; his heart knows nought but Him. God is the eye by which he sees, the hand with which he holds, and the tongue

with which he speaks. . . . Were he not in love, he would pass away. If his heart should be devoid of love for as much as a single moment, the dervish could not stay alive. Love is the dervish's life, his health, his comfort. Love ruins the dervish, makes him weep; union makes him flourish, brings him to life.[2]

The great Sufi poet Rumi described love as the only force that could transcend the bounds of reason, the distinctions of knowledge, and the isolation of normal consciousness. The love he experienced was not sensual pleasure. It might be more aptly described as love for all things, for creation itself. Love is a continually expanding capacity that culminates in certainty, in the recognition that in truth all beings are both loved and loving.

> Since hearing of the world of Love,
> I have given my life, my heart,
> And my eyes this way.
> At first, I believed that love
> And beloved are different.
> Now, I know they are the same. (Rumi[3])

The perception of God as the Beloved, common to both Christian and Sufi writings, comes from mystical experience. As you channel your energy into loving God, there appears to be a response of being loved in return. Just as in a personal relationship, the act of loving brings forth or awakens love in the other. According to an old Sufi saying, if you take two steps toward God, God runs to you.

A modern Sufi master writes: "The essence of God is love and the Sufi path is a path of love. . . . Love is to see what is good and beautiful in everything. It is to learn from everything, to see the gifts of God and the generosity of God in everything. It is to be thankful for all God's bounties" (Ozak, 1987, p. 7).

Sufis believe that when we come to a certain point along the path of love, God reaches out and begins to assist us by drawing us toward God's presence. As this occurs, we stop striving and begin to surrender, to allow ourselves to be helped and be taken in.

Service.   Service is the sister of devotion in Sufism. As our hearts open with love of God, we realize that all hearts yearn for God, and God is hidden in every heart. Once we realize that every heart contains God, then, as an essential aspect of our spiritual journey, we have to serve others.

One of the greatest services is to help heal the injured hearts of others. A Sufi master taught that "Every kind word or glance softens your heart, and every hurtful word or act closes or hardens your heart." To ignore God in the hearts of others is to separate ourselves from the union we so devoutly desire.

> If someone sits with me
> And we talk about the Beloved,
>
> If I cannot give his heart comfort,
> If I cannot make him feel better
> About himself and this world,

---

[2]Fadiman and Frager, *Essential Sufism*, p. 15.
[3]Author's translation.

Then, Hafiz,
Quickly run to the mosque and pray—
For you have just committed
The only sin I know. (Hafiz in Frager, 1999, p. 187)

In a well-known Sufi story, Harun al-Rashid was once walking through an orchard when he saw an old man planting date palms. He greeted him, and asked, "What are you doing, father?"

"As you see, I am planting date palms."

"How many years does it take a date palm to bear fruit?"

"Ten, twenty, thirty years. Some take as long as a hundred years."

"So you won't be able to eat the fruit of these palms you are planting."

"I may not live to see the day," said the old man, "but we eat from those trees our forefathers planted. So let us plant, that those who follow us may eat in turn!"

These words touched the caliph, and he tossed the old man a purse of gold coins.

The man took the purse, exclaiming, "I give praise to God, for the trees I planted here have borne fruit immediately!"

The caliph was so impressed by this that he gave him another purse of gold.

Said the old man, "I give praise to God! Trees normally bear fruit only once a year, but mine have produced two crops in one day!"

Throwing him yet another purse of gold, the caliph turned to his aide and said, "Quick, let us get away from here before this old man leaves us penniless."

Remembrance.   Remembrance of God fuels our devotion and service. The Sufis seek constant remembrance, never forgetting that we are in God's presence, constantly feeling God within us. As God says in the Qur'an, "I am closer to your than your own jugular vein." Prayer is practice of remembrance, as is meditation, spiritual chanting, and spiritual study.

> For everything there is a polish, and the polish of the heart is Remembrance of God. (Muhammad)

One basic Sufi spiritual practice is *Dhikrullah,* or Remembrance of God. This practice varies with different Sufi orders, but it generally includes repetition of one or more of the ninety-nine Divine Names. In many orders, Remembrance includes body movement, ranging from a simple movement of the head from right to left to the exquisite turning (called in the West, "whirling") of the Mevlevi dervishes. Some orders do repetition silently; others, aloud.

Community.   Sufi groups are like families. The teacher is the parent, and the dervishes are brothers and sisters. An ideal Sufi community replaces the sibling rivalry and poor parenting common in many real families with an opportunity to practice and experience patience, loving compassion, and service. The dervishes are mirrors to each other. We can learn to be patient with our own weaknesses when we see them in others, and we can also learn to focus more on each others' strengths and beauties, and less on each other's weaknesses.

Dervishes often think of each other as companions on a difficult and demanding journey. A man came to a famous Sufi teacher and asked, "True companions are scarce in these times. Where am I to find a companion in God?" The teacher replied, "If you want a companion to provide for you and to bear your burden, such are few and far between. However, if you want a companion in God whose burden you will carry and whose pain you will bear, then I have a multitude I can introduce you to."[4]

---

[4]James Fadiman and Robert Frager. 1997. *Essential Sufism.* San Francisco: HarperSanFrancisco. p. 61.

The Self (Nafs)

The Arabic term *nafs* means self or ego. It is a living process, rather than a static structure in the psyche. "The nafs is not a thing. The Arabic term is related to words for 'breath,' 'soul,' 'essence,' 'self,' and 'nature.' It refers to a process which comes about from the interaction of body and soul." (Ozak, 1987, p. 31)

At its lowest level, the self is a product of the self-centered consciousness—the narcissistic ego. The self must be transformed to reach the ideal. Like a wild horse, the nafs is powerful and virtually uncontrollable at first. As the self becomes trained, or transformed, it becomes capable of serving the individual.

> The nafs is not bad in itself. Never blame your nafs. Part of the work of Sufism is to change the state of your nafs. The lowest state is that of being completely dominated by your wants and desires. The next state is to struggle with yourself, to seek to act according to reason and higher ideals and to criticize yourself when you fail. A much higher state is to be satisfied with whatever God provides for you, whether it means comfort or discomfort, fulfillment of physical needs or not. (Ozak, 1987, p. 32)

The following categories of the self are based on Frager (1999) and other sources (Al-Ghazzali, 1963; Arasteh, 1973; Nurbakhsh, 1992; Ozak, 1981, 1987; Shafii, 1974; Trimingham, 1971).

The Tyrannical or Narcissistic Self.   This level has also been described as the "commanding self" or the "self that incites to evil." The **tyrannical self** seeks to dominate us and to control our thoughts and actions. At this level, the individual displays unbridled selfishness and no sense of morality or compassion. This level of self contains the narcissistic ego or lower personality. It is made up of powerful, and often unconscious, impulses, or drives. These drives dominate reason or judgment and are defined as the forces in one's nature that must be brought under control. They prevent one from following any path or discipline.

Descriptions of this level resemble descriptions of the id in psychoanalytic theory; the two concepts are closely linked to lust and aggression. Al-Ghazzali calls the drives of the tyrannical self the swine and the dogs of the soul—the sensual self behaves like swine, the ferocious self is like fierce dogs or wolves. Wrath, greed, sensual appetites, passion, and envy are examples of this stage of self. This is the realm of physical and egoistic desires. We are all dominated by these impulses at times, but most of us have moments of perspective in which we can see their tyranny.

At this level, people are like addicts in denial. Their lives are dominated by negative urges, yet they refuse to believe they have a problem. They have no hope of change, because they acknowledge no need for change.

The Regretful Self.   At the first level, we are unaware and unconscious. As the light of faith grows, we begin to see ourselves clearly, perhaps for the first time. We start to understand the negative effects of our self-centered approach to the world. This **regretful self** stage resembles Freud's concept of superego. It can be highly judgmental and self-blaming.

At this level, the individual remains dominated by wants and desires but repents from time to time and tries to follow higher impulses. This stage of inner struggle closely corresponds to the stage in the Zen picture "Catching the Ox." (See Figure 14.4, page 419.)

There is a battle between the nafs, the lower self, and the soul. This battle will continue through life. The question is who will educate whom? Who will become the master of whom? If the soul becomes the master, then you will be a believer, one who embraces Truth. If the lower self becomes master of the soul, you will be one who denies Truth. (Ozak, 1987, p. 4)

This level of self parallels aspects of the superego in psychoanalytic theory. It may entail excessive self-accusation, self-belittlement, or defensiveness, which appears in the form of excessive vanity. Typical manifestations include an insatiable hunger for praise, for recognition, or for control of others. "In this stage it is possible for one's motives to become so distorted that it is difficult to distinguish between fantasy and reality" (Beg, 1970). One of the strongest tendencies is hypocrisy. Armed with partial knowledge of higher ideals, individuals at this stage tend to pretend to what they have not yet achieved.

At this level, individuals lack the ability to alter their lives significantly. However, as they see their faults more clearly, their regret and their desire for change grow. They are like addicts beginning to realize the extent of their addiction and the pain they have caused themselves and others. Because the addiction is still so powerful, change requires far stronger medicine.

The Inspired Self.   The individual who has reached the level of the **inspired self** takes genuine pleasure in prayer, meditation, and other spiritual activities. Only now is the individual motivated by ideals such as compassion, service, and moral values. This stage marks the beginning of the real practice of Sufism. At earlier stages, the best anyone can accomplish is superficial understanding and mechanical worship.

Though the individual is not free of the power of desires and ego, the new level of motivation significantly reduces their power for the first time. It is essential to live according to these higher values; otherwise they will wither and die. Behaviors common to the inspired self include gentleness, compassion, creative acts, and moral action. Overall, a person impelled by the inspired self appears emotionally mature, respectable, and respected. This developmental stage can be the most dangerous. If the inspiration and energy of this stage feed the ego, the person can become inflated with pride and grandiosity. This is similar to the *mana* personality described by Jung. Someone who has touched powerful archetypes may gain great energy or *mana*, which then serves the ego instead of the self. The guidance of a sheikh is particularly important for someone going through this stage.

The Serene Self.   The seeker is now at peace, and the struggles of the earlier stages are basically over. The old desires and attachments are no longer binding. This level resembles the stage of gratitude and trust mentioned earlier; the **serene self** also corresponds to the stage shown in the Zen picture "Riding the Ox Home." (See Figure 14.6, page 421.) The ego-self begins to let go, allowing the individual to come closer to the Divine.

This level of self predisposes one to be liberal, grateful, and trusting. Individuals who accept difficulties with the same sense of equanimity with which they accept benefits may be said to have attained this level. Developmentally, this is a period of transition. The self can now begin to "disintegrate" and let go of all previous concern with self-boundaries; it can "reintegrate" as an aspect of the universal self (Arasteh, 1973).

> The radical division into good and bad can be the sickness of the Mind. (Erikson, 1964)

The Pleased Self.   At this stage, the individual is content not only with his or her lot but even with the difficulties and trials of life, realizing that they come from God. The state of the **pleased self** is quite different from our usual experience of the world, occupied primarily with seeking pleasure and avoiding pain. A Sufi story illustrates this state clearly.

> Sultan Mahmud of Ghazna once shared a cucumber with Ayaz, his most loyal and beloved servant. Ayaz was happily eating his half of the cucumber, but when the sultan bit into *his* half, it was so bitter he immediately spit it out.
>
> "How could you manage to eat something so bitter?" the sultan exclaimed. "It tasted like chalk or like bitter poison!"
>
> "My beloved Sultan," answered Ayaz, "I have enjoyed so many favors and bounties from your hand that whatever you give me tastes sweet to me."

Those whose love and gratitude to God are like Ayaz's love of his sultan have reached the stage of the pleased self.

> The path of Sufism is the elimination of any intermediaries between the individual and God. (Ozak, 1987, p. 1)

The Self Pleasing to God.   Those who reach this stage—the **self pleasing to God**—realize that all power to act originates in God, that they can do nothing by themselves. They no longer fear anything or ask for anything.

These individuals have achieved genuine inner unity and wholeness. Ibn 'Arabi calls this the stage of inner marriage, or union of self and soul. People struggle with the world because they experience *multiplicity*. A broken mirror creates a thousand different reflections of a single image. If the mirror could be made whole again, it would then reflect the single, unified image. Healing the multiplicity within themselves enables people to experience the world as whole and unified.

> Because someone has made up the word "wave," do I have to distinguish it from water? (Kabir, 1977, p. 29)

The Pure Self.   Those few who have attained this final level, that of the **pure self,** have transcended the self entirely. No ego or separate self remains, only union with God. At this stage, the individual has realized the truth "There is no god but God." The Sufi now knows that only the Divine exists, that there exists nothing other than God, and that any sense of individuality or separateness is an illusion. This is equivalent to the stage of *fana* described next.

Annihilation and Return

The Sufis describe two advanced states of consciousness—annihilation and return. The first is a state of union, or annihilation—**fana**—in which individual identity seems merged with the whole of reality. In this state, a person erects no barriers between the self and God, because it is clear that no barriers exist. A person has become like a drop of water that is aware of being part of the ocean or a column of air that is conscious of the wind.

The second aspect is a state of return, or persistence—**baqa**—in which one is part of the world but not concerned about one's wordly position or rewards. The awareness of the divine element in all things is so great that personal issues become secondary to caring for the rest of God's creation (Arberry, 1966, pp. 131–145; Ibn 'Arabi, 1981). The individual is in the world but separate from nothing in it.

> I laugh when I hear that the fish in the water is thirsty. (Kabir, 1977, p. 9)

In one sense, Sufism is essentially a path of self-transformation ending in fana and baqa. Arasteh and Sheikh (1989) describe the states of fana and baqa in psychological terms. *Fana* is the disintegration of one's narrow self-concept, social self, and limited intellect. *Baqa* is the reintegration of the Self, or rebirth as a whole, fully integrated human being.

DYNAMICS

Psychological Growth—Stages of Personal Development

Many Sufi teachers have described different stages in the course of personal development. Each stage trains or exposes different facets of the aspirant's character and perception. We will discuss each stage separately, but no single, linear pattern is typical of the actual experience of a Sufi student.

Initial Awakening.   This stage begins when a person finds the external world unsatisfying and decides to reevaluate his or her life. Such a realization often follows a personal crisis, sometimes coupled with bewilderment about the meaning of existence. **Initial awakening,** then, marks a fundamental reorientation of personal values.

Arasteh (1980), a psychiatrist and student of Sufism, writes that this stage is characterized by the desire to change. The seeker reexamines his or her life, a task that requires "strong discipline, constant identification, and transformation of undesirable values, interests, behaviours, thoughts, words, and deeds. *Undesirable* here refers to whatever hinders the seekers progress" (Arasteh, 1980, p. 53). The first step is to forgive all those by whom the seeker feels wronged. Sufism holds compassionate forgiveness as a powerful means of inner change and purification. Forgiveness is followed by repentance, or turning away from old, undesirable habits.

Patience and Gratitude.   At the stage of **patience and gratitude,** the individual (1) realizes that self-development takes time and (2) feels appreciation for the time granted. Patience surpasses passive acceptance of one's faults; it is perseverance, or the willingness to keep trying even when efforts at inner change are not immediately rewarded. A person reshapes his or her personality gradually, the way a tree is shaped, nourished, and pruned, again and again.

Patience, considered one of the greatest virtues, is essential for living in the present. Without patience, spiritual work is impossible. An impatient person focuses on the future, but prayer and meditation require present-centered, highly focused attention.

Patience is the key to putting one's faith in action, persevering until success is reached. Arasteh comments, "The psyche cannot be cleaned overnight: unlearning takes place gradually as the state of knowledge becomes no-knowledge" (1980, p. 68).

Gratitude is related to the understanding that all things come from God, including intelligence, health, and life itself. The highest level of gratitude is appreciation for everything one receives, whether pleasant or painful, whether one gains or one loses.

Fear and Hope.   Individuals seeking unity with the Divine experience **fear and hope.** This fear of God is not fear of being punished or being sent to hell, but rather the fear lovers feel of losing the love of their beloved. The Sufi master Shibli stated, "Each day that I was overcome with fear, the door of knowledge and insight opened to my heart" (in Shafii, 1985, pp. 183–184).

Hope allows one to see oneself clearly and honestly without becoming paralyzed. "The essence of Sufism is hope" (Shafii, 1985, p. 184). It is the hope that God will accept our small efforts at prayer, service, and the like. Sufi's hope, in spite of shortcomings, to progress on the spiritual path, the path that leads closer to God.

Self-denial and Poverty. In pursuit of spiritual attainment, the individual may practice **self-denial and poverty.** Self-denial means to abstain from wrong-doing, to avoid whatever the seeker believes is not in harmony with the spiritual path. The seeker develops self-awareness and learns to watch over his or her own desires and impulses. This leads to a state of detachment from the world, or nonattachment to our desires.

Nonattachment has also been described as a state of inner poverty. The seeker may be either poor or wealthy, but he or she is no longer attached to money or possessions. "When the heart is cleared (of all except God) poverty is not better than wealth nor is wealth better than poverty" (Hujwiri, 1959, p. 24). Significance lies in the loss of desire for everything except God. "The vacant heart [is] more important than the vacant hand" (Rice, 1964, p. 42). The seeker develops a heart and mind cleansed of everything and enters a state of simplicity and detachment.

In another sense, the Sufis seek to lose reliance on labels and concepts and to become empty. Arasteh writes that they seek to "attain a state of 'void,' to attain a zero point so that they could become related to any state of being and achieve 'everythingness'" (1980, p. 64).

Another word for Sufi is *faqir,* which comes from the Arabic root *faqr,* or poverty. Spiritual poverty is a heart empty of attachments to this world, a heart open and ready to be filled with God.

Trust in God. Individuals who place **trust in God** have accepted belief in the oneness of the Divine. They seek everything from God, not from the world. Sufis recognize the necessity of genuine effort, but believe success is only granted by the grace of God. In seeking a cure for illness, we take the medicines prescribed by a physician, but we know that is no guarantee; the cure is a gift from God.

Al-Ghazzali describes three degrees of trust. The first is the trust you might place in a skilled professional, such as a fine doctor or lawyer. The second is the trust of a child in its mother, a total reliance on the parent. The third is the complete submission of one's will, so that one is like a corpse in the hands of a washer of the dead. It involves no resistance to whatever happens, no expectation.

> This is not like a child who calls upon the mother, but like a child who knows deeply that even if he does not call for the mother, the mother will be totally aware of his condition and look after him. This is the ultimate degree of trust in God. (Al-Ghazzali in Shafii, 1985, p. 227)

This is a period of activity, not a time of indolence, passivity, or dependency. The balance between acting for oneself and trusting in the Divine is captured in a saying of Muhammad: "Trust in God but tie your camel first." Trust arises from assuming that your efforts are part of a larger system, the details of which you are unaware.

Love, Yearning, Intimacy, and Satisfaction. In the stage of **love, yearning, intimacy, and satisfaction,** the developing personality has only one desire, which is to love God. The Sufi realizes that this single desire is the only desire that ever existed. Arasteh writes, "One exists within the realm of the beloved, and manifests

Higher than the state of asceticism is the state wherein on the approach and departure of wealth the person remains unaffected equally. If it comes he is not glad and if it leaves him he is not sorry. (Al-Ghazzali, 1972, p. 206)

oneself in terms of the mechanism of 'love.' The Sufi is now able to practice the art of love which exists in the depth of the psyche . . . It is here that Sufi thought has made a great contribution, and unlike Darwin, Freud and Marx, whose doctrines were all based on the principles of conflict, Sufism experientially discovered and proved that the greatest mediator of rational and irrational conflicts in man, society and history was *love*" (1980, p. 98). Freud tells us that our psyches are bound to perpetual conflict; Sufism holds out the promise of full integration of the psyche. Arasteh writes of this integration, "superego, ego, and id (if indeed such a division exists in healthy people) finally becomes one creative victor" (1980, p. 121).

Satisfaction comes from knowing that all things, pleasant or unpleasant, come from God. When they enjoy love and a sense of intimacy with God, the Sufis cannot help but be satisfied with whatever comes to them in this world.

Intent, Sincerity, and Truthfulness.

The stage of **intent, sincerity, and truthfulness** is dominated by a concern for the intent, not the actual form, of action. According to a famous *hadith*, "Intention gives meaning to action."

Sheikh Muzaffer used the example of someone walking in a poor part of town and announcing, "These poor people desperately need a hospital. If I had a million dollars, I would immediately put it into a building fund for a hospital here." If the person is truly sincere in this wish—so that if he or she came into a million dollars, the money would immediately go into a hospital construction fund—then the announcement of intended generosity is equivalent to actually building the hospital. It is the sincerity of intention that counts. Whether one's actions succeed or not is God's will. It is one's inner intentions that give meaning to all actions.

Contemplation and Self-examination.

Many distractions might prevent one from **contemplation and self-examination** and thus render one unable to perceive inner reality. Sufi concerns parallel those voiced in Yoga and Buddhism with regard to clearing the mind. In a famous *hadith*, Muhammad teaches, "An hour of contemplation is worth a year of prayer."

One Sufi teacher visited another teacher who was in such deep contemplation the visitor could not even detect his breathing. After a long time, the man came out of this state, and his visitor asked, "From which great master did you learn this amazing depth of concentration?" The man responded simply, "From a cat watching a mouse hole. But the cat could concentrate better than I."

The Recollection of Death.

Contemplating death can be a powerful tool in releasing one from undesirable habits and attitudes. Thinking about our own death is an exercise in becoming more aware of our present experiences. It is a way to begin the process of personal growth.

Al-Ghazzali suggests the following exercise to engrave the awareness, or **recollection of death** into your consciousness:

> Remember your contemporaries who have passed away, and were of your age. Remember the honours and fame they earned, the high posts they held and the beautiful bodies they possessed, and today all of them are turned to dust. How they have left orphans and widows behind them and how their wealth is being wasted after them and their houses turned into ruins.
>
> No sign of them is left today, and they lie in the dark holes underneath the earth.
>
> Picture their faces before your mind's eye and ponder.

> Do not fix hopes on your wealth and do not laugh away life. Remember how they walked and now all their joints lie separated and the tongue with which they talked lightly is eaten away by the worms and their teeth are corroded. They were foolishly providing for twenty years when even a day of their lives was not left. They never expected that death shall come to them thus at an unexpected hour. (Al-Ghazzali, 1972, pp. 378–379)

Al-Ghazzali describes a cycle beginning with conversion and repentance and ending with reflection on death. It can easily go the other way: reflection on death leading to the psychological state that precedes conversion. Until recently, Western psychology has avoided the topic of death, perhaps because of our death-fearing culture.

Obstacles to Growth

The main obstacles to growth in Sufism are the lower self (nafs), which we discussed earlier, and heedlessness.

Man, like a sleepwalker who suddenly "comes to" on some lonely road, has in general no correct idea as to his origins or his destiny. (Shah, 1972f, p. 133)

Heedlessness (Forgetfulness). Sufis consider the inability to pay attention and to remember what we know as the cardinal problems of humanity. Such heedlessness supports all other human weaknesses and psychopathology. Inherent in our makeup is the tendency to lose sight of our divine origin; even as we remember we begin to forget.

People influenced by Sufi teachings indicate that the initial task is to wake up enough to be aware of one's predicament. Orage (1965) writes thus:

> Our present waking state is not really being awake at all. . . . It is, the tradition says, a special form of sleep comparable to a hypnotic trance. . . . From the moment of birth and before, we are under the suggestion that we are not fully awake; and it is universally suggested to our consciousness that we must dream the dream of this world—as our parents and friends dream it. . . . Just as in night-dreams the first symptom of waking is to suspect that one is dreaming, the first symptom of waking from the waking state—the second awakening of religion—is the suspicion that our present waking state is dreaming likewise. To be aware that we are asleep is to be on the point of waking; and to be aware that we are only partially awake is the first conditioning of becoming and making ourselves more fully awake. (p. 89)

As Harman (1967) concludes, "We are all hypnotized from infancy. . . . The apparent corollary is that we do not perceive ourselves and the world about us as they are but as we have been persuaded to perceive them" (p. 323).

personal reflection

DO YOU KNOW WHAT YOU LIKE, DO YOU LIKE WHAT YOU DO?

Here is an exercise to help you investigate your own heedlessness. Are you constantly aware of the choices and decisions you make?

You wake up in the morning and propose to get out of bed. Ask yourself whether you really wish to get up, and be candid about it.

You take a bath—because you like it or would you dodge it if you could?

You eat your breakfast—is it exactly the breakfast you like in kind and quantity? Are you eating *your* breakfast, or simply breakfast as defined by society? Do you, in fact, wish to eat at all?

You go to your office . . . or you set about the domestic and social duties of the day—would you freely choose to be where you are and do what you are doing? Assume that, for the present, you accept the general situation. Are you in detail doing what you like? Do you speak as you please to other persons? Do you really like or only pretend to like them? (Remember that it is not a question yet of acting on your likes and dislikes but only of discovering what they really are.)

You pass the day, every phase offering a new opportunity for self-questioning—do you really like this or not? The evening arrives, with leisure—what would you really like to do? What truly amuses you: theater or movies, conversation, reading, music, games, and which ones in particular?

We reiterate: In Sufism, doing what you like comes later. In fact, it can be left to take care of itself. The important thing is to know what you like. (Orage, 1965, p. 112)

A first step in overcoming heedlessness is to learn to recognize it in one's own life. It is as mundane as misplacing one's glasses or as troubling as an incident told about Norbert Weiner, the famous cybernetic researcher. One day he was walking along a path at the Massachusetts Institute of Technology when he met a colleague. They talked for a few minutes and, as they parted, Weiner asked his friend to tell him in which direction he had been walking when they met. Weiner could not recall if he had been on his way to lunch or if he had just finished it.

> Man is asleep, must he die before he wakes? (Muhammad)

STRUCTURE

Body

Al-Ghazzali says that one should consider the body as the carrier and the soul as the rider. "The soul should take care of the body, just as a pilgrim on his way to Mecca takes care of his camel; but if the pilgrim spends his whole time in feeding and adorning his camel, the caravan will leave him behind, and he will perish in the desert" (1964a, p. 49). Good health is encouraged because it allows outer service as well as inner work to proceed without impediment.

Both Islam and Sufism advocate caring for the body without becoming dominated by concern for it. They teach a middle ground that exists between asceticism and hedonism, an approach remarkably like that of Buddhism. "Do not sleep until you are unable to stay awake. Do not eat until you are hungry. Dress only to cover your body and to protect it from cold and from heat" (Ibn 'Arabi, 1992, p. 7).

Various Sufi schools employ exercises that entail a "fine-tuning" of the body and mind. The so-called whirling of the dervishes, a constantly turning movement, is the most widely known. "The objective is to produce a state of ritual ecstasy and to accelerate the contact of the Sufi's mind with the world-mind of which he considers himself to be a part" (Burke, 1966, p. 10). Sufi exercises may consist of movement, movement with music, or music alone.

> The Body too is a great and necessary principle, and without it the task fails and the purpose is not attained. (Rumi, 1972, p. 31)

The use of dance or movement to bring about mystical states is described by Burke (1975): "A dance is defined as bodily movements linked to a thought and a sound or a series of sounds. The movements develop the body, the thought focuses the mind, and the sound fuses the two and orientates them towards a consciousness of divine contact" (p. 49). This ecstatic state is a physical condition that allows certain subtle inner experiences to be felt and understood.

Social Relationships

Ibn 'Arabi stressed the importance of associating with others also on the spiritual path:

> It is best to separate yourself from people who do not believe in what you believe, who do not do what you do, and who are against your faith. Yet at the same time you should not think badly of them or condemn them for what they are. Your intention in ignoring them should be that you prefer the company of believers. (Ibn 'Arabi, 1992, p. 10)

The relationship between companions on the Sufi path is considered extremely important. The following is an explanation of the power of Sufi groups from a contemporary writer.

> Our tendency is toward personal independence, but in order to know our real Self we need to abandon the ego-protective behaviors that keep us in separation. We need to open ourselves to other beings in this milieu of Love. . . . Only as we begin to open to others in love can the isolated ego be transformed. (Helminski, 1992, p. 15)

Al-Ghazzali (1975) wrote that real friendship includes the following eight responsibilities:

You will not enter Paradise until you believe, and you will not believe until you love another. Let me guide you to something in the doing of which you will love one another: salute all and sundry among you. (Muhammad)

1. *Material aid.* You have an obligation to help your companions with food, or money, or other things they need for their own survival or development.
2. *Personal support.* "If they are sick, visit them; if they are busy, help them; if they have forgotten, remind them" (p. 33)
3. *Respect.* You should not complain of their faults to them or to others. Also, you should not give advice when you know it cannot be acted upon.
4. *Praise and attention.* You should praise the good qualities of your companions and let them know that you care for them.
5. *Forgiveness.* It is helpful to forgive others for their failings.
6. *Prayer.* You should pray for the well-being of your companions with the same fervor as you pray for your own well-being.
7. *Loyalty.* You should be firm in your friendships so that you can be depended on by those who put their trust in you.
8. *Relief from discomfort.* You should not create awkward or difficult situations that involve your companions. You should not be a burden to others.

Will

The term *will,* although used in Sufi writings, is elusive and defies a single definition. " 'Will,' to the Sufi, will vary in nature, quality and significance in direct relation to the stage which the aspirant has reached" (Khan, 1974). The question also arises of balance between free will and divine will.

Divine Will. In contrast to free will, *divine will* is described as a fundamental law of nature. A stone falls because it is obeying the divine will manifested as gravity. One definition of *saint* might be "one whose every action is in conformity with the divine will." *Islam* means "surrender," or surrender of one's limited personal will to divine will.

One modern teacher has explained divine will and personal will with the metaphor of an airplane trip. As an individual passenger, you can do virtually nothing that will affect the plane's arrival time. You have neither the skill nor the power to influence the flight itself. But you can decide whether or not to read or write, eat dinner, watch the movie, and so on. In short, you can use your personal will to have a pleasant and profitable time while on the plane, or not. The plane will arrive at exactly the same time in any case.

> Thy will be done
> On earth as it is in heaven.
> (Lord's Prayer)

Free Will. *Free will* is assumed to be part of human nature. Humanity is unique in its propensity and capacity to perform actions contrary to natural law and incompatible with physical, mental, or spiritual health. Unlike animals, we can turn away from our own best interests. One of the great goals of Sufism is to surrender our individual will to divine will.

> *The effort of attention by which we hold fast to an idea . . . is the secret of will.* (James, 1899, p. 91)

Emotions

Emotions orient consciousness either toward or away from knowledge of reality. A particular emotion is less important than its overall effect on one's behavior. Al-Ghazzali (1968a) recalls times of bliss and despair, both of which he saw as instrumental in his own realization.

Awareness of one's emotions is important. This awareness is itself transformative, as Fritz Perls and other therapists have recently discovered. "What is essential from you is to be heedful at all times, to be attentive to what comes into your mind and your heart. Think about and analyze these thoughts and feelings. . . . Beware of the wishes of your ego, settle your accounts with it" (Ibn 'Arabi, 1992, p. 7).

> Three things in life are destructive: anger, greed, and pride. (Muhammad)

Intellect

Al-Ghazzali's description of the intellect foreshadows the developmental models of Piaget (Inhelder & Piaget, 1958; Piaget, 1952). Al-Ghazzali distinguishes four stages of development. First is a drive for understanding, what Western psychology calls *curiosity* or the need for competence (White, 1959). The second, *axiomatic intellect,* is the capacity to understand logical relationships. The third element is *empirical knowledge,* the aspect concerned with external things and events. The fourth and last element to appear, the *developed intellect,* is a higher form of the original drive for understanding. This quality of the intellect guides inner development and allows a person to "conquer and subdue his appetite which hankers for immediate pleasure" (Al-Ghazzali, 1966, p. 228).

The developed intellect includes the heart as well as the head. It is an integrated way of understanding oneself, the world, and spiritual knowledge as well. Jelaladin Rumi (1207–1273) is a clear example of the integrated intellect. One of the world's greatest mystical poets, Rumi was also a gifted philosopher and founder of the Mevlevi Order, whose members are known as the whirling dervishes.

> If your thought is a rose, you are a rose garden; if it is a thorn, you are fuel for the bath stove. (Rumi in Helminski, 1992, p. 34)

Conventional learning that reflects a misunderstanding of the developed intellect's function can retard its abilities. Al-Ghazzali again and again upbraids his former scholastic colleagues for their unwillingness to use their learning to reach beyond the empirical and achieve real knowledge (Watt, 1971). He recounts that he needed to pierce his own intellectual training repeatedly with ecstatic and revelatory states until he understood enough to keep his intellect in balance.

Self

He who knows himself knows his Lord. (Muhammad)

Sufis describe the self in two ways. The first way is to see the self as a collection of socially determined, changeable roles—the self within society. The second is to see the true self, the core of one's being, distinct yet part of a larger entity. Sufi teaching encourages students to shift personal identification from the social self to the true self. As students identify more and more with their true selves, they accept themselves for who they are, they see their external attributes of personality (how they speak, how they eat, and so forth) in a new perspective. These attributes assume their natural place in the totality of the personality.

Teacher

But how will you ever know him as long as you are unable to know yourself? (Sanai, 1974, p. 10)

Arasteh and Sheikh (1989) comment that although the Sufi teacher–student relationship may seem hierarchical and authoritarian, the inner reality is quite different. In reality, two souls are communicating. One is a channel for a higher level of energy and inspiration. The other receives and progresses. The more the dervish progresses, the less guidance he or she requires. Eventually, the student's own heart provides all the guidance necessary.

The practices of Sufism are viewed as spiritual medicine and the sheikh as a spiritual physician. According to Chinese medicine, we become ill when our bodies get out of balance. Chinese medicine seeks not only to alleviate symptoms and cure illnesses, but also to foster balance and health, preventing illness. Similarly the practices of Sufism aim for a healthy spiritual balance so that inner wisdom and spiritual nature can blossom naturally.

Sufis view a teacher as a physician of the soul. Because few of us have the spiritual know-how to diagnose ourselves correctly, and fewer still to cure ourselves, we must turn to a teacher. A Sufi teacher determines what practices to prescribe for each student to help that student develop spiritually.

A young man once became the student of a Sufi teacher and was given the job of cleaning the latrines. His mother, a wealthy physician, asked the sheikh to give her son a more fitting task, and sent the teacher twelve Ethiopian slaves to clean the outhouses. The teacher replied, "You are a physician. If your son had an inflammation of the gall bladder, should I give the medicine to an Ethiopian slave instead of giving it to him?"

We can put a bandage on a cut, but we cannot operate on ourselves. Similarly Sufi students can engage in a certain amount of independent self-reflection and self-discipline, but major transformation requires the help, support, and advice of a guide. The outside help of a teacher is essential to transcend our boundaries and achieve real transformation.

The most important function of a Sufi teacher is to provide an atmosphere of love and trust for each dervish. The sheikh's unconditional love and trust in the dervish's capacity for spiritual growth are essential foundations for Sufi practice. In this atmosphere, the dervishes begin to heal their hearts of the pain and wounds experienced in this world. They gain the confidence to undergo the rigors of transformation, and develop the belief in their capacity for spiritual growth and their worthiness to seek and find God.

The Necessity of a Guide.   Why do Sufis consider a guide necessary? Mohammed Shafii, a psychiatrist knowledgeable in Sufi tradition, suggests the following reasoning:

> The Sufis feel that maturity cannot be achieved alone. They feel there is a need for guidance and discipline. The path is unknown, the night is dark and the road is full of danger. Dangers include preoccupation with selfishness, false visions, misinterpretations of mystical states, arrest in development, fixation in a particular state, appeal to various drugs to create false mystical experiences and not infrequently overwhelming anxiety and insanity. (1968, p. 11)

A guide has explored his or her own inner nature and is capable of leading others to explore their own inner spiritual depths. Such a teacher instructs from experience, as the following story points out:

> Nasruddin, a Sufi teacher, was serving as a local judge. A woman came to him with her son and complained that her son had an uncontrollable sweet tooth. She asked Nasruddin to tell the boy to stop eating sweets all the time. Nasruddin agreed and told her to come back in two weeks. When they returned, he said simply, "Young man, stop eating sweets! It is no good for you."
> The mother asked, "Why did you have us wait for two weeks? Couldn't you have said this to my son when we first came to you?"
> Nasruddin replied, "No I couldn't possibly have told that to your son two weeks ago. First, *I* had to stop eating sweets!

This story only seems funny because we are used to learning facts and talking about them without living by what we have learned. One requirement of a teacher is to practice what he or she teaches. Empty words help no one.

The Theory Firsthand

EXCERPT FROM *FORTY DAYS: THE DIARY OF A TRADITIONAL SOLITARY SUFI RETREAT*

The following passage from the diary of a Western woman, a Muslim and Sufi and also a prominent European psychologist, was written during a 40-day Sufi retreat.

The *zhikrs* [the practice of repetition of a sacred word or phrase] are becoming even deeper; in the truest sense of the word they are taking on "substance." This is where the inner peace unfolds, the peace described so beautifully by Islam as the tranquility of the heart. My head moves inside a column formed by my air body. Then I get the feeling that every back-and-forth motion of my head is spraying strings of this substance all over the room. Like water spraying from the hide of a wet dog when it shakes itself. Except that these strings have some kind of life of their own that draws them out farther and farther into the universe. Right above the heart region is where you feel it, as if pulling open curtains (veils?) on either side. With the steady, broad-stepping movements of a skater's legs—right, left, right, left....So is this the "polishing of the heart"?

Sometimes it feels as if I'm penetrating directly into the syllables of the holy formulas, into the sound that echoes silently within me. The greater the awareness, the more intense the experience is. The zhikr is showing me how to do zhikrs! The old precept comes to mind: "At first you act as if you're doing the zhikr. Then you do the zhikr. Then finally the zhikr does you." All at once I perceive this steering process as one of the "signs" of Allah: "He is closer to you than your jugular vein." Where can one perceive Him Who is immanent and transcendent if not in one's deepest insides? The signs of which the Holy Quran speaks are "on the horizons and within yourselves." Is that it? "His Heaven and His Earth cannot contain Him," says Islam, "only the [shiny, polished] heart of the believer has room for Him."

Suddenly it becomes painfully clear to me. There's really only one way: absolute surrender, absolute giving-up of wanting-for-oneself. The voluntary giving-up of "whatever is dearest." In the words of Hz. Mevlâna [Rumi]: "to take the step toward the lion in the lion's presence," to "jump into the fire," to "fall into the trap."

The Lion

So the reports of a lion reached every corner of the world. A man amazed by the rumors made his way to the forest from a faraway place to see the lion. For a whole year he endured the rigors of the journey, traveling from waystation to waystation. When he got to the forest and saw the lion from afar, he stood still and couldn't go a step closer. "What's this?" they said to him. "You came all this way out of love for this lion. This lion has the trait that if a person boldly comes up to him and strokes him lovingly, he will not hurt that person or do anything to him; but if someone is fearful and anxious, then the lion becomes furious at him; indeed he attacks some people meaning to kill them because they have a bad opinion of him. That being so, you've given yourself a year of trouble. Now that you've gotten close to the lion, you stand still. What kind of standing there is that?" No one had the courage to go a single step farther. They said, "All the steps we took up to now were easy. Here we can't take a step farther." Now, what Omar [one of the four Caliphs of Islam] meant by faith was this step, taking a step in the lion's presence toward the lion. This step is extremely rare; it is the part of the elect and God's close friends alone. It is the real step, the rest are only footprints. (Rumi)

...At some point, much later,...I experience the deepest and richest tranquility of the heart that I have ever felt....Now I have given everything, I have nothing left. Will I ever be able to stop crying? Only three weeks more [to the retreat], then they'll come and get me out. I wonder whether I can get myself back together by then.

And yet these few seconds of such a qualitatively utterly different, such an indescribable feeling of the peace of the heart are enough to strengthen me in the assumption that I'm on the right track. So I go on and on, until, between the tears and the exhaustion, I no longer know for sure whether I'm asleep or still praying. (Özelsel, 1996, pp. 54–56)

CHAPTER HIGHLIGHTS

- Not all Sufi teachings can be communicated in words, nor is there a single, systematic approach to the teachings. Sufism is often described as a path, a metaphor that suggests both an origin and a destination.
- The four basic principles in Sufi practice are (1) There are as many ways, involving transformation of the ego and service to creation, to reach truth (or God) as there are individuals. (2) To live in harmony with others we need an inner sense of justice and we must reduce our selfishness and arrogance. (3) One of the underlying principles of morality is love, which springs from self-work and expresses itself in service to others. (4) Self-knowledge is the cardinal truth that ripens into knowledge of God.
- Sufism is usually described as the mystical core of Islam, dating from about the seventh century as a major religious force.
- According to Ibn 'Arabi, Sufism has four stages of practice and understanding, each built upon the one before. The first is sharia (exoteric religious law); the second is tariqa (the mystical path); the third is haqiqa (truth); and the fourth is marifa (gnosis).

- The Sufis describe two states of advanced consciousness. The first is a state of annihilation or union (fana) and the second is that of persistence or return (baqa).
- Common to both Christian and Sufi writings, the perception of God as the Beloved comes from direct experience. It is said that if you take two steps toward God, God runs to you.
- Stages of psychospiritual growth include the following: initial awakening; patience and gratitude; fear and hope; self-denial and poverty; trust in God; love, yearning, intimacy, and satisfaction; intent, sincerity, and truthfulness; contemplation and self-examination; and the recollection of death.
- Heedlessness and the nafs, or lower self, are the main obstacles to growth in Sufism. The nafs is the source of most of our negative traits, such as pride, greed, anger, and hypocrisy. To transform the nafs into positive qualities is one of the great goals of Sufism.
- The nafs is a living process made up of impulses, or drives, to satisfy desires, which dominate reason or judgment. The process derives from the interplay of body and soul.
- The nafs has been categorized into the following levels of self: the tyrannical self, the regretful self, the inspired self, the serene self, the pleased self, the self pleasing to God, and the pure self.
- The teacher is considered a physician of the soul.

KEY CONCEPTS

Al-Ghazzali One of the most important figures in Islamic theology. He established a framework in which pathological, normal, and mystical behaviors are linked in a single, unified field of human experience. He also reinstated the elements of personal development and transpersonal experience into Islam.

Baqa State of return or persistence in which the individual is part of the world but unconcerned about his or her rewards or position in it. Baqa is reintegration as the universal self, or the activation of the individual's totality.

Contemplation and self-examination Meditation in order to perceive inner reality. The concerns of this stage, stilling and clearing the mind, are similar to those of Yoga and Buddhism.

Fana A state of union or annihilation in which individual identity seems merged with the whole of reality. Fana is the disintegration of the person's narrow self-concept, social self, and limited intellect. The experience of the individual is like a drop of water aware of being part of the ocean.

Fear and hope The sense of losing God (fear) and the anticipation that one's efforts will bring one closer to God (hope). The fear is akin to what lovers feel when they worry about losing their sweetheart. Hope allows one to see oneself clearly. One hopes that in spite of personal shortcomings, progress along the spiritual path is possible.

Haqiqa Truth, the third stage of Sufi practice. The term refers to the personal understanding of the inner meanings of the guidance and practices of the preceding stages, sharia and tariqa. All spiritual practice is imitation prior to this stage.

Initial awakening The beginning of a fundamental reorientation of personal values. It is often preceded by a personal crisis, after which the individual concludes that the external world is not as satisfying as it had once seemed.

Inspired self The third stage of the nafs, or ego. The individual is motivated, for the first time, by ideals such as compassion, service, and moral values. The power of the desires and the ego is reduced. This stage marks the beginning of the real practice of Sufism.

Intent, sincerity, and truthfulness Concern for the aim, or intent, of an action, rather than for the action itself. The individual experiences ever-increasing awareness of the inner meaning of events and less interest in observable behaviors.

Love, yearning, intimacy, and satisfaction The stage at which the developing personality has only the desire to love God. While enjoying a sense of intimacy with God, the individual derives satisfaction from knowing that all things come from the Divine.

Marifa Gnosis, the fourth stage of Sufi practice. A deep level of understanding, beyond haqiqa, it is the station of the great sages and saints, the messengers, and the prophets.

Patience and gratitude Willingness to accept the fact that efforts toward self-improvement are not immediately rewarded (patience) and appreciation for the fact that one is given time to make progress (gratitude). Gratitude is related to the belief that all things, whether pleasant or painful, come from God.

Pleased self The fifth stage of the nafs, or ego. The individual is contented with whatever happens, realizing that even pain and suffering come from the Divine.

Pure self The final stage of the nafs, or ego. It is equivalent to the stage of fana. The sense of "I" has been dropped. The Sufi now knows that only the Divine exists.

Recollection of death A potent practice in becoming more aware of one's present experiences, and a powerful tool in letting go of undesirable habits and attitudes.

Regretful self Second stage of the nafs, or ego. The individual is dominated by desires and wants but from time to time tries to follow higher impulses, as the negative effects of his or her self-centeredness become evident. This level of self is similar to the psychoanalytic concept of superego.

Self-denial and poverty Service to others rather than to oneself (self-denial) and freedom from attachment (poverty). Service is rendered in order to please God, not for any worldly rewards. The inner meaning of poverty is to be free of desire and attachment so that one may receive God.

Self pleasing to God The sixth stage of the nafs, or ego. The individual realizes that all power to act comes from God, that nothing can be done without divine help. It is the stage of genuine inner unity and wholeness.

Serene self Fourth stage of the nafs, or ego. The individual is at peace, and old desires and attachments are no longer binding.

Sharia The first of the four stages of Sufi practice. It consists of teachings of morality, ethics, and outer practice. The word means "road" in Arabic, and it refers to a route anyone can follow.

Tariqa The trackless path in the desert from oasis to oasis; not a visible road. The second stage of Sufi practice, it refers to the inner practice of the teachings.

Trust in God The stage at which the individual seeks everything from God. It is an active process, not passive or dependent. Trust arises from the assumption that one's efforts are part of a larger system, whose details are unknown.

Tyrannical self First stage of the nafs, or ego. The tyrannical self, like the id in psychoanalytic theory, seeks to dominate the individual's thoughts and behavior. This level reflects unbridled selfishness, narcissism, and no sense of morality or compassion. It is the tyranny of the least evolved aspects of the individual.

ANNOTATED BIBLIOGRAPHY

Al-Ghazzali, M. (1964). *The alchemy of happiness* (C. Field, Trans.). Lahore, Pakistan: Muhammad Ashraf.

> Part of his own abridgment of *The Revival of Religious Sciences*. This short, vivid book contains few references to purely Islamic ideas.

Al-Ghazzali, M. (1971). *Ghazzali's Ihya Ulum-Id-Din* (Alhaj Maulana Fazlul Karim, Trans.). Dacca, Bangladesh: Mission Trust.

> The only full translation of al-Ghazzali's *The Revival of Religious Sciences* available.

Al-Ghazzali, M. (1972). *The revival of religious sciences* (B. Behari, Trans.). Farnham, Surrey, England: Sufi.

> The best translation of the most important of al-Ghazzali's major works. Selections drawn primarily from the last half of *Ihya Ulum-Id-Din*.

Bakhtiar, L. (1987). *Sufi: Expressions of the mystic quest*. New York: Avon.

> A different approach; symbolic, geometric, and with beautiful illustrations.

Fadiman, J., & Frager, R. (Eds.). (1997). *Essential Sufism*. San Francisco: HarperSanFrancisco.

> A broad-ranging, accessible exploration of the treasures of Sufism. More than 300 beautiful and inspirational Sufi works, from thousand-year-old prayers to contemporary Sufi poetry.

Frager, R. (1999). *Heart, self, and soul: The Sufi psychology of growth, balance, and harmony*. Wheaton, IL: Quest Books.

> The first book by a Western psychologist to explore Sufism as a path for personal growth. Full of stories, poetry,

> meditations, exercises, and colorful everyday examples, this book will open the heart, nourish the self, and quicken the soul.

Ozak, M. (Al-Jerrahi). (1987). *Love is the wine*. (Edited and compiled by Sheikh R. Frager al-Jerrahi.) Putney, VT: Threshold Books.

> This book is derived from talks given in the United States by a contemporary Sufi master. It presents the depths of Sufi wisdom in a modern, highly accessible form.

Ozak, M. (Al-Jerrahi). (1988). *Irshad: Wisdom of a Sufi master*. Amity, NY: Amity House.

> A collection of discourses on Sufism, its practice and philosophy. For the serious student.

Shah, I. (1964). *The Sufis*. New York: Doubleday.

> Shah discusses the major traditional Sufi teachers, Sufism's major influences on Western thought, and central ideas of Sufi practice.

Shah, I. (1971). *The pleasantries of the incredible Mulla Nasrudin*. New York: Dutton.

> A collection of short, funny stories about the mulla, a folk hero who is the subject of numerous Sufi stories.

Web Sites

Sufism and Islam
www.arches.uga.edu/~godlas

> The best **web** site for information on Islam and on Sufism. Includes sections on Qur'an, hadith, and the Prophet

Muhammed, Islamic history, Muslim women and women's rights in Islam, and basic questions on Islam. Also an excellent introduction to Sufism, including definitions of key Sufi terms, discussions of the nafs, remembrance, Sufism in the West, as well as listings of Sufi Orders, and Sufi resources and books.

Jerrahi Order Site
www.jerrahi.org

This is the tradition on which much of this chapter is based. Available in Spanish and English, and includes information on Jerrahi books and writings and on-line reading on basic concepts and practices in Sufism.

REFERENCES

Al-Ghazzali, M. (1972). *The revival of religious sciences* (B. Behari, Trans.). Farnham, Surrey, England: Sufi.

Al-Ghazzali, M. (1975). *On the duties of brotherhood* (M. Holland, Trans.). London: Latimer.

Arasteh, A. R. (1973). Psychology of the Sufi way to individuation. In L. F. Rushbrook Williams (Ed.), *Sufi studies: East and West* (pp. 89–113). New York: Dutton.

Arasteh, A. R. (1980). *Growth to selfhood: Sufi contribution.* London: Routledge & Kegan Paul.

Arasteh, A., & Sheikh, A. (1989). Sufism: The way to universal self. In A. Sheikh & K. Sheikh (Eds.), *Eastern and Western approaches to healing.* New York: Wiley.

Arberry, A. J. (1966). *The doctrine of the Sufis.* Lahore, Pakistan: Shri Muhammad Ashraf. (Also, Cambridge: Cambridge University Press, 1977.)

Beg, M. A. (1970). A note on the concept of self, and the theory and practice of psychological help in the Sufi tradition. *Interpersonal Development, 1,* 58–64.

Burke, O. (1966). Travel and residence with dervishes. In R. Davidson (Ed.), *Documents on contemporary dervish communities.* London: Hoopoe.

Burke, O. (1975). *Among the dervishes.* New York: Dutton.

Erikson, E. (1964). *Insight and responsibility.* New York: Norton.

Frager, R. (1999). *Heart, self, and soul: The Sufi psychology of growth, balance, and harmony.* Wheaton, IL: Quest Books.

Harman, W. W. (1967). Old wine in new wineskins. In J. Bugental (Ed.), *Challenges of humanistic psychology* (pp. 321–334). New York: McGraw-Hill.

Helminski, K. (1992). *Living presence: A Sufi way to mindfulness and the essential self.* New York: Tarcher.

Hujwiri. (1959). *Kashf al-mahjub* (R. A. Nicholson, Trans.). London: Luzac.

Ibn 'Arabi, M. (1981). *Journey to the lord of power* (R. Harris, Trans.). New York: Inner Traditions.

Ibn 'Arabi, M. (1992). *What the seeker needs* (T. Bayrak al-Jerrahi & R. Harris al-Jerrahi, Trans.). Putney, VT: Threshold Books.

Inhelder, B., & Piaget, J. (1958). (A. Parsons & S. Milgrim, Trans.). *The growth of logical thinking from childhood to adolescence.* New York: Basic Books.

James, W. (1899). *Talks to teachers on psychology and to students on some of life's ideals.* New York: Holt, Rinehart and Winston. (Unaltered republication, New York: Dover, 1962.)

Jung, C. G. (1973). *C. G. Jung's letters* (G. Adler, A. Jaffe, & R. F. C. Hull, Eds.) (Vol. 1). Princeton, NJ: Princeton University Press.

Kabir. (1977). *The Kabir book.* Versions by Robert Bly. Boston: Beacon Press.

Khan, Pir Villayat. (1974). *Toward the one.* New York: Harper & Row.

Landinsky, D. (1996). *I heard God laughing: Renderings of Hafiz.* Walnut Creek, CA: Sufism Reoriented.

MacDonald, D. B. (1909). *The religious attitude and life in Islam.* Chicago: University of Chicago Press.

Nasr, S. (Ed.). (1987). *Islamic spirituality: Foundations.* New York: Crossroads.

Nicholson, R. A. (1964a). *The idea of personality in Sufism.* Lahore, Pakistan: Muhammad Ashraf.

Nicholson, R. A. (1964b). *Rumi, poet and mystic.* London: Allen & Unwin.

Nurbakhsh, J. (n.d.). *Sufism and psychoanalysis* (Parts 1 and 2). Unpublished papers, Department of Psychiatry, University of Tehran, Tehran, Iran.

Nurbakhsh, J. (1978). *In the tavern of ruin.* New York: Khaniqahi-nimatullahi.

Nurbakhsh, J. (1979). *In the paradise of the Sufis.* New York: Khaniqahi-nimatullahi.

Nurbakhsh, J. (1981). *Sufism: Meaning, knowledge and unity.* New York: Khaniqahi-nimatullahi.

Nurbakhsh, J. (1992). *The psychology of Sufism.* New York: Khaniqahi-nimatullahi.

Orage, A. R. (1965). *Psychological exercises and essays* (rev. ed.). London: Janus.

Ornstein, R. E. (1972). *The psychology of consciousness.* San Francisco: Freeman; New York: Viking Press.

Ozak, M. (Al-Jerrahi). (1981). The unveiling of love. (M. Holland, Trans.). New York: Inner Traditions.

Ozak, M. (Al-Jerrahi). (1987). *Love is the wine.* (Edited and compiled by Sheikh R. Frager al-Jerrahi). Putney, VT: Threshold Books.

Ozak, M. (Al-Jerrahi). (1988). *Irshad: Wisdom of a Sufi master.* Amity, NY: Amity House.

Özelsel, M. (1996). *Forty days: The diary of a traditional solitary Sufi retreat.* Brattleboro, VT: Threshold Books.

Piaget, J. (1952). *The origins of intelligence in children.* New York: International University Press.

Rice, C. (1964). *The Persian Sufis.* London: Allen & Unwin.

Rumi, Jalal al-Din. (1972). *Discourses of Rumi* (A. J. Arberry, Trans.). New York: Weiser.

Sanai, H. (1974). *The walled garden of truth* (D. L. Pendlebury, Trans.). London: Octagon.

Shafii, M. (1968). The pir (Sufi guide) and the Western psychotherapist. *R. M. Bucke Memorial Society Newsletter, 3,* 9–19.

Shafii, M. (1974). *Developmental stages in man in Sufism and psychoanalysis.* Unpublished manuscript.

Shafii, M. (1985). *Freedom from the self.* New York: Human Sciences Press.

Shah, I. (1964). *The Sufis.* New York: Doubleday.

Shah, I. (1972f). First statement. In L. Lewin (Ed.), *The diffusion of Sufi ideas in the West* (pp. 133–145). Boulder, CO: Keysign Press.

Trimingham, J. S. (1971). *The Sufi orders in Islam.* New York: Oxford University Press.

Watt, W. M. (1971). *Muslim intellectual: A study of Al-Ghazzali.* Edinburgh: University Press.

White, R. W. (1959). Motivation reconsidered: The concept of competence. *Psychological Review, 66,* 297–333.

credits

Text

P. 68: Harding, M. E., *The "I" and the "Not I"*. Copyright © 1974 by Princeton University Press. Reprinted by permission of Princeton University Press.

P. 84: From *Analytical Psychology: Its Theory and Practice* by C. G. Jung, copyright © 1968 by Heirs of C. G. Jung. Used with permission of Pantheon Books, a division of Random House.

P. 110: From Alfred Adler, *Social Interest: A Challenge to Mankind*, copyright 1964, Capricorn Books.

P. 135: From *Self Analysis* by Karen Horney. Copyright © 1942 by W. W. Norton & Company, Inc., renewed © 1970 by Marianne Eckardt, Renate Mintz, and Brigitte Swarzenski. Used with permission of W. W. Norton & Company, Inc.

P. 189: From *Identity: Youth and Crisis* by Erik H. Erikson. Copyright © 1968 by W. W. Norton & Company, Inc. Used with permission of W. W. Norton & Company.

P. 195: From *Childhood and Society* by Erik H. Erikson. Copyright © 1950, © 1968 by W. W. Norton & Company, Inc., renewed © 1978, 1991 by Erik H. Erikson. Used with permission of W. W. Norton & Company, Inc.

P. 233: From *Talks to Teachers on Psychology and to Students on Some of Life's Ideals* by William James. Copyright © 1962 by Dover Publications, Inc. Reprinted with permission.

P. 233: From *The Varieties of Religious Experience* by William James. Copyright © 1961 by Macmillan Publishing Company. Used with the permission of Scribner, a Division of Simon & Schuster, Inc.

P. 265: From *The Humanist,* July/August 1972. Copyright © 1972 by the B. F. Skinner Foundation. Reprinted by permission from the American Humanist Association.

P. 286: Reprinted from *Cognitive Therapy and Emotional Disorders* by Aaron Beck. By permission of International Universities Press, Inc. Copyright © 1976 by International Universities Press.

P. 287: From *The Embodied Mind: Cognitive Science and Human Experience* by Francisco Varela, Evan Thompson, and Eleanor Rosch. Copyright © 1991 by MIT Press. Reprinted with permission.

P. 334: Excerpt from *Comprehensive Textbook of Psychiatry,* Second Edition, by Harold J. Kaplan © 1995.

P. 368: From *Journal of Transpersonal Psychology,* Vol. 4, No. 2. Copyright © 1972 by Association for Transpersonal Psychology. Reprinted with permission.

P. 397: From *Radha: Diary of a Woman's Search* by Swami Sivananda Radha. Copyright © 1981 by Timeless Books. Reprinted with permission.

P. 432: From *The Wild, White Goose,* Volume I, by Rev. P. T. N. H. Jiyu-Kennett, Roshi (Mt. Shasta, CA: Shasta Abbey Press, 1977) pp. 81–95. Copyright © 1977 by Rev. P. T. N. H. Jiyu-Kennett, Roshi; copyright transferred to Shasta Abbey in 1998. Reprinted with permission from Shasta Abbey.

P. 455: From M. Ozelsel, *Forty Days: The Diary of a Traditional Sufi Retreat*. Originally published by Threshold Books. Reprinted with permission.

Photographs

Unless osherwise acknowledged, all photographs are the property of Prentice Hall.

P. xxiii: Courtesy Robert Frager
P. xxiv: Courtesy Renee Fadiman
P. 16 Corbis/Bettmann
P. 55 Yousuf Karsh/Woodfin Camp & Associates
P. 66 Paul Solomon/Woodfin Camp & Associates
P. 78 UPI/Corbis/Bettmann
P. 90 The Granger Collection
P. 105 AP Wide World Photos
P. 114 Dr. Marianne Horney Eckhardt, M.D.
P. 141 Courtesy Jean Baker Miller, The Stone Center, Wellesley College
P. 141 Courtesy Irene Pierce Stiver, The Stone Center, Wellesley College
P. 141 Courtesy Judith Jordan, The Stone Center, Wellesley College
P. 141 Courtesy Jan Surrey, The Stone Center, Wellesley College
P. 141 Jennifer Clements
P. 172 Jill Krementz, Inc.
P. 200 Library of Congress
P. 243 Ken Heyman/Woodfin Camp & Associates
P. 271 Aaron T. Beck, M.D.
P. 271 Albert Bandura
P. 291 Ohio State University Photo Archives
P. 311 Corbis/Bettmann
P. 341 Corbis/Bettmann
P. 349 Corbis/Bettmann
P. 351 AP Wide World Photos
P. 358 Anne Nielsen/Getty Images, Inc–Liaison
P. 359 Mark Antman/The Image Works
P. 374 Stockbyte
P. 382 David Young-Wolff/PhotoEdit
P. 388 R. Berriedale Johnson/Panos Pictures
P. 402 Cameramann International
P. 405 Dean Wong/The Image Works
P. 416 Sogen-sha Inc. Publishers
P. 417 Sogen-sha Inc. Publishers
P. 418 Sogen-sha Inc. Publishers
P. 419 Sogen-sha Inc. Publishers
P. 420 Sogen-sha Inc. Publishers
P. 421 Sogen-sha Inc. Publishers
P. 422 Sogen-sha Inc. Publishers
P. 423 Sogen-sha Inc. Publishers
P. 424 Sogen-sha Inc. Publishers
P. 425 Sogen-sha Inc. Publishers
P. 437 Jack Vartoogian

name index

Numbers in bold italic refer to names found in the Reference section at the end of each chapter.

subject index